T0135014

Lecture Notes in Computer Science   14028

Founding Editors

Gerhard Goos
Juris Hartmanis

Editorial Board Members

The series Lecture Notes in Computer Science (LNCS), including its subseries Lecture Notes in Artificial Intelligence (LNAI) and Lecture Notes in Bioinformatics (LNBI), has established itself as a medium for the publication of new developments in computer science and information technology research, teaching, and education.

LNCS enjoys close cooperation with the computer science R & D community, the series counts many renowned academics among its volume editors and paper authors, and collaborates with prestigious societies. Its mission is to serve this international community by providing an invaluable service, mainly focused on the publication of conference and workshop proceedings and postproceedings. LNCS commenced publication in 1973.

Vincent G. Duffy
Editor

Digital Human Modeling and Applications in Health, Safety, Ergonomics and Risk Management

14th International Conference, DHM 2023
Held as Part of the 25th HCI International Conference, HCII 2023
Copenhagen, Denmark, July 23–28, 2023
Proceedings, Part I

Springer

Editor
Vincent G. Duffy
Purdue University
West Lafayette, IN, USA

ISSN 0302-9743   ISSN 1611-3349 (electronic)
Lecture Notes in Computer Science
ISBN 978-3-031-35740-4   ISBN 978-3-031-35741-1 (eBook)
https://doi.org/10.1007/978-3-031-35741-1

This Springer imprint is published by the registered company Springer Nature Switzerland AG
The registered company address is: Gewerbestrasse 11, 6330 Cham, Switzerland

Foreword

Human-computer interaction (HCI) is acquiring an ever-increasing scientific and industrial importance, as well as having more impact on people's everyday lives, as an ever-growing number of human activities are progressively moving from the physical to the digital world. This process, which has been ongoing for some time now, was further accelerated during the acute period of the COVID-19 pandemic. The HCI International (HCII) conference series, held annually, aims to respond to the compelling need to advance the exchange of knowledge and research and development efforts on the human aspects of design and use of computing systems.

The 25th International Conference on Human-Computer Interaction, HCI International 2023 (HCII 2023), was held in the emerging post-pandemic era as a 'hybrid' event at the AC Bella Sky Hotel and Bella Center, Copenhagen, Denmark, during July 23–28, 2023. It incorporated the 21 thematic areas and affiliated conferences listed below.

A total of 7472 individuals from academia, research institutes, industry, and government agencies from 85 countries submitted contributions, and 1578 papers and 396 posters were included in the volumes of the proceedings that were published just before the start of the conference, these are listed below. The contributions thoroughly cover the entire field of human-computer interaction, addressing major advances in knowledge and effective use of computers in a variety of application areas. These papers provide academics, researchers, engineers, scientists, practitioners and students with state-of-the-art information on the most recent advances in HCI.

The HCI International (HCII) conference also offers the option of presenting 'Late Breaking Work', and this applies both for papers and posters, with corresponding volumes of proceedings that will be published after the conference. Full papers will be included in the 'HCII 2023 - Late Breaking Work - Papers' volumes of the proceedings to be published in the Springer LNCS series, while 'Poster Extended Abstracts' will be included as short research papers in the 'HCII 2023 - Late Breaking Work - Posters' volumes to be published in the Springer CCIS series.

I would like to thank the Program Board Chairs and the members of the Program Boards of all thematic areas and affiliated conferences for their contribution towards the high scientific quality and overall success of the HCI International 2023 conference. Their manifold support in terms of paper reviewing (single-blind review process, with a minimum of two reviews per submission), session organization and their willingness to act as goodwill ambassadors for the conference is most highly appreciated.

This conference would not have been possible without the continuous and unwavering support and advice of Gavriel Salvendy, founder, General Chair Emeritus, and Scientific Advisor. For his outstanding efforts, I would like to express my sincere appreciation to Abbas Moallem, Communications Chair and Editor of HCI International News.

July 2023   Constantine Stephanidis

HCI International 2023 Thematic Areas
and Affiliated Conferences

Thematic Areas

- HCI: Human-Computer Interaction
- HIMI: Human Interface and the Management of Information

Affiliated Conferences

- EPCE: 20th International Conference on Engineering Psychology and Cognitive Ergonomics
- AC: 17th International Conference on Augmented Cognition
- UAHCI: 17th International Conference on Universal Access in Human-Computer Interaction
- CCD: 15th International Conference on Cross-Cultural Design
- SCSM: 15th International Conference on Social Computing and Social Media
- VAMR: 15th International Conference on Virtual, Augmented and Mixed Reality
- DHM: 14th International Conference on Digital Human Modeling and Applications in Health, Safety, Ergonomics and Risk Management
- DUXU: 12th International Conference on Design, User Experience and Usability
- C&C: 11th International Conference on Culture and Computing
- DAPI: 11th International Conference on Distributed, Ambient and Pervasive Interactions
- HCIBGO: 10th International Conference on HCI in Business, Government and Organizations
- LCT: 10th International Conference on Learning and Collaboration Technologies
- ITAP: 9th International Conference on Human Aspects of IT for the Aged Population
- AIS: 5th International Conference on Adaptive Instructional Systems
- HCI-CPT: 5th International Conference on HCI for Cybersecurity, Privacy and Trust
- HCI-Games: 5th International Conference on HCI in Games
- MobiTAS: 5th International Conference on HCI in Mobility, Transport and Automotive Systems
- AI-HCI: 4th International Conference on Artificial Intelligence in HCI
- MOBILE: 4th International Conference on Design, Operation and Evaluation of Mobile Communications

List of Conference Proceedings Volumes Appearing Before the Conference

1. LNCS 14011, Human-Computer Interaction: Part I, edited by Masaaki Kurosu and Ayako Hashizume
2. LNCS 14012, Human-Computer Interaction: Part II, edited by Masaaki Kurosu and Ayako Hashizume
3. LNCS 14013, Human-Computer Interaction: Part III, edited by Masaaki Kurosu and Ayako Hashizume
4. LNCS 14014, Human-Computer Interaction: Part IV, edited by Masaaki Kurosu and Ayako Hashizume
5. LNCS 14015, Human Interface and the Management of Information: Part I, edited by Hirohiko Mori and Yumi Asahi
6. LNCS 14016, Human Interface and the Management of Information: Part II, edited by Hirohiko Mori and Yumi Asahi
7. LNAI 14017, Engineering Psychology and Cognitive Ergonomics: Part I, edited by Don Harris and Wen-Chin Li
8. LNAI 14018, Engineering Psychology and Cognitive Ergonomics: Part II, edited by Don Harris and Wen-Chin Li
9. LNAI 14019, Augmented Cognition, edited by Dylan D. Schmorrow and Cali M. Fidopiastis
10. LNCS 14020, Universal Access in Human-Computer Interaction: Part I, edited by Margherita Antona and Constantine Stephanidis
11. LNCS 14021, Universal Access in Human-Computer Interaction: Part II, edited by Margherita Antona and Constantine Stephanidis
12. LNCS 14022, Cross-Cultural Design: Part I, edited by Pei-Luen Patrick Rau
13. LNCS 14023, Cross-Cultural Design: Part II, edited by Pei-Luen Patrick Rau
14. LNCS 14024, Cross-Cultural Design: Part III, edited by Pei-Luen Patrick Rau
15. LNCS 14025, Social Computing and Social Media: Part I, edited by Adela Coman and Simona Vasilache
16. LNCS 14026, Social Computing and Social Media: Part II, edited by Adela Coman and Simona Vasilache
17. LNCS 14027, Virtual, Augmented and Mixed Reality, edited by Jessie Y. C. Chen and Gino Fragomeni
18. LNCS 14028, Digital Human Modeling and Applications in Health, Safety, Ergonomics and Risk Management: Part I, edited by Vincent G. Duffy
19. LNCS 14029, Digital Human Modeling and Applications in Health, Safety, Ergonomics and Risk Management: Part II, edited by Vincent G. Duffy
20. LNCS 14030, Design, User Experience, and Usability: Part I, edited by Aaron Marcus, Elizabeth Rosenzweig and Marcelo Soares
21. LNCS 14031, Design, User Experience, and Usability: Part II, edited by Aaron Marcus, Elizabeth Rosenzweig and Marcelo Soares

47. CCIS 1836, HCI International 2023 Posters - Part V, edited by Constantine Stephanidis, Margherita Antona, Stavroula Ntoa and Gavriel Salvendy

https://2023.hci.international/proceedings

Preface

Software representations of humans, including aspects of anthropometry, biometrics, motion capture and prediction, as well as cognition modeling, are known as Digital Human Models (DHM), and are widely used in a variety of complex application domains where it is important to foresee and simulate human behavior, performance, safety, health and comfort. Automation depicting human emotion, social interaction and functional capabilities can also be modeled to support and assist in predicting human response in real-world settings. Such domains include medical and nursing applications, work, education and learning, ergonomics and design, as well as safety and risk management.

The 14th Digital Human Modeling & Applications in Health, Safety, Ergonomics & Risk Management (DHM) Conference, an affiliated conference of the HCI International Conference 2023, encouraged papers from academics, researchers, industry and professionals, on a broad range of theoretical and applied issues related to Digital Human Modeling and its applications.

The research papers contributed to this year's volumes span across different fields that fall within the scope of the DHM Conference. The study of DHM issues in various application domains has yielded works emphasizing human factors and ergonomics based on human models, novel approaches in healthcare, and the application of Artificial Intelligence in medicine. Applications of interest are shown across many industries. Job design and productivity, robotics and intelligent systems are among the human-technology modeling and results reporting efforts this year.

Two volumes of the HCII 2023 proceedings are dedicated to this year's edition of the DHM Conference. The first volume focuses on topics related to human factors and ergonomics, job design and human productivity, as well as interaction with robots and exoskeletons. The second volume focuses on topics related to digital health, IoT and AI in medicine and healthcare, as well as modeling complex human behavior and phenomena.

Papers of these volumes are included for publication after a minimum of two single–blind reviews from the members of the DHM Program Board or, in some cases, from members of the Program Boards of other affiliated conferences. I would like to thank all of them for their invaluable contribution, support and efforts.

July 2023   Vincent G. Duffy

14th International Conference on Digital Human Modeling and Applications in Health, Safety, Ergonomics and Risk Management (DHM 2023)

Program Board Chair: **Vincent G. Duffy,** *Purdue University, USA*

- Karthik Adapa, *UNC-Chapel Hill, USA*
- Giuseppe Andreoni, *Politecnico di Milano, Italy*
- Mária Babicsné Horváth, *Budapest University of Technology and Economics, Hungary*
- Angelos Barmpoutis, *University of Florida, USA*
- André Calero Valdez, *University of Lübeck, Germany*
- Yaqin Cao, *Anhui Polytechnic University, P.R. China*
- Damien Chablat, *CNRS/LS2N, France*
- Anirban Chowdhury, *NMIMS University, India*
- H. Onan Demirel, *Oregon State University, USA*
- Yi Ding, Anhui *Polytechnic University, P.R. China*
- Manish K. Dixit, *Texas A&M University, USA*
- Lucia Donatelli, *Saarland University, Germany*
- Martin Fleischer, *Technical University of Munich, Germany*
- Martin Fränzle, *Oldenburg University, Germany*
- RongRong Fu, *East China University of Science and Technology, P.R. China*
- Afzal Godil, *NIST, USA*
- Wenbin Guo, U*niversity of Florida, USA*
- Jaana Hallamaa, *University of Helsinki, Finland*
- Sogand Hasanzadeh, *Purdue University, USA*
- Nicola Helfer, *KAN - Commission for Occupational Health and Safety and Standardization, Germany*
- Sandy Ingram, *University of Applied Sciences of Western Switzerland, Switzerland*
- Genett Isabel Jimenez Delgado, *Institucíon Universitaria de Barranquilla IUB, Colombia*
- Taina Kalliokoski, *University of Helsinki, Finland*
- Sougata Karmakar, *Indian Institute of Technology Guwahati, India*
- Najmeh Khalili-Mahani, *Concordia University, Canada*
- Steffi Kohl, *Zuyd University of Applied Sciences, The Netherlands*
- Nicola Francesco Lopomo, *Università degli Studi di Brescia, Italy*
- Alexander Mehler, *Goethe University Frankfurt, Germany*
- Manivannan Muniyandi, *IIT Madras, India*
- Peter Nickel, *Institute for Occupational Safety and Health of the German Social Accident Insurance (IFA), Germany*
- Miguel Ortiz-Barrios, *Universidad de la Costa CUC, Colombia*
- Thaneswer Patel, *North Eastern Regional Institute of Science and Technology, India*
- Manikam Pillay, *RESMEERTS, Australia*

- James Pustejovsky, *Brandeis University, USA*
- Qing-Xing Qu, *Northeastern University, P.R. China*
- Caterina Rizzi, *University of Bergamo, Italy*
- Deep Seth, *Mahindra University, India*
- Thitirat Siriborvornratanakul, *National Institute of Development Administration, Thailand*
- Beatriz Sousa Santos, *University of Aveiro, Portugal*
- Debadutta Subudhi, *IIT Madras, India*
- Youchao Sun, *Nanjing University of Aeronautics and Astronautics, P.R. China*
- Zhengtang Tan, *Hunan Normal University, P.R. China*
- Leonor Teixeira, *University of Aveiro, Portugal*
- Renran Tian, *IUPUI, USA*
- Joseph Timoney, *Maynooth University, Ireland*
- Alexander Trende, *German Aerospace Center (DLR), Germany*
- Dustin van der Haar, *University of Johannesburg, South Africa*
- Kuan Yew Wong, *Universiti Teknologi Malaysia, Malaysia*
- Shuping Xiong, *Korea Advanced Institute of Science and Technology, South Korea*
- James Yang, *Texas Tech University, USA*
- Azeema Yaseen, *Maynooth University, Ireland*
- Yulin Zhao, *Guangdong University of Technology, P.R. China*

The full list with the Program Board Chairs and the members of the Program Boards of all thematic areas and affiliated conferences of HCII2023 is available online at:

http://www.hci.international/board-members-2023.php

HCI International 2024 Conference

The 26th International Conference on Human-Computer Interaction, HCI International 2024, will be held jointly with the affiliated conferences at the Washington Hilton Hotel, Washington, DC, USA, June 29 – July 4, 2024. It will cover a broad spectrum of themes related to Human-Computer Interaction, including theoretical issues, methods, tools, processes, and case studies in HCI design, as well as novel interaction techniques, interfaces, and applications. The proceedings will be published by Springer. More information will be made available on the conference website: http://2024.hci.international/.

General Chair
Prof. Constantine Stephanidis
University of Crete and ICS-FORTH
Heraklion, Crete, Greece
Email: general_chair@hcii2024.org

https://2024.hci.international/

Contents – Part I

Job Design and Human Productivity

Interacting with Robots and Exoskeletons

Contents – Part II

IoT and AI in Medicine and Healthcare

Modeling Complex Human Behavior and Phenomena

Human Factors and Ergonomics

Simulation of Cable Driven Elbow Exosuit in Matlab

Sreejan Alapati[1,2], Deep Seth[1(✉)], and Yannick Aoustin[2]

[1] Department of Mechanical Engineering, École Centrale School of Engineering, Mahindra University, Hyderabad, India
{sreejan20pmee003,deep.seth}@mahindrauniversity.edu.in
[2] Nantes Université, École Centrale de Nantes, CNRS, LS2N, UMR 6004, 44000 Nantes, France
yannick.aoustin@ec-nantes.fr

Abstract. Exo-suit/Soft Exoskeletons are actuated using flexible actuators or cable driven systems. In a cable-driven exosuit, the routing of the cable needs to be defined mathematically to control the position of the joint. For an elbow exosuit, the actuation is applied to the elbow joint which has a single DoF. The generated movement takes place in the sagittal plane. To fabricate a cable-driven elbow exosuit, it is necessary to calculate the tension force in the string and the torque required at the elbow joint to select the cable and motor characteristics. The process of calculating these parameters are independent for any exosuit. A static model for a cable driven exo-suit has been presented. Using the model we have simulated the actuation of an elbow joint for an exosuit. The physical validation of the model will be done in future work.

Keywords: Elbow exosuit · soft exoskeleton · soft wearable device · simulation · elbow actuation

1 Introduction

Exosuits are soft wearable robotic devices that are used to assist the movement of limbs through power augmentation [1]. In the human body, several muscles work together in the actuation of joints and achieve complex motion of limbs to manipulate the environment around [2,3]. For an exosuit to achieve all the movements and to be able to assist every movement is difficult. However, few exosuit prototypes achieve assistance for multiple joints [4,5]. Considering the fact that assistance for rehabilitation and for repetitive tasks in the industries is sometimes required only at a single joint, the single joint exosuits are also significant to avoid musculoskeletal disorders. Single joint exosuit for rehabilitation [6] and assistance in industrial operations [7] have been fabricated earlier. Exosuits for the elbow joint are common among the rehabilitation devices and also among the wearable assistive devices used in industries [8]. This work presented in this paper is for a cable driven elbow exosuit that is being developed.

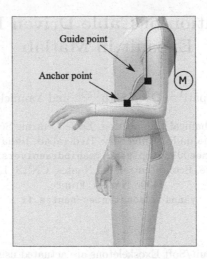

Guide point

Anchor point

M

Fig. 1. Elbow exosuit

Most of the elbow exosuits are actuated by a cable-driven mechanism, apart from pneumatic [9], passive and hybrid systems [10]. Different types of cables can be used for the actuation of an exosuit [11]. The design of the elbow exosuit mostly consists of an anchor point on the forearm which is pulled towards the guide point on the upper arm, for the actuation of the elbow joint [12], Fig. 1. The motor that assists in the actuation of the elbow joint is positioned on the back of the wearer or placed as a separate stationary device which is not on the wearer's body [5,13]. To control the angular position of the elbow joint, the actuation distance of the string between the guide point on the upper arm and the anchor point on the forearm should be known. Also to fabricate the elbow exosuit, the motor capacity required to actuate the elbow joint needs to be determined. These two parameters will be useful in the selection of the cable and the motor to fabricate the exosuit. These parameters depend on the construction and design of the exosuit device. The distance of the anchor point and guide point from the elbow joint, and the weight of the loaded arm are considered. Since these parameters change from one exosuit device to another, the modelling of one elbow exosuit is different from one another.

A static model can be considered to estimate the tension in the cable and the length of the cable to be actuated for the desired angular position. In a static model the inertial forces and centrifugal forces that exist during the actuation of the elbow exosuit are neglected. Also, the friction forces at the elbow joint are neglected. Earlier models use trigonometry and properties of triangles to obtain the relation between joint angular position [14,15]. Some of the mathematical models study the dynamics of the exosuit in a deeper sense [16]. Although many mathematical models exist for the actuation of a cable-driven elbow exosuit, the calculations that are necessary like the tension in the cable based on the weight loaded onto the exosuit, need to be calculated individually for each device. Also, the selection of cable is based on the tension forces generated while actuating the exosuit, which should be calculated independently for each exosuit. Apart from that, the amount of cable to be released also differs from one device to other because of the design and placement of anchor point and guide point. Even though these calculations vary, the actuation of cable-driven elbow exosuit however remains the same among these devices and lies in the sagittal plane. A mathematical relation with the freedom to vary the distance between anchor and guide points, the mass of the hand and forearm will allow to generalize the computation of tension in cable and thereby torque at the motor. Also the amount of cable to be released by the motor for actuation can be calculated.

This paper describes the mathematical model that calculates the parameters which aid in the fabrication of a cable-driven elbow exosuit. This paper is outlined as follows. Section 1 discusses the state of the art, Sect. 2 defines the objectives of the work presented and Sect. 3 presents the static model developed for the cable driven elbow exosuit. Further, Sect. 4, Sect. 5, Sect. 6 presents the results, discussion and the conclusion.

2   Objectives

Several mathematical models exist for the kinematic and dynamic analysis of the available elbow exosuits. These models define the movement of exosuit and control. However, some of these models do not explicitly calculate the tension generated in the cable used to actuate the joint. This parameter would be necessary in the selection of the string for the actuation. Also, this tension parameter can be used in the selection of a motor when the pulley diameter is known. This paper targets to develop a simple mathematical model which allows for the variability in the position of actuation points and calculate the parameters required in the fabrication of an exosuit for the elbow joint.

The idea is to input the parameters of the weight of the forearm (loaded/unloaded) and distance of the actuation points from the elbow joint; and output the calculated parameters of tension force experienced by the string, length of string to be actuated for that configuration.
The objective is to develop a mathematical model that can calculate the

- Tension force in the actuating cable
- Length of the cable to be actuated for any joint position.

3   Methodology and Model

The elbow joint flexes and extends in the sagittal plane, and hence a 2D mathematical model will be suitable. During the actuation of the elbow joint, in a cable-driven exosuit, the objective is to control the angular position of the joint. The elbow flexion and extension can be controlled by varying the amount of cable looped or released over the pulley at the motor. Another parameter that is required is to know the value of tension in the cable at the anchor point. This tension value will allow us to select a cable that can bear the tension forces at each position.

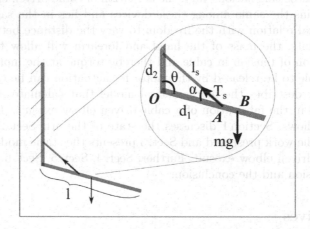

Fig. 2. Free body diagram of the Exosuit for elbow joint where m is mass of forearm and hand, T_s is tension in the cable, d_1 and d_2 are distances of guide point and anchor point from the elbow, l is the length of forearm and ls is the length of the cable between actuation points, θ is the joint angle and α is the angle made by cable with forearm

The free body diagram of the elbow joint exosuit actuation is shown in Fig. 2. Since the system forms a triangle, properties of that triangle can be used to solve for the length of the cable (l_s) for any flexion angle θ. By equating the moment generated by the force vector of mass and tension vector in the cable at the elbow joint, the tension in the cable (T_s) can be solved.

This mathematical model considers the position of the upper arm to be vertical and the elbow flexes concerning it. Also, the forearm is assumed to be homogeneous and weight is equally distributed, since it a static model. Hence, the weight of the forearm is assumed at the center of mass of the forearm. With the known value for the weight of the forearm and hand, the torque required at the elbow joint τ, to hold the forearm at an angular position 'θ' can be formulated as shown below.

$$\tau = \begin{cases} mg\frac{l}{2}\cos(-\frac{\pi}{2}+\theta), & \text{below horizontal position w.r.t ground} \\ mg\frac{l}{2}\cos(\frac{\pi}{2}-\theta), & \text{above horizontal position w.r.t ground} \end{cases} \quad (1)$$

The Eq. 1 is obtained by multiplying the perpendicular components of 'mg' and the distance from the centre of mass to the elbow joint. It can be observed that the values of τ will be the same even when the forearm is above and below the horizontal position. Hence, the torque required τ will be;

$$\tau = mg\frac{l}{2}\sin(\theta), \quad \text{for } \theta \text{ from }]0 \text{ to } \pi[\quad (2)$$

where, m - the mass of the forearm and hand
g - acceleration due to gravity
θ - flexion angle
l - length of forearm and hand

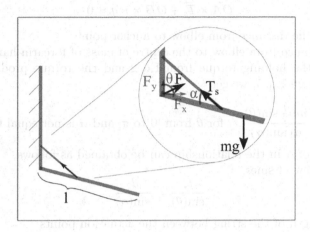

Fig. 3. Free body diagram of the forces at the elbow joint

This value of holding torque at the elbow joint τ, is the minimum amount of torque to be produced by the cable for the actuation of the forearm. The torque produced by the actuation of exosuit is because of the tension force T_s generated by the cable as shown in Fig. 2. Due to this tension force, reaction forces are also generated at the elbow joint. Since, the upper arm is assumed to be stationary, reaction forces F_x and F_y are generated at the elbow joint. From the Fig. 3, the sum of the vectors of reaction force at elbow, tension force in the cable and weight of the forearm-hand equals zero.

$$\vec{F} + \vec{T_s} + \vec{mg} = 0 \tag{3}$$

From the Eq. 3, we get the following equations of the reaction forces in x and y direction at the elbow joint.

$$F_x - |T_s| \sin(\alpha + \theta) = 0$$
$$F_y - |T_s| \cos(\alpha + \theta) = -mg \tag{4}$$

These reaction forces F_x and F_y will not produce any torque at the elbow joint. The torque is produced by the vertical component of cable tension τ_s which is $\tau_s \sin \alpha$.

The torque produced by the cable τ_s, with the known distance between the guide and anchor points from the elbow joint can be given as;

$$\tau_s = T_s \sin(\alpha) d_1 \tag{5}$$

where, T_s - Tension in the cable

d_1 - the distance between the actuation point and elbow

In static equilibrium the sum of the moment produced by the tension in the string and moment produced by the weight of forearm-hand equals zero.

$$\vec{OA} \times \vec{T_s} + \vec{OB} \times \vec{mg} = 0 \tag{6}$$

where, $\vec{OA}$ is the distance from elbow to anchor point

$\vec{OB}$ is the distance from elbow to the centre of mass of forearm-hand.

Equating the holding torque from Eq. 2 and the torque produced by the cable/string from Eq. 5, we get

$$T_s = \frac{mg\frac{l}{2}\sin(\theta)}{d_1 \sin(\alpha)}, \quad \text{for } \theta \text{ from }]0 \text{ to } \pi[\text{ and } \alpha \text{ is not equal to } 0 \tag{7}$$

The value of α in the relationship can be obtained as follows,

From the law of sines,

$$\frac{l_s}{\sin(\theta)} = \frac{d_2}{\sin(\alpha)} \tag{8}$$

where, l_s - length of the string between the actuation points

Since distances to the actuation points from the elbow d_1 and d_2 are known, the length of the string l_s can be calculated,

$$l_s = \sqrt{d_1^2 + d_2^2 - 2d_1 d_2 \cos(\theta)} \tag{9}$$

Since the length of the string cannot be negative, all the values generated from the above equation are positive.

From Eqs. 8 and 9, the relation between θ and α becomes,

$$\alpha = \sin^{-1}\left(\frac{d_2 \sin(\theta)}{\sqrt{d_1^2 + d_2^2 - 2d_1 d_2 \cos(\theta)}}\right), \quad \text{for } \theta \text{ from } 0 \text{ to } 180 \tag{10}$$

Although the equation can take values of flexion from 0 to 180°, the actual flexion of a human arm is different. From the anthropometric data the flexion of the human elbow joint for the 99 percentile man is 52° to 180° [17].

From the Eqs. 7 and 10, the tension force in the string for different weights of the forearm and hand can be calculated. Also, from the Eq. 9 the length of the string to be actuated by the motor for any given joint angle 'θ' can be calculated.

4   Results

To simulate the developed elbow exosuit actuation model, © MATLAB is used. To obtain the result from the model, the angle of the joint is considered to be flexing from 0° to 180°. An interval of 5° for the angles is taken to calculate the values of all the parameters at each position. The exosuit is considered to be unloaded and only the weight of the forearm and hand of a fully grown human is considered to be the weight that is required to be actuated. From the anthropometric data [17], the weight assumed was 2 kg at the centre of mass of the forearm for all the calculations here and results are obtained. And, the actuation points are assumed to be at a distance of 0.1 m to obtain the results when the simulations are run. The length of the forearm is assumed to be 0.3 m, which would be similar to a fully grown adult.

The joint position variable θ is related to all the other parameters involved in the actuation of the elbow joint, like the length of the cable to be actuated (l_s) and Tension in the cable (T_s) as described in the above static model. With the above-mentioned input parameters, the simulation in © MATLAB obtained the following values of Tension and length of the cable to be actuated.

The reaction forces at the elbow joint for the given configuration are predicted with the model and are shown in Figs. 4 and 5. It can be observed that reaction forces in the y direction are much higher than in the x direction at the elbow joint.

The modulus of the forces at the elbow joint for angular position from 0 to π is shown in Fig. 6. It can be pointed out that the curve is sigmoid in nature.

From the Eq. 7, the relation between the joint angle and the tension in the cable is obtained as shown in Fig. 7. The maximum tension value in the string for the assumed configuration is around 60 N. This value will be important in the selection of cable and any cable with can hold such tension force can be selected.

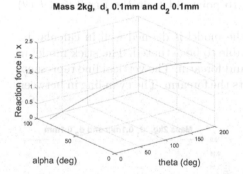

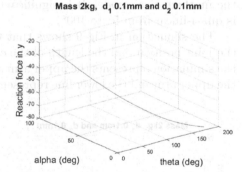

Fig. 4. Reaction force as a function if angle in x direction at elbow joint obtained from the Eq. 4

Fig. 5. Reaction force as a function of angle in y direction at elbow joint obtained from the Eq. 4

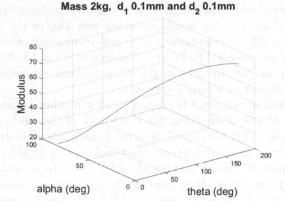

Fig. 6. Modulus of the forces F_x and F_y at the elbow joint

The relation between the variable angle θ of the elbow joint and the cable to be released/actuated by the motor is shown in Fig. 8. This graph is obtained from Eq. 9. From the figure, it can be observed that the maximum length of cable to be released by the motor in the given configuration would be 0.2 m. This parameter would be useful in designing the mechanism which should be able to release a string of 0.2 m for the complete actuation. To hold any position in between, the string to be released is also provided in the result generated by the mathematical model. It is significant to point out from the Fig. 8 that $l_s(\theta)$ is quasi-linear from 5° to 100°.

The simulation in Fig. 9 shows that the model is defined well in calculating the joint position and the length of the cable to be actuated. The stick model in the simulation represents the upper arm and forearm. The vertical line represents the upper arm and the lower line represents the forearm. The cyan line in between

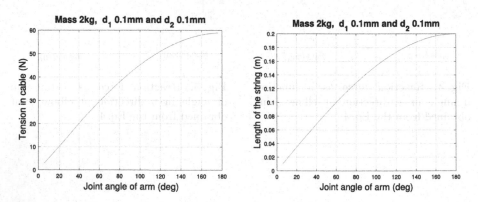

Fig. 7. Tension as a function of angle obtained from the Eq. 7

Fig. 8. Length as a function of angle obtained from the Eq. 9

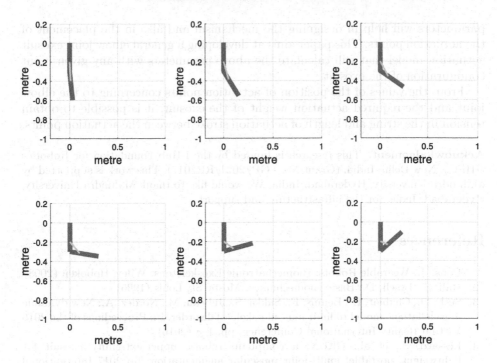

Fig. 9. Visualization of the elbow exosuit actuation shown in 2D space

represents the cable. It can be observed that when actuated the length of this cyan line is changed and it is always at tension as expected.

Although the validation of the model is not done physically, from the simulation it can be identified that the model predicts the movement of the elbow exosuit correctly.

5   Discussion

The above results provide the values of the parameters required in the fabrication of a cable-driven elbow exosuit. By changing the configuration of the exosuit, i.e., by changing the input parameters, it is possible to obtain new values for tension in the sting and actuation length of the string. By these parameters, the elbow exosuit can be designed to the newer configuration.

Future work can include the validation of this mathematical model by experimentation. Also, the approach used in developing the mathematical model to target the aid in the fabrication of an elbow suit can be adapted to a multiple DOF joint like the wrist.

6   Conclusion

In the fabrication of an elbow exosuit, it is necessary to know the tension generated in the string and the length of the string to be actuated by the motor. These parameters will help in designing the mechanism and also in the placement of the actuation points. This paper aims at developing a general elbow joint exosuit actuation model that will calculate the above parameters with any given input configuration of the exosuit.

From the values of the position of actuation points concerning to the elbow joint and the required actuation weight of the exosuit, it is possible to obtain tension in the string and length of actuation stroke between the actuation points.

Acknowledgement. This research is funded by the I-Hub Foundation for Robotics (IHFC), New Delhi, India. (Grant No. - GP/2021/RR/017). This work is supported by Mahindra University, Hyderabad, India. We would like to thank Mahindra University, Hyderabad, India, for the infrastructure and support.

References

1. Pons, J.: Wearable Robots: Biomechatronic Exoskeletons. Wiley, Hoboken (2008)
2. Hall, S., Lysell, D.: Basic Biomechanics. Mosby St, Louis (1995)
3. Seth, D., Chablat, D., Bennis, F., Sakka, S., Jubeau, M., Nordez, A.: New dynamic muscle fatigue model to limit musculo-skeletal disorder. In: Proceedings of the 2016 Virtual Reality International Conference, pp. 1–8 (2016)
4. Lessard, S., et al.: CRUX: a compliant robotic upper-extremity exosuit for lightweight, portable, multi-joint muscular augmentation. In: 2017 International Conference on Rehabilitation Robotics (ICORR), pp. 1633–1638 (2017)
5. Pont, D., et al.: ExoFlex: an upper-limb cable-driven exosuit. In: Silva, M.F., Luís Lima, J., Reis, L.P., Sanfeliu, A., Tardioli, D. (eds.) ROBOT 2019. AISC, vol. 1093, pp. 417–428. Springer, Cham (2020). https://doi.org/10.1007/978-3-030-36150-1_34
6. O'Neill, C., et al.: Inflatable soft wearable robot for reducing therapist fatigue during upper extremity rehabilitation in severe stroke. IEEE Robot. Autom. Lett. **5**, 3899–3906 (2020)
7. Kim, Y., Xiloyannis, M., Accoto, D., Masia, L.: Development of a soft exosuit for industrial applications. In: 2018 7th IEEE International Conference on Biomedical Robotics and Biomechatronics (Biorob), pp. 324–329 (2018)
8. Xiloyannis, M., et al.: Soft robotic suits: state of the art, core technologies, and open challenges. IEEE Trans. Robot. **38**, 1343–1362 (2022)
9. Thalman, C., Lam, Q., Nguyen, P., Sridar, S., Polygerinos, P.: A novel soft elbow exosuit to supplement bicep lifting capacity. In: 2018 IEEE/RSJ International Conference on Intelligent Robots and Systems (IROS), pp. 6965–6971 (2018)
10. Bardi, E., Gandolla, M., Braghin, F., Resta, F., Pedrocchi, A., Ambrosini, E.: Upper limb soft robotic wearable devices: a systematic review. J. NeuroEngineering Rehabil. **19**, 1–17 (2022)
11. Alapati, S., Seth, D.: Testing of different strings for their usability in actuation of exosuits. In: Duffy, V.G. (ed.) HCII 2022. LNCS, vol. 13319, pp. 3–15. Springer, Cham (2022). https://doi.org/10.1007/978-3-031-05890-5_1
12. Seth, D., Vardhan Varma, V.K.H., Anirudh, P., Kalyan, P.: Preliminary design of soft exo-suit for arm rehabilitation. In: Duffy, V.G. (ed.) HCII 2019. LNCS, vol. 11582, pp. 284–294. Springer, Cham (2019). https://doi.org/10.1007/978-3-030-22219-2_22

13. Li, N.: Bio-inspired upper limb soft exoskeleton to reduce stroke-induced complications. Bioinspiration Biomimetics **13**, 066001 (2018)
14. Harbauer, C., Fleischer, M., Nguyen, T., Bos, F., Bengler, K.: Too close to comfort? A new approach of designing a soft cable-driven exoskeleton for lifting tasks under ergonomic aspects. In: 2020 3rd International Conference on Intelligent Robotic and Control Engineering (IRCE), pp. 105–109 (2020)
15. Miranda, A., Yasutomi, A., Souit, C., Forner-Cordero, A.: Bioinspired mechanical design of an upper limb exoskeleton for rehabilitation and motor control assessment. In: 2012 4th IEEE RAS & EMBS International Conference on Biomedical Robotics and Biomechatronics (BioRob), pp. 1776–1781 (2012)
16. Langard, M., Aoustin, Y., Arakelian, V., Chablat, D.: Investigation of the stresses exerted by an exosuit of a human arm. In: Misyurin, S.Y., Arakelian, V., Avetisyan, A.I. (eds.) Advanced Technologies in Robotics and Intelligent Systems. MMS, vol. 80, pp. 425–435. Springer, Cham (2020). https://doi.org/10.1007/978-3-030-33491-8_50
17. Dreyfuss, H., Associates, H., Tilley, A.: The Measure of Man and Woman: Human Factors in Design. Whitney Library of Design (1993)

Experimental Research on Ergonomics Evaluation of HMDs

Kai An, Xu Wu$^{(\boxtimes)}$, Chongchong Miao, Lin Ding, and Guoqiang Sun

AVIC Aero Polytechnology Establishment, Beijing 100028, China
358964565@qq.com

Abstract. As a complex visual equipment worn on the pilot's head, HMD was a typical human-computer interaction equipment. Its ergonomic design had great impact on the safety and efficiency of personnel. Therefore, it was very important to carry out ergonomic evaluation of HMD. We proposed a comparative evaluation method of HMD ergonomics. By using Vienna Test System, pressure sensor and temperature sensor, the experiment collected the task performance, pressure measurement and temperature measurement data of personnel wearing HMD. Then the ergonomics of the two types of HMD were compared by statistical analysis. The method proposed in this study was beneficial to ergonomics evaluation of HMDs, and the data analysis results could provide references for HMD design and evaluation.

Keywords: HMD · ergonomics evaluation · task performance · pressure and thermal allocation

1 Introduction

HMD, known as Head-Mounted-Display, had played an important role in pilots' interaction in the cockpit. As the representative advanced display, HMD seemed to replace HUD (Head-Up-Display) in some ways. However, the optics features of display selection were indeed an essential consideration for cockpit design. The pilots always preferred comfortable experience with better performance of flight information processing, which was need to provide ergonomics proofs with evaluation and selection of HMDs. Therefore, an experimental study was developed to evaluate two types of HMDs in respective of behavior performance, head pressure allocation and thermal comfort under signal detection tasks.

2 Research Reviews

The head was critical composition of the human body, where the most complicated and vulnerable organs grew. The adaptability of HMDs with the pilots was a priority factor influencing flight performance and wearing comfort. Recent studies mainly concentrated on the HMD's interface design and multi-modal interaction with the pilots, but few were

V. G. Duffy (Ed.): HCII 2023, LNCS 14028, pp. 14–23, 2023.
https://doi.org/10.1007/978-3-031-35741-1_2

found in terms of the helmet pressure and thermal comfort of HMDs. Jia carried out a helmet pressure experiment to examine the impact of its weight on the pilot's neck muscles (Jia et al. 2012). Rueda studied the appropriate helmet lining structures under different conditions using simulation methods (Rueda et al. 2009). Sun analyzed the elastic modulus and Poisson's ratio of parietal bone, temporal bone and occipital bone in the human skull (Sun and Ma 1998). Further scholars conducted eye movement experiments to study the optimal comfort pressure ratio of pilot helmet (Ying et al. 2018). In thermal comfort studies, several studies experimentally analyzed the effects of sports helmets on various physiological parameters of the human body (Pang et al. 2013). Moreover, ISO/TC 159/SC 4 has proposed the "9241-300" serials of standards, which showed great interest of frontier display technology and ergonomics concern. Especially the latest released ISO 9241-380:2022 focused on HMD characteristics related to human-system interaction.

3   Methods

3.1   Experiment Design

Two designated HMDs of helicopter cockpit were selected as evaluation objects. HMD-A and HMD-B were different types of equipment in the same type of aircraft configuration. Compared to the HMD-A weighing about 3.1 kg, the HMD-B was slightly lighter (about 2.4 kg). HMD-A used EPS, sponge and cotton fabric liners, while HMD-B used EPS, sponge and COOLMAX liners.

12 participants from CAPE employees were recruited to perform Signal Detection Tests (SDTs) on VTS (Vienna Test System) platform. The experiment order was counter-balanced in Latin Square fashion. Each test lasted for 30 min with breaking interval of 10 min. Before the actual experiment, a short version of SDT was performed to obtain baseline results of each participant without wearing HMDs. The task performance indicators of this ergonomic evaluation were the Wrong Reaction and Response Time of the Signal Detection Tests (SDTs) on the VTS (Vienna Test System) platform.

The ergonomic evaluation also included pressure and thermal comfort measurements. Considering the shape characteristics of human head physiology, the pressure and temperature were not evenly distributed in the helmet when users wear HMD. Therefore, another valuable research we had conducted was to select appropriate and critical positions inside HMD and pasted pressure sensors and temperature sensors respectively. We could then use these sensors to measure the pressure and temperature of different points on the head while the user was wearing the HMD.

3.2 Experiment Task

As shown on computer screen, SDT interface contained randomly appearing black points on the white background (Fig. 1). The participants were required to press a button immediately when four nearby points were lined as a square, which was indicated the detection of signal. Both response time and wrong reaction were recorded in VTS to measure task performance of different HMDs.

Meanwhile, the helmet pressure and thermal allocation was measured by multi-modal sensors from Pliance & Ergolab supplies. Due to the current devices, the helmet pressure was adopted 10 sensors from evenly distributed positions (Fig. 2), and skin temperature was adopted only 4 sensors of coverage positions of vertex, forehead, lateral temporal, and occiput (Fig. 3). During the measurement of HMD internal pressure, the subjects were first seated in an upright posture, then wore a helmet and adjusted to the most comfortable state. After that, the ergonomics experimenter observed the stability of the data and recorded the stable pressure data after the data became stable. The thermal comfort measurement test inside the HMD was carried out synchronously with the SDT. The thermal comfort data before the execution of SDT and the thermal comfort data after SDT were recorded by the temperature sensor.

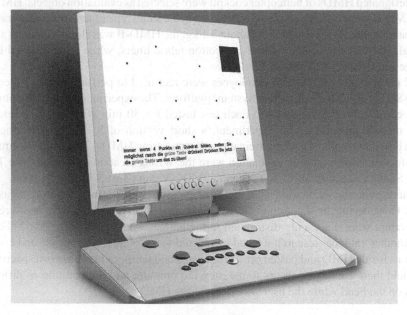

Fig. 1. SDT interface

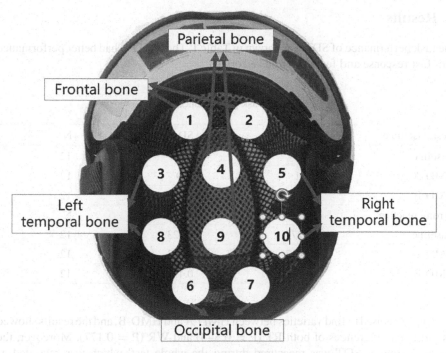

Fig. 2. Sensor positions of helmet pressure measurement

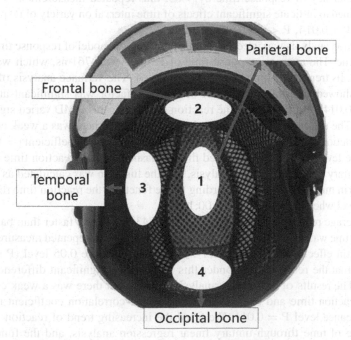

Fig. 3. Sensor positions of skin temperature measurement

4 Results

The task performance of SDT was shown in Table 1. The HMD-B had better performance with fast response and few detections errors.

Table 1. Task performance results

Response time	M (ms)	SD (ms)	N
Baseline	764	217	12
HMD-A	761	149	12
HMD-B	743	140	12
Wrong reaction	$M(\text{min}^{-1})$	$SD(\text{min}^{-1})$	N
Baseline	0.277	0.423	12
HMD-A	0.417	0.553	12
HMD-B	0.330	0.492	12

T-test was used to find varieties between HMD-A and HMD-B, and the results showed insignificant differences of both RT ($P = 0.343$) and WR ($P = 0.177$). Moreover, the response time of SDT was measured during the whole test, which was recorded as changing tendency of response time by VTS, thus repeated-measurement of ANOVA was performed to indicate significant effects of time interval on variety of response time of HMDs ($P = 0.014$; $P < 0.001$; $P = 0.029$).

Regression analysis was used to establish correlation model of response time changing with time. The average response time of HMD-A was 761ms, which was similar to baseline. Its trend over time was shown in Fig. 4. The variance analysis of repeated measures showed that the main effect of the time factor was significant at the 0.05 level ($P = 0.014$), indicating that the reaction time under this HMD varied significantly over time. The results of correlation analysis showed that there was a weak correlation between reaction time and time change, with linear correlation coefficient $r = 0.433$ and significance level $P = 0.021$. We fitted the increasing trend of reaction time over time through unitary linear regression analysis, and the function was calculated as "RT(s) = 0.003time (in mm) + 0.7177". According to the function, the reaction time reached the baseline level when the time reached 00:15:24.

The average response time of HMD-B was 743 ms, 21 ms faster than baseline. Its trend over time was shown in Fig. 5. The variance analysis of repeated measures showed that the main effect of the time factor was significant at the 0.05 level ($P < 0.001$), indicating that the reaction time under this HMD had a significant difference in time variation. The results of correlation analysis showed that there was a weak correlation between reaction time and time change, with linear correlation coefficient $r = 0.474$ and significance level $P = 0.011$. We fitted the increasing trend of reaction time with the passage of time through unitary linear regression analysis, and the function was calculated as "RT(s) = 0.004 time (in mm) + 0.6833". According to the fitting function, the reaction time reached the baseline level when the time reached 00:19:42.

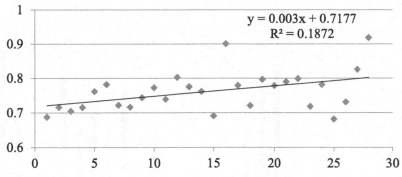

Fig. 4. Regression analysis of RT decline of HMD-A

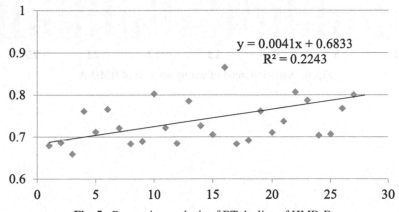

Fig. 5. Regression analysis of RT decline of HMD-B

The mean wrong reaction of HMD-A was 0.417 times, an increase of 50.5% over the baseline level (0.277 times). The variation trend of its wrong reaction over time was shown in Fig. 6. According to the results of repeated measurement analysis of variance, the main effect of time factor was significant at the 0.05 level ($P < 0.001$). This indicates that the wrong reaction of HMD-A varied significantly over time and presented a trend of periodic change.

The mean wrong reaction of HMD-B was 0.330 times, which was 19.1% higher than the baseline level (0.277 times). The variation trend of its wrong reaction over time was shown in Fig. 7. The main effect of the time factor was significant at the 0.05 level ($P < 0.001$). This indicates that the wrong reaction of HMD-B varied significantly over time and presented a trend of periodic change.

In addition, the helmet pressure and head temperature allocation were also measured and analyzed along with user experience interview. During the HMD-A test, the average pressure data of 12 subjects were shown in Fig. 8. The highest pressure values (10.02 kPa and 10.73 kPa, respectively) were found at 3 and 5 point in front of the head. The pressure values at 8 and 10 point behind the top of the head were followed by 4.34 kPa and 4.15 kPa, respectively. The pressure at 1 and 2 point on the forehead was low (4.39

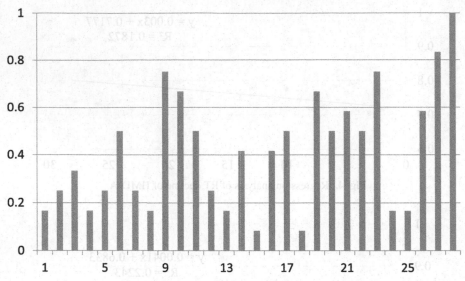

Fig. 6. Variation trend of wrong reaction of HMD-A

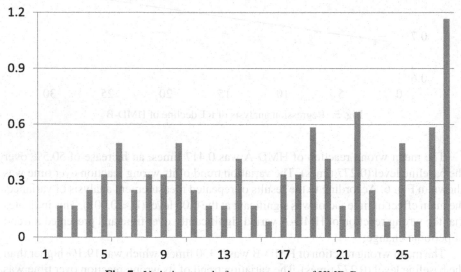

Fig. 7. Variation trend of wrong reaction of HMD-B

kPa and 2.52 kPa, respectively). The pressures measured at the remaining points were small.

During the HMD-B test, the average pressure test data of 12 subjects are shown in Fig. 9. The pressure values at 3 point (11.43 kPa), 5 point (7.04 kPa), 8 point (11.53 kPa) and 10 point (7.89 kPa) were the highest, followed by the pressure values at 1 point and 2 point (3.41 kPa and 2.75 kPa, respectively). The pressure values at other points were relatively small.

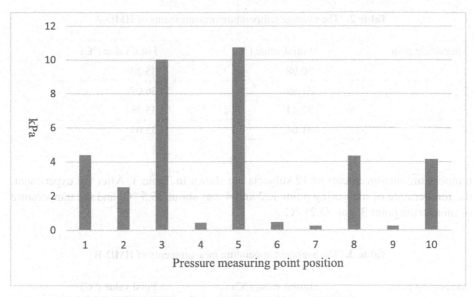

Fig. 8. The average pressure test data of HMD-A

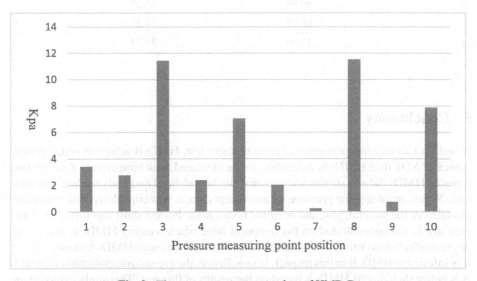

Fig. 9. The average pressure test data of HMD-B

When measuring the temperature of the HMD-A worn during the experiment, the average external temperature is 26.73 °C and always between 26 °C and 27 °C. The average temperature measurements of 12 subjects are shown in Table 2. At the end of experiment, the temperature of all measuring points was about 35.5 °C.

When measuring the temperature of the HMD-B in the wearing state, the average external temperature is 26.01 °C and always ranges from 26 °C to 27 °C. The average

Table 2. The average temperature measurements of HMD-A

Measuring point	Initial value (°C)	Final value (°C)
1	30.98	35.24
2	31.89	36.07
3	32.44	35.78
4	31.04	35.03

temperature measurements of 12 subjects are shown in Table 3. After the experiment, the temperature of measuring point 1, 2 and 4 was about 35.5 °C, and the temperature of measuring point 3 was 33.21 °C.

Table 3. The average temperature measurements of HMD-B

Measuring point	Initial value (°C)	Final value (°C)
1	30.87	35.27
2	30.68	35.25
3	28.95	33.21
4	31.79	35.71

5   Conclusions

Based on this mission performance measurement test, HMD-B achieved better performance of SDT than HMD-A. According to the measured head temperature data, the two types of HMDs did not significantly exceed the human head and body surface temperature. When analyzing the pressure measurement data, it was considered that the elastic modulus of the parietal, jaw, and occipital bones in the human skull was different. If the pressure is too concentrated on the temporal bone when wearing HMD, it may cause physiological discomfort. The pressure measurement results of HMD-A showed that it was inferior to HMD-B in this respect. In conclusion, the ergonomic evaluation of HMD-B is better than that of HMD-A based on the results of this test. This study explored the ergonomic evaluation method of HMD, but it was worth further conducting follow-up studies, such as selecting the experimental design close to the real task, and analyzing the correlation between stress and task performance.

References

ISO/TR 9241-380:2022, Ergonomics of human-system interaction - Part 380: Survey result of HMD (Head-Mounted Displays) characteristics related to human-system interaction

Jia, X.H., Mao, J.B., Wang, R.C., et al.: Effect of helmet mass and mass center on neck muscle strength in military pilots. J. Med. Biomech. **27**(4), 416–420 (2012)

Rueda, F., Cui, L., Gilchrist, M.D.: Optimization of energy absorbing liner for equestrian helmets. Part I: layered foam liner. Mater. Des. **30**(9), 3405–3413 (2009)

Pang, T.Y., Subic, A., Takla, M.: A comparative experimental study of the thermal properties of cricket helmet. Int. J. Ind. Ergon. **43**(2), 161–169 (2013)

Sun, Q.L., Ma, H.S.: Experimental study on testing of elastic modulus and Poisson coefficient for human skull. Test Technol. Test. Mach. **38**(1), 94–95 (1998)

Ying, X., Xin, Z., Ludan, Z., et al.: Research on pressure comfort of pilot's helmet. Space Med. Med. Eng. **31**(4), 452–457 (2018)

A Platform for Long-Term Analysis and Reporting of Sitting Posture

Rafael de Pinho André[✉], Almir Fonseca, Kayo Yokoyama, Lucas Westfal,
Luis Laguardia, and Marcelo de Souza

Fundação Getúlio Vargas, Rio de Janeiro, Brazil
rafael.pinho@fgv.br
https://emap.fgv.br/en

Abstract. Worldwide, recent changes in the work environment affected workspace ergonomics conditions over long periods of time. This extended period of bad ergonomic conditions hindered the ability to maintain good posture, aggravating the postural challenges of the typical office worker that spends 15 h seated each day and leading to a surge of the prevalence of lower back and neck pain. Bad posture initially leads to muscle, disc, and joint pain, and can evolve to serious conditions. Therefore, the monitoring of spatial and temporal characteristics of the hip and back is of utmost importance for injury prevention. We developed an IoT platform that employs a sensor fusion array methods to collect specific postural information during long term usage. The collected data was used to assemble a Postural Dashboard, employing data visualization and Exploratory Data Analysis (EDA) to provide descriptive statistics data and allow the investigation of a user's long-term postural patterns.

Keywords: Health and Ergonomics · IoT Computing and Sensing · Postural Data Visualization

1 Introduction

The Coronavirus pandemic has dramatically altered the work environment of a large group of workers worldwide, affecting workspace ergonomics conditions over a long period of time. Lockdown and social distancing moved the workforce from the ergonomically planned desks and chairs of our offices to the improvised beds, sofas, and dinner tables of our homes. This extended period of bad ergonomic conditions hindered the ability to maintain good posture, aggravating the postural challenges of the typical office worker that spends 15 h seated each day and leading to a surge of the prevalence of lower back and neck pain. Works, such as [17] and [12], point out a twofold increase of the prevalence of knee pain injuries, whereas works such as [3] show a threefold increase of the prevalence of lower back pain and injuries. Knee and hip pain have been associated with numerous orthopedic pathologies and injuries of the back and lower limbs. The lack of physical conditioning, a factor as common as bad ergonomic conditions during the Coronavirus pandemic, can aggravate this process. Work ergonomics encompasses diverse factors, such as chair ergonomics, desk ergonomics, screen ergonomics, lightning and body awareness. This work focuses on improving chair ergonomics and enhancing postural awareness.

Good posture, predominantly characterized by the neutral spine and knee position, with aligned shoulders, spine, and hips, improves health by reducing the stress on the joints, muscles, and ligaments, whereas bad posture initially leads to muscle, disc, and joint pain. Then, if the posture pattern is not amended, pain can evolve to serious, or even permanent, conditions affecting the blood vessels, the nerves around the spine area or the morphological development of the spine [8]. Therefore, the monitoring of hip and back pressure distribution and the spatial and temporal characteristics of hip and back positioning abnormalities is of utmost importance for injury prevention. Common methods employed by health professionals for the diagnosis of back pain are physical exams, which mostly include (a) an examination of the spine and posture, (b) the execution of simple movement patterns, such as bending or lifting the legs and (c) a reflexes, muscle strength, and sensation test. Some cases might require imaging, blood or even urine tests, which are neither accessible nor affordable to a large group of individuals.

As discussed in [15], Human Activity Recognition (HAR) research on posture information has seen an intense growth during the last ten years, with applications mostly focused on mobile healthcare and ergonomics. Researchers investigate the recognition of human movement behaviors and stationary patterns to better understand our actions and their context, helping people perform better in their daily life or professional activities. Traditionally, the equipment used to track and process these patterns and behaviors were invasive, expensive and unsuited for outdoor experiments, but the development of Internet of Things (IoT) and wearable technologies allowed researchers to investigate HAR related questions without the constrains of a laboratory environment.

We developed an IoT platform that employs a sensor fusion array methods to collect specific postural information during long term usage. The IoT platform comprises three components: a backrest monitor, a seat monitor and the controller unit. The backrest monitor is built upon a cover made of comfortable and breathable material that can be used for extended periods of time without discomfort for the user. It acquires data from the lumbar and thoracic regions of the back. The seat monitor is built upon a cover of the same material and is used to acquire data from the sacrum region of the back and the thighs. The raw data collected from force sensitive resistor (FSR) sensors and stretch sensors used on both components is streamed to an application server for processing and storage. The dataset was used to assemble a Postural Dashboard, employing data visualization and Exploratory Data Analysis (EDA) to provide descriptive statistics data and allow the investigation of postural patterns and trends.

Section Related Work presents related work and a brief literature review of HAR-related lower back studies. The design of the IoT platform, sensors deployment and replication information are shown on section Building the IoT

Platform. Section Postural Data Visualization shows the postural dashboard and data visualizations developed from the acquired data. Conclusion and future work are discussed on section Conclusion and Future Work.

2 Related Work

This section presents an analysis of research projects that collect hip, lumbar spine and thoracic spine data to support posture analysis, diagnosis and feedback. We conducted a review of the related works in four steps: (i) definition of a research question and its sub questions, (ii) formulation of a search query string, (iii) definition of exclusion criteria and (iv) completion of a quantitative and qualitative data analysis. The research question posed in this work is: What are the IoT sensor-based research projects conducted for the analysis of sitting patterns to help prevent or treat posture-related injuries? This research question was broken down into four sub-questions:

- What spinal areas were the focus of the data collection?
- What sensor fusion – types, quantities and locations of the sensors – was employed?
- Was the data employed on reports or dashboards?

We formulated a query string and executed it on relevant databases such as, although not limited to, ACM Digital Library, IEEE Xplore and Springer Link. We noticed that many works investigate upper body posture, mainly focusing on the relation of NSP (Neck/shoulder pain) and sitting posture, or propose an upper body posture recognition classifier. Although we recognize the relevance of the analysis of the thoracic and cervical spine regions for our platform, we excluded from our review all research that did not encompass lumbar spine and hip posture analysis.

After applying the exclusion criteria, we were able to group the surveyed works into three distinct research categories: postural classifiers and design and evaluation of sensors.

2.1 Postural Classifiers

In [9], researchers developed a prototype chair to collect seat and backrest data for the building of a NN (Neural Network) classifier for 11 posture classes. A similar work employed pattern recognition techniques commonly used in computer and robot vision to sitting posture classification, using a pressure distribution map [16]. A more recent work uses six flex sensors to build a posture recognition system for an office chair that can categorize between 11 posture classes employing a two-layer ANN (Artificial Neural Network) [5]. These studies, and many others such as [1,6,11], use the same approach - building a pressure sensor array and employing machine learning models classifiers. Some researchers, such as [18], evaluate the effectiveness of feedback methods for posture guidance on office chairs. Few studies provide detailed hardware or model information.

2.2   Design and Evaluation of Sensors

The work in [10] states that the use of textiles makes unobtrusive, comfortable, lightweight, and washable sensors possible. The research presents a textile pressure sensor designed for measuring pressure distribution on the human body, made from electrodes built with conductive textiles and arranged on both sides of a compressible spacer. A more recent study develops a force sensor made of piezoresistive conductive film [7]. The force sensor was designed with multiple layers and includes a conductive foil and an insulation cover, and employed on a force sensor platform. In [4], researchers fabricate an all-textile capacitive pressure sensor arrays made of a polyurethane foam, fabric and electrically-conducting yarn for chair seats and backrests. Some works, such as [2], present alternatives other than pressure sensors. A common method is the usage of POF (Plastic Optical Fiber) sensors for monitoring spinal posture.

3   Building the IoT Platform

On this Section, we describe the stages followed to develop the IoT Platform: prototyping the IoT device and implementing the IoT infrastructure for data collection.

3.1   IoT Device Prototype

On this subsection, we present the IoT prototype and the infrastructure devised to collect user postural data. To allow for the reproduction of this research, we provide detailed hardware information - types, quantities and models - for each component and comprehensive diagrams of the circuit.

We followed the prototyping principles discussed in [13], designing a low-power IoT device with only a power button that requires minimal interaction with the user. This allowed for ease and extended operation during the experiments. The prototype uses the seat and backrest to deploy the sensors, as discussed on section Introduction, and comprises three components: (i) a backrest cover that houses the lumbar and thoracic pressure sensors, (ii) a seat cover that houses the sacrum and thigh pressure sensors and (iii) an external hardware shelf, placed on the back of the chair, that houses the microcontroller and the Analog-to-Digital Converters (ADCs).

The backrest cover and the seat cover are similar components, housing the FSR sensors and allowing for the acquisition of a user's postural data. We used the FSR 402 and the FSR 406 of the FSR 400 Series, by Interlink Electronics - PTF (Polymer Thick Film) devices that exhibit a decrease in resistance as the force applied to their active surface increases - and Amphenol FCI Clincher Connectors to avoid melting or distorting the silver traces of each component. As in [14], to create a variable voltage for the ADC inputs of each sensor, we embedded twelve $3.3\,K\Omega\frac{1}{4}\,W$ static resistors in the circuit. The backrest cover houses four FSR 406 sensors and the seat cover houses eight FSR 402 sensors - their distribution is shown in Fig. 1.

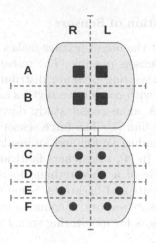

Fig. 1. FSR sensor distribution.

The main component of the external hardware shelf is the SparkFun Smart Thing Plus, a microcontroller from Sparkfun with an integrated 802.11b/g/n WiFi 2.4 GHz transceiver and a dual-mode Bluetooth® (classic and low-energy) that collects data from the seat and the backrest sensor arrays and transmits the data to the remote database. For the ADCs, we used the Texas Instruments ADS1115, a low-power 16-Bit system-in-package component that is capable of I^2C communication with the Sparkfun microcontroller. The SparkFun Smart Thing Plus microcontroller and its board, along with the ADCs and static resistors mentioned above, were positioned on a breadboard to allow for easy tinkering and replacement of components. The prototype is powered by a 2,200 mAh lithium ion battery pack by Sparkfun Electronics, that enables fast replacement for extended use. We employed single-point calibration for the FSR sensors; however, we did not take any measures to address the sensor drift over time during the test of this prototype because there no deviation was detected before each test. The schematic of the external hardware shelf is shown in Fig. 2.

Recommended ergonomic chairs are (i) made from first-class materials - breathable, cushioned and firm -, (ii) ergonomically designed - fit to the contours of a user's body, with a revolving five-point wheelbase - and (iii) adjustable - allowing for the user to set:

- Seat height, width and depth
- Seat tilt
- Backrest lumbar support and recline
- Armrests height, width and depth
- Headrest height and depth

These ergonomic chairs, although preferable, are not accessible to the majority of the world's office workforce. With affordability as a main requirement to allow for a greater reach of the proposed work, the external hardware shelf and

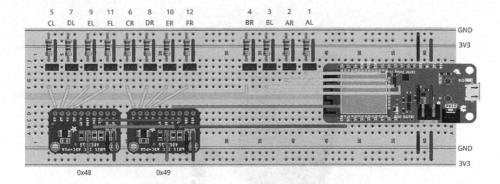

Fig. 2. Hardware diagram of the main component.

the covers were deployed over a standard desk chair with no other feature than a limited height adjustment. The prototype is shown in Fig. 3.

3.2 The IoT Infrastructure for Data Collection

The software model used in this work improves on the model proposed in [13] and [14]. The embedded software running on the microcontroller is responsible for acquiring, structuring and transmitting the sensor data over WiFi to the Firebase NOSQL database. The conceptual model is shown in Fig. 4.

During the data acquisition, a stream of unprocessed sensor signals is built from the combination of the seat's sensors and the backrest's sensors, and it is stored in the microcontroller in JSON format. This raw data combines twelve FSR sensors using 2 Hz sampling rate. During the prototype's test different sample rates up 15 Hz were evaluated - we chose the sampling that yielded the best visualization results while maintaining adequate power consumption. The JSON formatted data was periodically sent to the application server in small packages to reduce energy and data usage.

4   Postural Data Visualization

On this Section, we describe the usage of the data pipeline to devise a postural dashboard - developed with Python and the Dash Open Source Framework.

4.1   Pressure Heat Map

The standard heat map visualization depicts the average pressure measured by each sensor of the seat and the backrest during a sitting bout, representing the postural trends of the user. The graph is shown in Fig. 5.

We provide a date selector to allow for the investigation of the user's posture during specific observation ranges. This dashboard component offers an auto-play function for easy of use, and is shown in Fig. 6.

Fig. 3. Chair, seat and backrest covers

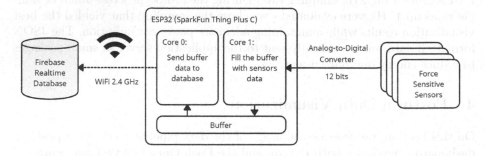

Fig. 4. Conceptual model of the IoT Platform.

Sensor data

Last update: 2023-03-06 19:52:57
☑ Heatmap ☑ Bars

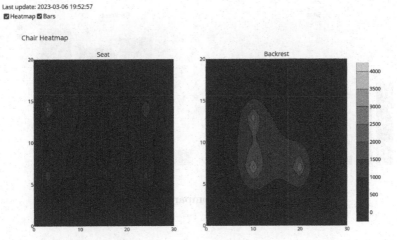

Fig. 5. Average pressure distribution.

Time interval selector

| 02/20/2023 | 02/22/2023 | 00:00:00 | 23:59:59 | 7664 frames selected |

Data per captured frame

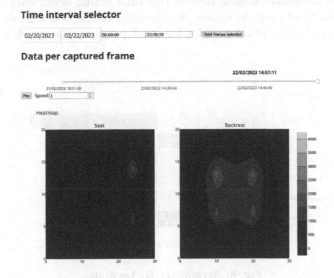

Fig. 6. Pressure distribution selector.

4.2 Pressure Comparison by Location

This graph provides information regarding each sensor of the seat and the backrest. The bars depict the pressure intensity on a chair location on a selected time frame, and the graph is shown in Fig. 7.

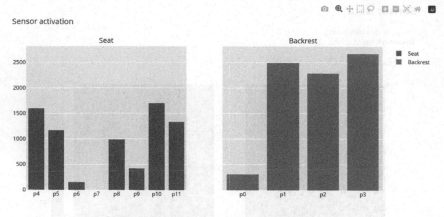

Fig. 7. Pressure comparison by location.

4.3   Asymmetry

This postural dashboard section depicts real-time sitting asymmetry of the hips and the lumbar and thoracic spines. As discussed on Section Introduction, this is one of the most important metrics for good posture. The graph is shown in Fig. 8.

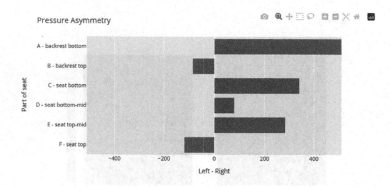

Fig. 8. Asymmetry By Location.

5   Conclusion and Future Work

This work reports an ongoing research of an IoT platform for long-term posture monitoring and reporting. The collected data is summarized in a postural dashboard, assembled to enhance the diagnosis efficacy of health professionals when treating thoracic, lumbar and hip pain and conditions. As discussed on Section Introduction, the alignment of shoulders, spine, and hips are key to maintaining good posture, and understanding the type, severity and frequency of slumping and asymmetric posture can lead to a faster and more precise diagnosis.

The current contributions to date are:

- A reproducible IoT device blueprint for lumbar and hip posture data collection;
- A platform model for exploratory data analysis using back and hip posture information for the investigation of a user's postural history; and,
- A postural dashboard tailored to help health professionals perform better physical exams and support the diagnosis process.

Currently, we are developing a new version of the IoT prototype with a sensor fusion array to allow for the exploration of the effect of different features on the posture. This new version of the prototype has improved batteries and battery management for extended usage and data collection. We are currently working with certified health professionals to devise metrics and statistical models to (i) provide diagnosis support, (ii) real-time posture feedback to users and (iii) symmetry analytics to the Postural Dashboard. For that goal, we plan on conducting an experiment with a diverse volunteer base to collect enough data to train and validate the models.

References

1. Cho, H., Choi, H.J., Lee, C.E., Sir, C.W.: Sitting posture prediction and correction system using arduino-based chair and deep learning model. In: 2019 IEEE 12th Conference on Service-Oriented Computing and Applications (SOCA), pp. 98–102 (2019). https://doi.org/10.1109/SOCA.2019.00022
2. Dunne, L.E., Walsh, P., Smyth, B., Caulfield, B.: Design and evaluation of a wearable optical sensor for monitoring seated spinal posture. In: 2006 10th IEEE International Symposium on Wearable Computers, pp. 65–68 (2006). https://doi.org/10.1109/ISWC.2006.286345
3. Freburger, J., et al.: The rising prevalence of chronic low back pain. Arch. Intern. Med. **169**(3), 251–258 (2009)
4. Gleskova, H., Ishaku, A.A., Bednár, T., Hudec, R.: Optimization of all-textile capacitive sensor array for smart chair. IEEE Access **10**, 48615–48621 (2022). https://doi.org/10.1109/ACCESS.2022.3171231
5. Hu, Q., Tang, X., Tang, W.: A smart chair sitting posture recognition system using flex sensors and FPGA implemented artificial neural network. IEEE Sens. J. **20**(14), 8007–8016 (2020). https://doi.org/10.1109/JSEN.2020.2980207
6. Ishaku, A.A., et al.: Flexible force sensors embedded in office chair for monitoring of sitting postures. In: 2019 IEEE International Conference on Flexible and Printable Sensors and Systems (FLEPS), pp. 1–3 (2019). https://doi.org/10.1109/FLEPS.2019.8792250
7. Lee, B.W., Shin, H.: Feasibility study of sitting posture monitoring based on piezoresistive conductive film-based flexible force sensor. IEEE Sens. J. **16**(1), 15–16 (2016). https://doi.org/10.1109/JSEN.2015.2480600
8. Li, C., et al.: Sagittal imbalance of the spine is associated with poor sitting posture among primary and secondary school students in China: a cross-sectional study. MC Musculoskelet. Disord. **23** (2022). Article number: 98. https://doi.org/10.1186/s12891-022-05021-5

9. Martins, L., et al.: Intelligent chair sensor. In: Iliadis, L., Papadopoulos, H., Jayne, C. (eds.) EANN 2013. CCIS, vol. 383, pp. 182–191. Springer, Heidelberg (2013). https://doi.org/10.1007/978-3-642-41013-0_19

10. Meyer, J., Arnrich, B., Schumm, J., Troster, G.: Design and modeling of a textile pressure sensor for sitting posture classification. IEEE Sens. J. **10**(8), 1391–1398 (2010). https://doi.org/10.1109/JSEN.2009.2037330

11. Mutlu, B., Krause, A., Forlizzi, J., Guestrin, C., Hodgins, J.: Robust, low-cost, non-intrusive sensing and recognition of seated postures. In: Proceedings of the 20th Annual ACM Symposium on User Interface Software and Technology, UIST 2007, pp. 149–158. Association for Computing Machinery, New York (2007). https://doi.org/10.1145/1294211.1294237

12. Nguyen, U., et al.: Increasing prevalence of knee pain and symptomatic knee osteoarthritis. Ann. Intern. Med. **155**(11), 725–732 (2011)

13. de Pinho André, R., Diniz, P.H., Fuks, H.: Bottom-up investigation: human activity recognition based on feet movement and posture information. In: iWOAR 2017 (2017)

14. de Pinho André, R., Diniz, P.H., Fuks, H.: Investigating the relevance of sensor selection: recognition of ADLs based on feet movement and posture information. In: Sensor Devices 2018 (2018)

15. de Pinho André, R., Raposo, A., Fuks, H.: Using foot and knee movement and posture information to mitigate the probability of injuries in functional training. In: Duffy, V.G. (ed.) HCII 2019. LNCS, vol. 11581, pp. 153–169. Springer, Cham (2019). https://doi.org/10.1007/978-3-030-22216-1_12

16. Tan, H., Slivovsky, L., Pentland, A.: A sensing chair using pressure distribution sensors. IEEE/ASME Trans. Mechatron. **6**(3), 261–268 (2001). https://doi.org/10.1109/3516.951364

17. Wallace, I., et al.: Knee osteoarthritis has doubled in prevalence since the mid-20th century. Proc. Natl. Acad. Sci. U. S. A. **114**(35), 9332–9336 (2017)

18. Zheng, Y., Morrell, J.B.: Comparison of visual and vibrotactile feedback methods for seated posture guidance. IEEE Trans. Haptics **6**(1), 13–23 (2013). https://doi.org/10.1109/TOH.2012.3

Design and Development of a Novel Wearable System for Assessing the Biomechanical and Psychological Risk of the Healthcare Worker

Carla Dei[1] , Giulia Stevanoni[2], Emilia Biffi[1] , Fabio Storm[1] ,
Nicola Francesco Lopomo[3] , Paolo Perego[2] , and Giuseppe Andreoni[1,2(✉)]

[1] Bioengineering Laboratory, Scientific Institute IRCCS "E. Medea", Lecco, Bosisio Parini,
Italy
carla.dei@lanostrafamiglia.it, giuseppe.andreoni@polimi.it
[2] Dipartimento di Design, Politecnico di Milano, Milano, Italy
[3] Dipartimento di Ingegneria dell'Informazione, Università degli Studi di Brescia, Brescia, Italy

Abstract. The state of emergency caused by Covid19 increased the risk of biomechanical and psychological problems among healthcare workers and assumed the need to implement a strategy to prevent these. Adopting tools for monitoring parameters related to the previously mentioned risks can be a valid solution to avoid or reduce work-related physical disorders and stress level. The present work describes the design of a multiparameter system for the hospital environment aimed to monitor the musculoskeletal effort and estimate the stress level required to the healthcare workers. The main challenge was to design a wearable system that does not obstacle or disturb the healthcare worker in his/her work activities. The final set-up is the result of a structured co-design in which doctors, nurses and therapists were involved in a focus group, in order to identify the user requirements considering the needs of each profession. The focus group also served to analyze the activities performed by each category of operators selected (nurse, physical therapist and doctors). An emerging key point was that the final device has to adapt to the healthcare operators' work routine without changing it or adding other tasks. In conclusion, the focus group allowed to collect user requirements to design a multicomponent wearable to monitor physical and mental wellbeing in healthcare workers.

Keywords: Healthcare workers · mental wellbeing · physical strain

1 Introduction

The prevention of both biomechanical and psychological risk and the health of the healthcare workers are an essential and priority element also in light of the episodes of burnout and overload that occurred during the pandemic emergency [1]. Health professionals are indeed more likely to experience mental health problems than the general population; in particular, pediatric nurses, physicians and physiotherapists show burnout, anxiety

V. G. Duffy (Ed.): HCII 2023, LNCS 14028, pp. 35–47, 2023.
https://doi.org/10.1007/978-3-031-35741-1_4

and moderate/severe depression as common mental conditions [2, 3]. The COVID-19 pandemic has exacerbated this trend, with 22% of healthcare workers experiencing moderate depression, anxiety, and post-traumatic stress disorder during its peak [4]. Extensive evidence suggests that the healthcare quality and safety strongly depend on workers wellbeing [5]. Tackling mental health problems of the working-age population is crucial because of their negative impact on individuals, families and societies [6].

For what concerns musculoskeletal disorders, they are frequent health disorders and with a great potential for production losses in healthcare professionals [7]. Nurses and physical therapists are the professionals most afflicted by these health issues due to the frequent physical contact with patients [8, 9]. These practices are indeed physically demanding, involving repetitive tasks, high force manual techniques for treating patients, techniques that exert direct pressure on certain joints during the treatment, awkward positioning of joints during certain maneuvers and prolonged constrained postures [9].

In this context, it is mandatory to prepare appropriate tools for assessing and monitoring the health of healthcare workers, even in their various functions.

For the biomechanical factors, the MAPO index has been proposed as a useful tool to assess the risk of work-related musculoskeletal disorders [10], but few applications are shown in the literature findings. About stress and psychological effort, the basic noninvasive techniques for monitoring these conditions are based on Heart Rate Variability analysis (HRV) [11] or Electrodermal activity, with several limitations due to the difficult data processing and calibration of the signals with respect to emotional state detection. Recently some methodologies using wearable systems (wristbands, smartwatches or armbands) and artificial intelligence techniques showed promising results [12]. No integrated approaches are presented.

On these premises, we have identified the need of designing a wearable system that could provide a set of quantitative measurements of different aspects of workplace ergonomics for the main involved clinical operators: medical doctors, nurses and physical therapists. The system requirements were defined by means of a codesign session conducted with a Focus Group (FG).

FG, compared to other qualitative group interview techniques, allow to collect, within the group dynamics, in-depth and enriched opinions that often remain unexplored using other data collection methods, such as individual interviews [13]. In this facilitating environment, the people recruited are encouraged to discuss different experiences and points of view to gather not only "what you think" or "what you feel", but also the underlying reasons for that behavior/thought. Participants are encouraged to talk to each other, asking questions, exchanging anecdotes and generating comments on other people's points of view and experiences; this facilitates the elaboration of ideas [14, 15]. The purpose of a FG is to investigate the motivation that influences feelings, attitudes and behaviors on a given topic; its peculiarity consists in generating in a short time a large amount of data based on the synergy of group interaction [16]. The FG methodology, formulated by Merton et al. in 1946 [17], was originally applied in the advertising and marketing field, but in recent years it has also become very popular in the healthcare field [18, 19], using group discussion to generate and collect data on a specific topic.

This paper aims at describing the co-design of a multiparameter monitoring system for the hospital environment able to monitor in real-time the time needed by each patient for her/his assistance/care, the musculoskeletal and physiological effort of the clinical operators, and the estimation of the stress level/mental effort of the health professional.

2 Materials and Methods

Participatory design was the methodology adopted for the system design in a codesign session to define the system requirements. In fact, in particular in the clinical setting where the acceptance of innovations by operators is crucial for their deployment into the clinical practice, co-design results to be a win-win model and an appropriate development strategy.

2.1 Study Setting

The authors conducted the study at IRCCS E. Medea, that is the research section of the Association "La Nostra Famiglia", a no-profit organization of social utility whose purpose is to promote and safeguard health care, education and services for people with special needs. The Medea Institute, Placed in Bosisio Parini (Lecco, Italy), Creates synergies between scientific research and clinical activity through innovative rehabilitation interventions for people with disabilities, especially in the developmental age.

The extensive experience in the rehabilitation of pediatric patients takes advantage of a close cooperation among clinicians, physiotherapists, engineers and psychologists, bridging the gap between a human centered vision and technical applications. At Medea, which is the main rehabilitation center of Association La Nostra Famiglia, there are 46 clinicians, 24 physical therapists, 55 nurses, divided into two clinical areas: the neuro-rehabilitation Unit and Psychopathology Unit.

2.2 Participants and Recruitment

The recruitment was done at the neuro-rehabilitation Unit of the Scientific Institute IRCCS E. Medea on a voluntary basis. physiatrists, nurses and physical therapists were enrolled in the study.

2.3 Data Collection and Analysis

A data collection protocol was prepared through a consultative process among three researchers. The protocol was set-up as a structured presentation (Fig. 1) and after showing a short introduction about the project and the goals, it presented the main factors, elements, component of the system: at the end of each phase the suitable tools (free interviews, think aloud, charts with body map - for the design of sensors placement, device positioning and to identify existing discomfort issues in the current situation - questionnaire with Likert scale scoring) were administered to the participants for data collection.

The protocol focused on the following specific themes:

- The expected functions and features of the wearable device, both from a design point of view, such as sizes, comfort, and aesthetics, and from a more technical one

▌Tell us your experience

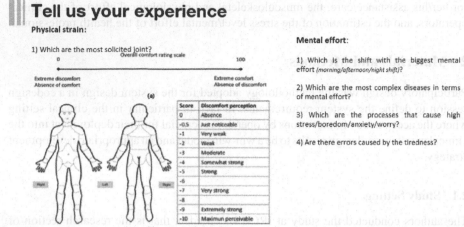

Physical strain:

1) Which are the most solicited joint?

Mental effort:

1) Which is the shift with the biggest mental effort *(morning/afternoon/night shift)*?

2) Which are the most complex diseases in terms of mental effort?

3) Which are the processes that cause high stress/boredom/anxiety/worry?

4) Are there errors caused by the tiredness?

Fig. 1. Example from the presentation shared during the focus group for the mental effort recognition.

concerning the positioning of the sensors for monitoring various parameters such as heart rate, respiratory rate, and motion detection;

- A focus on technologies useful for the collection and monitoring of data about the interaction between healthcare workers and patients, like Radio Frequency Identification (RFID) or Beacon systems;
- An indirect task analysis for each professional role involved regarding the discomfort and physical and psychological stress due to the environment, the type of work, and the procedures performed.

The FG was conducted by four researchers, one senior researcher in Design and Technology, one senior researcher in technological innovations in rehabilitation, mental health and human factors and two junior researchers with an expertise in Design.

The FG was videorecorded. Subsequently, the salient contents of the discussion were extracted according to a classical qualitative methodology of thematic analysis. Three researchers independently listened to the recordings in order to note the main themes verbalized by the focus group participants. Subsequently, the themes were discussed collectively in order to identify the qualitative dimensions capable of summarizing the themes that emerged.

At the end of the FG, each participant was asked to identify a general discomfort/fatigue rating and, on a body map, the location and intensity (on a scale from 0 to −10) of physical strain. Due to the small sample size, these data were analyzed only qualitatively.

3   Results

3.1   Participants

In the first FG, we enrolled 4 participants, 1 physiatrist, 1 nurse and 2 physical therapists. Table 1 shows demographic characteristics of the participants.

Table 1. Demographic data of the participant

Subject	Job title	Gender	Age
S1	Clinician	F	60
S2	Nurse	F	47
S3	Physical Therapist	M	37
S4	Physical Therapist	M	40

3.2   End Users' Point of View

The first outcomes of the FG consisted of the identification of three main topics that the design of such a system should consider: (1) work organization, (2) caregiver-patients interaction, and (3) caregiver-parent interaction. Figure 2 shows a map of the topic and sub-topics that emerged during the FG. Table 2 presents also some quotes related to discussed topics thanks to the think aloud process.

Work Organization. The first topic that the personnel highlighted was organization, considering several aspects: environment, time, and people. The discussion revealed that today spaces and the environment are affecting working conditions. The working environment and the climatic conditions inside cause stress. From the focus group, it emerged that bad conditions such as excessive heat or cold, and lack of natural light can affect the stress of the healthcare worker. By spaces we mean all those areas used to carry out the various medical procedures and, from the focus group, it emerged that they contribute to the discomfort of the medical staff. One of the spaces that create the most cognitive stress is the double room. Nurses complain of this type of organization because it is necessary to frequently transfer one of the two patients during routine procedures or, simply, when one of the two is sick. Other Causes of Cognitive Stress Are shared spaces during physical therapy which can lead to patient distraction and make the physiotherapy session difficult. About this factor a request for a system able to monitor environmental conditions or stress related to these conditions, or a garment with thermoregulation properties should be well considered.

Another issue that emerged during FG was the distribution of nurses during the different shifts (morning, afternoon, and evening) in relation to the number of patients they have to manage. This is another cause of both cognitive and physical stress.

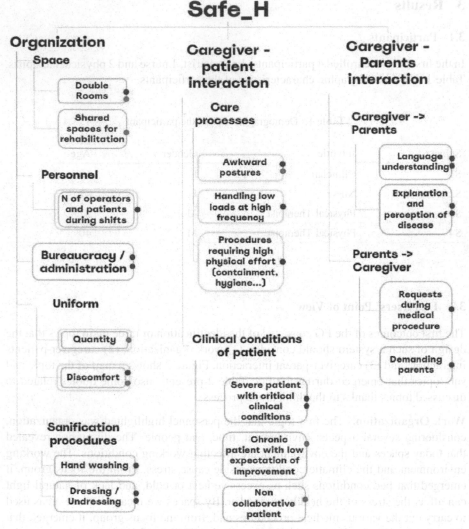

Fig. 2. Map of topics and sub-topics that emerged during the FG. Yellow boxes represent physical stress while blue boxes represent cognitive stress. The colors of the dots represent the caregiver category: purple = nurse, green = physical therapists, and blue = doctor.

Caregivers also discussed about bureaucracy and administration, that was defined as a boring task that takes up a lot of time. Due to this particular theme, caregivers concluded in the FG that they not to want a very demanding additional device.

Another aspect that affects physical and cognitive stress is related to the uniforms. During the focus group, it emerged that while Personal Protective Equipment (PPE) is provided to both nurses and physical therapists, the latter are not given uniforms. Another element of discomfort is the fabric and the shape of the uniform, both of the previously mentioned users find the uniform uncomfortable, some due to lack of pockets and some

Table 2. Identified themes and sub-theme after FG discussion

Themes	Sub-themes	Aspects	Quotes
Organization	Spaces	Double rooms	Intolerance has increased, also towards double rooms. It was already present before, now it has increased exponentially
		Shared spaces for rehabilitation	There are peaks of crowding. From 10.30 am to 2.00 pm, it may be difficult finding a room where to do the rehabilitation activity
	Personnel	Number of operators and patients during shifts	The night for some is considered a quiet moment, for others, instead, a source of stress because they are alone with 28 patients
	Bureaucracy / administration		The stress associated with bureaucracy. Covid has accentuated this aspect. Minutes lost recording
	Uniform	Quantity	Not provided
		Discomfort	The uniforms were not elastic, there were no pockets in the scrub trousers but only in the scrub top
	Sanification procedures	Hand washing	Matter of rolling up your sleeves
		Dressing / Undressing	We wear single use coat to be changed for each patient, over our uniform
Caregiver-patient interaction	Care processes	Awkward postures	When a medication lasts 45 min, in the end, even the body has been affected, perhaps even just for the position held

(*continued*)

Table 2. (*continued*)

Themes	Sub-themes	Aspects	Quotes
		Handling low loads at high frequency	In the pediatric sector, physical effort in moving patients is not very relevant because they are lightweight
		Procedures requiring high physical effort	Physical restraint: I have several colleagues who at the end of the blood sampling say that even their shoulders hurt
	Critical conditions of patient	Severe patient with critical clinical conditions	There is cognitive stress in clinical treatment of transferred patient because their therapy may be complex to manage
		Chronic patient with low expectation of improvement	Boredom especially in patients who arrive in very chronic conditions
		Non collaborative patient	A child never stands still during sampling blood
Caregiver-Parents interaction	Caregiver - > Parents	Language understanding	Not knowing the patient's language
		Explanation and perception of disease	A child with a rare disease may not be as difficult to clinically manage as a child with acquired brain damage, but it is not easy to make the concept understandable to parents
	Parents - > Caregiver	Requests during medical procedure	During the blood sampling, I heard the parent say: - I recommend only one hole!
		Demanding parents	Managing the parent, his needs and his difficulties, sometimes causes some stress

due to too rigid materials that limit movement. Finally, sanification procedures were also described as cause of mental effort. The nurse described the procedure of hand sanification, which has also some implication on uniform (that must be comfortable enough to roll up the sleeves) and the duty of not wearing rings and bracelets. Furthermore, all the caregivers underlined the need of dressing different clothes before entering the patient's room, depending on the bacterial/viral contamination of each patient and undressing at the end of the visit/procedure/rehabilitation. This was described as a cause of mental effort.

Caregiver-Patient Interaction. Secondly, the FG focused on the interaction between caregiver (clinician, physical therapist or nurse) and patient. This topic was sub-divided in two macro areas: "care process" and "clinical condition of patient".

"Care process" refers to activities and tasks requiring physical effort to healthcare operators. Researchers proposed to assess the interaction between the caregiver and the patient's bed, but it emerged the needs of assessing the interaction with the patient him/herself. The suggestion to use RFID technology was highlighted by the discussion among FG participants. Maintaining awkward postures, handling low loads at high frequency were identified as the most physically demanding activities. Hygiene, medications and containment are other activities identified as causes of physical stress.

In particular, the nurse and physical therapists involved in the focus group agreed that the lumbar and back region was the most physically stressed; for physical therapists interacting with children, the knees are also stressed because rehabilitation activities are usually performed on the floor. The overall physical strain rating scale confirmed the location of major effort (Fig. 3). Concerning the intensity of the physical strain, the physical therapists rated with -1 and -6 the knees and both with -3 the back region. The nurse indicated also the shoulders and wrists but did not rate the intensity of the strain. Finally, the clinician said they usually do not suffer from physical effort. This topic, as shown in Fig. 3, is not so relevant for the clinicians who do not experience much physical effort with patients but are more mentally/ emotionally stressed by their health condition. "Clinical condition" refers to the health condition and behavior of the patient involved in the therapy. A chronic pathology makes the clinical process more difficult to manage and requires a lot of mental effort from doctors and nurses who have to control the situation avoiding worsening of patient's condition. On the other side, a patient who does not improve or who is not cooperative can become a source of stress for the physical therapist.

Caregiver-Parents Interaction. The last theme touched during the focus group is related to the interaction between caregiver and the patient's family.

The first point debated is the caregiver's problem in relating to the parents. One problem that raised concerns is the correct explanation of the disease to the family members. Indeed, being emotionally involved, caregivers declared that they tend to perceive some diseases as more severe than they are. This problem is common to figures such as clinicians and nurses causing them cognitive stress. This situation is aggravated by the linguistic difficulty in communicating with relatives. In addition to the previously mentioned problems, there are some relational and communication problems of the relatives towards the caregiver. One of the causes of cognitive stress is due to demanding parents who continuously ask for clarifications/explanations. On the other hand, there are parents who are very demanding during some medical procedures such as blood sampling.

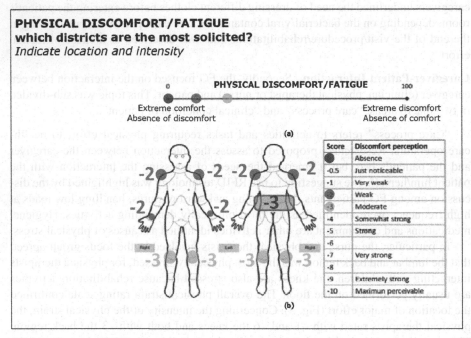

Fig. 3. The body map to investigate the level of physical discomfort/fatigue. The participant has to indicate in the image the zone afflicted by the disease, specifying the intensity (on a scale from 0 to –10). The colors of the dots represent the caregiver category: purple = nurse, green = physical therapists, and blue = doctor.

3.3 Definition of Technical Requirements

The topics emerged during the FG were used- when possible - to define the system requirements, the first outcome of the codesign activity.

Considering that all the caregivers declared to suffer from both mental and physical effort, the first requirement was to have a set of sensors to monitor physical strain and another one to measure physiological data related to mental wellbeing.

Considering the theme related to the uniform and to the environmental discomfort, the second requirement was to have a breathable garment having the following features:

– It must support the monitoring of the caring effort for the operators though an embedded RFID system (passive on patient, active on caregivers) which evaluates the average time-per-patient;
– It must support the assessment of the biomechanical load of the healthcare worker both daily and related to each single patient (triggered by RFID) using a set of inertial

units in the wearable garment and corresponding to simplified biomechanical model (e.g. by MAPO index or similar);

– It has to integrate the assessment of the operator's stress level through the recording of parameters from the Autonomous Nervous System like Heart Rate Variability (HRV) and respiratory rate. This implies the adoption of 1 ECG lead by means of at least two textile electrodes embedded in the smart garment. Measuring the HRV will provide an index for mental wellbeing assessment. Time-domain parameters will be used as main indicators of the effort/arousal status for short term analysis and feedback, while a more complete data processing adding also frequency domain parameters could be done on the off-line downloaded data.

The sensorized garment can be integrated by a wearable bracelet for clinicians and physical therapists. Figure 4 shows possible configurations for each healthcare workers.

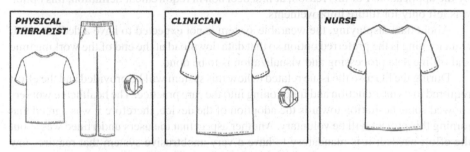

Fig. 4. Possible configurations of the monitoring system divided by healthcare operator. Each configuration is proposed taking into consideration the needs expressed by the focus group participants. The common element among these three set-ups is the sensorized t-shirt.

4 Discussion

In this work, we present the definition of the requirements phase through a codesign methodology to develop a smart solution for monitoring the physical, cognitive and organizational effort of caregivers in a rehabilitation hospital setting. In addition, the user's preferences about a data presentation interface (online for the wearable or linked app, or webapp for a remote PC connection) that can display collected data and provide some services. Codesign method (that we exploited in the form of the FG) allowed to highlight three main categories of working conditions: organization, relationship with the patient, and relationship with the patient's relatives.

Among the participants in the FG, the major interest was dedicated to the assessment of cognitive stress, which turn out to be the predominant aspect for the working environment and conditions. The stress level can be obtained through the acquisition of HRV. Another solution could have been the measurement of the electrodermal activity (EDA), but, in our case, this latter would be not applicable because of the positioning of the sensors onto the fingers. Environmental conditions certainly have impact on the work experience: FG participants identify environmental temperature as an important aspect to be added in the sensors set.

Starting from the expressed needs, the main system configuration should include sensors to monitor the cognitive stress more than the physical effort. The physical component of the work analysis is important for the nurse about the upper limbs and for the physical therapists focusing on both upper and lower limbs. To this purpose, the system could also embed some EMG sensors for the main muscles of the corresponding anatomical districts of the body (biceps and triceps for the upper limbs, rectus femuri and anterior tibialis together with gastrocnemii and soleus for the lower limbs - the gluteus maximus could be interesting but its measurement was considered too obtrusive); this datum would integrate the kinematic measures so improving the overall reliability, but it is would be worth of consideration during the development phase that it would imply a very complex hardware configuration thus affecting the ecological monitoring required by the application. For this reason, at first decision in requirement definition, this option was left only for future improvements.

About data displaying, the wearable system is not expected to have a dedicated UI. Data logging is the preferred option so that data download at the end of the working time and offline data processing and visualization is to be done.

During the FG also the issue related to how this system will be provided and the effort required to its introduction and functioning into the care practice. The healthcare workers showed some hesitation towards the adoption of the device, therefore it was agreed that joining this project will be voluntary. Another aspect that the users underlined was about the effort needed: it is mandatory to have a very unobtrusive system that requires low effort and works autonomously without requiring further actions/inputs.

Finally, data protection and privacy issues were discussed at the end of the FG: all users agreed in the anonymous data sharing to monitor the working conditions at general level and to highlight possible problems. The possibility to have a personal dashboard was considered interesting.

5   Conclusions

This paper discusses the first results from a Codesign activity to develop a wearable system for monitoring health and wellbeing condition of healthcare worker in a rehabilitation hospital setting. From a methodological point of view, we have reached a further demonstration of the validity of the participatory design approach to define reliable and precise product-system specifications. The next steps are the development of two further FGs, one targeted to the UX/UI for the visualization mode and related applications, and the second focused on the development of possible corporate welfare services.

The current activity has two limitations: the first one is the low number of participants and the second is the specificity of the hospital. In fact, the analyzed context is a pediatric rehabilitation hospital, so attention for results generalization has to be considered.

References

1. Lasalvia, A., Amaddeo, F., Porru, S., et al.: Levels of burn-out among healthcare workers during the COVID-19 pandemic and their associated factors: a cross-sectional study in a tertiary hospital of a highly burdened area of north-east Italy. BMJ Open 11(1) (2021)
2. Robba, H.C.S., Costa, A.A., Kozu, K.T., Silva, C.A., Farhat, S.C.L, Ferreira, J.C.D.O.A.: Mental health impacts in pediatric nurses: a cross-sectional study in tertiary pediatric hospital during the COVID-19 pandemic. Revista Latino-Americana de Enfermagem 30 (2022)
3. Burri, S.D., et al.: Risk factors associated with physical therapist burnout: a systematic review. Physiotherapy 116, 9–24 (2022)
4. Li, Y., Scherer, N., Felix, L., Kuper, H.: Prevalence of depression, anxiety and post-traumatic stress disorder in health care workers during the COVID-19 pandemic: a systematic review and meta-analysis. PLOS ONE 16(3) (2021)
5. Bodenheimer, T., Sinsky, C.: From the triple aim to quadruple aim: care of the patient requires care of the provider. Ann Fam Med. 12, 573–576 (2014)
6. Leka, S., Nicholson, P.J.: Mental health in the workplace. Occup. Med. 69(1), 5–6 (2019)
7. Davis, K.G., Kotowski, S.E.: Prevalence of musculoskeletal disorders for nurses in hospitals, long-term care facilities, and home health care: a comprehensive review. Hum. Factors 57(5), 754–792 (2015)
8. de Araújo Vieira, E.M., da Silva, J.M.N., Leite, W.K.D.S., Lucas, R.E.C., da Silva, L.B.: Team workload and performance of healthcare workers with musculoskeletal symptoms. Int. J. Environ. Res. Publ. Health 20(1), 742 (2022)
9. Milhem, M., Kalichman, L., Ezra, D., Alperovitch-Najenson, D.: Work-related musculoskeletal disorders among physical therapists: a comprehensive narrative review. Int. J. Occup. Med. Environ. Health 29(5), 735–747 (2016)
10. Battevi, N., Menoni, O., Ricci, M.G., Cairoli, S.: MAPO index for risk assessment of patient manual handling in hospital wards: a validation study. Ergonomics 49(7), 671–687 (2006)
11. Valderas, M.T., Bolea, J., Laguna, P., Vallverdú, M., Bailón, R.: Human emotion recognition using heart rate variability analysis with spectral bands based on respiration. Annu. Int. Conf. IEEE Eng. Med. Biol. Soc. 2015, 6134–6137 (2015)
12. Shu, L., Yu, Y., Chen, W., Hua, H., Li, Q., Jin, J., Xu, X.: Wearable emotion recognition using heart rate data from a smart bracelet. Sensors (Basel), 20(3), 718 (2020)
13. Doody, O., Slevin, E., Taggart, L.: Focus group interviews part 3: analysis. Br. J. Nurs. 22, 266–269 (2013)
14. Halliday, M., Mill, D., Johnson, J., Lee, K.: Let's talk virtual! Online focus group facilitation for the modern researcher. Res. Soc. Adm. Pharm. (2021)
15. Kitzinger, J.: Qualitative research: introducing focus groups. BMJ 311, 299–302 (1995)
16. Rabiee, F.: Focus-group interview and data analysis. Proc. Nutr. Soc. 63, 655–660 (2004)
17. Merton, R.K., Kendall, P.L.: The focused interview. Am. J. Sociol. 51(6), 541–557 (1946)
18. Wong, L.P.: Focus group discussion: a tool for health and medical research. Singapore Med. J. 49(3), 256–261 (2008)
19. Woodyatt, C.R., Finneran, C.A., Stephenson, R.: In-person versus online focus group discussions: a comparative analysis of data quality. Qual. Health Res. 26, 741–749 (2016)

The Impact of Smart Glasses on Commissioning Efficiency Depends on the Display Device Used

Daniel Friemert[1], Martin Laun[1(✉)], Christopher Braun[1], Nicolai Leuthner[1],
Rolf Ellegast[2], Christoph Schiefer[2], Volker Harth[3], Claudia Terschüren[3],
Kiros Karamanidis[4], and Ulrich Hartmann[1]

[1] Department of Mathematics and Technology, Koblenz University of Applied Sciences,
Joseph-Rovan-Allee 2, 53424 Remagen, Germany
laun@hs-koblenz.de

[2] Institute for Occupational Safety and Health of the German Social Accident Insurance, 53757
Sankt Augustin, Germany

[3] Institute for Occupational and Maritime Medicine (ZfAM), University Medical Centre
Hamburg-Eppendorf (UKE), Hamburg, Germany

[4] Sport and Exercise Science Research Centre, School of Applied Sciences, London South Bank
University, London, UK

Abstract. As the digitalization of the industry moves forward, some technologies are awarded the role of high-impact technologies, which could change the way this industry works for good, setting new standards for productivity. Popular literature and everyday news feed often deem smart glasses as one of these critical technologies to change the world of many industries, especially the world of logistics. The purpose of this study was to examine the impact of utilizing smart glasses on work process and efficiency in the context of order picking in a controlled laboratory setting. A study comparing the errors and performance rates of 26 adults in a simulated picking task using three different smart glasses, a tablet, and a handheld scanner for visual instructions was conducted. A repeated measures ANOVA was conducted to examine the commissioning times. On average, the fewest errors were made with the tablet. Regarding the assistance systems, the fastest gripping time corresponded to the tablet ($9.57 \, s \pm 2.16 \, s$). In the statistical analysis, there were significant differences between the smart glasses in terms of picking and gripping times. The observed effects presented in this study are dependent on the hardware implementation. This means that the results of other studies on the efficiency of smart glasses must be thoroughly evaluated, focusing on the model type, and should not be generalized to smart glasses in the logistics industry.

Keywords: Smart Glasses · Human-Computer-Interaction · Efficiency

1 Introduction

The number of studies assessing the efficacy of smart glasses in the workplace is limited, and the results are partially inconsistent (Friemert et al. 2020; Günthner et al. 2009; Holz et al. 2020; Laun et al. 2022; Lee and Hui 2018; Rejeb et al. 2021; Rodriguez et al. 2021;

© The Author(s), under exclusive license to Springer Nature Switzerland AG 2023
V. G. Duffy (Ed.): HCII 2023, LNCS 14028, pp. 48–57, 2023.
https://doi.org/10.1007/978-3-031-35741-1_5

Stelter 2019). Vidovič and Gajšek (2020) focused on pick errors that occur during the use of pick-by-vision systems. They aimed to evaluate the impact of smart glasses on the error rate and type of error. A literature review and laboratory study were conducted to address their research question. Only two studies have utilized multiple pick-by-vision systems. The literature review revealed that error rates ranged from 0% to 9.75%. Vidovič and Gajšek (2020) concluded that pick-by-vision systems positively affect the error rate as they enable early detection. The nature of the errors was found to be dependent on the configuration of the systems. Theoretically, the systems could be extended by multiple control phases to reduce the number of errors to zero. Theis et al. (2015) studied the effect of different display types on processing times during an assembly task. They found that the display type significantly influenced work performance, measured in terms of task completion time. Ishio et al. (2017) investigated the impact of smart glasses on work efficiency during information search tasks. Their primary focus was to determine if the efficiency improvement depended on the user's age. Participants received visual search tasks with information projected onto the smart glasses, as well as a control condition with the information presented on paper. Results showed that while the percentage of correct answers was similar for all age groups when using paper instructions, the rate of correct answers was significantly higher for all groups when using smart glasses. Kim et al. (2019) concluded that a graphical representation of information reduced task completion time and decreased the number of errors compared to a text-based representation. In their study, Rodriguez et al. (2021) sought to determine the impact of instruction delivery method on performance and usability during a building task. A sample of 63 participants was randomly assigned to one of three experimental conditions, which involved the use of paper instructions, step-by-step text instructions presented on smart glasses, and step-by-step text and auditory instructions presented on smart glasses. The results indicated that the task was completed more efficiently with the paper instructions compared to the two forms of digital instruction. However, few empirical studies have been conducted to examine the impact of various assistance systems on reducing picking errors, improving picking and grasping time. This exploratory study is intended to increase understanding of the impact of various assistance systems on efficiency and serve as a starting point for further research in this area.

2 Methods

2.1 Participants

In this study, 26 subjects (21 males and 5 females) with a mean age of 35.0 ± 10.3 years and a range of 16 to 55 years participated after providing written informed consent. Two subjects were excluded from the evaluation due to language difficulties. The mean height of the subjects was 174.1 ± 9.2 cm, and the mean weight was 80.7 ± 19.7 kg. Eight subjects reported having a prior medical condition. Most of the participants were right-handed (23 out of 24), with one being left-handed. Ten subjects reported having a visual impairment, but none of them relied on visual aids during the measurements. Thirteen of the subjects were not native German speakers, but they had an average of 13.2 ± 10.8 years of experience with the language. Six participants had no school-leaving qualification, four had a secondary school leaving certificate, seven had a secondary modern school-leaving certificate, two had a general higher education entrance qualification, and five had a university degree. Eighteen of the subjects had prior experience in logistics, averaging 5.2 ± 7.2 years. None of the participants had prior experience with smart glasses.

2.2 Experimental Design and Task Description

In this study, we employed three monocular smart glasses, a tablet, and a handheld scanner. The tablet and handheld scanner served as reference systems for the smart glasses and were used for comparison as they are common systems for order picking. The smart glasses used were two from the manufacturer Vuzix: the Vuzix M400 (M400) and the Vuzix Blade (Blade), and the Google Glass Explorer Edition (Glass). All three smart glasses have displays for presenting virtual information, with the Blade and Glass having see-through displays. The tablet used was the Lenovo Tab M10, and the handheld scanner was the MC3300 model from Zebra. The smart glasses and tablet were all connected to a Proglove Mark 2 scanner glove for scanning purposes. All systems utilized the same custom software.

The study was conducted in a mock-up order picking workspace, with a square area of approximately 18 m^2. It consisted of six shelves, two in the center and four on the sides, as illustrated in Fig. 1. The starting base was located in one of the corners of the room, and shelves were identified by ascending numbers from 1 to 6. Each shelf was divided into four compartments identified by capital letters A to D, where A represents the top shelf and D represents the bottom shelf. The warehouse was stocked with 48 different small products, each assigned a code and placed on the shelf below in a fixed place system.

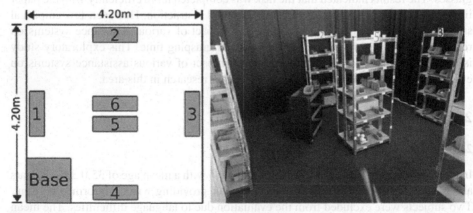

Fig. 1. Schematic (left) and real representation (right) of the picking workstation. The experimental setup is displayed from the base's point of view, which corresponds to the starting point of every picking task. With the wheeled conveyance device each of the six shelves is approached once within a picking task.

At the beginning of the measurement day, each participant was administered an introductory questionnaire, followed by instructions. The participants then performed a specific picking task using each of the five assistance systems. After using each assistance system, a questionnaire was completed. This was followed by a ten-minute break. After the final break, the participants completed a final questionnaire. The use of the assistance systems was randomized according to the Latin Square design, with the order of the five different picking tasks being identical for each participant. The picking task was performed manually using the picker-to-goods method. The task consisted of eight orders, each requiring the picking of six products. Across all assistance systems, each of the 48 total products was picked once. Within each order, one product had to be picked from each of the six shelves. The order of the shelves was randomized. The participants were equipped with a wheeled conveyance device and used the tablet, which was placed firmly transversely on the device, to display the task information conveyed via the assistance system. This information included the shelf number, compartment identification, product name, and quantity, and was displayed in the same manner for all assistance systems.

Participants received feedback on whether they had scanned the correct product, and the information for the next product was provided after a successful scan. The assistance systems were solely controlled through scanning, and before the picking task, participants had to perform a practice trial with each system. The order of the picking task was as follows: the participant started at the base and moved to the designated shelf with the wheeled conveyance device, where the product to be picked was scanned and the corresponding number of pieces were taken and stored in a box on the device. The participant repeated this process until all six products of an order were picked, then returned to the base, where the timing ended and the order was completed. The order was checked for accuracy, but the participant was not informed of any errors, and this was repeated until the entire picking task was completed.

2.3 Data Analysis

The objective of this study was to determine the effectiveness of various assistance systems through the evaluation of objective parameters, including picking and gripping times and picking errors. The picking time was defined as the total duration required for scanning and placing items into a carrier box. The subjects performed five picking tasks in a fixed order, with the recorded parameters presented in relation to these tasks. Each task consisted of eight picking times for each assistance system, which were then averaged to obtain a single picking time per subject per assistance system. To assess the existence of a learning effect on picking tasks, the duration of the measurements was analyzed. The assistance systems were deployed in five randomized sequences, and a linear trend line correction was utilized to ensure comparability between the systems with regards to errors, picking times, and gripping times. The correction was adjusted for the fifth task, which was believed to exhibit the maximum learning effect. The gripping times were analyzed using the seventh and eighth orders of each respective task to determine the maximum learning effect for each assistance system, yielding an average gripping time. The time intervals were calculated using the Widaan software, resulting in an average of twelve picking times per subject per assistance system.

2.4 Statistics

The errors were analyzed using descriptive analysis. The picking and gripping times were subjected to a repeated measures analysis of variance (rmANOVA), with the assistance systems serving as the factor levels and the significance level set at $\alpha = 0.05$. The normality of the picking and gripping times was assessed using the Shapiro-Wilk test ($\alpha = 0.05$), and sphericity was assumed based on the results of the Mauchly test ($\alpha = 0.05$). In the event that the rmANOVA revealed statistically significant differences, post-hoc tests were conducted. The Spearman correlation method was utilized to examine linear correlations between parameters such as the age and logistics experience of the subjects and the mean picking times ($\alpha = 0.05$). Given the exploratory nature of the study design, no adjustments were made to the significance level of the statistical tests. The statistical analysis was conducted using IBM-SPSS-Statistics 27 software.

3 Results

3.1 Errors

During the measurements, the 24 subjects completed 5760 picks, during which 88 errors were recorded. On average, each subject made $F = 0.73 \pm 0.75$ errors per picking task (for 48 picks), with almost 94% of the errors being quantity errors. Occasionally, an incorrect product was also picked. The first picking task accounted for 28.4% of the total errors, while only 9.1% could be attributed to the last task (refer to Table 1). The correction for the observed learning effect is used to calculate the mean errors (f^*) across all subjects for each assistance system. On average, the highest number of errors was made with the glass (0.58 ± 0.97) and the fewest with the tablet (0.25 ± 0.34). The corresponding mean values and standard deviations are listed in Table 2. The mean values are presented as error rates, which refer to 48 picks and are expressed as a percentage. Thus, for each assistance system, the error rate is a maximum of 1.21%.

3.2 Times

The average picking time for the first picking task was 117.04 ± 24.71 s, while for the last task it was 94.13 ± 17.98 s (refer to Table 1). The observed learning effect is depicted in Fig. 2. The correction was used to calculate the average picking time (t^*) across all test subjects for each assistance system (refer to Table 2). On average, picking was fastest with the tablet (87.78 ± 17.21 s) and slowest with the M400 (95.96 ± 19.48 s), as shown in Fig. 2.

The results of the repeated measures ANOVA indicate that there is a statistically significant difference in the picking times among the assistance systems ($F(4, 92) = 4.35$, $p = 0.003$, $\eta^2 p = 0.16$). The post-hoc tests reveal that there are significant differences ($p < 0.001$) in picking times between the tablet and the M400 (-8.18 95% CI [-12.02, -4.34]), the Glass and the M400 ($p = 0.005$, -6.09, 95% CI [-10.13, -2.06]), and the Blade and the M400 ($p = 0.019$, -4.81, 95% CI [-8.76, -0.87]).

Table 1 presents the average gripping times for the first and last tasks, respectively, 11.85 ± 2.79 s and 10.59 ± 2.2 s. The learning effect is depicted in Fig. 3. The results

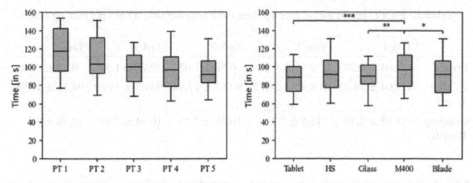

Fig. 2. Picking time t per picking task PT (left) and picking time t* per assistance system (right) in seconds. Based on the observed trend of the picking time with respect to PT, a correction was made leading to the picking time t*. The statistically significant differences were annotated using asterisks (* $p < 0.05$, ** $p < 0.01$, *** $p < 0.001$).

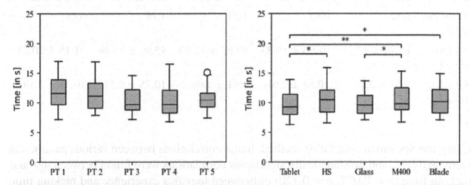

Fig. 3. Gripping time tG per picking task (left) and gripping time tG* per assistance system (right) in seconds. The corrected gripping time tG* is a result of the observed trend of the gripping time tG with respect to PT. The statistically significant differences were annotated using asterisks (* $p < 0.05$, ** $p < 0.01$, *** $p < 0.001$).

show that the fastest gripping time was recorded for the tablet (9.57 ± 2.16 s) and the slowest for the M400 (10.75 ± 2.57 s), as illustrated in Fig. 3.

The results of the repeated measures analysis of variance (rmANOVA) indicate a significant difference between the assistance systems in terms of gripping time ($F(4, 92) = 3.75$, $p = 0.007$, $\eta^2 p = 0.14$), with the effect size being classified as large. The post-hoc tests show significant differences in the gripping times between the tablet and the M400 ($p = 0.003$, -1.18, 95% CI $[-1.93, -0.43]$), the tablet and the HS ($p = 0.017$, -1.07, 95% CI $[-1.93, -0.21]$), and the tablet and the Blade ($p = 0.030$, -0.74, 95% CI $[-1.40, -0.08]$). Additionally, a significant difference ($p = 0.033$) is observed between the Glass and the M400 (-0.84, 95% CI $[-1.60, -0.07]$).

The mean percentage of gripping times tG* relative to picking time t* for the different assistance systems falls within a range of 1.85%. The tablet has the lowest mean percentage of gripping time ($63.95 \pm 3.70\%$) and the M400 has the highest ($65.80 \pm 4.97\%$).

Table 1. Error f (per 48 picks), picking time t and gripping time tG in s per picking task.

	Task 1	Task 2	Task 3	Task 4	Task 5
Error f	1.04 ± 1.30	0.96 ± 1.12	0.58 ± 1.02	0.75 ± 1.39	0.33 ± 0.70
Picking Time t	117.04 ± 24.71	108.96 ± 24.25	99.67 ± 17.94	95.83 ± 19.69	94.13 ± 17.98
Gripping Time tG	11.85 ± 2.79	11.5 ± 2.77	10.38 ± 2.26	10.44 ± 2.68	10.59 ± 2.2

Table 2. Error f* (per 48 picks), error rate, picking time t* and gripping time tG* in s per assistance system.

	Tablet	HS	Glass	M400	Blade
Error f*	0.25 ± 0.34	0.31 ± 0.48	0.58 ± 0.97	0.57 ± 0.73	0.33 ± 0.65
Error rate [%]	0.52	0.64	1.21	1.18	0.68
Picking time t*	87.78 ± 17.21	91.96 ± 19.23	89.87 ± 15.80	95.96 ± 19.48	91.15 ± 20.15
Gripping time t_G*	9.57 ± 2.16	10.64 ± 2.61	9.91 ± 1.98	10.75 ± 2.57	10.31 ± 2.39

Using the Spearman correlation method, linear correlations between various parameters were analyzed, and no statistically significant correlations were found between age and picking time ($\rho = 0.077$, $p = 0.720$) or between logistics experience and picking time ($\rho = 0.128$, $p = 0.550$).

4   Discussion

The results of the study indicate that there is no significant difference in efficiency between smart glasses and reference systems. The error rate for the assistance systems was found to be within a range of 0.52–1.21%. The lowest error rates were observed in the reference systems. This study did not apply weighting to the errors, as the weighting is expected to vary among companies. Companies must evaluate the investment costs of implementing the new technology, the operational costs that include error rate costs, and the increase in profit resulting from possible increases in efficiency. Other studies report error rates within a similar range for pick-by-vision-based assistance systems in order picking (Vidovič and Gajšek 2020). In the industry, the typical error rates for conventional picking methods (excluding pick-by-vision) are around 0.4% on average, with an error rate of 0.1% being considered optimal (Günthner et al. 2009). The error rates found in this study exceed the error rates of conventional picking systems. It is typical to see higher error rates in laboratory conditions (Günthner et al. 2009). One possible factor is the experience of the subjects, of which 18 out of 26 in this study had picking experience. In addition, the subjects are required to be highly focused due to the short path times and frequent consecutive picks (Reif 2009). Picking small individual parts, as commonly found in the warehouse in this study, can also increase the likelihood of errors. The results of the study suggest that with increased usage of the assistance systems, a decrease in error rate can be expected. On average, each assistance system was used for approximately 20 min. There were variations in the error rate among the smart glasses. The Blade had an error rate within the range of the reference systems, while the M400 and the Glass showed almost double the number of errors. The smart glasses were comparable in terms of control and software, as they were identical. However, the Blade displayed information directly in the user's field of vision, while the M400 and Glass had their displays in the upper right area, which required additional effort for the user to view. Further research is necessary to explore this issue. A uniform difference between the reference systems and the smart glasses in terms of picking time is not discernible. A significant difference was observed between the tablet and the M400, with the latter being the slowest assistance system. The HS was the only assistance system that did not allow for hands-free work, but there were no significant differences found between it and the other assistance systems. Our study does not confirm the advantage of hands-free working, which is commonly expected from the use of smart glasses. The comparison of the smart glasses among each other showed significant differences between the M400 and the other two. Picking was significantly slower with the M400, which was also the heaviest of the three and had occasional slipping problems that required repositioning by the subject. This issue may be related to the weight distribution of the M400. The display of the M400, which was connected directly to the right temple and could be adjusted in three different axes, was occasionally changed by repositioning and needed to be corrected. Such problems were not observed with the Blade and the Glass, which did not have any adjustment options or only had one axis of adjustment, respectively. No uniform difference was observed between the reference systems and smart glasses in terms of grasping time. Significant differences were found between the tablet and the M400 and between the HS and the Blade. The hands-free mode of operation with the tablet may have enabled faster grasping compared to the HS, which had to be put down occasionally during the process. The supposed advantage of hands-free operation with the M400 and the Blade may have been relativized by other factors, leading to significant differences. Furthermore, a significant difference was observed between the Glass and the M400. The reason for this difference is unclear, but it is consistent with the significant difference found between these two systems in terms of picking time. Overall, the M400 was found to have the slowest picking time. Typically, grasping times are within a range of 2 to 10 s (Reif 2009). The grasping times with all the assistance systems were towards the upper end of this range, which may be attributed to several factors such as the repeated picking of small parts. The picking time can be analyzed into its component elements, which include the base time, dead times, gripping time, and travel time across all items in an order (Reif 2009). According to the VDI Guideline 3657, the gripping time typically constitutes 25 to 40% of the picking time. However, in the study, the gripping time accounts for 65% of the total picking time for all assistance systems. This higher value is likely a result of the study design, which eliminates the base time and minimizes travel times. Despite having the fastest overall picking time, the tablet has a similar proportion of gripping time to the other assistance systems, indicating that the improvement in picking time is not solely due to a reduction in gripping time, but also a reduction in dead times and/or travel time. A learning effect is observed in both the error rate and the picking and gripping times. The cause of this effect is unclear but may be attributed to the consistent use of identical software across the assistance systems and the unchanging experimental setup and task structure throughout the study. It is possible that the subjects became acclimated to the factors influencing the learning effect over the course of the measurement period. Additionally, it should be noted that the study's results are limited by the fact that the effects of smart glasses were only analyzed after a thirty-minute usage period. Therefore, it remains uncertain if the findings can be generalized to scenarios where individuals use the technology for extended periods of time.

5 Conclusion

In the current study, the efficacy of five different assistance systems, including three smart glasses, in a laboratory setting was evaluated using a mixed group of subjects. The results of the study indicate that making generalized conclusions about the efficiency of smart glasses in the context of order picking is limited, even under controlled laboratory conditions. The findings suggest that the use of new technical components does not necessarily result in improved process performance. Future evaluations of the efficiency of assistance systems should focus on specific models rather than device type. Additionally, in large warehouse operations, the interaction with the assistance system is only a minor portion of the working time and is dominated by other factors such as travel times between products. Hence, the potential benefits of using smart glasses may not be realized in these environments. It is recommended to implement strict scientific testing criteria prior to the introduction of new technology in order to obtain reliable results regarding efficiency and error rates.

Availability of Data and Materials. The datasets used and analyzed during the current study are available from the corresponding author on reasonable request.

Declaration of Competing Interest. All authors declare that they have no known competing financial interests or personal relationships that could have appeared to influence the work reported in this paper.

Acknowledgments. This study was funded by the German Employers' Liability Insurance Assocation 'BGHW' (Berufsgenossenschaft Handel und Warenlogistik).

References

Friemert, D., et al.: What is the state of smart glass research from an OSH viewpoint? a literature review. In: Duffy, V.G. (ed.) HCII 2020. LNCS, vol. 12199, pp. 346–364. Springer, Cham (2020). https://doi.org/10.1007/978-3-030-49907-5_25

Günthner, W.A., Blomeyer, N., Reif, R., Schedlbauer, M.: Pick-by-vision: augmented reality supported order picking. Res. Rep. Technische Universität München (2009)

Holz, A., Herold, R., Friemert, D., Hartmann, U., Harth, V., Terschüren, C.: Zentralblatt für Arbeitsmedizin, Arbeitsschutz und Ergonomie **71**(1), 24–28 (2020). https://doi.org/10.1007/s40664-020-00394-7

Ishio, H., Kimura, R., Miyao, M.: Age-dependence of work efficiency enhancement in information seeking by using see-through smart glasses. In: Proceedings of the 12th International Conference on Computer Science and Education (ICCSE) (S. 107–109). Springer, Houston (2017)

Kim, S., Nussbaum, M., Gabbard, J.: Influences of augmented reality head-worn display type and user interface design in performance and usability in simulated warehouse order picking. Appl. Ergon. **74**, 186–193 (2019). https://doi.org/10.1016/j.apergo.2018.08.026

Laun, M., Czech, C., Hartmann, U., Terschüren, C., Harth, V., Karamanidis, K., Friemert, D.: The acceptance of smart glasses used as side-by-side instructions for complex assembly tasks is highly dependent on the device model. Int. J. Indus. Ergon. 90, 103316 (2022). ISSN 0169-8141. https://doi.org/10.1016/j.ergon.2022.103316

Lee, L.-H., Hui, P.: Interaction methods for smart glasses: a survey. IEEE Access **6**, 28712–28732 (2018). https://doi.org/10.1109/ACCESS.2018.2831081

Reif, R.: Entwicklung un Evaluierung eines Augmented Reality unterstützten Kommissioniersystems. Dissertation, TU München (2009)

Rejeb, A., Keogh, J.G., Leong, G.K., Treiblmaier, H.: Potentials and challenges of augmented reality smart glasses in logistics and supply chain management: a systematic literature review. Int. J. Prod. Res. 1–30. Taylor & Francis (2021)

Rodriguez, F.S., Saleem, K., Spilski, J., Lachmann, T.: Performance differences between instructions on paper vs. digital glasses for a simple assembly task. Appl. Ergon. **94**, 103423 (2021). https://doi.org/10.1016/j.apergo.2021.103423. 5, Epub 8 April 2021, PMID: 3383952

Stelter, R.: Kommissionierung – Eine Analyse von aktuellen Kommissionierverfahren unter besonderer Berücksichtigung ihrer Effizienz. Schriftenreihe des Lehrstuhls für Logistikmanagement Nr. 1, Universität Bremen (2019)

Theis, S., Mertens, A., Wille, M., Rasche, P., Alexander, T., Schlick, C.: Effects of data glasses on human workload and performance during assembly and disassembly tasks. In: Proceedings of 19th Triennial Congress of the IEA, Melbourne (2015)

Vidovic, E., Gajsek, B.: Analysing picking errors in vision picking systems. Logistics Sustain. Transp. **11**(1) (2020). https://doi.org/10.2478/jlst-2020-0006

Digital Twin Modelling for Human-Centered Ergonomic Design

Micah Wilson George[1]([✉]), Nandini Gaikwad[1], Vincent G. Duffy[1],
and Allen G. Greenwood[2]

[1] Purdue University, West Lafayette IN-47906, USA
{georg179,ngaikwad,duffy}@purdue.edu
[2] FlexSim Software Products, Canyon Park Technology Center, Orem UT-84097, USA
allen.greenwood@flexsim.com

Abstract. Simulation turns out to be one of the most important aspects of ergonomics, as it allows testing the interaction of the people and the system before they are brought into effect to improve the design process. Digital Twin is a concept that utilizes simulation to implement the representation of the model of a system or product in a virtual manner so that its purpose and working can be analyzed and evaluated before bringing it into the real world to serve its purpose as expected. This report focuses on how Digital Twin is a powerful industrial tool and explains its distinct properties along with its applications through case studies that provide explanations for the required methodology to implement Digital Twin in a simulation software called FlexSim. The results show how important it is in today's world to carry out proper simulations, i.e., implementing the Digital Twin to provide critical solutions in workplace ergonomics and other areas.

Keywords: Simulation · Digital Twin · Ergonomics

1 Introduction

Simulation refers to the replication of any system or process occurring in the real world, in a virtual environment. The evolution of the world has brought about a change in how we can perceive and predict the goals of engineering. Simulation enables one to visualize how their outcome would look or function in the real world. It helps in analyzing the performance and efficiency of the products/machines/systems which in the industry, help in the optimization of outputs, in turn leading to profitability. It is a powerful tool that offers an opportunity to study practical industrial systems in a laboratory environment with plenty of room for experimentation. Digital Twin makes use of this simulation for the virtual representation of real-world processes and systems. Its basic utilization is for the purpose of simulation of systems, testing of systems, integration, and keeping a check on them, along with ensuring their maintenance for an acceptable working lifecycle to produce efficient and optimal outputs.

The basic component of a Digital Twin is the simulation model which is synthesized using simulation software that enables engineers to fabricate appropriate representation

V. G. Duffy (Ed.): HCII 2023, LNCS 14028, pp. 58–69, 2023.
https://doi.org/10.1007/978-3-031-35741-1_6

of the processes and systems in a computer-generated environment, regulated with the help of mathematical equations and data which are already inbuilt into the simulation software. Proper conclusions can be derived after observing the interaction between the models and the real system. These can be further analyzed to implement the required changes and improvements to guarantee the better working of the system and to provide finer performance values. There are various simulation softwares which are available these days. Some of them are FlexSim, Arena, Solidworks, Autodesk Fusion 360, Solid Edge, Simulink, Ansys, SIMIO, etc.

Digital Twin in ergonomics, provides the ability to test the interaction of the people and the system before they are brought into effect to increase the optimality. This stands by what is said in Chapter 26: Mathematical Modeling in Human-Machine System Design and Evaluation [1] of the Handbook of Human Factors and Ergonomics: "Engineers want to know why certain phenomena occur in a real system. With simulation, we can deconstruct the system and take a partial, or even microscopic examination of system behavior to determine why a phenomenon occurs. We can also control system input or output and identify system properties from their transfer function."

In this report, emphasis has been provided on the FlexSim simulation software and how it utilizes the concept of Digital Twin to understand its effects in the field of ergonomics and the whole industry in general. There are numerous recent documentations based on Digital Twin which make it evident that there is a significant amount of research and development going on in this domain. A few of the articles have been reviewed below which have contributed to the successful completion of this report all the while maintaining the integrity of the information.

1.1 A Subsection Sample

The domain of Digital Twin has been one of the growing topics in the field of research and development. There have been numerous articles and research papers published which have reviewed and analyzed this concept. Here we review the literature of some of the articles out of the many, as cited above.

Production and manufacturing processes require strict monitoring of the whole system for improved performance, efficiency, working conditions, and estimated results. Data collection, simulation, and ergonomic assessment form the basic framework for the process of decision-making to improve the desired outcomes using Digital Twin. Using Digital Twin, ergonomics can be evaluated rapidly and in a more accurate manner than the ones assessed using manual methods [2].

Increasingly adaptable and efficient processes can be integrated and developed using the Digital Twin. This can help in the manufacturing of products that are high in quality, low in cost, and require less time to produce. Research could be carried out to integrate the Digital Twin and the virtual environment to ensure a realistic behavior depicted by the actual system [3].

Human-centered design of workplaces uses ergonomic performance as a key factor for assessment and evaluation. Digital Twins are capable of simulating workstations in assembly lines to evaluate their ergonomic indexes hence saving time and cost as shown in the FCA (Fiat Chrysler Automobiles) case study [4].

The FCA follows a design framework involving Digital Twins as validating tools for creating rapid digital prototypes of assembly stations through a closed-loop development process [4]. Here ergonomics becomes an important design variable and no longer a constraint. Digital Twin also becomes the digital controller of real-world systems [5] where it simulates operating conditions of production systems and optimizes settings to improve ergonomics and also predict contingencies in various dimensions (Figs. 1, 2 and 3).

2   Bibliometric Analysis

Steps involved-

1. Coined keywords - "Digital Twin", search strings – "Digital Twin AND Ergonomics".
2. Ran keywords and search strings through Google Ngram and Scopus.
3. Leading tables were identified to select articles of interest.

From the Bibliometric analysis, it becomes clear that the topic of Digital Twins is an emerging field with plenty of evolutionary nuances. The large volume of research done in this area is made evident through Google Ngram and Scopus search results from using keywords like "Digital Twin"/ "Digital Twin AND Ergonomics" providing insightful tables showing documents by year, author, country/territory, affiliation, type and funding sponsors as shown in Figs. 4, 5, 6 and 7.

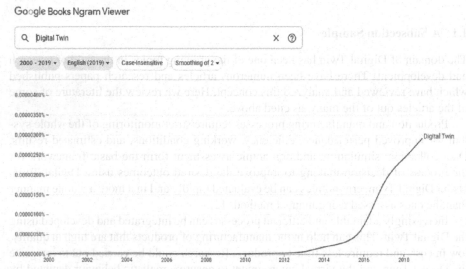

Fig. 1. Google Ngram results for "Digital Twin" shows that it's an emerging topic gathering momentum each year [6]

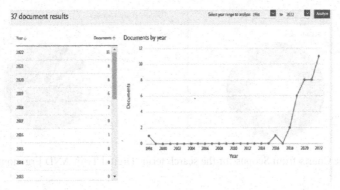

Fig. 2. Scopus analysis for documents by year for "Digital Twin AND Ergonomics" validates the Google Ngram finding shown above [7]

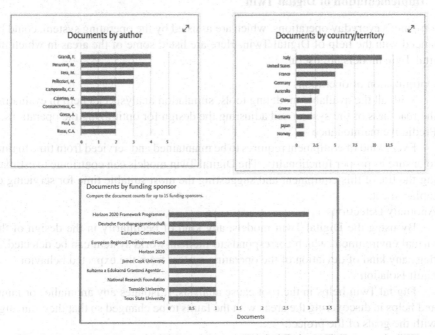

Fig. 3. Bar plots from Scopus for search term "Digital Twin AND Ergonomics" [7]

The leading tables from Scopus indicate that the majority of the research related to the search string "Digital Twin and Ergonomics" is concentrated in the engineering domain with European countries at the forefront along with the USA. Relevant articles used in this report were selected based on the number of citations and prominence of authors as indicated in the leading tables.

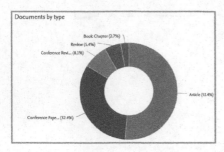
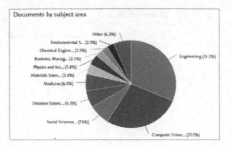

Fig. 4. Pie Charts from Scopus for the search term "Digital Twin AND Ergonomics" [7]

3 Applications

3.1 Implementation of Digital Twin

A company's everyday operations, which are assisted by the operating system, could be enhanced with the help of Digital Twin. Here are listed some of the areas in which the Digital Twin models are useful:

- Optimization of operations -
  With all the available modeling tools, simulation analysis can help in evaluating the readiness of the system and adjusting the design for optimizing the operations.
- Predictive maintenance -
  Every kind of equipment requires to be maintained and serviced from time to time to ensure its proper functionality. The Digital Twin models can contribute to estimating the life of this equipment and suggesting the most suitable time for servicing or replacement.
- Anomaly Detection -
  By using the Digital Twin models, any kind of peculiarity in the design of the virtual environment which corresponds to the real-world system can be detected. It flags any kind of deviation of the operating system from the expected behavior.
- Fault Isolation -
  Digital Twin helps in the root cause analysis. It isolates any anomalies or faults and helps in discovering the areas with the faults to be changed so that they can align with the goals of the project.

3.2 Implementation of FlexSim

FlexSim is a 3D simulation software capable of creating simulation models that can help in: analyzing, predicting, visualizing business systems across industries like manufacturing, mining, healthcare, warehousing, logistics, etc.

It has an open architecture that is favorable for constructing Digital Twins, as the models auto-build from captured and generated data. It also seamlessly connects with databases and is compatible with machine learning and artificial intelligence with VR-based immersive user experience.

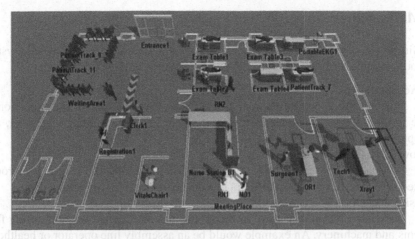

Fig. 5. FlexSim model of a healthcare setup [8]

3.3 Digital Twin in FlexSim

FlexSim-enabled Digital Twin virtually represents the setup and behavior of physical systems in 3D models that can help answer questions or provide improvements based on different inputs and layouts. It can automatically load data during regular intervals and run AI-powered simulations using reinforcement algorithms to send recommendations to the user regarding any change that needs to be made to the actual system.

Fig. 6. VR-enabled FlexSim Digital Twin [9]

4 Methodology

FlexSim 3D models consist of objects that are commonly used for any business system but could assume different meanings or purposes. Some of these objects are-

- Fixed Resources -
    Objects with specific functions remain stationary throughout the execution of the model. A few examples are- Source, Queue, Processor, Sink, Combiner, and Separator.
- Flow Items –
    Objects that move around in the model. They are moved downstream through fixed resources. Example- customers in a queue, boxes in a warehouse, etc.
- Task Executors –
    These are objects that move in the model and are capable of transporting flow items and machinery. An example would be an assembly line operator or healthcare worker.

A basic model will comprise these elements and will be connected as shown in Fig. 10 for the movement of resources in the desired direction.

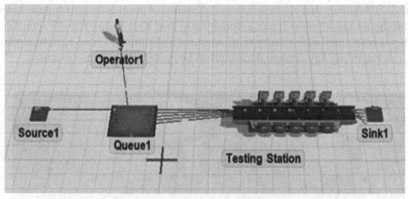

Fig. 7. A simple FlexSim model consisting of a Source, Queue, Processor (Testing Station), Sink, and Operator.

The Fixed Resources can have various types of Inter-arrival times for the flow objects based on the type of distribution like exponential, triangular, logarithmic, normal, etc.

This adds to the variability in the model and helps understand critical nuances that occur in real-world systems(Figs. 8 and 9).

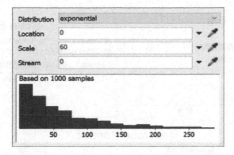

Fig. 8. Inter-arrival time distribution selection

5 Case Study

Two types of models are presented as case studies to depict the analyzing capabilities of FlexSim that could serve well in creating Digital Twins.

5.1 Material Handling System (Uniform Material Type)

The object utilization of a Material Handling system was studied and the average WIP (Work in Progress) content was calculated for a source following exponential distribution and a processor/testing station following triangular distribution. Refer to Fig. 12.

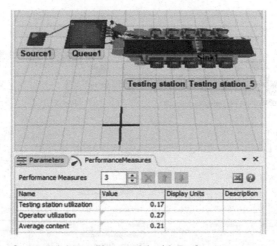

Fig. 9. Material Handling model with Performance measures

State Bars are an important feature in FlexSim depicting object utilization levels as the simulation model runs. Figure 13 below shows State Bars for all the testing stations, operators, and the dynamic average WIP content.

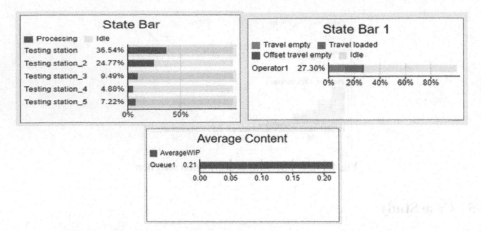

Fig. 10. FlexSim State Bars showing utilization levels and Average WIP

5.2 Material Handling System (Different Material Types)

A material handling system dealing with different types of materials (color coded as red, blue, green, and yellow) was analyzed (refer to Fig. 14) to find the object utilization and other performance measures. This model involved the usage of pallets to combine materials using Combiners and separators to separate and segregate them in the end from the pallets. Conveyors were also used to move the material downstream (Fig. 11).

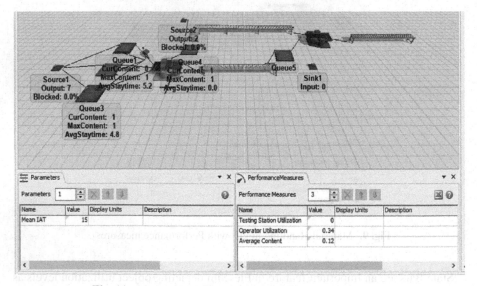

Fig. 11. Material Handling model for different material types

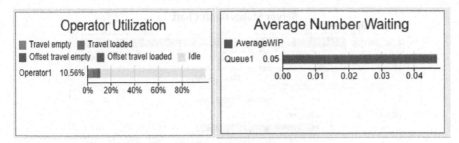

Fig. 12. State Bars show the operator's utilization and the average number of materials waiting to be moved downstream from the Queue.

5.3 Queuing System

Server utilization of a queuing system FlexSim model was studied to analyze the percentage of balked and reneged customers. The number of servers and their serving time windows was varied to compare the number of balked and reneged customers, server utilization, and average wait time in both cases.

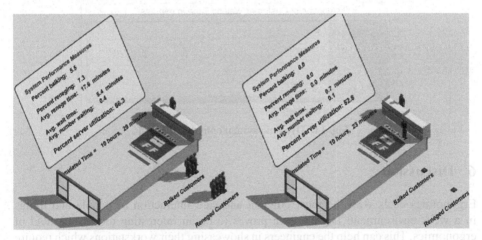

Fig. 13. Queuing system comparison-One server vs Two server

The dynamic output status of the system as the model runs is shown through Gantt charts, Utilization bars, and Bar plots as shown below.

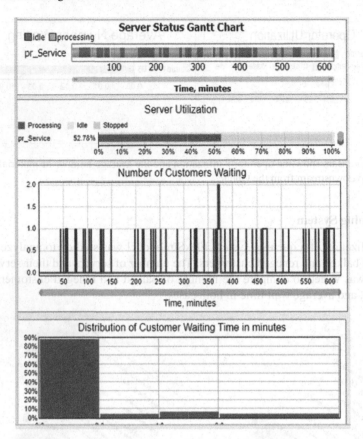

Fig. 14. Dynamic system output dashboard

6 Discussion

Ergonomics deals with the most efficient and safe interaction of people and things in a work environment. Digital Twin proves to be an interesting tool in the field of ergonomics. This can help the engineers in showcasing their workstations which require the performance of simulation so that the safety and ergonomics assessments can be carried out. Warehouses, workstations, tools, machines, operators, sensors, etc. can be designed using the Digital Twin and their working can be evaluated. Moreover, under ergonomic studies, the movements and postures of the operators can also be gauged by employing digital human models [10].

The basic models made using FlexSim provide an idea of how Digital Twins can be enabled for system simulations. The Case studies shown earlier are classroom examples for showing the possibilities of implementing a Digital Twin in business systems. The material handling system case study provides an example of how Digital Twins can calculate dynamically the average WIP content in manufacturing industries to understand the distribution process along with object utilization levels. While the queuing system case study shows how a FlexSim-enabled Digital Twin provides the percentage server utilization and average wait times.

The operator or server utilization from both case studies provides an idea about the ergonomic performance of the setups as it can help identify fatigue levels and other types of physical or cognitive ergonomic stresses. The size of the operator can be changed along with the dimensions of other stationary objects like Source, Conveyor, and Queue which can affect the operator's utilization levels. These factors are crucial when designing workplaces and FlexSim-enabled Digital Twins with VR immersive experience can help pinpoint design flaws in labor-intensive setups and ultimately improve the ergonomic index of the workplace.

7 Conclusion

Simulation enables one to visualize how their outcome would look or function in the real world. It helps in analyzing the performance and efficiency of the products/machines/systems which in the corporate world, help in the optimization of outputs, in turn leading to profitability. Simulation using Digital Twin helps analyze workplace ergonomics and creates better designs for human workers' safety, health, and comfort.

Digital Twin allows testing the interaction of the people and the system before they are brought into effect to increase optimality. The FlexSim experience was very enriching as it was presented and experienced as a powerful industrial tool. It enables users to design, visualize and analyze complex systems spanning across industries. The most exciting part about FlexSim was the Digital Twin, which it can seamlessly create.

References

1. Wu, C., Arbor, A.: Part 5 human performance mathematical modeling in human – machine what is an ideal mathematical model the applications of mathematical performance (2021)
2. Greco, A., Caterino, M., Fera, M., Gerbino, S.: Digital twin for monitoring ergonomics during manufacturing production. Appl. Sci. (Switzerland) **10**(21), 1–20 (2020). https://doi.org/10.3390/app10217758
3. Havard, V., Jeanne, B., Lacomblez, M., Baudry, D.: Digital twin and virtual reality: a co-simulation environment for design and assessment of industrial workstations. Prod. Manuf. Res. **7**(1), 472–489 (2019). https://doi.org/10.1080/21693277.2019.1660283
4. Caputo, F., Greco, A., Fera, M., Macchiaroli, R.: Digital twins to enhance the integration of ergonomics in the workplace design. Int. J. Ind. Ergon. **71**(January), 20–31 (2019). https://doi.org/10.1016/j.ergon.2019.02.001
5. Fera, M., et al.: Towards digital twin implementation for assessing production line performance and balancing. Sensors (Switzerland), **20**(1) (2020). https://doi.org/10.3390/s20010097
6. Google Ngram: Digital Twin. https://books.google.com/ngrams/
7. Scopus: Digital Twin and Ergonomics. https://www.scopus.com/home.uri
8. FlexSim: Welcome to FlexSim HealthCare. FlexSim Problem Solved
9. FlexSim: FlexSim + Digital Twin. FlexSim. https://www.flexsim.com/digital-twin/
10. Weistroffer, V., Keith, F., Bisiaux, A., Andriot, C., Lasnier, A.: Using physics-based digital twins and extended reality for the safety and ergonomics evaluation of cobotic workstations. Front. Virtual Real. **3**(February), 1–18 (2022). https://doi.org/10.3389/frvir.2022.781830

Wearables and Mixed Reality in Applied Ergonomics: A Literature Review

Xiyun Hu(✉), Runlin Duan, Ziyi Liu, and Vincent G. Duffy

Purdue University, West Lafayette, IN 47906, USA
{hu690,duan92,liu1362,duffy}@purdue.edu

Abstract. Wearable technology and mixed reality (MR) have gained significant attention in recent years due to their potential to improve industrial ergonomics. Wearable technology can enable real-time monitoring and feedback of workers' physiological and biomechanical parameters, while MR can provide visual, auditory, and haptic feedback to support training and assessment of ergonomic risk factors. This review aims to provide an overview of the current use of wearable technology and MR in applied ergonomics. We first provide an overview of the general concepts and technologies underlying wearable technology and MR by gathering a bibliography using Publish or Perish on various datasets. Then the metadata of the bibliography is analyzed with BibExcel, VOSviewer, Citespace, MAXQDA, and regression analysis. The current applications of wearable technology and MR in the assessment and improvement of industrial ergonomics are also reviewed. Finally, we discuss the challenges and future directions for the use of wearable technology and MR in industrial ergonomics.

Keywords: Wearable Technology · Mixed Reality · Ergonomics · Data Mining

1 Introduction

Ergonomics is the science of designing and adapting work and environments to fit the needs of people [18]. In recent years, there has been an increasing interest in the use of wearable technology and mixed reality as tools for ergonomic applications [17,20]. Wearable technology refers to devices that are worn on the body and can measure and transmit data on various physiological and physical parameters [11,22]. Mixed reality (MR) refers to the integration of virtual and physical environments, allowing for the overlay of digital information on the real world [14]. Both technologies have the potential to provide real-time, rich data on human performance and behavior, which can be used to improve the effectiveness of ergonomic interventions [12,19].

Ergonomics research on wearables and mixed reality has focused on improving the design and usage of these technologies to minimize pain and strain on the body while maximizing their usefulness and usability. The design of the gadgets themselves is a primary focus of ergonomics research on wearables and MR.

Fig. 1. Word Cloud of the article keywords in wearables, mixed reality, and ergonomics

For instance, research has been undertaken on the appropriate size, shape, and positioning of wearable gadgets, as well as the design of mixed-reality headsets and other devices, in order to reduce pain and strain on the body. Focus is also placed on the user interface of wearable and mixed reality devices, including the design of buttons and displays and the utilization of natural gestures and motions for interaction.

In addition to the design of the devices, research into the ergonomics of wearables and mixed reality has also focused on how these technologies are utilized. This includes studies on the possible negative consequences of prolonged usage, such as eye strain and neck pain, as well as methods for mitigating these effects.

Figure 1 shows the keywords in these three areas. Despite the potential of wearable technology and mixed reality for ergonomic applications, there is a lack of information on the specific effects of these technologies on the effectiveness of ergonomic interventions and how they compare to traditional ergonomic methods. Therefore, this study aims to review the current state of research on the use of wearable technology and mixed reality for ergonomic applications. By conducting a literature search and analyzing the data using statistical inference techniques, we aim to provide a comprehensive overview of the current state of research on this topic and identify future research directions (Fig. 2).

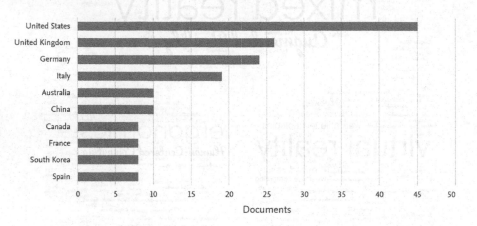

Fig. 2. Publication by country or territory. Data collected on Scopus with the keyword "wearables", "mixed reality" and "ergonomics"

2 Purpose of Study

This review's main goal is to provide a thorough data mining study of the current use of wearable technology and mixed reality (MR) utilization in the field of applied ergonomics. Through the use of various data mining techniques, including bibliometric analysis, we seek to:

- Demonstrate the application of data mining techniques to elucidate the general concepts and technologies underlying wearable technology and MR
- Examine the current applications of these technologies in the assessment and improvement of applied ergonomics
- Identify the challenges and future directions for the use of wearable technology and MR in this field

This study intends to be a useful resource for scholars, practitioners, and policymakers interested in the application of wearable technologies and MR in applied ergonomics. We intend to promote more research and development in this vital and quickly expanding sector by emphasizing the present state of the art and future directions.

3   Research Methodology

This report utilized various software to collect and analyze the bibliography data. In this section, all the techniques used in the review will be presented and discussed. Table 1 includes all the software used for this report.

Table 1. Softwares used in the report separated by their function

Category	Software		
Dataset	Google Scholar [3]	Scopus [5]	Web of Science [8]
Data Mining	Publish or Perish [4]		
Visualization	Citespace [1]	VOSviewer [7]	Google Ngram [2]
Analysis	Excel Regression Analysis		

Firstly, a literature search was conducted to identify relevant studies on the use of wearable technology and mixed reality for ergonomic applications. The search was conducted using the keywords "wearable technology," "mixed reality," and "ergonomics" in the following databases: Google Scholar, Scopus, and Web of Science. The search was limited to articles published in two periods: 2001–2010 and 2011–2020. From the literature search, we identified a total of 36 articles that were included in our bibliography for further analysis. By combining the three keywords and using Publish or Perish to search, we were able to identify 10 authors that have the most articles in the overlapping area, from which we selected the top 5 to analyze in detail.

The data from the bibliography were analyzed using statistical inference techniques, including regression analysis and comparison of means. The analysis was conducted using Excel, which is a widely used software tool for statistical analysis. The bibliography was visualized using Citespace and VOSviewer, two software tools for visualizing and analyzing scientific literature. To examine the trend of research on wearable technology and mixed reality in applied ergonomics over time, we used Google Ngram, a tool that allows for the analysis of the frequency of words or phrases in books. All the studies included in the bibliography were published in peer-reviewed journals and followed ethical guidelines for research involving human subjects. The results of the study were reported in accordance with the guidelines for scientific reporting, including the use of tables and figures to present the data clearly and concisely. The bibliography and data analysis code was also made available as supplementary materials.

3.1   Data Mining

Table 2 presents the number of search results from the two time periods. Except for the result count for "Ergonomics" in google scholar, comparing inside the dataset, all the other keywords have more articles in the 2011–2020 decade.

Table 2. Number of papers found in the different datasets from previous two decades

Time Period	Dataset		
	Google Scholar	Scopus	Web of Science
Wearable Technology			
2001–2010	36,100	2,100	1,473
2011–2020	217,000	25,655	19,877
Mixed Reality			
2001–2010	95,300	2,286	2,075
2011–2020	157,000	8,204	8,020
Ergonomics			
2001–2010	232,000	13,249	8,289
2011–2020	150,000	24,090	20,760

3.2   Engagement Measure

Vicinitas [6] is a Twitter data tracking tool. It can also analyze the engagement of several keywords given a period of time. The keyword to analyze for this review is wearables. Figure 3 shows the engagement timeline of that keyword. Although it is from a short period, this trend indicates that the topic remains relevant to the general users. The growth of the fitness tracker market has contributed to the trend, as more and more people have started using these devices to track their physical activity and health metrics.

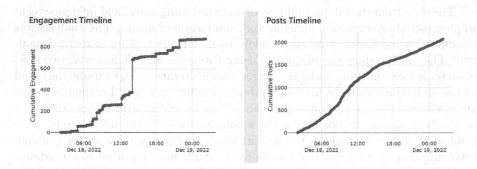

Fig. 3. Vicinitas [6] engagement timeline for keyword "wearables"

3.3   Trend Analysis

In this section, we analyzed the overall trend of the selected topic in the academic area by taking a closer look in the datasets: Google Scholar, Scopus, and Web of Science.

Figure 4 visualizes the change in publications in the wearables and ergonomics area on Web of Science. From 2004 to 2023, the number of publications per year is increasing. It shows that this combined area is emerging after 2015.

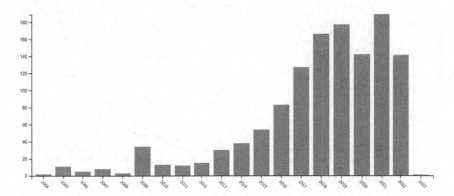

Fig. 4. Publication by year. Data collected on Web of Science with the keyword "wearables" and "ergonomics"

Figure 5 shows the documents published by year in the combined area of the three topics: wearables, mixed reality, and ergonomics. Notice that it has a sudden spike in the year 2020. The reason behind that might be COVID-19 promotes research that focuses on remote or non-physical-contact cooperation, where mixed reality falls in this scope.

Figure 6 shows the overall trend of the change in frequency of the three keywords (Wearable Technology, Mixed Reality, Ergonomics) throughout 1940–2019. It is observable that the frequency of "Ergonomics" decreased starting around the year 2000 and increased again after 2010. The frequencies of the other two words slowly increase overall. But after 2010, the increased amount became larger. That period coincides with the second increase period of "Ergonomics". For this reason, we decide to analyze the literature in two separate periods: 2001–2010 and 2011–2020.

Combining the three keywords and searching using Publish or Perish in Google Scholar, we found the following 10 authors have the most published articles in the overlapping area (Fig. 7). It is also worth mentioning that the top 3 authors shared some research interests–augmented reality in surgery.

Table 3 shows the leading papers in the topic area. It is noticeable that their applications are related to health care and surgery.

Documents by year

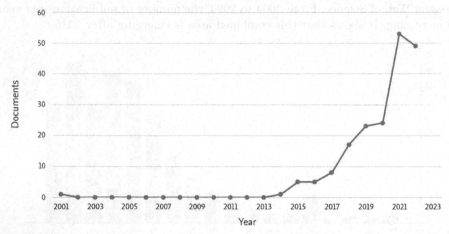

Fig. 5. Publication by year. Data collected on Scopus with the keyword "wearables", "mixed reality" and "ergonomics"

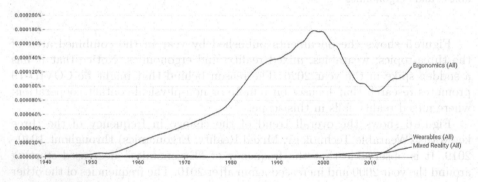

Fig. 6. Google Ngram keyword trend from year 1940 to 2020

4   Results

4.1   Co-citation Analysis

Co-citation analysis is a method of analyzing the relationships between different scientific papers or other documents based on the citations that they share. It is used to identify the key papers or ideas in a particular field, and to understand the way that knowledge is disseminated and shared within that field [10].

Using the keywords "Wearables" AND "Mixed Reality" AND "Ergonomics" to collect 186 articles from Scopus, Fig. 8 depicts the co-citation analysis in VOS Viewer. The graph illustrates the relationship between the three reach areas by displaying the co-cited paper in the area. Table 4 shows the author, title, and year for the cited references.

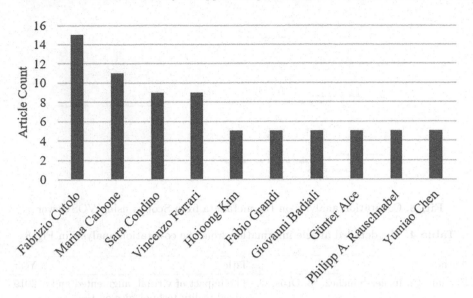

Fig. 7. Top 10 author from the 500 google scholar search result

Table 3. Leading Papers from the Scopus search for the topic

Authors	Title	Citation
Slam, S.M.R., et al.	The internet of things for health care: A comprehensive survey	1759
Heath, R.W., et al.	An Overview of Signal Processing Techniques for Millimeter Wave MIMO Systems	1605
Piwek, L., et al.	The Rise of Consumer Health Wearables: Promises and Barriers	591
Son, D., et al.	An integrated self-healable electronic skin system fabricated via dynamic reconstruction of a nanostructured conducting network	547
Farahani, B., et al.	Towards fog-driven IoT eHealth: Promises and challenges of IoT in medicine and healthcare	547

4.2   Content Analysis

By extracting the relationship of the articles in Scopus, Fig. 9 shows the connection between the keywords inside the article. While wearables, mixed reality, and ergonomics are three different fields, their content are overlapping based on the co-occurrence of the keywords.

Figure 10 depicts CiteSpace's cluster analysis of 1313 publications retrieved on Web of Science using the keywords "Wearables" OR "Mixed Reality" OR "Ergonomics." The result demonstrates that distinct publications are intercon-

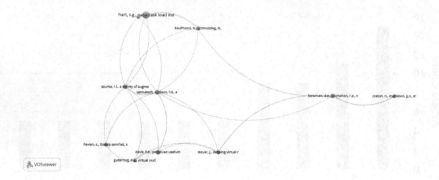

Fig. 8. Co-citation analysis on the metadata from Scopus using VOSviewer

Table 4. The detailed article information from the co-citation analysis in Fig. 8

Authors	Title	Year
Flavián, C., Ibáñez-Sánchez, S., Orús, C.	The impact of virtual, augmented and mixed reality technologies on the customer experience	2019
Guttentag, D.A.	Virtual reality: applications and implications for tourism	2010
Bowman, D.A., McMahan, R.P.	Virtual reality: How much immersion is enough?	2007
Hart, Sandra G	Nasa-Task Load Index (NASA-TLX); 20 Years Later	2006
Venkatesh, V., Davis, F.D	A theoretical extension of the technology acceptance model: Four longitudinal field studies	2000
Azuma, R.T.	A survey of augmented reality	1997
Craton, N., Matheson, G.O.	Training and clinical competency in musculoskeletal medicine. Identifying the Problem	1993
Steuer, J.	Defining virtual reality: Dimensions determining telepresence	1992
Davis, F.D.	Perceived usefulness, perceived ease of use, and user acceptance of information technology	1989

nected and grouped based on the top 10 terms in their keywords. These keywords are associated with mixed reality applications, wearable fabrications, wearable-related sensors, and their respective applications.

Figure 11 demonstrates the dramatic increase in the number of references cited. As indicated in the graph, the majority of burst start times have occurred during the previous five years, indicating that the issue of interest is relatively young and has undergone significant advancements in recent years.

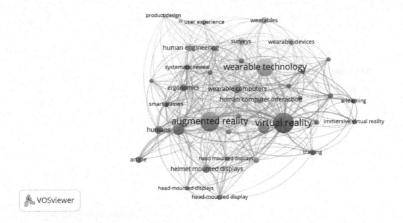

Fig. 9. Content analysis on the metadata from Scopus using VOSviewer

Vicinitas was utilized to construct a word cloud. Figure 12 displays the word cloud generated by searching "wearables" on Vicinitas. Vicinitas is software capable of tracking and analyzing Twitter terms. Large font indicates that the word is often used. "Digital", "gaming", "nft", "platform", "extension", and "future" are the most often used phrases associated with "wearables."

4.3   Regression Analysis

To further analyze the difference between datasets, we conducted regression analysis [9] on the citation of the top 5 authors from different datasets and the citation of the selected 36 papers from different datasets and time periods.

Table 5 collects the number of citations of the authors from different datasets. Google Scholar has the most citation for all the authors followed by Scopus. And Wed of Science has the least citation. By performing a regression analysis inside Excel, the result is shown in appendix Fig. 15.

Table 5. Citation count of five leading authors from different datasets

Author	Citation Count		
	Google Scholar	Scopus	Web of Science
Fabrizio Cutolo	1429	665	853
Marina Carbone	1107	604	607
Sara Condino	1111	561	543
Vincenzo Ferrari	3448	1645	1,272
Hojoong Kim	690	504	191

The regression result $R^2 = 0.998$ shows that the Eq. 1 is a good fit for the data. GS means Google Scholar, SC means Scopus, and WS means Web of

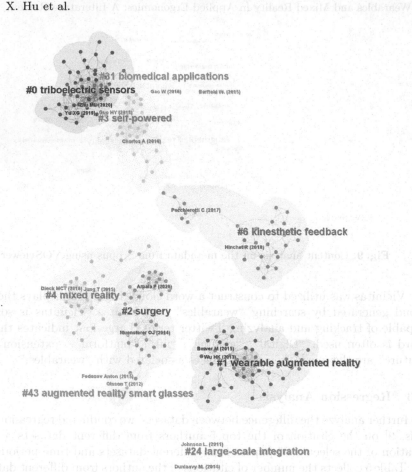

Fig. 10. Cluster analysis on the metadata from Scopus using Citespace

Top 5 References with the Strongest Citation Bursts

References	Year	Strength	Begin	End	2001 - 2022
Wu HK, 2013, COMPUT EDUC, V62, P41, DOI 10.1016/j.compedu.2012.10.024, DOI	2013	3.31	2015	2017	
Muensterer OJ, 2014, INT J SURG, V12, P281, DOI 10.1016/j.ijsu.2014.02.003, DOI	2014	4.63	2016	2019	
Leue M.C., 2015, INFORM COMMUNICATION, V0, PP463, DOI 10.1007/978-3-319-14343-9, 34, 10.1007/978-3-319-14343-9, 34, DOI	2015	3.69	2016	2018	
Dieck MCT, 2018, CURR ISSUES TOUR, V21, P154, DOI 10.1080/13683500.2015.1070801, DOI	2018	4.19	2018	2019	
Pacchierotti C, 2017, IEEE T HAPTICS, V10, P580, DOI 10.1109/TOH.2017.2689006, DOI	2017	5.55	2019	2022	

Fig. 11. Citation burst on the metadata from Scopus using Citespace

Science.

$$GS = -315.83 + 1.76SC + 0.68WS \qquad (1)$$

The coefficient p-values (SC = 0.0058 < 0.05, WS = 0.051 > 0.05) show that the citation count in Scopus is significantly related to Google Scholar, while we

Word Cloud

Fig. 12. World Cloud with the keyword "wearables" search from Vicinitas

can not reject the null hypothesis for Web of Science. The reason behind that might be not enough data samples. By inspecting the original data further, we found that the citation count for author Hojoong Kim is much lower in Web of Science compared with Scopus. It could be considered an outlier.

Table 6 shows the citation count of 36 articles from different periods and datasets. Numbers 1 and 2 stand for the period 2001–2010 and 3 and 4 for 2011–2020.

Table 6. Citation of selected paper

Dataset & Time Period	Citation Count		
	Wearable Technology	Mixed Reality	Ergonomics
GS1	75	132	116
GS2	560	753	140
GS3	130	425	558
GS4	557	263	104
SC1	952	1581	5944
SC2	898	324	3189
SC3	2683	1279	492
SC4	1759	634	885
WS1	482	336	875
WS2	1262	466	560
WS3	1246	2470	330
WS4	2551	324	311

Using the citation count of papers in wearable technology as Y and Mixed Reality and Ergonomics as Xs. The regression analysis (appendix Fig. 16) shows that it is highly unlikely that the citation counts of articles from those three areas are related (p-value $= 0.38$, $0.70 > 0.05$) to each other. It possibly indicates that the 36 papers selected do not contain overlap in area.

5   Discussion

From the literature review, we learned that the keyword ergonomics got much more search history from 1940 to 2019. In contrast, mixed reality and wearable technology saw an increasing trend after 2000. The difference between the search frequencies on the three keywords is reasonable. Researchers have been focusing on the ergonomic problem for a long time since ergonomics covers not only human-computer interactions but also considers the factors of human interactions with other machines and devices. The increasing frequency of mixed reality and wearable technology increased during the past two decades because of the hardware breakthrough during this time. The new form of visualization techniques brings the attention of the researchers to mixed reality, and the mobile phone and internet of things (IoT) open the potential of using wearable devices in a border scenario.

Considering the keywords wearable technology and mixed reality. There is also a significant difference in the number of papers published during 2001–2010 and 2011–2020. The increasing trend is because of the development of IoT and virtual reality techniques. During that period of time, the research society experienced a tremendous increase in computational resources. The inclination on the computational ability leverage the production and consumption of data. And with the support of data, and the requirement for data processing, more research has been conducted on mixed reality and wearable devices.

During the data-gathering stage, we also noticed that the current applications for the three areas are closely related to healthcare and surgery. Given the small amount of paper found in that direction, further research can be done to investigate the role of wearables and mixed reality in the healthcare context.

In addition, the regression analysis in Table 5 and Table 6 suggests that the citation count for these keywords differs significantly between the different datasets, with Google Scholar having the highest citation count for all authors and articles. This may be due to the fact that Google Scholar is a more widely used and well-known database, leading to more citations for the articles indexed within it (Fig. 13).

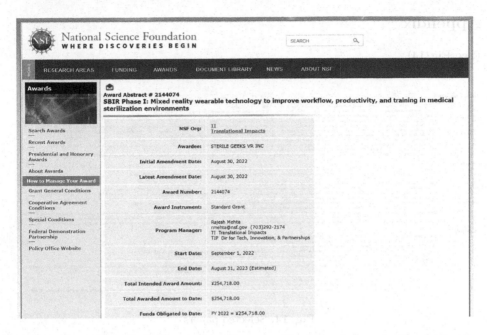

Fig. 13. An NSF award for mixed reality wearable technology research starting in 2022 [13]

6   Conclusion

Overall, the results suggest that the study of Wearable Technology, Mixed Reality, and Ergonomics has seen a significant increase in popularity over the past two decades, with a particular focus on the use of these technologies in applied ergonomics. The research done in these areas is often related. Further research could explore the reasons for this increase and how these technologies are being used to improve ergonomic design and practices.

7   Future Work

The wearable device and the mixed reality bring opportunities to create an immersive experience for users. The immersive experience is especially useful for education, training, and improving productivity. The NSF award for mixed-reality wearable technology research focuses on using mixed reality to improve workflow, productivity, and training in medical sterilization environments [13]. Future work on the wearable device must tackle the challenges and opportunities of integration between multiple users and multiple devices [16]. It requires hardware developments, such as soft materials for creating sensors and controllers [15]. Another direction includes creating a novel visualization and interaction system to support multiple users' collaboration using wearables and mixed reality devices [21]. Overall, wearable devices and mixed reality are still under development, and more studies are required to reveal their application in ergonomic design and practices.

Appendix

(See Fig. 14).

Wearable Technology	
GS1	Rutherford, Jesse Jayne. "Wearable technology." IEEE Engineering in Medicine and Biology Magazine 29, no. 3 (2010): 19-24.
GS2	Dul, Jan, and W. Patrick Neumann. "Ergonomics contributions to company strategies." Applied ergonomics 40, no. 4 (2009): 745-752.
GS3	Godfrey, Alan, Victoria Hetherington, Hubert Shum, Paolo Bonato, N. H. Lovell, and Sam Stuart. "From A to Z: Wearable technology explained." Maturitas 113 (2018): 40-47.
GS4	Wilson, John R. "Fundamentals of systems ergonomics/human factors." Applied ergonomics 45, no. 1 (2014): 5-13.
SC1	Chlamtac, Imrich, Marco Conti, and Jennifer J-N. Liu. "Mobile ad hoc networking: imperatives and challenges." Ad hoc networks 1, no. 1 (2003): 13-64.
SC2	Duan, Xiangfeng, Chunming Niu, Vijendra Sahi, Jian Chen, J. Wallace Parce, Stephen Empedocles, and Jay L. Goldman. "High-performance thin-film transistors using semiconductor nanowires and nanoribbons." Nature 425, no. 6955 (2003): 274-278.
SC3	Gao, Wei, Sam Emaminejad, Hnin Yin Yin Nyein, Samyuktha Challa, Kevin Chen, Austin Peck, Hossain M. Fahad et al. "Fully integrated wearable sensor arrays for multiplexed in situ perspiration analysis." Nature 529, no. 7587 (2016): 509-514.
SC4	Islam, SM Riazul, Daehan Kwak, MD Humaun Kabir, Mahmud Hossain, and Kyung-Sup Kwak. "The internet of things for health care: a comprehensive survey." IEEE access 3 (2015): 678-708.
WS1	Kim, Dae-Hyeong, and John A. Rogers. "Stretchable electronics: materials strategies and devices." Advanced materials 20, no. 24 (2008): 4887-4892.
WS2	Hu, Liangbing, Mauro Pasta, Fabio La Mantia, LiFeng Cui, Sangmoo Jeong, Heather Dawn Deshazer, Jang Wook Choi, Seung Min Han, and Yi Cui. "Stretchable, porous, and conductive energy textiles." Nano letters 10, no. 2 (2010): 708-714.
WS3	Stoppa, Matteo, and Alessandro Chiolerio. "Wearable electronics and smart textiles: A critical review." sensors 14, no. 7 (2014): 11957-11992.
WS4	Gao, Wei, Sam Emaminejad, Hnin Yin Yin Nyein, Samyuktha Challa, Kevin Chen, Austin Peck, Hossain M. Fahad et al. "Fully integrated wearable sensor arrays for multiplexed in situ perspiration analysis." Nature 529, no. 7587 (2016): 509-514.
Mixed Reality	
GS1	Costanza, Enrico, Andreas Kunz, and Morten Fjeld. "Mixed reality: A survey." In Human machine interaction, pp. 47-68. Springer, Berlin, Heidelberg, 2009.
GS2	Pan, Zhigeng, Adrian David Cheok, Hongwei Yang, Jiejie Zhu, and Jiaoying Shi. "Virtual reality and mixed reality for virtual learning environments." Computers & graphics 30, no. 1 (2006): 20-28.
GS3	Benford, Steve, and Gabriella Giannachi. Performing mixed reality. Mit Press, 2011.
GS4	Speicher, Maximilian, Brian D. Hall, and Michael Nebeling. "What is mixed reality?." In Proceedings of the 2019 CHI conference on human factors in computing systems, pp. 1-15. 2019.
SC1	Pawson R, Greenhalgh T, Harvey G, et al. Realist review-a new method of systematic review designed for complex policy interventions[J]. Journal of health services research & policy, 2005, 10(1_suppl): 21-34.
SC2	Jarmon, Leslie, Tomoko Traphagan, Michael Mayrath, and Avani Trivedi. "Virtual world teaching, experiential learning, and assessment: An interdisciplinary communication course in Second Life." Computers & Education 53, no. 1 (2009): 169-182.
SC3	Ionescu C, Papava D, Olaru V, et al. Human3. 6m: Large scale datasets and predictive methods for 3d human sensing in natural environments[J]. IEEE transactions on pattern analysis and machine intelligence, 2013, 36(7): 1325-1339.
SC4	Chen, Min, and Yixue Hao. "Task offloading for mobile edge computing in software defined ultra-dense network." IEEE Journal on Selected Areas in Communications 36, no. 3 (2018): 587-597.
WS1	Sale, Joanna EM, Lynne H. Lohfeld, and Kevin Brazil. "Revisiting the quantitative-qualitative debate: Implications for mixed-methods research." Quality and quantity 36, no. 1 (2002): 43-53.
WS2	Zhou, Feng, Henry Been-Lirn Duh, and Mark Billinghurst. "Trends in augmented reality tracking, interaction and display: A review of ten years of ISMAR." In 2008 7th IEEE/ACM International Symposium on Mixed and Augmented Reality, pp. 193-202. IEEE, 200
WS3	Newcombe, Richard A., Shahram Izadi, Otmar Hilliges, David Molyneaux, David Kim, Andrew J. Davison, Pushmeet Kohi, Jamie Shotton, Steve Hodges, and Andrew Fitzgibbon. "Kinectfusion: Real-time dense surface mapping and tracking." In 2011 10th IEEE
WS4	Potkonjak, Veljko, Michael Gardner, Victor Callaghan, Pasi Mattila, Christian Guetl, Vladimir M. Petrović, and Kosta Jovanović. "Virtual laboratories for education in science, technology, and engineering: A review." Computers & Education 95 (2016): 309-327.
Ergonomics	
GS1	Beevis, David. "Ergonomics—costs and benefits revisited." Applied ergonomics 34, no. 5 (2003): 491-496.
GS2	Stone, Robert, and Rory McCloy. "Ergonomics in medicine and surgery." Bmj 328, no. 7448 (2004): 1115-1118.
GS3	Murrell, K. Ergonomics: Man in his working environment. Springer Science & Business Media, 2012.
GS4	Catanzarite, Tatiana, Jasmine Tan-Kim, Emily L. Whitcomb, and Shawn Menefee. "Ergonomics in surgery: a review." Female pelvic medicine & reconstructive surgery 24, no. 1 (2018): 1-12.
SC1	Armitage C J, Conner M. Efficacy of the theory of planned behaviour: A meta-analytic review[J]. British journal of social psychology, 2001, 40(4): 471-499.
SC2	Winter, David A. Biomechanics and motor control of human movement. John Wiley & Sons, 2009.
SC3	Gold, Christian, Daniel Damböck, Lutz Lorenz, and Klaus Bengler. ""Take over!" How long does it take to get the driver back into the loop?." In Proceedings of the human factors and ergonomics society annual meeting, vol. 57, no. 1, pp. 1938-1942. Sage CA: Lo
SC4	Hancock, Peter A., Deborah R. Billings, Kristin E. Schaefer, Jessie YC Chen, Ewart J. De Visser, and Raja Parasuraman. "A meta-analysis of factors affecting trust in human-robot interaction." Human factors 53, no. 5 (2011): 517-527.
WS1	Punnett, Laura, and David H. Wegman. "Work-related musculoskeletal disorders: the epidemiologic evidence and the debate." Journal of electromyography and kinesiology 14, no. 1 (2004): 13-23.
WS2	Haslam, Roger A., Sophie A. Hide, Alistair GF Gibb, Diane E. Gyi, Trevor Pavitt, Sarah Atkinson, and Alexander Roy Duff. "Contributing factors in construction accidents." Applied ergonomics 36, no. 4 (2005): 401-415.
WS3	Young, Mark S., Karel A. Brookhuis, Christopher D. Wickens, and Peter A. Hancock. "State of science: mental workload in ergonomics." Ergonomics 58, no. 1 (2015): 1-17.
WS4	Dul, Jan, Ralph Bruder, Peter Buckle, Pascale Carayon, Pierre Falzon, William S. Marras, John R. Wilson, and Bas van der Doelen. "A strategy for human factors/ergonomics: developing the discipline and profession." Ergonomics 55, no. 4 (2012): 377-395.

Fig. 14. Selected papers

SUMMARY OUTPUT								
Regression Statistics								
Multiple R	0.99916712							
R Square	0.998334934							
Adjusted R Squai	0.996669868							
Standard Error	62.85440923							
Observations	5							
ANOVA								
	df	*SS*	*MS*	*F*	*gnificance F*			
Regression	2	4737469	2368734	599.5768	0.001665			
Residual	2	7901.354	3950.677					
Total	4	4745370						
	Coefficients	*andard Err*	*t Stat*	*P-value*	*Lower 95%*	*Jpper 95%*	*ower 95.0%*	*pper 95.0%*
Intercept	-315.8314043	61.99488	-5.09448	0.036437	-582.574	-49.0889	-582.574	-49.0889
Scopus	1.759581171	0.13429	13.10288	0.005774	1.18178	2.337383	1.18178	2.337383
Web of Science	0.681703272	0.160254	4.253884	0.051066	-0.00782	1.371222	-0.00782	1.371222

Fig. 15. Regression analysis of the citation of the 5 authors

SUMMARY OUTPUT							
Regression Statistics							
Multiple R	0.299248						
R Square	0.089549						
Adjusted R	-0.11277						
Standard E	906.0798						
Observatio	12						
ANOVA							
	df	*SS*	*MS*	*F*	*ignificance F*		
Regressio	2	726742.9	363371.5	0.442607	0.655623		
Residual	9	7388825	820980.6				
Total	11	8115568					

	Coefficients	*andard Err*	*t Stat*	*P-value*	*Lower 95%*	*Upper 95%*	*ower 95.0%*	*pper 95.0%*
Intercept	885.8871	408.3977	2.169177	0.058191	-37.9727	1809.747	-37.9727	1809.747
Mixed Rea	0.377718	0.407715	0.926427	0.378397	-0.5446	1.300032	-0.5446	1.300032
Ergonomic	-0.06444	0.163191	-0.39487	0.702131	-0.4336	0.304724	-0.4336	0.304724

Fig. 16. Regression analysis of the citation of the 36 papers

References

1. Citespace. http://cluster.cis.drexel.edu/~cchen/citespace/
2. Google ngram. https://books.google.com/ngrams/
3. Google scholar. https://scholar.google.com/
4. Publish or perish. https://harzing.com/resources/publish-or-perish
5. Scopus. https://www.scopus.com/
6. Vicinitas. https://www.vicinitas.io/
7. Vosviewer. https://www.vosviewer.com/
8. Web of science. https://www.webofknowledge.com/
9. Freund, R.J., Wilson, W.J., Sa, P.: Regression Analysis. Elsevier, Amsterdam (2006)
10. Gmür, M.: Co-citation analysis and the search for invisible colleges: a methodological evaluation. Scientometrics **57**(1), 27–57 (2003)
11. Godfrey, A., Hetherington, V., Shum, H., Bonato, P., Lovell, N., Stuart, S.: From A to Z: wearable technology explained. Maturitas **113**, 40–47 (2018)
12. Incekara, F., Smits, M., Dirven, C., Vincent, A.: Clinical feasibility of a wearable mixed-reality device in neurosurgery. World Neurosurg. **118**, e422–e427 (2018)
13. Jones, S.: SBIR phase I: mixed reality wearable technology to improve workflow, productivity, and training in medical sterilization environments (2022). https://www.nsf.gov/awardsearch/showAward?AWD_ID=2144074
14. Kenn, H., Bürgy, C.: "Are we crossing the chasm in wearable AR?": 3rd workshop on wearable systems for industrial augmented reality applications. In: Proceedings of the 2014 ACM International Symposium on Wearable Computers: Adjunct Program, ISWC 2014 Adjunct, pp. 213–216. Association for Computing Machinery, New York (2014). https://doi.org/10.1145/2641248.2645641

15. Koelle, M., Nicolae, M., Nittala, A.S., Teyssier, M., Steimle, J.: Prototyping soft devices with interactive bioplastics. In: Proceedings of the 35th Annual ACM Symposium on User Interface Software and Technology, pp. 1–16 (2022)

16. Mueller, F.F., et al.: Next steps for human-computer integration. In: Proceedings of the 2020 CHI Conference on Human Factors in Computing Systems, pp. 1–15 (2020)

17. Rowen, A., Grabowski, M., Rancy, J.P., Crane, A.: Impacts of wearable augmented reality displays on operator performance, situation awareness, and communication in safety-critical systems. Appl. Ergon. **80**, 17–27 (2019)

18. Salvendy, G., Karwowski, W.: Handbook of Human Factors and Ergonomics. Wiley, Hoboken (2021)

19. Speicher, M., Hall, B.D., Nebeling, M.: What is mixed reality? In: Proceedings of the 2019 CHI Conference on Human Factors in Computing Systems, pp. 1–15 (2019)

20. Stefana, E., Marciano, F., Rossi, D., Cocca, P., Tomasoni, G.: Wearable devices for ergonomics: a systematic literature review. Sensors **21**(3), 777 (2021)

21. Wang, C.H., Tsai, C.E., Yong, S., Chan, L.: Slice of light: transparent and integrative transition among realities in a multi-HMD-user environment. In: Proceedings of the 33rd Annual ACM Symposium on User Interface Software and Technology, pp. 805–817 (2020)

22. Zeagler, C.: Where to wear it: functional, technical, and social considerations in on-body location for wearable technology 20 years of designing for wearability. In: Proceedings of the 2017 ACM International Symposium on Wearable Computers, ISWC 2017, pp. 150–157. Association for Computing Machinery, New York (2017). https://doi.org/10.1145/3123021.3123042

Enhancing Ergonomic Design Process with Digital Human Models for Improved Driver Comfort in Space Environment

Md Tariqul Islam[1], Kamelia Sepanloo[1], Ronak Velluvakkandy[1], Andre Luebke[2], and Vincent G. Duffy[1(✉)]

[1] Purdue University, West Lafayette, IN 47904, USA
{islam70,ksepanlo,rvelluva,duffy}@purdue.edu
[2] Human Solutions of North America, Morrisville, NC 27560, USA
aluebke@human-solutions.com

Abstract. The primary focus of this research is to develop digital human models (DHM) that include accurate posture and motion prediction models for a diverse population. The posture and motion prediction models currently employed in DHMs must be adapted and improved based on actual motion data in order to provide validity for simulations of challenging dynamic activities (Ahmed et al. 2018). Additionally, if accurate models for predicting human posture and motion are developed and applied, they can be combined with psychophysical and biomechanical models to provide a deeper understanding of dynamic human performance and population-specific limitations, and these new DHM models will eventually serve as a useful tool for ergonomics design. In this line, we are making an effort to forecast driver comfort and postures when designing a mars rover's seat and peripherals using RAMSIS software. The core of RAMSIS is a highly accurate three-dimensional human model that is built on anthropometry databases from around the globe and can simulate humans with a variety of body measurements. To assess comfort during the design process, we employ a variety of additional analysis techniques, including those for comfort studies, eyesight, reachability, and force.

Keywords: Ergonomic Analysis · Digital Human Modeling · RAMSIS · Simulation

1 Introduction and Background

Early in the media and entertainment business, digital human modeling (DHM), a technology for replicating human interaction with a product or workplace in a virtual environment, was introduced. The manufacturing, agriculture, healthcare, transportation, and aviation industries are rapidly adopting this technology to proactively assess human performance and its constraints. However, DHM's applicability in designing ergonomic products and work environments for the space environment is restricted. Since new-generation simulators are used in training for spacecraft launch, flight, and landing,

V. G. Duffy (Ed.): HCII 2023, LNCS 14028, pp. 87–101, 2023.
https://doi.org/10.1007/978-3-031-35741-1_8

distributed simulation is essential for modeling complex systems. Astronauts now spend hours practicing in simulators for every minute they spend in space, so they are comfortable with the scheduled tasks and can respond quickly to unforeseen circumstances. They rehearse their own decisions and learn to predict the reactions of their teammates, which is crucial for successfully overcoming an unanticipated issue in space. In addition, simulations are essential for testing flights and peripherals since this is where everything comes together.

After multiple iterations of development and testing, the results are analyzed to optimize designs for specific situations. To achieve the required scalability, the design strategy leverages the benefits of having several layered architectures and more flexible middleware solutions. This virtual review approach is effective for producing user-centered products by adding human factor concepts at an early stage of design, which decreases design time and enhances product quality. Several distributed simulation research projects have focused on web-based worldwide cooperation and its structures for improved model implementation.

To represent the real world in simulations, a simplified model that captures the actions conducted during a process or the phenomena that emerge throughout a process might be utilized (Litwin and Stadnicka 2019). The term "model" can apply to any component of the human; however, it most commonly refers to a mathematical instrument for the simulation (typically in software, which makes the simulation digital) and prediction of some aspect of human performance and future results. This area is limited to the use of human models in physical design, for instance, in human factors engineering. Typically, this design endeavor involves human interface design, and the computer models employed are based on anthropometric data (Digital Human Modeling, n.d.). The chance for students to observe a process in action is usually limited. As a result, simulations can be used to study the behavior of processes. In today's engineering workspaces, modeling, simulation, and computational tools are commonly used to aid in the research and design of systems. Because of this, modeling and simulation capabilities have been included in several scientific and engineering fields as analytical tools to improve the understanding of complex phenomena and as predictive tools to evaluate the viability of new designs (Magana 2017).

Professionals can effectively augment theoretical and experimental methodologies to the discovery and innovation processes in engineering workplaces by using modeling and simulation. Engineering education policymakers and practitioners, among other stakeholders, have stressed the need for educational researchers and educators to consider strategies to integrate students into the activities of professional science and engineering through modeling and simulation. Recent advancements in computer technology over the past 20 years have made it easier to build computer simulations for ergonomics. One of the primary use of digital human modeling (DHM) simulations is to rate the productivity of human operators. DHM can also be used in conjunction with computer-aided design to evaluate the ergonomics of product design (CAD). Simulation can aid in the evaluation of an ergonomic design by offering a preliminary evaluation of ergonomic characteristics in a simulated or virtual environment. A crucial aspect of enabling simulation in ergonomic-related investigations is the capacity to assess alternative state-of-the-art solutions or the impact of advancements from an ergonomics standpoint. Another important component of ergonomic design to consider is human-centered design (HCD). To better address user needs, HCD emphasizes iterative system development while guaranteeing that end users and stakeholders are actively involved in the design process (Margetis et al. 2021).

While healthier populations live longer and are more productive, it also helps to the advancement of the economy (Vardell 2020) and is, therefore, one of the most important aspects of human well-being. Workers usually engage in some form of physical exercise at work, and certain job duties need continuous manual effort. An ergonomically sound workplace can minimize musculoskeletal pain, increase efficiency and productivity, cut expenses associated with production, and promote overall well-being (Chim 2019). More advanced tools are now required to move heavier goods, equipment, and materials throughout the workplace as needs for job sites have increased. The introduction of the mars rover addressed this need in the space environment. These vehicles are frequently used for exploration and carrying out routine research tasks in the space environment. However, the rover must be properly designed to meet all the needs of an astronaut, where the needs cover a broad range of physical, cognitive, and research needs. A poorly designed rover may be uncomfortable for the operator and will not accomplish the intended research objectives. For a mars rover, like any other, seat design is one of the most crucial steps among all other design considerations. Long durations of time spent riding on uneven terrain with poorly designed seat characteristics can result in repetitive use injuries to the musculoskeletal system, much as those experienced by forklift users, according to research (Collins et al. 1999). Musculoskeletal injuries, such as sprains, tears, strains, discomfort, and pain, account for roughly 52% of reported injuries for 10,000 workers posing a serious risk to human health (*U.S. Bureau of Labor Statistics*, n.d.).

For safe working conditions, it is essential to build an ergonomically sound work environment. A comfortable workplace that fosters a positive work atmosphere can increase productivity. Consequently, the primary objective of this work is to comprehend in detail how astronauts will interact with the environment of the Mars rover and to include this understanding in the design. To improve the physical ergonomics of workstations, the discipline of ergonomics is becoming more and more dependent on the digital human modeling of workers (Bäckstrand et al. 2007). In this study, we utilized RAMSIS, a market-leading simulation tool, to evaluate the ergonomics of the Digital Human Model using this 3D CAD manikin tool that simulates the real world. With the use of visualization employing digital human models, the decision-maker in an organization can better appreciate the potential implications of design alterations using this tool. This evaluation modality is inexpensive and more effective than traditional physical ergonomic modeling techniques. Engineers can modify the surroundings of workstations and evaluate how ergonomic changes will affect human operators using computer-aided design software applications like RAMSIS.

2 Problem Statement

In this paper, we demonstrated the use of RAMSIS software to simulate astronauts' posture while driving the mars rovers and assess their comfort accordingly. To ensure effective accommodation of these users from the onset of the design process, RAMSIS's primary aim is to provide designers with a realistic representation of occupants in their CAD model, both in terms of anthropometry and posture. Therefore, we first model a set of boundary manikins inside the vehicle with the optimal posture. To reduce discomfort to an appropriate level for all manikins, this work focused on evaluating the level of comfort experienced by rover operators of different body sizes (i.e., 5th, 10th, 20th, 30th, 40th, 50th, 60th, 70th, 80th, 90th, and 95th percentage body measurements) and the adjustment ranges required for several aspects of the driver's seat, driver's touchscreen, comfort, visibility, blind spot, and readability in the space environment.

3 Procedure

The following steps have been taken in this work to conduct analysis:

1. Creating task-specific boundary manikins
2. Transferring the boundary manikins to the car seat
3. Analyzing and improving the seat adjustment range to guarantee that all percentile manikins can reach the primary controls comfortably.
4. Evaluation of the passenger's level of comfort as well as the position, reach and reach of the touch screen
5. A review of the driver's visibility when using controls
6. A discussion of the center of gravity for both the body and the passenger's suit.
7. A description of restricted motion conditions, external forces (such as the driver's anatomy and the steering wheel), and internal body pressure against the suit.

Before getting into the analysis using RAMSIS, we first conducted several bibliometric analyses on different platforms using the keywords "Ergonomic Analysis, Digital Human Modeling, Simulation" From Scopus, 88 research articles were screened by the website (shown in Fig. 1).

The connected research networks were also identified by using VOS Viewer (Fig. 2). Bibliometric networks are generated and visualized using this software. These networks, which include journals, researchers, and individual publications, can be constructed through citation, bibliographic linkage, co-citation, and co-authorship relationships. The largest cluster was found in the bibliometric network and came from the research group of Hanson and Lamkull. Furthermore, it was surprising to see how many research teams were engaged in the same area of study but did it independently and with little collaboration.

Fig. 1. Bibliometric analysis of Scopus articles

3.1 Boundary Manikin Creation

RAMSIS software allows us to create any target group, define size, gender, population, and age-specific features, and model them in 3D in the context of the environment. Figure 3 depicts the software's platform.

In addition, several roles (such as driver and passenger) can be allocated to RAMSIS manikins, each of which is familiar with its typical posture and movement patterns. RAMSIS calibrates task- and role-specific postures according to the interior of the vehicle. Figure 4 depicts four manikins posed as a driver, a passenger, and a standing individual. As our design process focuses primarily on driver comfort, we developed manikins with driver roles for this study.

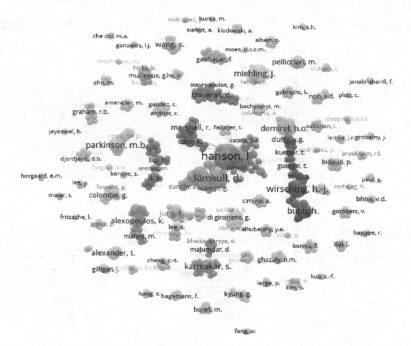

Fig. 2. Bibliometric analysis of research networks using VOS Viewer

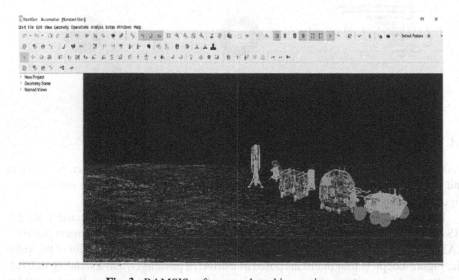

Fig. 3. RAMSIS software and working environment

To accommodate the large range of human body sizes, we considered different body sizes for our driver's position. For example, we selected a 5th percentile male body, gave it the label "5th percentile man," and assigned it the role of "driver." Similarly,

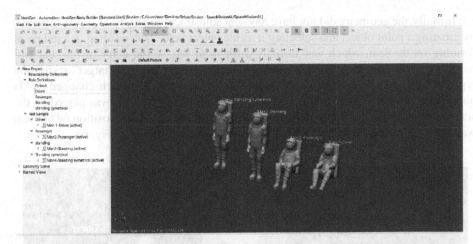

Fig. 4. Manikins in 4 different roles

we assigned the driver role to all the manikins of different percentiles (i.e., 5th, 10th, 20th, 30th, 40th, 50th, 60th, 70th, 80th, 90th, and 95th percentage body measurements) (Fig. 5). We kept the other options as they defaulted in the additional options section.

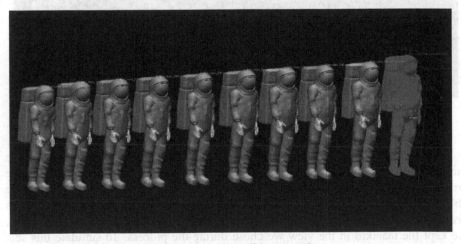

Fig. 5. Boundary manikin generation

3.2   Placement of the Manikin in the Seat

The rover seat design should be flexible enough to accommodate all ranges of manikins or people in real life. That is why we put different use case-based constraints to the seat at this stage. Here, flexible seat design means that the manikin must be able to reach the paddle, the screen, and other navigating equipment, which was designed to ensure a safe and comfortable ride.

Initially, the geometry did not have any seat adjustment function. This was achieved by creating a point object and selecting it as the object field. This resulted in a red point forming on the seat, which was initially difficult to see, so the color of the seat was modified. Next, the "define constraints" icon was clicked, and the "target" restriction type was selected, followed by "manikin comp" and "PHPT," which changed to "H point" automatically. The point object was clicked, and the manikin was placed on the seat automatically when apply was pressed. However, the manikin's position on the seat was not well-defined and should have been in the center of the seat (Fig. 6).

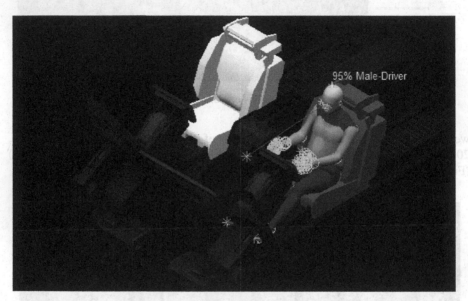

Fig. 6. Placement of the manikin in the rover seat

We used the keyboard keys "T" for top, "F" for front, and "L" for left view in the model window. So, to fix the seating alignment, we clicked on the manikin, chose the "translate" icon, and then in the translation mode, chose "relatively/vector." We were able to then enter particular X, Y, and Z values to move the manikin in relation to its present location. By hitting the "T," "L," and "R" keys appropriately for our needs, we kept the manikin in the view we chose during the process. To simulate this seat adjustment, we drew one line in the forward direction, allowing the seat to move back and forward in accordance with the needs of the person occupying it. To achieve this, we employed a tool feature. When we chose the "analysis" tab, "calculate body point," "add," and "PHPT" in the body point fields sequentially, a new point was generated at the boundary of the person's heap. After clicking the newly formed point, we duplicated another point by clicking "edit" > "copy" > "edit" > "paste." Next, we moved the x-axis position by 200 mm using the translate icon. Next, we clicked "create geometry" on the geometry tab once more, choosing the "point to point" line type while selecting the initial and last points we had already generated. We were able to establish a line for horizontal seat adjustment in this way.

Then, using the "define restrictions" option, we added another constraint to the newly created H point, just as we had done with the first point. The line that was just created served as the environment object in this new constraint, allowing us to guarantee that the manikin can move anywhere along the line. After choosing the line, we selected the "create" and "posture calculation" tabs. By doing so, the manikin could now sit with its back against the seat line. We must choose the line length when building this restriction so that the manikin can touch the touchscreen and the necessary control hardware.

We did not have any shoes on our manikin at this point and to do so, we opened object properties with the right mouse button, navigated to additional options > shoe model, selected "workboot" as the type, and then clicked apply to activate the shoe. At that point, we added another constraint to restrict the left heel of the manikin's movement in the XY plane. To view the points, we were creating beforehand, we had to turn off the texture. Then we selected geometry > point > construct on object and clicked to designate a point on the base. Then, by selecting Geometry > Create Geometry > Plane > Point and Vectors, we generated a plane. The first vector should be the x-axis and the second vector will be the y-axis, and the point should be the point we generated previously. We then added a new restriction to ensure that the shoe's heel stays above the surface we made. To accomplish this, we chose constraints > define restrictions > manikin comp. Here, we had to choose the lowest position on the left heel, labeled "Left Heel" in the Manikin comp. The plane that we previously generated was selected in the environment object before we clicked the "posture calculation" icon and the "start" button. So, the plane was marked on the heel of the manikin. We repeated the process with regard to the identical restriction for the right heel (Fig. 7).

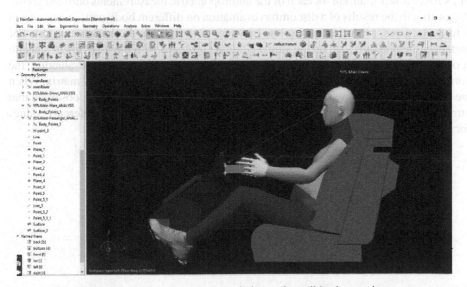

Fig. 7. Touch screen adjustment restriction and manikin shoe assignment

To prevent the feet from touching the steering sidebar in the XZ plane, we added more constraints in the following stage, similar to how we did for the heel. To do that, we first built the surface via the aforementioned method (first creating one point using geometry and then creating one plane using point and vectors where the vectors will be X and Z axis this time). At this point, we selected the "define restrictions" button, the "limit surface" restriction type, and the "left Inner Ball" small yellow point on the left heel of the manikin. We entered "Negative Y direction" in the orientation field and added a 50 mm offset. At this point, the manikin tilts if we calculate posture, and the right foot will encroach on the steering sidebar. In order to prevent it, we added additional restrictions by clicking on define restrictions, restriction type (pelvis rotation), selecting "tilt sideways," clicking "update to current angle," and then clicking on posture calculation. We were still getting the right feet inside the steering bar at this point. To prevent it, we implement the identical offset constraint that we did for the left feet, except this time the constrained surface is the right side of the steering wheel bar instead of the left.

3.3   Comfortability Assessment

We defined a plane (200 mm * 50 mm) in the XZ plane for the display touch screen adjustment for both hands for the manikins in the following phase. Then, to ensure that the driver can access the touchscreen while seated, constraints were put in place. At this point, we copied all the constraints we created for this particular manikin and used a special paste to apply them to all the manikins of various sizes. Then, with the posture calculation active, all of the manikins of different sizes were seated on the rover seat with the previously mentioned predefined restrictions.

Figure 8 displays the results of the discomfort assessment tests performed on the mars rover driver manikin for each of the anthropometric measurements outlined above. According to the results of a discomfort evaluation on different body parts, a value from 1 to 8 are given, where 1 denotes the most comfort and 8 is the lowest comfort. For instance, the pressure load on the spinal column correlates with the assessment's health score and therefore, a lower health value is preferred. According to the evaluation, the current seat design provides all of the manikins with a good comfortability matrix. When we compared the achieved comfortability values to reference values, we observed that our proposed system ensures a value that is lower than or equal to the reference values for all the manikins.

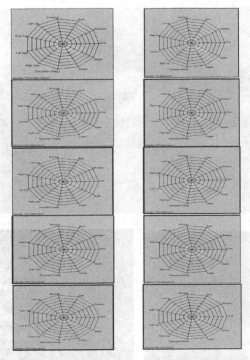

Fig. 8. Comfort assessment for the manikin's of varying anthropometric measurements

We also adjusted the manikin's neck posture to ensure that it was looking at the touch screen. Figure 9 shows the posture of the neck and body when staring at the screen. We also evaluated the smallest font size necessary for the manikin to comfortably read the content on the touch display. As seen in Fig. 9 (right), this analysis indicates that the display's minimum font size should be 1.98 mm in width and 3.02 mm in height.

A picture of the 95th-percentile driver's field of vision is shown in Fig. 10. Parts of the windshield glass structure block the driver's forward vision when looking down, creating an awkwardly angled blind spot. Due to this blind zone, the driver may find it difficult to control the vehicle safely. As a result, the driver may compromise the safety of the rover and the object in that blind region. This suggests that the windshield design has to be modified to improve visibility to the front left corner.

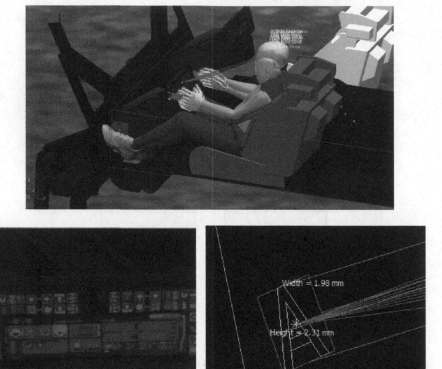

Fig. 9. Neck posture (top) displaying gazing point (bottom left), and minimum font size (bottom right) of the manikin

The 95th and 5th percentile manikins' left, and right arms were likewise assessed for reachability. Figures 11 show that, for both percentiles, the touchscreen is within the manikin's reach, ensuring that the existing design will meet the needs of all other manikins since it is already accommodating two extreme examples of manikin sizes. Here, the 95th percentile male's reachability is represented by the larger half sphere, while the 5th percentile male's reachability is represented by the smaller half sphere.

3.4 Proposed Design Changes

Based on the data and corresponding analysis, we recommend an adjustable touchscreen monitor which can move in the XZ axis where relative X and Y movement values should be at least 200 mm in the X direction and 50 mm in the Y direction. In addition, the front windshield should be redesigned as due to the support structure of the left side glass, there is a big blind spot which may compromise the safe operation of the vehicle in the mars environment.

Fig. 10. Visibility study and blind spot detection

Fig. 11. Left and right arm reachability for 95th and 5th percentile manikin

4 Discussion

In this study, we demonstrated the capabilities of RAMSIS digital human modeling software for the design and evaluation of a Mars rover's seat and peripherals. However, the same approach can be applied to a wide variety of applications, such as passenger vehicles, forklifts, and workstation design. Therefore, similar studies can be conducted on various applications in order to make informed decisions on the design and user comfort.

The current study was done with the assumption that the driver was not wearing a space suit inside the rover. Nevertheless, based on our investigation, we created the seat adjustment so that the driver could sit on the rover while wearing the suit. However, the substantial weight of the suit will cause the astronaut's center of gravity to shift from where it is currently, therefore this must be considered when analyzing movement while wearing the suit. Currently, since the manikin was not thought to be wearing a suit, the center of gravity would be in the front as opposed to when the manikin was wearing a suit, where the extra weight of the suit would cause the center of gravity to shift backward. RAMSIS allows us to conduct this further analysis. This might be one effective way to continue this work in the future. This knowledge would be beneficial in addition to a question-and-answer session with a RAMSIS representative once an initial demonstration is finished so that users can troubleshoot any outstanding problems with their help. Additionally, more discussion is required regarding the numerous studies conducted and the correct interpretation of the results. Our interpretation of this data may deviate from its intended use because, specifically, the visual field analysis at the back of the rover was not covered during the demos for the current study.

5   Future Work

The surrogate modeling strategy utilized in the DHM research provides a time- and resource-efficient alternative to conventional reactive ergonomics approaches. The computational method proposed in this study does not require the presence of an HFE expert in order to conduct experiments and evaluate early design concepts. In contrast, executing task simulations with idea product models in DHM can provide the benefit of iterating digitally on design concepts (Ahmed et al. 2018).

Anthropometry is a key part of DHM-based product design and workplace evaluation. Various anthropometric databases are incorporated in RAMSIS software to obtain the manikin for the targeted population in the simulation process; however, in the current version of RAMSIS, we are limited to the Germany and Germany 2004 databases, so expanding the database would allow us to model a manikin that is more representative of the population as a whole. We have not shown the feasibility and effectiveness of the design method in this article. This is essential for industries to conduct a validation study comparing the results received from our model, which includes a functional Mars-rover prototype, with the results obtained from people using a simulator setup.

Implementing artificial intelligence (AI) to produce or synthesize models, gaining acceptability, is a second possibility for future work. Currently, AI's use is restricted to particular performance analysis, although this is gradually changing. The relationship between actual humans and digital humans will strengthen over time. It will go beyond observing a computer-based manikin. However, such integration of technology for the space environment is currently restricted and would require substantial collaboration between ergonomists and designers to develop. DHM users must comprehend human variability and its impact on design, the implications of variable and unpredictable human behavior, the extent to which the models are indicative of a particular capacity, and the ramifications of contemplating a plan univariately (Rabelo et al. 2013).

References

Ahmed, S., Gawand, M.S., Irshad, L., Demirel, H.O.: Exploring the design space using a surrogate model approach with digital human modeling simulations. In: Proceedings of the ASME Design Engineering Technical Conference,1B-2018 (2018). https://doi.org/10.1115/DETC201886323

Bäckstrand, G., et al.: Ergonomics analysis in a virtual environment. Int. J. Manufact. Res. **2**(2) (2007). https://doi.org/10.1504/IJMR.2007.014645

Chim, J.M.Y.: 6Ws in ergonomics workplace design. In: Bagnara, S., Tartaglia, R., Albolino, S., Alexander, T., Fujita, Y. (eds.) IEA 2018. AISC, vol. 824, pp. 1282–1286. Springer, Cham (2019). https://doi.org/10.1007/978-3-319-96071-5_129

Collins, J.W., Smith, G.S., Baker, S.P., Warner, M.: Injuries related to forklifts and other powered industrial vehicles in automobile manufacturing. Am. J. Indus. Med. **36**(5) (1999). https://doi.org/10.1002/(SICI)1097-0274(199911)36:5<513::AID-AJIM3>3.0.CO;2-K

Digital Human Modeling. (n.d.). NASA Technical Reports Server (NTRS)

Litwin, P., Stadnicka, D.: Computer modeling and simulation in engineering education: intended learning outcomes development. In: Hamrol, A., Grabowska, M., Maletic, D., Woll, R. (eds.) MANUFACTURING 2019. LNME, pp. 169–184. Springer, Cham (2019). https://doi.org/10.1007/978-3-030-17269-5_12

Magana, A.J.: Modeling and simulation in engineering education: a learning progression. J. Profess. Issues Eng. Educ. Pract. **143**(4) (2017). https://doi.org/10.1061/(ASCE)EI.1943-5541.0000338

Margetis, G., Ntoa, S., Antona, M., Stephanidis, C.: Human-centered design of artificial intelligence. Handbook Hum. Factors Ergon. (2021). https://doi.org/10.1002/9781119636113.ch42

Rabelo, L., Sala-Diakanda, S., Pastrana, J., Marin, M., Bhide, S., Joledo, O., Bardina, J.: Simulation modeling of space missions using the high level architecture.Model. Simul. Eng. (2013). https://doi.org/10.1155/2013/967483

U.S. Bureau of Labor Statistics (n.d.). IIF News Releases

Vardell, E.: Global Health Observatory Data Repository. Med. Ref. Serv. Q. **39**(1) (2020). https://doi.org/10.1080/02763869.2019.1693231

Improving Facility Layout Using an Ergonomics and Simulation-Based Approach

Krittika J. Iyer[✉], Nandini Narula, Marlyn Binu, and Vincent G. Duffy

Purdue University, West Lafayette, IN 47906, USA

{iyer151,nnarula,mbinu,duffy}@purdue.edu

Abstract. In today's world, a sizable portion of small and medium sized businesses deal with various issues relating to productivity. These can be in the form of machine conditions, bottlenecks, material handling delays and various others issues. However, the success of the businesses depends on work efficiency and productivity. With new engineering techniques, one can design, develop, and implement better facility layouts that can help with both efficiency and productivity. The FlexSim software is used to develop these better facility layouts by simulating the machine areas and plant operations. It is also used to test and analyze the performance of the remodeled facility layouts under various scenarios. Each run of a modified version of the simulation shows changes in productivity and performance. By using simulations, we find a better and a more economical alternative to simply increasing the efficiency of every machine. In this paper, we investigate how discrete plant layouts affect the manufacturing process's production limits.

Keywords: Ergonomics · Facility Layout · Efficiency · Simulation · FlexSim · REBA

1 Introduction and Background

Operational efficiency can be influenced by several factors, like planning and control, inventory management, job design, capacity, maintenance, et cetera. Simulation-based techniques can help improve operational efficiency on these factors. Another key factor is worker health and safety, which, if neglected, can lead to costly delays. Ergonomically designed facilities can address this issue efficiently, thereby greatly enhancing the overall operational efficiency of the system. It is therefore particularly important to include ergonomics in facility design.

1.1 Literature Review

- Kanse et al. concluded that by analyzing the parameters like manpower, machine process time, machine setup time, layout, production rate, etc., simulation software gave information about the effect of modification of system layout [1].

- Sugandi et al. presented analytical methods and simulation techniques of a maintenance unit like XYZ Industry's access and processing times by contrasting the current system with the FlexSim software model. Since the software has a higher level of computational complexity, the model would be much more accurate with this software [2].
- Kulkarni et al. examined variables such as the workforce, machine process time, machine setup time, layout, production rate, etc. and showed how the effects of changing the system layout can be determined with the aid of simulation software [3].
- Deros et al. (2011) found from their study that the current assembly workstation at the company they examined needed to be redesigned to eliminate awkward postures and anthropometric mismatches to lower musculoskeletal disorders (MSD) problems and improve productivity among assembly workers [5].
- Delgado et al. proposed an integrated model that enhanced the layout of the entire facility, including the workstations, and ensured appropriateness for both the layout and the workstation because of taking real dimensions into account [6].
- Qin LI et al. applied Systematic Layout Planning (SLP) and FlexSim simulation software to carry out reasonable adjustments and optimization design for the workshop facility layout, achieving the goal of reducing the logistics distance and logistics cost, improving production proficiency, and lowering the equipment cost [7].

1.2 Ergonomics and Its Importance

Soon after the industrial revolution, Scientific Management principles took a significant hold on work environments. It aimed to improve the economic efficiency of organizations and labor productivity. However, it met with criticism as it did so with a focus on technology rather than human factors of organizations. It soon led to the start of the Human Relations era, where human aspects of working environments and conditions became more focused and improved workplace conditions significantly. The idea behind it was that if people were comfortable in the workplace, their efficiency would improve, thus also improving the efficiency of the organization as a whole.

Ergonomics is the "study of people's efficiency in their working environment." It aims to increase the elements of efficiency and comfort in the workplace and is often accomplished by designs that go unnoticed by most people. They could be in the form of appropriate heights of a workstation, number of workstations, mobility of work garments et cetera.

Efficiency in organizations is a prime driver of its long-term success. As such, any method to increase the efficiency of an organization is important. The ergonomics of a workplace can help directly increase a workplace's efficiency. Therefore, a great deal of importance must be placed on the ergonomic design of a workplace environment. A lack of attention to ergonomics of a workplace can cause disastrous results. An example in real life can be found in that of the Boeing 737 Max - a lack of attention to human factors led to a crash and costing the lives of 157 passengers!

1.3 What is Simulation?

The idea behind simulations is simple. It provides a manner of visualizing a workplace design and checking its efficiency before resources have been used to implement the design on a large scale. Various software have been designed to aid in this. Some examples are FlexSim, RAMSIS, SimSolid, SOLIDWORKS, Teamcenter, Navisworks, Autodesk Fusion 360, Simulink. In this project, we will make use of the FlexSim simulation software.

1.4 FlexSim

Understanding FlexSim. FlexSim is software used for Discrete Event Simulation and is easy to use. It allows users to create three-dimensional computer simulation models of real-life systems. Experiments can then be run on these models. A set of performance reports help users identify problems with the model. It can thus be tweaked until the desired results are achieved. Doing so helps eliminate issues by encouraging users to think of alternative solutions.

Some important terms related to FlexSim must first be understood.

Flow items: These are dynamic objects that move through a model. For example, in a real factory, items that flow through the factory would be packages, pallets, manufacturing parts etc. These items, on the virtual platform of FlexSim are called Flow items.

FlexSim objects: To construct a simulation model, various building blocks must be used. These building blocks are referred to as FlexSim objects. In a real factory setting, these items would be objects such as a queue, source, conveyors, separators, et cetera. These items, on the virtual platform of FlexSim, are called FlexSim objects. These objects are in the Object Library grid panel on the left side of the FlexSim window.

Ports: To simulate the flow of FlexSim items from one FlexSim object to the next, the FlexSim objects must relate each other. This is done through connecting the ports on each object. FlexSim objects have input and output ports. Typically, the output port of an object is connected to the input port of the next object. Once the connection is established, flow items can move from one object to the next.

Process Flow: Once FlexSim objects have been connected through their ports, FlexSim flow items can move on them. This movement of items on various objects is referred to as process flow. In other words, a series of processing, queuing, and transportation stages in the FlexSim model is referred to as Process Flow.

Using FlexSim. As we learned from [8], once the model to be made has been decided upon, using FlexSim involves the following steps:

1. Create FlexSim objects for the model. This can be done by dragging and dropping the desired objects into the FlexSim model view window.
2. The user must connect the various FlexSim objects by their ports to define the process flow. To connect one object to the next, the user must press and hold the 'A' key, left click on the first object, then drag the mouse to the second object and release.

3. Once objects have been connected, the user must input data into the model. Examples of this data are processing times, resource demands, source item types, operation time, queue capacity, arrival rates, and so on. This can be done by double clicking on FlexSim objects and entering the details on the pop-ups that appear.
4. Once the model has been created, the user must click on the 'Run' button to start the simulation.
5. The user can then examine the results received and analyze them.
6. Based on the results, the user can make tweaks and changes to the model to enhance the results according to the user's needs.

Kanse et al. [1] showed a flowchart explaining the above process, starting with selecting a layout, then collecting data, building a simulation model, and then applying iteration conditions. If the model is validated, analyze the result, otherwise, start the process again.

1.5 Bibliometric Analysis

The analysis is done to see the trends of the topic being researched. The key specifiers used are "simulation, facility layout, and ergonomics." The results showed 1470 articles. The first category we used was to check papers published by year. The result showed that the first paper mentioning the specified keywords dated back to 1960 and some papers are yet to be published and will be in 2023 as shown in Fig. 1.

The category chosen next was to check the score of the paper using cite score. The cite score (which shows the impact of articles) of the article published in "Human Factors and Ergonomics in Manufacturing" was 3.0 out of 5.0 in 2021 (Fig. 2).

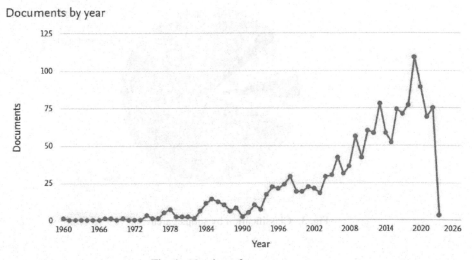

Fig. 1. Number of papers per year

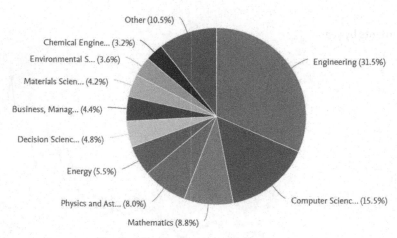

Human Factors and Ergonomics In Manufacturing
Formerly known as: The International journal of human factors in manufacturing
Scopus coverage years: from 1996 to Present
Publisher: Wiley-Blackwell
ISSN: 1090-8471   E-ISSN: 1520-6564
Subject area: (Engineering: Industrial and Manufacturing Engineering) (Social Sciences: Human Factors and Ergonomics)
Source type: Journal

View all documents >   Set document alert   Save to source list   Source Homepage

CiteScore 2021
3.0

SJR 2021
0.457

SNIP 2021
0.873

CiteScore   CiteScore rank & trend   Scopus content coverage

Improved CiteScore methodology
CiteScore 2021 counts the citations received in 2018–2021 to articles, reviews, conference papers, book chapters and data
papers published in 2018–2021, and divides this by the number of publications published in 2018–2021. Learn more >

CiteScore 2021

3.0 -   493 Citations 2018 - 2021
          163 Documents 2018 - 2021
Calculated on 05 May, 2022

CiteScoreTracker 2022 ⓘ

3.1 -   490 Citations to date
          158 Documents to date
Last updated on 05 October, 2022 • Updated monthly

Fig. 2. Cite score showing the impact of articles

The division of categories into subcategories makes it easier to find articles using subtopics. Engineering has the most articles that are related to the keywords that were used, which demonstrates how closely related it is to ergonomics, flexible manufacturing systems, and human factors. Figure 3 illustrates how documents are categorized according to various subject areas.

Documents by subject area

Other (10.5%)
Chemical Engine... (3.2%)
Environmental S... (3.6%)
Materials Scien... (4.2%)
Business, Manag... (4.4%)
Decision Scienc... (4.8%)
Energy (5.5%)
Physics and Ast... (8.0%)
Mathematics (8.8%)
Engineering (31.5%)
Computer Scienc... (15.5%)

Fig. 3. Classification by subject area

Figure 4 illustrates how documents are categorized according to their various sources per year.

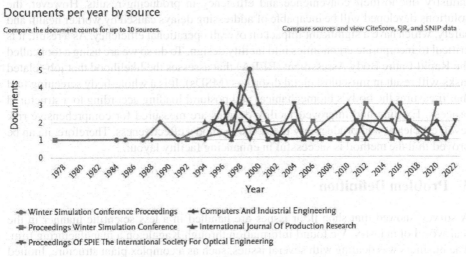

Fig. 4. Documents per year by source

The number of nations that have contributed research to the following subtopic facilitates the sharing of documents and is shown in Fig. 5. It can be seen from Fig. 5 that the United States is the top contributor with well over 350 papers thereby building a robust research network that allows multiple authors to work together.

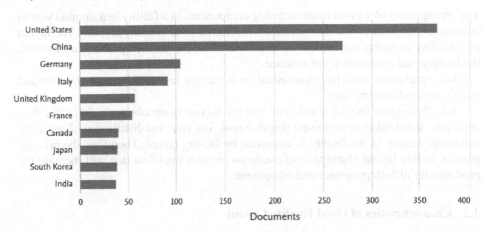

Fig. 5. Documents by country or territory

2 Objectives

The use of simulation-based techniques in facility layout has become popular in the industry due to their convenience and efficiency in producing results. However, the solutions developed will be incapable of addressing delays caused by worker health and safety, which have a significant impact on overall operational efficiency. As a result, it is critical to incorporate ergonomics into facility design. To do so we are using a tool called the Rapid Entire Body Assessment (REBA) that assessses the likelihood that job-related tasks will result in musculoskeletal disorders (MSDs). It is a whole-body screening tool that measures the body's biomechanical and postural loading according to a structured process. Existing and improved facility designs are measured for comprehensive risk level, efficiency, and productivity to test the method's effectiveness. Therefore, it can be proved that the method is successful in enhancing facility layout.

3 Problem Definition

A survey showed that shop floor issues are handled in a less scientific manner in the real world of industry. We found information through Kaggle on a manufacturing firm. The business was dealing with several issues, such as a complex plant structure, limited room for material handling, repetitive material retracing, and longer component cycle times. Given these challenges, the current project work tries to approach the issues in a more scientific manner by utilizing technologies like simulation software. The goal of this work is performance enhancement through modeling and simulation considering the parameters. We are looking into the manufacturing of dye plates.

4 Facility Layout

4.1 Introduction

The arrangement of various manufacturing components in a facility in a suitable way to accomplish targeted production outcomes is referred to as "facility layout". The layout of a facility considers the amount of space available, the finished product, user safety, the facility, and operational convenience.

An organization must pay close attention to facility layout to have an effective and efficient manufacturing unit.

A well-designed facility makes sure that production materials, tools, and labor flow smoothly and steadily at the lowest possible cost. The physical distribution of space for economic activity in the facility is examined by facility layout. Therefore, the primary goal of facility layout planning is to create an optimal workflow that will increase the productivity of both personnel and equipment.

4.2 Characteristics of Good Facility Layout

Good facility layout has several useful characteristics that are listed below:

• Effective and efficient use of available floor space

- The timely transportation of work from one location to another
- Effective use of production capacity
- Reduced material handling costs
- Utilize labor efficiently
- Reduced accidents
- Provide volume and product flexibility
- Provide ease of supervision and control
- Provide employees for safety and health
- Allow easy maintenance of machines and plants.
- Improve productivity

An organization can achieve the above-mentioned objective by ensuring the following:

- Better training of the workers and supervisors.
- Creating awareness about health hazard and safety standards
- Optimum utilization of workforce and equipment
- Encouraging empowerment and reducing administrative and other indirect work.

4.3 Factors Affecting the Facility Layout

There are several variables that affect how a facility is laid out and designed. The layout of a facility is influenced by these variables, which vary by industry. Following is a list of these elements guided by prior research [2]:

1. Nature of the product: Plant layout is influenced by the type of product that will be manufactured there. A line architecture would be more appropriate for moving small, light products from one machine to another with the least amount of time and effort. For large, hefty objects, a stationery layout would be appropriate. Process layout is ideal in situations where a wide range of non-standardized items are produced.
2. Production volume: If standardized goods are produced on a large scale, a line layout ought to be chosen. When manufacturing is driven by customer orders, a functional layout is ideal. Low-volume work production is best suited for it.
3. Location of the site: The selection of a particular plan is influenced by the topology and size of the site. The goal is to use space as efficiently as possible. The layout ought to work with the factory structure. The layout is further impacted by the placement of stairways, parking lots, elevators, and storage areas.
4. When using noisy, heavy machines, a stationary layout is preferred. Such massive equipment can be mounted on the ground. The placement of machinery should have enough room, and there should be enough room between them, to prevent accidents.
5. Climate: Temperature, illumination, and ventilation should be considered while deciding on the type of layout. The above factors should be considered to improve the health and welfare of employees.
6. Service facilities: The design should consider the employees' well-being and comfort. There ought to be sufficient access to restrooms and drinking water. There should be enough room for workers to walk about freely.

7. Safety of employees: While deciding on a particular type of layout, the safety of employees should be given importance. The layout should provide for obstruction-free floors, non-slippery floors, protection against dangerous fumes, excess heat, strong odors etc.

8. Type of production: There are several layout plans that are employed depending on the type of production. When creating non-standard items in response to job demands, a functional process outlet is ideal. A line plan would be suitable for the large-scale production of standardized products.

9. Type of process: In the case of intermittent types of production (bicycle manufacturing, electronics), functional layout is suitable. For synthetic types of production (cement and automobile industries), line layout is preferable.

10. Management policies: The management's policies about the type of product, quality, volume of production, level of plant integration, type of production, potential for future expansion, etc., determine the layout that should be used.

5 Methodology

5.1 Basic Data Collection

Plant or Framework Survey: Analyzes or reviews the current framework to decide on the various methods of simulation. Kanse et al. [1] used a plant layout in their study that we referenced. The existing facility layout they used has been re-drawn and shown in Fig. 6 for reference.

Collection of basic data: The collection of simulation information involved that data is gathered according to the simulation target and data with respect to the framework's beginning state.

The framework that integrates ergonomics and plant layout simulation in designing an efficient facility layout, on which the current study is based, is shown by Delgado et al. [6] in their Figure 2.1, page 94. In each stage of the model, variables are found. Process, ergonomics, and plant layout are all related to these factors. Process variables are considered in Process Analysis, and Ergonomic Variables are considered in Risk Assessment and Workstation Design. If the workstation design is improved, we move to plant layout simulation, which uses plant layout variables. We conduct a plant layout analysis, and determine whether the layout design has improved. A case study is used to test the effectiveness of a meta method such as production, worker, and workstation variation should be carefully considered when analyzing the data. Additionally, the division of this method considers elements related to process analysis, ergonomics, and layout simulation.

Process Variables. The process variables include productive and non-productive time, the distance that workers must travel between stations, productivity (units/hour), resource utilization, and the number of units produced. They are related to process cycle time, which is simply the total amount of time needed to move a unit of work from the start to the finish of a physical process. These are reliant on the production and the process itself

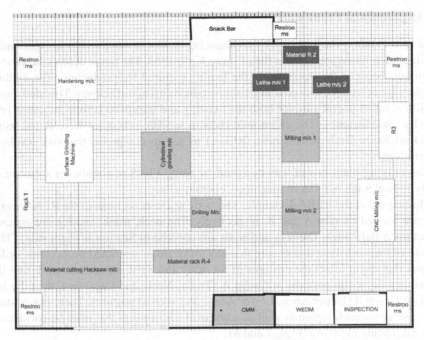

Fig. 6. Existing Plant Layout used as the basis for the FlexSim Analysis (Adapted from [1])

and have a direct impact on the size or dimension of the tested company's production floor.

Ergonomics Variable. The anthropometry of the workers and their workstations, the dimensions and spaces of the workstations, the weight handled and the coupling, as well as physical environmental factors that have an impact on productivity like lighting, air/ventilation, temperature, and noise, are all examples of ergonomic variables. Ergonomics also considers body posture and awkward positions, with a focus on the neck, arm, wrist, legs, and truck. The impact of these variables on the health, safety, and productivity of the workers can be summarized as being related to them. To ascertain what activities and other elements raise ergonomic risks in workers, these variables are analyzed. These can vary from one production or process to another because they are so heavily reliant on the workers, their activities, the process, the workstations, and the physical environment.

Plant Layout Variables. The model's final set of variables, which have to do with plant layout, includes process cycle time (both productive and unproductive), resource utilization, productivity rate expressed in units per hour, total units produced, total distance traveled, and process efficiency. Using FlexSim software, these variables are all measured. The revised workstation dimensions, the layout shapes, and the area of the production floor all changed.

5.2 Experimental Framework

Kanse et al. [1] show the framework for enhancing facility layout through an ergonomics and simulation-based approach in their Figure 3, page 863. The figure depicts the various movements between the machines in the facility required for production. The method considers factors related to ergonomic risks, productivity, and efficiency. This study used FlexSim simulation software for both the existing and improved layouts to gauge productivity and efficiency. The ergonomic risks in specific processes were found using the Rapid Entire Body Assessment (REBA) to set up comprehensive risk levels in workstations.

The existing plant layout was designed by using FlexSim simulation software. It clearly indicates the number of machines, operators, etc.

Making use of the REBA-Example: The body segment sections of the REBA worksheet are located on tabs A and B, respectively. The neck, trunk, and leg are covered in Section A (left side). The arm and wrist are covered in Section B (right side). This division of the worksheet makes sure that any awkward or restricted neck, trunk, or leg postures that might affect the postures of the arms and wrist are considered during the assessment. Score the postures in Group A (Trunk, Neck, and Legs) first, then the left and right Group B (Upper Arms, Lower Arms, and Wrists) postures. There is a posture scoring scale for each region as well as additional adjustments that must be considered when calculating the score (Figs. 7 and 8).

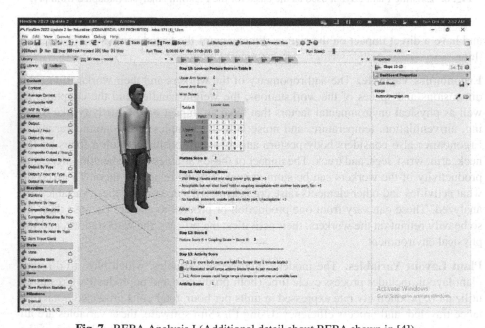

Fig. 7. REBA Analysis I (Additional detail about REBA shown in [4])

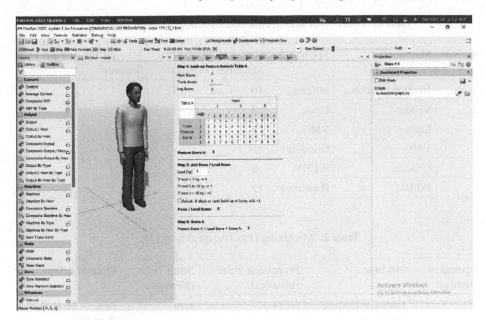

Fig. 8. REBA Analysis II

Here, we use FlexSim simulation software to simulate the trial work. First, choose the 01 part for trial and error, and support the simulation of the current design model. After that, input the part's information and apply different conditions or cycles to that design. At the very last, conduct an investigation into the results. Selected as a part of exploratory work: M- Section Plates. Trial-and-error steps: A) Summary and Information Variety: Review Fig. 6's representation of the assembling unit's current plant design first. After some time, by embracing Time to focus on the procedure, gathers the information about the machining. Tables 1 and 2 have information including the following items: machining time, setup time, machine-to-machine distance, etc. Each activity's handling time is the best component in the assembly system. Every activity has a specific processing time that allows producers to reduce costs while increasing benefits and client satisfaction. We choose two components from the assembling unit for this trial-and-error process based on the cycle time that was previously examined. B) Remake currently used format with simulation software: FlexSim simulation software is used to plan the current plant design. It clearly displays the number of computers, administrators, and other information. Provide input data for each machine's handling and setup time, machine distance, and other values shown in Tables 1 and 2 (as observed in [1]).

Table 1. Data of Machine-to-Machine Distance (Adapted from [1])

Sr. No	Machine 1	Machine 2	Distance between two Machines (Meters)	Material Travel Time in Seconds
1	Hacksaw Machine	Milling 2	10	80
2	Milling	Lathe	3	32
3	Lathe	VMC	4	42
4	VMC	Grinding	11	95
5	Grinding	WEDM	9	60
6	WEDM	Hardening	12	120

Table 2. Machining Data (Adapted from [1])

Operation Number	Machine	Processing Time (Minutes)	Setup Time (Minutes)	Operation Type
1	Hacksaw Cutting Machine	60.14	4.99	Setup – Manual Processing – Automatic
2	Vertical Milling Machine	180	15	Manual
3	Lathe Machine	86.70	17.8	Manual
4	CNC Machine	29.72	2.95	Setup – Manual Processing – Automatic
5	Surface Grinding Machine	183.5	10.25	Setup – Manual Processing – Automatic
6	WEDM Machine	260.68	31.3	Setup – Manual Processing – Automatic
7	Hardening Machine	120	20	Setup – Manual Processing – Automatic
8	Inspection	15	20	Setup – Manual

6 Results and Discussions

Kanse et al. [1] show that by simulating the current layout using FlexSim with the input parameters, an output of 17 parts in a week was obtained. In their figure 5, they display a Gantt Chart showing the conditions of different machines for ideal, setup, operating, processing, blocked and transport. They [1] obtain the following results (reproduced here for ease of understanding) (Table 3):

Table 3. Result of 6-day week, considering two eight-hour shifts (Adapted from [1])

Object	Class	Stat Input	Stat Output
Source 1	Source	0	124
Hack Saw Machine	Processor	124	23
Milling Machine 1	Processor	23	22
Lathe	Processor	22	21
VMC	Processor	21	20
Grinding	Processor	20	19
WEDM	Processor	19	18
Hardening	Processor	18	17
Inspection	Processor	17	17
Sink	Source	17	17

Simulation Design for Improved Efficiency. The simulation model offers a response to the inquiry i.e., the number of machines that are truly expected in the process to keep the production cycle working appropriately. The simulation model ought to be used in the framework for examinations to impact parameters in the full process. FlexSim Simulation Software is used.

6.1 Iteration 1

Placement of Machines According to Process or Workstation

For the first iteration, Kanse et al. [1] added an extra machine to improve production. They say that instead of operators remaining idle, their efficiency can be used in production to improve the productivity of the whole system. By running the iteration with the extra added machine, they obtained results showing an output of **46** production parts in a week – a significant improvement. A section of their results table (obtained from FlexSim) has been reproduced below to aid understanding (Table 4).

6.2 Iteration 2

In the second iteration, Kanse et al. [1] change the layout of the machines on FlexSim and apply the information parameters. After running the simulation model, a look at the results shows that the changed design gives an output yield of **56** production parts in a week – an improvement over iteration 1. A section of their results table (obtained from FlexSim) has been reproduced below to aid understanding (Table 5).

Table 4. Result of 6-day week, considering two eight-hour shifts (Adapted from [1])

Object	Class	Stat Input	Stat Output
Source 2	Source	0	1352
MCM	Processor	1352	356
Milling Machine	Processor	356	122
Lathe	Processor	122	122
CNC MCH	Processor	122	123
Grinding	Processor	123	65
WEDM	Processor	65	35
Hardening MCH	Processor	35	38
Inspection	Processor	38	46
Sink16		46	**46**
Operator 1	Sink	0	0
Operator 2	Operator	0	0
Operator 3	Operator	0	0
Operator 4	Operator	0	0
	Operator	0	0

Table 5. Result of 6-day week, considering two eight-hour shifts (Adapted from [1])

Object	Class	Stat Input	Stat Output
Source 2	Source	0	1352
MCM	Processor	1352	356
Milling Machine	Processor	356	122
Lathe	Processor	122	122
CNC MCH	Processor	122	123
Grinding	Processor	123	65
WEDM	Processor	65	35
Hardening MCH	Processor	35	42
Inspection	Processor	42	54
Sink16		54	**56**
Operator 1	Sink	0	0
Operator 2	Operator	0	0
Operator 3	Operator	0	0
Operator 4	Operator	0	0
	Operator	0	0

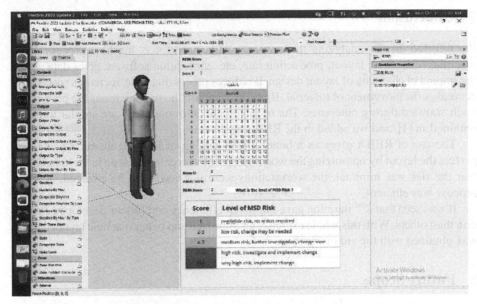

Fig. 9. REBA Analysis II (Displaying Level of MSD Risk)

As seen in Fig. 9, the REBA score is 2 which shows minimal risk and that a change may be needed in the workstations but is not necessary. Hence, it is seen that perfecting the layout without any changes to the workstations works as effectively.

Finally, the overall results obtained by Kanse et al. [1], are reproduced in Table 6:

Table 6. The consolidated results table from FlexSim for M-Bracket Die Plate. Key information for the analysis is shown in the Production Quantity column (Adapted from [1])

Layout	Remarks	Production Quantity
Existing	Simulation done on existing layout	37
1st Iteration	Rearrange machines	46
2nd Iteration	Extra Machine Added	56

End-product: From the aforementioned Four Parts results contrasting and existing format, it was determined that by actions of machines in the workstation and additionally adding another machine (where generally bottleneck issues are recognized), the production amounts increased implying that process time shrinks, leading to an increase in efficiency.

7 Conclusion

We inferred that by analyzing the parameters like workforce, machine process time, machine setup time, layout, production rate, etc., simulation software gives data about the impact of changing of layout design. It reduces processing time, increases space, and decreases the movement of material. By using FlexSim the two iterations are presented. Each shows differing outcomes. The results obtained in our study are similar to those obtained in [1], and we added in the REBA analysis.

The use of REBA gives us a better understanding of how ergonomically we can perfect the layout by optimizing the workstations. However, it was seen in the simulation that the risk was minimal, the workstations were not needed to be changed, and the process was efficient.

It was seen that 2nd iteration gave improved efficiency and further developed execution than others. With this whole exercise, an improved and better machine layout design was obtained with the aid of FlexSim.

8 Future Scope

Using FlexSim, Rapid Entire Body Assessment (REBA) and the learnings from this study, we can create simulation models for new and diverse and complex layouts. The results of these can be utilized in improving every process and overall efficiency. As Lean practices are starting to take hold of industries, we can use the learnings from this study to help in the lean transformation of shop floors, and help management implement the same. We can aid in better time saving and improvement, foresee problems to implementation and work towards solving them.

Acknowledgements. The authors acknowledge the contribution of Professor Allen Greenwood, Mississippi State University, for having made the FlexSim software freely available to us, and training us in its use.

References

1. Kanse, A.B., Patil, A.T.: Manufacturing plant layout optimization using simulation. Int. J. Innov. Sci. Res. Technol. **5**(10) (2020). www.ijisrt.com
2. Sugandhi, S., Sisodiya, P.S., Soni, M., Scholar, R., Professor, A., Professor, A.: Optimization of process layout for maintenance unit of XYZ industry using FlexSim simulation software (2017). www.ijsdr.org12
3. Patil, R.J., Kubade, P.R., Kulkarni, H.B.: Optimization of machine shop layout by using FlexSim software. In: AIP Conference Proceedings, vol. 2200 (2019). https://doi.org/10.1063/1.5141203
4. A Step-by-Step Guide Rapid Entire Body Assessment (REBA) (n.d.). www.ergo-plus.com
5. Deros, B.M., Khamis, N.K., Ismail, A.R., Jamaluddin, H., Adam, A.M., Rosli, S.: An ergonomics study on assembly line workstation design. Am. J. Appl. Sci. **8**(11), 1195–1201 (2011)
6. Delgado, J.E., Cecilia, M., Carlos, C.: Facility layout improvement model using ergonomics and layout simulation (n.d.)

7. Li, Q., Liu, H.: Workshop facility layout optimization design based on SLP and Flexsim. Int. J. Simul. Syst. Sci. Technol. (2016). https://doi.org/10.5013/ijssst.a.17.08.08
8. Garrido, J.M.: Introduction to Flexsim. In: Garrido, J.M. (ed.) Object Oriented Simulation, pp. 31–42. Springer, Boston (2009). https://doi.org/10.1007/978-1-4419-0516-1_3

A Smart Sensor Suit (SSS) to Assess Cognitive and Physical Fatigue with Machine Learning

Ashish Jaiswal[✉][iD], Mohammad Zaki Zadeh, Aref Hebri,
Ashwin Ramesh Babu, and Fillia Makedon

The University of Texas at Arlington, Arlington, TX, USA
ashish.jaiswal@mavs.uta.edu

Abstract. Fatigue is a loss in cognitive or physical performance due to physiological factors such as insufficient sleep, long work hours, stress, and physical exertion. It adversely affects the human body and can slow reaction times, reduce attention, and limit short-term memory. Hence, there is a need to monitor a person's state to avoid extreme fatigue conditions that can result in physiological complications. However, tools to understand and assess fatigue are minimal. This paper primarily focuses on building an experimental setup that induces cognitive fatigue (CF) and physical fatigue (PF) through multiple cognitive and physical tasks while simultaneously recording physiological data. First, we built a prototype sensor suit embedded with numerous physiological sensors for easy use during data collection. Second, participants' self-reported visual analog scores (VAS) are reported after each task to confirm fatigue induction. Finally, an evaluation system is built that utilizes machine learning (ML) models to detect states of CF and PF from sensor data, thus providing an objective measure. Our methods beat state-of-the-art approaches, where Random Forest performs the best in detecting PF with an accuracy of 80.5% while correctly predicting the true PF condition 88% of the time. On the other hand, the long short-term memory (LSTM) recurrent neural network produces the best results in detecting CF in the subjects (with 84.1% accuracy, 0.9 recall).

Keywords: fatigue · cognitive fatigue · physical fatigue · multi-modal sensors · machine learning

1 Introduction

Fatigue is a state of weariness that develops over time and reduces an individual's energy, motivation, and concentration. Fatigue can be classified into three types: Acute fatigue is caused by excessive physical or mental exertion and is alleviated by rest. Changes in circadian rhythm and daily activities influence Normative fatigue. In contrast, Chronic fatigue is primarily caused by stress or tension in the body and is less likely to be relieved by rest alone. While various factors influence human fatigue in the real world, factors affecting sleep and the circadian system have a high potential to contribute to fatigue [23].

Severe or chronic fatigue is usually a symptom of a disease rather than the result of daily activities. Some conditions, such as Multiple Sclerosis (MS) [24], Traumatic Brain Injury (TBI) [9], and Parkinson's Disease (PD) [18], have fatigue as a significant symptom. Physical and cognitive fatigue are the two types of fatigue. Physical fatigue (PF) is most commonly caused by excessive physical activity and is usually associated with a muscle group or a general feeling of fatigue in the body [12]. Cognitive fatigue (CF), on the other hand, can occur as a result of intense mental activity, resulting in a loss of cognition with decreased attention and high-level information processing [28]. In the real world, however, there is no clear distinction between what causes both types of fatigue. Workers with heavy machinery, for example, may require both cognitive skills and physical labor to complete a task that may induce both PF and CF simultaneously.

Researchers have previously attempted to assess both types of fatigue separately by approaching them differently. One of the most common methods of studying fatigue is to analyze the participants' subjective experience by having them fill out surveys rating their current state of fatigue. Although these methods have successfully quantified human fatigue, they are frequently prone to human bias and poor data collection methods. For example, an aviation study [10] discovered that 70–80 percent of pilots misrepresented their fatigue level. As a result, relying solely on a subjective measure from the participants may raise safety concerns. It is where physiological sensors, which provide objective measures of fatigue, come into play. To study fatigue, data collected from sensors such as electrocardiograms (ECG) [20], electroencephalograms (EEG) [22], electrodermal activity/galvanic skin response (EDA/GSR) [14], and electromyograms (EMG) [13] have been commonly used.

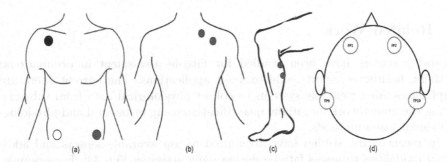

Fig. 1. Sensor placements on the human body (a) **ECG**: right shoulder, the left and the right hip forming Einthoven's triangle [15] (b) **EDA/GSR** electrodes on the left shoulder to record the skin conductivity, (c) **EMG** electrodes recording muscle twitches from the right calf, (d) **EEG** sensor positions in the 10–10 electrode system used by MUSE. It records data from the TP9, AF7, AF8, and TP10 positions in the system.

In this paper, we created an experimental setup that includes multiple standardized cognitive tasks (N-Back tasks [8,17,19]) and a physical task (running on a treadmill [16,30]) to induce both CF and PF simultaneously. When the participants completed each of the assigned tasks, data modalities such as ECG (for heart rate variability), EMG (for muscle activation), EDA/GSR (for skin conductivity and emotional arousal), and EEG (for electrical brain signals) were recorded. We combined multiple physiological data modalities to assess both CF & PF and correlate objective measures from the sensors with the participants' self-reported subjective visual analog scores (VAS). The self-reported scores were analyzed to verify the induction of fatigue in the participants. Finally, several statistical features were extracted from the collected signals, and machine learning (ML) models were trained to predict the participant's fatigue levels. The significant contributions of the paper are highlighted as follows:

- A novel experimental setup that integrates standardized cognitive and physical tasks to induce fatigue and record multivariate physiological sensor signals to analyze the state of fatigue in a subject
- Ablation study to understand what combination of sensors produces the best results in detecting both cognitive and physical fatigue
- Statistical feature extraction and machine learning models to classify the state of fatigue from sensor data using different window sizes technique
- A well-accumulated dataset of EEG, EDA/GSR, EMG, and ECG signals from 32 healthy subjects with their self-reported fatigue states is presented. To access the dataset, visit [Dataset Link].

The rest of the paper is structured as follows: We present the related work in Sect. 2. Then, Sect. 3 explains the data collection process followed by data processing techniques for different sensor data in Sect. 4. We then describe the experiments and methods we inherited in our project along with the obtained results in Sect. 5. Finally, we conclude the paper and propose future work in Sect. 6.

2   Related Work

Wearable sensors have been studied for fatigue assessment in occupational settings, healthcare, sports, and exercise applications. The current literature emphasizes using wearable systems to collect physiological data from subjects, laying the groundwork for fatigue quantification using behavioral and physiological signal-based methods.

In recent years, studies have attempted to use wearable sensors and additional modalities to assess fatigue during daily activities [5,6,33]. For example, Aryal et al. [4] used wearable sensors to record heart rate, skin temperature, and EEG to assess fatigue in construction workers. In addition, Maman et al. [38] conducted a study that focused on detecting physical fatigue by measuring heart rate and analyzing body posture during various physical tasks. Similarly, in [2], the authors presented a new operator-fatigue analysis and classification method based on heart rate variability (HRV) using low-cost wearable devices that identified the operator's alertness/fatigue states. Finally, not being limited to constrained experimental setups, the authors in [7] collected ECG and Actigraphy data from free-living environments to assess objective fatigue based on self-reported scores.

Although most studies have focused solely on CF or PF, some researchers have attempted to study both types of fatigue concurrently. For example, Marcora et al. [27] discovered that mental fatigue affects exercise tolerance, while Xu et al. [39] proposed that physical activities affect mental fatigue. Similarly, a single wearable sensor that measures acceleration and ECG during a self-paced trial run was used to assess CF and PF by [37]. In addition to wearable sensors, work has been done to determine CF from visual data such as fMRI scans [21, 40].

A review of fatigue sensors [1] found out that motion (MOT), electroen-cephalogram (EEG), photoplethysmogram (PPG), electrocardiogram (ECG), galvanic skin response (GSR), electromyogram (EMG), skin temperature (Tsk), eye movement (EYE), and respiratory (RES) sensors were the most effective. Among the proposed fatigue quantification approaches, supervised machine learning models were found to be dominant. This paper expands on previous research to look into wearable sensors for fatigue assessment. While previous research has primarily focused on assessing CF or PF separately, our research combines multiple physiological sensors to assess CF and PF at a larger scale.

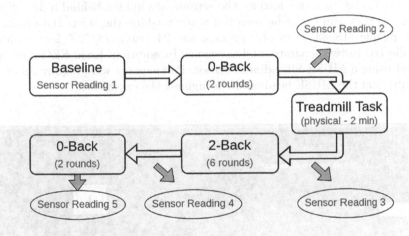

Fig. 2. Flow diagram of the tasks performed by a participant.

3 Data Collection

We built an experimental setup around a custom-built wearable t-shirt (Pneumon) (presented in Fig. 5) that was used to record physiological data using the attached sensors, and a MUSE S headband [29] (as shown in Fig. 6). In Fig. 4, although additional sensors are connected to the shirt, such as Microphone, Breathing Band, and Oximeter, we ignored those signals for fatigue detection as they added negligible value to our analysis in this paper. The suit is made using a

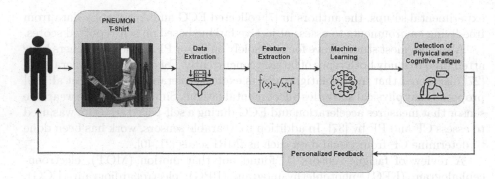

Fig. 3. System Flow Diagram: Data collection using the sensors attached on the PNEU-MON t-shirt and MUSE S worn by one of the participants while performing tasks presented in Fig. 2. Features extracted from the recorded signals were used to train ML models for detection of state of CF and PF.

stretchable Under Armour shirt [3]. The advantage of using a shirt with embedded sensors is its ease of use during data collection and practical application during day-to-day use. In addition, the sensors are hidden behind a detachable covering, so they can easily be removed while washing the shirt. Data from 32 healthy people (18–33 years old, average age 24 years, 28/72% female/male) were collected in two separate study sessions. In addition, brain EEG data was collected using a MUSE S headband sensor. Participants were required to wear the t-shirt and the MUSE headband throughout the experiment.

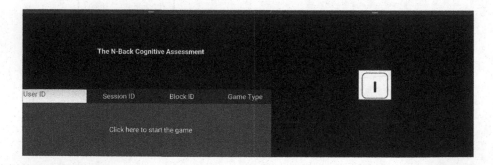

Fig. 4. Graphical User Interface built for the N-Back tasks with an example image of a letter during a game round on the right.

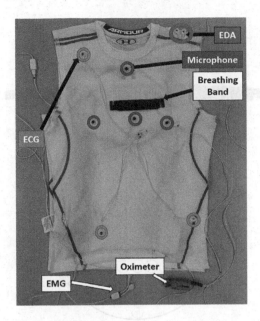

Fig. 5. A prototype of the sensor shirt (inside-out view): Physiological sensors are embedded in the shirt and remain in contact with the subject's torso during data collection using adhesive tapes. Multiple sensory signals are collected using different combinations of the sensors present. **In this paper, we do not use the microphone, oximeter, and breathing band signals.**

The researchers began by taking a baseline reading from the sensors while the subject stood still for one minute. The experiment aimed to induce CF and PF while collecting sensory data throughout the process. Next, the participants were asked to perform multiple sets of N-Back tasks to cause CF, as shown in Fig. 2. As observed by the participant, the GUI of the N-back game is shown in Fig. 4. In these tasks, the subject is shown a series of letters, one after the other. The subject's goal is to determine whether the current letter matches the letter presented N steps back. If it does, the subject must perform the specified action (pressing the space bar on the keyboard). Finally, to induce PF in the subjects, they were asked to run for 2 min on a treadmill (speed - 5mph, incline - 10%). Additional data was collected (sensor reading 3 in Fig. 2) after the subjects stood still for 90 s after completing the physical task.

The study was divided into two sessions on separate days for each participant. Subjects were asked to come in the morning for one session and in the evening for another. It eliminated the effect on the data caused by the time of the day. The tasks performed in both sessions were identical, the only difference being the order they were completed. The first session followed the flow depicted in Fig. 2, whereas the second session prioritized the cognitively challenging 2-Back game before the physical task. It dismisses PF's reliance on CF and allows us to collect

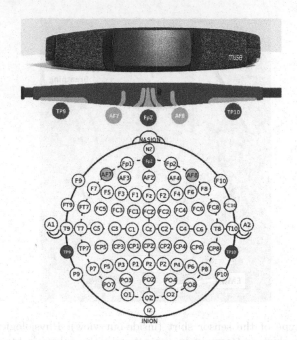

Fig. 6. Electrode placement comparison between MUSE and the international 10–20 system. Top: Commercial MUSE S Headband. Bottom: 10–20 Electrode Placement System

more robust data for analysis. Each round of 0-back and 2-back tasks lasted between 80.4 s and 144.3 s, respectively (on average) during the data collection process.

Participants were asked to complete a brief survey indicating their current physical and cognitive fatigue levels following each task. In addition, they reported visual analog scale (VAS) scores ranging from 1 to 10 for the following questions:

1. Describe your overall tiredness on a scale of 1–10.
2. How physically fatigued/tired do you feel on a scale of 1–10?
3. How cognitively fatigued do you feel on a scale of 1–10?
4. How sleepy or drowsy do you feel on a scale of 1–10?

Figure 8 depicts the distribution of self-reported VAS scores after each task. We divided the scores from 1 to 10 into three categories for simplification while plotting: None (<4), Moderate (≥ 4 and =7), and Extreme (>7). Most participants gradually began to feel cognitively fatigued after completing each task. In fact, after the fourth block, CF appears to be induced in more than 80% of the subjects (Fig. 8(d)), supporting the hypothesis on which we based our experimental setup. Similarly, as shown in Fig. 8(c), the physical task was able to induce at least moderate PF in more than 90% of the subjects (c). Thus, data collected during the fourth and fifth blocks of the study were considered a state for CF in the participants, whereas data collected immediately following the physical task was considered a PF condition. Of course, there may be some biases in the subjective scores collected. However, the majority of the scores recorded from the participants (as shown in Fig. 8) support the hypothesis on which the whole experiment was based.

4 Data Processing

4.1 EEG

We used the MUSE S headset to collect EEG signals while the subjects performed different tasks during the experiment. It consists of 4 electrodes (AF7, AF8, TP9, TP10) that are in contact with other regions of the head, as shown in Fig. 1(d). EEG signals quantify electrical activity in the brain. These signals are generally decomposed into five frequency bands: alpha, beta, delta, gamma, and theta, as shown in Fig. 7, where each band signifies a different state of the brain. For example, delta waves occur in the frequency range of 0.5 Hz 4 Hz and are present during deep sleep, while beta waves occur 13 Hz 30 Hz and are associated with active thinking. Similarly, other waves are associated with – alpha waves (8–12 Hz): normal awake conditions, gamma waves (30–80 Hz): sensory perception integration; and theta waves (4–7 Hz): drowsiness and early stages of sleep. In addition, 50–60 Hz frequencies were processed beforchand to avoid power line interference on the signals.

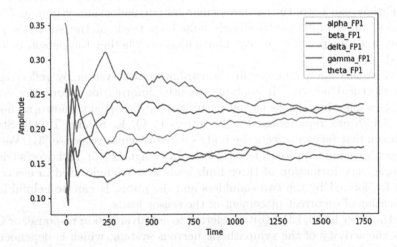

Fig. 7. Raw Amplitude plot of Frequency bands extracted from the electrode at AF7 position (on MUSE) from a sample raw EEG signal from one of the subjects. The readings were collected during one of the 2-Back tasks undergoing for a little under 3 min.

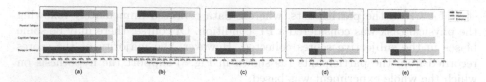

Fig. 8. Likert plots for survey responses from subjects after each block of tasks (before taking the sensor readings) as shown in Fig. 2. (a) Initial survey at the start of the session showing that less to no fatigue was found in most of the participants. (b) Response after the first 0-Back task and before sensor reading 2 showed a slight increase in CF for some participants. (c) Response after the treadmill task verifying that PF is induced in most of the participants. (d) Response after the first 2-Back task indicating a prominent increase in CF (e) Shows that CF continues to be persistent even during the easier 0-Back task

The different EEG bands and the raw signals were streamed by the MUSE SDK using a UDP server and were recorded from all four electrodes in a csv file. We calculated statistics such as mean, standard deviation, min, max, and median using the sliding window technique for each band from the respective electrodes for feature extraction.

4.2   ECG, EDA, and EMG

Physiological sensors were used in the wearable t-shirt, as shown in Fig. 3 to simultaneously collect ECG, EDA, and EMG signals during the entire experiment. Fatigue can harm the cardiovascular system, endocrine system, and brain. Therefore, these multi-modal signals help keep track of the subject's physical state and can provide quality information on whether the person is feeling fatigued.

ECG signals show changes in the cardiovascular system by reflecting the heart's electrical activity. It contains essential information about the cardiac pathologies affecting the heart, characterized by five peaks known as fiducial points, which are represented by the letters P, Q, R, S, and T [34]. Studies have shown that fatigue affects the body's cardiovascular response [31]. We used Einthoven's triangle approach to record the ECG signals [15]. Eithoven's triangle is an imaginary formation of three limb leads in a triangle used in electrocardiography, formed by the two shoulders and the pubis. It can be helpful in the identification of incorrect placement of the sensor leads.

On the other hand, EDA (often referred to as galvanic skin response, or GSR) reflects the activity of the sympathetic nervous system, which is dependent on physiological and emotional activation by measuring the skin conductivity of the body. EDA signals can also be reflective of the intensity of our emotional state. Therefore, measuring this signal allows us to identify psychological or emotional arousal episodes. Finally, EMG signals record the change in voltage between two electrodes during muscle contraction and relaxation. PF has been shown to affect muscle activity and can lead to reduced muscle activation [36].

To remove unwanted noise from the ECG signals, we used Pan and Tompkins QRS detection algorithm [32]. First, we cleaned the signals using a high-pass Butterworth filter with a fixed cut-off frequency of 0.5 Hz. After this, a notch filter was applied to the cleaned signal to remove components 50 Hz frequency and avoid power line interference. Next, RR intervals were extracted using the R_Peaks from the signal and were cleaned by removing the outliers. The missing values were substituted using the linear interpolation method. Finally, 113 time-domain and frequency-domain features, including heart rate variability (HRV) metrics, were extracted to train ML models.

EDA signals were first passed through a low-pass Butterworth signal with a cut-off frequency 3 Hz. EDA signals can be decomposed into two components: phasic and tonic [11]. Since the phasic component of the EDA signal is the faster-changing element of the signal based on physiological changes due to a stimulus, it was extracted for processing. Skin Conductance Response (SCR) peaks were extracted as features from the cleaned EDA signals. Similarly, time domain and frequency domain features were extracted from the EMG signals. Most of the feature extraction was carried out using the package named Neurokit2 [26] for all three signals.

5   Experimentation and Results

We extracted 100 statistical features from EEG signals and 169 combined features from ECG, EDA, and EMG to train the ML models. Based on the responses accumulated from the participants (in Fig. 8), data collected in sensor readings 1, 2, and 3 (before the 2-Back tasks in Fig. 2) were labeled as "No CF" condition. In contrast, the data recorded during the final two readings (4 and 5, i.e., after the 2-Back rounds) were labeled as "CF" conditions. Similarly, data recorded right after the physical task (sensor reading 3) was marked as a "PF" condition when the subjects stood still. Meanwhile, readings 4 and 5 were not considered for PF analysis.

For training, instead of processing the entire signal for a task as a single input, we split the time signal into multiple slices based on different window sizes (5 s, 10 s, and 20 s). Each signal slice was labeled the same as the original signal label, and features were extracted. It also increased the number of input data points to the ML models during training. However, we also tested the models with entire signal blocks as inputs. Similarly, during inference, the input signal was broken down into smaller slices based on the window size chosen during training, and each slice was classified as one of the classes by the model. Finally, the whole signal block was classified based on the higher count of the class among the classified slices. This technique makes the model more robust toward any noise or outliers in the signals, as noise contained in some slices may not contribute much to the final classification result.

The entire dataset was randomly split into train (70%, 22 subjects), validation (15%, five subjects), and test (15%, five subjects) sets. We used stratified sampling while splitting the dataset to prevent dealing with an unbalanced

Table 1. Detection of Cognitive Fatigue (CF) with EEG Features only

Model	Accuracy (Window Size)				Avg. Recall
	5s	10s	20s	Full Block	
Log Reg	69.7%	72.6%	71.3%	62.3%	0.76
SVM	73.1%	73.3%	71.7%	69.4%	0.81
RF	72.3%	**81.9%**	79.1%	76.3%	**0.89**
LSTM	69.8%	71.8%	73.8%	**81.9%**	0.82

Table 2. Detection of Cognitive Fatigue (CF) with ECG + EDA + EMG Features

Model	Accuracy (Window Size)				Avg. Recall
	5s	10s	20s	Full Block	
Log Reg	69.8%	70.1%	67.2%	65.3%	0.69
SVM	71.2%	71.7%	70.8%	70.1%	**0.73**
RF	74.8%	**76.3%**	72.1%	70.9%	0.71
LSTM	62.2%	63.7%	68.9%	70.1%	0.69

Table 3. Detection of Physical Fatigue (PF) with ECG + EDA + EMG Features

Model	Accuracy (Window Size)				Avg. Recall
	5s	10s	20s	Full Block	
Log Reg	72.2%	72.2%	68.2%	62.9%	0.74
SVM	76.1%	79.6%	75.2%	73.1%	0.86
RF	79.9%	**80.5%**	77.6%	77.2%	**0.88**
LSTM	64.2%	64.8%	62.7%	68.9%	0.79

Table 4. Detection of Cognitive Fatigue (CF) with EEG + ECG + EDA + EMG Features

Model	Accuracy (Window Size)				Avg. Recall
	5s	10s	20s	Full Block	
Log Reg	64.0%	66.9%	66.1%	60.4%	0.69
SVM	70.3%	74.6%	74.5%	70.3%	0.79
RF	67.9%	77.2%	76.8%	74.5%	0.81
LSTM	71.3%	74.2%	74.8%	**84.1%**	**0.90**

dataset. In addition, 5-fold cross-validation was performed for each of the models. Four different ML models: Logistic Regression (Log Reg.), Support Vector Machines (SVM), Random Forest (RF), and Long Short-Term Memory (LSTM) recurrent neural network, were used in the analysis. We used multiple combinations of features extracted from the signals to predict fatigue.

Since EEG signals represent brain activity related to cognitive functions, initially, only features extracted from the EEG data were used to predict CF, as shown in Table 1. Similarly, we used features extracted from the physiological sensors (ECG, EDA, and EMG) to train models that predict both CF and PF, as presented in Tables 2 and 3. Finally, features from all the data modalities were combined and normalized for the detection of CF, represented by Table 4. For results in Table 4, we applied Principal Component Analysis (PCA) [35] to reduce dimensions to 189 features for the best results from the ML models.

The first three models (Log Reg., SVM, and RF) were trained using the features extracted from the signals. However, an LSTM model (with 256 hidden layers) was trained on the raw signals directly as it can process time-series data. We used the same window-based approach to train the LSTM models, where the input size for the EEG signals was t x 20 × 1 (five frequency bands from each of the four electrodes). On the other hand, ECG, EDA, and EMG signals were combined to form t × 3 × 1 inputs. Finally, the LSTM was trained on t × 23 × 1 inputs for all signals combined. Here, "t" represents the number of timesteps in the signal, which varies based on the window size.

Table 5. Comparison of different models with the state-of-the-art algorithms

Fatigue Type	Model	Accuracy	Avg. Recall	Ref.
Physical	RF	71.85	0.72	[25]
Physical	cCNN + RF	71.40	0.73	[25]
Physical	**RF (Ours)**	**80.50**	**0.88**	Table 3
Cognitive	RF	64.69	0.65	[25]
Cognitive	RF	66.20	0.66	[25]
Cognitive	**LSTM (Ours)**	**84.1**	**0.90**	Table 4

The average recall (Avg. Recall) presented in all four tables is the average recall for the "Fatigue" condition (either cognitive or physical) obtained across 5-fold cross-validation for each model. The best value obtained for each model among different window sizes was considered. With a CF prediction accuracy of 81.9%, RF performs the best using only the EEG features in Table 1. We can see that it correctly predicts CF conditions 89% of the time. Recall is an essential metric since our primary goal is to detect actual fatigue conditions in the subjects and avoid false negatives.

Similarly, RF seems to outperform the rest of the models when trained with features from ECG, EDA, and EMG to detect both CF and PF with respective accuracies of 76.3% (recall=0.71) and 80.5% (recall=0.88). Also, the window size of 10s works the best for feature-based models, while the LSTM model performs the best when provided with the entire block of signal collected. Based on Table 4, LSTM performs the best when all four modalities are combined and the whole signal block is provided to the model. Hence, for the detection of CF, feature engineering can be avoided entirely with four modalities combined and processed directly with an LSTM network.

Finally, there is only one study by Luo et al. [25] that deals with fatigue detection in human subjects using wearable sensors. Their pilot study looked at multiple digital data sources on physical activity, vital signs, and other physiological parameters and their relationship to subject-reported non-pathological physical and mental fatigue in real-world settings. They demonstrated how multimodal digital data could be used to inform, quantify, and augment subjectively collected non-pathological fatigue measures. Based on the performance of their methodology with ours in Table 5, we can see that our methods outperform their approaches in detecting both physical and cognitive fatigue with models RandomForest (RF) and LSTM, respectively.

6   Conclusion

This paper presents one of the preliminary works that utilizes a unique combination of physiological (ECG, EDA, EMG) and brain (EEG) sensors to detect CF and PF simultaneously. The flow of the tasks designed for data collection successfully induced CF (> 80% participants) and PF (> 90% participants) based on the reported subjective VAS scores from the participants. While the Random Forest classifier performed the best in detecting PF, the success of the LSTM model in predicting CF eliminates the need for extensive data preprocessing and feature extraction. Overall, the best models in the system failed to detect actual PF in less than 12% of the cases (recall=0.88) and CF in less than 10% (recall=0.90), with promising results. Similarly, our models outperform state-of-the-art models in detecting cognitive and physical fatigue. Further research directions will include visual sensor data to analyze facial expressions and gait movement, which will aid in better prediction of fatigue. Additionally, including subjects with severe conditions impacted by fatigue can benefit the study in detecting symptoms related to those diseases.

References

1. Adão Martins, N.R., Annaheim, S., Spengler, C.M., Rossi, R.M.: Fatigue monitoring through wearables: a state-of-the-art review. Front. Physiol. 2285 (2021)
2. Al-Libawy, H., Al-Ataby, A., Al-Nuaimy, W., Al-Taee, M.A.: HRV-based operator fatigue analysis and classification using wearable sensors. In: 2016 13th International Multi-Conference on Systems, Signals & Devices (SSD), pp. 268–273. IEEE (2016)
3. Armour, U.: Men's ua heatgear armour sleeveless compression shirt. https://www.underarmour.com/en-us/p/tops/mens_ua_heatgear_armour_sleeveless_compression_shirt/1257469.html
4. Aryal, A., Ghahramani, A., Becerik-Gerber, B.: Monitoring fatigue in construction workers using physiological measurements. Autom. Constr. 82, 154–165 (2017)

5. Babu, A.R., Cloud, J., Theofanidis, M., Makedon, F.: Facial expressions as a modality for fatigue detection in robot based rehabilitation. In: Proceedings of the 11th PErvasive Technologies Related to Assistive Environments Conference, pp. 112–113 (2018)
6. Babu, A.R., Rajavenkatanarayanan, A., Brady, J.R., Makedon, F.: Multimodal approach for cognitive task performance prediction from body postures, facial expressions and EEG signal. In: Proceedings of the Workshop on Modeling Cognitive Processes from Multimodal Data, pp. 1–7 (2018)
7. Bai, Y., Guan, Y., Ng, W.F.: Fatigue assessment using ECG and actigraphy sensors. In: Proceedings of the 2020 International Symposium on Wearable Computers, pp. 12–16 (2020)
8. Bailey, A., Channon, S., Beaumont, J.: The relationship between subjective fatigue and cognitive fatigue in advanced multiple sclerosis. Mult. Scler. J. 13(1), 73–80 (2007)
9. Belmont, A., Agar, N., Hugeron, C., Gallais, B., Azouvi, P.: Fatigue and traumatic brain injury. In: Annales de réadaptation et de médecine physique, vol. 49, pp. 370–374. Elsevier (2006)
10. Bendak, S., Rashid, H.S.: Fatigue in aviation: a systematic review of the literature. Int. J. Ind. Ergon. 76, 102928 (2020)
11. Braithwaite, J.J., Watson, D.G., Jones, R., Rowe, M.: A guide for analysing electrodermal activity (EDA) & skin conductance responses (SCRS) for psychological experiments. Psychophysiology 49(1), 1017–1034 (2013)
12. Chaudhuri, A., Behan, P.O.: Fatigue in neurological disorders. The Lancet 363(9413), 978–988 (2004)
13. Cifrek, M., Medved, V., Tonković, S., Ostojić, S.: Surface EMG based muscle fatigue evaluation in biomechanics. Clin. Biomech. 24(4), 327–340 (2009)
14. Dawson, M.E., Schell, A.M., Courtney, C.G.: The skin conductance response, anticipation, and decision-making. J. Neurosci. Psychol. Econ. 4(2), 111 (2011)
15. Einthoven, W., Fahr, G., De Waart, A.: On the direction and manifest size of the variations of potential in the human heart and on the influence of the position of the heart on the form of the electrocardiogram. Am. Heart J. 40(2), 163–211 (1950)
16. García-Pérez, J.A., Pérez-Soriano, P., Llana Belloch, S., Lucas-Cuevas, Á.G., Sánchez-Zuriaga, D.: Effects of treadmill running and fatigue on impact acceleration in distance running. Sports Biomech. 13(3), 259–266 (2014)
17. Guastello, S.J., Reiter, K., Malon, M., Timm, P., Shircel, A., Shaline, J.: Catastrophe models for cognitive workload and fatigue in n-back tasks. Psychology, and Life Sciences, Nonlinear Dynamics (2015)
18. Hagell, P., Brundin, L.: Towards an understanding of fatigue in Parkinson disease. J. Neurol. Neurosurg. Psychiatr. 80(5), 489–492 (2009)
19. Hopstaken, J.F., Van Der Linden, D., Bakker, A.B., Kompier, M.A.: A multifaceted investigation of the link between mental fatigue and task disengagement. Psychophysiology 52(3), 305–315 (2015)
20. Huang, S., Li, J., Zhang, P., Zhang, W.: Detection of mental fatigue state with wearable ECG devices. Int. J. Med. Inform. 119, 39–46 (2018)
21. Jaiswal, A., Babu, A.R., Zadeh, M.Z., Makedon, F., Wylie, G.: Understanding cognitive fatigue from FMRI scans with self-supervised learning. arXiv preprint arXiv:2106.15009 (2021)
22. Jap, B.T., Lal, S., Fischer, P., Bekiaris, E.: Using EEG spectral components to assess algorithms for detecting fatigue. Expert Syst. Appl. 36(2), 2352–2359 (2009)

23. Ji, Q., Lan, P., Looney, C.: A probabilistic framework for modeling and real-time monitoring human fatigue. IEEE Trans. Syst. Man Cybern. Part A Syst. Humans **36**(5), 862–875 (2006)
24. Krupp, L.B., Alvarez, L.A., LaRocca, N.G., Scheinberg, L.C.: Fatigue in multiple sclerosis. Arch. Neurol. **45**(4), 435–437 (1988)
25. Luo, H., Lee, P.A., Clay, I., Jaggi, M., De Luca, V.: Assessment of fatigue using wearable sensors: a pilot study. Digit. Biomark. **4**(1), 59–72 (2020)
26. Makowski, D., et al.: NeuroKit2: a Python toolbox for neurophysiological signal processing. Behav. Res. Methods **53**(4), 1689–1696 (2021). https://doi.org/10.3758/s13428-020-01516-y
27. Marcora, S.M., Staiano, W., Manning, V.: Mental fatigue impairs physical performance in humans. J. Appl. Physiol. **106**(3), 857–864 (2009)
28. Meier, B., Rothen, N., Walter, S.: Developmental aspects of synaesthesia across the adult lifespan. Front. Hum. Neurosci. **8**, 129 (2014)
29. MUSE: Muse s - the next generation of muses. https://choosemuse.com/muse-s/
30. Myles, W.S.: Sleep deprivation, physical fatigue, and the perception of exercise intensity. Med. Sci. Sports Exerc. (1985)
31. Nelesen, R., Dar, Y., Thomas, K., Dimsdale, J.E.: The relationship between fatigue and cardiac functioning. Arch. Intern. Med. **168**(9), 943–949 (2008)
32. Pan, J., Tompkins, W.J.: A real-time QRS detection algorithm. IEEE Trans. Biomed. Eng. 230–236 (1985)
33. Ramesh Babu, A., Zadeh, M.Z., Jaiswal, A., Lueckenhoff, A., Kyrarini, M., Makedon, F.: A multi-modal system to assess cognition in children from their physical movements. In: Proceedings of the 2020 International Conference on Multimodal Interaction, pp. 6–14 (2020)
34. Richley, D.: New training and qualifications in electrocardiography. Br. J. Card. Nurs. **8**(1), 38–42 (2013)
35. Ringnér, M.: What is principal component analysis? Nat. Biotechnol. **26**, 303–304 (2008)
36. Rota, S., Morel, B., Saboul, D., Rogowski, I., Hautier, C.: Influence of fatigue on upper limb muscle activity and performance in tennis. J. Electromyogr. Kinesiol. **24**(1), 90–97 (2014)
37. Russell, B., McDaid, A., Toscano, W., Hume, P.: Predicting fatigue in long duration mountain events with a single sensor and deep learning model. Sensors **21**(16), 5442 (2021)
38. Sedighi Maman, Z., Alamdar Yazdi, M.A., Cavuoto, L.A., Megahed, F.M.: A data-driven approach to modeling physical fatigue in the workplace using wearable sensors. Appl. Ergon. **65**, 515–529 (2017)
39. Xu, R., et al.: How physical activities affect mental fatigue based on EEG energy, connectivity, and complexity. Front. Neurol. **9** (2018)
40. Zadeh, M.Z., Babu, A.R., Lim, J.B., Kyrarini, M., Wylie, G., Makedon, F.: Towards cognitive fatigue detection from functional magnetic resonance imaging data. In: Proceedings of the 13th ACM International Conference on PErvasive Technologies Related to Assistive Environments, pp. 1–2 (2020)

Application of Ramsis Digital Human Modeling to Human Factors in Space

Kevin Jin[✉], Mackenzie Richards[✉], and Kevin Lee[✉]

Purdue University, West Lafayette, IN 47906, USA
{jin393,richa453,lee2721}@purdue.edu

Abstract. This paper will cover using Ramsis for simulating and modeling a new Mars site. Ramsis is a 3D computer-aided design (CAD) modeling software used to design vehicle interiors and manikin positioning. Other related applications are reachability, seat belt routing, and field of view limitations. Our paper covers the procedures used to create manikins, optimize seat range, evaluate location/visibility, and other relevant ergonomic-related analyses. Comfortability and visibility analysis were also conducted on Mars rover usage. The paper will also cover simulation research, bibliometric analyses, discussion, and future work. References will be listed at the end.

Keywords: Ramsis · Digital Human Modeling · Ergonomics Analysis · Simulation

1 Introduction

1.1 Ramsis Introduction

With the rise of fully automated cars, safety has become an increasingly concerning factor in vehicle design and management. Ramsis, a CAD software, enables engineers to model the safety and use features of vehicles. Prototypes are simulated in a virtual environment to determine vehicle functionality and evaluate overall vehicle design. Ramsis and other digital modeling software have numerous benefits, including timeliness of simulation, cost reductions, and accuracy analysis (Meulen, 2007). These benefits justify the investment in vehicle software modeling, addressing many challenges for ergonomic engineers and human factor researchers.

2 Overview of Report Contents

2.1 Problem Statement

Digital human modeling has long been used to design and evaluate the ergonomics of cars. Using simulation software like Ramsis allows designers to create better-designed systems that work with a wide range of body types. These analyses are easier to conduct with simulation and can occur earlier in the design process before prototypes are

V. G. Duffy (Ed.): HCII 2023, LNCS 14028, pp. 135–146, 2023.
https://doi.org/10.1007/978-3-031-35741-1_11

made, saving time and money. As newer and more advanced products and technologies are introduced, human design and ergonomics are further linked together. While those two factors work to meet safety and comfort requirements, they will result in low production costs and an increase in sales. It will also result in better product ratings with fewer discrepancies as well as setting a foot towards new advancement in the era within the field (Chaffin, 2001). Ergonomics and human design will evaluate the productivity and reliability of any finished design without bias. Human modeling-type simulation is important for applied ergonomics for a variety of reasons. Product and system design require significant research to understand intricacies and proper use. According to "Digital Human Modeling for Vehicle and Workplace Design," engineers need to know early in the design process how effectively and efficiently humans will be able to interact with them." Simulation modeling assists in understanding how systems work in their designated environment, allowing for life-size scaling after ergonomic analysis is considered. In the context of space human factors, an emerging area of ergonomics, existing simulation software must be applied to the new challenges outer space brings.

2.2 Procedure

The first step in using Ramsis to analyze ergonomic situations in a space human factors context was learning the basics of the software. The authors were able to familiarize themselves with the process of digital human modeling and ergonomics analysis, through extensive research and applying skills toward manikin development. To perform an ergonomics analysis on astronauts interacting with a Mars rover, a boundary manikin was created using the "test sample" function under ergonomics analysis. Default options were selected and the manikin's posture and joints were able to be manipulated. Boundary manikins were created using standard settings, which will be adjusted for percentile compositions later in this analysis. Next, the manikin was placed into the rover as a driver and a passenger was added. Figure 1 shows these manikins situated inside the vehicle in seated positions.

Once the manikins were in place using a built-in option, the ergonomics analysis could begin. To do this, the first metric evaluated was the seat adjustment range. The goal was to create a range in which all percentile manikins had a comfortable reach to the rover's main controls. The smallest female and largest male manikins available in the Ramsis German population database were used to cover the entire spectrum of percentiles in the population. This method captures 90% of the population, allowing the ergonomic design to be marketed nearly to everyone. Figure 2 shows the comfort analysis of these manikins. Upon additional evaluation, each limb remains in the "comfort range." If accommodations for larger individuals were considered, there may be significantly more discomfort, as the manikins are already adjusted to optimal positions.

The next method of ergonomics analysis was to evaluate the location, reach, and comfort of the touchscreen controls for the passenger. Two built-in functions were used to determine joint angle limitations and joint capacity. These measurements determine the maximum distance a manikin can move within the rover and the reachability of manikins to the appropriate locations within the structure. Upon further analysis, some of the smaller manikins are unable to reach across the rover to the screen, whereas larger manikins have definitive dimension constraints. Testing was conducted for 90–95% of

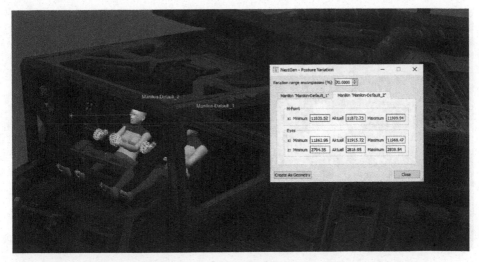

Fig. 1. Default German Ramsis manikins in Mars rover as driver and passenger.

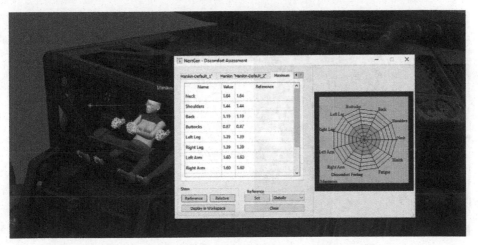

Fig. 2. Comfort analysis for smallest and largest manikins in the Mars rover.

the population, using the built-in German modeling data. Figures 3 and 4 show the results of these calculations.

Finally, the visibility for both the driver and passenger when inside the rover was evaluated. The limits of visual fields function in Ramsis were used to display the vision radius of each manikin for both eyes. Visibility does not seem to be limited while operating the rover, since both manikins can see the Mars base adequately. This was determined using the sight limit function to display that drivers can detect the object of interest, the Mars base in this case, in their visual field shown by the visual cone. Figure 5 shows this visual cone for both the driver and the passenger. Overall, there do not seem to be sight limitations. However, other factors such as glare, window tint, and

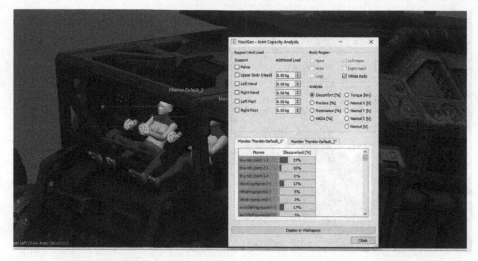

Fig. 3. Joint capacity analysis for the passenger to the touch screen.

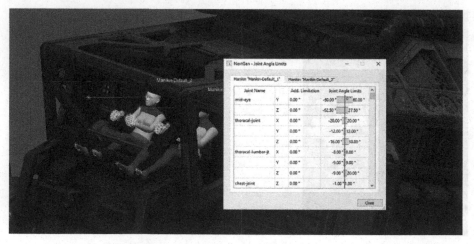

Fig. 4. Joint angle limit analysis for the passenger to the touch screen.

atmospheric conditions may play a role. There are numerous safety risks associated with impaired visibility, a topic of discussion for future research. On Mars, there are numerous factors to consider. Risks include environment, heat, ventilation, safety equipment, wind, workspace quality, window quality, and suit composition. These factors may all play a role in determining overall visibility for drivers, as the simulation is unable to capture all these factors. Simulating more environmental distractions may aid in future research using Ramsis.

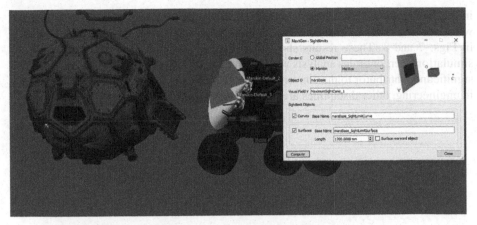

Fig. 5. Visual analysis and cones for Mars rover driver and passenger.

2.3 Results

Based on the ergonomics analysis conducted, the seats and controls of the rover must be highly adjustable. This will allow for comfortable accommodation of passengers from both ends of the size spectrum, 5th percentile females and 90th percentile males. A high level of adjustability also improves safety, as personal protective equipment like space suits and the vehicles used to traverse new planets must fit an individual extremely well and exactly as intended. As indicated in Figs. 3 and 4, the reachability is undesirable for both the smallest and largest members of the population. This is the result of a fixed display that does not allow for ergonomically important adjustments to be made. The seating position of the passengers is not an issue, as the comfortability analysis results are within the acceptable range for all manikins tested. Visibility is also not an issue for the vehicle itself, but consideration must be made for the helmet passengers will be wearing when on the surface of Mars. No matter how good the visibility of the vehicle is, a helmet that blocks vision is what the passengers will be seeing out of, so its design must be carefully considered. Safety and comfort must both be considered for final designs. According to an article in Sage Journals, there are "several items involving tradeoffs between safety and comfort." Engineers must properly consider environmental conditions to optimize suit parameters within a budget. This is relevant in future sections of this report, during the analysis of center of gravity and force.

2.4 Bibliometric Analysis

A bibliometric analysis of existing literature on simulation and applied ergonomics was conducted to gain insight into the current climate of these applications of simulation. First, several databases were selected to search for relevant articles, including Scopus and Dimensions. These databases were searched with two sets of keywords: "ergonomics analysis" AND "simulation" and "ergonomics" AND "vehicle design" AND "simulation modeling." For the first set of keywords, Scopus yielded 78 results. The leading table analysis of these publications is shown in Fig. 6. Using these same search parameters in the Dimensions AI database, a much larger number of publications was presented, with 84,297 results to analyze. The leading table analysis of these results is shown in Figs. 7 and 8. These results show that there is increasing interest in the topic of simulation to ergonomics analysis with a spike in 2019. The University of Michigan is a significant contributor to the conversation, and while it is more commonly talked about in engineering, other disciplines are also interested in the application.

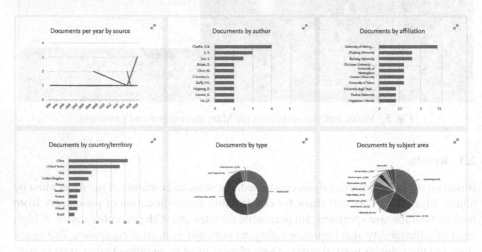

Fig. 6. Meta-data analysis from "ergonomics analysis" AND "simulation" papers in Scopus.

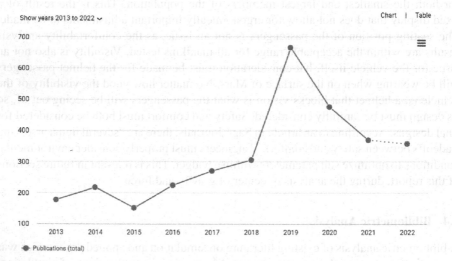

Fig. 7. Number of "ergonomics analysis" AND "simulation" publications by year as presented by the Dimensions database.

Using the second set of keywords as the search parameters in Scopus, only one publication was found as shown in Fig. 9. The paper, "Guide and documentation system to support digital human modeling applications," was written in 2006 and discusses a method with which to reduce discrepancies and errors in digital human modeling. This

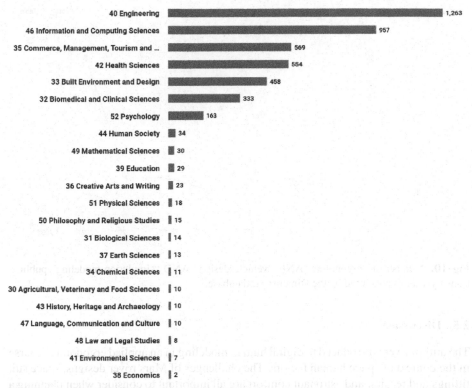

Fig. 8. Categories and number of papers within each category for "ergonomics analysis" AND simulation" publications in Dimensions AI.

was also the only result when searching Web of Science, but Dimensions yielded 574 results. There is also increasing interest in this set of keywords in a recent spike as shown in Fig. 10.

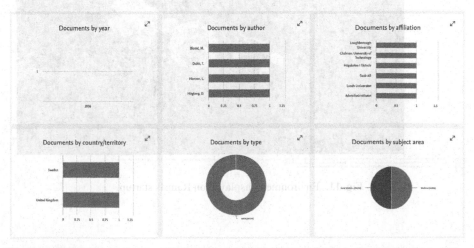

Fig. 9. Leading table Scopus result for "ergonomics" AND "vehicle design" AND "simulation modeling."

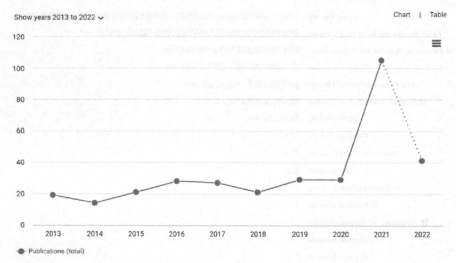

Fig. 10. Number of "ergonomics AND "vehicle design" AND "simulation modeling" publications by year as presented by the Dimensions database.

2.5 Discussion

The authors were introduced to digital human modeling in an applied ergonomics course in the context of space human factors. The challenges of Mars rover designs, space suit fittings and repairs, and astronaut comfort are all important to consider when planning a manned trip to Mars. Ramsis was used to fit a manikin to a space suit and in the driver's seat of a vehicle. Figure 11 shows the initial environment used to introduce the authors to the Ramsis software.

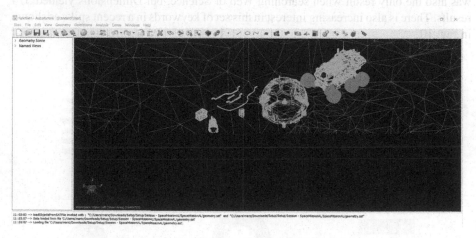

Fig. 11. Environment displayed on Ramsis startup.

One challenge faced when completing the analysis for this assignment was effectively using the Ramsis software, as the mechanics of creating a manikin and manipulating its skeletal points was a new concept to grasp. This took considerable troubleshooting and rewatching of the tutorial videos and sessions provided. Once the initial hurdle of understanding how Ramsis human modeling works, the ergonomics analysis is intuitive and can be applied to other vehicles and environments.

Based on the ergonomics analysis results of this assignment, the Mars rover should have an adjustable control display screen as well as an adjustable seat. This would allow for the comfortable operation of the vehicle for a wider range of the population. With an increase in customizability for passengers, the rover also becomes safer. Space is hard on the bodies of astronauts. It is known that bone loss occurs in space, but effective methods of reducing its effects have yet to be determined (Greenleaf). With how little is known about effective methods of reducing bone loss, it is important to take every available opportunity to reduce the effects of joint strain and damage that are known. By creating a more inclusively fitting vehicle, the strain on astronauts' bodies is reduced and safety is increased.

The center of gravity for a passenger wearing a suit would be different from the center of gravity of a passenger not wearing a spacesuit. Since a suit has weight and mass added onto the passenger, it will have a greater force acting on the suit, and the center of gravity will be different from that of the passenger without a suit. A space suit is also a different shape than a human not wearing bulky gear. This changes the weight distribution and therefore the center of gravity. To calculate the difference in center of gravity using Ramsis the evaluation would need to be done twice, once with a standard passenger and once with the passenger wearing a spacesuit. For the purposes of this report, the calculations were made using a standard manikin with no external suit. In order to accurately perform an ergonomics analysis, the proposed suit design would need to be modeled in Ramsis and fit specific manikins. These modifications would alter the comfort level, reach, and percentage of users operable for the rover. With this suit in the software, an ergonomics analysis of the Mars rover could be tailored specifically to a vehicle, person, and mission.

For motion conditions on the Mars rover, a couple of risks must be analyzed to determine safety compatibility with suits and machinery. To begin, inner pressure within the suit may affect the user's upper extremities. A study between July 2002 and July 2003 conducted a study of training sessions with extravehicular mobility units. Over 50% of participants had injuries or suit fit problems involved in their upper extremities, including "hand in 122 cases, the elbow in 14 cases, and the shoulder in 66 cases" (Viegas, 2004). From this study, additional research needs to be conducted on the long-lasting impact of extensive extraterrestrial vehicle travel. Participants in the study have also been identified with nerve damage, including "cell necrosis, apoptosis, axonal microtubular transport degeneration, or segmental demyelination." These neuropathic degenerations require extensive and continuous examination of Mars Rover passengers. Conditions may change between Earth and Mars, especially considering the gravitational and atmospheric differences. The longevity of studies and intensity of vehicle use are also additional factors that must be ergonomically analyzed.

Outer forces of the steering wheel may also yield risk under improper training or harsh conditions. In a Swedish study, ergonomic engineers found that 55% of males and 64% of females hold their hand position above 10 and 2 o'clock. These extended hand positions "might affect spinal posture and thereby increase backset distance, which influences neck injury risk in impacts" (Jonsson, 2011). Though the study focused on automotive transportation on Earth, results may apply to the Mars rover, as the vehicle structure is similar. From the study analyzed, there seems to be agency in drivers to reduce outer force trauma and minimize injuries. An article examining blunt cardiac injury in traffic incidents came to a similar conclusion. Various simulations were carried out for thorax-to-steering impact at different heights. Results indicated that "contact force was decreased when the inclination angle was decreased." These results can be further extrapolated to conclude outer force risk, which may pose a threat to drivers. However, results indicate that these risks can be reduced by additional ergonomic research.

For both outer and inner pressure forces on passengers, risks can be mitigated with proper training. For degenerative conditions that may occur in outer space, additional exercise training may reduce the deterioration of muscular strength, increase cognitive performance, and prolong bone loss risk (Greenleaf, 1989). Vehicle collision risk can also be reduced with proper driving techniques and additional safety protocols established for Mars rovers. Both external and internal forces can be analyzed ergonomically for potential risks and can be reduced accordingly.

2.6 Future Work

As human design is a key factor in designing any prototypes regarding space missions, multiple types of research are done and recorded on NSF as well as awards pertaining to such research. Before designing a spaceship or space transmission machine, it is necessary to understand humans' musculoskeletal systems. Researchers from Rutgers University have been awarded by NSF for their research on such topic of the musculoskeletal system and their goals were as follows: Allow real-time calibration through overlay between fluoroscopic images and optical images; Automatically reconstruct 3D bone models from CT and MRI scans in real-time; Automatically estimate 3D in vivo bone movement through 2D/3D registration; Automatically establish 3D bone coordinated systems and convert the 3D in vivo movement into 3D joint kinematics; Fuse the accurate joint kinematics, whole body kinematics, muscle activation, and body reaction forces and visualize all the information on digital human models. (Referred from the Award page listed in references. Rita Rodriguez, the primary researcher and program manager from NSF, has made her point clear that algorithms of human bodily functions are far more important than doing any other operations on machinery. There must be steps to be taken prior to any research or procedures in order for an operation to be successful. She and her team plan on taking CT and MRI as well as X-Ray of the musculoskeletal system in a real-time space setting to prevent any injuries or limitations an astronaut could have in space.

Future publications based on this research are infinite. It will not only involve industrial engineers and aerospace engineers, but it will also bring forth biologists as well as psychologists to the field. Topics of discussion could lead to publications involving the biological and psychological limitations of humans in space. Since outer space is full of uncertainty, researchers can only perform experiments in space-like settings that most closely imitate space. Each experiment could lead to different results and various findings. The most anticipated publication from this award seems to be how to prevent injuries considering space human factors.

2.7 Experience

Bibliometric analysis is an important feature in research due to the opportunity of exploring large quantities of scientific data and synthesizing results from such data. Further analysis using said tools can be seen in Professor Duffy's chapter on "Human Digital Modeling in Design," where analysis in CiteSpace, VOSviewer, NGram, and other bibliometric software is used. The authors applied the same concepts to conduct analysis on a variety of topics ranging from ergonomics to statistics. There is a clear link between the applications used in class and the reports synthesized in industrial fields (Fig. 12).

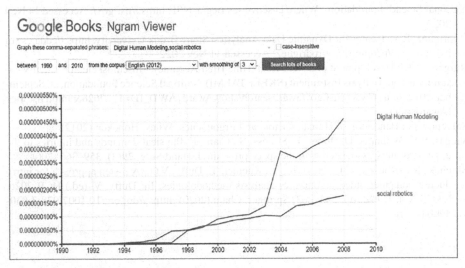

Fig. 12. NGram Viewer in Salvendy Handbook, portraying search results of Digital Human Modeling and Social Robotics over time.

Other similar figures are seen throughout ergonomic papers, primarily the Handbook of Human Factors and Ergonomics, indicating the relationship between key subjects and citation analysis. From prior experience, the team has used similar software to model data via an educational medium. For future research, proper citation and data visualization tools are useful for communicating information effectively. Within the professional space, the team has used Powerpoint and other presentation software to monitor changes and provide updates. Applying the lessons learned throughout ergonomic research and bibliometric analysis remains evidently crucial for career success.

References s

Cassenti, D.N., Scataglini, S., Rajulu, S.L., Wright, J.L.: Advances in Simulation and Digital Human Modeling. Springer, Cham (2022). https://doi.org/10.1007/978-3-030-51064-0

Award Search. National Science Foundation. https://www.nsf.gov/awardsearch/simpleSearchRes ult?queryText=human%2Bmodeling. Accessed 11 Nov 2022

Chaffin, D.B., Nelson, C.: Digital Human Modeling for Vehicle and Workplace Design. Society of Automotive Engineers, Warrendale (2001)

Greenleaf, J.E., Bulbulian, R., Bernauer, E.M., Haskell, W.L., Moore, T.: Exercise-training protocols for astronauts in microgravity. J. Appl. Physiol. **67**(6), 2191–2204 (1989)

Hanson, L., Blomé, M., Dukic, T., Högberg, D.: Guide and documentation system to support digital human modeling applications. Int. J. Ind. Ergon. **36**(1), 17–24 (2006)

Jonsson, B.: Hand position on steering wheel during driving. Traffic Inj. Prev. **12**(2), 187–190 (2011)

Meulen, P., Seidl, A.: Ramsis – the leading cad tool for ergonomic analysis of vehicles. In: Duffy, V.G. (ed.) ICDHM 2007. LNCS, vol. 4561, pp. 1008–1017. Springer, Heidelberg (2007). https://doi.org/10.1007/978-3-540-73321-8_113

National Science Foundation - Where Discoveries Begin. NSF. https://nsf.gov/. Accessed 14 Nov 2022

Rodriguez, R.V.: Center for Dynamic Data Analytics. Stony Brook University. https://cdda.cs.sto nybrook.edu/people/rita-v-rodriguez. Accessed 11 Nov 2022

Rutgers: MRI: Development of a Near-Real-Time High-Accuracy Musculoskeletal System Measurement and Analysis Instrument (SKELETALMI). National Science Foundation, 20 September 2012. https://www.nsf.gov/awardsearch/showAward?AWD_ID=1229628&Historica lAwards=false

Salvendy, G.: Handbook of Human Factors and Ergonomics. Wiley, Hoboken (2012)

Viegas, S.F., Williams, D., Jones, J., Strauss, S., Clark, J.: Physical demands and injuries to the upper extremity associated with the space program. J. Hand Surg. **29**(3), 359–366 (2004)

Sinchuk, K., Hancock, A.L., Hayford, A., Kuebler, T., Duffy, V.G.: A 3-step approach for introducing computer-aided ergonomics analysis methodologies. In: Duffy, V. (ed.) HCII 2020. LNCS, vol. 12198, pp. 243–263. Springer, Cham (2020). https://doi.org/10.1007/978-3-030-49904-4_18

Ergonomics Research of Domestic Vehicle Cab Central Control System Based on Entropy Method

Qingchen Li[1(✉)] and Yongxin Wu[2]

[1] School of Art Design and Media, Nanjing University of Science and Technology, Nanjing 210094, People's Republic of China
adrean@163.com

[2] School of Design, Jianghan University, Wuhan 430056, People's Republic of China

Abstract. The ergonomics of the central control system of household automobile cab has a great influence on the operation of automobile. In order to better evaluate the ergonomics of the central control system of automobile cab, the ergonomics evaluation index system of automobile cab is studied. 5 drivers were selected to evaluate 4 models; According to the composition of the cab, the ergonomics evaluation index system of the central control system was divided into 4 first-level indexes and 22 second-level indexes, and then the evaluation and quantitative research were carried out. An ergonomic evaluation method based on entropy method was proposed. The evaluation information of each index was collected by Likert scale and combined with entropy method to obtain the objective factor weights, which provided a reference method for comparing the advantages and disadvantages of different design schemes and models, and explored the ergonomic indexes and weight distribution affecting the central control system of automobile cab. At the same time, it can also find the index that the driver has higher requirements for ergonomic design in the vehicle central control system, as well as the optimal ergonomic model.

Keywords: Automotive ergonomics · Cab central control system · Entropy value method · Evaluation index · ergonomics

The family car central control system mainly includes the dashboard of the center console, the auxiliary dashboard of the driver's side channel, the combination instrument and the steering wheel, etc. It is an important component of the vehicle's information display and vehicle control, and also an important device for the driver to obtain the vehicle's state information. Ergonomics evaluation of the central control system of a car is a factor affecting the ergonomics of the driver. In the process of driving, the driver and the central control system of the cab constitute a man-machine system. Reasonable ergonomics design of the central control system can ensure the safe driving of the driver.

1 Overview

1.1 Automotive Ergonomics

Ergonomics is the study of human, machine, environment and their relationship between the edge of interdisciplinary subjects, such as engineering and technology, anthropometry, human anatomy, physiology, psychology, safety engineering, behavioral science, anthropology and environmental science [1]. The International Society of Ergonomics defines ergonomics as: Ergonomics is the study of human anatomy, physiology, psychology and other aspects of the various factors in a work environment; The study of the interaction between man and machine and the environment. The study of how productivity, health, safety, and comfort are taken into account in work, family life, and vacation.

The purpose of ergonomics is firstly to improve the efficiency and efficiency of people's work and other behaviors; secondly, to improve the value of people, such as increasing safety, reducing fatigue and pressure, improving comfort, increasing job satisfaction and improving the quality of life; thirdly, to solve the mutual relationship between people, machines and environment and optimize the system.

Automotive ergonomics is an important branch of ergonomics, it takes the human (driver and passenger)—vehicle—environment system as the object, to improve the driver's working conditions and passenger comfort as the core, to human safety, health, comfort, efficient as the goal, so that the overall performance of the whole system to achieve the best. Mainly studies the relationship between people, cars and the environment.

1.2 Ergonomics of Vehicle Cab Central Control System

The vehicle cab central control system is the interaction space between the driver and the vehicle as well as the medium and equipment of information interaction between man and machine. Its research content is a part of vehicle ergonomics, its ergonomics level is related to the driver information acquisition and operation efficiency.

With the improvement of automobile aesthetics and the development of electronic control technology, the functions of central control system are becoming more and more abundant. In the driver—vehicle—environment system, the driver is the core object of ergonomics research. The man-machine ergonomics of automotive central control system is human-centered. It studies how the vehicle central control system meets the driving needs and provides information that is easy to be recognized and understood. Reliable and convenient operation; Create a safe and comfortable human—car—environment system [2]. At present, the evaluation of the design of the cab central control system mainly comes from the subjective feelings of the driver, but because of the uncertainty of human psychology and physiology, the evaluation of man-machine ergonomics also has a certain ambiguity. Therefore, it is of great significance to propose a set of relatively objective and effective ergonomic evaluation methods for automotive central control design.

1.3 The Entropy Value Method

As early as 1865, the German physicist T. Clausuis put forward the concept of entropy. In 1948, C. E. Shannon introduced entropy into information theory, representing the measure of uncertainty. The smaller the information carrying capacity of data, the greater the uncertainty, and the greater the entropy. The lower the entropy. The principle of the entropy method is to judge the dispersion degree of the index and the size of the information carrying capacity according to the entropy value of each index. The larger the entropy value, the smaller the dispersion degree, the less effective information, the smaller the influence on the comprehensive evaluation, and the smaller the weight. On the contrary, the larger the weight. Entropy method, carried by the use of each evaluation index and the amount of information on the whole the influence degree of the evaluation system, to comprehensively judge the effectiveness of the various indicators and its importance, and make an objective and fair evaluation system according to the objective facts of empowerment, has higher weight value credibility, to ensure the objectivity and accuracy of the result.

The main calculation steps of entropy method are as follows:

1) First of all, standardization is carried out:

$$y_{ij} = \frac{x_{ij} - x_{i\,min}}{x_{i\,max} - x_{i\,min}} \tag{1}$$

where, y_{ij} is the JTH index of the i_{th} unit after dimensionless processing, and x_{ij} is the original value of the JTH index of the i_{th} unit.

2) Standardization of definitions:

$$Y_{ij} = \frac{y_{ij}}{\sum\limits_{j=1}^{n} y_{ij}} \tag{2}$$

3) The index information entropy value e and the information utility value d, The information entropy value of the i_{th} index is

$$e_i = -\frac{1}{In_m} \sum\limits_{i=1}^{m} Y_{ij} In Y_{ij} \tag{3}$$

The Information utility value is

$$d_i = 1 - e_i \tag{4}$$

4) The weight of the evaluation index: the information utility value is the largest, indicating that the more important the index is, the more important it is to the evaluation. Finally, the weight of the j index is

$$W_i = \frac{d_i}{\sum\limits_{i=1}^{m} d_i} \tag{5}$$

5) Comprehensive evaluation:

$$F = \sum w_i y_{ij} \tag{6}$$

1.4 Related Research

Automobile cabin design of control system plays an important role for the safety of the vehicle. In the paper "Driver's Hand Reach and Interface and Cab Size Comprehensive Factor G", Wen Wufan et al. from Jilin University proposed a rational detection formula for detecting the layout of operating buttons in the cab, and a design formula for driver's hand reach and measuring table [3]. Xu Weitong et al. analyzed the influencing factors of ergonomic design of civil aircraft cockpit touch display system based on the basic ergonomic principles, and initially constructed the ergonomic evaluation index system of civil aircraft touch display system, which provided references for the design and evaluation of the system [4]. Based on the ergonomic design and comprehensive evaluation of aircraft cockpit, Wang Wenjun from Northwestern Polytechnical University constructed the framework of the ergonomic design and comprehensive evaluation system of aircraft cockpit, and put forward the corresponding solutions [5]. Song Haijing from Nanjing University of Aeronautics and Astronautics improved the traditional expert scoring method, established a comprehensive evaluation index system of civil aircraft cockpit ergonomics, and obtained the comprehensive evaluation result by fuzzy mathematics [6]. Zhang Fuyong used BP neural network to evaluate the human-machine interface of automobile Cab Display Control System in his study, and developed the corresponding interface evaluation software for comprehensive evaluation [7]. Through the literature research, found that the current evaluation system of the whole cabin control system of the evaluation is less, therefore, this article will to household car central ergonomics evaluation index system of evaluation and quantitative research, carries on the comprehensive overall evaluation, also found that the driver for ergonomic design in the vehicle control system to demand higher index.

2 Evaluation Index System

2.1 Index Design

Ergonomic evaluation of central control system in cab involves cab space, layout and so on. The establishment of evaluation index system is the premise and foundation of effective overall evaluation of central control system.

In this paper, through the systematic, integral and scientific description of the central control system of the automobile, according to the structure of the automobile cab, the ergonomics evaluation index system of the central control system of the cab is constructed. The ergonomics evaluation index system of the central control system is divided into two parts: 4 first-level indicators (based on function and composition: combination instrument, instrument panel, steering wheel and sub-instrument panel) and 22 second-level indicators (such as spatial layout, size, icon, visual field, manipulation force and operation texture, etc.). The specific indicators are shown in Fig. 1.

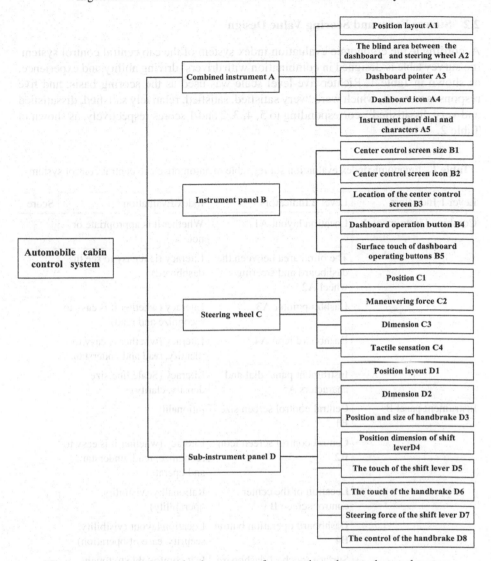

Fig. 1. Ergonomic index evaluation system of automotive cab central control system

2.2 Survey Form and Scoring Value Design

According to the ergonomic evaluation index system of the cab central control system, the survey table is designed in combination with drivers' driving ability and experience, as shown in Table 1. Richter five-level scale was used as the scoring basis, and five responses were set, which were "very satisfied, satisfied, relatively satisfied, dissatisfied and very dissatisfied", corresponding to 5, 4, 3, 2 and 1 scores respectively, as shown in Table 2.

Table 1. Ergonomic index evaluation survey table of automotive cab central control system

Level 1 Indicators	Level 2 Indicators	Index Evaluation	Score
Combined instrument A	Location layout A1	Whether it is appropriate or not	
	The blind area between the dashboard and steering wheel A2	Literacy (is it easy to see the dashboard)	
	Dashbo pointer A3	Literacy (whether it is easy to recognize and read)	
	Dashboard icon A4	Literacy (whether is easy to identify, read and understand)	
	Instrument panel dial and characters A5	Literacy (Scale line size, density, clarity)	
Instrument panel B	Central control screen size B1	rationality	
	Central control screen icon B2	Literacy (whether it is easy to recognize, read, understand, and operate)	
	Location of the center control screen B3	Rationality (visibility, operability)	
	Dashboard operation button B4	Location layout (visibility, security, ease of operation)	
	Surface touch of dashboard operating buttons B5	Is it comfortable to touch	
Steering wheel C	Position C1	Whether the position layout is reasonable (comfortable position)	
	Maneuvering force C2	Flexibility of operation	
	Dimension C3	Is it fit and comfortable to grip	
	Tactile sensation C4	Is it comfortable to touch	

(*continued*)

Table 1. (*continued*)

Level 1 Indicators	Level 2 Indicators	Index Evaluation	Score
Sub-instrument panel D	Position layoutD1	Whether the location layout is reasonable (visibility, safety, comfortable position)	
	Dimension D2	Whether it is suitable, convenient and comfortable to operate	
	Position and size of handbrake D3	Whether it is appropriate or not	
	Position dimension of shift lever D4	Is it fit and comfortable to grip	
	The touch of the shift lever D5	Is it comfortable to touch	
	The touch of the handbrake D6	Is it comfortable to touch	
	Steering force of the shift lever D7	Flexibility of operation	
	The control of the handbrake D8	Flexibility of operation	

Table 2. Scores of Richter Scale

Subjective feeling	Very satisfied	Be satisfied	Relatively satisfied	Not satisfied	Very dissatisfied
Score	5	4	3	2	1

2.3   Evaluation Steps

In this paper, 4 kinds of household small car models in the market are selected as the test samples, and 5 drivers with certain professional knowledge and driving experience are selected. The evaluation adopts the form of questionnaire. Firstly, the purpose of this study and relevant background information are introduced to the drivers participating in the evaluation. Drivers are required to drive a certain distance on the specified road surface and pay attention to the use of instrument panel and steering wheel during the driving process. Each index that affects driver ergonomics is graded. After completing the investigation of one car, the second car was randomly selected to drive, and the third and fourth car were successively investigated (Fig. 2).

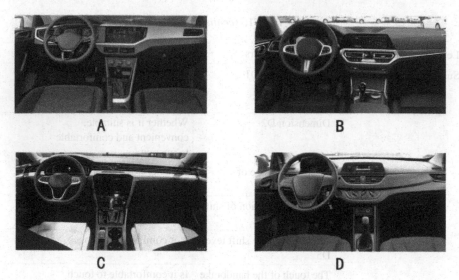

Fig. 2. Cab central control system of four models

2.4 Evaluation Results

According to the survey of five drivers (a, b, c, D and e) after experiencing four types of driving, the score value of the display control interface of each vehicle is shown in the Table 3. It can be seen that the score of each index of type B car is higher, that of type A car and type C car is not much different, and that of type D car is slightly lower.

According to Eqs. 1 and 2, dimensionless processing is carried out on the index score data of each vehicle type.

Then, according to Eqs. 3 and 4, the information entropy value, information utility value and weight of the index (Table 4), and the score of each index (Table 5 and Table 6) are obtained.

Table 3. Index score table of each vehicle type

Type A																						
	A1	A2	A3	A4	A5	B1	B2	B3	B4	B5	C1	C2	C3	C4	D1	D2	D3	D4	D5	D6	D7	D8
a	3	4	4	3	3	3	4	4	4	3	2	3	3	4	3	3	4	3	2	3	3	3
b	4	3	4	3	4	4	3	3	3	3	3	4	4	5	3	3	4	3	3	3	3	2
c	3	3	4	2	4	4	2	4	3	3	4	3	4	3	4	3	3	4	3	3	4	3
d	2	2	3	3	3	3	4	3	3	4	3	4	4	4	3	3	4	4	3	3	4	3
e	3	4	3	2	3	4	3	4	3	3	3	4	4	5	3	3	3	3	2	3	3	3

(continued)

Table 3. (*continued*)

Type B

	A1	A2	A3	A4	A5	B1	B2	B3	B4	B5	C1	C2	C3	C4	D1	D2	D3	D4	D5	D6	D7	D8
a	4	4	4	4	5	5	5	4	5	4	4	4	4	5	5	4	4	4	4	4	5	4
b	5	4	5	4	4	4	4	5	5	4	4	4	4	5	5	5	5	5	4	4	5	4
c	3	4	5	3	4	4	3	4	3	4	3	5	4	4	4	5	4	5	5	4	4	3
d	4	5	5	4	5	4	5	3	4	4	5	5	5	4	5	4	5	4	4	4	5	4
e	4	5	5	4	5	4	4	5	5	5	5	5	5	5	5	4	5	5	4	5	4	4

Type C

	A1	A2	A3	A4	A5	B1	B2	B3	B4	B5	C1	C2	C3	C4	D1	D2	D3	D4	D5	D6	D7	D8
a	3	4	3	3	3	4	4	4	3	3	4	4	3	4	4	3	4	4	4	4	4	3
b	3	4	4	3	3	3	4	4	3	3	4	4	3	3	4	4	4	3	4	4	3	4
c	4	4	4	3	4	3	5	3	3	4	3	3	4	3	3	4	4	4	4	4	4	4
d	4	4	4	3	4	4	3	3	4	3	4	3	4	4	3	4	5	4	5	3	3	3
e	3	3	3	3	2	3	3	3	3	3	3	4	3	3	3	4	4	3	4	4	3	3

Type D

	A1	A2	A3	A4	A5	B1	B2	B3	B4	B5	C1	C2	C3	C4	D1	D2	D3	D4	D5	D6	D7	D8
a	3	4	4	3	3	2	3	2	4	3	4	4	3	3	3	3	4	3	2	3	3	3
b	2	3	4	3	2	3	3	3	3	3	3	3	3	3	2	2	4	3	3	3	3	2
c	1	3	4	3	2	2	2	3	3	1	3	4	2	1	2	2	3	3	3	3	3	3
d	2	3	4	3	2	3	3	3	2	2	3	4	3	3	3	3	4	3	3	2	3	3
e	4	3	4	3	3	2	3	3	2	3	4	3	3	3	2	2	4	3	2	3	3	3

Table 4. Entropy value, information utility value and weight of indicators

	Entropy value	Information utility value	Weight
A1	0.965751822	0.034248178	0.018919978
A2	0.961527231	0.038472769	0.021253801
A3	0.918528882	0.081471118	0.045007701
A4	0.950178496	0.049821504	0.027523268
A5	0.906608289	0.093391711	0.051593084
B1	0.922317049	0.077682951	0.042914976
B2	0.940809021	0.059190979	0.032699317
B3	0.963574055	0.036425945	0.020123058
B4	0.938474884	0.061525116	0.033988782
B5	0.972864993	0.027135007	0.014990396

(continued)

Table 4. (*continued*)

	Entropy value	Information utility value	Weight
C1	0.958436866	0.041563134	0.022961034
C2	0.85620113	0.14379887	0.07943989
C3	0.965670222	0.034329778	0.018965057
C4	0.971961178	0.028038822	0.015489697
D1	0.915847992	0.084152008	0.046488726
D2	0.92067656	0.07932344	0.043821244
D3	0.918528882	0.081471118	0.045007701
D4	0.733451583	0.266548417	0.147251344
D5	0.905177922	0.094822078	0.052383273
D6	0.963064359	0.036935641	0.020404634
D7	0.694134639	0.305865361	0.168971498
D8	0.946054459	0.053945541	0.02980154

Table 5. Scores of index A1–B5

		A1	A2	A3	A4	A5	B1	B2	B3	B4	B5
A	a	0.0126	0.0142	0.0225	0.0138	0.0258	0.0143	0.0218	0.0201	0.0227	0.0100
	b	0.0189	0.0071	0.0225	0.0138	0.0516	0.0286	0.0109	0.0101	0.0113	0.0100
	c	0.0126	0.0071	0.0225	0.0000	0.0516	0.0286	0.0000	0.0201	0.0113	0.0100
	d	0.0063	0.0000	0.0000	0.0138	0.0258	0.0143	0.0218	0.0101	0.0113	0.0150
	e	0.0126	0.0142	0.0000	0.0000	0.0258	0.0286	0.0109	0.0201	0.0113	0.0100
B	a	0.0126	0.0142	0.0225	0.0138	0.0516	0.0429	0.0218	0.0201	0.0227	0.0150
	b	0.0126	0.0142	0.0225	0.0275	0.0516	0.0286	0.0218	0.0201	0.0340	0.0100
	c	0.0126	0.0142	0.0450	0.0138	0.0516	0.0143	0.0109	0.0201	0.0113	0.0150
	d	0.0189	0.0213	0.0225	0.0275	0.0258	0.0286	0.0218	0.0101	0.0227	0.0150
	e	0.0189	0.0071	0.0225	0.0275	0.0516	0.0286	0.0218	0.0201	0.0227	0.0150
C	a	0.0126	0.0142	0.0000	0.0138	0.0258	0.0286	0.0218	0.0201	0.0113	0.0100
	b	0.0126	0.0142	0.0225	0.0138	0.0258	0.0143	0.0218	0.0201	0.0113	0.0100
	c	0.0189	0.0142	0.0225	0.0138	0.0516	0.0143	0.0327	0.0101	0.0113	0.0150
	d	0.0189	0.0142	0.0225	0.0138	0.0516	0.0286	0.0109	0.0101	0.0227	0.0100
	e	0.0126	0.0071	0.0000	0.0138	0.0000	0.0143	0.0109	0.0101	0.0113	0.0100
D	a	0.0126	0.0142	0.0225	0.0138	0.0258	0.0000	0.0109	0.0000	0.0227	0.0100
	b	0.0063	0.0071	0.0225	0.0138	0.0000	0.0143	0.0109	0.0101	0.0113	0.0100
	c	0.0000	0.0071	0.0225	0.0138	0.0000	0.0000	0.0000	0.0101	0.0113	0.0000
	d	0.0063	0.0071	0.0225	0.0138	0.0000	0.0143	0.0109	0.0101	0.0000	0.0050
	e	0.0189	0.0071	0.0225	0.0138	0.0258	0.0000	0.0109	0.0101	0.0000	0.0100

Table 6. Scores of index C1–D8

		C1	C2	C3	C4	D1	D2	D3	D4	D5	D6	D7	D8
A	a	0.0000	0.0000	0.0095	0.0116	0.0155	0.0146	0.0225	0.0000	0.0000	0.0102	0.0000	0.0149
	b	0.0077	0.0794	0.0190	0.0155	0.0155	0.0146	0.0225	0.0000	0.0175	0.0102	0.0000	0.0000
	c	0.0153	0.0000	0.0190	0.0077	0.0310	0.0146	0.0000	0.1473	0.0175	0.0102	0.1690	0.0149
	d	0.0077	0.0794	0.0190	0.0116	0.0155	0.0146	0.0225	0.1473	0.0175	0.0102	0.1690	0.0149
	e	0.0077	0.0794	0.0190	0.0155	0.0155	0.0146	0.0000	0.0000	0.0000	0.0102	0.0000	0.0149
B	a	0.0077	0.0794	0.0190	0.0116	0.0310	0.0292	0.0225	0.1473	0.0349	0.0204	0.1690	0.0298
	b	0.0153	0.0794	0.0190	0.0077	0.0465	0.0438	0.0225	0.1473	0.0349	0.0102	0.1690	0.0149
	c	0.0077	0.0794	0.0190	0.0116	0.0310	0.0292	0.0225	0.1473	0.0349	0.0204	0.1690	0.0149
	d	0.0153	0.0794	0.0190	0.0116	0.0310	0.0292	0.0000	0.1473	0.0349	0.0204	0.0000	0.0298
	e	0.0230	0.0000	0.0190	0.0077	0.0465	0.0146	0.0225	0.0000	0.0349	0.0204	0.1690	0.0298
C	a	0.0153	0.0794	0.0095	0.0116	0.0310	0.0146	0.0225	0.1473	0.0349	0.0204	0.1690	0.0149
	b	0.0153	0.0794	0.0095	0.0077	0.0310	0.0292	0.0225	0.0000	0.0349	0.0204	0.0000	0.0298
	c	0.0077	0.0000	0.0190	0.0077	0.0155	0.0292	0.0225	0.1473	0.0349	0.0204	0.1690	0.0298
	d	0.0153	0.0000	0.0190	0.0116	0.0155	0.0292	0.0450	0.1473	0.0524	0.0102	0.0000	0.0149
	e	0.0077	0.0794	0.0095	0.0077	0.0155	0.0292	0.0225	0.0000	0.0349	0.0204	0.0000	0.0149
D	a	0.0153	0.0794	0.0095	0.0077	0.0155	0.0146	0.0225	0.0000	0.0000	0.0102	0.0000	0.0149
	b	0.0077	0.0000	0.0095	0.0077	0.0000	0.0000	0.0225	0.0000	0.0175	0.0102	0.0000	0.0000
	c	0.0077	0.0794	0.0000	0.0000	0.0000	0.0000	0.0000	0.0000	0.0175	0.0102	0.0000	0.0149
	d	0.0077	0.0794	0.0095	0.0077	0.0155	0.0146	0.0225	0.0000	0.0175	0.0000	0.0000	0.0149
	e	0.0153	0.0000	0.0095	0.0077	0.0000	0.0000	0.0225	0.0000	0.0000	0.0102	0.0000	0.0149

According to Formula 5, the comprehensive evaluation of each sample is obtained, as shown in Table 7. The final scores of A, B, C and D are as follows: Type B has the highest score and is the best ergonomic model in this evaluation. The scores of type A cars and type C cars were in the middle, with a difference of 0.54 points. The scores of D cars were the lowest, and they were the worst in ergonomics.

Table 7. Scores of each sample

Vehicle type	Driver	Score	Total score
A	a	0.276534989	2.231077235
	b	0.386576528	
	c	0.610254935	
	d	0.647420983	
	e	0.3102898	

(continued)

Table 7. (*continued*)

Vehicle type	Driver	Score	Total score
B	a	0.838865844	3.743143597
	b	0.853436771	
	c	0.795629574	
	d	0.632034003	
	e	0.623177404	
C	a	0.728597365	2.777397924
	b	0.446208808	
	c	0.707262613	
	d	0.563517314	
	e	0.331811823	
D	a	0.322081987	1.176148475
	b	0.181294543	
	c	0.194398954	
	d	0.279209816	
	e	0.199163175	

3 Discuss

3.1 Combination Instrument

According to the score, drivers think that type B and type C are the most suitable, while type D is relatively poor. Model B is the easiest to see the instrument panel, the blind area between the instrument panel and the steering wheel is the smallest, while model A has the most blind area, which affects the observation of instrument information during driving. The best dashboard icon reader is the Model B, the worst is the Model A; B type car instrument panel dial and characters, instrument panel pointer reading ability is the best; Type A and Type C have the lowest number of cars, while Type D is the worst.

For the five indicators of the combined instrument, the driver thinks that the reading of the instrument dial, the character and the instrument pointer in the combined instrument are the most important and occupy a large weight. Scales and Pointers are devices that indicate important parameters and conditions during vehicle running. First of all, their display mode should have high reliability and stability, and the display of relevant signals should be clear. Therefore, it is necessary to select and design the scale, characters and Pointers of the instrument panel reasonably. In addition, it is necessary to choose reasonable shape and color collocation to make them coordinate with each other, shorten the reading time and reduce the misreading rate.

Dashboard dial and character type, direction, length and width should be appropriate, too small is not conducive to reading, degree accuracy and speed are low; If it is too large, the dial size will increase, the spatial layout is not reasonable, and the reading effect will be reduced. The shape of the pointer should be concise, and its shape should be designed according to the principle of tip, flat tail and medium width. At the same time, the color of the pointer should be in sharp contrast with the color of the instrument panel, but should be consistent or coordinated with the color of the scale line and characters, so as to facilitate the driver's reading.

3.2 The Dashboard

According to the score, drivers think the center screen size of Model B is the most reasonable, followed by Model A and Model C, and model D is the worst. Screen icon Type B car C car score higher, the best reading, D car is lower, the center control screen position of type B car is the best, A car and C car number, three in the visibility and operation of the score is not different; The most reasonable and convenient layout of dashboard operation buttons is type B, type A and type C have the same score, and D is the worst. In terms of the tactile comfort of dashboard operation button surface, Model A, B and C have the same score, while model D is the worst.

For the five indicators of the instrument panel, the driver thinks that the size of the center control screen is reasonable, the visibility of the instrument panel operation button, the safety and whether it is easy to operate are relatively important, accounting for a large weight.

3.3 The Steering Wheel

According to the score, drivers think that the steering wheel position of Model B and C is the most comfortable, followed by model D, and Model A is the worst. In terms of steering steering force, model B is the most flexible, and model A, C and D have the same score; The steering wheel size of type B car is the most suitable and the grip is the most comfortable. The scores of type A car and type C car are not much different. On the comfort of steering wheel surface, car A is the best, car B and C have the same score, and car D is the worst.

For the four indicators of steering wheel, the driver thinks that the flexibility of steering wheel operation and the position of steering wheel are more important and occupy a large weight. Steering wheel is the most frequent hand control equipment operated by drivers. Reasonable layout of steering wheel position and Angle and selection of appropriate steering wheel size can reduce the fatigue of drivers' hands and upper arms during driving. The layout of the steering wheel should fully consider the driver's seat adjustment space. In addition, in addition to the geometry of the steering wheel, it is also necessary to consider that it is within the range of human comfort.

3.4 Auxiliary Instrument Panel

According to the score, in terms of position layout and rationality, the driver thinks that the sub-instrument panel is the most comfortable position in B car, followed by A car, C car, D car comfort is the worst; In terms of size, Model B and model C had the best score, while model A and D were worse. Hand brake position size C car is the most suitable, B type of car; The position and size of shift lever of type B car are the most reasonable and the most convenient to operate, followed by C car and A car. Shift lever and handbrake touch is the best car B, C; Shift lever and hand brake control force, B car operation is the most flexible, A, C car score followed by more flexible, compared with the worst type D car.

For the seven indicators of the sub-instrument panel, the driver thinks that the flexibility of the shift lever operation and the rationality of the position are more important and occupy a large weight. In the process of vehicle driving, gearshift usually need to choose the big power to manipulate, and drivers in the use of the gearshift, eyes is generally pay attention to the road ahead, operate at the same time, so the gearshift shall be set up in the pilot of the elbow under the oblique position, on the road, so the driver can accurately and quickly by touch. In the design, we also need to consider the shape and size of the joystick grip, should conform to the size of the human hand.

4   Conclusion

According to the comprehensive score of weight score, the ergonomic design of cab central control system of type B is the best, and the ergonomic design of cab central control system of car A and car C can meet the basic requirements of drivers, and there is little difference between the scores of the two cars. Model D had the lowest overall score. The car price of Type B is significantly higher than that of other vehicles. Comparatively, its configuration and spatial layout are more perfect, while Type D has the lowest price and is the most economical and practical.

To the ergonomic design of automotive cab control system of evaluation, combining the theory of man-machine engineering and related standards, develop automotive cab control system ergonomics evaluation index, with auto combination instrument vice the dashboard, the steering wheel, instrument panel, and the main components such as the research object, to build the bridge control system of evaluation index system, A quantitative comprehensive evaluation is also carried out. It provides a reference method for comparing the advantages and disadvantages of different design schemes and models, and also can find the indicators that drivers have higher requirements for the ergonomic design of vehicle central control system.

However, the ergonomic design evaluation of the central control system in the cab studied in this paper is only a preliminary discussion, and further research is needed. For example, other factors affecting the driving efficiency, such as driving time and road conditions, have not been fully taken into account, and further in-depth research will be carried out in the future to further improve it.

References

1. Lv, J., Chen, J., Xu, J.: Ergonomics. Tsinghua University Press, Beijing (2009)
2. Zhou, Y., Mao, E.: Vehicle Ergonomics. Beijing Institute of Technology Press, Beijing (1999)
3. Wen, W., Du, Z.: Comprehensive factor G of driver's reach and interface and cab size. Autom. Eng. 01 (1991)

4. Xu, W., Zhang, Y., Dong, L.: Research on the ergonomic evaluation index system of civil aircraft cockpit touch display system. Avionics **52**(02) (2021)
5. Wang, W.: Key technologies of ergonomic design and comprehensive evaluation for aircraft cockpit. Northwestern Polytechnical University, Xi'an (2017)
6. Song, H., Sun, Y., Lu, Z.: Research and application of civil aircraft cockpit ergonomics comprehensive evaluation method. Aircr. Des. **30**(04) (2010)
7. Zhang, F.: Human-machine interface evaluation of vehicle cab display control system. Harbin Engineering University, Harbin (2007)
8. He, J.: A comparative study on user experience evaluation of different types of vehicle HMI interface based on multiple indexes. Zhejiang Sci-Tech University (2018)
9. Zheng, W., Zhong, L., Chen, J., Chen, W.: Research on graphical interface display of automobile digital dashboard. J. Xiamen Univ. Nat. Sci. Ed. **48**(6), 830–834 (2009)
10. Yan, C., Yu, Q.: Design and ergonomic evaluation of vehicle instrument based on human factor. China Saf. Sci. J. **17**(10), 62–66, 176 (2007)
11. Fu, B., Liu, W., Wang, Q., et al.: Experimental study on the size ergonomics of touch screen keys in vehicle-mounted display control terminal. Veh. Motor Technol. (02), 45–48 (2015)
12. Feng, F.: Research on automobile cab evaluation system based on ergonomics. School of Mechatronics Engineering, Northeastern University, Shenyang (2008)
13. Zaidel, D.M.: Specification of a methodology for investigating the human factors of advanced driver in-formation systems (Technical report TP 11199 (E)), Road Safety and Motor Vehicle Regulation, Transport Canada, Ottawa, Canada. 30 Reid, G.B.and Nygren (1991)
14. Zheng, Z.Y., Liu, J., Li, Y.: Comprehensive evaluation of Marine industry in Donghai Region based on entropy method. East China Econ. Manag. (33), 09 (2019)

Investigating the Time Dependency of Elbow Flexion Angle Variations in Real and Virtual Grabbing Tasks Using Statistical Parametric Mapping

Nils Mayat[1], Stella Adam[1], Mahmood Alkawarit[1], Anika Weber[1,2], Jan P. Vox[3], Krzysztof Izdebski[4], Thomas Schüler[4], Karen Insa Wolf[3], and Daniel Friemert[1]([⊠])

[1] Department of Mathematics and Technology, University of Applied Science Koblenz, Joseph-Rovan-Alle 2, 53424 Remagen, Germany
friemert@hs-koblenz.de
[2] Institute Sport and Exercise Science Research Centre, School of Applied Sciences, London South Bank University, 103 Borough Road, London SE1 0AA, UK
[3] Division Hearing, Speech and Audio Technology HAS, Fraunhofer Institute for Digital Media Technology IDMT, Marie-Curie-Str. 2, 26129 Oldenburg, Germany
[4] Halocline GmbH & Co. KG, Netter Platz 3, 49090 Osnabrück, Germany

Abstract. In this paper, we explore the differences in movement between real life and virtual reality. To gather data for our study, 23 healthy adults were asked to move a box with their right hand in both a real life setting and virtual environment. The movements were captured using a marker-based motion capture system consisting of eight cameras. We analyzed the elbow flexion and angular velocity during object manipulation tasks in both virtual reality and the real-world using Statistical Parametric Mapping. The VR environment caused differences in the flexion angle and an decrease in the angular velocity compared to the real environment for the majority of the task duration. The findings suggest that VR environments can affect the kinematics of object manipulation and should be considered when designing VR interfaces for manual tasks.

The results of our study also provide new insights into the ways in which movement is impacted by virtual reality. Our findings have implications for a range of fields, including virtual reality technology, human-computer interaction, and sports science. By better understanding the differences between real-life and virtual movement, we can help to improve the design and use of virtual reality systems.

Keywords: motion tracking · virtual reality · statistical parametric mapping

1 Introduction

Musculoskeletal injuries and disorders are a prevalent issue in many workplaces, with awkward postures at work being a major contributing factor (Amell und Kumar 2001; Kjellberg et al. 2016). Therefore, it is in the interest of employers to evaluate and create

V. G. Duffy (Ed.): HCII 2023, LNCS 14028, pp. 162–174, 2023.
https://doi.org/10.1007/978-3-031-35741-1_13

new ergonomic workplaces to reduce the risk of these injuries and disorders (Punnett und Wegman 2004). One method of risk assessment is through evaluating joint movements in body postures and motion sequences and utilizing virtual reality (VR) technology and motion capture systems during simulated work processes (Simonetto et al. 2022). This allows for the calculation of joint angles and assessment of individual body regions, as well as the simulation and optimization of the work environment for ergonomic design (McAtamney und Nigel Corlett 1993). While implementing changes in a physical workplace may be costly and labour-intensive, VR technology offers high flexibility and the ability to make quick and easy adaptations (Gabajová et al. 2021). Additionally, VR technology allows for the capture of body postures through tracker positions, with past studies finding good agreement with motion capture systems in certain body regions (Vox et al. 2021; van der Veen et al. 2019). Therefore, utilizing VR technology in the assessment and design of ergonomic workplaces can be a valuable tool in reducing the risk of musculoskeletal injuries and disorders among employees. To ensure a valid transfer of analysis in VR to reality, the difference between motion in VR and reality should be well understood. However, there have been studies showing differences and similarities in movements in VR and reality (Friemert et al. 2018). When examining a VR-based assembly task simulator for its ability to assess physical risk factors in ergonomics, results showed that subjects experienced more discomfort in VR, despite having fewer constrained postures and mostly lower levels of muscle activity (Pontonnier et al. 2014). In their study, (Whitman et al. 2004) showed that VR can be compared to a similar experimental task in a real environment when only the range of motion is measured, not velocities or accelerations. Biomechanical data is often presented as a temporal one-dimensional (1-D) continua (Naouma und Pataky 2019) as homologous data over a 1-D domain of 0–100% (Sadeghi et al. 2003). A common analysis method is to compress the data to a zero-dimensional (0-D) metric, such as local extrema (Pataky et al. 2015b) or mean values However, this approach may not be ideal as it may not capture the full complexity of the 1-D data. For example, using the mean as a 0-D parameter would lose the information that a trajectory lies above the mean in the first part of the time series and below the mean in the second part. Additionally, most research questions need to be answered not only on a null-hypothesis which is based on one extracted metric, but rather on the whole time-series (Naouma und Pataky 2019). Another bias when using 0-D metrics is that most test hypothesis pertain on 1-D trajectories and therefor a 1-D model of randomness is needs to be employed (Pataky et al. 2015b; Pataky et al. 2013). To address this problem, (Pataky et al. 2013)) proposed the use of statistical parameter mapping (SPM) as a technique for analysing 1-D time series. SPM was originally developed for use in neuroimaging to control false positives (Worsley et al. 1992). It has been validated for hypothesis testing for 1-D data (Pataky 2016) and has been used on different types of biomechanical data (Ridder et al. 2015; Robinson et al. 2015; Nüesch et al. 2019; Serrien et al. 2015). SPM involves calculating a test statistic field (e.g. F or t) and using random field theory (RFT) to identify clusters where the test statistic field exceeds a calculated threshold. SPM has the capability to identify variations in movement patterns over time, enabling the formulation of temporal risk assessments based on movement, in addition to simply posture evaluation.

This study aims to investigate the differences in motion between real and VR environments while performing spatially oriented tasks, such as the task of rearranging objects on a shelf. The proposed methodology employs an experimental design and statistical analysis of time-series data of the elbow flexion angle, using RFT and the test statistic continua of a linear mixed model (LMM) to compare the data.

2 Methods

2.1 Subjects

In the current study, 26 young healthy adults (16 males, 10 females) participated with informed consent. All subjects were free of neurological or musculoskeletal impairments that might have affected movements or cognitive function. They all had normal or corrected-to-normal vision. The group consisted of subjects between 21 and 27 years (age: 22.80 ± 1.54 yrs; height: 1.75 ± 0.07 m; mass: 74.92 ± 12.28 kg; mean $\pm$ standard deviation). The study was approved by the ethics committee of the University of Applied Sciences Koblenz through whitelisting and met all requirements for human experimentation in accordance with the Declaration of Helsinki (World Medical Association, 2013). Three of the 26 measured subjects were excluded due to incomplete data collection because of technical problems. Therefore 23 subjects were included in the comparison analysis.

2.2 Experimental Setup and Procedures

A marker-based motion capture system consisting of eight cameras (Oqus 7/Oqus 5, Qualisys, Gothenburg, Sweden) was utilized to acquire kinematic data at a sampling rate of 100 Hz. 48 markers were placed at anatomic landmarks directly on the skin (Qualisys Animation Marker Set). Qualisys software was used for calibration, gap filling, and inverse kinematics to derive the kinematic data and skeleton data. Subjects wore a head-mounted display (HMD) with six Vive trackers (one at each foot, one at navel height, one at the sternum, one at each upper arm near the elbow) to allow visualization of their body in the virtual environment. The subjects also held Vive controllers for grasping objects in the virtual environment. The virtual environment in the HMD was created using the Unity game engine (version 2018 LTS) and an avatar based on Vive tracker data and final inverse kinematics was used to visualize the body. Anthropometric data were measured for each subject and the size of the avatar was adjusted accordingly.

The experimental setup in the real world was mirrored in the VR environment and the controls were set up so that the experiment could be conducted in the same way. It included a shelf with 16 compartments on four levels, the height of which was adjusted to the subjects' anthropometry. This configuration of the shelf was chosen because it is a wide representation of different industrial tasks, ranging from sorting to assembly. Anthropometric data were collected according to (Jürgens et al.) (1998). The width of the shelves remained the same for all subjects. To avoid additional occlusions during data recording of the motion capture system, the vertical shelf limits were indicated by markings on the base plate and each compartment was numbered. The shelf was set to

Fig. 1. On the left side the instructions are shown on the smartboard while on the right side the shelf is shown in reality.

the following heights: 1st level: body height, 2nd level: shoulder height – 10% of arm length, 3rd level: shoulder height – 140% of arm length, 4th level: the floor. The subjects' task was to sort a hand-sized, light package on the shelf, using only their right hand. A total of three packages were used, which differed in colour. The smartboard (SMART Board 6065, SMART Technologies ULC, Calgary, Canada) with the respective task was located behind the subject so that the subject had to turn around for each new task. The colour of the package as well as its old and new position was displayed in a graphical representation (Fig. 1 and 2). Each task resulted in a different type of rearrangement and thus a different movement execution. Grabbing in VR was simulated by pressing a button on the controller. All subjects performed the same tasks in reality and VR. In total, the objects were rearranged 43 times each in the VR and the real environment.

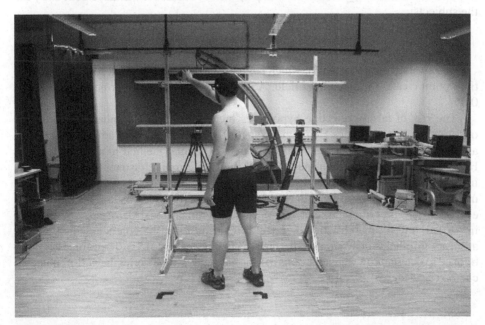

Fig. 2. A subject performing a task in the real life environment. The package must be grabbed with the right hand.

2.3   Data Analysis and Statistics

The Qualisys data was used to construct a body model with Qualisys' skeletal solver. The proprietary motion analysis tool Winkel Daten Analyse (WIDAAN, German for "angle data analysis") (Ellegast et al. 2010; Vox et al. 2021) was used to calculate joint angles. WIDAAN maps the movement data on body model called "the Dortmunder" (Jäger et al. 2001). It uses the individual anthropometric dimensions of the respective subject for angle calculation.

For further data analysis, only the data where the subjects moved the package between compartments were used. Thus, the analyzed movement consisted of the subject grabbing the object, moving it and letting go of it. The flexion angle of the right elbow (α) was analyzed (meaning 0° when the arm is stretched fully). It was filtered using the Butterworth filter which is a common linear filter in biomechanical signals. The data should be filtered with a cutoff frequency between 3–10 Hz which should be applied two times, in forward and reverse directions (Crenna et al. 2021). A 10 Hz cutoff frequency was chosen to preserve the signals information. For this the functions butter and filtfilt from scipy's signal library were used (Virtanen et al. 2020).

The angular velocity was calculated from the filtered angle data. For further analyses only the absolute values of the angular velocity (ω) were analyzed. All time-series were temporally normalized to the length of the movement, so that each time series consists of 101 points (0–100%), using B-splines from the scipy interpolate library (Virtanen et al. 2020).

For each time point a linear mixed effect regression model (LMM) was computed using python's library statsmodels (Seabold und Perktold 2010). The type of movement and the subjects were fitted as random effects and the condition (Real/VR) was fitted as fixed effect. The models were fitted to Eq. 1, where i stands for the movement and j for the subjects:

$$Y_{ij} = \beta_0 + \beta_1 Condition\_VR + b_{1i} Movement_i + b_{2j} Subject_j + \epsilon_{ij} \tag{1}$$

The t values of the factor β_0, which compares the influence of VR to Real, for each time point creates the so called t field. A two tailed t test was performed with α set at 0.05.

The risk of falsely rejecting hypotheses increases with the number of simultaneous tests performed (James Hung und Wang 2010). The Bonferroni adjustment, which assumes independence among multiple tests, is a popular method to account for this. However, when tests are non-independent, the Bonferroni adjustment can lead to an increase in false negatives (Pataky et al. 2015b). A possible solution to this bias is the use of RFT. RFT can be utilized to establish thresholds for test statistic continua (Pataky et al. 2013). It "describes the behaviour of smooth n-dimensional Gaussian continua, and in particular the probability that they will produce test statistic continua which exceed arbitrary thresholds in arbitrary experiments" (Pataky et al. 2015a). Therefore, RFT can be used to determine in which portions of a biomechanical time-series the null-hypothesis can be rejected.

Using the rft1d package (Pataky 2016), the threshold t^* was computed so that identically smooth Gaussian fields would reach it in only 5% of identical, repeated experiments (Pataky et al. 2015a). Rft1D first estimates the field smoothness and then calculates the critical threshold using an inverse survival function. It computes the critical threshold at a Type I error rate of α. After that the p values for each cluster are calculated. If the t field exceeds t^* the null hypothesis can be rejected. To generalize the findings a cohens'd (from here on out denoted as d_C) was computed for every time point to demonstrate the effect size. The complete workflow for the SPM can be seen in Fig. 3.

Fig. 3. Workflow for the SPM

Additionally, an LMM was computed for the duration a subject needed for the movement. The same LMM was used, only that the predicted variable Y was the duration of the movement. In all LMMs the variance structure for the subjects was chosen to be variance components and for the movements heterogenous compound symmetry in order to describe the underlying patterns of variation caused by the variance and correlation in the response variables.

All computations were done using Python 3.9.7 with following packages and version numbers: pandas: 1.3.4, statsmodels: 0.13.2, numpy: 1.21.6, rft1d: 0.2.0.

3 Results

In Fig. 4, mean and standard deviation (SD) curves are presented for three distinct movements of an object. The movements depicted include from left to right column: moving the object from the uppermost right compartment to the uppermost left compartment, moving the object from the upper middle right compartment to the upper middle left compartment, and moving the object from the lowest and furthest right compartment to the highest and rightmost compartment. The first row of the figure displays the angle in degrees, the second row shows the angular velocity in degrees per second, and the third row illustrates the absolute angular velocity in degrees per second. The x-axis is represented by normalized time in percentage.

The results of the LLM analysis for the durations revealed a statistically significant effect of the predictor variable ($t = 10.897; p = 0.001$). The estimated coefficient for the predictor variable β_1 was 0.318, with a standard error of 0.029. This suggests that the use of VR technology results in slower movements, as indicated by the positive coefficient for the predictor variable.

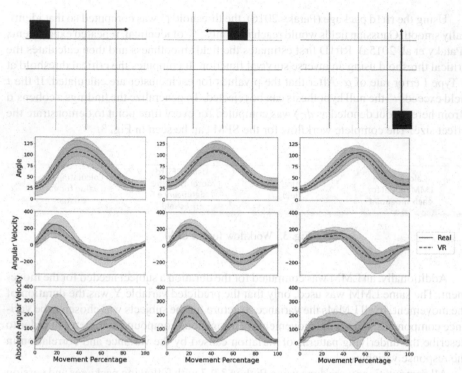

Fig. 4. Three examples of elbow flexion angles, velocities, and absolute velocities. All curves are showing mean and sd over all subjects. The three displacements are shown above.

Figures 5 and 6 show the results of the SPM. The upper plots display the t-field for the angle and absolute angular velocity, respectively. The y-axis displays the t-value and the x-axis depicts the time in movement percentage. The red dashed lines indicate the t-threshold computed by the RFT. The $t*$ value shows at what height the threshold is located. The grey area indicates regions where the t-value demonstrates a statistically significant result. The p-values displayed in the plots represent the probability that a cluster of the same extent (i.e. time length) would occur from a random Gaussian field at the calculated threshold (Friston 2011). The lower plots depict the d_C on the y-axis, where the red areas indicate regions where the t-field exceeds the calculated threshold.

The results of the statistical analysis indicate that there are three clusters of significant differences in the angle measurements (Fig. 3), located at the intervals of 0 to 27% (p = 0.001), 39 to 57% (p = 0.006), and 72 to 100% (p < 0.001). The t-values in the first and last intervals are above the upper threshold, indicating that the use of VR in this setup results in an increase in angle elbow flexion in these intervals. Conversely, the t-values in the middle interval are below the lower threshold, indicating that the use of VR technology results in a decrease in angle measurements in this interval.

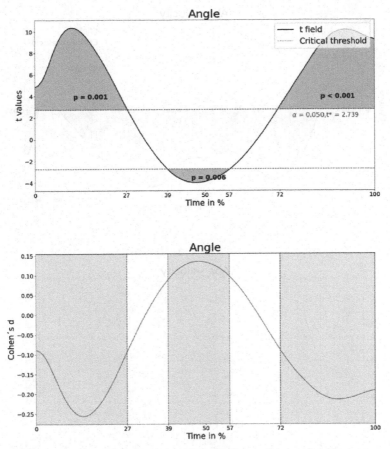

Fig. 5. SPM Results of the elbow flexion angle. In the upper plot the t field is shown and in the lower plot the cohen's d is shown.

The results of the statistical analysis of the absolute velocity indicate that there are four clusters of significant differences in the absolute angular velocity measurements (Fig. 4), located at the intervals of 0% (p = 0.0249), 2 to 9% (p = 0.003), 13 to 90% (p < 0.001), and 96 to 100% (p = 0.011). Only in the second cluster the t field lays above the threshold, suggesting that the movement in VR was completed at a faster rate than in real-world conditions. Conversely, the t-values in the other clusters are below the threshold, indicating that the use of VR results in a decrease in absolute velocity measurements in these intervals. The continuous cluster throughout the middle of the movement shows that throughout most of the movement the movement velocity in VR lays below the one in real which is in accordance with the results of the LMM of the movement durations.

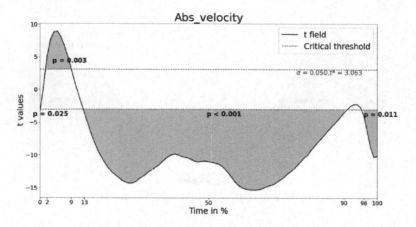

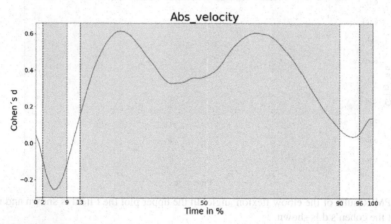

Fig. 6. SPM Results of the absolute angular velocity. In the upper plot the t field is shown and in the lower plot the cohen's d is shown.

4   Discussion

The aim of the present study was to investigate the differences in elbow flexion angle and angle velocity during object manipulation tasks in VR and real environments. When rearranging an object, the main body movement is done with the arm. Therefore, the elbow flexion angle of the right arm was chosen for further analysis.

The angles displayed in the Fig. 2 exhibit a shifted cosine trajectory, which is consistent with the movement pattern of taking an object out of a shelf, pulling it closer to the body, and placing it back in the shelf. Using SPM, the results revealed significant differences in both angle and absolute angular velocity between the two conditions. Specifically, the elbow flexion angle was found to be higher during the beginning and ending phases of the movement in VR compared to the real-world condition but was lower during the middle phase of the movement. These findings suggest that subjects adopted a different movement strategy in VR, characterized by a higher flexion of the elbow during object grasping and releasing, and a lower flexion of the arm during object manipulation. One potential explanation for these differences is that estimating the distance between the object and the hand-held handle may be more challenging in VR. Additionally, the use of the handle in VR may only require it to be in close proximity to the object, rather than in direct contact, which could account for the observed differences in movement strategy.

The results of the analysis of absolute angular velocity revealed the presence of four significant clusters of data points. Only one of these indicates a significantly higher absolute angular velocity in VR while most of the t continua lays below the lower threshold. The absolute velocity curves for both conditions exhibited a 'M' shape, as illustrated in Fig. 2. However, it should be noted that the first cluster only contains the first percent of the movement and is barely significant. It indicates that the starting velocity in the real environment lays above the starting velocity of the movements in VR. During the latter part of this initial phase, the velocity in the real-world condition was found to be higher, resulting in a higher peak velocity. This corresponds to the portion of the movement in which the object is moved from its starting position closer to the body. From here on out the angular velocity under the real-world condition is above the absolute angular velocity under the condition of VR. After the first peak both velocity curves show a local minima in the middle of the movement. This corresponds to the movement phase in which the object is being moved while being closer to the body. Also, in the second half the movement in real is carried out faster. A second peak in the absolute velocity curves occurred, when the object is moved from the body to the shelf.

A possible explanation for the observed pattern in the field of absolute angular velocity could be that it indicates subjects' different levels of movement awareness in a VR environment to hold the object safely during VR interaction. The uncertainty of how to move in the VR environment may contribute to the lower angular velocity curve for the majority of the movement. We struggle to explain why the onset of the movement in VR is faster than under real life condition. A far-fetched explanation could be the subjects perception of the physical properties of the environments and therefore expecting a different (perhaps lower) risk of colliding with objects e.g. the shelf in the VR environment.

The results of this study are consistent with the LMM analysis of the duration of the movement. The velocity curves in VR were found to be lower than the velocity curves of the movement in the real-world condition. The duration of the movement in VR was 0.318 ± 0.029 s longer than in the real-world condition, which is consistent with previous literature (Wang et al. 2011; Cherni et al. 2020).

Using SPM on 1-D time series of the elbow flexion angle it was possible to detect the intervals where there were statistically significant differences in the movement. If only the duration had been analysed, it would not have been possible to detect the underlying differences in the time series, especially in the angle curves.

5 Limitations

The study assumed that the variance in movement among subjects was similar, as clear instructions were given and the shelf was normalized to the subjects' anthropometry. However, it is acknowledged that subjects may still exhibit variation in their movements despite given instructions.

Although implementing grabbing virtual objects through the usage of VR controllers is widely in the scientific literature it has to be stated the controller can extend the reach of the participant depending on how it is used. Therefor future studies where this effect might influence the results of OSH risk assessment or impactful analysis we advise to control the hand and controller position to account for this effect when analysing arm posture in VR.

Furthermore, the study only analysed one body angle, recognizing that movements typically involve a combination of movements in different body angles. A more comprehensive analysis of movement adaptation in VR could be achieved by analysing multivariate time series of different body angles. Although, it is acknowledged that when moving an object in a shelf, elbow flexion is a prominent part of the movement and thus, justifies a single analysis.

Another limitation of the study is the analysis of a single task. Movements analysed when using VR, especially in ergonomics, typically involve a wide variety of tasks. The generalizability of the findings from analysing the specific task of object manipulation in a shelf to other movements may be limited. Nevertheless, a high proportion of industrial tasks require grabbing and object manipulation.

In total, 43 different movements were analysed, which is considered a relatively high number when compared to the number of subjects. It is acknowledged that each movement was only carried out once by each subject, and that an option could be to analyse fewer movements but carried out multiple times by each subject. The approach shown here may reduce generalizability of the results.

6 Conclusion

The objective of the current study was to examine the variations in elbow flexion angle and angular velocity during object manipulation tasks in VR and real-world conditions. Subjects performed object manipulation tasks in a three-story shelf under both conditions. While the trajectories of the elbow flexion angle where similar in VR and the real environment, the SPM analyses revealed that subjects held the object closer to the body and displayed greater angular velocity in real-world conditions as compared to VR. VR risk assessment continuous to be a good addition or even replacement for risk assessment under real life conditions. Although, to developer further it has to account for time dependent differences to improve assessment reliability. It was demonstrated that SPM is an adequate tool for this analysis. Further research may benefit from incorporating multivariate analyses of multiple body angles and various types of movements.

References

Amell, T., Kumar, S.: Work-related musculoskeletal disorders: design as a prevention strategy. A review. J. Occup. Rehabil. **11**(4), 255–265 (2001). https://doi.org/10.1023/a:1013344508217

Cherni, H., Métayer, N., Souliman, N.: Literature review of locomotion techniques in virtual reality. IJVR **20**(1), 1–20 (2020). https://doi.org/10.20870/IJVR.2020.20.1.3183

Crenna, F., Rossi, G.B., Berardengo, M.: Filtering biomechanical signals in movement analysis. Sensors **21**(13), 4580 (2021). https://doi.org/10.3390/s21134580

Ellegast, R., Hermanns, I., Schiefer, C.: Feldmesssystem CUELA zur Langzeiterfassung und-analyse von Bewegungen an Arbeitsplätzen, vol. 375. GRIN Verlag, München (2010)

Friemert, D., Saala, F., Hartmann, U., Ellegast, R.: Similarities and differences in posture during simulated order picking in real life and virtual reality. In: Duffy, V.G. (ed.) DHM 2018. LNCS, vol. 10917, pp. 41–53. Springer, Cham (2018). https://doi.org/10.1007/978-3-319-91397-1_4

Friston, K.J.: Statistical Parametric Mapping. The Analysis of Functional Brain Images. Elsevier Science, Burlington (2011). https://ebookcentral.proquest.com/lib/kxp/detail.action?docID=282095

Gabajová, G., Krajčovič, M., Matys, M., Furmannová, B., Burganová, N.: Designing virtual workplace using unity 3D game engine. AT **7**(1), 35–39 (2021). https://doi.org/10.22306/atec.v7i1.101

Jäger, M., Luttmann, A., Göllner, R., Laurig, W.: "The dortmunder" - biomechanical model for quantification and assessment of the load on the lumbar spine. SAE Trans. **110**, 2163–2171 (2001). http://www.jstor.org/stable/44731090

James Hung, H.M., Wang, S.-J.: Challenges to multiple testing in clinical trials. Biometrical J. **52**(6), 747–756 (2010). https://doi.org/10.1002/bimj.200900206

Jürgens, H.W., Matzdorff, I., Windberg, J.: Internationale anthropometrische Daten als Voraussetzung für die Gestaltung von Arbeitsplätzen und Maschinen (1998)

Kjellberg, K., Lundin, A., Falkstedt, D., Allebeck, P., Hemmingsson, T.: Long-term physical workload in middle age and disability pension in men and women: a follow-up study of Swedish cohorts. Int. Arch. Occup. Environ. Health **89**(8), 1239–1250 (2016). https://doi.org/10.1007/s00420-016-1156-0

McAtamney, L., Corlett, E.N.: RULA: a survey method for the investigation of work-related upper limb disorders. Appl. Ergon. **24**(2), 91–99 (1993). https://doi.org/10.1016/0003-6870(93)900 80-S

Naouma, H., Pataky, T.C.: A comparison of random-field-theory and false-discovery-rate inference results in the analysis of registered one-dimensional biomechanical datasets. PeerJ **7**, e8189 (2019). https://doi.org/10.7717/peerj.8189

Nüesch, C., Roos, E., Egloff, C., Pagenstert, G., Mündermann, A.: The effect of different running shoes on treadmill running mechanics and muscle activity assessed using statistical parametric mapping (SPM). Gait Posture **69**, 1–7 (2019). https://doi.org/10.1016/j.gaitpost.2019.01.013

Pataky, T.C.: RFT1D: smooth one-dimensional random field upcrossing probabilities in Python. J. Stat. Soft. **71**(7), 1–22 (2016). https://doi.org/10.18637/jss.v071.i07

Pataky, T.C., Robinson, M.A., Vanrenterghem, J.: Vector field statistical analysis of kinematic and force trajectories. J. Biomech. **46**(14), 2394–2401 (2013). https://doi.org/10.1016/j.jbiomech.2013.07.031

Pataky, T.C., Vanrenterghem, J., Robinson, M.A.: Two-way ANOVA for scalar trajectories, with experimental evidence of non-phasic interactions. J. Biomech. **48**(1), 186–189 (2015a). https://doi.org/10.1016/j.jbiomech.2014.10.013

Pataky, T.C., Vanrenterghem, J., Robinson, M.A.: Zero- vs. one-dimensional, parametric vs. non-parametric, and confidence interval vs. hypothesis testing procedures in one-dimensional biomechanical trajectory analysis. J. Biomech. **48**(7), 1277–1285 (2015b). https://doi.org/10.1016/j.jbiomech.2015.02.051

Pontonnier, C., Samani, A., Badawi, M., Madeleine, P., Dumont, G.: Assessing the ability of a VR-based assembly task simulation to evaluate physical risk factors. IEEE Trans. Vis. Comput. Graph. **20**(5), 664–674 (2014). https://doi.org/10.1109/TVCG.2013.252

Punnett, L., Wegman, D.H.: Work-related musculoskeletal disorders: the epidemiologic evidence and the debate. J. Electromyogr. Kinesiol. Off. J. Int. Soc. Electrophysiological Kinesiol. **14**(1), 13–23 (2004). https://doi.org/10.1016/j.jelekin.2003.09.015

De Ridder, R., Willems, T., Vanrenterghem, J., Robinson, M.A., Roosen, P.: Lower limb landing biomechanics in subjects with chronic ankle instability. Med. Sci. Sports Exerc. **47**(6), 1225–1231 (2015). https://doi.org/10.1249/MSS.0000000000000525

Robinson, M.A., Vanrenterghem, J., Pataky, T.C.: Statistical parametric mapping (SPM) for alpha-based statistical analyses of multi-muscle EMG time-series. J. Electromyogr. Kinesiol. Off. J. Int. Soc. Electrophysiological Kinesiol. **25**(1), 14–19 (2015). https://doi.org/10.1016/j.jelekin.2014.10.018

Sadeghi, H., Mathieu, P.A., Sadeghi, S., Labelle, H.: Continuous curve registration as an intertrial gait variability reduction technique. IEEE Trans. Neural Syst. Rehabil. Eng. **11**(1), 24–30 (2003). https://doi.org/10.1109/TNSRE.2003.810428

Seabold, S., Perktold, J.: Statsmodels: Econometric and Statistical Modeling With Python (2010). https://www.researchgate.net/publication/264891066_Statsmodels_Econometric_and_Statistical_Modeling_with_Python

Serrien, B., Clijsen, R., Blondeel, J., Goossens, M., Baeyens, J.-P.: Differences in ball speed and three-dimensional kinematics between male and female handball players during a standing throw with run-up. BMC Sports Sci. Med. Rehabil. **7**(1), 27 (2015). https://doi.org/10.1186/s13102-015-0021-x

Simonetto, M., Arena, S., Peron, M.: A methodological framework to integrate motion capture system and virtual reality for assembly system 4.0 workplace design. Saf. Sci. **146**, 105561 (2022). https://doi.org/10.1016/j.ssci.2021.105561

van der Veen, S.M., Bordeleau, M., Pidcoe, P.E., France, C.R., Thomas, J.S.: Agreement analysis between Vive and Vicon systems to monitor lumbar postural changes. Sensors **19**(17) (2019). https://doi.org/10.3390/s19173632

Virtanen, P., Gommers, R., Oliphant, T.E., Haberland, M., Reddy, T., Cournapeau, D., et al.: SciPy 1.0: fundamental algorithms for scientific computing in Python. Nat. Methods **17**(3), 261–272 (2020). https://doi.org/10.1038/s41592-019-0686-2

Vox, J.P., Weber, A., Wolf, K.I., Izdebski, K., Schüler, T., König, P., et al.: An evaluation of motion trackers with virtual reality sensor technology in comparison to a marker-based motion capture system based on joint angles for ergonomic risk assessment. Sensors **21**(9) (2021). https://doi.org/10.3390/s21093145

Wang, C.-Y., Hwang, W.-J., Fang, J.-J., Sheu, C.-F., Leong, I.-F., Ma, H.-I.: Comparison of virtual reality versus physical reality on movement characteristics of persons with Parkinson's disease: effects of moving targets. Arch. Phys. Med. Rehabil. **92**(8), 1238–1245 (2011). https://doi.org/10.1016/j.apmr.2011.03.014

Whitman, L.E., Jorgensen, M., Hathiyari, K., Malzahn, D.: Virtual reality: its usefulness for ergonomic analysis. In: Proceedings of the 2004 Winter Simulation Conference (2004)

Worsley, K.J., Evans, A.C., Marrett, S., Neelin, P.: A three-dimensional statistical analysis for CBF activation studies in human brain. J. Cerebral Blood Flow Metab. Off. J. Int. Soc. Cerebral Blood Flow Metab. **12**(6), 900–918 (1992). https://doi.org/10.1038/jcbfm.1992.127

An Experimental Study of the Psychological Effects of Vision Loss for Practical Application to Windowless Cockpits

Yuki Mekata[✉] [ID], Nagisa Hashimoto, and Miwa Nakanishi

Keio University, 3-14-1 Hiyoshi, Kohoku-Ku Yokohama, Kanagawa, Japan

Abstract. In recent years, technology presenting views using cameras and sensors has been promoted in aircraft and automobiles. Since sudden vision loss can occur in the event of a malfunction, concerns exist not only about the effects of the loss itself but also about psychological effects such as pilots' or drivers' upset or mental strain. Although studies have been conducted from a performance perspective, no studies have examined the psychological effects of vision loss. Therefore, in this study we assessed the psychological effects of vision loss for the reliability design of windowless cockpits while considering human factors. We used a simulator experiment involving controlling the altitude and attitude of an aircraft to examine the psychological effects of various ranges and duration of loss. Our results showed that the psychological effects of the range of loss were significant, and these were not significantly affected by whether vision was restored. Therefore, once vision loss occurs, even if for a short duration, psychological effects follow. In addition, the range of one-third or less for forward field of view vision loss may be acceptable, and thus, designing system partitioning and other aspects using this value may lead to improved reliability.

Keywords: Human factors · Reliability design · Vision loss

1 Introduction

In recent years, technology presenting views using cameras and sensors has been developed for aircraft and automobiles. In particular, in aircraft a windowless cockpit is used, with a large screen instead of windows. For example, the X-59, NASA's quiet supersonic aircraft, substitutes a monitor for forward field of view (FOV), and Airbus's windowless cockpit presents forward FOV using a large screen [1, 2]. It is expected that the improvement of visibility and situational awareness by using image processing and also the reduction in aircraft weight from a decline in the use of glass will be desirable [2].

However, since sudden vision loss can occur in the event of a malfunction, concerns exist not only about the effects of the loss itself but also about psychological effects such as pilots' or drivers' upset or mental strain. Several studies have examined direct visibility limitations. For example, in motor vehicle driving and walking, participants coped by reducing driving speed [3] but also increased object misidentification [4].

Although these studies were conducted from a performance perspective, no study has examined the psychological perspective. It is important to clarify how the magnitude of psychological effects can vary depending on the range and duration of the vision loss, which ultimately can lead to reliability design that considers human factors. Therefore, this study aims to clarify the magnitude of the psychological effects of various conditions of vision loss.

2   Method

2.1   Experimental Task

We conducted the experiment as a flight task in a virtual three-dimensional space using a simulator indicating the operation of an aircraft with a FOV that was replaced by a camera monitor image. Participants controlled the direction of the aircraft with a joystick and maneuvered it for 5 min to pass a circular target of a specific color (Fig. 1). Two circular targets always appeared in the space, and a new target appeared when one target was passed. The speed was set to a constant velocity. The task's objective was to ensure safe maneuvering without violations in altitude and attitude, including altitude falling below 1,000 and attitude deviating from the instrument's standard range (20° per side).

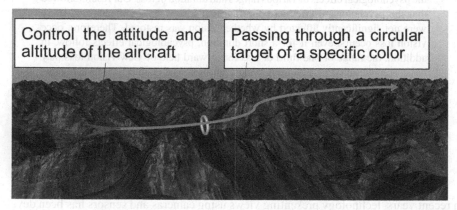

Fig. 1. Overview of the experimental simulation task.

Fig. 2. Example of the experimental screen

2.2   Experimental System and Environment

The FOV was presented by three 65-in. Displays (TH-65EF1J, Panasonic Corp.), and the viewing angle was 50° vertically and 255° horizontally. Participants operated the direction of the aircraft with a joystick controller (Logitech Extreme 3D Pro, Logicool Co. Ltd.). Each maneuvering task lasted 5 min and was performed 15 times. The instrument in front of the participants showed information such as aircraft altitude and attitude. Figure 2 shows the experimental screen, and Fig. 3 shows the experimental environments and the information displayed on the instrument screen.

2.3   Experimental Conditions

We set the conditions as the differences in range and duration of vision loss. The range varied within one-sixth to two-thirds of the forward FOV, and the four conditions were set as one-sixth, one-third, one-half, and two-thirds of the FOV. Figure 4 shows examples of the experimental screen while vision loss occurred, with the areas where the loss occurred shown in black. We set the loss so that it did not occur within one-sixth of each of the left and right edges of the viewing area. In addition, we set patterns for the duration of the loss: one condition in which vision was restored after 15 s when a restore button was pressed and the other in which vision was not restored when the button was pressed. A button on the joystick controller was assigned as the "restore" button, and it was necessary for the participants to perform the restore operation by pressing this button regardless of whether restoration was successful.

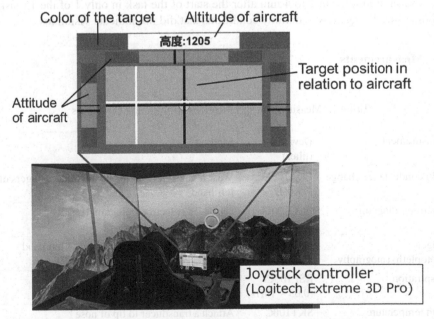

Fig. 3. Experimental environments and instrument display.

one – sixth

one – third

one – half

two – third

Fig. 4. Examples of vision loss in the experiment.

On the basis of these settings, eight conditions were established with a combination of range of vision loss and restoration success. The participants were instructed about the possibility of vision loss and were not informed of the conditions. Vision loss occurred at a random timing from 1 to 4 min after the start of the task in only 1 of the 15 tasks, and the other 14 tasks were dummy conditions that did not indicate vision loss.

2.4 Measurements

Table 1. Measurement specifications of physiological indices

Measurement	Device (filter)	Method
Skin conductance change	EDA100C (~1.0Hz)	Wear a transducer on index and middle fingers of left hand
Electrocardiogram	ECG100C (0.5 ~ 35Hz)	Three-lead electrocardiogram (LeadII)
Finger photoplethysmography	PPG100C (0.5 ~ 10Hz)	Wear a transducer on ring finger of left hand
Respiration	RSP100C (0.05 ~ 10Hz)	Wear a band around abdomen
Skin temperature	SKT100C (~1.0Hz)	Attach a transducer to tip of nose

Since the sympathetic nervous system (SNS) is known to be activated when an individual is upset or under a mental strain [5, 6], we recorded physiological indices (i.e., skin conductance level, electrocardiogram, finger photoplethysmography, respiration, skin temperature), and related these indices to the autonomic nervous system by using MP150, EDA100C, ECG100C, PPG100C, RSP100C, and SKT100C (BIOPAC Systems, Inc.). Table 1 shows the indices' measurement specifications. We calculated skin conductance level, heart rate, amplitude of pulse wave, respiration rate, and nose skin temperature as the indicators of psychological effects. In these, skin conductance level and heart and respiration rates can increase and the amplitude of pulse wave and nose skin temperature can decrease when the SNS is activated.

In addition, during the tasks, we constantly recorded the altitude and attitude of the aircraft controlled by the participants, and determined if both were within the standard range. Furthermore, we recorded the subjective assessment of workload (WL) using NASA-TLX [7, 8] after each task. From the rating scores of six titles (i.e., mental demand, physical demand, temporal demand, effort, performance, frustration level), we calculated the weighted WL (WWL) scores and used these to evaluate WL.

2.5 Procedure

Participants performed the tasks 15 times. Before each task, participants completed a closed-eye rest for 1 min. After performing the task for 5 min, the participants responded to a subjective assessment by NASA-TLX regarding task WL. Vision loss occurred in only 1 task of 15, and the task in which the loss occurred was randomized for each participant. In the tasks in which the loss occurred, it did so at random times within a range of 1–4 min after the task's beginning. In addition, the participants were not informed about the timing of the loss.

2.6 Participants

The 17 participants were ages 21–24 years (eight men, nine women). Each participant was assigned to two different conditions, and four or five participants were assigned to each condition. Each participant performed only one condition per day, and the repeated experiments were performed on the other days. Participants were instructed to refrain from consuming alcohol and caffeine from the day before the experiment and to practice good sleep hygiene. This study was approved by the Research Ethics Review Committee of Keio University Faculty of Science and Technology. Informed consent was obtained from each participant.

3 Results

3.1 Evaluation by Physiological Indices

We standardized the evaluation indicators of each physiological index with the resting state as the reference according to Eq. (1), where x was the mean of the data in the analysis interval, $\bar{x}$ was the mean of the data at rest with the eyes closed immediately before the task, and σ was the standard deviation of the data.

$$Z = (x - \bar{x})/\sigma \tag{1}$$

We calculated the indicator of psychological effect (*PE*) according to Eq. (2). We calculated the mean value of 1 min after vision loss (Z_{after}) relative to the mean value of 1 min before the loss (Z_{before}) as an index reflecting the psychological effects.

$$PE = Z_{after} - Z_{before} \qquad (2)$$

In addition, for comparison, we calculated the indicators of change in the dummy conditions (Z_d) according to Eq. (3). The mean value of the difference between before and after 1 min at the same time of the onset of vision loss were calculated and averaged over 14 times.

$$Z_d = \sum\nolimits_{i=1}^{14} \left(Z_{i,after} - Z_{i,before}\right)/14 \qquad (3)$$

Figures 5 and 6 show the results of respiration rate and skin conductance level. From the findings of two-way analysis of variance (ANOVA), the effect of range was significant for respiration rate and marginally significant for skin conductance level, suggesting that the larger the range of vision loss, the greater the psychological effects. However, from the results of the two-way ANOVA, the effects of the presence or absence of vision resto-ration was not significant, suggesting that even a brief vision loss can have PE. For heart rate, amplitude of pulse wave, and skin temperature, no significant effects occurred for range and restoration, nor did differences occur in psychological effects across conditions. In addition, in comparison to the dummy condition, the values for the condition of two-thirds showed a trend toward greater change in both respiration rate and skin conductance level; respiration rate also showed a trend toward greater change in the condition of one-half. These results suggest that, even in the case of vision loss, which can lead to upset and mental strain, a range of loss of about one-third of the forward FOV may be acceptable.

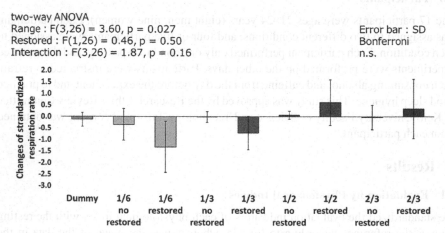

Fig. 5. Change of standardized respiration rate after vision loss occurred and the change of value in dummy conditions

3.2 Subjective Assessment

We calculated the WL indicator of according to Eq. (4). Relative to the maximum (WWL_{max}) and minimum (WWL_{min}) WWL scores in the dummy condition, we calculated the relative values of the WWL scores in the condition of vision loss (WWL).

$$WL = (WWL - WWL_{max})/(WWL_{max} - WWL_{min}) \qquad (4)$$

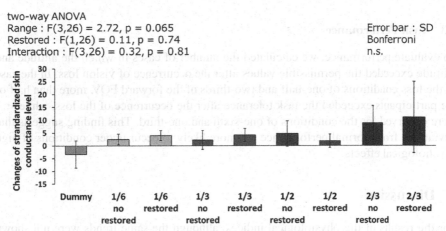

two-way ANOVA
Range : $F(3,26) = 2.72$, $p = 0.065$
Restored : $F(1,26) = 0.11$, $p = 0.74$
Interaction : $F(3,26) = 0.32$, $p = 0.81$

Error bar : SD
Bonferroni
n.s.

Fig. 6. Change of standardized skin conductance level after vision loss occurred and the change of value in dummy conditions

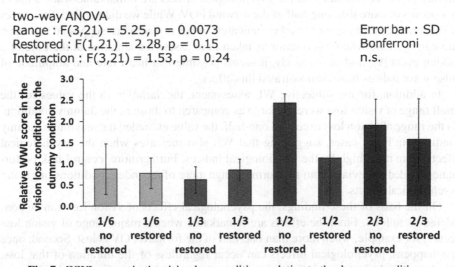

two-way ANOVA
Range : $F(3,21) = 5.25$, $p = 0.0073$
Restored : $F(1,21) = 2.28$, $p = 0.15$
Interaction : $F(3,21) = 1.53$, $p = 0.24$

Error bar : SD
Bonferroni
n.s.

Fig. 7. WWL scores in the vision loss conditions relative to the dummy conditions

Figure 7 shows the results of relative WWL scores. From the results of two-way ANOVA, the effect of range was significant, confirming the same trend as that observed in the evaluation by the physiological indices, and the effect of the presence or absence of vision restoration was not significant. In addition, because the value was > 1 when the range of vision loss was greater than one-half, the results were similar to those obtained by the physiological indices, which showed that a range of loss of about one-third of the forward FOV was acceptable.

3.3 Task Performance

To evaluate performance, we calculated the number of cases in which the altitude and attitude exceeded the permissible values after the occurrence of vision loss. In the case of the loss conditions of one-half and two-thirds of the forward FOV, more than half of the participants exceeded the task tolerance after the occurrence of the loss, while < 1 were observed for the conditions of one-sixth and one-third. This finding suggests that deviations from normal performance are more likely to occur under conditions of high psychological effects.

4 Discussion

For the results of the physiological indices, although the same trends were not shown in all indicators, the effect of range of vision loss was significant for respiratory rate and skin conductance level. In particular, the results from the comparison with the dummy condition indicate that the psychological effects are remarkable when a major loss occurs of more than one-half of the forward FOV. While we did not find differences in PE across conditions for the other indicators, other research has suggested that heart rate can decrease when information is taken in to assess the situation at the time of a sudden event [9], and in our study, it seems possible that heart rate and amplitude of pulse wave indices have demonstrated this effect.

In addition, for the subjective WL assessment, the variation in the values for the small range of vision loss were not large as compared to those in the dummy condition. As the range of vision loss exceeded one-half, the value exceeded the maximum dummy condition in many cases, suggesting that WL also increases when the psychological effects were rated high by the physiological indices. Furthermore, control task performance tended to deviate from the normal range more often under conditions of greater psychological effects.

On the basis of these findings, the psychological effects of vision loss can be considered as follows. First, the effects are remarkable when a major range of vision loss occurs, for example, when more than one-half of the forward FOV is lost. Second, once loss happens, psychological effects can occur regardless of the duration of that loss. Third, even if the loss is only for a short time, the psychological effects of that loss can affect WL and performance.

5 Conclusion

This study investigated the PE of vision loss to achieve the reliability design of a windowless cockpit considering human factors. Our results suggest that even a vision loss of a short duration can lead to pilot upset or mental strain. However, a loss of one-third or less of forward FOV may be acceptable, and so designing system partitioning and other aspects on the basis of this value when setting operational regulations such as the minimum equipment list may lead to improved reliability.

References

1. Randall, E., Williams, S., Kibler, K., Arthur, T.: eXternal vision system development and testing for X-59 low boom flight demonstrator. AIAA **2020–3087**, 1–16 (2020)
2. Zaneboni, J., Saint Jalmes, B.: Aircraft with a cockpit including a viewing surface for piloting which is at least partially virtual. In: U.S. patent no. 2014/0180508. (2014)
3. Wood, J.M., Troutbeck, R.: Effect of restriction of the binocular visual field on driving performance. Ophthal. Physiol. Optic **12**, 291–298 (1992)
4. Alfano, P.L., Michel, G.F.: Restricting the field of view: perceptual and performance effects. Percept. Mot. Skills **70**, 35–45 (1990)
5. Simono, F., Ohsuga, M., Terashita, H.: Method for assessment of mental stress during hightension and monotonous tasks using heart rate, respiration and blood pressure. Japanese J. Ergon. **34**(3), 107–115 (1992)
6. Nakagawa, C., Akiu, N., et al.: Basic study on assessment of state of the drivers based on physiological indices. RTRI Rep. **33**(1), 5–10 (2019)
7. Hart, S.G., Staveland, L.E.: Development of NASA-TLX (task load index): results of empirical and theoretical research. Adv. Psychol. **52**, 139–183 (1988)
8. Haga, S., Mizukami, N.: Japanese version of NASA task load index: sensitivity of its workload score to difficulty of three different laboratory tasks. Japanese J. Ergon. **32**(2), 71–79 (1996)
9. Nakagawa, C., Akiu, N., et al.: Basic study on changes of the autonomic indices when a train driver becomes unsettled in driving. Japanese J. Ergon. **52**(Supplement), S322–S323 (2016)

Human Factors in Interface Design of Electronic Control Systems for Mechanical Equipment in Stage and Studio Automation

Peter Nickel[(✉)] (iD)

Department of Accident Prevention: Digitalisation – Technologies, Institute for Occupational Safety and Health of the German Social Accident Insurance (IFA), Sankt Augustin, Germany
peter.nickel@dguv.de

Abstract. Increasing digitalization and automation are pushing for redesign of human-system interfaces, not only in industrial production. On stages and in studios, the transition from analog to digital interfaces of event technology is ongoing, technical systems of several generations are operated simultaneously, and references to findings from human factors and ergonomics are little prominent. A review of potentially relevant national and international literature, standardization, and information materials to support the design and evaluation process provided some generic but few specific indications. Human factors and ergonomics design principles refer to the task, the interaction and the information interfaces with generic requirements and recommendations to be specified for stage and studio automation. Examples from sets of design principles focusing on human information processing are applied to work scenarios in the domain and illustrate translation in the specified contexts. The procedure paves the way to permeate stage and studio automation towards digital transformation with state-of-the-art human factors and ergonomics.

Keywords: Task interface · Interaction interface · Information interface · Occupational safety and health · Human information processing · Human-system interaction · Event technology

1 Introduction

Increasing digitization and automation are influencing the design of user interfaces of machines and technical equipment not only in industrial production. In the area of stages and studios, the change from analog to digital human-machine interfaces of event technology is an ongoing process. In practice, humans involved operate in parallel with technical systems and devices of several generations. Indications for application of findings from human factors and ergonomics for human-centered design of interfaces do not seem very obvious. This phenomenon is often part of a process towards digital transformation ranging from digitization over digitalization to digital transformation [1]. While digitization is meant to indicate a conversion of signals and technology from analog into digital format, during digitalization digital data and technology is used to automate data handling and process optimization. On top evolves digital transformation by creating new business opportunities through the use of digitalization including digitization.

The process towards digital transformation closely links to technology and business development in the context of industry 4.0 and does not always consider humans involved in or concerned with transformation processes and working conditions involved. From a human factors and ergonomics perspective already simple conversions from analog to digital displays and lacking analysis of human tasks and appropriate redesign can lead to deterioration of human task performance. This is because tasks of human operators referring to perception in human information processing are differentially affected by digitization or digitalization. Digital in contrast to analog information presentation on displays improves performance for tasks requiring reading measured values but reduces performance for tasks requiring checking readings and for tasks requiring monitoring changes in measured values [2, 3]. Concerns regarding industry 4.0 as a paradigm driven by technological opportunities and with limitation concerning work force and operational demands in practice resulted in new conceptualizations with enhancements and expansions towards industry 5.0 (see e.g., [4]).

Technical effort by itself does neither determine nor guarantee performance quality on stages and in studios, however, prearrangements, rehearsals and performance nowadays would be rather limited [5]. When human factors and ergonomics in addition to functional safety requirements play a substantial role for the design of technical equipment along with user interfaces, performance on stages and in studios including related activities will contribute to human safety and health for all persons directly and indirectly involved.

In this work domain, several human-machine interfaces are used to monitor and control technical equipment belonging to technical systems inclusive attachment parts in event and production facilities (e.g., theaters, open-air stages, studios, stage areas). The main purposes of mechanical equipment used in event technology substantially lay in highly dynamic transportation, stage design, and design of scene effects. More recently, control consoles for technical systems have also been introduced in theaters, for example, to move lighting bridges, point and scenery hoists, stage doors, revolving stages, platforms, and orchestra pits of the upper and lower machinery [5–7]. Control consoles for sound, lighting and video systems do not control the upper and lower machinery, but digitalization meanwhile allows to directly control and to a certain extent also to move individual spotlights or loudspeakers distributed over stages and studios, for example. In addition, interlocking control consoles for mechanical stage movements with those for sound, lightning, and video systems can enable automatic tracking of a hoisted projection screen while the dynamic video projection is running. Control consoles become user interface standard of electronic control systems for mechanical and other equipment in stage and studio automation.

Human-centered design of control consoles or other types of displays and control actuators shall be designed according to human requirements of work tasks and conditions in the work system to execute and perform the tasks. This allows for significant contributions from perspectives of human and system performance as well as occupational safety and health (OSH). Scientific findings and practical experience from human factors and ergonomics provide a profound basis to present suitable requirements and recommendations for design of user interfaces of electronic control systems for mechanical equipment used in event technology. This has the potential to improve system performance and system safety while at the same time support human-system interaction in a process towards digital transformation in the domain.

2   From Generic to Specific Design Requirements in Human Factors and Ergonomics

Several design requirements and recommendations for user interfaces under the perspective of human factors and ergonomics related to occupational safety and health are documented in national and international literature (e.g., [8, 9]). However, content often is presented rather general and therefore translation into requirements and recommendations for the work domain of stages and studios is desired, especially when specifically addressing user interfaces of electronic control systems for mechanical equipment used in event technology. Basically, a design process aligned with the concept of work system design in human factors and ergonomics (e.g., [9, 10]) includes task analysis, evaluation, and design, and combines existing scientific findings on the design of displays and control actuators for user interfaces and information presentation.

The situation is similar in national and international standardization with several specifications in general form (e.g., [2, 10–17]) and others adjusted more specifically to the application domain (e.g., [18]). Thus, some basic human factors and ergonomics principles for the design of the task, the interaction, and the information interfaces are introduced and elaborated in standards (e.g., [12, 14, 16]). Specific guidance by standards for event technology interface design addresses among others human factors and ergonomics design requirements and recommendations and gives some examples of hazards and risks, e.g., due to lack of consideration of ergonomic aspects in the design of user interfaces [18].

Standardization referring to content from human factors and ergonomics also often points out a close relationship to OSH regarding risk assessments and preventive measures required for manufacturers of machines and work equipment of event technology and for operating companies such as stages and studios (e.g., [19–23]). Although OSH regulations are different across countries, the hierarchy of controls has been well-established and appears similar across countries and application contexts. Embedded in procedures for risk assessments, it guides selection of effective measures in OSH prevention with an emphasis on prevention through work system design, following levels according a 'STOP!' principle [3, 23, 24]. OSH interventions shall call for the higher levels of control by *s*ubstitution or *t*echnical measures since levels lower in hierarchy such as *o*rganizational, *p*ersonnel and *i*nformational measures are assumed to be decreasingly or less effective, albeit often required.

Some bond of human factors and ergonomics with OSH becomes evident for example with the legally binding requirements of the German Social Accident Insurance [21, 22] for event and production venues for scenic presentation, which are concretized and explained by supplementary provisions [7]. Reference is made in the provision for example, to the securing of the upper and lower machinery of stages against unintentional movements, which must be prevented by design. Measures for safe operation are included, which explicitly enclose and refer to the design of displays and control elements to be based on human information processing requirements such as conformity with expectations of operators (e.g. [14]) and thus draw on basic findings from human factors and ergonomics (e.g., [3, 8, 9, 25]).

The design of control consoles for stage automation is challenging with regard to stage technology, performance requirements, and the tasks of operators [5]. Some example requirements and recommendations referring to OSH and human factors and ergonomics are presented as follows.

- Computer-controlled systems for mechanical equipment shall meet functional safety requirements.
- Safety reasons require human operators to follow movement sequences by direct sight; under specific circumstances this might be possible with closed-circuit television. Control consoles shall be set up at locations that allow for continuous visual feedback from and communication with location of action.
- Simultaneous control of several hoists should be designed for two master switches provided for two-handed use. Control consoles should be as compact as possible, with menu-selectable displays showing only the work areas required for the task at hand. As display and for menu selection touchscreens are often used.
- Control console user interface design should support independent operation of individual hoists in combination with operation of several groups of hoists (for different types of battens or pipes, for example).
- Control console user interface design should enable the operator to reliably implement complex motion sequences in short time intervals. The assignment of control levers to individual stage suspension barrels and keyboards for target specifications shall be concise, consistent, and clear. Control consoles should allow to save inputs and process sequences and recalling them during performances.
- Control consoles shall be designed to enable reliable and safe interruption of initiated motion sequences at any time. Master switches with automatic return to zero position can be used, on/off switches shall not be used.
- The control system cannot overrun limit positions of hoists. In limit positions, automatic switch-off also occurs if the master switch is not returned to zero position in time or if macros do not consider timely switch-off.
- A set deceleration ramp at set target speeds stops hoists regardless of the deflection of the master switch. Hoists accelerate over preset acceleration ramps even if the master switch is moved faster. Hoist overloading, unintentional position changes, etc. shall be prevented.

Design requirements according to human factors and ergonomics for control consoles for sound, lighting, and video technology match those for mechanical stage equipment in case operator tasks and related processing procedures are similar. However, special risks when operating mechanical stage equipment sometimes result in different task interface design requirements from human factors and ergonomics and especially regarding occupational safety.

3 Task, Interaction, and Information Interface Design Requirements in Stage and Studio Automatization

Often, at stages and in studios, different generations of machinery and interface technology exist in parallel in such a way that, for example, the stage technology is still operated analogously via rope-operated counterweight rigging system and the lighting technology is operated at digitalization level via lighting control consoles [5, 6]. Because of the specific tasks and the conditions under which they are carried out, this area of work with display units also makes demands on the design of interfaces regarding human factors and ergonomics that go beyond those more commonly known for the office and administrative domains. Therefore, human task interfaces, interaction interfaces, and information interfaces rather require addressing general demands for monitoring and control operations and specific demands for operating stage and studio automation technology with electronic control systems for mechanical equipment (e.g., [26, 27]).

Tasks such as word processing and calculation in the office and administration area are usually not bound to specific workplaces and workstations and can naturally be interrupted at any time. If typing errors during word processing or erroneous input in calculations occur, error tolerant system design may detect flaws and suggests improvements or in case this is detected by the worker he/she can use the undo function. In these cases, and most often even without corrections, errors do not result in hazardous situations or accidents. Processes external in terms of content, structure, and time to human-computer interaction in the office to a relatively low extent tend to have an impact on human task performance. However, consideration of human factors and ergonomics design requirements have a high impact on human task performance and OSH [28].

Due to other tasks, for example in the process industries, there are also other requirements for the design of the human task interfaces, human-computer interaction, and information presentation. Monitoring and control of processes are often linked to specific workplaces in control centers and custom-built user interfaces in a control room. Operators are requested to continuously perform their monitoring and control tasks (possibly by changing personnel) and are relatively strongly influenced in terms of content, structure, and time by external processes, e.g., inherently dynamic process plant. In case of typing errors or erroneous input the use of undo functions is neither available nor suitable because operator activities have direct consequences to potentially hazardous external processes under control. Other precautions for interface design to avoid and prevent from reasonably foreseeable misuse are required [27]. Also in this work domain, consideration of general as well as specific human factors and ergonomics design requirements have a high impact on human task performance and OSH [17, 26, 27].

In principle, modes of task performance as mentioned above can be found in interface design for stage and studio automation. For stage performances, among others stacks for the lighting design and sets for the stage technology are elaborately created and composed, programmed, and reviewed in trigger tables. The running of set suits is then monitored and controlled in parallel with rehearsals and performance as external drivers for continuous operator task performance. Also, in studios some work is depending on and bound to processes running in parallel and other is not. Studio work includes cutting, mixing and subtitling recordings at editing stations. Time-bound and oriented towards announcements from the life television director or camera switching, programs are continuously monitored and controlled in the control room over the duration of the program.

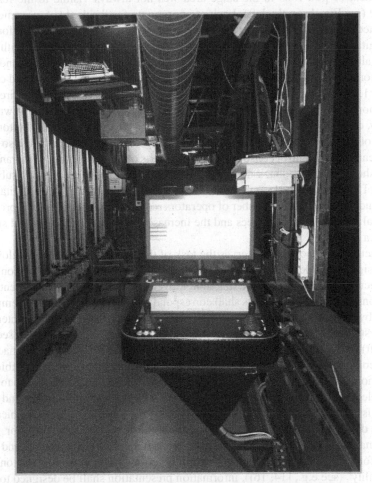

Fig. 1. Control console mounted on running rails on the working gallery for driving the upper and lower machinery of the Bonn Opera House. [Photo: Peter Nickel]

Human factors and ergonomics requirements for the design of technical equipment for monitoring and control thus refer first to the task interfaces and next to interaction and information interfaces (e.g., [3, 9, 12, 29]). A shift from manual labor or activities with analog interfaces towards user interfaces of electronic controls of mechanical equipment of stage and studio automation results in changes of work tasks of the employees, which require redesign according to relevant principles of task design.

According to one of the principles of task design, "contribute to process" (e.g., [3, 12, 29]), system design shall enable the operator to assess quality and quantity of his/her own task performance and, if necessary, adjust performance accordingly. Still nowadays, movement of battens or pipes as part of stage technology are rope-operated with the counterweight rigging systems on demand by several employees. When wire rope hoists were operated by different employees during performances by announcement, the range of movement of pull rods in the stage area was not always visible to the respective employee (see Fig. 1, on the left). Lack of appropriate feedback about movements due to restricted view resulted in operator uncertainty about quality of task performance. When digitalization results in stage automation operated by user interfaces with control consoles all movements of the upper and lower machinery (e.g., platforms and hoists) are monitored, controlled, and driven via mobile and/or permanently installed consoles (see Fig. 1, on the right). From the gallery railing the stage is visible by direct view and via monitors (as in the top left of Fig. 1). Pre-programmed sets can be flown and, if necessary, corrective action can be taken, e.g., via master switch or brake buttons or, in the event of imminent danger, via an emergency stop. With the system design so that the operator can see the control console and moving parts of the machinery with transported load, he/she receives feedback about quality of task performance. Besides substantial changes of employees' tasks and conditions to perform the tasks, other digitalization consequences are a reduced number of operators required, the reduction of a proportion of physical strain of the employees and the increase of a proportion of mental strain, to name but a few.

Interaction interface design serves the task of the operator and should follow interaction design principles. According to the principle of interaction design "conformity with expectations" (e.g., [14]), the function, movement, and position of elements of the control console including displays shall correspond to the expectations of the employees and thereby pick up on population stereotypes. With the rope-operated counterweight rigging system rope hoists were numbered and arranged along the gallery wall (see Fig. 1, on the left), but referred to different e.g., rod and leaf hoists of the upper machinery. With the control console, a stage topographical illustration of the hoists is possible on the console monitor with appropriate orientation of the monitor in relation to the topology, correct selection via the console touch display is facilitated, and monitoring and control of hoists is made easier with an overhead view of the stage. The topographical view should be designed matching the mental model of the control console operator.

Information interface design serves the interactions for operator tasks and should follow information design principles. According to the principle of information design "detectability" (see e.g., [14, 16]), information presentation shall be designed to enable the operator to perceive quickly and clearly. Markings for various wire rope hoists at the monitor of the control console shall be presented with approximately 20' arc minutes height, legibly displayed with high figure to background contrast, clearly distinguishable from one another and, if possible, appear in expected areas of the display. Detectability would be supported in the present example if the monitor tilt provided a right-angle top view, and a negative representation on the display was used appropriate to the lightning conditions of the working environment.

Presented design principles for the task, the interaction, and the information interface are examples taken from sets available in context relevant standards (e.g., [2, 11–17]) representing several scientific findings in human factors and ergonomics (e.g. [8, 9]). As the selection can give only suggestions about how to select generic principles and translate them to the application domain at hand, information about how to include the principles in the design process are provided by references.

4 Discussion and Conclusions

Technical development in stage and studio automation is dynamic. The design of human-machine interfaces faces an evolution from digitization over digitalization towards digital transformation. Few stages and studios still fully operate at analog levels. Most started into evolution towards digital transformation and integrated some digital technologies for stage and studio automation at digitalization level with challenges for adapting design requirements from human factors and ergonomics as well as occupational safety. Some events such as concerts or shows already operate at digital transformation level with business models for highly automated performances.

Based on the concept of work system design and a design that is based on interfaces through tasks, interactions and information exchange processes, ample findings from human factors and ergonomics are readily available to be used for the field of event technology [3, 9]. This has been illustrated by general design principles for the task interface, the interaction interface and the information interface translated for stage and studio automation. Requirements for the design and evaluation of interfaces and suitable approaches to solutions can thus be developed for the wide range of tasks in which human-machine interfaces of electronic control systems for mechanical work equipment in event technology are used.

At present, the scope of human factors and ergonomic knowledge included in standardization (e.g., [18]) and regulations of accident insurance institutions (e.g., [7]) must be described as fragmented and not very conspicuous – especially in comparison to scientific findings and knowledge available to be translated for this area of event technology. Therefore, an active and constructive influence of human factors and ergonomics is needed in the future world of work, in which interfaces are informed by digitalization and automation and in which interface design related to processes of human information processing is required and should be promoted.

References

1. Buer, S.-V., Fragapane, G.I., Strandhagen, J.O.: The data-driven process improvement cycle: using digitalization for continuous improvement. IFAC PapersOnLine **51–11**, 1035–1040 (2018). https://doi.org/10.1016/j.ifacol.2018.08.471
2. EN 894-2: Safety of machinery - Ergonomics requirements for the design of displays and control actuators - Part 2: Displays (A1:2008). CEN, Brussels (2008)
3. International Social Security Association, International Prevention Section of the ISSA on Machine and System Safety, Human Factors Working Group. https://www.safe-machines-at-work.org/human-factors/. Accessed 10 Feb 2023
4. Newman, W.P., Winkelhaus, S., Grosse, E.H., Glock, C.H.: Industry 4.0 and the human factor – a systems framework and analysis methodology for successful development. Int. J. Prod. Econ. **233**, 107992 (2021). https://doi.org/10.1016/j.ijpe.2020.107992
5. Grösel, B.: Bühnentechnik. Mechanische Einrichtungen [Stage technologies. Mechanical equipment]. De Gruyter, Berlin (2022)

6. Campbell, D.: Technical Theater for Nontechnical People. Allworth Press, New York (2016)
7. DGUV Rule [Regel] 115-002: Staging and production facilities for the entertainment industry [Veranstaltungs- und Produktionsstätten für szenische Darstellung]. DGUV, Berlin (2018)
8. Schmidtke, H., Jastrzebska-Fraczek, I.: Ergonomie. Daten zur Systemgestaltung und Begriffsbestimmungen [Ergonomics. System design data and definitions]. Hanser, München (2013)
9. Lee, J.D., Wickens, C.D., Liu, Y., Ng Boyle, L.: Designing for people. An introduction to human factors engineering. CreateSpace, Charleston (2017)
10. EN ISO 6385: Ergonomics principles in the design of work systems (ISO 6385: 2016). CEN, Brussels (2016)
11. EN 614-1: Safety of machinery - Ergonomic design principles - Part 1: Terminology and general principles (A1:2009). CEN, Brussels (2009)
12. EN 614-2: Safety of machinery - Ergonomic design principles - Part 2: Interactions between the design of machinery and work tasks (A1:2008). CEN, Brussels (2008)
13. CEN/TR 614-3: Safety of machinery - Part 3: Ergonomic principles for the design of mobile machinery. CEN, Brussels (2010)
14. EN 894-1: Safety of machinery - Ergonomics requirements for the design of displays and control actuators - Part 1: General principles for human interactions with displays and control actuators (A1:2008). CEN, Brussels (2008)
15. EN 894-3: Safety of machinery - Ergonomics requirements for the design of displays and control actuators - Part 3: Control actuators (A1:2008). CEN, Brussels (2008)
16. EN 894-4: Safety of machinery - Ergonomics requirements for the design of displays and control actuators - Part 4: Location and arrangement of displays and control actuators. CEN, Brussels (2010)
17. EN ISO 10075-2: Ergonomic principles related to mental workload - Part 2: Design principles (ISO 10075-2: 1996) [under revision]. CEN, Brussels (2000)
18. EN 17206: Entertainment technology - Machinery for stages and other production areas - Safety requirements and inspections (AC:2021). CEN, Brussels (2021)
19. EU Machinery Directive 2006/42/EC of the European Parliament and the Council of 17 May 2006 on machinery and amending Directive 95/16/EC (recast). Off. J. Eur. Union L 157, 24-86 (2006)
20. EN ISO 12100. Safety of machinery - General principles for design - Risk assessment and risk reduction (ISO 12100:2010). CEN, Brussels
21. DGUV Vorschrift [Regulation] 17: Veranstaltungs- und Produktionsstätten für szenische Darstellung [Staging and production facilities for the entertainment industry.]. DGUV, Berlin (1998)
22. DGUV Vorschrift [Regulation] 18: Veranstaltungs- und Produktionsstätten für szenische Darstellung [Staging and production facilities for the entertainment industry.]. DGUV, Berlin (1997)
23. EU OSH Framework Directive 89/391/EEC of 12 June 1989 on the introduction of measures to encourage improvements in the safety and health of workers at work (with amendments 2008). Off. J. Eur. Union L 183, 1-8 (1989)
24. Nickel, P., et al.: Human-system interaction design requirements to improve machinery and systems safety. In: Arezes, P.M. (ed.) AHFE 2019. AISC, vol. 969, pp. 3–13. Springer, Cham (2020). https://doi.org/10.1007/978-3-030-20497-6_1
25. Proctor, R.W., Vu, K.-P.L.: Location and arrangement of displays and control actuators. In: Karwowski, W., Szopa, A., Soares, M. (eds.) Handbook of Standards and Guidelines in Human Factors and Ergonomics, pp. 30.1–30.12. CRC Press, Boca Raton (2021)
26. Nachreiner, F., Nickel, P., Meyer, I.: Human factors in process control systems: the design of human–machine interfaces. Saf. Sci. 44, 5–26 (2006). https://doi.org/10.1016/j.ssci.2005.09.003

27. Bockelmann, M., Nachreiner, F., Nickel, P.: Bildschirmarbeit in Leitwarten - Handlungshil-fen zur ergonomischen Gestaltung von Arbeitsplätzen nach der Bildschirmarbeitsverordnung (F2249) [VDU work in control centers - Guidelines for the ergonomic design of work systems in accordance with the EU directive VDU work.]. baua, Dortmund (2012)

28. DGUV Rule [Regel] 215-401: Office business sector [Branche Bürobetriebe.]. DGUV, Berlin (2018)

29. DGUV Information 215-450: Softwareergonomie [Human factors and ergonomics of software systems]. DGUV, Berlin (2021)

Quantitative Characterization of Upper Limb Intensity and Symmetry of Use in Healthcare Workers Using Wrist-Worn Accelerometers

Micaela Porta⑩, Giulia Casu, Bruno Leban⑩, and Massimiliano Pau⁽⊠⁾ ⑩

Department of Mechanical, Chemical and Materials Engineering, University of Cagliari,
09123 Cagliari, Italy
Massimiliano.pau@unica.it

Abstract. Due to the continuous and prolonged exposure to highly physically demanding tasks, healthcare workers (HCWs) are at risk to develop low back and upper limb (UL) musculoskeletal disorders (MSD). Since repetitiveness and movement asymmetries have been hypothesized to play an important role on the development of UL-MSD, in this study we propose an approach based on the use of wearable accelerometers to quantitatively characterize the main features of UL use during actual working tasks. To this aim, we tested thirty full-time professional HCWs which operate in wards characterized by different profiles of risk assessed using the "Movement and Assistance of Hospital Patients" (MAPO) technique. During a regular shift day, their activity was simultaneously monitored both using wrist-worn accelerometers and direct visual observation. Accelerations were processed to calculate several metrics associated with intensity and symmetry of use of UL. The results showed that among the daily routine activities, patient hygiene requires the most intense use of the UL, while meal distribution is the most asymmetrical. The knowledge of intensity and asymmetry of UL use associated to specific working tasks might represent a useful tool to highlight potentially harmful condition and plan suitable ergonomic interventions.

Keywords: Wearable · Accelerometer · Upper Limb · Health care workers

1 Introduction

Health care represents one of the major employment sectors in Western countries. In, particular, in the European Union it accounts for approximately 10% of all workforce, with a significant predominance of female gender (~80%) [1]. Due to the intrinsic complexity of the health system, health care workers (HCWs) face a challenging environment characterized by extremely diverse job demands, which encompasses physical, mental, psychological, and social aspects. The physical effort required by daily routine activities like lifting and moving carts and devices, moving patients, changing patient positions, supporting patient ambulation, dragging wheelchairs, provide hygienic care to patients, etc. is relevant, and HCWs also spend a significant time in standing position or walking.

V. G. Duffy (Ed.): HCII 2023, LNCS 14028, pp. 194–204, 2023.
https://doi.org/10.1007/978-3-031-35741-1_16

Such tasks are associated to one or more risk factors for the development of musculoskeletal disorders (MSD), a fact which poses HCWs among workers at the highest level of risk for MSD [2] with a yearly prevalence of 55% for low back disorders and of 44% and 26% respectively for shoulders and upper limb (UL) [3]. For this reason, the accurate assessment of the ergonomic risk for HCWs represent a critical issue.

In the last twenty-five years, such issue has been faced by some countries (particularly those of the Latin America, Iberian Peninsula and Italy) using a dedicated approach called "Movement and Assistance of Hospital Patients" (MAPO)[4]. This method, using a "traffic light" paradigm defines, on the basis of factors like work organization, average frequency of handling, type of patients, equipment, environmental conditions and the training of the operators, the class of exposure to risk associated to manual patient handling by means of the "MAPO index" as follows:

- MAPO index "green" when the value is in the range 0.5 and 1.5. Absent or negligible risk;
- MAPO Index "yellow" for values in the range 1.51–5.00. Moderate risk;
- MAPO Index "red" for values exceeding 5.00. High risk.

The effectiveness of such index was confirmed by several multicentric studies [4–7], which all reported a positive association between increasing levels of MAPO index and the number of episodes of acute low back pain. In contrast, to the best of our knowledge, less information is available regarding the correlation between MAPO index and the risk to develop MSD of the UL. This is probably because most research on the prevention of MSD in HCWs focuses its attention on the analysis of low back symptoms while UL-MSD and their relationship with different aspects of the working task, generally received less consideration.

Taking into consideration the relationship between HCWs' job demands and MSD [8–10], and recalling that repetitiveness and movement asymmetries, have been hypothesized to play an important role on the development of UL-MSD [11], we proposed here a methodological approach based on quantitative objective data obtained through wearable sensors with the following dual aim 1) to understand if levels of physical activity and UL use (in terms of duration, asymmetry and intensity) measured during an actual work shift differ in hospital wards characterized by increasing MAPO index and 2) to characterize the UL use in terms of intensity and symmetry during the execution of basic tasks commonly performed by HCWs.

To achieve such goals intensity, duration, and (a)symmetry of UL use will be assessed following the approach originally proposed in case of individuals with neurological conditions [12, 13] and recently applied in ergonomic contexts [14]. UL use parameters will be calculated starting from data recorded by two wrist worn accelerometers in a sample of HCWs during their regular shifts, and thus in the most ecological possible conditions.

2 Materials and Methods

2.1 Participants

Thirty HCWs (24 F, 6 M), employed at the University Hospital "Policlinico Universitario, D. Casula" (University of Cagliari, Italy) were recruited for the study on a voluntary basis. They were assigned to wards characterized by different MAPO index as follows: 10 to Green MAPO wards, 9 to Yellow MAPO wards and 11 to Red MAPO wards. Participants' demographic and anthropometric characteristics are reported in Table 1.

All HCWs, regardless of the ward to which they belong, were routinely assigned to the same series of tasks which include patient hygiene; patient transfer (e.g., wheelchair and bed handling) and meal distribution. The study was carried out in compliance with the ethical principles for research expressed in the Declaration of Helsinki and its later amendments.

Table 1. Demographic and Anthropometric characteristics of the participants. Values are expressed as mean (SD)

	Green MAPO	Yellow MAPO	Red MAPO
Age (years)	49.5 (5.2)	55.4 (5.3)	44.0 (8.2)
Height (cm)	162.9 (5.9)	162.8 (7.9)	161.6 (9.9)
Body Mass (kg)	60.2 (7.2)	64.6 (11.8)	59.6 (16.2)

2.2 Experimental Protocol

HCWs were required to wear for 4 consecutive hours two (one for each wrist) tri-axial accelerometers (Actigraph GT3X-BT, Acticorp Co., Pensacola, Florida, USA), previously employed in occupational contexts to assess the physical activity performed [10, 14, 16–18] as well as UL inclination [19]. In addition, each participant was continuously monitored by a trained observer to record type and duration of each performed task.

At the end of the acquisition period, the raw accelerations (collected at 30 Hz frequency) were downloaded to a PC via USB cable and processed to assess the following aspects associated to the HCWs duty.

1. Amount and intensity of the occupational physical activity. In this case the raw acceleration were processed using the dedicated software Actlife v6.13.4 (Acticorp Co., USA), to obtain the number of travelled steps per hour and the percentage of time spent at different levels of physical activity. In particular, physical activity was classified as light (<3 MET), moderate (3–6 MET) and vigorous (>6 MET) using the set of cut-points proposed by Hildebrand et al. [20]
2. Intensity and symmetry of UL use. In this case the raw data were processed accordingly to the associated task. In particular, the acceleration time-series were segmented on 1-min basis, then labelled accordingly to the corresponding task recorded by the

observer and finally merged. The obtained signals were subsequently processed with a custom routine developed in Matlab (R2019a, MathWorks, Natick, Massachusetts, USA) to calculate the Bilateral Magnitude, the Use Ratio (UR) [21] and the Magnitude Ratio (MR) [21, 22] parameters defined as follow:

$$\text{Bilateral Magnitude} = \sqrt{a_x^2 + a_y^2 + a_z^2}_{DL} + \sqrt{a_x^2 + a_y^2 + a_z^2}_{NDL}. \qquad (1)$$

The Bilateral Magnitude represent a proxy measure of the overall intensity required to perform the task.

$$UR = \frac{\text{Minutes of Use}_{NDL}}{\text{Minutes of Use}_{DL}} \qquad (2)$$

The UR is a measure of symmetry/asymmetry of UL use in terms of duration, an UR = 1 indicates that the dominant and non-dominant UL are used for the same amount of time, an UR > 1 indicates that the non-dominant limb is used for longer period whit respect to the dominant one and vice-versa for an UR < 1

$$MR = \frac{\sqrt{a_{x-axis}^2 + a_{y-axis}^2 + a_{z-axis}^2}_{NDL}}{\sqrt{a_{x-axis}^2 + a_{y-axis}^2 + a_{z-axis}^2}_{DL}} \qquad (3)$$

The MR is a measure of symmetry/asymmetry of UL use in terms of intensity, a MR = 0 indicates that the dominant and non-dominant UL are used at the same intensity; a MR > 1 indicates that the non-dominant UL worked more intensely than the dominant UL and vice-versa for a MR < 1.

In formulas (1), (2) and (3) x, y, z indicate the three planes of motion, NDL indicates the non-dominant limb and DL indicates to the dominant limb.

2.3 Statistical Analysis

Amount and intensity of the occupational physical activity.

To investigate the existence of possible differences in the physical activity performed by HCWs employed in ward with different MAPO index two different statistical analyses were performed:

1. One-way Analysis of Variance (ANOVA) on the overall number of steps (dependent variable) and the group (i.e., green, yellow or red MAPO ward) as independent variable;
2. One-way Multivariate Analysis of Variance (MANOVA) on the percentage of time spent at different intensity (i.e., light, moderate, vigorous) as dependent variables and the group (i.e., green, yellow, or red MAPO ward) as independent variable.

Intensity and symmetry of UL use

To characterize the UL use during the performance of the three main tasks associated to HCWs' duty and to investigate possible differences among ward characterized by different MAPO index, as well as possible differences associated to the feature of the task itself, we performed two different analyses one for the UR (that is a time parameter) and one for the Bilateral Magnitude and the MR (that are both intensity parameters):

1. Two-way ANOVA setting UR as dependent variable, and task type (i.e., patient hygiene, patient transfer and meal distribution) and group (green, yellow, or red MAPO ward) as independent variables.
2. Two-way MANOVA setting Bilateral Magnitude and MR as dependent variables, and task type (i.e., patient hygiene, patient transfer and meal distribution) and group (green, yellow, or red MAPO ward) as independent variables.

The level of significance was set at $p = 0.05$ and the effect of size was assessed using the eta-squared (η^2) coefficient. Where necessary, univariate ANOVAs were carried out as a post-hoc test on the adjusted group means, reducing the level of significance to p $= 0.0166$ (0.05/3) for physical activity intensity-related parameters and to p = 0.025 (0.05/2) for UL intensity parameters. All analyses were performed using the IBM SPSS Statistics v.20 software (IBM, Armonk, NY, USA).

3   Results

As regard amount and intensity of the occupational physical activity, the statistical analysis did not reveal any significant difference in terms of both number of travelled steps $[F(2,28) = 2.406, p = 0.109, \eta^2 = 0.445]$ and percentage of time spent at different level of intensity of physical activity $[F(6,52) = 0.736, p = 0.623,$ Wilks' $\lambda = 0.85, \eta^2 = 0.259]$ (see Fig. 1 and 2).

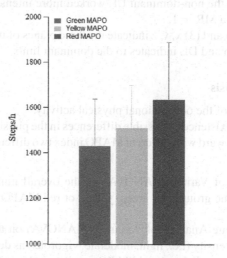

Fig. 1. Number of travelled steps per hour for each group of workers.

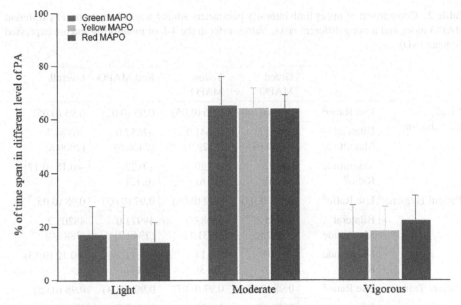

Fig. 2. Percentage of time spent in different level of physical activity for each group of workers.

The results which refer to intensity and symmetry of UL use are reported in Table 2. Below are summarized the main findings which emerged from the statistical analysis.

- As regard UR parameter, no significant differences were found between wards characterized by different MAPO index [$F(2,153) = 0.031$, $p = 0.970$, $\eta^2 = 0.055$], but the analysis indicated a significant main effect associated to the task type [$F(2,153) = 3.576$, $p = 0.030$, $\eta^2 = 0.656$]. In particular, the post-hoc analysis revealed that meal distribution is the most asymmetrical task, with an UR mean value of 0.95 compared to 0.98 for both patient hygiene and patient transfer tasks.
- As regards intensity parameters, the statistical analysis detected a significant main effect for both group and task type. In particular, for group $F(4,296) = 3.932$, $p = 0.004$, $\eta^2 = 0.050$, and for task type $F(4,296) = 39.424$, $p < 0.001$, $\eta^2 = 0.396$. The "group" post-hoc analysis revealed that the mean value of Bilateral Magnitude in the Yellow MAPO ward was significantly lower (mean Bilateral Magnitude = 34982.6) with respect to both the Red (mean Bilateral Magnitude = 41892.6) and the Green MAPO (mean Bilateral Magnitude = 38857.5) wards. No significant differences were found for the MR parameter.

The "task type" post-hoc analysis revealed that patient hygiene in the most intense activity compared to meal distribution and patient transfer as indicated by the Bilateral Magnitude mean values (48205.2, 36874.7, 29353.4 respectively), while meal distribution is the most asymmetrical as indicated by the MR mean values (−0.17) compared to patient hygiene (−0.10) and patient transfer (−0.07).

Table 2. Comparison of upper limb intensity parameters among ward characterized by different MAPO index and among different tasks. Values refer to the 4-h of monitoring and are expressed as mean (SD)

		Green MAPO	Yellow MAPO	Red MAPO	Overall
Meal Distribution	Use Ratio[a]	0.95 (0.04)	0.96 (0.05)	0.95 (0.02)	0.95 (0.05)
	Bilateral Magnitude	39091.9 (6244.0)	32641.0 (8129.9)	42857.0 (7426.6)	36874.7 (7900.8)
	Magnitude Ratio[b]	−0.17 (0.20)	−0.20 (0.16)	−0.22 (0.12)	−0.18 (0.17)
Patient Hygiene	Use Ratio[a]	0.99 (0.03)	0.99 (0.06)	0.97 (0.05)	0.98 (0.05)[*]
	Bilateral Magnitude	49465.7 (6831.8)	45683.0 (7831.1)	49971.0 (7949.7)	48205.2 (7888.0)[*, †]
	Magnitude Ratio[b]	−0.10 (0.16)	−0.14 (0.13)	−0.11 (0.11)	−0.12 (0.13)
Patient Transfer	Use Ratio[a]	0.98 (0.05)	0.97 (0.07)	0.99 (0.04)	0.98 (0.05)[*]
	Bilateral Magnitude	28014.9 (9817.2)	26623.8 (7613.3)	32849.7 (5527.1)	29353.4 (8096.6)[*]
	Magnitude Ratio[b]	−0.07 (0.17)	−0.09 (0.20)	−0.06 (0.15)	−0.08 (0.18)[*]

The symbol * denotes statistically significant difference with respect to Meal distribution task. The symbol † denotes statistically significant difference with respect to Patient Transfer task. [a] Lower values indicate superior activity on the dominant limb. [b] Negative (positive) values indicate superior activity intensity on the dominant (non-dominant) limb. Higher negative (positive) values correspond to higher unbalance towards the dominant (non-dominant) limb.

4 Discussion and Conclusion

The objective instrumental assessment of the physical effort performed by HCWs during a regular shift (expressed in terms of UL use and physical activity profile) in combination with the MAPO method, might represent an effective approach to support the accurate assessment of physical exposure and thus support the actions aimed to prevent the development of MSD in HCWs. In this study we try to verify such possibility by deriving a series of metrics associated with UL use as well as amount and intensity of the overall physical activity performed during a regular shift in a cohort of HCWs assigned to wards characterized by different risk for low back acute pain as indicated by the MAPO index.

Our results suggest that, although the statistical significance was not achieved, there is a trend as regards the association between the number of travelled steps and the ward to which they belong. In particular, the number of steps increases with increasing MAPO index, a result which would indicate that MAPO is also, to some extent, representative of the overall physical engagement. It is noteworthy that the number of steps calculated in this study (1500 steps per hour on average) is higher with respect to what reported in previous similar studies (between 800 and 1100 per hour) probably due to differences in sensor placement (wrist vs hip) [10, 16, 22].

As regards the accelerometric-derived parameters representative of UL use, we found similar values of MR and UR across all wards. This suggest that HCWs adopt similar strategies in terms of dominant and non-dominant limb use which are not dependent from the level of risk associated with the ward in which they operate but rather from the kind of performed tasks. We also observed that the intensity of UL use (expressed in terms of bilateral magnitude) was lower for workers employed in the wards labelled as yellow MAPO with respect to both workers employed in the green and red MAPO wards. This result seems to indicate that the MAPO classification might underestimate the exposure to physical risk factors in wards associated with the lowest level of risk.

Regarding the feasibility of use of the proposed setup to characterize UL intensity and symmetry during tasks commonly performed by HCWs, the obtained results appear promising. In particular, we found that patient hygiene task is the most demanding when compared to both patient transfer and meal distribution. However, meal distribution was found the most asymmetrical task (both in terms of time and intensity of use) as a predominant use of the dominant limb (as indicated by an UR value of 0.95 and a MR value of −0.17) was calculated. In contrast, patient hygiene and transfer were the most symmetrical activities with an UR value close to 1 and a MR value close to zero. To the best of our knowledge no previous study have quantitatively analyzed HCWs tasks during regular shifts to identify specific features potentially associated to the development of UL-MSD, even though the association between job characteristics and risk of development of UL-MSD has been investigated, particularly as regards factors such as: repetitiveness, patient handling, non-neutral posture, and hand dominance. For instance, Alexopulus et al. [23] analyzed the relationship between physical risk factors at work and musculoskeletal complains on 420 HCWs using a questionnaire, finding a statistically significant correlation between shoulder pain and strenuous shoulder movement and repetitiveness of tasks. Abdalla et al. [24] analyzed 9 tasks commonly performed by HCWs (e.g., handling the bed cranks, disposal of materials, bed bath, placing patient in bed etc.) using the Rapid Entire Body Assessment (REBA) method. They found that all the tasks were characterized by an excessive biomechanical exposure of both spine and UL. Leifer et al. [25] found that, among anesthetists, possible risk factors for the development of UL disorders were: years of experience and right-handedness. The relevance of this latter aspect, rarely considered, was attributed to the ergonomic design of the equipment, that induced a different use of the right and left hand.

Task-related risk factors for the development of UL-MSD are scarcely studied in health care professions despite the high prevalence of such disorders in this category of workers. For this reason, we believe that the proposed approach, which provides information about job demands in terms of physical activity and intensity and symmetry/asymmetry of UL use, may effectively support actions for the risk prevention. Through these data, and in particular, exploiting the detailed knowledge about the way the various tasks originated different patterns of UL use, it would be possible to develop suitable prevention programs aimed to reduce the cumulative exposure to specific physical factors, reorganizing sequence and duration of the activities regularly performed by HCWs.

Some limitations of the study should be acknowledged. This methodology does not allow to have information about the magnitude of the loads associated with any performed activity, a variable which is known to play a significant role in the UL exertion. Moreover, the HCWs' sample was predominantly composed by women, thus we cannot rule out the existence of gender differences in UL use during performance of tasks (this aspect was found relevant in previous similar studies [26, 27]). On the other hand, such percentage is representative of the actual gender ratio in health care professions in Europe [1].

In conclusion, the knowledge of intensity and asymmetry of UL use associated to specific working tasks allows to highlight potentially harmful condition that can be controlled planning ergonomic interventions, such as structuring the work shift avoiding excessive repetitions of the same task or instructing workers to use both arms in order to avoid an excessive use of the dominant UL.

References

1. de Kok, J., et al.: European Agency for Safety and Health at Work. 2019. Work-related musculoskeletal disorders: prevalence, costs and demographics in the EU European Risk Observatory Report. EU OSHA (2019). https://osha.europa.eu/en/publications/work-related-musculoskeletal-disorders-prevalence-costs-and-demographics-eu/view. https://doi.org/10.2802/66947
2. Eurofound, Sixth European Working Conditions Survey – Overview report (2017 update), Publications Office of the European Union, Luxembourg (2017)
3. Davis, K.G., Kotowski, S.E.: Prevalence of musculoskeletal disorders for nurses in hospitals, long-term care facilities, and home health care: a comprehensive review. Hum. Factors 57(5), 754–792 (2015). https://doi.org/10.1177/0018720815581933
4. Battevi, N., Consonni, D., Menoni, O., Ricci, M. G., Occhipinti, E., Colombini, D.: Application of the synthetic exposure index in manual lifting of patients: Preliminary validation experience. [L'applicazione dell'indice sintetico di esposizione nella movimentazione manuale pazienti: Prime esperienze di validazione] Medicina Del Lavoro 90(2), 256–275 (1999)
5. Battevi, N., Menoni, O., Ricci, M.G., Cairoli, S.: MAPO index for risk assessment of patient manual handling in hospital wards: a validation study. Ergonomics 49(7), 671–687 (2006)
6. Battevi, N., Menoni, O.: Screening of risk from patient manual handling with MAPO method. Work 41(Suppl. 1), 1920–1927 (2012). https://doi.org/10.3233/WOR-2012-0408-1920
7. Cantarella, C., et al.: MAPO method to assess the risk of patient manual handling in hospital wards: a validation study. Hum. Factors 62(7), 1141–1149 (2020). https://doi.org/10.1177/0018720819869119
8. Jung, K., Suh, S.: Relationships among nursing activities, the use of body mechanics, and job stress in nurses with low back pain. J. Muscle Joint Health 20(2), 141–50 (2013). https://doi.org/10.5953/JMJH.2013.20.2.141
9. Trinkoff, A.M., Le, R., Geiger-Brown, J., Lipscomb, J., Lang, G.: Longitudinal relationship of work hours, mandatory overtime, and on-call to musculoskeletal problems in nurses. Am. J. Ind. Med. 49(11), 964–971 (2006). https://doi.org/10.1002/ajim.20330
10. Chang, H.E., Cho, S.: Nurses' steps, distance traveled, and perceived physical demands in a three-shift schedule. Hum. Resour. Health 20(1) (2022) https://doi.org/10.1186/s12960-022-00768-3

11. Kucera, J.D., Robins, T.G.: Relationship of cumulative trauma disorders of the upper extremity to degree of hand preference. J. Occup. Med. **31**(1), 17–22 (1989)

12. Bailey, R.R., Klaesner, J.W., Lang, C.E.: Quantifying real-world upper-limb activity in nondisabled adults and adults with chronic stroke. Neurorehabil. Neural Repair **29**(10), 969–978 (2015). https://doi.org/10.1177/1545968315583720

13. Pau, M., et al.: Use of wrist-worn accelerometers to quantify bilateral upper limb activity and asymmetry under free-living conditions in people with multiple sclerosis. Mult. Scler. Relat. Disord. **53**, 103081 (2021). https://doi.org/10.1016/j.msard.2021.103081

14. Porta, M., Leban, B., Orrù, P.F., Pau, M.: Use of bilateral wrist-worn accelerometers to characterize upper limb activity time, intensity and asymmetry of use in physically demanding and sedentary working task. Int. J. Ind. Ergon. **92**, 103359 (2022). https://doi.org/10.1016/j.ergon.2022.103359

15. Schall, M.C., Jr., Fethke, N.B., Chen, H.: Working postures and physical activity among registered nurses. Appl. Ergon. **54**, 243–250 (2016). https://doi.org/10.1016/j.apergo.2016.01.008

16. Kwiecień-Jaguś, K., Mędrzycka-Dąbrowska, W., Czyż-Szypenbeil, K., Lewandowska, K., Ozga, D.: The use of a pedometer to measure the physical activity during 12-hour shift of ICU and nurse anaesthetists in poland. Intensive Critical Care Nurs. 55 (2019). https://doi.org/10.1016/j.iccn.2019.07.009

17. Porta, M., Orrù, P.F., Pau, M.: Use of wearable sensors to assess patterns of trunk flexion in young and old workers in the metalworking industry. Ergonomics **64**(12), 1543–1554 (2021). https://doi.org/10.1080/00140139.2021.1948107

18. Korshøj, M., et al.: Validity of the Acti4 software using ActiGraph GT3X+accelerometer for recording of arm and upper body inclination in simulated work tasks. Ergonomics **57**(2), 247–253 (2014). https://doi.org/10.1080/00140139.2013.869358

19. Hildebrand, M., Van Hees, V.T., Hansen, B.H., Ekelund, U.: Age group comparability of raw accelerometer output from wrist- and hip-worn monitors. Med. Sci. Sports Exerc. **46**(9), 1816–1824 (2014). https://doi.org/10.1249/MSS.0000000000000289

20. Lang, C.E., Waddell, K.J., Klaesner, J.W., Bland, M.D.: A method for quantifying upper limb performance in daily life using accelerometers. J. Visualized Exp. (122), 55673 (2017). https://doi.org/10.3791/55673

21. Bailey, R.R., Klaesner, J.W., Lang, C.E.: An accelerometry-based methodology for assessment of real-world bilateral upper extremity activity. PLoS ONE **9**(7), e103135 (2014). https://doi.org/10.1371/journal.pone.0103135

22. Li, J., Sommerich, C., Lavender, S., Chipps, E., Stasny, E.: Subjective and objective estimation of physical activities on the lower extremities for inpatient staff nurses and their lower extremity musculoskeletal discomfort. Paper presented at the Proceedings of the Human Factors and Ergonomics Society, 2017-October, pp. 1017–1021 (2017). https://doi.org/10.1177/1541931213601737

23. Alexopoulos, E.C., Burdorf, A., Kalokerinou, A.: Risk factors for musculoskeletal disorders among nursing personnel in Greek hospitals. Int. Arch. Occup. Environ. Health **76**(4), 289–294 (2003). https://doi.org/10.1007/s00420-003-0442-9

24. Abdalla, D.R., Sisconeto de Freitas, F., Chieregato Matheus, J.P., Porcatti de Walsh, I.A., Bertoncello, D.: Postural biomechanical risks for nursing workers. Fisioterapia em Movimento **27**(3) (2014). https://doi.org/10.1590/0103-5150.027.003.AO13

25. Leifer, S., Choi, S.W., Asanati, K., Yentis, S.M.: Upper limb disorders in anaesthetists – a survey of association of anaesthetists members. Anaesthesia **74**(3), 285–291 (2019). https://doi.org/10.1111/anae.14446
26. Dahlberg, R., Karlqvist, L., Bildt, C., Nykvist, K.: Do work technique and musculoskeletal symptoms differ between men and women performing the same type of work tasks? Appl. Ergon. **35**(6), 521–529 (2004). https://doi.org/10.1016/j.apergo.2004.06.008
27. Kjellberg, K., Lagerström, M., Hagberg, M.: Work technique of nurses in patient transfer tasks and associations with personal factors. Scand. J. Work Environ. Health **29**(6), 468–477 (2003). https://doi.org/10.5271/sjweh.755

Human Ergonomic Assessment Within "Industry 5.0" Workplace: Do Standard Observational Methods Correlate with Kinematic-Based Index in Reaching Tasks?

Emilia Scalona[1]([✉]) [iD], Doriana De Marco[2], Pietro Avanzini[2],
Maddalena Fabbri Destro[2], Giuseppe Andreoni[3], and Nicola Francesco Lopomo[4]

[1] Dipartimento di Specialità Medico-Chirurgiche, Scienze Radiologiche e Sanità Pubblica,
Università degli Studi di Brescia, Brescia, Italy
emilia.scalona@unibs.it

[2] Istituto di Neuroscienze, Consiglio Nazionale delle Ricerche, Parma, Italy

[3] Dipartimento di Design, Politecnico di Milano, Milan, Italy

[4] Dipartimento di Ingegneria dell'Informazione, Università degli Studi di Brescia, Brescia, Italy

Abstract. This work aimed to investigate the contribution of each single joint during the execution of whole-body reaching tasks to the overall discomfort of the worker evaluated through standard observational methods.

Forty-five healthy volunteers were asked to reach and rotate 2 spheres placed on a custom-made rack in standardized positions, i.e., above the head and one at floor level at the center side. Whole-body kinematics was acquired via a system based on wearable inertial measurement units, which represent proper enabling technologies within human-centered "Industry 5.0" context. Standard ergonomic scales including RULA (Rapid Upper Limb Assessment), REBA (Rapid Entire Body Assessment), and MMGA (Method for Movement and Gesture Assessment), were assessed for each subject and each sphere position. Moreover, a quantitative index based on actual joint kinematics, i.e., the W1 index, was computed for each joint angle involved in the task. Pearson's correlation analysis was performed for W1 relative to each joint with respect to RULA, REBA, and MMGA scores.

Considering REBA and MMGA scores, the most comfortable reaching areas were the ones in which the sphere was positioned at the top; in contrast, the lowest positions evidenced the most increased discomfort indexes. The RULA did not result sensitive to the different positions, while REBA and MMGA seemed to be more influenced by the range of motion of the lower limb joint angles than the upper limb ones.

This study underlines the necessity to focus on multiple potential contributors to work-related musculoskeletal disorders and underlines the importance of subject-specific approaches toward risk assessment by exploiting quantitative measurements and wearable technologies.

Keywords: Ergonomics assessment · Wearable technologies · Kinematic monitoring · Risk assessment · Standard scales

V. G. Duffy (Ed.): HCII 2023, LNCS 14028, pp. 205–214, 2023.
https://doi.org/10.1007/978-3-031-35741-1_17

1   Introduction

Work-related musculoskeletal disorders (WMSDs) have been reported to be a leading cause of sick leave in many occupations [1]. Despite improvements in the workplace also due to the introduction of several enabling technologies, including exoskeletons and robots, workers still suffer from repetitive arm movements and strenuous postures [2]. Due to the presence of "hybrid" manufacturing lines that involve workers in increasingly complex activities, the work intensity has been growing within the context of "Industry 4.0" [3]. Consequently, a human-centric approach called "Industry 5.0" has been proposed recently to mitigate these problems and promote occupational well-being [4–6]; indeed, health and welfare burdens must be considered when applying policies aimed at minimizing WMSD risks. At present, to prevent WMSDs, the best practice is to properly evaluate the exposure to risk factors focusing on a class of workers in a defined environment during the realization of specific tasks characterizing their shift; following this analysis, it is mandatory to plan ergonomic interventions, such as the workplace redesign [7].

In this context, a large number of observational methods, which are widely used in industry and manufacturing activities, have been presented in the last decades; however, most of these approaches involve a direct visual observation of workers during their activities [8, 9]. The ergonomic risk scales are methods for assessing musculoskeletal load and the risk of developing musculoskeletal disorders, by analyzing a particular aspect or a specific activity; by way of example but not limited to, we can mention: i) the NIOSH method, that evaluates carrying and lifting activities [10]; ii) the OCRA approach that deals with low loads at high frequency [11]; iii) the OWAS [12], RULA [13], and REBA[14] that evaluate posture and movements; in particular, the last two methods represent the main applied approaches for ergonomic risk assessment. On the other hand, these two methodologies present several limitations and have the main disadvantage to require a field expert who have to perform a time-consuming analysis of the postures.

Over the years some progress has been made to overcome the limits of these methods, leading - for example - to the definition of the MMGA (Method for Movement and Gesture Assessment) approach [15], i.e., a quantitative method for discomfort classification based on the LUBA [16] but addressing the whole body kinematics; the enabling technologies used for defining the MMGA are indeed the systems used for human motion analysis, which provide information concerning both static posture and dynamic movements.

However, the use of "discrete" parameters could be a limitation considering the inherent variability that exists in the ways individuals can complete a specific working task; in fact, most of the movements we perform during daily life activities involve different muscles and the coordination of multiple joints. In order to provide a wider perspective, recently, Lorenzini *et al.*, proposed a multi-index framework based on kinematic and dynamic parameters estimated via wearable technologies and specifically characterizing each joint and related degrees-of-freedom [17]; however the authors did not provide cues concerning possible relations between standard assessment methodologies and joint-specific metrics.

Therefore, in this work we hypothesized that joint displacement (W_1) could be a paradigmatic kinematic index that highlights the multifactor factors that determine workers' overall discomfort. The goal of this study was to examine the contribution that W_1 played in the overall discomfort of the worker during the execution of whole-body reaching tasks by using standard observational methods and scores. In this way, we wanted to underline the need for quantitative and subject-specific approaches to characterize occupational risks more accurately and, therefore, guide proper mitigating strategies.

2 Materials and Methods

2.1 Participants

Forty-five healthy volunteers (33 females, 12 males, mean age 25.1 years old) were enrolled in the study. All the subjects reported no previous history of neurological disorders or recent orthopedic injuries. All subjects were right-handed according to the Edinburgh Handedness Inventory [18]. Each participant provided written informed consent before the experimental sessions. The local ethics committee approved the study (Comitato Etico dell' Area Vasta Emilia Nord, 10084, 12.03.2018), which was conducted according to the principles expressed in the Declaration of Helsinki.

2.2 Experimental Setup

Subjects were asked to perform motor tasks which consists of reaching and manipulating soft spheres (6 cm diameter) placed on a 2x1 meters rack, formed by 3 rows and 3 columns, adapting the experimental paradigm proposed by Andreoni et al. [15].

Inter-column distances were set at 40 cm. The soft spheres placed in the three rows were moved in a specific position of the rack, according to the anthropometric measures of the subject: the three in the lower position were always placed 6 cm above the floor; the three in the middle position were placed in correspondence to the participant's pelvis height; the three in the top positions were moved in correspondence to participant's height plus 10 cm. The experimental setup is reported in Fig. 1 and only spheres in the upper-central (UC) and lower-central (LC) positions were used for this study.

The subjects stand still in front of the rack with the feet behind a reference cross placed considering the length of the forearm plus 30 cm, to make the task more challenging.

2.3 Testing Procedure

The experimental procedure required that the participants perform a reach and grasp task addressing the manipulation of each sphere, consisting of three times clockwise rotations with the right hand. The task was repeated five times for each position of the spheres.

Each movement started from a static standing position with the arms by their side and the subject was asked to perform the task without crossing the reference line and without lifting their feet completely off the ground. An example of the subject's posture at the end of the reaching phase for the two positions is reported in Fig. 1.

Fig. 1. Experimental setup; spheres on the right and left sides were not used for this study.

2.4 Motion Tracking

Whole-body kinematics was acquired by using a full-body motion tracking system based on inertial measurement units - IMUs (MVN Link and Biomech Awinda, XSens, The Netherlands). The motion trackers were positioned within the suit according to the protocol required by the manufacturer; in particular, 17 sensors were positioned on the subject to capture the movement of the following 23 body segments, which included the head, neck, eighth and tenth thoracic vertebra, third and fifth lumbar vertebra, right and left shoulder, right and left arm, right and left forearm, right and left hand, pelvis, right and left thigh, right and left shank, right and left foot, and right and left forefoot. Before starting the recording session, a calibration procedure was performed to align the motion trackers to the anatomical segments of the subject. The movement was acquired by using a sampling frequency of 240 Hz. Joint kinematics in terms of joint angles was exported for custom analysis.

2.5 Data Analysis

Three-dimensional joint angles were extracted from exported files via custom processing and analysis pipeline (Matlab2018a; MathWorks Inc.). Before additional data processing, the start and end frames for each trial were determined. In particular, we focused only on the reaching phase which was segmented according to the tangential velocity of the hand [19]; the temporal boundaries of the reaching phase were identified as the times at which the hand velocity surpasses and returns below 5% of the peak velocity (reaching start and end, respectively). Subsequently, each joint angle curve was segmented according to the reaching duration and then ergonomic scores were computed.

The RULA index was calculated by assigning a score to each segment considering the values of the joint angles at the end of the reaching phase. The final RULA score is a single score that represents the level of MSD risk for the job task being evaluated. The minimum RULA score is equal to 1, and the maximum RULA score is equal to 7, representing negligible risk and very high risk, respectively.

The REBA worksheet is used to evaluate required or selected body posture, forceful exertions, type of movement or action, repetition, and coupling. Using the REBA worksheet, a score was assigned for each of the following body regions: wrists, forearms, elbows, shoulders, neck, trunk, back, legs, and knees. After the data for each region is collected and scored, tables on the form are then used to compile the risk factor. REBA scores range from 1 (no discomfort) to 15 (maximum discomfort).

The MMGA index accounts for three factors: a) the joint angles kinematics; b) an articular coefficient of discomfort for each joint; c) a coefficient estimating the "weight" of the ergonomic contribution of each joint to the movements. Unlike the RULA and REBA indices, MMGA is not calculated at a specific time point but takes into account the entire movement. The MMGA scoring considers the contribution of both the upper and the lower body segments and weights their intervention according to the mass involved. High values of MMGA indicated great ergonomic discomfort.

Once defined the overall repetition was, RULA and REBA indices were estimated and MMGA scores were calculated for each subject, each sphere position, and each trial and then averaged among trials.

Moreover, the kinematic-based displacement index W_1 was computed for paradigmatic joints, considering its absolute values and the joint angle's upper and lower boundaries, respectively, which can be found in the literature [20]. The aim of monitoring the joint displacement is to detect wherever the body configurations that subjects adopt to perform their tasks are not ergonomic. This index ranges from 0 to 1 and 1 indicates that the joint is in proximity to the maximum limits and this range of motion (ROM) should be avoided. The joint displacement was computed for the following joint angles: trunk_pelvis abduction, trunk_pelvis rotation, trunk_pelvis flexion/extension, right shoulder ab/adduction, right shoulder intra/extrarotation, right shoulder flexion/extension, right elbow rotation, right elbow flexion/extension, right wrist flexion/extension, right and left hips ab/adduction, right and left hips intra/extrarotation, right and left hips flexion/extension, right and left knees flexion/extension, right and left ankle dorsi/plantarflexion. W_1 was averaged among trials as well.

Pearson's correlation analysis was performed for the values of W_1 relative to each joint with respect to the obtained RULA, REBA, and MMGA scores, so to assess their sensitivity with respect to the contribution of each individual joint.

3   Results and Discussion

Figure 2 reported the average score for RULA, REBA, MMGA, and displacement indices concerning the lowest and highest positions. The average scores of RULA were 6.08 (±0.56) and 5.97 (±0.33), whereas focusing on REBA we obtained a score of 10.04 (±0.72) and 7.46 (±0.71), respectively; from the analysis of MMGA, the score was 424.75 (±44.62) for the lower and 190.42 (±21.72) for the highest position.

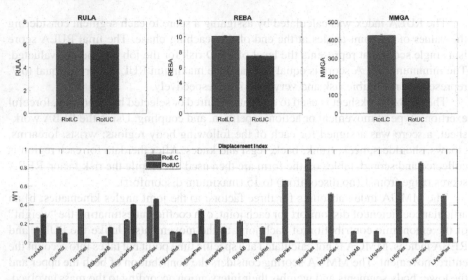

Fig. 2. Mean and standard error of RULA, REBA, MMGA, and single joint discomfort indices W_1 for each position. Bars in cyan represent the lowest position (LC), while bars in red are relative to the highest positions (UC).

Considering both REBA and MMGA scores, the most comfortable reaching areas were the ones in which the target sphere was positioned at the top. In contrast, the lowest rows evidenced the most increased discomfort indexes. Surprisingly, the RULA index did not highlight any difference between the tasks devoted to reaching the sphere positioned at the highest level with respect to that placed at the lowest one, highlighting a lack of sensitivity towards this kind of task.

As we expected, and as it was confirmed by the analysis of W_1, the movements toward the highest vs lowest positions recruited body segments differently. In fact, the W_1 allows for detection wherever the human current body configuration lays within specific sections of the human range of motion, which should be avoided (e.g., in proximity to the maximum limits). In general, in the UC movements, participants mainly stressed the lateral bending of the trunk, the shoulder, and the elbow, while different grades of the hip, knee, and ankle flexion characterized the movements toward the LC positions (Fig. 2). Figure 3 shows an example of how the average shoulder and knee joint angles differ in the two tasks, especially in amplitude at the end of the reaching phase. It is possible to notice that participants expressed higher shoulder flexion in the movement toward the upside with respect to the ones on the low side. On the contrary, higher grades of knee flexion characterize the movement in the lower part of the rack.

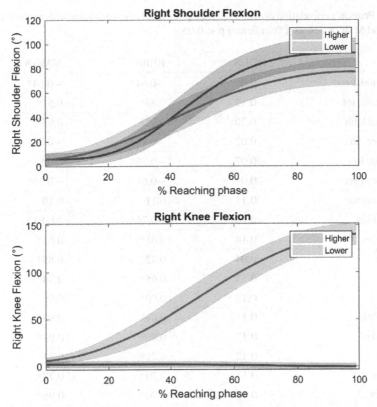

Fig. 3. Mean and standard deviation among the subject of the normalized joint angle curves. Right shoulder flexion curves relative to the task in the higher and lower position is depicted on the top. Right knee flexion is depicted at the bottom of the figure. Curves in cyan represent the lowest position (LC), while curves in red are relative to the highest positions (UC).

Focusing on the correlation analysis, the main results are reported in Table 1.

In this frame, the RULA index does not significantly correlate with any W_1, further underling the lack of sensitivity of this assessment method with respect to these specific tasks. On the other hand, both REBA and MMGA negatively correlate with trunk bending, all shoulder rotations, and elbow flexion ($r < -0.65$, $p < 0.01$); further, both indices positively correlate with trunk tilt and all rotations of the lower limbs' joint angles ($r > 0.65$, $p < 0.01$).

Finally, RULA seemed to be not sensitive to the different positions, whereas REBA and MMGA seem to be more influenced by the range of motion of the lower limbs' joint angles than the upper limbs' ones.

Table 1. Pearson's correlation coefficient among W_1 relative to each joint with respect to RULA, REBA, and MMGA scores. (*) indicates $p < 0.05$.

W_1	RULA	REBA	MMGA
Pelvis_trunk bend	0.09	−0.64*	−0.64*
Pelvis_trunk rot	0.12	0.37*	0.51*
Pelvis-trunk tilt	0.20	0.92*	0.95*
RShoulder Ab	0.02	−0.72*	−0.75*
RShoulder Rot	−0.07	−0.76*	−0.86*
RShoulder Flex	−0.01	−0.61*	−0.76*
RElbow prono	0.11	0.11	0.10
RElbow Flex	−0.13	−0.79*	−0.87*
RWrist Flex	0.14	0.61*	0.63*
RHip Ab	0.04	0.72*	0.85*
RHip Rot	0.17	0.65*	0.74*
RHip Flex	0.13	0.90*	0.96*
RKnee Flex	0.11	0.89*	0.97*
RAnkleFlex	0.17	0.86*	0.91*
RHip Ab	0.12	0.71*	0.81*
RHip Rot	0.11	0.70*	0.77*
RHip Flex	0.13	0.90*	0.96*
RKnee Flex	0.10	0.88*	0.96*
RAnkleFlex	0.16	0.87*	0.91*

4   Conclusions

The aim of this study was to determine the contribution of each joint to overall worker discomfort, as measured by standard observational methods and scores, during the execution of manipulative tasks and so as to identify which standard ergonomic index is more sensitive to the variations to the position of individual body parts.

From the main findings obtained in this study emerged that the RULA index was indeed not sensitive to the different tasks required to reach the sphere placed at different positions; on the other hand, both REBA and MMGA seemed to be more influenced by the range of motion of the lower limb joint angles than the upper limb ones.

In light of these findings, there is the need to focus on multiple potential contributors to WMSDs, and emphasize the importance of subject-specific approaches to risk assessment that utilize quantitative measurements and wearable technology, both of which are key enabling approaches within the context of "Industry 5.0".

Hence, by monitoring how often and how long these body configurations are maintained, it is possible to determine if a potential ergonomic risk exists.

References

1. Eurofound First findings: Sixth European working conditions survey (2015)
2. Manghisi, V.M., Uva, A.E., Fiorentino, M., Bevilacqua, V., Trotta, G.F., Monno, G.: Real time RULA assessment using Kinect v2 sensor. Appl. Ergon. **65**, 481–491 (2017). https://doi. org/10.1016/j.apergo.2017.02.015
3. Myrelid, A., Olhager, J.: Hybrid manufacturing accounting in mixed process environments: a methodology and a case study. Int. J. Prod. Econ. **210**, 137–144 (2019). https://doi.org/10. 1016/j.ijpe.2019.01.024
4. Xu, X., Lu, Y., Vogel-Heuser, B., Wang, L.: Industry 4.0 and industry 5.0—inception, conception and perception. J. Manuf. Syst. **61**, 530–535 (2021). https://doi.org/10.1016/j.jmsy. 2021.10.006
5. Leng, J., et al.: Industry 5.0: prospect and retrospect. J. Manuf. Syst. **65**, 279–295 (2022). https://doi.org/10.1016/j.jmsy.2022.09.017
6. Maddikunta, P.K.R., et al.: Industry 5.0: a survey on enabling technologies and potential applications. J. Ind. Inf. Integr. **26**, 100257 (2022). https://doi.org/10.1016/j.jii.2021.100257
7. Bortolini, M., Gamberi, M., Pilati, F., Regattieri, A.: Automatic assessment of the ergonomic risk for manual manufacturing and assembly activities through optical motion capture technology. Procedia CIRP **72**, 81–86 (2018). https://doi.org/10.1016/j.procir.2018.03.198
8. Li, G., Buckle, P.: Current techniques for assessing physical exposure to work-related musculoskeletal risks, with emphasis on posture-based methods. Ergonomics **42**, 674–695 (1999). https://doi.org/10.1080/001401399185388
9. David, G.C.: Ergonomic methods for assessing exposure to risk factors for work-related musculoskeletal disorders. Occup. Med. (Chic. Ill) **55**, 190–199 (2005). https://doi.org/10. 1093/occmed/kqi082
10. Murphy, M.A., Willén, C., Sunnerhagen, K.S.: Kinematic variables quantifying upper-extremity performance after stroke during reaching and drinking from a glass. Neurorehabil. Neural Repair **25**, 71–80 (2011). https://doi.org/10.1177/1545968310370748
11. Colombini, D., Occhipinti, E.: Preventing upper limb work-related musculoskeletal disorders (UL-WMSDS): New approaches in job (re)design and current trends in standardization. Appl. Ergon. **37**, 441–450 (2006). https://doi.org/10.1016/j.apergo.2006.04.008
12. Karhu, O., Kansi, P., Kuorinka, I.: Correcting working postures in industry: a practical method for analysis. Appl. Ergon. **8**, 199–201 (1977). https://doi.org/10.1016/0003-6870(77)90164-8
13. McAtamney, L., Nigel Corlett, E.: RULA: a survey method for the investigation of work-related upper limb disorders. Appl. Ergon. **24**, 91–99 (1993). https://doi.org/10.1016/0003-6870(93)90080-S
14. Hignett, S., McAtamney, L.: Rapid entire body assessment (REBA). Appl. Ergon. **31**, 201–205 (2000). https://doi.org/10.1016/S0003-6870(99)00039-3
15. Andreoni, G., Mazzola, M., Ciani, O., Zambetti, M., Romero, M., Costa, F., Preatoni, E.: Method for movement and gesture assessment (MMGA) in ergonomics. In: Duffy, V.G. (ed.) ICDHM 2009. LNCS, vol. 5620, pp. 591–598. Springer, Heidelberg (2009). https://doi.org/ 10.1007/978-3-642-02809-0_62
16. Kee, D., Karwowski, W.: LUBA: an assessment technique for postural loading on the upper body based on joint motion discomfort and maximum holding time. Appl. Ergon. **32**, 357–366 (2001). https://doi.org/10.1016/S0003-6870(01)00006-0
17. Lorenzini, M., Kim, W., Ajoudani, A.: An online multi-index approach to human ergonomics assessment in the workplace. IEEE Trans. Hum.-Mach. Syst. **52**, 812–823 (2022). https://doi. org/10.1109/THMS.2021.3133807
18. Oldfielf, R.C.: The assesment and analysis of handedness: the Edimburgh inventory. Neuropsychologia **9**, 97–113 (1971). https://doi.org/10.1007/978-0-387-79948-3_6053

214   E. Scalona et al.

19. Michaelsen, S.M., Jacobs, S., Roby-Brami, A., Levin, M.F.: Compensation for distal impairments of grasping in adults with hemiparesis. Exp. Brain Res. **157**, 162–173 (2004). https://doi.org/10.1007/s00221-004-1829-x
20. Whitmore, M., Boyer, J., Holubec, K.: NASA-STD-3001, space flight human-system standard and the human integration design handbook. In: Proceedings of the Industrial and Systems Engineering Research Conference (2012)

Challenges for Standardized Ergonomic Assessments by Digital Human Modeling

Kerstin Schmidt(✉), Paul Schmidt, and Anna Schlenz

BioMath GmbH, Friedrich-Barnewitz-Str. 8, 18119 Rostock, Germany
Kerstin.schmidt@biomath.de

Abstract. Today, many existing and emerging Digital Human Models (DHM) are available. These tools are increasingly used both by research institutions and private companies. Applications in the field of occupational health and safety were analyzed by systematically reviewing international scientific literature. The review results demonstrate the diversity of applied models, tools, methods, and data formats. Currently, merging and evaluating various study data is nearly impossible. This review helps to understand the hurdles and challenges on the way to standardization of digital ergonomic assessment tools.

Keywords: Digital Huma Modeling · ergonomic assessment · occupational health and safety

1 Introduction

Digital Human Modeling supports the design of both usable products (virtual product planning, product engineering, usability) and safe, healthy, and competitive work processes (virtual process planning, manufacturing engineering) and makes an important contribution to preventive occupational health and safety [1]. Computer-aided ergonomic assessments support product development regarding the consideration of ergonomic requirements, such as those arising from legal requirements, and the suitability of the product for a target population. They also help in process development, especially when considering existing requirements for work systems and workflows. Employee-specific characteristics can be given greater consideration in the design of product and work systems, and better harmonized with workload [2], physical stress can be reduced.

Digital human models (DHM), which are placed in an environment and then manipulated to determine work science parameters, are at the heart of digital ergonomic assessments (Fig. 1). The individual components (CAD systems, DHM, Motion Capture systems MoCap) each have an enormous variety of software solutions from different developers, which makes it difficult to disseminate and compare results or exchange research ideas. To understand the hurdles and problems for standardization of interfaces and file formats, this diversity was analyzed and systematized in a review.

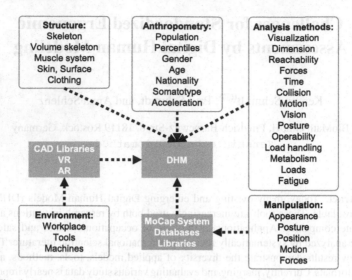

Fig. 1. Interaction of different components in digital ergonomic assessments

2 Methods

The literature search was conducted according to the principles of a scoping review. A scoping review addresses an exploratory research question that aims to capture key concepts, types of evidence, and research gaps related to a particular domain or field through systematic search, selection, and synthesis of existing knowledge [3]. In general, scoping studies may aim to quickly capture the key concepts underlying an area of research and the main sources and types of evidence available and may be conducted particularly when an area is complex or has not been extensively studied [4].

The methodology of scoping reviews is not as strongly defined in guidelines as is the case for systematic reviews. Nevertheless, some methodological publications have established themselves as standard [4–8].

The method is used to identify relevant literature regardless of the study design. Therefore, scoping reviews also consider gray literature in particular, which is also searched for using a systematic approach [9].

The scoping review was carried out in 5 steps:

- Step 1: Define the research question(s)
- Step 2: Systematic search for relevant studies
- Step 3: Study selection according to predefined inclusion/exclusion criteria
- Step 4: Data extraction and processing
- Step 5: Compilation, synopsis, and report of results

2.1 Definition of the Research Question

The objective of the review was to search for occupational science knowledge related to digital human models and the digital acquisition, assessment, and representation of biomechanical data. The literature search aimed to identify publications (on studies, research projects) that analyzed human work/movements using digital human models and evaluated them regarding the design of ergonomic products and socio-technical work systems. The focus was on the aspect of data formats and interfaces.

This review question was of the DMO type with three key elements Data (D); Models (M); and Outcomes (O), see Table 1.

Table 1. Key elements of the search question

Key element	Specification
Data	Motion data, biomechanical data, interfaces, data formats vision, measurements, force, action, time, paths,... Occupational medicine, occupational safety
Methods	Digital ergometry, digital human models, biomechanical model calculations, kinematic models, visualization methods
Outcomes	Work design, occupational science findings

2.2 Systematic Search for Relevant Studies

A comprehensive literature search in English in electronic databases was carried out on the international state of the art in science and research. First, the search terms were defined, then the search query derived from the search terms was submitted to the selected databases (PubMed, Scopus, Web of Science). Furthermore, a search for gray literature was conducted via Google Advanced Search. In addition, the websites of institutions dealing with the topic (e.g. AnyBody Technology, Bundesanstalt für Arbeitsschutz und Arbeitssicherheit BAuA) were searched for gray literature/project reports. Afterwards, a backward reference search was performed manually using key publications (especially reviews). All identified publications were managed in the reference management software Citavi[1], indicating their source (literature database, free search, web pages, reverse search).

2.3 Study Selection According to Predefined Inclusion/Exclusion Criteria

In addition to the key elements, further selection criteria were applied for the selection of suitable publications (Table 2).

The articles were selected in two steps: first, the titles and abstracts of the identified references were screened primarily against the inclusion criteria and the exclusions were documented. Then, the full texts of the manuscripts were screened.

To assess the methodological quality of the studies, a critical evaluation of their scientific robustness was performed. There are several tools for assessing the quality of studies, both for assessing published studies (reporting guidelines) and for assessing the

---

[1] Citavi 6 for Windows, Copyright © 2022 by Swiss Academic Software GmbH. All rights reserved.

Table 2. Selection criteria

Key element	Specification
Year of publication	after 2010 (exception: description of data formats)
Language of publication	English, German
Type of publication	Journal article, review, project report, university or government paper
Place of study	no restriction
Access to publication	full text

risk of bias in studies (risk of bias assessment tools). For this review, four criteria were defined that related to the quality and informativeness of the studies with respect to the review question:

- Q1: Is the study described completely and understandably?
- Q2: Are the methods presented in a complete and understandable way?
- Q3: Are the systems used described completely and comprehensibly?
- Q4: Are the results of the study described in detail?

Each of these criteria was scored on a scale from -1 to 1 (-1 no, 0: partially, 1: yes). The individual scores were added to a sum score to exclude studies with a sum score lower than 2.

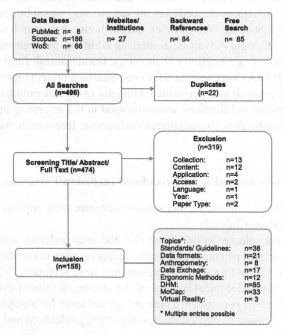

Fig. 2. Flow chart of search and selection process

The selection and assignment of categories were documented in the literature management system. The selection process was documented in a flow chart according to PRISMA [10–12], see Fig. 2.

2.4 Data Extraction and Processing

For the included studies in the subject areas of file formats, data exchange, DHM and MoCap, the information on the three key elements Data (D); Models (M) and Outcomes (O) were extracted.

- Data: file formats reported in the publication, interfaces.
- Methods: DHM, MoCap systems used in the study.
- Outcomes: ergonomic procedures applied in the study.

2.5 Compilation, Synopsis, and Report of the Results

The included studies and extracted information are described in the following.

3 Results

3.1 Digital Human Models DHM

There can be more than one answer to the question "What is DHM?" as the term has different connotations and nuances depending on the area of interest. Even in the technical field, DHM can have different meanings - from computer avatars to anatomical models [13]. In contrast to previous traditional definitions that focus predominantly on software applications and ergonomic assessments, [13] define DHM in a holistic view that promotes system and design level perspectives as part of the domain definition:

A research domain that focuses on synthesizing and applying theory, principles, methods, and technology from a wide range of disciplines that enables computational visualization, modelling, and simulation of human-systems interactions to facilitate the prediction and optimization of well-being and performance.

Since the 1960s, about 150 different commercially available or scientific DHMs with heterogeneous properties, capabilities, underlying algorithms, anthropometric and biomechanical datasets have been developed for different purposes [14, 15]. This complicates both the comparison of results and the transfer of validated research concepts into commercially distributed DHM software systems, which would broaden their user base. In Sect. 4 of their book "Homo sapiens digitalis - Virtuelle Ergonomie und digitale Menschenmodelle" [16] describe 90 digital human models that can be used in occupational science and ergonomics. In addition, other directories or reviews of digital human models exist [13, 17, 18].

[19] distinguishes four domains of DHM (Fig. 3):

- anthropometric models (e.g. JACK, Safework/Human Builder, RAMSIS, SANTOS)
- biomechanical models (e.g. ADAMS, SIMPACK, Dynamicus, CASIMIR, AnyBody Modelling System AMS)
- cognitive models (e.g. ACT-R, Soar, QN-MHP, PARDIC, PELOPS)
- physiological-medical models (e.g. HUGO, Cosmodrive).

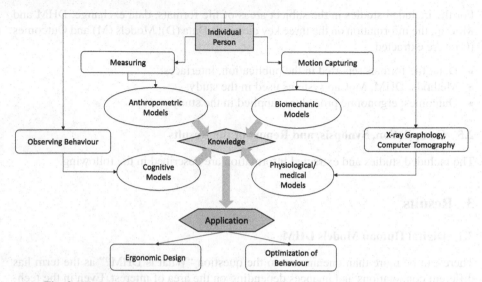

Fig. 3. Figure 2 Overview of DHM generation and application (adapted from [19])

Anthropometric human models are based on the variability of body measurements of people in a population and are used for metric planning or assessment of body-related equipment, postures, and space requirements, while biomechanical models are intended to simulate human movements. The task of cognitive models is to predict the behaviour of the information technology interaction between humans and machines. Physiological medical models play an important role in medical patient care and the representation of body functions, ranging from DNA and protein functions to cells, soft tissues, organs, and anatomy.

The literature further shows - based on the application - different taxonomies of DHM:

- characteristics of application: artistic (animation, visualization, information) vs. scientific (anthropometric, empirically and computationally driven, cognitive) [13]
- application fields:

  - animation, media, and games
  - anatomy and medicine
  - 3D CAD and modelling
  - finite element or multibody dynamics [13]

- application fields:

  - clothing,
  - ergonomics
  - biomechanical behaviour
  - crowd simulator
  - medical [20].

Some widely used DHM are listed in Table 3, the list does not claim to be exhaustive but lists models that have been described/used in studies identified in this search.

Table 3. Listing of Digital Human Models described in the identified papers

Short name	Domain	Operator	Country	Website	Platform/ System
3D Human Model	anthropometric	Delft University of Technology, SLIMDESIGN	NL	https://3dhumanmodel.com/	Solidworks, CREO, CATIA and NX
3DSSPP	anthropometric	University of Michigan, since 2020 VelocityEHS | Humantech	US	https://www.ehs.com/solutions/ergonomics/3d-sspp/	Stand-alone or as AutoCAD-Integration
AMS	biomechanical	AnyBody Technology A/S	DK	www.anybody.com	Stand-alone Software
Apolinex	anthropometric	Rafal Michalski	PL	http://rafalmichalski.com/software--apolinex-description.php	AutoCAD
ARMO	biomechanical	G-sport, Inc	JP	https://www.gsport.co.jp/p_l_armo_e.html	Stand-alone Software

(continued)

Table 3. (*continued*)

Short name	Domain	Operator	Country	Website	Platform/ System
BoB	biomechanical	BoB Biomechanics Ltd	UK	https://www.bob-biomechanics.com/	Stand-alone Software
CADHUMAN	anthropometric	Cadhuman		https://www.cadhuman.com/	Solidworks, Catia, Autodesk Inventor, creo Pro Engíneer, Solid Edge, UGS NX
CASIMIR	anthropometric	Wölfel Engineering GmbH + Co. KG	DE	https://www.woelfel.de/	E-Preprocessor HyperMesh®, FE-Solver SIMULIA Abaqus
CharAT	anthropometric	ESI Software Germany GmbH (ehem. IC.IDO/ VHE GmbH)	DE	https://www.esi-group.com/products/virtual-reality	Stand-alone Software
Creo Manikin	anthropometric	PTC Inc	US	http://www.creomanikin.com/	CREO
DPE	anthropometric	Dassault Systems	FR	https://www.3ds.com/products-services/delmia/	Delmia Process Engineer
Ema	anthropometric	imk automotive GmbH	DE	www.imk-automotive.de	Stand-alone, modular program core for different platforms

(*continued*)

Table 3. (*continued*)

Short name	Domain	Operator	Country	Website	Platform/ System
Human Builder	anthropometric	Dassault Systèmes	FR	http://cat iadoc. free.fr/ online/ CAT IAfr_C2/ hbrugC ATIAfrs. htm	CATIA, ENOVIA, DELMIA
HumanCAD	anthropometric	NexGen Ergonomics	CA	http:// www. nexgen ergo. com/erg onomics/ hum ancad. html	Stand-alone, SolidWorks
HumanShape	anthropometric	University of Michigan	UC	http:// humans hape. org/	Stand-alone Software
IMMA	biomechanical	fleXstructures GmbH	DE	https:// flexstruc tures.de/ pro dukte/ ips- imma/	Stand-alone Software
LifeMOD	biomechanical	LifeModeler, Inc	US	www.lif emo deler. com/pro ducts/lif emod	MD ADAMS
MakeHuman	anthropometric	MakeHuman Community	-	http:// www. makehu mancom munity. org/	Open-Source Tool

(*continued*)

Table 3. (*continued*)

Short name	Domain	Operator	Country	Website	Platform/ System
Mixamo	anthropometric	Adobe Systems Incorporated	US	https://www.mixamo.com/	Stand-alone Software
OpenSim)	biomechanical	National Center for Simulation in Rehabilitation Research	US	https://opensim.stanford.edu/	Open-Source Tool
Poser	anthropometric	Bondware Inc	US	https://www.posersoftware.com/	Stand-alone Software
RAMSIS	anthropometric	Human Solutions GmbH	DE	https://www.human-solutions.com/de/produkte/ramsis-allgemein/index.html	stand-alone, CATIA, Tecnomatix, Autodesk
SAMMIE	anthropometric	SAMMIE CAD Ltd	UK	https://www.lboro.ac.uk/microsites/lds/sammie/dhm.html	Stand-alone Software
Santos	anthropometric	SantosHuman Inc	US	www.santoshumaninc.com	Stand-alone Software
SIMM	biomechanical	Musculographics	US	-	Stand-alone Software
ViveLab	anthropometric	ViveLab Ergo Plc	HU	https://www.vivelab.cloud/software	Stand-alone Software

Some of these DHM exist as standalone solutions, while others are directly integrated with CAD and PLM (Product Lifecycle Management) systems.

The wide variability of existing digital human models concerns the naming of segments or joints, the definition of global and local coordinate systems and degrees of freedom (DoF) of joint and segment motion, and the embedded anthropometric and biomechanical data [14], for more details see Sect. 3.6.

3.2 Anthropometry

Today, most DHM programs have anthropometric libraries of body measurements (from manual or 3D scanned measurements) that allow statistical breakdown and grouping of populations (e.g., 5th percentile of US males). Most DHM software programs use the surveys ANSUR and Civilian and European Surface Anthropometry Resource Project - CAESAR. These databases allow developers to create and scale CAD models and dummies according to anthropometric measurements representing different population groups [13]. The detail, representativeness, and quality of (occupational) analyses performed with DHM depend on the detail, representativeness, and quality of the anthropometric data fed into the system.

3.3 Motion Capture Systems

[21] distinguish five types of motion control of DHM:

- key frame methods: manual adjustment of each key pose of a DHM and interpolation of key poses to produce continuous motion,
- motion capture methods: drive DHMs using motion data captured from real people,
- model-driven methods: construction of motion functions for human motion and generation of continuous motion by inputting various parameters into the motion functions,
- motion synthesis methods: processing and synthesis of stored motion data to generate the desired motions for DHMs,
- motion planning methods: use of random sampling used to solve the problem of motion generation for DHMs in complex environments and tasks, mainly used in the field of robotics.

Key frame and motion capture methods are the main motion control methods used in the manufacturing industry.

Motion capture methods require motion data of a human for transfer to a digital human model; motion capture (MoCap) involves recording such data. MoCap systems can be optical (camera-based) or non-optical (sensor-based). The optical systems work either with or without markers.

Table 4 lists the MoCap systems identified in the studies search, the list by far is not exhaustive but lists systems that were described/used in studies identified in this search.

Motion data collected with MoCap systems are stored in extensive databases offered by commercial and research institutes (e.g. CMU Graphics Lab Motion Capture Database, Cologne Motion Capture Database, Emotional Body Motion Database,

Table 4. List of MoCap-Systems described in the identified papers

Name	Operator	Country	Website
ART Motion Capture-System	Advanced Realtime Tracking GmbH & Co. KG (ART)	DE	https://ar-tracking.com/de/solutions/ergonomics
CodaMotion	CodaMotion Ltd	UK	https://codamotion.com/
GTeleMyo 2400 DTS System	Noraxon	US	https://www.noraxon.com/
Leap Motion Controller	ultraleap	US	https://www.ultraleap.com/product/leap-motion-controller/
Microsoft Kinect	Microsoft	US	https://azure.microsoft.com/de-de/products/kinect-dk/#faq
Motion Analysis Corporation	Santa Rosa	US	https://motionanalysis.com/
Octolus Rift/ Meta Quest	Meta	US	https://motionanalysis.com/
OptiTrack	NaturalPoint, Inc	UA	https://optitrack.com/
Perception Neuron	Noitom Ltd.	UA	https://neuronmocap.com/pages/perception-neuron-studio-system
Polaris Vega	NDI Europe GmbH	DE / CN	https://www.ndieurope.com/de/produkte/optische-mess-systeme/
Polaris Vicra	NDI Europe GmbH	DE / CN	https://www.ndieurope.com/de/produkte/optische-mess-systeme/
Qualisys	Qualisys AB	SE	https://www.qualisys.com/
SIMI	Simi Reality Motion Systems GmbH	DE	http://www.simi.com/de/home.html
Smart DX	BTS Bioengineering	IT	https://www.btsbioengineering.com/products/smart-dx-motion-capture/?gclid=EAIaIQobChMIi9q_zJaA-wIVRePmCh21kAEYEAAYASAAEgLNVvD_BwE
Vicon Nexus	Vicon Motion Systems Ltd	UK	https://www.vicon.com/software/nexus/

(continued)

Table 4. (*continued*)

Name	Operator	Country	Website
Virtools	Dassault Systèmes	FR	https://www.3ds.com/products-services/3dvia/
Xsens MTw Awinda	Xsens Technologies B.V.	NL	https://www.xsens.com/products/mtw-awinda
Xsens MVN Animate	Xsens Technologies B.V.	NL	https://www.xsens.com/products/mvn-animate

Archive of Motion Capture As Sur-face Shapes, HDM05, Human Motion Dynamics on Actuation Level, HumanEva-I, Interactive Emotional Dyadic Motion Capture Database, KIT Whole-Body Human Motion Database, Mocap Club, SFU Motion Capture Database). These databases contain many different types of actions, and each action can have many variants. The aggregation and integration of existing data into a unified and structured database system is not easy and there is currently no unified solution for collecting motion capture data from different sources into one database. However, direct use of motion data in DHM tools requires proper indexing of the motions for automatic selection and retrieval; thus, DHM tools are not able to use this data efficiently [22].

3.4 Ergonomic Assessment Procedures

Ergonomic assessment procedures can be categorized according to different questions:

- 3D visualization of anthropometric problem areas and collisions
- Vision analysis (analysis of field of view and field of vision, determination of hidden objects)
- Reachability analysis (investigation of reaching e.g. operating levers)
- Dimensional analysis (determination of distances or movement spaces)
- Posture and strength analysis (evaluation of postures and various loads), e.g. Diskomfort, OWAS, RULA, REBA
- Load handling analysis, e.g. NIOSH, Snook & Ciriello
- Gait analysis
- Energy consumption/metabolism analysis
- Fatigue analysis, e.g. CUELA
- Time analysis, e.g. MTM
- a.o.

Depending on the objective of the development, one or more of the methods are integrated into the DHM in one or the other constellation. No DHM can perform all analyses, so for a comprehensive assessment multiple (incompatible!) DHM needs to be applied.

3.5 Data Formats

[23] basically distinguish between three file formats:

- File formats for geometric information (static 3D solids, anthropometric data),
- File formats for kinematic and kinetic data (hierarchical skeletal structures or marker motions),
- File formats of comprehensive data such as geometry, dynamics, and structure.

Various quasi-standards (formats that are commonly used for data exchange without being officially recognized as a standard) exist, such as ASF/AMC [24], BVH [25], GMS [26], C3D [27], COLLADA [28], or X3D [29–36], some of which are being pushed by the games and film industries in conjunction with motion capture.

File Formats for Data of 3D Objects (Solids). DHM systems use static 3D data to integrate workplace design, tools, machines, and the environment from external software, such as computer-aided design (CAD) systems. For the exchange of static 3D data within DHM systems, it is useful to have a manufacturing-neutral, well documented, standardized format. For a real-time simulation, it is advantageous to choose a small file format rather than a very detailed one [23]. Commonly used data formats are:

- IGES (Initial Graphics Exchange Specification), a vendor-neutral file format for data exchange between CAD systems, registered as a standard with the American National Standards Institute (ANSI) ANS Y14.26M-1981
- OBJ (Object), open file format for saving three-dimensional geometric shapes
- JT (Jupiter), 3D model format developed as an open, high-performance, compact and persistent storage format for very large compilations of product data, standardized under ISO 14306:2017
- STEP (Standard for the Exchange of Product model data), international standard (ISO 10303-1; ISO 10303-21) for the exchange of 3D data
- STL (Stereo Litographie or Standard Tesselation Language), File format for rapid prototyping and computer-aided manufacturing.

File Formats for Kinematic and Kinetic Data. Typically, the motion capture vendor is the deciding factor for using a particular file format. Since different vendors have developed their own file formats, it is unlikely to convince them to adhere to a single standard format. HTR from Motion Analysis, ASF/AMC from Acclaim, BVA/BVH from Biovision, and V/VSK from Vicon are examples of commercially available vendor-based MoCap file formats.

- ASF/AMC (Acclaim Skeleton File/Acclaim Motion Capture), the ASF file defines the skeleton hierarchy, the properties of the joints and bones, and optionally provides shape data. The AMC file describes the motion related to the skeleton defined in the ASF file
- BVH (Biovision Hierarchical Data), a de facto standard in the animation community, first section [Hierarchy] contains a joint-based hierarchy and angle constraints for the skeleton, the second section [Motion] contains the number of frames, frame rates and motion data

- C3D, often used in the biomechanical motion capture community, can be used in the most popular computer environments Matlab (MathWorks) and LabView (National Instruments)
- HTR (Hierarchical Translation-Rotation), provides a hierarchical skeleton structure, with rotation, translation and scaling information for each segment.

File Formats of Comprehensive Data.

- COLLADA (COLLAborative Design Activity), XML-based, open standard format for the exchange of digital assets between applications
- FBX ("Filmbox"), one of the most important 3D exchange formats used by many 3D tools.

3.6 Interfaces

Data exchange between anthropological and biomechanical DEM is of interest for ergonomic evaluation of biomechanical parameters as additional information [37–39]. At the very least, the blending of cognitive, anthropometric, and biomechanical models would be beneficial for the application of DHM to product design and production processes [19]. With biomechanical models, postures are evaluated not only according to a categorical scoring system or a traffic light scheme, but also according to internal muscle forces as a function of external conditions [37]. Another area where data exchange protocols are of interest is in improving motion simulation [22]. However, despite numerous approaches, there is no universal solution for data exchange between different DHM and between DHM and other systems [1, 14, 22, 23, 40].

A data transfer between components of digital ergonomics is conceivable (Fig. 4):

- between CAD and DHM for providing environmental data within DHM software applications,
- between different DHM to combine the independent properties of different DHM to perform a complete ergonomic analysis,
- from MoCap to DHM to transfer recorded posture and motion data to the DHM,
- between different MoCap.

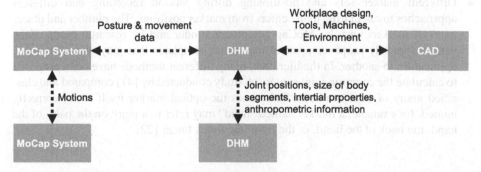

Fig. 4. Interfaces between system components and data exchange

Aspects of Data Exchange. Comprehensive data exchange between different DHM is complicated by different hierarchical structures of the human skeleton, different file formats, different naming conventions, different marker placement, different degrees of freedom (DoF) in certain joints, different orientations, and ranges of motion of joints, different orientation and rotation of global and local coordinate systems, and different scaling units [22]. The variety of applications and the fact that they originated from different scientific groups led to a chaos of conventions in the naming of bones, joints, and body features.

When exchanging data between DHM, several areas need to be considered [37]:

Anthropometry. Anthropometric data concern body length and width measurements, such as height, foot and leg length, hip and shoulder width, hand width, waist circumference, and skeletal measurements. To ensure consistent results from DHM studies, it would be helpful to refer to existing international standards for anthropometric data or computer manikins, such as ISO 7250-1, ISO 7250-2, ISO 15535, ISO 15536-1, ISO 15536-2, and ISO/IEC 19774. Standards for volumetric (relating to the volume of bodies) anthropometric measures have yet to be established [37].

Scaling. Different conventions are used in motion data files imported or exported from the various DHM. Common units for longitudinal displacement are either metric [mm, cm, m] or [inches] and [feet]. Degrees or radians are usually used for specifying rotation angles. Due to regional preferences and different hardware solutions or software applications, standardized units for DHM motion data are difficult to achieve [37].

Biomechanics (Kinematics and Forces). Kinematic data describing motions are an essential part of the data exchange between DHM. However, several incompatibilities may occur:

- Non-uniform structures of the body skeleton. In the context of digital human modeling, a common element of all articulated bodies is a body skeleton ("rig"). A body skeleton is a set of hierarchical rigid segments connected by joints that realize the movements of the human body. At fixed segment lengths, motion can be defined by a series of changes in joint angles that determine the orientation of each segment relative to its proximal segment. The configuration of these hierarchical structures is not uniformly defined in virtual humans [22].
- Different marker sets and positioning during motion recording and different approaches to calculating joint centers from marker positions. The number and placement of markers vary by MoCap equipment vendor and by research group. Each vendor typically proposes a set of marker set templates that may differ from one application to another. In the literature, many different methods have been proposed to calculate the common joint centers. A study conducted by [41] compared and classified many of these methods. Sometimes the optical marker itself is not correctly named, for example, a marker named "hand" may refer to a mark on the palm of the hand, the back of the hand, or the tip of the index finger [22].

- Different number of degrees of freedom (DoF) in the joints. In general, a segment in space can be completely defined by six parameters (three translational and three rotational). For articulated bodies, it is advisable to also consider a length factor that determines the length changes of each segment during animation. However, when providing a set of hierarchical segments with 7 degrees of freedom (DoF) for each segment, one must deal with enormous complexity and computational redundancies. Most MoCap systems can constrain one or more of these DoF. However, this can lead to mismatches between the DHMs [22].
- Different global position (and translation of a body in space) and local position (and translation of limbs and body segments over joints). Fixed bones or virtual joints are the bones/joints that have no degree of freedom. The reason for defining such a joint is usually to create a constant offset relative to the parent joint without using translation daters in the transformation matrix. For the movement of the parent joint to the child joint two different methods (transformation matrix, definition of a dummy segment) can be used [22].
- Differences in the conventions for the order of rotation. When using motion capture data for DHM applications, in most cases a conversion to the joint-specific conventions of the manikin is required. In motion capture files as well as in DHM tools, the use of the Euler convention for defining rotation angles and the orientation of segments in space is widespread, but just not a defined standard. There are other methods for defining object orientation in space, such as rotation matrices, vector gels, and quaternions [22].
- Different definitions of the basic pose. Basic pose, key pose or neutral pose are common terms, but they do not have a uniform meaning in the field of motion capture (a standing pose with arms open almost 90 degrees to the side (called T-pose), a standing pose with arms next to the body in a relaxed position, etc.) [22].
- Gravity axis convention. Some applications prefer the -Y direction to represent the gravity direction, while others use the -Z direction as the gravity axis. There is also no agreement between standards on the direction of gravity relative to the global coordinate system. For example, the ISO 15536-2 (2007) standard suggests the Z-axis, while the H-Anim (2006) standard suggests the Y-axis as the upward direction [22].
- Differences in the common coordinate system. For a hierarchical joint body, local coordinate systems for each joint are required to solve the forward kinematic equations. Once these joint coordinate systems are defined, not only are the orientation and displacement of each subordinate joint determined with respect to the parent joint, but the orientation of the distal segment (direction of the bone) is also defined [22].

Reaction force data in biomechanical analyses are important for inverse dynamic calculations to determine internal body forces and moments. However, only a few file formats take external forces into account. The exchange of force data via other file formats is not standardized and therefore complicated. In some cases, a lot of sophistication and higher programming effort is required [37].

Data Exchange Procedures

Interfaces Between DHM. In the last years, some interfaces for data exchange between different DHM systems have been developed (Table 5). What they all have in common are the individual, tailor-made solutions [23].

Table 5. Studies in which data exchange between DHM was realized.

Authors	Title	Year	Ergonomics	Systems	Interface
Paul, G.; Lee, W. C	Interfacing Jack and Anybody: Towards anthropometric musculoskeletal digital human modeling	2011	n.s	AMS; Jack	Interface Program
Jung, M.; et al.	Integrating biomechanical manikins into a CAD environment	2013	Posture; forces	SolidWorks Assembly, AMS	Interface
Krüger, D.; Wartzack, S	Towards CAD integrated simulation of use under ergonomic aspects	2014	Forces	CAD model; OpenSim	interface between OpenSim and CAD Creo/ Parametric
Peters, M., et al.	Biomechanical Digital Human Models: Chances and Challenges to Expand Ergonomic Evaluation	2018	Load handling	AMS; ema	BVH data
Peters, M.; Wischniewski, S	Evaluation of physical workload using simulation versus motion capturing data for biomechanical models	2020	Load handling	AMS; ema	BVH data
Ulherr, A. & Bengler, K	Umfassende Diskomfortbewertung für Autoinsassen durch Simulation: UDASim	2016	Diskomfort	AMS; CASIMIR; RAMSIS	Interface platform

Pooling/Master Modell. Some studies propose migrating different skeletons into each other via a standard or reference skeleton (Table 6).

Import of MoCap-Daten into DHM. The publications mention a variety of MoCap systems that are used to record motions for further processing in DHM systems (Table 7).

Table 6. Studies in which a standard or reference skeleton was proposed.

Authors	Title	Year	Method
Aberman, K., et al.	Skeleton-aware networks for deep motion retargeting	2020	Pooling/Unpooling
Monzani, J.-S., et al.	Using an intermediate skeleton and inverse kinematics for motion retargeting	2000	Intermediate Skeleton
Terlemez, Ö., et al.	Master motor map (MMM) – framework and toolkit for capturing, representing, and reproducing human motion on humanoid robots	2014	Master Motion Map
Azad, P., et al.	Toward a unified representation for imitation of human motion on humanoids	2007	Master Motion Map

Table 7. Studies in which data exchange between MoCap data and DHM was realized.

Authors	Title	Year	Ergonomics	Systems	Formats
Alexander, N.; et al.	Effect of different walking speeds on joint and muscle force estimation using AnyBody and OpenSim	2021	Gait; Forces	Nexus → AMS, → OpenSim	GRF-Daten, Filter
Asadi, F.; Arjmand, N	Marker-less versus marker-based driven musculoskeletal models of the spine during static load-handling activities	2020	Load handling	Kinect, Nexus → AMS	n.s
Babicsné Hor-váth, Mária; et al.	Early results of a usability evaluation of two digital hu-man model-based ergonomic software applying eye-tracking methodology comparison of the usability of Vi-veLab and Jack software	2019	Posture -lyse, RULA	Xsens → Jack, → ViveLab	n.s

(continued)

Table 7. (*continued*)

Authors	Title	Year	Ergonomics	Systems	Formats
Behjati, M. & Arjmand, N	Biomechanical assessment of the NIOSH lifting equation in asymmetric load-handling activities using a detailed musculoskeletal model	2019	Load handling; NIOSH	Nexus → AMS	n.s
Deuse, Jochen; et al.	A customizable digital human model for assembly system design	2016	Posture-lyse, REBA	Kinect → DHM	C# Code
Fonk, R., et al.	Hand motion capture from a 3D leap motion controller for a musculoskeletal dynamic simulation	2021	Motion	LMC → AMS	Python-based interface, BVH, AnyScript
Kong, Y.-K., et al.	Ergonomic assessment of a lower-limb exoskeleton through electromyography and Anybody modeling system	2022	Posture	Xsens → AMS	n.s
Nimbarte, A. et al.	Biomechanical loading of the shoulder complex and lumbosacral joints during dynamic cart pushing task	2013	Load handling	Nexus → AMS	C3D
Peters, M. & Wischniewski, S	Evaluation of physical workload using simulation versus motion capturing data for biomechanical models	2020	Load handling	Perception Neuron → AMS; → ema	BVH

(*continued*)

Table 7. (*continued*)

Authors	Title	Year	Ergonomics	Systems	Formats
Seiferheld, Bo	Biomechanical investigation of a passive upper extremity exoskeleton for manual material handling	2021	Forces	Xsens → AMS	BVH
Tröster, M., J., et al.	Biomechanical analysis of stoop and free-style squat lifting and lowering with a generic back-support exoskeleton model	2022	Load handling	Qualisys → AMS	C3D
Tröster, M., et al.	Biomechanical model-based development of an active occupational upper-limb exoskeleton to support healthcare workers in the surgery waiting room	2020	Load handling	Qualisys → AMS	n.s
Zhou, J	Physical stresses on caregivers when repositioning patients in bed	2020	Load handling	n.s. → AMS	n.s
Hermsdorf, H.; et al.	Bewertung digital erfasster Bewegungen mit Dynamicus	2016	Posture; Forces	ART → Dynamicus	Dynamicus/Recorder
Walther, M.; Muñoz, B.T	Integration of time as a factor in ergonomic simulation	2012	Posture, Forces, Load handling, EAWS	ART → Dynamicus	n.s

(*continued*)

Table 7. (*continued*)

Authors	Title	Year	Ergonomics	Systems	Formats
Caporaso, T.; et al.	Digital human models for gait analysis: Experimental validation of static force analysis tools under dynamic conditions	2017	Gait	BTS SMART-DX → Jack	open data exchange format (i.e., C3D)
Choi, N.-C; Lee, S.H	Discomfort evaluation of truck ingress/egress motions based on biomechanical analysis	2015	Posture	Vicon → LifeMOD	slf data
Chang, J., et al.	Muscle fatigue analysis using opensim	2017	Gait	Motion Analysis Corporation → OpenSim	n.s
Hamner, S. R., et al.	Muscle contributions to propulsion and support during running	2010	Forces; gait	Motion Analysis Corporation → OpenSim	n.s
Trinler, U.; Baker, R	Estimated landmark calibration of biomechanical models for inverse kinematics	2018	Gait	Nexus → OpenSim	n.s

3.7 Standards

Scope of Standardization. According to [14], it is fundamentally important to have a uniform human anatomical structure, with defined global and local coordinate systems, consistent naming and numbering of limbs or joints with their corresponding uniform degrees of freedom. Furthermore, a DHM standard procedure and a parametric model for linking anthropometric databases (DIN EN ISO 15535 [42]) with a defined DHM human structure must be considered in order to create representative proportions for a selected population. It must also be ensured that available anthropometric data (DIN EN ISO 7250-1 [43]) can be used to calibrate the digital human model.

A DHM standard data model should include an input section that contains information describing the model structure, parameterization of structural components (e.g., limb size, range of motion), anthropometric assumptions, fixed points, and kinematic drivers, and an output section that documents the nature and results of simulations performed with a DHM [14].

Status of Standardization. In July 2011, the International Ergonomics Association (IEA) Technical Committee on Human-simulation and Virtual Environments established a DHM standardization subcommittee to provide a framework for standardizing digital human models [14]. However, headwinds quickly arose, after which the project was dropped. Meanwhile, informaticians from the gaming and video fields have entered the field of DHM and have taken their standards with them or established them very quickly. This could also be built upon for work science.

Standards for digital humans have been developed in the Working Group on Anthropometry and Biomechanics of ISO Technical Committee TC 159 (Ergonomics). Another standardization activity on digital human modelling in ISO TC 133 relates to clothing sizing [44].

The International Organization for Standardization (ISO) provides ISO 15536, a basic standard for computer manikins with degrees of freedom of articulation. ISO 15536 Part 1 contains the principles and terminology of digital humans and ISO 15536 Part 2 contains verification and validation methods for commercially available digital human systems. The detailed standard ISO 7250 provides the standard of terminology and measurement methods for body dimensions, ISO 15535 refers to human body dimensions and their storage in databases.

In recent years, 3D scanning systems have been used for digital modelling of humans and size determination. Therefore, TC 159 has set the standards for quality control of 3D scanning systems. ISO 20685 [45] provides quality thresholds for scan-derived measurements to ensure comparability with traditional anthropometry.

The ISO 18825 series contains the terminology of the virtual human body. The body dimensions required for sizing clothing are not included in the ergonomic standard DIN EN ISO 7250-1; therefore, another standard, ISO 8559, was introduced. ISO 8559-1 contains many circumferential dimensions, while ISO 7250-1 mainly contains longitudinal limb dimensions and functional dimensions (e.g. seat height, forward reach).

General recommendations for body coordinate systems and kinematic data have been agreed upon by the International Society of Biomechanics (ISB) [46]. The ISB also provides recommendations for standardizing the reporting of kinematic data [47, 48].

The Institute of Electrical and Electronics Engineers (IEEE) is one of the largest organizations developing international "forum" standards. In 2015, IEEE established a new technical committee to standardize the processing of 3D body data for apparel. Several working groups are developing standards for terminology, quality, metadata format, security and privacy, and business interfaces.

As one of the most important rule-setters, the VDI e.V. publishes up to 250 VDI guidelines per year. The standard VDI 4499-4 [49] introduces digital human models in the context of factory planning, especially ergonomic workplace design, and highlights the main legal aspects of human modelling. The digital modelling of working humans in combination with work equipment in a work environment (i.e. with machines, plants, transport equipment, etc.) is described in order to analyze and evaluate ergonomic, work methodical and time-economic aspects [50].

The HAnim Working Group develops and demonstrates the international standard for Humanoid Animation (HAnim). ISO/IEC 19774 (ISO/IEC 19774-1; ISO/IEC 19774-2) specifies a system for representing humanoids in a network-enabled 3D graphics and multimedia environment (including names, positions, joints, hierarchies, relationships, mapping, data structures). The H-Anim standard (ISO/IEC 19774-1; ISO/IEC 19774-2) proposes to consider models with different degrees of articulation (LOA). The degree of articulation (LOA) represents the complexity and level of detail of the joints of a humanoid skeletal hierarchy and can be used to generate different movements based on the joints.

HAnim supports a variety of articulated figures - including anatomically correct human models - with haptic and kinematic interfaces to enable shareable skeletons, bodies, and animations. ISO/IEC 19774 contains the complete normative and in-formative information for specifying an abstract human form.

4 Conclusions

Standardization of digital human models is being worked on by various actors, but so far valid nouns are mainly limited to anthropometry. Fundamentally important would be a uniform human anatomical structure, with defined global and local coordinate systems, consistent naming and numbering of limbs or joints with their corresponding uniform degrees of freedom (DHM standard procedure). The ISO 19774 standard, which contains detailed ideas about designations, positions, joints, hierarchies, relationships, mapping, and data structures that can serve as the basis for an "intermediate" standard or reference skeleton when transferring from one DHM to another or as a "master" skeleton for merging and evaluating existing data, is proving to be a trendsetter for an interface standard format in the field of digital ergonomics.

Although, some recommendations and approaches can be found in the literature, establishing standards for data exchange between different DHM and between DHM and other systems is and remains challenging.

References

1. Wischniewski, S.: Delphi Survey: Digital Ergonomics 2025. In: Delphi Survey: Digital Ergonomics 2025; (2013)
2. Offensive Mittelstand, editor. Personenbezogene digitale Ergonomie (2018)
3. Colquhoun, H.L., Levac, D., O'Brien, K.K., et al.: Scoping reviews: time for clarity in definition, methods, and reporting. J. Clin. Epidemiol. **67**(12), 1291–1294 (2014). https://doi.org/10.1016/j.jclinepi.2014.03.013. PMID: 25034198

4. Arksey, H., O'Malley, L.: Scoping studies: towards a methodological framework. Int. J. Soc. Res. Methodol. **8**(1), 19–32 (2005). https://doi.org/10.1080/1364557032000119616

5. Daudt, H.M., van Mossel, C., Scott, S.J.: Enhancing the scoping study methodology: a large, inter-professional team's experience with Arksey and O'Malley's framework. BMC Med. Res. Methodol. **13**(48) (2013). https://doi.org/10.1186/1471-2288-13-48

6. Hidalgo Landa, A., Szabo, I., Le Brun, L., Owen, I., Fletcher, G., Hill, M.: An evidence-based approach to scoping reviews. Electron. J. Inf. Syst. Eval. **14**(1), 46–52 (2011)

7. Levac, D., Colquhoun, H.L., O'Brien, K.K.: Scoping studies: advancing the methodology. Implement Sci. **5**, 69 (2010). https://doi.org/10.1186/1748-5908-5-69. PMID: 20854677

8. Tricco, A.C., Lillie, E., Zarin, W., et al.: PRISMA extension for scoping reviews (PRISMA-ScR): checklist and explanation. Ann. Int. Med. **169**(7): 467–473 (2018). https://doi.org/10.7326/M18-0850. PMID: 30178033

9. Godin, K., Stapleton, J., Kirkpatrick, S.I., Hanning, R.M., Leatherdale, S.T.: Applying systematic review search methods to the grey literature: a case study examining guidelines for school-based breakfast programs in Canada. Syst. Rev. **4**, 138 (2015). https://doi.org/10.1186/s13643-015-0125-0. PMID: 26494010

10. Liberati, A., Altman, D.G., Tetzlaff, J., et al.: The PRISMA statement for reporting systematic reviews and meta-analyses of studies that evaluate health care interventions: explanation and elaboration. PLoS Med. **6**(7), e1000100 (2009). https://doi.org/10.1371/journal.pmed.1000100. PMID: 19621070

11. Moher, D., Liberati, A., Tetzlaff, J., Altman, D.G.: Preferred reporting items for systematic reviews and meta-analyses: the PRISMA statement. PLoS Med. **6**(7), e1000097 (2009). https://doi.org/10.1371/journal.pmed.1000097. PMID: 19621072

12. Page, M.J., McKenzie, J.E., Bossuyt, P.M.M., et al.: The PRISMA 2020 statement: an updated guideline for reporting systematic reviews. Syst. Rev. **10**(1) (2021). https://doi.org/10.1186/s13643-021-01626-4

13. Demirel, H.O., Ahmed, S., Duffy, V.G.: Digital human modeling: a review and reappraisal of origins, present, and expected future methods for representing humans computationally. Int. J. Hum.-Comput. Interact. **38**(10), 897–937 (2022). https://doi.org/10.1080/10447318.2021.1976507

14. Paul, G.E., Wischniewski, S.: Standardisation of digital human models. Ergonomics **55**(9), 1115–1118 (2012). https://doi.org/10.1080/00140139.2012.690454. PMID: 22676278

15. Mühlstedt, J.: Digitale Menschmodelle. In: Bullinger-Hoffmann, A.C., Mühlstedt, J. (eds.) Homo sapiens digitalis - Virtuelle Ergonomie und digitale Menschenmodelle, pp. 73–182. Springer Vieweg (2016)

16. Bullinger-Hoffmann, A.C., Mühlstedt, J. (eds.) Homo sapiens digitalis - Virtuelle Ergonomie und digitale Menschenmodelle. Springer Vieweg (2016)

17. Wolf, A., Miehling, J., Wartzack, S., et al.: Virtuelles Planen und Bewerten menschlicher Arbeit. Arbeitsmedizin, Sozialmedizin, Umweltmedizin: ASU, Zeitschrift für medizinische Prävention **54**(6) (2019)

18. Duffy, V.G. (ed.): Handbook of Digital Human Modeling: Research for Applied Ergonomics and Human Factors Engineering. CRC Press, Boca Raton (2009)

19. Bubb, H.: Why do we need digital human models? In: Scataglini, S., Paul, G.E. (eds.) DHM and Posturography, pp. 7–32 (2019)

20. Regazzoni, D., Rizzi, C.: Virtualization of the human in the digital factory. In: Kenett, R.S., Swarz, R.S., Zonnenshain, A. (eds.) Systems Engineering in the Fourth Industrial Revolution, pp. 161–189. Wiley (2019)

21. Zhu, W., Fan, X., Zhang, Y.: Applications and research trends of digital human models in the manufacturing industry. Virtual Reality Intell. Hardw. **1**(6), 558–579 (2019). https://doi.org/10.1016/j.vrih.2019.09.005

22. Keyvani, A., Lämkull, D., Bolmsjö, G., Örtengren, R.: Considerations for aggregation of motion-captured files in structured databases for DHM applications. In: Considerations for Aggregation of Motion-Captured Files in Structured Databases for DHM Applications (2013)
23. Bonin, D., Wischniewski, S., Wirsching, H.-J., Upmann, A., Rausch, J., Paul, G.E.: Exchanging data between digital human modeling systems - a review of data formats. In: Exchanging Data Between Digital Human Modeling Systems - A Review of Data Formats (2014)
24. Schafer M. Internal technical memo #39 [online]: Acclaim Advanced Technologies Group (1994). http://www.darwin3d.com/gamedev/acclaim.zip
25. Meredith, M., Maddock, S.: Motion capture file formats explained (2001)
26. Luciani, A., Evrard, M., Couroussé, D., Castagné, N., Cadoz, C., Florens, J.-L.: A basic gesture and motion format for virtual reality multisensory applications. arXiv (2010)
27. Motion Lab Systems. The C3D file format user guide (2008). https://www.c3d.org/docs/C3D_User_Guide_2008.pdf
28. Khronos Group. COLLADA – Digital Asset Schema Release 1.5.0 (2008). https://www.khronos.org/files/collada_spec_1_5.pdf
29. ISO. Information technology - Computer graphics, image processing and environmental data representation - Extensible 3D (X3D) encodings - Part 3: Compressed binary encoding; 2015 (2015). https://www.iso.org/standard/60504.html
30. ISO. Information technology — Computer graphics, image processing and environmental data representation — Extensible 3D (X3D) encodings — Part 2: Classic VRML encoding; 2015 (2015). https://www.iso.org/standard/60503.html
31. ISO. Information technology — Computer graphics, image processing and environmental data representation — Extensible 3D (X3D) encodings — Part 1: Extensible Markup Language (XML) encoding; 2015 (2015). https://www.iso.org/standard/60502.html
32. ISO. Information technology — Computer graphics, image processing and environmental data representation — Extensible 3D (X3D) — Part 2: Scene access interface (SAI); 2015 (2015). https://webstore.iec.ch/publication/23241
33. ISO. Information technology — Computer graphics, image processing and environmental data representation — Extensible 3D (X3D) — Part 1: Architecture and base components; 2013 (2013). https://www.iso.org/standard/60760.html
34. ISO. Information technology — Computer graphics and image processing — Extensible 3D (X3D) language bindings — Part 3: Part 3: C; under development under development. https://www.iso.org/standard/83751.html
35. ISO. Information technology — Computer graphics and image processing — Extensible 3D (X3D) language bindings — Part 2: Java; 2006 (2006). https://www.iso.org/standard/38020.html
36. ISO. Information technology — Computer graphics and image processing — Extensible 3D (X3D) language bindings — Part 1: ECMAScript; 2006 (2006). https://www.iso.org/standard/33915.html
37. Peters, M., Wischniewski, S., Paul, G.E.: DHM data exchange protocols. In: Scataglini, S., Paul, G.E. (eds.) DHM and Posturography, pp. 663–670 (2019)
38. Peters, M., Quadrat, E., Nolte, A., et al.: Biomechanical digital human models: chances and challenges to expand ergonomic evaluation. In: International Conference on Human Systems Engineering and Design 2018 (2018)
39. Paul, G.E., Lee, W.C.: Interfacing Jack and Anybody: towards anthropometric musculoskeletal digital human modeling. In: Wang, X., Bubb, H. (eds.) Interfacing Jack and Anybody: Towards Anthropometric Musculoskeletal Digital Human Modeling (2011)
40. Wegner, D., Chiang, J., Kemmer, B., Lämkull, D., Roll, R.: Digital human modeling requirements and standardization. In: Digital Human Modeling Requirements and Standardization. SAE International400 Commonwealth Drive, Warrendale (2007)

41. Ehrig, R.M., Taylor, W.R., Duda, G.N., Heller, M.O.: A survey of formal methods for determining the centre of rotation of ball joints. J. Biomech. **39**(15), 2798–2809 (2006). https://doi.org/10.1016/j.jbiomech.2005.10.002. PMID: 16293257

42. DIN. Allgemeine Anforderungen an die Einrichtung anthropometrischer Datenbanken; 2013 (2013). https://www.din.de/de/mitwirken/normenausschuesse/naerg/veroeffentlichungen/wdc-beuth:din21:167441816

43. DIN. Wesentliche Maße des menschlichen Körpers für die technische Gestaltung - Teil 1: Körpermaßdefinitionen und -messpunkte: ISO 7250-1; 2017 (2017). https://www.din.de/de/mitwirken/normenausschuesse/naerg/veroeffentlichungen/wdc-beuth:din21:280954281

44. Mochimaru, M.: Standards and norms. In: Scataglini, S., Paul, G.E. (eds.) DHM and Posturography, pp. 659–661 (2019)

45. DIN. 3D-Scanverfahren für international kompatible anthropometrische Datenbanken - Teil 1: Prüfprotokoll für aus 3D-Scans extrahierte Körpermaße; 2019 (2019). https://www.din.de/de/mitwirken/normenausschuesse/naerg/veroeffentlichungen/wdc-beuth:din21:298746990

46. Wu, G., Cavanagh, P.R.: ISB recommendations for standardization in the reporting of kinematic data. J Biomech **28**(10), 1257–1261 (1995). https://doi.org/10.1016/0021-9290(95)00017-C

47. Wu, G., van der Helm, F.C.T., Veeger, H.E.J., et al.: ISB recommendation on definitions of joint coordinate systems of various joints for the reporting of human joint motion - Part II: shoulder, elbow, wrist and hand. J. Biomech. **38**(5), 981–992 (2005). https://doi.org/10.1016/j.jbiomech.2004.05.042. PMID: 15844264

48. Wu, G., Siegler, S., Allard, P., et al.: ISB recommendation on definitions of joint coordinate system of various joints for the reporting of human joint motion—part I: ankle, hip, and spine. J. Biomech. **35**(4), 543–548 (2002). https://doi.org/10.1016/s0021-9290(01)00222-6

49. VDI. Digitale Fabrik - Ergonomische Abbildung des Menschen in der Digitalen Fabrik. Berlin: Beuth Verlag; 2015 (2015). https://www.vdi.de/richtlinien/details/vdi-4499-blatt-4-digitale-fabrik-ergonomische-abbildung-des-menschen-in-der-digitalen-fabrik

50. Zülch, G.: Ergonomische Abbildung des Menschen in der Digitalen Fabrik – Die neue VDI-Richtlinie 4499-4 (2013)

Assessing Ergonomics on IPS IMMA Family of Manikins

Manuela Vargas[1], Maria Pia Cavatorta[2], Valerio Cibrario[1(✉)], Enrica Bosani[3], and Meike Schaub[4]

[1] Flexstructures Italia Srl, Corso Castelfidardo 30/A, 10129 Turin, Italy
{manuela.vargas,valerio.cibrario}@flexstructures.de
[2] Department of Mechanical and Aerospace Engineering, Politecnico di Torino, Corso Duca degli Abruzzi 24, 10129 Turin, Italy
maria.cavatorta@polito.it
[3] Whirlpool Management, EMEA, Via Aldo Moro 5, 21024 Varese, Italy
enrica_bosani@whirlpool.com
[4] fleXstructure GmbH, Trippstadter Street 110, 67663 Kaiserslautern, Germany
meike.schaub@flexstructures.de

Abstract. Europe's growing focus on the health and safety of workers in an aging society is driving a structural approach to ergonomics assessment in the early phase of product and process design. In this respect, Digital Human Model (DHM) software programs can help anticipate the design process criticalities and lead to an optimal solution for workplace design, work cycle content and compliance with the health and safety requirements of ISO and CEN standards. This paper presents the results of the research project D-HUMMER funded by EIT Manufacturing (project number 22294). The project builds on the software IPS IMMA to implement a module for holistic ergonomics risk assessment that can provide designers with some recommended ways to proceed based on the level of risk. A workstation from Whirlpool refrigeration factory has been used as a concrete industrial use case. The IMMA family manikins' model was used for a complete and reliable ergonomics assessment of the target population and to disclose potential anthropometric mismatches. The implementation of a holistic ergonomics assessment inside a DHM software such as IPS IMMA makes it easier for companies to apply proactive ergonomics. The use of a family of manikins allows considering the variety among human operators by running one simulation.

Keywords: Digital Human Model (DHM) · Ergonomic assessment · Family of manikins

1 Introduction

Operators' health and well-being at work are crucial factors of social sustainability in industry. Musculo-Skeletal Disorders (MSDs) are one of the most common work-related ailments (European Agency for Safety and Health at Work 2019). This wide range of inflammatory and degenerative conditions affect the back, neck, shoulder, upper and lower limbs, causing pain and reducing strength and motility (Roquelaure 2018). In more chronic cases, MSDs can lead to disability and the necessity to give up work (Bhattacharya and McGlothlin 2012; Punnett and Wegman 2004).

Throughout Europe, MSDs affect millions of workers and cost employers billions of euros. Prevention of MSDs through good ergonomics is key to keep a stable and motivated workforce, which is paramount in Western aging societies. The presence of MSDs accelerates the degenerative process due to aging, which affects the biomechanical tolerance to high weights and/or high-frequency activities (Bouziri et al. 2022).

Often ergonomics interventions are reactive to discomfort or pain reported during work activities in already-built workstations. These kinds of interventions are costly and often limited to managerial changes. A more effective approach is proactive ergonomics that looks for solving problems in advance, possibly in the design phase where significant changes are still possible at a limited cost. Applying ergonomics principles into design not only helps targeting MSDs but also improves productivity and worker's efficiency.

Digital Human Modeling (DHM) is a powerful tool for proactive ergonomics. Digital environments help designers assess the risk and performance of human work by simulating human behavior in the interaction with the virtual background. The visualization tool makes the simulation visually realistic (Demirel et al. 2022) and helps identifying the potential physical risks factors in the workstation and the work task such as awkward postures, high-force exertions, and high-frequency movements with no need for physical prototypes.

Real-life work tasks are composed of different types of activities and risk factors. It is then key that the ergonomics assessment considers all factors that contribute to the physical workload. Many ergonomics assessment methods target one type of activity only, i.e. manual material handling or repetitive movements, and the body segment most at risk for the analyzed work activity, i.e. back or upper limbs respectively. Holistic approaches on the contrary wish to take into account the different types of work activities that the worker performs during the shift and that all together may influence the worker's exposure to risk. EAWS is a holistic method developed by researchers from the University of Darmstadt to evaluate the biomechanical loads of the whole body and of the upper limbs (Schaub et al. 2012, 2013). The method is broadly used in different sectors such as industrial manufacturing, automotive, aerospace, and defense as a tool for workplace design and ergonomics assessment.

Ergonomics assessment methods like EAWS originated as observational methods. In other words, they are designed to be used by an analyst that observes the worker performing the task and fills the evaluation worksheet. These types of analyses are normally performed by an expert since they are not easy to apply and intra- and inter-variability can introduce bias in the scoring. The necessity for expert analysis and the intra- inter-variability issues have brought the idea of implementing ergonomics assessment methods into DHM software programs. DHM have the potential to allow for performing a more objective and reproducible evaluation of the task, for carrying out the ergonomic assessments of the different activities present during a work shift, for evaluating different setups also in the early phases of the design process without the need for an expert to perform the assessment.

This paper presents part of the work developed within the research project D-HUMMER funded by EIT Manufacturing (project number 22294). D-Hummer stands for A Digital Human Model for Ergonomic Workplace Layout and Optimized Production Process. The project builds on the software IPS IMMA to implement a module for holistic ergonomics assessment in order to automatize in a virtual environment a method that originated as observational. This module will assist engineers in optimizing workplace design while ensuring proper ergonomics for operators. A workstation from Whirlpool refrigeration factory has been used as a concrete industrial use case.

2   DHM Tool and Use Case

IPS IMMA (Intelligently Moving Manikins) tool is a DHM software program endowed with advanced path-planning techniques. These techniques ensure good repeatability of simulations, positioning the manikin in an ergonomic reliable posture, avoiding collision with the workplace and the manikin itself, and fulfilling constraints due to grasping and viewing requirements (Brolin 2014). Additionally, the IPS IMMA anthropometric module uses the multivariate and PCA (Principal Component Analysis) approach to create manikins that allow for keeping the anthropometric diversity of the target population (Brolin et al. 2011, 2012, 2019). The manikin family is an innovative feature of IPS IMMA that allows building a customized family of manikins with different anthropometries and simultaneously running the simulation for the entire family.

Part of the evaluation of a workstation is to verify it through an ergonomics assessment. The manikin family enables the user to perform in one run the ergonomics assessments for the entire family of manikins. In other words, the user can determine the level of the biomechanical load for different members of the workers' population simply by setting up one simulation (Brolin 2014, 2016; Brolin et al. 2012, 2019).

Currently, IPS IMMA is endowed with two ergonomics assessment methods, the Rapid Upper Limb Assessment (RULA) and the Rapid Entire Body Assessment (REBA) (fleXstructures 2020) that focus mainly on the evaluation of postures. In contrast to these methods, EAWS provides the possibility to combine the different hazards for biomechanical overload, such as postures, forces, frequency, in an overall risk score, thus allowing for a comprehensive risk evaluation of the entire work task while maintaining a correlation with ISO and CEN standards. In particular, the whole-body score of EAWS considers four sections, where each section evaluates the different types of hazards and activities that can be found in a work task. Fig. 1 shows the EAWS structure and its reference to the standards.

As described in Schaub et al. (2012, 2013), Section 1 is for the evaluation of working postures and movements with low additional physical efforts. Section 2 is for the evaluation of action forces of the whole body (>40 N) or hand-finger system (>30 N) and Section 3 is for the evaluation of manual materials handling activities (>3 kg). Loads less than 3 kg, hand-finger action forces of less than 30 N and whole body forces of less than 40 N are classified low physical effort and are included in Section 1. Sections 1, 2 and 3 are mutually exclusive, meaning that 'whole body' load situations are rated in one of the sections either. Section 0 is for Extra Points arising from special load situations that are not dealt by the other sections, such as working on moving objects or with low accessibility.

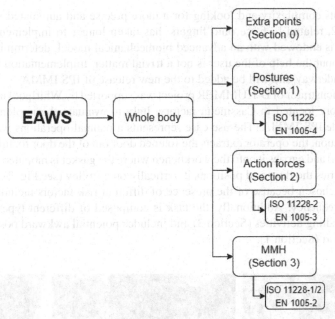

Fig. 1. EAWS whole body: structure and reference to standards. (Adapted from Schaub et al. 2013)

The implementation of EAWS in IPS IMMA was carried out following the EAWS guidelines to ensure that the assessment was implemented correctly. The EAWS version that has been implemented is v1.3.6. The implementation was carried out in the most possible automated way, minimizing the user inputs.

Section 1 is fully automated. IPS IMMA analyzes the recorded joint angles and positions of the body segments throughout the entire simulation and categorizes each posture into one of the standard posture classes defined by EAWS. Time of back bending forward or working with hands at or above shoulder level can therefore be assessed in an objective and efficient way while running the simulation.

Information regarding action forces and objects weights needs to be input by the user to complete the ergonomics assessment of Section 2 and 3. Information on the frequency parameter is also required for manual material handling activities, since the assessment in Section 3 of EAWS refers to the whole shift, while the simulation is normally limited to one cycle. Sections 1, 2 and 3 of EAWS are mutually exclusive and the software recognizes automatically which section to use depending on the characteristics of the activities that are present in the work task. Due to the nature of Section 0, user inputs are necessary to calculate the Extra Points.

Due to its complexity and looking for a more precise and automated way, line 17 of Section 2, related to force onto fingers, has taken longer to implement. Although IPS IMMA is endowed with an advanced biomechanical model, determining the hand posture without the help of the user is not a trivial matter. Implementation of line 17 is currently underway and will be added to the new release of IPS IMMA.

The demonstrator of D-HUMMER project was supported by Whirlpool in the Refrigeration factory located in Cassinetta factory, Italy to evaluate the implementation of EAWS inside IPS IMMA. The use case represents a manual operations workplace. In this workstation, the operator extracts the foamed door out of the door foaming machine (called drum) and carries it onto the workbench where the gasket is mounted. Finally, the operator carries the door and positions it vertically on a trolley (see Fig. 2). This workstation was chosen because of the presence of different risk factors including posture, force and frequency. Additionally, the task is composed of different types of manual material handling activities (Section 3) and includes potential awkward postures at low physical effort (Section 1).

Fig. 2. Workplace activity.

The D-HUMMER demonstrator was focused on the creation of the existing workplace within the IPS IMMA platform and on the evaluation of the ergonomics assessment with EAWS using the software. A common situation in the manufacturing industry is the lack of digital data on the environment and machinery. This is because 3D CAD data are not always available, especially for older production lines. In order to tackle this issue, the workstation environment was acquired through an on-site point cloud acquisition (see Fig. 3), via topometric optical projection, with usage of an optical high precision rotary laser system. It was based on a 3D optical scanning with Artec Eva system, which detects color and movement sequences (16 3D images/s). The post-processing gave.e57 files of the detected parts, which were then imported inside IPS IMMA, after a cleaning activity of the CAD model (see Fig. 4).

Fig. 3. Point cloud acquisition.

Fig. 4. Point cloud of the workstation inside IPS IMMA.

3 Results and Discussion

An example of how EAWS results are displayed in IPS IMMA is shown in Fig. 5 and Fig. 6. When working with a family of manikins, a summary table with all the information is shown (see Fig. 5.). The software provides a general overview of the ergonomics evaluation for each manikin in separate rows and the specific section or item of EAWS in separate columns.

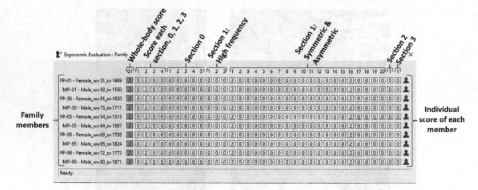

Fig. 5. Example of EAWS results for a family of manikins inside IPS IMMA.

Family   ×

2 **Whole Body Score**

| 0 Extra | 2 Postures | 0 Action Forces | 0 Loads |

Extra

| 0 0a | 0 0b | 0 0c |
| 0 0d | 0 0e |

Dynamic Postures

| 0 Frequency - Bent Forward | 0 Frequency - Kneeling or Crou | 0 Frequency - Arm Liftings |

Static Postures > 4s

2 1 - Standing and Walking	0 2 - Standing, Confined space	0 3 - Back - Bent Forward	0 4 - Back - Strongly Bent Forwa
0 5 - Elbow Above Shoulder Lev	0 6 - Hands Above Head Level	0 7 - Sitting With Back Support	0 8 - Sitting With No Back Supp
0 9 - Sitting Bent Forward	0 10 - Sitting Elbow Above Shou	0 11 - Sitting Hands Above Heac	0 12 - Kneeling or Crouching
0 13 - Bent Forward	0 14 - K/C with Elbow Above Sh	0 15 - Lying	2 (a) Sum
0 Trunk Rotation Sum	0 Lateral Bend Sum	0 Far Reach Sum	0 (b) Sum

Action Forces

| 0 Action Forces |

Loads

| 0 Loads |

Export Data   Close

Fig. 6. Example of EAWS results for a single manikin inside IPS IMMA.

The user has the option to visualize the score for each manikin individually. In this case (see Fig. 6) the software provides in detail the score for each item of the extra points section and for the static and dynamic postures of Section 1. The score for Section 2 and Section 3 is shown in case action forces and manual material handling activities are present in the working cycle. The whole-body score is displayed following the traffic light color code according to EAWS guidelines. Green implies no increased risk for strain-related MSDs, yellow ought to be investigated further, red needs immediate attention and should be analyzed in detail (Schaub et al. 2012).

By clicking on the squares with the score of each line or section, a graph will pop up showing in what part of the simulation the specific line or section is active. Figure 7. Shows an example of when the manual material handling section is active during the simulation (yellow section) and the posture assumed by the manikin in two moments during the manual handling activities. These graphs use the same color-coded system to guide the designers in recognizing the moments where the workers could be at potential risk. Since different manikins use diverse motions and are likely to assume different postures based on their stature, the ergonomics evaluation varies between manikins.

The EAWS score can be exported as a text file by just clicking on the button "Export data". This allows the user to have access to the result data and to perform additional analysis.

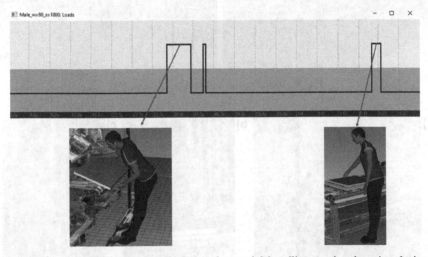

Fig. 7. Example of the graph when the manual material handling section is active during the simulation.

For the present study, the family of manikins was created based on the stature and weight of the actual workers at the refrigerator workstation (4 females and 1 male).

The IPS IMMA anthropometric module allows creating customized manikins using available anthropometric data. It is also possible to make use of the internal databases to create a family of manikins that typically covers from the very small (P5 female) to the very tall (P95 male) in order to understand hazards related to reachability, postural comfort, and others anthropometry-related factors within the working population. Table 1 reports the stature and weight of each worker at the refrigerator workstation. Figure 8. Shows the initial scene of the simulation and includes the created family of manikins.

Table 1. Main anthropometric data for the actual workers of the refrigerator workstation.

N°	Gender	Stature (mm)	Weight (Kg)
1	Female	1580	58
2	Female	1600	52
3	Female	1620	60
4	Female	1650	75
5	Male	1800	80

Fig. 8. Initial scene and family of manikins.

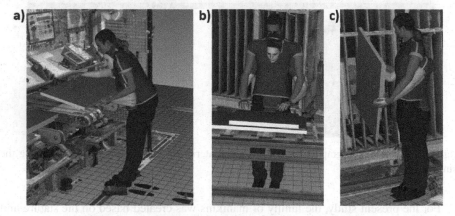

Fig. 9. Simulation of the work cycle inside IPS IMMA.

The entire work cycle at the refrigeration workplace was simulated to include the different working activities. Figure 9 depicts moments of the main activities in the task. Figure 9a shows the operator extracting the foamed door out of the door foaming machine (called drum), highlighting the degree of back bending forward requested to the operator for extracting the door. The awkward posture combined with the frequency of the handling activity represents a potential risk that needs to be assessed. Figure 9b depicts the operator at the workstation where the gasket is mounted. This operation can be quite critical for small users as visible in Fig. 2, requiring significant back bending forward and arm far reach. Running the simulation on the family of manikins can help understanding how a different height of the working tables may reduce the strain on operators. Different grasping techniques can also be analyzed and simulated. Finally, Fig. 9c shows the operator placing the door on the trolley. In this last part of the task, there are no criticalities for the adopted postures for all users although it is recommendable to evaluate the potential risk of the overall manual material handling activity considering that there are several handling activities within the task.

Table 2. EAWS results for the simulation of the refrigerator workstation.

	Section 1	Section 3					Whole body score
	Line 1	Load points	Posture points OR1	Posture points OR2	Frequency points	Score Section 3	
Female-1580	2.0	1.3	4.0	4.0	6.9	36.4	38
Female-1650	2.0	1.3	2.0	4.0	6.9	29.5	31
Male-1800	2.0	1.0	2.0	2.0	6.9	21.1	23

Table 2 synthetizes the EAWS results for the shortest and tallest female manikins as well as for the male manikin. For all manikins, the major criticality is in the manual material handling activities (Section 3). The factors that generate the high score are the adopted postures, especially for the shortest users, and the frequency of the repositioning.

Figure 10 illustrates the posture at the origin of the first lift, i.e. when the operator extracts the foamed door out of the drum. For the shortest female manikin, arms are at shoulder level, leading to four points for posture. For the tallest female and the male operators' arms are at normal working height, although some degree of back bending is requested to grasp the door on both sides, leading to two points for posture. For the second lift, only the male manikin is tall enough to maintain arms at normal working height. All female manikins are requested to lift with arms at shoulder level and are characterized by four points for posture (see Table 2). The posture classes identified by the software for the different manikins matched those selected by the Whirlpool analyst.

In compliance to European standards, the EAWS method assigns higher load points to female operators for the same mass lifted. The better posture at the origin of the lifts and the lower load points are the reason why the male manikin receives the lowest EAWS score. The shortest female manikin on the contrary receives the highest score.

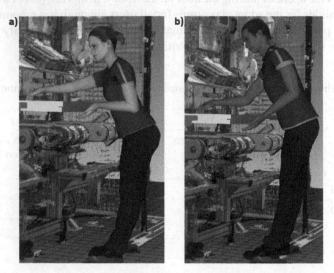

Fig. 10. Posture at the origin of the first lift, a) smallest female, b) male manikin.

In the postural section (Section 1), all manikins receive 2 points. Also for this section, the score given by the software matched the assessment performed by the Whirlpool analyst. The simulation allowed highlighting some difficulties for the shortest female manikin due to the height of the working tables and cassettes, especially compared to the male manikin (Fig. 11). However, for this specific workstation no operation requires prolonged static postures (that exceeds the 4-s threshold) or high-frequency movements that would lead to additional scores in Section 1. For all manikins, the 2 points of Section 1 come from the standing position that EAWS evaluates in line 1 of this section.

It is in any case important to emphasize the benefits offered by the IPS IMMA family of manikins to evaluate in one simulation how different percentiles interact with the workstation. Observing and assessing different operators in production can be time consuming and is rarely done.

Looking at the results in general, it is clear that the task is more suitable for tall workers as they are able to adopt better postures when grasping and handling the refrigerator door. Changing the height of worktables could help reduce strain for smaller workers as well. Workplace optimization can be easily performed using the family of manikins, and the new ergonomics assessment can be evaluated for the entire family in a single simulation.

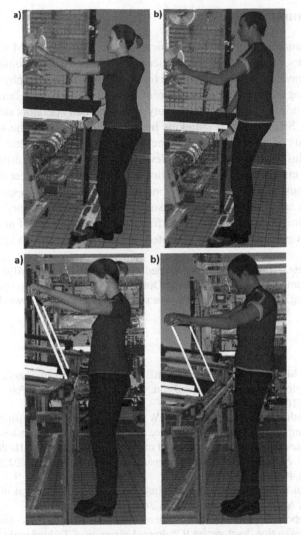

Fig. 11. Far reaching and arm posture, a) smallest female, b) male.

New workstations are currently being tested to confirm the validity of the results and refine the ergonomics evaluation and visualization of the output in the software. The results are encouraging and show that the scores provided by the software match those of experienced users, including identifying what portions of the task to assess in which section. The results also show that the software is accurate in measuring angles and posture holding time, and that it can correctly classify EAWS posture classes for different manikins and reveal critical postural issues that might not be detected by observing an individual operator at the workplace.

4 Conclusions

The implementation of a holistic ergonomic assessment inside a DHM software like IPS IMMA facilitates companies in the application of proactive ergonomics. Evaluations done in digital environments eliminate the time and cost required by physical prototypes and enable testing the workspace for different operators. The use of a family of manikins in IPS IMMA allows considering the variety among human operators simultaneously in one simulation. Since different manikins interact differently with the workplace environment in terms of postures and movements, the ergonomics evaluation results vary between manikins, highlighting different levels of physical strain for different operators. Assessing such changes through observational evaluation on different operators would be very time consuming and is rarely done in industries. In this respect, DHM tools like IPS IMMA are particularly useful also for workstation design and improvements. Workplace optimization can be easily performed using the family of manikins, and the new ergonomics assessment can be evaluated for the entire family in a single simulation.

Acknowledgments. This work has been carried out within the D-HUMMER (Digital Human Model for Ergonomic Workplace Layout and Optimized Production Process) project, funded by EIT Manufacturing, Project number 22294. The support is gratefully acknowledged.

References

Bhattacharya, A., McGlothlin, J.D.: Occupational ergonomics. In: Bhattacharya, A., McGlothlin, J.D. (eds.), Taylor & Francis Group (2nd edn, vol. 2, Issue 4). Taylor & Francis Group (2012). https://doi.org/10.1201/b11717

Bouziri, H., Descatha, A., Roquelaure, Y., Dab, W., Jean, K.: Can we distinguish the roles of demographic and temporal changes in the incidence and prevalence of musculoskeletal disorders? A systematic review. In: Scandinavian Journal of Work, Environment and Health, vol. 48, Issue 4, pp. 253–263. Nordic Association of Occupational Safety and Health (2022). https://doi.org/10.5271/sjweh.4018

Brolin, E.: Design of a digital human modelling module for consideration of anthropometric diversity. Adv. Appl. Digital Hum. Model. (2014)

Brolin, E.: Anthropometric diversity and consideration of human capabilities - Methods for virtual product and production development [Chalmers University of Technology] (2016). http://publications.lib.chalmers.se/records/fulltext/232940/232940.pdf

Brolin, E., et al.: Creation of the IMMA manikin with consideration of anthropometric diversity. In: 21st International Conference on Production Research (2011). https://www.researchgate.net/publication/247778095

Brolin, E., Högberg, D., Hanson, L.: Description of boundary case methodology for anthropometric diversity consideration. Int. J. Hum. Factors Model. Simul. 3(2), 204 (2012). https://doi.org/10.1504/ijhfms.2012.051097

Brolin, E., Högberg, D., Hanson, L., Örtengren, R.: Development and evaluation of an anthropometric module for digital human modelling systems. Int. Jo. Hum. Factors Model. Simul. 7(1), 47 (2019). https://doi.org/10.1504/ijhfms.2019.102178

Demirel, H.O., Ahmed, S., Duffy, V.G.: Digital human modeling: a review and reappraisal of origins, present, and expected future methods for representing humans computationally. Int. J. Hum.-Comput. Interact. **38**(10), 897–937 (2022). https://doi.org/10.1080/10447318.2021.1976507

European agency for safety and health at work. Work-related MSDs: prevalence, costs and demographics in the EU. In: European Statistics on Accidents at Work. European Health (2019). http://europa.eu

fleXstructures. (2020). Digital Assembly Planning and Ergonomics, flexstructures GmbH Kaiserslautern. Digital Assembly Planning and Ergonomics. https://flexstructures.com/solutions/digital-assembly-planning-and-ergonomics/

Punnett, L., Wegman, D.H.: Work-related musculoskeletal disorders: the epidemiologic evidence and the debate. J. Electromyogr. Kinesiol. 14(1), 13–23 (2004). https://doi.org/10.1016/j.jelekin.2003.09.015

Roquelaure, Y.: Musculoskeletal disorders and psychosocial factors at work (2018)

Schaub, K., Kugler, M., Bierwirth, M., Sinn-Behrendt, A., Bruder, R.: Prevention of MSD by means of ergonomic risk assessment (tools) in all phases of the vehicle development process. Work 41(SUPPL.1), 4409–4412 (2012a). https://doi.org/10.3233/WOR-2012-0738-4409

Schaub, K., et al.: Ergonomic assessment of automotive assembly tasks with digital human modelling and the "ergonomics assessment worksheet" (EAWS). Int. J. Hum. Fact. Model. Simul. 3, 398–426 (2012b)

Schaub, K., Caragnano, G., Britzke, B., Bruder, R.: The European assembly worksheet. Theor. Issues Ergon. Sci. 14(6), 616–639 (2013). https://doi.org/10.1080/1463922X.2012.678283

Improving Ergonomic Training Using Augmented Reality Feedback

Diego Vicente[1] , Mario Schwarz[2] , and Gerrit Meixner[2(✉)]

[1] Centro de Informática Médica y Telemedicina (CIMT), Universidad de Chile, Santiago de Chile, Chile
diego.vicente@ug.uchile.cl
[2] Usability and Interaction Technology Laboratory (UniTyLab), Heilbronn University, Heilbronn, Germany
{mario.schwarz,gerrit.meixner}@hs-heilbronn.de

Abstract. Work-related musculoskeletal disorders are costly to economies and society, and are the most common work-related health problems. In the European Union and the United States, 30–40% of workers reported work-related musculoskeletal disorders at least in the last decade. Effective ergonomics interventions can be difficult and expensive to implement, leaving administrative measures such as rest breaks, job rotation, and ergonomic training as the main interventions. However, traditional ergonomic training often lacks effectiveness due to design flaws. With advancements in technology, motion capture and pose estimation technologies based on Augmented Reality and Virtual Reality have been proposed as solutions, but these still have limitations such as they are not participative and are not conducted in the actual workplace. This study aimed to evaluate the effectiveness and usability of an AR pose estimation prototype intended for use as real-time visual feedback in ergonomic training at the workplace. Mediapipe Pose, a computer vision solution from Google, was used to project holograms on the bodies of participants based on a custom Rapid Upper Limb Assessment calculation on shoulders, elbows, neck and back. The participants performed a simulated task and were randomly assigned to one of two groups for practical training. AR Group (n = 5) received AR pose estimation ET with a big screen to provide visual feedback to detect postural exposures and improve technique. The Control group (n = 4) received feedback from an ergonomics specialist. The effectiveness of each ET intervention was measured using a custom time-weighted Rapid Upper Limb Assessment-based score showing positive results from both interventions, the AR pose intervention and the Control Group. The usability of the AR prototype was evaluated using the Post-study System Usability Questionnaire and Bipolar Laddering which resulted in both positive and negative points which are going to be used as input for future improvement of the AR prototype. The results of the study showed promising results in terms of the AR pose estimation prototype being effective in transferring knowledge into behavior. Overall, the AR group showed a greater learning effect than the control group. However, these results have to be taken with caution in relation to the number of participants. The study may contribute to enhancing the outcomes of ET and expanding the field of study on its potential impact on health and safety culture in organizations. The improved prototype will be tested in a real occupational context to further assess its effectiveness.

Keywords: Ergonomics training · Augmented Reality · Computer Vision

1   Introduction

Musculoskeletal disorders (MSDs) include a wide range of inflammatory and degenerative conditions that affect muscles, tendons, ligaments, joints, peripheral nerves, and blood vessels. They may arise from diseases affecting the musculoskeletal system, sports activities, or from work. If MSDs are related to risk factors present in the workplace, they are referred to as work-related musculoskeletal disorders (WRMSDs), which can arise from either a mechanical overload on a specific part of the musculoskeletal system capable of causing accumulated trauma over time associated with insufficient rest for physiological recovery, or from a single overload that exceeds the tissue's resistance, causing an injury [1–3]. Upper limb and back WRMSD are the most common, affecting shoulders (e.g., rotator cuff syndrome: shoulder impingement syndrome, subacromial impingement syndrome, subacromial bursitis, rotator cuff tendonitis, and rotator cuff tears both partial- or full-thickness); elbows (e.g., lateral and medial epicondylitis); wrist, hands, and fingers, which includes both hand-wrist tendinitis, tenosynovitis, carpal tunnel syndrome, ulnar tunnel syndrome and trigger fingers [1–3]. MSDs remain the most frequent health problem among workers in both the United States and the European Union countries, even after various efforts and initiatives have been implemented to address the issue [1,2,4,5]. Back pain complaints reached 43% in the European Union in 2015, with upper extremities at 41% and lower extremities at 29% [4]. The same year, the International Labour Organization estimated that WRMSD represented 40% of the global cost in compensation for work-related injuries and diseases [6]. In Nordic countries, the direct cost was estimated at between 2.7% and 5.2% of the Gross Domestic Product in 2003, and between 15.2% and 22.2% if all associated costs were included [1].

There are many classes of risk factors for WRMSD but the most important are biomechanicals in relationship with task requirements, such as strength, repetitiveness, non-neutral anatomic postures, static postures, and external compression forces; also organizational and psychosocial factors such as employment conditions, daily duration of different tasks and job, working pace imposed by production line, payment systems (salary according to the quantity produced), low decision capacity for rest breaks, among others; environmental factors such as cold temperature and vibration exposures are also important [1–3]; there are also relevant both personal and non-work-related factors such as age, previous clinical history, physical capabilities, gender, sports, and leisure activities, and inadequate postural habits, among others [1–3]. Evidence shows that workers who are simultaneously exposed to both biomechanical and organizational/psychosocial factors have more probability to report symptoms compared to being exposed separately to each of them [1]. The most effective programs for managing ergonomic risks to reduce the hazards of WRMSD follow the "Hierarchy of Preventive Measures" approach, which advocates for either eliminating or substituting the hazard by physically removing it or replacing it with a lower-risk alternative [7], but it can be difficult to implement in established work processes. Engineering controls include mechanical assist devices, fixtures, and lighter-weight packaging materials [7], which also involve redesigning production lines, furniture, and tools accordingly to the anthropometry of the population but it can also be difficult to implement. Administrative controls are practices and policies for workers to follow until engineering controls become feasible, such as reducing the length of shifts, job rotation, more breaks, varying tasks, and employee training such as Ergonomics Training (ET) [7]. In the context of either difficult interventions or high residual risk after control measures implementation, the risk exposure ends up being prolonged in time. In consequence, administrative controls become the main interventions [1,2,8] which sometimes are not enough to reduce the WRMSD incidence [4,5]. ET is the fourth most important element in an ergonomics program [7,9], but traditional ET use to have several design flaws since are usually low-engaging expository lectures, conducted in training rooms rather than on the job site [10–12], they usually contain PowerPoint presentations or posters with generic images or videos representing «correct posture» and «incorrect postures» which are often scenes as reference but not necessarily related to the work performed [10,11]. That tends to reduce its effectiveness in terms of transferring knowledge to workers' behaviors related to control measures adoption and its persistence in the workplace.

A systematic review [11] showed that ET programs targeted at visually engaging workers and allowing for practice sessions were effective at achieving a long-term reduction in WRMSD in computer users. Moreover, Denadai et al. [9] carried out an ET by providing a 40-minute theoretical lecture followed by a group video analysis of the participants to minimize the risk of WRMSD, and also, they provided a booklet with pictures of participants classifying the adopted postures as adequate or at risk. The intervention was capable to obtain a reduction in both, biomechanical exposure evaluated with a custom assessment checklist based on Rapid Upper Limb Assessment (RULA) [13], as well as musculoskeletal symptoms in the neck and upper limbs in a poultry company. Consistent with the above, the more engaging training is designed the better the knowledge acquisition that leads to transfer learning and the reduction in lost time injuries [9,11].

In that sense, the progress in technology such as artificial intelligence and interaction devices, motion capture, and computer-based pose estimation technologies are constantly improving to open up new opportunities for Augmented Reality (AR) and Virtual Reality (VR) solutions which are becoming very active fields for research [14–17]. Casey et al. [12] stated that immersive virtual environments and gamification can improve ET by increasing interest, inducing strong emotions, and facilitating stronger neuronal connections in the amygdala; so that these advancements can help to enhance the learning experience of physical skills and motor movements through immersive scenarios that provide real-time feedback capable to improve the effectiveness of transfer learning into behavior [12,14,16]. Two research tools for usability assessment usually applied in the development process of either AR or VR are the Post-Study System Usability Questionnaire (PSSUQ) [18] and Bipolar Laddering (BL) [19]. This work assesses the preliminary effectiveness and usability of a prototype for AR pose estimation designed to be used as visual feedback in ET at the workplace.

The research questions that lead the study are: How does the effectiveness of the prototype fare in terms of immediate transfer of knowledge to behavior compared to an engaging participatory video analysis, followed by video demonstrations? How can this prototype solution be improved based on user experience and feedback?

2   Methods

2.1   AR Pose Estimation Prototype

Used Technologies and Virtual Skeleton Model. MediaPipe is a set of open-source, ready-to-use, extensible, and customizable cross-platform machine learning solutions developed by Google, available in C++, Python, Android, and iOS. One of its solutions is MediaPipe Pose, which is a high-fidelity pose estimation tool that uses Google's research BlazePose [20]. The system takes as input an RGB image or video frames and produces as output a list of 3D locations (pose_landmarks) of key anatomical points for a person in the image, which usually indicate the position of certain joints, in the following format [x, y, z, Visibility]. The [x] and [y] values represent the normalized coordinates between [0.0, 1.0] with respect to the width and height of the image (w × h) respectively; [z] Represents the depth of the key anatomical point, with the midpoint between both hips as the origin [0.0, 0.0, 0.0]. The z coordinate is a value in "image pixels" like [x] and [y]. Negative values indicate a position between the camera and the midpoint between the hips, and positive values indicate a position behind the midpoint between the hips. The [Visibility] is a value between [0.0, 1.0] and denotes the probability that the key anatomical point is located within the frame and not occluded by another part of the body or another object. The model tracks the pose in two steps: using a detector (Fig. 1a and Fig. 1b), the algorithm locates the person's face and pose region of interest (ROI) within the frame, then the tracker predicts the pose reference points and segmentation mask within the ROI using the cropped ROI frame as input 2. In video use cases, the detector is only invoked when needed, for example, for the first frame and when the tracker could not identify the presence of the body posture in the previous frame. For other video frames, the pipeline derives the ROI from the pose reference points of the previous frame.

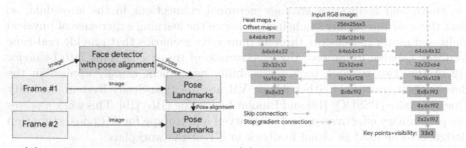

(a) Mediapipe Pose detection model.   (b) Convolutional neural network structure

Fig. 1. Extracted from [20]

The application was developed using Python, leveraging libraries such as CSV, math, and NumPy to process the human pose estimation data from Mediapipe Pose. The 3D positions of key anatomical points were used to build a virtual skeleton model. The midpoint between the hips served as the origin, and the midpoint between the shoulders defined the trunk vector as the body's centerline. Vectors of body segments and local anatomical axes were calculated as the result of subtracting the 3D positions of the joints that form them. For example, the right arm segment was obtained by subtracting the coordinates of the right shoulder and right elbow. Similarly, the three main axes of each joint were calculated to identify the three anatomical planes at a local level, for example, an x-axis was defined as the vector from the origin to the left hip, the related y-axis was defined as the trunk vector, and the z-axis was calculated using the cross product between x and y axes. At this point, the main procedure can be summarized as follows: Step 1, set joint landmarks according to coordinates position. This is determined based on the number and topology of Mediapipe landmarks, as depicted in Fig. 2; Step 2, define joint local axis coordinate system. The joint local axis coordinate system is established by using the NumPy np.subtract method for calculations as explained above; Step 3: Calculate angles between bones vectors and 3D joint local coordinate axes. At this point the Python code was debugged by streaming data to Unity Hub to implement C# functions in Python, including adaptations such as "Vector3.Angle", "Vector3.SignedAngle", and "Vector3.ProjectOnPlane" functions for angle calculations. The angles between the bone vectors and joint coordinate axis were calculated, specifically for the shoulders the relationship between 3D planes and the arm for angle calculation was taken from [21]. In the case of elbows, neck, and back the angles are calculated between bones or projected vectors as follows: the angle calculation for neck flexion/extension was evaluated by defining two vectors, the first vector_neck results from subtraction between the midpoint between shoulders and points to the custom Mid-Head landmark (midpoint between ears), and the second, by the subtraction of the midpoint between shoulders and the origin at the midpoint between hips but negative

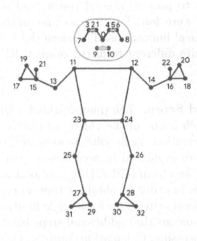

Mediapipe's topology:
0. Nose; 1. Left eye inner; 2. Left eye;
3. Left eye outer; 4. Right eye inner;
5. Right eye; 6. Right eye outer; 7.
Left ear; 8. Right ear; 9. Mouth left;
10. Mouth right; 11. Left shoulder;
12. Right shoulder; 13. Left elbow; 14.
Right elbow; 15. Left wrist; 16. Right
wrist; 17. Left pinky #1 knuckle; 18.
Right pinky #1 knuckle; 19. Left index #1 knuckle; 20. Right index #1
knuckle; 21. Left thumb #2 knuckle;
22. Right thumb #2 knuckle; 23. Left
hip; 24. Right hip; 25. Left knee; 26.
Right knee; 27. Left ankle; 28. Right
ankle; 29. Left heel; 30. Right heel; 31.
Left foot index; 32. Right foot index.

Fig. 2. Mediapipe Pose «landmarks» and output enumeration. Extracted from [20]

(opposite direction), which means it starts from the midpoint between shoulders
and points up vertical, a third vector starting from midpoint between shoulders
and pointing to the left shoulder was used for the axis and plane definition. Similar to this, the back flexion was calculated as the angle between two vectors: the
first starts from the midpoint of the feet pointing to the origin, and the other
vector is the trunk vector as described above and the axis vector starting from
the origin and pointing to the left hip.

Planning and Implementation. The initial plan of the project was to adapt
and improve on an existing application that was built with Google Mediapipe.
The main points planned were an adaptation to work with an AR device,
improved angle calculation and visuals, as well as better feedback according
to RULA criteria. At the beginning, the application was supposed to be built
and deployed on the Microsoft Hololens 2 AR device. The main advantage of
this approach was thought to be a mobile and hands-free experience. However,
this approach soon proved to be out of scale for this type of project as it introduced a lot of potential problem sources while trying to run the existing code
and systems on the Hololens in a standalone version. After that, the new solution was built for a laptop with a wireless smartphone acting as the camera, so
that the improved mobility features can be retained. This change also provided
other benefits as reduced cost for hardware as more common devices could be
used, as well as a shared screen that allows multiple people to view the same
experience without needing multiple AR devices. The evaluation planned to
include an adapted RULA scoring system to provide a numerical score to
recorded postures, but adjustments had to be made as the original RULA method

is not designed for continuous real-time evaluation. Landmark accuracy of certain body parts was not accurate enough to provide a good result, and some features like wrist movement or strength were found to be too inaccurate to include in the scoring system due to technical limitations. Therefore the implemented scoring system ended up being quite different from the original RULA system.

Custom Time-Weighted RULA-Based Score. The time-weighted RULA-based score calculation was updated at each frame of the video. To reduce the jittering from Mediapipe on landmark detection, each joint is averaged over the last 3 detected positions. The joints are evaluated in accordance with the posture criteria for both angles and score taken from RULA [13], this joint score includes the elapsed time in its calculation in order to obtain a time-weighted score. Figure 3 shows the shoulder's assessment criteria for both angle limits and score rating based on image-scores only. It means that additional steps like "1a" present in Fig. 3 were all discarded from processing. Calculation consists of a sum of time-weighted RULA-based scores for each joint at every frame, and then the result is divided by the number of joints. This average, called "AverageScore", is calculated each frame and then is added to the "TotalScore" which is based on all previous frames since the start of the recording in a cumulative way. Finally a "RoundedScore" is calculated at the end of the video or real-time camera processing by taking the total score and dividing it by the duration of the video.

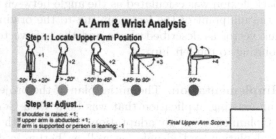

Fig. 3. RULA-Based posture, score criteria and colors assignations for shoulders. Steps 1a were discarded in our design (adding +1 if shoulder and so on). Image adapted from RULA Employee Assessment Worksheet [13].

2.2 Post-Study System Usability Questionnaire and Bipolar Laddering (BL)

The PSSUQ is a type of questionnaire used to evaluate the usability of a system or application after it has been used by participants in a study. It consists of multiple questions that can be attributed to one of three categories. In this study, version 2 of the questionnaire has been used which consists of 19 questions. Each question is positively formulated and ranges from 1 (strongly agree) to 7 (strongly disagree), therefore a lower value indicates a better experience using the system. System Usefulness is derived from questions 1 through 8, Information Quality is derived from questions 9 through 15 and Interface Quality is derived from questions 16 to 18. Question 19 is reserved for the overall satisfaction with the tested system. Values have been rounded to 3 decimal places. The mean category scores of an analysis of the PSSUQ from 2002 [22] are provided for comparison.

Bipolar Laddering was used to extract informative opinions directly from the study participants by asking for their positive and negative thoughts on the prototype based on the work of [19].

2.3 Study Design

An invitation to participate in the study was sent by an email to the students of the Computer Science faculty of Heilbronn University. The individual contacts were made and they were invited to join the study. On the individual study days, the procedure was the following:

1. **Pre-training individual video recordings of simulated occupational task**
   Participants were individually asked to perform a simulated occupational task while video recordings were taken, one by one. In this task, a crate with 11 half-filled plastic bottles (about 250 ml each), had to be transported to a table, an then picked each bottle out of the crate and put it on the table. After that, they picked each bottle back into the crate to fill it again and transported the crate back to the original position on the floor, followed by the participant returning back to the starting point. This task was chosen based on simplicity, visibility of joints for evaluation, postural requirements such as the need for bending down to pick up the crate and flexion, and abduction of shoulders to pick up the bottles and put them over the table.
2. **Theoretical Ergonomics Training lecture**
   A 40-minute theoretical ET lecture was provided by an ergonomics specialist to simulate an industrial setting and to give the participants a basic understanding of ergonomics, how WRMSD can occur, among the content included: basic human anatomy and upper limbs biomechanics of shoulder, elbows, neck, and back in relationship with the most common WRMSD.
3. **Dividing participants into groups**
   The random group allocation was made by asking the participants to build a line, and then every other participant was told to move to either the Control Group or the AR group location.
4. **Control Group and AR group practical training**
   The Control Group participated in a practical lecture which started with a task analysis provided by the ergonomics specialist followed by instructions about how to improve the working technique, and then the task was practiced while talking feedback was provided by the ergonomist mainly but the group participation was allowed to discuss the performance. In parallel, the AR group participated in a practical lecture using the AR system streamed to

a big screen, so each participant was able to see their own body joints with holographic spheres which turned into traffic light colors to provide real-time visual feedback like a mirror with holograms. The groups were separated by removable walls that had been previously set up.

5. **Pre-training individual video recordings of simulated occupational task**

Same as in step 1, but after the lecture and training in order to compare data processing with step 1.

6. **Filling out PSSUQ and BL questionaires**

PSSUQ questionnaires were given to participants in the AR group. However, two participants from the Control Group filled out the PSSUQ questionnaire due to an excess of copies available, but their answers were mistakenly included with the AR Group results, affecting the accuracy. Due to the anonymous testing, their answers couldn't be separated from the AR Group results. BL questionnaires were given to participants in the AR group and each one of them was interviewed to deepen into the topics and write the results manually on the paper.

2.4 Data Acquisition, and Processing

The data collected from PSSUQ and BL was digitized into google drive spreadsheets for further analysis. The experiments from AR system and video processing were run on a Laptop Dell XPS-13–9310, Ubuntu 20.04.1 LTS (Processor: 11th Gen Intel® Core™ i7-1165G7 @ 2.80 GHz × 8; Memory: 15.3 Gib; Graphics: Mesa Intel® Xe Graphics (TGL GT2)). The AR video processing script was coded in Python 3.8.10. Since the frame rate of Mediapipe Pose deploying videos depends on processing power, we were interested in testing the overall performance of the prototype, so we decided to run the experiments on a "common-home" computer. The script consisted of running each video 10 times by using a "for loop", the same process was done 10 times in total in order to reach 100 times (due to processing power, it was not possible to run all the experiments within a big 100 times "for loop"). After each 10 times loop, a CSV file was obtained and saved for later data processing. The data processing pipeline was coded in Python and implemented within the Google Colaboratory service, the script included the following libraries: Pandas, NumPy, and SciPy; graphs were displayed using libraries such as Matplotlib and Seaborn within the same pipeline script. The procedure consisted of importing all the data from CSV files to build a big Pandas Dataframe object, then the data was sorted and filtered to run normality tests of samples and within-participant comparison before and after intervention by using, respectively, stats.normaltest and stats.ttest_ind functions where statistical significance was assessed with a p-value ≤ 0.001.

The average change pre- and post-intervention of all participants within each group were obtained using the stats.norm.fit function for 100 samples from each participant's videos, but further comparison between was limited by reduced number of participants.

3   Results

Figure 4 shows the resulting display of a video being processed. Semi-transparent holographic spheres over the following landmarks (Fig. 4a) which turn into traffic light colors are deployed into the screen to provide real-time visual feedback like a mirror with holograms. Similar images to Fig. 4b were able to see by the participants when the practical ET was done with the AR intervention group. A "TotalScore" is shown on the screen as a time-cumulative score obtained at each frame which depends on both the posture risk exposure and video duration. An "AverageScore" is shown as the result of the actual frame.

The main features of the Prototype are described as follows:

- Video Input: Recorded videos of people performing their job can be processed and evaluated to obtain different scores.
- Camera Input: Instead of using recorded videos, any computer-recognized camera can be used as an input source for live evaluation. For the purpose of the study, a Smartphone (Samsung Galaxy S10 lite) was used as a mobile webcam.
- Landmarks Detection: Based on the Landmarks provided by Mediapipe, the landmarks have been reorganized to better suit our needs. As seen in Fig. 4, the Midd-Head was custom calculated (explained in Subsect. 2.1)
- Angle Calculation: The program is internally calculating the angles based on the RULA system. The calculated angles are used as a base for the final score.
- Visual Feedback: Depending on the angle calculation the semitransparent holograms covering both shoulders, elbow, neck, and back change their overlay color from green (good) over yellow and orange to red (bad). This provides quick visual feedback without overwhelming detail. Grey lines and circles represent landmarks like joints and bones that were not included in the evaluation but are still included for visual orientation
- Scoring System: The current "AverageScore", as well as the "TotalScore" are displayed in the top left of the screen beside information about the frame rate of the application. A "RoundedScore" is calculated at the end of the video.

3.1   Data from Video Processing

The participant's video recording after random assignation following the theoretical lecture was: ARGroup = [3,5,7,8,10], and controlGroup = [1,2,4,6], the number identified both videos and participants. Since our interest was to evaluate if the set of samples from each video being processed 100 times was distributed normally or not, our evaluation showed that participant n°4 after intervention

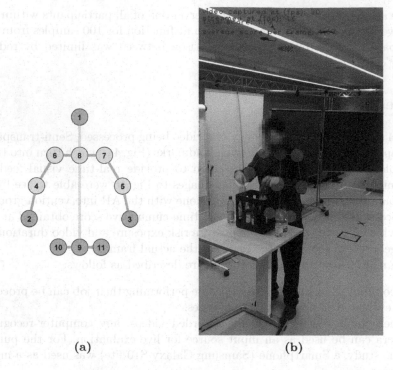

(a)   (b)

Fig. 4. 4a shows the AR Prototype landmark used in this solution: 1. The resulting landmarks are 1. Midd-Head (custom calculated); 2. Left Hand; 3. Right Hand; 4. Left Elbow; 5. Right Elbow; 6. Left Shoulder; 7. Right Shoulder; 8. Shoulder Center; 9. Hip center; 10. Left Hip; 11. Right Hip; 4b shows the resulting display of a video being processed with holographic spheres with traffic light colors and "TotalScore" and "AverageScore" for each frame.

(ControlGroup) was the only video processing that resulted in a "non-normally distributed" set of samples, showing an outlier sample in "TotalTime" (Fig. 5a) (statistic= 50.490, p-value = 1.087e-11) and "TotalScore" (Fig. 5b) (statistic = 51.982, p-value = 5.156e-12), but it is important to remark that, the "RoundedScore" (Fig. 5c) of the same video resulted in a normally distributed set of samples (statistic = 1.1135 p-value = 0.573), which is important since "RoundedScore" was designed to be independent of video duration or data processing power. Figure 5 shows the results as a histogram of probability density from running the AR-Pose algorithm 100 times in the video of participant n°4 after intervention explained above.

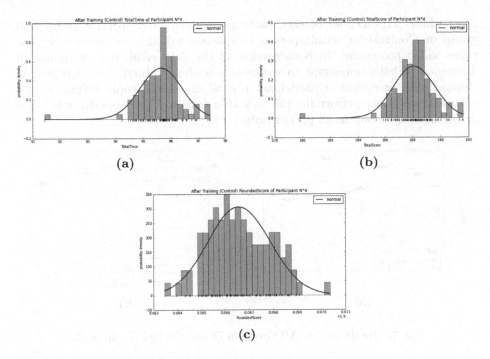

(a)   (b)

(c)

Fig. 5. Example of «RoundedScore» Histogram of probability density from running the AR-Pose algorithm 100 times after the intervention. Note that the power processing of the computer affects frame rate of Mediapipe processing and video output, which has influence on 5a "TotalTime", generating an outlier data seen only at the video of participant n°4; 5b "TotalScore" of the same participant is also affected, but in 5c "RoundedScore" calculation was a custom design intended to be independent of video duration or power processing of the computer.

3.2 Within Participant Pre-intervention Vs Post-intervention Comparison

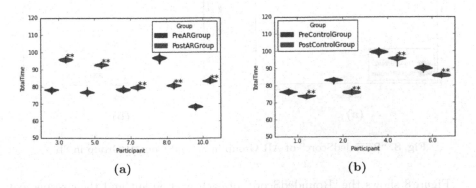

(a)   (b)

Fig. 6. "TotalTime" of AR Group in 6a and Control Group in 6b

Fig. 6 shows "TotalTime" of each participant and their respective group (AR group or Control) for within-person comparison taking into account the 100 times video processing. In both groups all the data resulted in a significant difference. What's important to notice is a tendency about the "direction" of change: with exception of participant n°8 all the other people within the AR group lasted longer performing the task after training. The opposite was found in the Control Group in all participants.

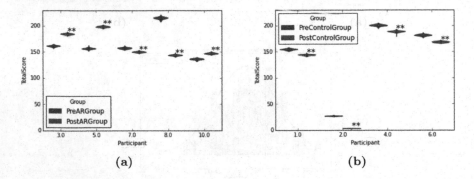

Fig. 7. "TotalScore" of AR Group in 7a and Control Group in 7b

Figure 7 shows "TotalScore" of each participant and their respective group (AR group or Control) for within-person comparison taking into account the 100 times video processing. In both groups, all the data resulted in a significant difference. Since the "TotalScore" is influenced by video duration and pose estimation it's important to notice the same tendency as "TotalTime" in participants n°3, n°5, and n°10; participants n°7 and n°8 reduced it's "TotalScore". In the control group in all participants improved reducing their "TotalScore".

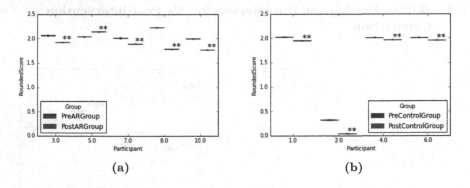

Fig. 8. "RoundedScore" of AR Group in 8a and Control Group in 8b

Figure 8 shows the "RoundedScore" of each participant and their respective group (AR group or Control) for within-person comparison taking into account the 100 times processed video. In both groups, all the data resulted in a significant difference. Almost, all participants had a decrease in "RoundedScore", which equals an improved posture during the task, except for participant n°5 in the AR group that had a worse score than before the training. However, the average decrease in "RoundedScore" was still **47.7%** higher in the AR group (**0.167**) compared to the control group (**0.113**), even with participant n°5 values included. Overall, the AR group showed in average a greater learning effect than the control group.

3.3   Post-Study System Usability Questionnaire

System Usefulness. The best score in this category were questions n°2 and n°7. Participants liked how easy to use the system is and how quickly they could use it. The worst scoring question was number 5, which might be explained by the fact that the question doesn't apply as the task was never done while the instant feedback system was running. Another explanation might be that using the system took time and concentration away from the task for learning purposes and slowed down the task completion. The total System Usefulness score was **2.286**, which is **0.514** points better than the mean score found in the PSSUQ study (**2.80**) [22]. The category score is based on the average of the following individual question scores.

Number	Question	Answers	Average Score (1–7)
1	"Overall, I am satisfied with how easy it is to use this system."	7	2.143
2	"It was simple to use this system."	7	1.857
3	"I could effectively complete the tasks and scenarios using this system."	7	2.286
4	"I was able to complete the tasks and scenarios quickly using this system."	7	2.714
5	"I was able to efficiently complete the tasks and scenarios using this system."	7	2.857
6	"I felt comfortable using this system."	7	2.286
7	"It was easy to learn to use this system."	7	1.857
8	"I believe I could become productive quickly using this system."	7	2.286

Information Quality. The best score in this category was question 13, which means participants liked the way the visual overlay was easy to understand and tied in with the most liked aspects of the System Usefulness category. The worst scoring question was number 10, which could be attributed to a difficulty adjusting correctly when a bad posture was detected, or when the tracking was lost behind an object for example. The total Information Quality score was

2.221, which is **0.799** points better than the mean score found in the PSSUQ study (**3.02**) [22]. The category score is based on the average of the following individual question scores.

Number	Question	Answers	Average Score (1–7)
9	"The system gave error messages that clearly told me how to fix problems."	7	2.714
10	"Whenever I made a mistake using the system, I could recover easily and quickly."	6	3.429
11	"The information (such as on-line help, on-screen messages and other documentation) provided with this system was clear."	6	2
12	"It was easy to find the information I needed."	6	2.167
13	"The information provided for the system was easy to understand."	6	1.5
14	"The information was effective in helping me complete the tasks and scenarios."	6	2.286
15	"The organization of information on the system screens was clear."	6	1.857

Interface Quality. The best score in this category was question number 16, as the interface was seen as pleasant. The worst score in this category was question number 17. The total Interface Quality score was **2.357**, which is **0.133** points better than the mean score found in the PSSUQ study (**2.49**) [22]. The category score is based on the average of the following individual question scores.

Number	Question	Answers	Average Score (1–7)
16	"The interface of this system was pleasant."	6	2.167
17	"I liked using the interface of this system."	6	2.571
18	"This system has all the functions and capabilities I expect it to have."	6	2.333

Total Score (PSSUQ). The total score is determined by an average of all the 19 questions, including the 19th question "Overall, I am satisfied with this system." which does not belong to any other category. For the 19th question, 7 answers have been submitted which result in an average score of 2.571. The total average of all 19 questions is **2.284**, which is **0.536** points better than the mean score found in the PSSUQ study (**2.82**) [22]. Each individual category and the resulting total score performed better than the corresponding score from the PSSUQ study. Therefore the prototype seems to have been better received by the participants than most other PSSUQ-tested applications.

3.4   Bipolar Laddering (BL)

Bipolar Laddering was used to extract informative opinions directly from the study participants by asking for their positive and negative thoughts on the prototype, instead of already providing the options for them to rate like in the PSSUQ. The result is a list of different positive and negative points which are given an impact score and the reason those points are important. Of the low number of participants, there were few common elements. In the following, the positive and negative elements have been summarized and merged into the main feedback points.

Positive prototype elements:

- The system provides real-time, live detection of posture.
- The system tracks the user's behavior and provides instant feedback on bad posture.
- It is based on previous research.
- The prototype guides the user to a better posture.
- The system is easy to understand and provides clear visual feedback on the location of posture problems.

The positive elements showcase the strengths of the prototype and what is working well for the users. The real-time live detection of posture, the instant feedback, the ease of use, and the clear visual feedback all contribute to a positive user experience and highlight the potential for the prototype to be effective in improving posture.

Negative prototype elements:

- The system could benefit from additional UI elements, such as angle information and arrows to guide correction.
- The box could be heavier for a more realistic feel.
- The dots marking the joints could be easier to see, less transparent, and smaller to improve visibility.
- There is a lack of instructions on how to use the system.
- More cameras may be needed to more accurately determine the user's posture.
- The system does not consider unique body types and may not accurately detect all users.
- Tests should be run to determine differences in detection between men and women.
- The back feedback could be made larger and generally more visible.

– The exact score is hard to see and could be improved with changes in color and size.

The negative elements identify areas for improvement and potential problems with the prototype. The lack of clear information on proper posture and the difficulty in correcting positions are both important to address because they may impact the effectiveness of the prototype in helping users improve their posture. Additionally, the perceived limitations experienced by some users in the accuracy of landmark detection attributed to either different body types or men and women differences are important considerations to keep in mind as a need for further research to make the prototype as inclusive and effective as possible.

By taking these positive and negative elements into consideration, the application can be improved to better meet the needs of the users and effectively help them improve their posture. This can be done by incorporating additional UI elements, such as angle information and arrows to guide correction, and making improvements to the visual feedback, such as making the exact score easier to see and more stable. Different methods could be used to improve landmark detection like a more robust machine learning pose estimation algorithm.

4   Discussion

An interesting aspect of the results is that just one set of samples from the video processing had a non-normal distribution, which is unexpected because in this instance the video processing was way faster than the other 99 times.

Regarding Time and Score results, there was a tendency for the majority of participants in the AR group to perform for a longer time if compared to their previous results. We propose that AR Group people were trying to integrate and actually learn a different motor pattern and it takes more time to perform better, similar to learning a new sport or a new dance. The opposite was found in the Control Group in which all participants reduced their performance time "TotalTime". Participant n°8 reduced both its "TotalTime", "TotalScore" and also the "RoundedScore" and this is the kind of behavior to be expected in people who actually improve their motor pattern and motor learning by getting skilled at work by performing a safer technique. In the case of the control group they performed significantly faster ("TotalTime") in comparison to their previous results, but the "RoundedScore" didn't show as much reduction. In general, this means that guided feedback intervention was also effective but a more robust comparison is limited due to the reduced number of participants which is not enough to be able to provide conclusive evidence of differences when compared between groups.

This prototype was built also with the intention of integrating some of the evidence for producing ET within the most engaging category, according to the meta-analysis of Burke et al. in 2006 [10]. Burke's work divided the engagement of training methods in occupational health and safety into three categories: the most engaging, which includes behavioral modeling, practical demonstrations, and dialogue; the most engaging methods are three times more effective than the least effective methods in promoting knowledge and skill acquisition. Practical demonstrations and behavioral simulations with active participation from students and trainers were recommended as they go beyond one-way feedback and encourage students to reflect on their actions, which is considered important for knowledge acquisition and training transfer. We decided to introduce gamification characteristics from scoring systems trying to enable creativity from future users and research which can also boost engagement by providing more detailed performance feedback and personalized training feedback [12]. Our prototype gathers those ideas from research and mixes them with common practices from different disciplines such as in gym and dance where people usually look at their motor performance in mirrors for visual feedback and to improve their motor patterns. AR pose solution is quite similar but it includes semitransparent holograms covering specific landmarks which changes the overlay color to provide feedback about posture performance. From the PSSUQ we decided to highlight questions with a better score such as "The information provided for the system was easy to understand.", scoring 1.5; and the worse score "Whenever I made a mistake using the system, I could recover easily and quickly", scoring 3.429, which if combined with Bipolar Laddering results such as "The system could benefit from additional UI elements, such as angle information and arrows to guide correction"; "here is a lack of instructions on how to use the system". Those answers are indicative of a lack of user-guidance information. By looking at the negative points (Back feedback too small; Exact score hard to see), the improved version must increase the font size, change the font colors and use a bigger screen or projected images, as well as include more instructions related to feedback in order to optimize the workflow and correct the posture.

4.1 Future Works

The results indicate that AR has the potential to enhance the ET effectiveness in terms of transferring the learned knowledge into behavior for each participant compared with themselves before intervention. The majority of ET group participants showed a longer time required to perform a task and at the same time showed a reduction of "RoundedScore" as indicative of improved motion strategies. This AR prototype needs to be improved based on feedback from the AR Group, so we decided that a future release should include arrows or another indicator of which direction the stance should be corrected in order to improve. Also, we consider implementing and testing the AR prototype using different machine learning pose estimation algorithms to overcome both jittering and occluded landmark estimation. After that, an improved version of a more elaborate study with a larger number of participants in a more realistic working environment should be conducted. Feedback from the questionnaires should be also taken into account when developing new versions of the solution. Other applications of AR for ET could be tested as well. For example, it could be either tested with people who recently started to feel musculoskeletal symptoms for the purpose of reeducation or tested with people working in jobs with a high risk of

WRMSD. Overall there is a huge potential to improve the health and well-being of workers which can be achieved by introducing new technologies combining AR applications to make ET much more effective.

Acknowlegdements. We would like to express our sincere gratitude to the Deutscher Akademischer Austauschdienst (DAAD) for their collaborative relationship with Heidelberg University, Heilbronn University, and Universidad de Chile, and for awarding the internship scholarship that enabled us to undertake this work. We would also like to thank the members of UniTyLab - University of Heilbronn and the Centro de Informática Médica y Telemedicina (CIMT) of the Universidad de Chile for their invaluable guidance, support, feedback, and expertise, which helped us to improve our work. Finally, we extend our special thanks to Prof. Dr. Steffen Härtel from CIMT, and Director of the Magister en Informatica Médica at the Universidad de Chile, for making this opportunity possible.

References

1. Niu, S.: Ergonomics and occupational safety and health: An ILO perspective. Appl. Ergon. **41**(6), 744–753 (2010)
2. Punnett, L., Wegman, D.H.: Work-related musculoskeletal disorders: the epidemiologic evidence and the debate. J. Electromyogr. Kinesiol. **14**(1), 13–23 (2004)
3. Bernard, B.P., Putz-Anderson, V.: Musculoskeletal disorders and workplace factors; a critical review of epidemiologic evidence for work-related musculoskeletal disorders of the neck, upper extremity, and low back. National Institute for Occupational Safety and Health. (97B141) (1997). https://www.cdc.gov/niosh/docs/97-141/pdfs/97-141.pdf?id=10.26616/NIOSHPUB97141
4. European agency for safety and health at work and IKEI and Panteia. Work-related musculoskeletal disorders: prevalence, costs and demographics in the EU. Publications Office (2019)
5. Bureau of labor statistics. Fact Sheet | Occupational injuries and illnesses resulting in musculoskeletal disorders (MSDs). U.S. Department of Labor (2022). https://www.bls.gov/iif/factsheets/msds.html Accessed 29 Nov 2022
6. International labour organization. Global trends on occupational accidents and diseases; (2015). https://www.ilo.org/legacy/english/osh/en/story_content/external_files/fs_st_1-ILO_5_en.pdf Accessed 03 Nov 2022
7. The national institute for occupational safety and health (NIOSH). WMSDs Step 4: Implement your Ergonomic Program (2022). https://www.cdc.gov/niosh/topics/ergonomics/ergoprimer/step4.html Accessed 29 Nov 2022
8. Nicholson, A., Smith, C., Mitchell, A., et al.: Cost-benefit studies that support tackling musculoskeletal disorders. Health and Safety Executive (HSE). Research report (2006)
9. Denadai, M.S., Alouche, S.R., Valentim, D.P., Padula, R.S.: An ergonomics educational training program to prevent work-related musculoskeletal disorders to novice and experienced workers in the poultry processing industry: a quasi-experimental study. Appl. Ergon. **90**, 103234 (2021)
10. Burke, M.J., Sarpy, S.A., Smith-Crowe, K., Chan-Serafin, S., Salvador, R.O., Islam, G.: Relative effectiveness of worker safety and health training methods. Am. J. Public Health **96**(2), 315–324 (2006)

11. Etuknwa, A.B., Humpheries, S.: A systematic review on the effectiveness of ergonomic training intervention in reducing the risk of musculoskeletal disorder. J. Nursing Health Stud. **03**(02) (2018). https://doi.org/10.21767/2574-2825.1000032
12. Casey, T., Turner, N., Hu, X., Bancroft, K.: Making safety training stickier: a richer model of safety training engagement and transfer. J. Saf. Res. **78**, 303–313 (2021)
13. McAtamney, L., Corlett, E.N.: RULA: a survey method for the investigation of work-related upper limb disorders. Appl. Ergon. **24**(2), 91–99 (1993)
14. Diego-Mas, J.A., Alcaide-Marzal, J., Poveda-Bautista, R.: Effects of using immersive media on the effectiveness of training to prevent ergonomics risks. Int. J. Environ. Res. Public Health **17**(7), 2592 (2020)
15. Rauh, S.F., Koller, M., Schäfer, P., Meixner, G., Bogdan, C., Viberg, O.: MR On-SeT: a mixed reality occupational health and safety training for world-wide distribution. Int. J. Emerg. Tech. Learn. (iJET). **16**(05), 163 (2021)
16. da Silva, A.G., Winkler, I., Gomes, M.M., Pinto, U.D.M.: Ergonomic analysis supported by virtual reality: a systematic literature review. In: 2020 22nd Symposium on Virtual and Augmented Reality (SVR), IEEE (2020)
17. Desmarais, Y., Mottet, D., Slangen, P., Montesinos, P.: A review of 3D human pose estimation algorithms for markerless motion capture (2020)
18. Sauro, J., Lewis, J.R.: Standardized usability questionnaires. In: Quantifying the User Experience, Elsevier, pp. 185–248 (2016). https://doi.org/10.1016/b978-0-12-802308-2.00008-4
19. Pifarreacute, M., Sorribas, X., Villegas, E.: BLA (Bipolar Laddering) applied to YouTube. Performing postmodern psychology paradigms in user experience field. In: Advanced Technologies. InTech; (2009). https://doi.org/10.5772/8233
20. Bazarevsky, V., Grishchenko, I., Raveendran, K., Zhu, T., Zhang, F., Grundmann, M.: BlazePose: on-device real-time body pose tracking (2020)
21. Manghisi, V.M., Uva, A.E., Fiorentino, M., Bevilacqua, V., Trotta, G.F., Monno, G.: Real time RULA assessment using Kinect v2 sensor. Appl. Ergon. **65**, 481–491 (2017)
22. Lewis, J.: Psychometric evaluation of the PSSUQ using data from five years of usability studies. Int. J. Hum. Comput. Interact. **09**(14), 463–488 (2002)

BGHW Warehouse Simulation – Virtual Reality Supports Prevention of Slip, Trip and Fall (STF) Accidents

Christoph Wetzel[1]([⊠]) [iD], Andy Lungfiel[2] [iD], and Peter Nickel[2] [iD]

[1] German Social Accident Insurance Institution for the Trade and Logistics Industry (BGHW), DGUV Expert Committee 'Trade and Logistics' (FBHL), Mannheim, Germany
c.wetzel@bghw.de

[2] Department of Accident Prevention: Digitalisation – Technologies, Institute for Occupational Safety and Health of the German Social Accident Insurance (IFA), Sankt Augustin, Germany
andy.lungfiel@dguv.de

Abstract. Falls caused by tripping, slipping and missteps are an accident hotspot in both the professional and private environment. In addition to structural defects such as slippery floors or tripping hazards, the causes are often found in objects lying around and dirt, which could be avoided. Order and cleanliness are also well-known occupational safety measures, but they do not work across the board. In the area of occupational safety and health (OSH), employees can be sensitized to hazards and their consequences in a professional context and motivated to behave in a safe manner. The project 'BGHW Warehouse Simulation' packs an old topic into new technologies – virtual reality (VR) – to reawaken interest in the problem. The aim is that the hazard is eliminated directly by the employee or at least a warning is pronounced, or a report is sent to the superior. Trainers support the application in supervised discussions. The development of an instructional application is presented following a structural design approach. The design of the VR technology considers the Warehouse Simulation as an initial approach with more to come in different application domains. Experiences from the use of the simulator refer to different stakeholders and are presented and discussed. Considerations for further revisions are summarized.

Keywords: Instructional design · Gamification · Game-based learning · Slip · trip and fall accident · Virtual reality · Human-system interactions · Omnidirectional treadmill

1 Introduction

Falls of humans caused by tripping, slipping and missteps are an accident hotspot in both the professional and private environment [1, 2]. According to national and international statistics, about one fifth of accidents go down to accidents involving slips, trips, and falls (STF) and therefore result in high priority prevention in occupational safety and health (OSH) [3–5]. In addition to structural defects such as slippery floors or tripping hazards, the causes are often found in objects lying around and dirt, which could often be avoided [6–8].

V. G. Duffy (Ed.): HCII 2023, LNCS 14028, pp. 276–289, 2023.
https://doi.org/10.1007/978-3-031-35741-1_21

The problem itself is not new, quite the opposite. Order and cleanliness are also well-known occupational safety measures [6, 9], but they do not work across the board. In the area of occupational safety, employees can be sensitized to hazards and their consequences in a professional context and motivated to behave in a safe manner.

With this intention the German Social Accident Insurance Institution for the trade and logistics industry (BGHW) initiated a research and development project. A major part of the project packs an old topic into new technologies - virtual reality - to re-awaken interest in the problem. In collaboration with the Institute for Occupational Safety and Health of the German Social Accident Insurance (IFA) the 'BGHW Warehouse Simulation' ('BGHW Lagersimulator') should be developed, an instructional application that is supported by a virtual reality (VR) simulation environment to attract attention of employees towards suitable measures to combat STF accidents.

1.1 STF Prevention

OSH prevention is mainly organized along the internationally established hierarchy of controls (STOP model) [10–13]. Top level controls intend to substitute hazards and in the context of fall prevention they strive for alternative walking routes without obstacles or hazards. At second level, technical controls include measures such as designing work areas without steps and laying out of anti-slip floors [7, 8, 14]. In principle, measures at the two upper levels once implemented, eliminate, or reduce STF hazards effectively for many employees and pedestrians.

Lower-level controls also contribute to protection of persons concerned and its impact as additional control is of high value for improvements in OSH. Third level organizational controls apply measures on organizing work activities and include measures such as walking on official paths, organizing cleaning and winter services as well as tidying up work areas; sometimes called good housekeeping [6, 9]. Lowest level control use measures with effective acts on personnel that include for example wearing work shoes as personal protective equipment and attending behavioral training programs intended to improve safe behavior and reduce the consequences of accidents [7, 8, 14].

1.2 VR in OSH and in STF Prevention

VR technologies have a long tradition and a firm standing in supporting instructional design and training [15–17]. In education sciences, appropriate design of VR simulation environments supporting human-system interactions allow bridging to instructional design and constructivism. Learners actively construct knowledge through interactions rather than passively taking in information. Knowing does rather not occur by administration of information but is an adaptive process organizing the learner's experiential environment.

The application of VR technologies in trainings in STF prevention, i.e., through behavioral-based prevention measures is still popular [18]. VR techniques offer potential solutions by potentially supporting an increase in trainees' engagement and understanding by affording them experiential learning in safety-related scenarios [19]. In addition, trainees with specific caution can be exposed dangerous virtual environments with the risk of actual physical harm being rather low [20].

Some of the studies on development and implementation of VR in training environments demonstrate, however, that it might not always be that easy [21, 22]. Due scientific findings and experiences gained with VR simulation support over recent years, a human factors concept for a framework for structured development of virtual environments (SDVE, [23]) has been developed and successfully applied in different fields of application (e.g., [24]).

2 Application Requirements and Concept Development

Improvement of awareness of employees are assumed a crucial component in the prevention of STF accidents. Instructional design combined with a tailored VR simulation environment should support the endeavor to improve accident prevention at work. A human factors framework for structured development of virtual environments (SDVE, [23]) is used to organize an iterative process of developing a target-oriented VR application environment supporting STF accident prevention. SDVE follows stages presented as following.

Definition. The initial stage of the SDVE framework defines the endeavor. The application aims at improving awareness of employees for the prevention of STF accidents at work. However, the technical structure of the application should be generic regarding potential domains of application, e.g., the structure should allow to easily switch between domains, while it should be domain specific regarding preventive measures and instructional designs to reach out to prospective employees at work.

Requirement Analysis. Analyses in this stage refer to tasks and stakeholders. Analyses cover the task environment of the employees as well as hazards typical in every day working routines. Stakeholder analyses should refer to people that will use the application or will setup and maintain the technical equipment as well as address, instruct and interact with participants before, during and after use of the instructional application.

Specification and Integration of Human-System Interaction. Human-system interaction plays an integral part in the instructional context to support the aim of the application. Interactional processes will be spelled out for the instructional context by scenario specifications and storyboarding and may also reveal potential limitations for instructional requirements as well as potential free space for additional instructional content.

Development of the VR Simulation Environment. Hardware specifications and software development are the core elements of the given stage in SDVE. While technical developments on the one hand closely follow scenario specifications and storyboarding, on the other hand the development process may provide alternative solutions and refinements in human-system interaction appropriate for instructional design.

Implementation as Instructional Application. The implementation stage amalgamates the instructional design with the developed VR simulation environment to allow for target-oriented human-system interaction.

Evaluation of Goals. A final evaluation is required to find out about effects of the instructional application in practice and it should be able to demonstrate whether the aim of the application as defined at the beginning of the SDVE framework has been reached.

3 Technical Conversion and VR Application Design

The given section will inform about the development of the application 'BGHW Warehouse Simulation'. The results will be presented according to SDVE [23] stages with an emphasis on the technical development of the VR simulation environment.

3.1 Definition

The instructional application aimed at motivating interest for occupational safety and health focusing on STF prevention at work and at sensitizing employees in companies, at fairs and prevention events for active involvement in prevention activities. The structure for developing the VR simulation environment was intended to be generic in terms of covering a broader range of domains such as logistics, retail trade, and mail carrier or delivery services while at the same time being domain specific to address appropriate measures to prevent STF accidents and to address instructional designs to reach out to intended employees involved. Application development started in the logistics domain with the 'BGHW Warehouse Simulation' addressing rather typical scenarios in STF accident prevention. This instructional application was implemented in a show truck, the 'BGHW mobil' that also contained other stations for OSH prevention such as an inclining ramp for experiencing different slip resistance of shoes to be driven to companies, fairs, and prevention events for active involvement of employees in preventions of STF accidents.

3.2 Requirement Analysis

Stakeholder analyses identified three parties to be involved in application use: users in the company (e.g., employees, safety experts, management), the instructors as well as the maintenance engineers. The intended user population consisted of varying groups of employees in companies, at fairs and prevention events.

Users in the specific context for the initial instructional application 'BGHW Warehouse Simulation' were required to perform tasks in an intralogistics environment such as deliveries, stocktaking, schedule merchandise, activities for maintaining the facilities, cleaning staff, to name but a few.

Instructors overseeing use of the applications were required to prepare and start or stop technical operation of equipment, to motivate and instruct employees during use of the simulation, to involve individual participants and groups in discussions about typical scenarios at their own workplaces, their experiences with STF hazards, and opinions about what could be done to prevent accidents. With groups of employees interested in participation, the setup of the application allowed to opt for time limited use and for feedback about chosen measures for prevention during virtual activities in the intralogistics simulation environment.

Maintenance engineers for the technical application provided onboard software and hardware updates including development, testing and roll-out.

3.3 Specification and Integration of Human-System Interaction

In the specific context for the initial application 'BGHW Warehouse Simulation' employees as users were required to perform tasks in inhouse storages, outside loading platforms and administrative areas of intralogistics. Several suggestions for design were taken from an OSH compendium of the BGHW and available as an internet platform to inform educational and instructional purposes on work processes in automation-driven intralogistics with special emphasis on safe and healthy human-system interactions [25]. In addition, design ideas resulted from visits in logistic centers and from experiences gained during inspections in intralogistics. Accident analyses in intralogistics available to the BGHW [5, 6] also served scenario specification for the instructional environment. This allowed to identify and to outline typical accident scenarios in the context of STF and to collect and arrange causes of accidents. Based on up-to-date information available about the intralogistics domain, the simulation environment of intralogistics including a selection of typical accident scenarios could be created. On top, information available served supporting employees with suggestions for potential measures or controls for prevention in human-system interaction [5, 6].

The story to encounter several accident scenarios was through walking activities for task performance in intralogistics such as warehouse, administration or loading ramp. Users are asked to freely move within the intralogistics environment. While walking through different sections employees faced obstacles on the floor, derangements of warehouse stock and other items or situations causing potential risks for STF accidents. When they identified scenarios with potential risk, they were able to ignore and follow their destination in the warehouse or to deal with the situations by selection of the scenario. In the latter case they were asked to choose among four alternative actions ranging from for example bringing back fallen stock to the storage rack through informing colleagues about potentially hazardous situations down to ignoring the scenario and go on as if nothing had happened. Every encounter in scenarios called the employee for active decisions about measures of prevention but also informed about possible alternatives available among which most suitable.

Since the instructional environment should motivate prospective employees, techniques of VR were chosen to model a dynamic VR simulation first of an intralogistics domain and in future in other domains. Selection of technical VR equipment for supporting human-system interaction followed basic human factors and ergonomics design requirements and strongly aimed to avoided human impairments and health and safety risks (e.g. [26, 27]). A treadmill was required for locomotion in the dynamic VR simulation since work environments in intralogistics are spacious and instructional requirements called for employees walking freely in all parts of the spacious environment.

3.4 Development of the VR Simulation Environment

Hardware specifications and software development are the core elements of the given stage in SDVE. While technical development on the one hand closely follows scenario specification and storyboarding, the development process on the other hand may provide alternative solutions and refinements in human-system interaction appropriate for instructional design.

Design of the VR Software. The development of the VR simulation environment was implemented using Unity software (Unity Technologies, USA). A simplified class diagram in unified modeling language (UML) for the design of the virtual environment is presented in Fig. 1. The "HazardManager" reads all relevant information such as description of hazards and measures in from a central file in Microsoft Excel format (Microsoft Cooperation, USA). This file is organized to take any number of scenarios and hazards, however, in an active simulation environment or application, only one scenario can be active at a time, which in turn can contain any number of hazards. All hazards within one scenario are automatically recognized and initialized based on information from the Microsoft Excel file. The upload of information from a central file in Microsoft Excel format, in addition had the advantage, that extensions and modifications are possible without accessing the Unity software system.

The design as described in the UML class diagram (see Fig. 1) makes the simulation application flexible and above all language independent. Any number of Microsoft Excel files can be created in various languages. This made it possible to provide user menus in simulation environments with specified languages according to the Microsoft Excel file selected. At start of program, all files are automatically recognized and available for selection in an initial menu (Fig. 2, see "select Excel file"). In Unity, scenarios and hazards are assigned as "Components" [28] to a "GameObject" [28]. The components have an ID as their most important property, which is used to initialize them with the help of the "HazardManager". A "GameObject" can be a 3D model of any complexity. Figure 3 shows the hierarchy in Unity. Hazards or scenarios are independent of an environment and therefore, making them easily interchangeable.

When a hazardous situation in the simulation environment was identified by the user and he/she decided to address the scenario, selection of the scenario by the user presented a menu as shown as an example in Fig. 4. With the perspective of the target of the overall VR simulation environment the focus was given on rather typical activities according to knowledge available from safety experts at work as well as OSH inspectors. In addition, the employee should get the option to learn during interaction by finding hazardous situations and selecting among measures.

The example menu in Fig. 4 presents the typical structure and shows the name the hazard, a description, and a picture of the source of the hazard and asks what the user would like to do. Every menu contains four options with responses to the hazard, of which one response is 'ignore' and three responses are possible actions for the employee. Ignoring is the worst option from a health and safety perspective, as the hazard is not removed and remains present to the same extent. This option will be highlighted in red after selection. The employee should learn that taking the initiative and actively combat hazards is always possible. Therefore, the remaining three options contain active, appropriate measures with solutions different in quality. More than one option can be selected by the employee and will be highlighted in green. At the end of the menu there are also two buttons to confirm and cancel the procedure.

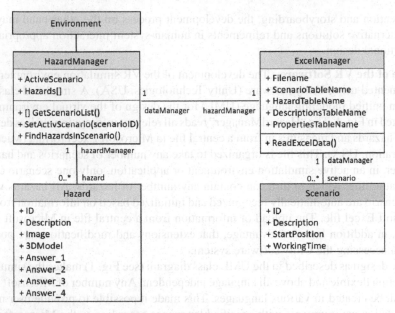

Fig. 1. UML class diagram.

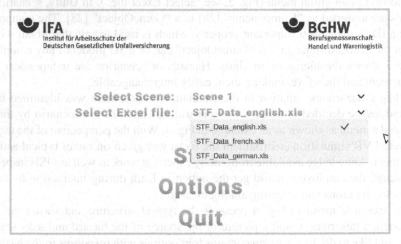

Fig. 2. Initial menu with options to select central file in Microsoft Excel format.

Information given in the menu are automatically retrieved from the Microsoft Excel file. The intention for designing user interfaces was to keep the interaction process simple, i.e., without animations or point systems for selected options. Decision making for the user after identification of potentially hazardous scenarios avoided overtaxing.

Design of the VR Hardware. For navigation and interaction in the virtual environment, several interaction interfaces have been integrated. The VR application enables

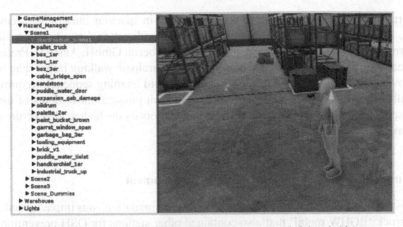

Fig. 3. Hierarchy of the Unity program structure (left hand side).

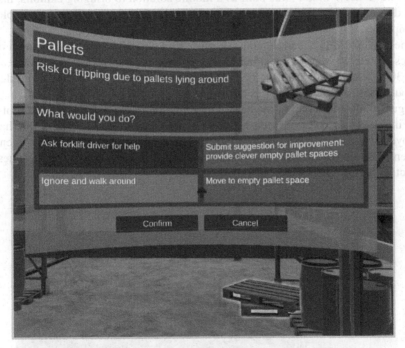

Fig. 4. Menu for response for identified a hazardous situation.

use of mouse and keyboard, but also use of a head-mounted display (HMD) such as the VIVE Pro (HTC Corporation, Taiwan) including VIVE controllers and optionally a VIVE Tracker. Controllers served for hazard identification, for cleaning up elements lying around and selecting a menu to select measures for combating the hazards. In addition, controllers were used to navigate in the virtual intralogistics environment by teleportation. To allow for closer to reality walking in spacious intralogistics environments, the VR application also interfaced to an omnidirectional treadmill or walking platform enabling full movement in 360 degrees (Cyberith GmbH, Austria). Preference to a treadmill was given e.g., to include close to naturalistic walking rather than opting for movements initiated by VIVE controllers, to avoid learning sequences required for controlling movements via VIVE controllers, to limit physical movements of users to small space, and to attract attention to users and visitors by the technical structure of the treadmill.

3.5   Implementation of the Instructional Environment

The instructional environment 'BGHW Warehouse Simulation' was implemented in the show truck 'BGHW mobil' that also contained other stations for OSH prevention such as an inclining ramp for experiencing different slip resistance of shoes (Fig. 5, right hand side). The 'BGHW mobil' was built as a mobile solution to bringing exhibits, instructional design, and preventive measures to places the target population, i.e., employees in companies.

The 'BGHW Warehouse Simulation' presents a typical work environment in intralogistics. While walking in the simulation environment, employees could come across about 30 different STF hazards to be presented in different hazardous situations flexibly distributed across the intralogistics environment.

Figure 6 illustrates one of the hazardous situations and presents an open roof-light in an intralogistics hall with rain already entering the floor. To address this hazard, employees were required to select among different options (see Fig. 4, with menu for different hazardous situation) and were involved in discussions with colleagues and instructors during 'BGHW mobil' presentation.

Fig. 5. 'BGHW mobil' with exhibits for STF prevention.

Fig. 6. Scenario with wet puddle due to open roof-light and risk for STF accident.

3.6 Evaluation of Goals

Instructional design combined with a tailored VR simulation environment should support the endeavor to improve prevention of STF incidents and accidents at work. An evaluation would be helpful for finding out about effects of the instructional environment in practice and for demonstrating whether the instructional aim as defined according to the beginning of the SDVE has been reached.

Although a systematic and empirical evaluation is not yet available, feedback from onsite use of 'BGHW mobil' including the 'BGHW Warehouse Simulation' has been very positive. The 'BGHW mobil' is very well booked by companies from the logistics domain for OSH events such as OSH prevention days or company picnics at the premises (see Fig. 7). In addition, the 'BGHW mobil' has been supporting accident prevention at OSH related fairs and OSH performances. The application of the 'BGHW Warehouse Simulation' has been very favorite according both instructors and safety experts presenting the 'BGHW mobil' at events.

Employees were motivated to engage in STF prevention by VR as new technology and by active human-system interactions in scenarios that represent their own work environment. Activities usually resulted in lively discussions about STF hazards at work with groups of employees, company safety representatives as well as trade unions, managers, and company owners. In general, the message to personally get involved and always having options to combat STF accidents has been very much supported and with the given instructional environment it has been possible to involve much more employees than usual in active prevention activities. This suggests that awareness for related hazards increased, at least for users so far involved, and employees improved sensitivity towards preventive actions and controls.

Maintenance engineers have not been required often except for updating the VR environment and minor adjustments of VR technologies used and aesthetic repairs for the software system. Since employees sometimes call for presenting more lively scenarios in intralogistics, an upgrade is currently under development. More complex environments and improved HMDs, however, require more computing power. Hardware updates are rather easy since standard components from gaming are used and can therefore be changed according to requirements. Recently, the motion platform has also been revised. Treadmill walking has been improved by slightly tilting the floor and initial tests suggested that adaptation to virtual walking on the platform is easier.

Fig. 7. Rollout of the 'BGHW Warehouse Simulation' [29].

4   Discussion and Conclusions

High numbers of accidents across sectors of industry and services call for mobilization of the full range of the hierarchy of control in STF prevention. In addition to substitutional, technical, and organizational measures available, controls addressing personnel level are very laborious to be effective for those concerned [5, 6, 14]. In general, however, personnel level controls have the potential to reinforce those controls higher in the hierarchy [10, 12]. The 'BGHW Warehouse Simulation' has been launched to support preventive activities in intralogistics. Since there are several different jobs and work tasks with specific hazards in the retail and logistics industry, it was decided even before the technical development of this first VR-based instructional environment began to make it scalable so that it could be used in alternative domains in the future.

Development of the instructional application followed the SDVE process [23] and successfully aimed at gaining sensitivity for STF accidents at work and to put this across to employees in their daily working routines. This has been achieved by offering a broad range of practical options for active involvement in prevention at work and by allowing to arrange for implementation in the virtual environment. According to feedback available for the 'BGHW Warehouse Simulation' it could be assumed that participants gained experiences and expanded knowledge on preventive measures by experiential human-system interaction in the virtual environment and by engagement in discussion with instructors and colleagues. However, systematic evaluations would be required to provide more systematic and meaningful feedback with more specific recommendations how to further improve the instructional concept amalgamated with the VR simulation environment.

Positive feedback for the 'BGHW mobil' with the 'BGHW Warehouse Simulation' and other STF preventive activities has created strong demand for extending the simulation environment to other domains in trade and logistics industry, such as convenience stores in the retail trade [30] as well as newspaper carriers in the delivery sector. While the instructional application for the retail trade is going to be launched soon, the application for the delivery sector is still in preparation.

References

1. Hsiao, H.: Fall prevention and protection: a public health matter. In: Hsiao, H. (ed.) Fall Prevention and Protection. Principles, Guidelines, and Practices, pp. 3–17. CRC Press, Boca Raton (2017)
2. Di Pilla, S.: Slip and fall controls for pedestrian and community safety. In: Hsiao, H. (ed.) Fall Prevention and Protection. Principles, Guidelines, and Practices, pp. 321–339. CRC Press, Boca Raton (2017)
3. DGUV: Statistik. Arbeitsunfallgeschehen 2021. Deutsche Gesetzliche Unfallversicherung (DGUV), Berlin (2022). [publikationen.dguv.de/widgets/pdf/download/article/4590]
4. Eurostat: Accidents at work – statistics on causes and circumstances. https://ec.europa.eu/eurostat/statistics-explained/index.php?title=Accidents_at_work_-_statistics_on_causes_and_circumstances#Contact_mode_of_injury. Accessed 17 Feb 2023
5. Schäfer, K., Klockmann, H.-C., Wetzel, C., Mahlberg, J.: Schwere Arbeitsunfälle im Handel und in der Warenlogistik. DGUV Forum 11(2022), 9–17 (2022)
6. Wetzel, C.: Sturzunfälle. Es ist noch immer gut gegangen – oder eben nicht! Sicher ist sicher 12/2022, pp. 528–533 (2022). https://doi.org/10.37307/j.2199-7349.2022.12.06
7. DGUV Information 208–181: Maßnahmen zur Vermeidung von Stolper-, Rutsch- und Sturzunfällen. German Social Accident Insurance (DGUV), Berlin (in preparation)
8. Mewes, D.: Slips, trips and falls. OSHwiki networking knowledge [https://oshwiki.eu/wiki/Slips,_trips_and_falls. Accessed 17 Feb 2023
9. Alli, B.O.: Fundamental principles of occupational health and safety. International Labour Organization (ILO), Geneva (2008)
10. Lehto, M.R., Cook, B.T.: Occupational health and safety management. In: Salvendy, G. (ed.) Handbook of human factors and ergonomics, pp. 701–733. Wiley, Hoboken (2012)
11. EU OSH Framework Directive 89/391/EEC of 12 June 1989 on the introduction of measures to encourage improvements in the safety and health of workers at work (with amendments 2008). Official Journal of the European Union L 183, 29/06/1989, pp. 1–8 (2008)
12. International Social Security Association, International Prevention Section of the ISSA on Machine and System Safety, Human Factors Working Group. https://www.safe-machines-at-work.org/human-factors/work-organisation-design-issues/osh-and-work-system-design. Accessed 17 Feb 2023

13. DGUV Information 208–041: Bewertung der Rutschgefahr unter Betriebsbedingungen. German Social Accident Insurance (DGUV), Berlin (2019)
14. Wetzel, C., Windhövel, U., Mewes, D., Ceylan, O.: Slipping on pedestrian surfaces: methods for measuring and evaluating the slip resistance. Int. J. Occup. Saf. Ergon. (JOSE) 21(3), 256–267 (2015). https://doi.org/10.1080/10803548.2015.1081767
15. Schmorrow, D., Cohn, J., Nicholson, D.: The PSI handbook of virtual environments for training and education. Vol. 1: Learning, requirements, and metrics. Praeger Security International, Westport (2009)
16. Nicholson, D., Schmorrow, D., Cohn, J.: The PSI handbook of virtual environments for training and education. Vol. 2: VE components and training technologies. Praeger Security International, Westport (2009)
17. Cohn, J., Nicholson, D., Schmorrow, D.: The PSI handbook of virtual environments for training and education. Vol. 3: Integrated systems, training evaluations, and future directions. Praeger Security International, Westport (2009)
18. Simeonov, P.: Fall risk associated with restricted and elevated support surfaces. In: Hsiao, H. (ed.) Fall Prevention and Protection. Principles, Guidelines, and Practices, pp. 119–140. CRC Press, Boca Raton (2017)
19. Lawson, G., Shaw, E., Roper, T., Nilsson, T., Bajorunaite, L., Batool, A.: Immersive virtual worlds: multi-sensory virtual environments for health and safety training (University of Nottingham Research report). Institution of Occupational Safety and Health, Wigston (2019)
20. Nickel, P., Lungfiel, A., Trabold, R.-J.: Reconstruction of near misses and accidents for analyses from virtual reality usability study. In: Barbic, J., D'Cruz, M., Latoschik, M.E., Slater, M., Bourdot, P. (eds.) Virtual Reality and Augmented Reality. LNCS, vol. 10700, pp. 182–191. Springer, Cham (2017). https://doi.org/10.1007/978-3-319-72323-5_12
21. Simpson, B.D., Cowgill, J.L., Gilkey, R.H., Weisenberger, J.M.: Technological considerations in the design of multisensory virtual environments: how real does it need to be? In: Hale, K.S., Stanney, K.M. (eds.) Handbook of Virtual Environments: Design, Implementation, and Applications, pp. 313–333. CRC Press, Boca Raton (2015)
22. Champney, R.K., Carroll, M., Surpris, G., Cohn, J.: Conducting training transfer studies in virtual environments. In: Hale, K.S., Stanney, K.M. (eds.) Handbook of Virtual Environments: Design, Implementation, and Applications, pp. 781–795. CRC Press, Boca Raton (2015)
23. Eastgate, R.M., Wilson, J.R., D'Cruz, M.: Structured development of virtual environments. In: Hale, K.S., Stanney, K.M. (eds.) Handbook of Virtual Environments: Design, Implementation, and Applications, pp. 353–390. CRC Press, Boca Raton (2015)
24. Gomoll, K., Nickel, P., Huis, S.: Development of a VR based qualification module in trainings on risk assessments according to the EU Directive on Safety of Machinery. In: Proceedings of the 9th International Conference on Safety of Industrial Automated Systems (SIAS 2018), Oct 10–12, 2018, INRS, Nancy, France, pp. 306–311 (2018)
25. BGHW – Das sichere Lager (im Kompendium für Arbeitsschutz). https://www.bghw.de/arbeit sschutz/wie-wir-sie-im-arbeitsschutz-unterstuetzen/das-sichere-lager. Accessed 17 Feb 2023
26. Wickens, C.D., Hollands, J.G., Banbury, S., Parasuraman, R.: Engineering Psychology and Human Performance. Pearson, Upper Saddle River (2013)
27. ISO 9241–394: Ergonomics of human-system interaction — Part 394: Ergonomic requirements for reducing undesirable biomedical effects of visually induced motion sickness during watching electronic images. ISO, Geneva (2020)
28. Unity script references. https://docs.unity3d.com/ScriptReference. Accessed 17 Feb 2023
29. BGHW: In diesem Lkw steckt was drin. BGHW aktuell 3/2019, 18–21 (2019). https://www. bghw.de/medien/bghw-aktuell-die-zeitschrift-fuer-mitgliedsbetriebe/bghw-aktuell-03-19/ bghw-aktuell-3-19. Accessed 17 Feb 2023

30. Project of the Institute Occupational Safety and Health of the German Social Accident Insurance (IFA) commissioned by the German Social Accident Insurance Institution for the trade and logistics industry (BGHW) on 'Accident prevention in retail scenarios supported by virtual reality techniques'. https://www.dguv.de/ifa/forschung/projektverzeichnis/ifa517 3.jsp. Accessed 17 Feb 2023

The Low Back Fatigue Research Based on Controlled Sedentary Driving Tasks

Xiang Wu[1](✉), Tianfeng Xu[1], Yeqi Wu[1], Ziyan Dong[1], Xinran Liu[1],
Xiangyu Liu[2](✉), and Li Xu[1](✉)

[1] School of Art Design and Media, East China University of Science and Technology, Shanghai, China
y81220077@mail.ecust.edu.cn
[2] College of Communication and Art Design, The University of Shanghai for Science and Technology, Shanghai, China

Abstract. Studies have found that sedentary behavior is a potential causative factor for diabetes, cardiovascular disease, cancer, and skeletal muscle disease. Physical activity has been shown to have a relationship between sedentary behavior and cardiovascular disease and cancer mortality and reduce the incidence of cardiovascular disease and cancer caused by sedentary behavior. However, the likelihood of Musculoskeletal Disorders (MSKD) in sedentary populations remains high, with lower back pain (LBP) becoming a typical symptom of MSKD in sedentary people. For more highly sedentary populations, such as long-haul truck drivers, coach drivers, and cab drivers, long-term passive sedentariness puts the prevalence of low back pain in occupational drivers at 84%, professional drivers are a frequent or high-risk group for low back pain. Muscle fatigue from prolonged sedentary activity increases drivers' risk of MSKD and LBP. In this study, we used high-density sEMG (HD-sEMG) to represent the muscle fatigue condition of ES (erector spinae) and LDM (Vastus Medialis) in the LB (lower back) region during a simulated driving task and for the comparison of fatigue (including fatigue onset and recovery) in sedentary and non-sedentary populations, to provide a comprehensive understanding of microscopic fatigue mechanisms. Our result showed that Heat treatment after fatigue was effective for both long-term sedentary and non-long-term sedentary people, and the recovery effect of heat treatment for non-long-term sedentary people was better than that for long-term sedentary people, which may be because long-term inactive on the fatigue resistance of ES and LDM muscles.

Keywords: Muscle fatigue · Long-term Sedentary · Non-long-term sedentary · surface electromyogram · Truck · Heat

1 Introduction

Nearly 58% of the world's population spends a third of their lives working, and these driving jobs are the most dangerous of all [1]. One study was conducted in Malaysia by Tamrin [2]. Found a very high prevalence of skeletal muscle pain among bus drivers.

A subsequent survey found that most of these WMSDs (Work-related Musculoskeletal Disorders) did not improve over the next seven years. In a study by Balasubramanian and Jagannath, significant physiological fatigue was found in the TM (trapezius medial), ES, and LDM of motorcyclists during 60 min of motorcycle driving. The LD and ES muscles are important muscle groups in the LB region, and current research has focused less on muscle fatigue in the LD and ES muscle regions of drivers during car driving. Therefore, the study of fatigue onset mechanisms and fatigue recovery measures of LD and ES during driving is essential for alleviating and improving muscle fatigue in the LB region of drivers and is potentially valuable for addressing LBP, and even MSKD, in driver groups that multiple factors may cause.

In studying the mechanisms of fatigue onset, previous studies have demonstrated that looking at synchronization between composite MU spike trains by MU discharge synchronization can explain fatigue-induced neural mechanisms in microscopic aspects.

Specifically, the synchronization of the MUs can be divided into four specific frequency bands, Delta (1–4 Hz), Alpha (8–12 Hz), Beta (15–30 Hz), and Gamma (30–60 Hz) [3]. Each band represents a discrepant origin. The Delta band may represent a "common driver" in the neural control system, suggesting that the activation of the MU may be influenced by the same source [4]. The alpha band, considered a physiological and pathological tremor indicator, may also increase after isometric fatigue and post-fatigue [5]. Beta and gamma represent cortical and subcortical oscillations [6].

In a previous study, MU spike trains were also successfully decomposed from HD-sEMG using fast-ICA to calculate the synchronization of simultaneous active MU in different frequency ranges. And it was found that the synchronization of each frequency band was significantly increased under two muscle fatigue-induced contractions, the isometric muscle-fatigue task, and the dynamic muscle-fatigue task. The corresponding results suggest that the mechanism of biceps fatigue is more relevant to the muscle rather than to the specific job [7]. In the present experiment, we focused on an isometric muscle-fatigue task and emotional muscle-fatigue task in LD and ES region muscles to verify whether fatigue mechanisms in LD and ES muscles are muscle rather than task-specific related.

The previous results showed that after the treatment with Microwave diathermy, the elbow flexor strength appeared to be significantly weakened, resulting in a significant reduction in electrical activity in the studied muscle areas. This can, to a certain extent, indicate that microwave diathermy of the biceps reduces the flexion and extension strength of the elbow, as well as the signs of muscle fatigue in the biceps [8]. In the presented study, we did not use Microwave diathermy apparatus (EFROM 2.45 G MICROWAVE) [8]. We used an external heat source type thermostatic heating device for external heat treatment of the power to understand the effect of heat treatment on fatigue recovery time by comparing the fatigue recovery time of all subjects with heat (A2/B2/C2/D2) and without heat (A1/A3/B1/B3/C1/C3/D1/D3). Indirectly, the effect of external heat treatment on fatigue recovery was understood.

2 Material and Methods

2.1 Participants

A total of 20 volunteers were recruited for the experiment. All 20 volunteers had no neuromuscular impairment or skeletal muscle damage in the lower back area. The characteristics of the participants are shown in Table 1. Before the start of the experiment, all participants were informed of the procedure and signed an informed consent form.

Each of the 20 volunteers will be divided into a long-term sedentary group and a non-long-term sedentary group after questioning based on the following definitions; Sedentary was defined as any waking behavior characterized by consumption ≤ 1.5 METs (Metabolic equivalent of task) while in a sitting or reclining position, i.e., for more than five days in a week, sitting in the awake state lasts ≥ 8 h/day or lasts 2 h/day without getting up and moving or changing sitting posture, such as most desk jobs, watching TV, and driving are considered as sedentary behaviors. Long-term sedentary behavior was defined as persistent behavior lasting more than three months for ≥ 20 days/month.

Table 1. The characteristics of the participants.

Subject ID	Gender	Age	Height (cm) and Weigh (kg)	Group*
1	Female	23	161 cm, 56 kg	I
2	Male	22	183 cm, 65 kg	I
3	Female	23	164 cm, 48 kg	II
4	Female	22	161 cm, 50 kg	II
5	Female	23	160 cm, 52 kg	II
6	Male	26	174 cm, 68 kg	I
7	Female	24	160 cm, 64 kg	I
8	Female	24	167 cm,59 kg	I
9	Female	22	158 cm, 42 kg	I
10	Male	22	173 cm, 63 kg	II
11	Male	26	183 cm, 70 kg	II
12	Male	22	183 cm, 62 kg	I
13	Female	22	152 cm, 55 kg	I
14	Female	23	162 cm, 49 kg	I
15	Male	23	170 cm, 55 kg	I
16	Male	24	175 cm, 70 kg	II
17	Female	22	163 cm, 52 kg	II
18	Female	22	165 cm, 53 kg	II
19	Male	25	174 cm, 72 kg	II
20	Male	21	172 cm, 66 kg	II

Note: *Group I refers to the long-term sedentary group; Group II refers to the long-term inactive group

2.2 Experimental Procedure

Before the start of the experiment, 20 volunteers performed dynamic and isometric force tasks in an orderly manner during the investigation. The active task and isometric task are described in Fig. 1,

And the experimental grouping is presented in Fig. 2.

Before the start of the experiment, all subjects were collected through questionnaires about their age, gender, and daily sedentary degree and were divided into a long-term inactive group (Group I: 10) and a non-long-term sedentary group (Group II: 10) according to their daily passive degree.

Subjects in both group I and group II were required to perform dynamic and isometric tasks. During the overall experiment, the subjects performed the isometric task - vertical sedentary movement and the dynamic task - unilateral foot single-point stepping movement in an orderly manner. In contrast, the surface EMG signals of the subjects were recorded. Twenty subjects were divided into 10 participants in Group I (long-term sedentary group) and 10 participants in Group II (non-long-term inactive group) as required by the definition of long-term passive. Participants were asked to perform an exhausting movement task in each trial, either sitting upright in silence or stepping on one foot at one point. Each test was performed for more than 2 min until the subjects stopped independently. The upright sitting task required the issue to simulate the torso posture in everyday straight driving, i.e., with the hands naturally flat and the body stationary and upright until the subject felt lumbar fatigue and stopped voluntarily. The single-foot single-point pedaling task required the issue to simulate the natural action of stepping on the gas pedal in driving, i.e., to complete the single-foot single-point pedaling action at a frequency of 20 times/minute from the natural state (the angle between the surface of the foot and the ground is about 30°) until the state of stepping on the bottom (the surface of the foot is almost parallel to the floor). Verbal cues were provided during the single-leg, single-point pedaling task to stabilize the subject's pedaling frequency. In the two consecutive experiments, 10–15 min of rest time was provided to avoid the accumulation of fatigue, and the rest time could be extended appropriately according to the subjects' requirements. Recovery time. Each task was repeated three times, and each rest for groups A, B, C, and D was labeled as (A1\A2\A3) (B1\B2\B3) (C1\C2\C3) (D1\D2\D3) at the time of the repeated rest, and (A2\B2\C2\D2) of them was set to a constant temperature of 40 °C for heat application, comparing (A1\A2\A3) (B1\B2\B3) (C1\C2\C3) (D1\D2\D3) in terms of recovery time. During the experiment, an experimental assistant was assigned to provide verbal cues for the single-leg, single-point pedaling task and the safety of the testing process. A final sample of 120 will be obtained for this experiment (2 groups * 10 people * 3 repetitions * 2 tasks = 120 samples).

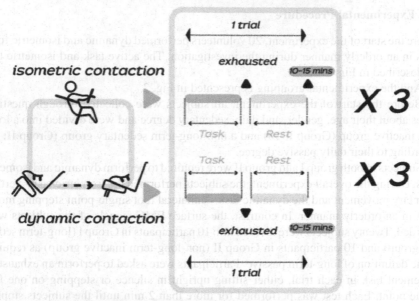

Fig. 1. The experimental process.

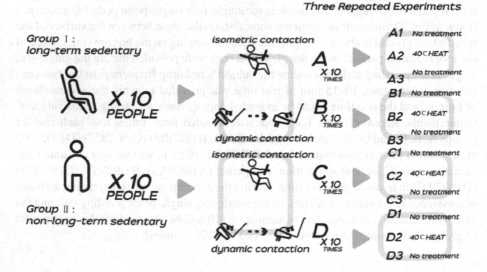

The diagram of experimental grouping

Fig. 2. The diagram of experimental grouping.

2.3 EMG Recording

Before the experiment, subjects will be asked to perform a preview of the dynamic and static tasks at the beginning of the formal investigation to determine the location of the firing muscles, as well as to help the researchers find the right site for muscle signal acquisition. A 64 HD-sEMG electrode array was placed at the junction of the ES and LD; the position was presented in Fig. 3 before data collection to ensure that muscle signals from both the ES and the LDM electrode placement were explored sufficiently before the experiment to minimize the effects of anatomical differences between participants. HD-sEMG was recorded by a Sessantaquattro system (OT Bioelettronica, Italy) with a gain of 1000, a sampling frequency of 2000 Hz. After subjects failed to perform the required isometric and dynamic tasks for each experiment, the data were saved.

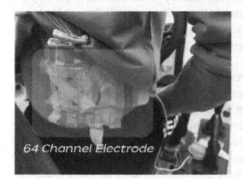

Fig. 3. The placement of 64 electrodes.

2.4 Data Analysis

Scope of Pre- and Post-fatigue
Before data processing, we set a 10-s pre-fatigue and 5-s post-fatigue window to segment HD-sEMG, with the initial window before the task starts as the pre-fatigue state and the window before resting at the end of the job as the post-fatigue state. The initial windows for the execution of the last two functions in the three repetitions of the task were considered to have been fully rested sufficiently.

3 Result

Our results demonstrated an increase in the HD-sEMG activations in both dynamic and isometric tasks. During the data analysis, our variables were dynamic task, isometric task, pre-fatigue corresponding to post-fatigue. The overall conclusions were as follow: The HD-sEMG activation for the post-fatigue condition were consistently higher than those for the pre-fatigue condition under all conditions.

Heat application therapy is widely used in recovery from muscle fatigue and even as an effective means of recovery from muscle strain. The use of electromyographic signals is an excellent indicator to determine the state of the muscle, and fatigue as a character is an essential factor affecting the state of the force.

Microwave diathermy is performed before exercise therapy techniques. Its purpose is to increase blood flow, remove by-products of inflammatory processes, and improve joint range of motion by reducing stiffness, increasing collagen fiber extensibility, and enhancing soft tissue elasticity [12]. This therapeutic modality provides heat to the soft tissues in a somewhat satisfactory manner for the prevention and treatment of musculoskeletal injuries [13].

In the experiments of Wagner Menna Pereira et al. [14], it was demonstrated that microwave therapy on the biceps reduces the flexion strength of the elbow and the signs of muscle fatigue in the biceps. However, in studies on muscle fatigue recovery, there are few studies on the recovery from heating the muscles in the lower back region. Few studies have mentioned the recovery effect of simple, immediate heat treatment on fatigue. In the experiment, 20 subjects were asked to perform two tasks three times each, i.e., a total of 3*20 = 60 data and the data were presented in Table 2. The experiment included the following variables: dynamic task corresponding to isometric task, fatigue recovery time, and subject population type (sedentary or non-sedentary).

When the fatigue recovery time and three recovery treatments were fixed, (A1/B1) (C1/D1) (A2/B2) (C2/D2) (A3/B3) (C3/D3) were taken as mean values, and the time required for three recoveries (A1/B1/C1/D1), (A2/B2/C2/D2), (A3/B3/C3/D3) were compared. The natural recovery of 20 subjects the effects of natural recovery and heat recovery of 20 participants were presented in Fig. 4. When comparing the long-term sedentary heat treatment recovery group with the non-long-term sedentary heat treatment recovery group and the long-term sedentary natural recovery group with the non-long-term sedentary natural recovery group, the mean values of (A1/A3/B1/B3) (C1/C3/D1/D3) and (A2/B2) (C2/D2) for the long-term sedentary group and the non-long-term sedentary group were compared. The fatigue recovery effects of the long-term sedentary group and the non-long-term sedentary group are presented in Fig. 5. It was shown in Fig. 5, and it can be seen that: 1) Heat treatment was effective for both the long-term sedentary group and the non-long-term sedentary group, and 2) The non-long-term sedentary group showed a better recovery effect, both in terms of recovery from heat treatment and natural recovery, which may represent the fatigue resistance of ES and LDM muscle groups in the non-long-term sedentary group compared to the long-term sedentary group. Sufficient evidence is needed for further experimental investigation.

Table 2. Statistical table of fatigue rest time.

Subject ID	Isometric task			Dynamic task		
	A1/C1	A2/C2	A3/C3	B1/D1	B2/D2	B3/D3
1	220.31	96.9	198.25	173.67	121.6	167.05
2	173.67	140.6	167.05	279.72	159.84	240.46
3	112.84	23.33	77.64	93.25	59.39	73
4	66.05	55.09	66.71	96.43	36.43	79.96
5	104	42.48	153.22	129.94	106.77	151.35
6	265.77	202.45	176.72	265.63	126.92	159.89
7	369.7	327.62	361.37	355.04	189.28	347.5
8	231.44	158.36	201.27	194.83	116.52	146.58
9	155.73	95.45	192.85	187.37	88.16	277.57
10	160.93	69.24	178.88	164.41	95.36	105.8
11	96.5	45.95	67.57	74.56	59.16	97.8
12	173.96	97.36	185.71	344.86	189.64	279.04
13	176.36	91.99	186.36	194.2	106.68	286.68
14	73.03	51.53	116.68	171.6	57.19	106.05
15	359.51	238.13	511.64	214.57	105.3	349.58
16	80.39	60.14	105.7	89.51	54.2	114.21
17	102.42	74.09	121.88	125.84	69.07	129.07
18	85.09	68.02	108.26	166.82	124.28	127.98
19	98.44	77.7	125.46	129.33	70.21	126.23
20	114.76	81.88	142.57	104.52	76.72	102.64

Note: All figures in the above table are in seconds

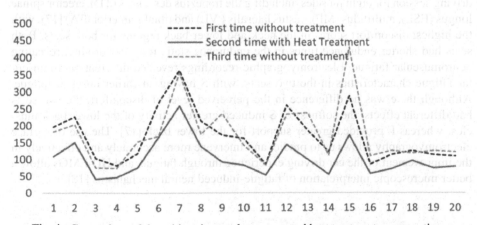

Fig. 4. Comparison of the subjects' natural recovery and heat treatment recovery time.

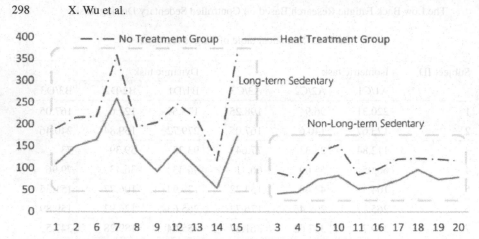

Fig. 5. Comparison of fatigue recovery effect between the long-term sedentary group and non-long-term sedentary group.

4 Product Design Expectation

4.1 Relevant Product Design

In the current product design, especially in the improvement of the driving experience of cars, the focus is on reducing the damage caused by the driver's prolonged passive, sedentary behavior and solving a series of problems caused by fatigue [15]. In Jangwoo and Shinsuk's study, drivers steered the steering wheel through kinematically constrained arm movements during daily driving, and such repetitive arm movements led to muscle fatigue and even neuromuscular damage [16]. The steering wheel design achieves a natural torsional motion by adding additional degrees of freedom to the driver's steering motion [16]. In an experiment by Mathieu Lecocq et al. comparing the effects of two different seats (S-soft and F-hard) on neuromuscular fatigue and discomfort during prolonged driving, surface electromyography (sEMG) was recorded throughout the driving session for eight muscles, including the trapezius descensus (TD), erector spinae longus (ESL), multifidus (MF), vastus lateralis (VL) and tibialis anterior (TA) [17], with the highest discomfort scores in the neck and lower back regions for both seats. Both seats had shorter endurance times in the endurance static test after driving, revealing neuromuscular fatigue. Electromyographic recordings revealed different neuromuscular fatigue characteristics in the two seats, with S having an earlier onset of fatigue. Although there was no difference in the perceived level of discomfort, the two seats had different effects: the softness of S induced greater activity of the lower back muscles, whereas F provided greater support for the lower back [17]. The use of surface electromyography allows us to predict and intervene more accurately and effectively in the improvement of the car driving experience through fatigue, and HD-EMGs allow a better microscopic interpretation of fatigue-induced neural mechanisms [18].

4.2 Product Design

HD-EMGs provide a better perspective for studying fatigue-induced neural mechanisms, and alpha bands, considered indicators of physiological and pathological tremors, may also increase after fatigue, as decomposed by MU spike trains [5]. Vibration during driving is also an important factor in lower back pain in professional drivers [19]. According to the experiment results, the fatigue recovery time of both ES and LDM was shortened after heat treatment in both long-term sedentary and non-long-term sedentary populations, and the fatigue recovery time in the non-long-term sedentary population was shorter than that in the non-long-term sedentary population under the same circumstances. Therefore, we designed the product to alleviate muscle fatigue and possibly lower back pain of ES and LDM muscle groups during driving using EMG interval monitoring and heat treatment. The renderings of the product were presented in Fig. 6 Fig. 7 and Fig. 8.

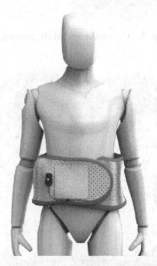

Fig. 6. Product design and human-computer interaction.

The product can be charged for heat treatment and is equipped with an EMG device, which can detect muscle fatigue in the ES and LDM areas of the user at intervals and record the corresponding muscle fatigue level in real-time. Suitable heat treatment makes long-term sedentary people and non-long-term sedentary people can play a role in relieving fatigue no matter the task of any driving process. However, the product still needs continuous improvement. Firstly, the consideration of the human-machine relationship of the product may need more research to determine further. Secondly, the product for fatigue detection and user fatigue level and the details of heat treatment control. The visualization can be additionally linked to the interface interaction design. Thirdly, the current appearance of the product is more inclined toward medical products; if the product is used in daily life, the shape of the product can be more enjoyable.

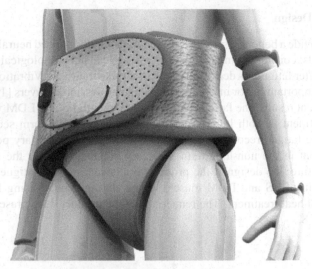

Fig. 7. Upward view of the product.

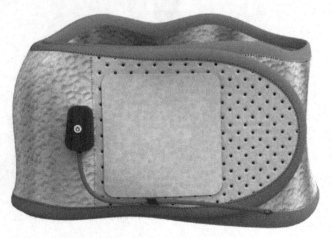

Fig. 8. Front view of the product design.

5 Conclusion

In the experimental study, significant increases were observed in MU synchronization in Delta, Alpha, Beta, and Gamma bands during the execution of both tasks. The results indicate that the microscopic fatigue mechanisms of the ES and LDM muscle groups in the lower back region do not vary depending on the contraction task, which provides new insights into the muscle fatigue in the lower back region of the driver during driving. In the fatigue recovery phase of subjects performing an exhaustive dynamic and isometric task, the long-term and non-long-term sedentary populations showed differences. The muscle fatigue of both long-term and very long-term sedentary people was better relieved under the treatment of heat recovery, which provides more possibilities for drivers' temporary fatigue due to long-term passive inactive. This offers the opportunity for more recovery means.

Acknowledgment. This work is sponsored by the Shanghai Sailing Program (22YF1430800).

References

1. Lalit: The prevalence of musculoskeletal disorders among bus drivers in Tricity. Int. J. Physiotherapy **2** (2015). https://doi.org/10.15621/ijphy/2015/v2i5/78244
2. Tamrin, S.B.M., et al.: The association between risk factors and low back pain among commercial vehicle drivers in peninsular Malaysia: a preliminary result. Ind. Health **45**, 268–278 (2007). https://doi.org/10.2486/indhealth.45.268
3. Farina, D., Merletti, R., Indino, B., Nazzaro, M., Pozzo, M.: Surface EMG crosstalk between knee extensor muscles: experimental and model results. Muscle Nerve. **26**, 681–695 (2002). https://doi.org/10.1002/mus.10256
4. Deluca, C., Erim, Z.: Common drive of motor units in the regulation of muscle force. Trends Neurosci. **17**, 299–305 (1994). https://doi.org/10.1016/0166-2236(94)90064-7
5. Hyvarinen: Fast and robust fixed-point algorithms for independent component analysis. IEEE Trans. Neural Netw. **10**, 626–634 (1999). 10.1109/ 72.761722
6. Tecchio, F., Porcaro, C., Zappasodi, F., Pesenti, A., Ercolani, M., Rossini, P.M.: Cortical short-term fatigue effects assessed via rhythmic brain–muscle coherence. Exp. Brain Res. **174**, 144–151 (2006). https://doi.org/10.1007/s00221-006-0432-8
7. Liu, X., et al.: Changes in synchronization of the motor unit in muscle fatigue condition during the dynamic and isometric contraction in the Biceps Brachii muscle. Neurosci. Lett. **761**, 136101 (2021). https://doi.org/10.1016/j.neulet.2021.136101
8. Pereira, W.M., Ferreira, L.A.B., Rossi, L.P., Kerpers, I.I., Grecco St, L.A.C., de Paula, A.R., Oliveira, C.S.: Influence of heat on fatigue and electromyographic activity of the biceps Brachii muscle. J. Bodyw. Mov. Ther. **15**, 478–484 (2011). https://doi.org/10.1016/j.jbmt.2011.04.007
9. Negro, F., Muceli, S., Castronovo, A.M., Holobar, A., Farina, D.: Multi-channel intramuscular and surface EMG decomposition by convolutive blind source separation. J. Neural Eng. **13**, 026027 (2016). https://doi.org/10.1088/1741-2560/13/2/026027
10. Farina, D., Merletti, R., Enoka, R.M.: The extraction of neural strategies from the surface EMG. J. Appl. Physiol. **96**, 1486–1495 (2004). https://doi.org/10.1152/japplphysiol.01070.2003
11. Dai, C., Shin, H., Davis, B., Hu, X.: Origins of common neural inputs to different compartments of the extensor digitorum communis muscle. Sci. Rep. **7**, 13960 (2017). https://doi.org/10.1038/s41598-017-14555-x
12. Thompson, L.V.: Effects of age and training on skeletal muscle physiology and performance. Phys. Ther. **74**, 71–81 (1994). https://doi.org/10.1093/ptj/74.1.71
13. Valouchová, P., Lewit, K.: Surface electromyography of abdominal and back muscles in patients with active scars. J. Bodyw. Mov. Ther. **13**, 262–267 (2009). https://doi.org/10.1016/j.jbmt.2008.04.033
14. Pereira, L.: Avaliação da atividade eletromiográfica e da força isométrica máxima do tibial anterior após aplicação de crioterapia. Universidade Do Vale Do Paraíba, São Paulo (2008)
15. Nurwahidah, A.: Ergonomics risk analysis of public transportation drivers (study case: public transportation drivers in Makassar city). IOP Conf. Ser. Mater. Sci. Eng. **505**, 012138 (2019). https://doi.org/10.1088/1757-899X/505/1/012138

16. Park, J., Park, S.: Reduction of arm fatigue and discomfort using a novel steering wheel design. Int. J. Precis. Eng. Manuf. **15**(5), 803–810 (2014). https://doi.org/10.1007/s12541-014-0403-0

17. Lecocq, M., et al.: Neuromuscular fatigue profiles depends on seat feature during long duration driving on a static simulator. Appl. Ergon. **87**, 103118 (2020). https://doi.org/10.1016/j.apergo.2020.103118

18. McManus, L., Hu, X., Rymer, W.Z., Suresh, N.L., Lowery, M.M.: Muscle fatigue increases beta-band coherence between the firing times of simultaneously active motor units in the first dorsal interosseous muscle. J. Neurophysiol. **115**, 2830–2839 (2016). https://doi.org/10.1152/jn.00097.2016

19. Wilder, D., Magnusson, M.L., Fenwiek, J., Pope, M.: The effect of post e seat suspension design discomfort back m le fatig duri simulated truck driving. Appl. Ergon. **25** (1994)

An Experimental Study of the Comfort of Stroke Rehabilitation Gloves Based on ANSYS

Yanmin Xue[1], Liangliang Shi[1(✉)], Qing Liu[2], and Suihuai Yu[3]

[1] School of Art and Design, Xi'an University of Technology, Xi'an, Shaanxi, China
2040129833@qq.com
[2] School of Automation and Control Engineering, Xi'an University of Technology, Xi'an, Shaanxi, China
[3] Industrial Design and Research Institute, Northwestern Polytechnical University, Xi'an, Shaanxi, China
ysuihuai@vip.sina.con

Abstract. In recent years, stroke diseases show a trend of rapid population growth and younger age, and impaired hand function is one of the main manifestations of stroke, and the market demand for rehabilitation gloves has expanded. In order to study the comfort of stroke rehabilitation gloves, the influence of different shapes of finger sleeves of tendon rehabilitation gloves on patient comfort was analyzed by finite element simulation, and guidance was provided for the comfort design of rehabilitation gloves. Combined with the existing research and market products of rehabilitation gloves, the factors affecting the comfort of rehabilitation gloves were analyzed; Using the finite element simulation method, the contact pressure generated between the finger sleeve and the finger of the tendon glove was simulated by static analysis, and five different modeling schemes were established according to the existing finger sleeve form, and the influence of finger sleeve size, shape, wrapping degree and other factors on the comfort of finger pressure was analyzed. Through the analysis and comparison of the finite element simulation results between different finger sleeve schemes and fingers, it is finally concluded that (1) generally soft fabrics have better pressure comfort than exoskeletons finger sleeves, and no matter what form of finger sleeves, longer sizes can reduce the pressure on fingers; (2) Increasing the fit between the exoskeleton finger sleeve and the finger surface can effectively improve the pressure comfort of the finger sleeve, and the hollow feature is easy to cause excessive contact pressure on the finger; (3) The contact pressure between the finger sleeve and the finger is less when the fixed parts are fully covered. This paper uses the finite element simulation analysis method to analyze the pressure comfort of tendon gloves, verifies the application value of the finite element method in product comfort design, and provides effective support for the comfort design and development of tendon rehabilitation gloves.

Keywords: Stroke · Rehabilitation gloves · Ansys · Finite element · Comfort

V. G. Duffy (Ed.): HCII 2023, LNCS 14028, pp. 303–314, 2023.
https://doi.org/10.1007/978-3-031-35741-1_23

1 Introduction

According to the China Stroke Prevention and Control Report 2019 [1], with the accelerated aging and urbanization of society, the prevalence of unhealthy lifestyles among residents, and the widespread exposure to cerebrovascular disease risk factors, the disease burden of stroke in China has an explosive growth trend and shows a rapid increase in low-income groups, significant gender and geographic differences, and a trend toward rejuvenation. Impaired hand function is one of the main manifestations of stroke. The dysfunction is often characterized by flexion contracture, predominant flexor tone of the hand, difficulty in extending the interphalangeal and metacarpophalangeal joints, loss of fine motor functions such as grip, lateral pinch, palmar and finger pairs, as well as loss of tactile and proprioceptive functions and loss of feedback perception of movement. According to scientific studies, the average person performs about 1,500 gripping movements per day, which is an important tool for communication with the external environment [2]. As a result, assistive devices for hand rehabilitation have emerged to replace the rehabilitation practitioner in helping patients to perform repetitive higher-intensity rehabilitation training, increasing rehabilitation efficiency and improving rehabilitation outcomes.

At present, most of the research on rehabilitation gloves at home and abroad focuses on functional hardware and mechanical structure, but often neglects the wearing comfort, color design and shape of rehabilitation gloves. These aspects are closely related to ergonomics. If the design is unreasonable or not considered, it will lead to a decline in user experience, reduce work efficiency, increase safety risks, and even lead to patients' resistance to using rehabilitation products. As for the hand rehabilitation market, domestic rehabilitation products are too homogeneous and homogenous in form, often choosing pneumatic control design and ignoring other possibilities. The design of rehabilitation gloves should take into account the special characteristics of patients' special diseases and their special psychological states, and improve the comfort experience of rehabilitation gloves from the user experience, so as to better help patients recover their hand functional deficits.

2 Overview of Rehabilitation Gloves

Research on hand rehabilitation robots first originated in Europe and the United States, and at the beginning of the 21st century, there were productized hand rehabilitation robots abroad, such as the hand exoskeleton robot from Carnegie Mellon University [3] and the hand motion-assisted rehabilitation robot developed by Gifu University [4], Japan. Traditional rehabilitation gloves can be broadly classified into rigid exoskeleton type and flexible wearable type according to their structures, among which the flexible wearable type has been developing faster in recent years due to its light weight and good fit with human hands. And from the type of drive mechanism contains three main categories: rigid linkage mechanism, pneumatic \ hydraulic mechanism and tendon drive structure [5]. The rigid linkage mechanism is usually composed of metal or 3D printed rigid rods, which is more accurate and intuitive for finger control, but the relative volume and weight is larger, and the wearability is poor; the pneumatic/hydraulic mechanism is mainly composed of a pump supplying air/liquid pressure, a control valve and an inflatable elastic actuator, and the actuator is mainly made of rubber or silicone, without complicated transmission components and good suppleness, which is the current market The tendon-based rehabilitation robot first appeared in early 2010, and its design can be regarded as the bionic of human hand structure, through the internal structure of human hand movement analysis, imitating the structure of tendons, muscles and ligaments during hand movement to design, its structural composition mainly includes artificial tendons, tendon fixation path components and wearable parts, artificial tendons are fixed by path The artificial tendon is fixed on the surface of the wearable glove by the path component, and the motor drives the tendon to realize the movement of the finger, which is small in size, light in weight and simple in structure, and very suitable for productization. At present, pneumatic is the most common type of rehabilitation gloves, but tendon gloves also have good market prospects, and their market application should receive more attention in the future.

3   The Comfort Study of Rehabilitation Gloves

3.1   Analysis of the Hand Characteristics of Stroke Patients

As one of the important organs of the human body, the hand is an important tool for human life at the beginning, which can realize complex and delicate movements, including pinching, grasping, gripping, etc. Its fine and sensitive motor senses are of great importance. Anatomical studies have shown that the human hand is mainly composed of the carpal, metacarpal and finger bones and the muscles connected to them, and contains many arteries, nerves, ligaments and so on. A single human hand consists of 29 bones, 123 ligaments, 48 nerves, 35 muscles and more than 30 arteries, making its composition quite complex [6]. In terms of the motor characteristics of the hand, the main motor joints include the metacarpophalangeal (MCP), proximal phalangeal (PIP), and distal phalangeal (DIP) joints, of which the metacarpophalangeal joint can be flexed and extended and abducted, while the phalangeal joint can only be flexed and extended, and these movements are mainly achieved by the tendons attached to the finger bones.

The main etiology and clinical manifestations of hand dysfunction in stroke patients include three aspects [7]. First, the affected hand is in a state of flaccid paralysis caused by hypotonia, with complete loss of motor function, no random movements, no joint responses and no synergistic movements, and occasional micro-contraction of the major muscles, but not able to cause any effective activity; second, the affected hand spasm caused by abnormal muscle tone, specifically It is characterized by hand curling, finger flexion and rotation forward. The spasticity lasts for a long time and can lead to complications such as difficulty in hand free movement and finger flexion deformity; thirdly, some patients may suffer from a partial sensory deficit in the affected hand, including partial perceptual deficit and deficit in position and motion perception, which significantly affects the sensory and motor functions of the affected hand.

3.2   Factors Affecting the Comfort of Rehabilitation Gloves

At present, the function of the rehabilitation gloves is to drive the fingers of the affected hand to bend and stretch by means of pneumatic and electric motors, and the movement process mainly occurs in the fingers, relying on the binding module of the fingers to transmit force and thus control the activities of the fingers. The general soft rehabilitation gloves on the market are mainly fixed and adapted to the hand by means of Velcro, and the size of the glove will affect the comfort of driving and movement of the fingers; in addition, the fingers will inevitably receive pressure from the binding components during movement, and the material of the glove will also affect the tactile perception of the patient's hand. Therefore, in the comfort design of rehabilitation gloves, the ergonomic analysis is mainly based on the product size adaptation, binding pressure and material selection.

- **Size adaptation.**

As the patient's hand is driven by the glove to perform various movements, the rehabilitation glove should have a good fit with the affected hand to achieve high man-machine synergy, and should also have a suitable gap to facilitate the patient's posture adjustment during the wearing process to reduce the pressure of tight binding during the movement. For general glove sizing, only the length and width of the hand are usually considered, but the variability of other hand sizes is ignored. Some studies have shown that for different regions, even if the length and width are approximately the same, there are considerable differences in the proportion of the various parts of the human hand. The three obvious characteristics of the palm and fingers were found to have a higher proportion of thumb, index finger or little finger, and then through analysis and experimentation, three types of hand shapes were finally summarized as thumb dominant, average and ring small dominant [8].

These studies can also be applied to the design of the size adaptability of rehabilitation gloves. During the research of related products, it was found that the current consideration of the size of rehabilitation gloves is that some large enterprises will provide personal customization services for patients, so that patients can get more suitable rehabilitation products; on the other hand, the size design of ordinary gloves is followed, and the rehabilitation gloves are roughly divided into S-L, etc. On the other hand, the size of the rehabilitation gloves are divided into S-L and so on, which can match the geometric size of different hands within a certain range, which causes the same size gloves to be worn by different patients with large gaps between their fingers, thus affecting the efficiency of the human-machine synergy between the rehabilitation gloves and the patients. Therefore, the size adaptability design of rehabilitation gloves should add a certain range of adjustability in the finger part that is easy to produce differences, in order to adapt to patients with the same hand size but different hand shapes.

- **Binding pressure**

The binding parts are the flexible support formed by the wrapping parts that act on the limbs, waist or back of wearable products such as exoskeletons in order to achieve man-machine matching and synergistic movement with the human body [9]. For the rehabilitation gloves, the binding parts are mainly concentrated in the wrist, fingers, tiger mouth and other parts. Commonly used binding methods include Velcro, buckles, adjustable straps, bar buckles, etc., of which Velcro and bar buckles are the more commonly used binding methods.

The binding pressure is the force generated by the vertical action of the binding parts on the skin surface of the human body when wearing the product, and a moderate force can often effectively improve the synergy between the product and the human body and the degree of human-machine matching. The finger area is the most frequent and extensive part of the patient's rehabilitation training, and it is subject to stronger binding pressure. Moderate binding pressure can ensure the fit between the fingers and the rehabilitation glove and improve the efficiency of movement, while excessive binding pressure can increase the pressure on the soft tissues of the hands and affect the blood flow of the capillaries on the surface of the hands, resulting in an uncomfortable use experience. Therefore, the design of the finger area should take into account the surface pressure of different shapes and materials on the finger area, so as to reduce the binding pressure on the finger area as much as possible and distribute the pressure reasonably while ensuring the efficiency of human-machine cooperation.

- **Material selection**

The material selection of rehabilitation products is one of the most important aspects of the design process, especially for wearable rehabilitation products. In the whole process of rehabilitation training, the tactile sensation generated by the contact between the flexible material and the skin of the affected hand will affect the comfort of the product. The flexible material chosen for the rehabilitation glove should meet the skin-friendly, soft and other characteristics, but also should have a certain mechanical stiffness to support the synergistic movement between the glove and the hand. In addition, the breathability and friction coefficient of the material should be considered to avoid discomfort such as stuffiness and sweating of the patient's hand. At present, the materials commonly used in rehabilitation gloves include SBR neoprene, OK cloth, silicone, PP material, etc. Among them, SBR and OK cloth are often used in pneumatic rehabilitation gloves, and silicone and PP material are often used in tendon-driven rehabilitation gloves.

4 Based on the Tendon Drive Mechanism Finite Element

Tendon-driven soft exoskeleton rehabilitation gloves are relatively simple and easy to control the force transmission, and by combining the artificial tendon-driven structure with the soft gloves made of fabric, the compactness of the wearable part can be improved and a more comfortable wearing experience can be obtained. This type of product motion control is mainly through the artificial tendon fixed in the soft glove surface path components, and finally fixed in the fingertip area, by pulling the other end of the artificial tendon to transfer the force to the fingertip to achieve finger movement, and currently due to the late development of this type of rehabilitation gloves, there is no more mature marketable products, most of them remain in the laboratory stage. In the overall form of rehabilitation gloves, there are two types of gloves, one is the exoskeleton form using a single material such as PP and silicone to fix the parts, which is in direct contact with the hand (see Fig. 1) [10]; the other is the soft fabric form with the fixation parts anchored on fabric (see Fig. 2) [11]. In this process, the fingertip area is the main part to bear the force transmission, and it is also the part of the hand with the most sensitive sense of touch, so it is easy to produce discomfort caused by bad the shape and material of the finger cap, the fixed part in direct contact with the fingertip, are the main factors that affect the size and uniformity of the pressure on the fingertip. The FEM simulation method is used to analyze the pressure of the finger and the finger cap.

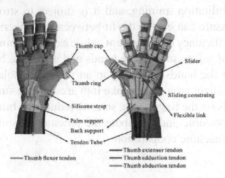 

Fig. 1. The exoskeleton form   **Fig. 2.** The soft fabric form

4.1 Pre-model Construction

The establishment of an accurate and reasonable simulation model is the key factor for the finite element simulation of simulated pressure. In this study, we mainly focus on the contact pressure simulation on the fingertip area, so we consider to intercept only the middle finger of the hand model for analysis, and at the same time, considering the difficulty of problem analysis and calculation time, we divide the middle finger into two layers of different materials, such as bone and soft tissue (see Fig. 3).

Fig. 3. Finger double layer simulation model

The modeling scheme of the finger cap is designed for five kinds according to the above two different forms of exoskeleton and soft fabric, and the modeling is simplified, only need to meet the simulation requirements. The two forms of Program 1, Program 2 and Program 3 are short, medium and long sizes respectively, and the size difference is between 4–5 mm, so as to compare the influence of the size factor on the finger contact pressure; Program 4 of the exoskeleton category adds hollow features, and the inner wall of Program 5 is basically the same as the finger shape, which has the most ideal fit, Meanwhile, the Program 3, Program 4 and Program 5 sizes are the same, so as to observe the effect of hollow out and fit on the finger contact pressure compared with other schemes; the soft fabric Program 4 and Program 5 follow the size of Program 2 to change the degree of covering of the fixed parts, and the effect of the degree of covering on the finger contact pressure was analyzed by comparing the results of Program 3, 4 and 5 (see Fig. 4 and 5).

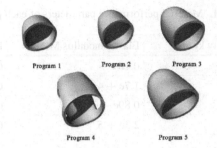

Fig. 4. Exoskeleton class program model

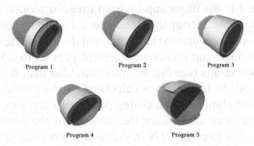

Fig. 5. Soft fabric class program model (grey is fabric)

4.2 ANSYS Workbench Finite Element Analysis

In order to verify the pressure comfort of the finger sleeve program, this study uses the Workbench simulation platform developed by ANSYS to perform a static analysis of the contact pressure between different program and the finger. Firstly, after importing the simulation models constructed in advance into Workbench, the material property parameters of the different models need to be set. According to the literature [12, 13], human skin as well as subcutaneous tissues including muscles exhibit low stiffness under small strain, while the stiffness increases exponentially when the strain increases, so the hyperelastic behavior should be used for material properties, and the soft tissue material properties are defined by the Ogden hyperelastic material model. Meanwhile, the skin is the main pressure sensing organ of the finger in this study, so the soft tissue material properties are adopted from the skin material properties of the hand; the muscle and finger cap are set as flexibles, and their material nonlinear behavior is considered, and the corresponding material properties are set; the finger cap is made of PP material, which is commonly used for 3D printing, and the fabric is simulated by carbon fiber material. The material parameters of each model are shown in Table 1.

Since the distal end of the finger of the exoskeleton type is in direct contact with the finger cap and the corresponding friction is generated between the two contact surfaces when driving the tendon, the contact is set as friction contact with a friction coefficient of 0.3, while the fabric type is set as friction contact between the fabric and the finger, and the fixed part is set as binding contact with the fabric to simulate the actual effect; at the same time, a fixed support is set at one end of the finger to prevent the finger from

Table 1. Material performance parameters of each part.

Materials	Density kg/m^3	Elastic modulus MPa	Font size and style
Soft Tissue	1000	0.18	0.42
Bone	1185	1.7e + 4	0.3
PP	900	0.89e + 3	0.42
Carbon Fiber	1800	2.3e + 5	0.2–0.4

slipping. In addition, according to the actual working condition, the motion constraint should also be applied to the finger cap to avoid irregular motion such as rotation; in terms of mesh division, considering the simulation calculation speed and accuracy, the overall model cell mesh size is divided into 1mm, and the part where the contact between the finger tip and the finger cap is encrypted separately is set to 0.5mm to improve the accuracy of simulation results (see Fig. 6); after that After that, the initial contact state between the finger and the finger cap is calculated by the contact tool to avoid rigid body displacement and eliminate the existing penetration and gap, so as to reduce the additional penetration stress and ensure the accuracy of the results. After the above settings are completed, a force of 10 N in the direction normal to the cross-section is applied to the finger cap to simulate the tendon tension during the finger movement, and the solution is performed.

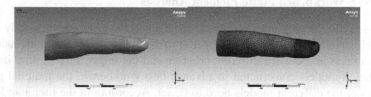

Fig. 6. Finger part meshing

4.3 Analysis of Simulation Results

Pressure comfort is an important factor affecting the comfort of wearing rehabilitation gloves. Excessive pressure will cause excessive pressure on the muscles of the hands, thus causing muscle fatigue and reducing the comfort experience. In addition, the uniformity of pressure distribution also affects the wearing comfort. The final simulations under the same boundary load conditions resulted in the magnitude and distribution of the pressure on the fingertips of each program, as shown in Figs. 7 and 8 for the exoskeleton and the soft fabric. The common point of the two is that the area with the greatest pressure is basically concentrated in the abdomen of the fingertip, and gradually spreads around. At the same time, it can be observed that the pressure diffusion area is larger in the abdomen and the back is smaller, which indicates that the middle finger abdomen bears more pressure during the pulling process.

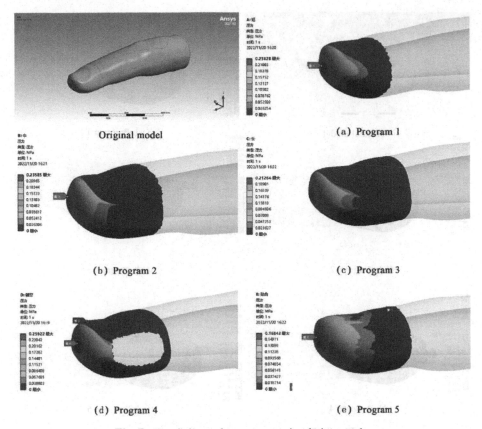

Fig. 7. Exoskeleton class pressure simulation results

- **Exoskeleton class simulation analysis.**

According to the simulation results, there is no contact pressure in the hollow part of Program 4 because there is no contact, and the contact pressure is the largest compared with Scheme 3, indicating that adding the hollow out feature under the same conditions will increase the contact pressure between the finger and the finger sleeve. Compared with the results of Program 1 (short size), Program 2 (medium size) and Program 3 (long size), the pressure value of the short size of Program 1 is significantly increased, which indicates that too short finger sleeve will lead to the increase of contact pressure; From the perspective of pressure distribution, compared with Program 3 and other Programs, Program 5 has a very reasonable and uniform pressure distribution and the lowest pressure value, which indicates that the ideal fit helps to evenly distribute the pressure on the finger, significantly reduce the pressure value, and improve the wearing comfort.

- **Soft fabric class simulation analysis.**

The change of pressure magnitude from Program 1 to Program 3 of the soft fabric category reflects the effect of size change on finger pressure, where Program 3 (long

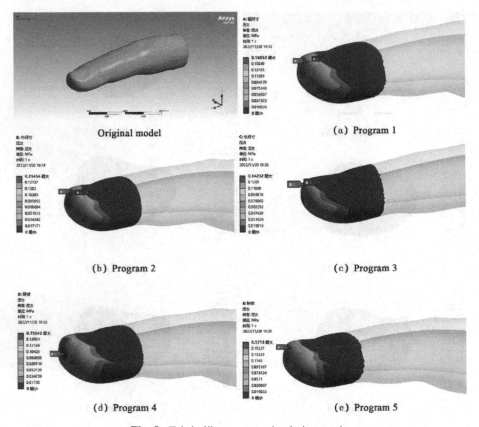

Fig. 8. Fabric-like pressure simulation results

size) has a smaller pressure, and the result is consistent with the exoskeleton category, so the fixed parts on the fabric should be selected with longer size more suitable; Program 2, Program 4 and Program 5 (The package degree is a full package, a half and a quarter, respectively)have gradually increasing pressure values, which indicates that the contact pressure on the finger caused by the fully wrapped fixed parts is smaller, and the specific pressure values The specific pressure values change as shown in Fig. 9.

In general, whether exoskeleton or soft fabric, the smaller finger pressure requires its fixed parts to be designed with longer size; from the overall trend of pressure value changes, The pressure value of the exoskeleton scheme 5 (with ideal fit) has decreased very significantly, which indicates that the fit degree of the finger sleeve shape and the surface shape of the human finger has a great influence on the contact pressure of the finger; the pressure value of the fabric Program 5 (One-quarter parcel)is the largest, indicating that the reduction in the degree of fixed parts wrapping will affect the pressure comfort of the finger area. In addition, compared with the exoskeleton class, the soft fabric is more supple for the contact pressure caused by the finger is smaller, so from the point of view of finger comfort, the soft fabric form is more in line with the needs of the user to wear.

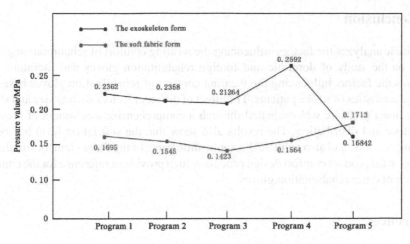

Fig. 9. Variation of pressure values for both forms

5   Discussion

From the results of finite element simulation, the shape, material and size of the finger cover affect the finger pressure comfort. By choosing the optimal finger cover solution (soft fabric form, longer size) in the design of tendon-driven gloves, the finger surface contact pressure can be significantly reduced, thus enhancing the comfort experience of rehabilitation gloves. Finite element simulation methods have been widely used in research on human comfort and have a great role in product development to obtain data on deformation, displacement and contact area of human tissues at low cost to guide the design of product solutions. In recent years, the research on hand comfort mainly focuses on the comfort of hand tools, including hand grip posture, pressure distribution, grip force size and operational flexibility, etc. For example, Gregor et al. [12] developed a finite element hand model, which can simulate the grip and motion of the hand using finite element simulation technology and provide quantitative results for product ergonomics analysis; Kazuki et al. [14] have studied the relationship between hand grip comfort and contact pressure and hand posture.

In the current studies of stroke rehabilitation gloves, few of them have addressed the aspect of comfort in use, and most of them have focused on structural hardware and control algorithms. Therefore, the article studies the existing rehabilitation glove products, analyzes the comfort influence factors, and applies the finite element simulation method to the comfort design research of the product using the tendon-actuated glove as an example, and evaluates the comfort influence of different solutions through quantitative simulation results, effectively confirming the role of finite element simulation in the product comfort design process. Due to the complexity of human tissue biomechanics, the hand simulation experiments conducted in the article only focus on the static simulation analysis of the fingers, ignoring the simulation changes in the dynamic process of the hand, and a dynamic digital model of the hand should be developed in the future to more realistically reflect the interaction between the hand and the product and guide the comfort design of the product.

6 Conclusion

The article analyzes the factors influencing the wearing comfort of rehabilitation gloves based on the study of domestic and foreign rehabilitation gloves and literature, and analyzes the factors influencing the wearing comfort of rehabilitation gloves based on the characteristics of stroke patients. The effect of different factors such as size and shape on the finger pressure was evaluated through a comprehensive assessment of pressure magnitude and distribution. The results also show that the soft fabric form has better wearing comfort, and also validate the application value of the finite element simulation method in the product comfort design process, which provides a reference for the comfort research of other rehabilitation gloves.

References

1. Summary of the China stroke prevention and control report 2019. Chinese J. Cerebrovasc. Dis. **17**(05), 272–281 (2020)
2. Zheng, J.Z., Rosa, S.D.L., Dollar, A.M.: An investigation of grasp type and frequency in daily household and machine shop tasks. In: IEEE International Conference on robotics and Automation, Shanghai, CN, pp. 4169–4175. IEEE Press (2011)
3. Pu, S.W., Tsai, S.Y., Chang, J.Y.: Design and development of the wearable hand exoskeleton system for rehabilitation of hand impaired patients. In: 2014 IEEE International Conference on Automation Science and Engineering, Taipei, CN, pp. 996–1001. IEEE Press (2014)
4. Kawasaki, H., Ito, S., Ishigure, Y., et al.: Development of a hand motion assist robot for rehabilitation therapy by patient self-motion control. In: IEEE International Conference on Rehabilitation Robotics, Noordwijk, NL, pp. 234–240. IEEE Press (2007)
5. Tran, P., Jeong, S., Herrin, K.R., Desai, J.P.: Review: hand exoskeleton systems, clinical rehabilitation practices, and future prospects. IEEE Trans. Med. Robot. Bionics **3**(3), 606–622 (2021). https://doi.org/10.1109/TMRB
6. Gao, X.L., Yu, E.H.: Human anatomy (2003)
7. Zhou, Y.F., Wang, D.Q., Li, H.W., Liu, J.X.: Research progress of hand mobility disorders after stroke. China Rehabil. 151–154 (2017)
8. Vergara, M., Agost, M.-J., Bayarri, V.: Anthropometric characterisation of palm and finger shapes to complement current glove-sizing systems. Int. J. Ind. Ergon. **74**, 102836 (2019)
9. Ming, Z.W., Gan, J., Luo, W.X., Wang, M.Q.: Exploring the safety and comfort design of active exoskeleton strapping system. Design **33**(18), 134–136 (2020)
10. Chen, W., Li, G., Li, N., et al.: Soft exoskeleton with fully actuated thumb movements for grasping assistance. IEEE Trans. Rob. **38**(4), 2194–2207 (2022). https://doi.org/10.1109/TRO.2022.3148909
11. Popov, D., Gaponov, I., Ryu, J.-H.: Portable exoskeleton glove with soft structure for hand assistance in activities of daily living. IEEE-ASME Trans. Mechatron. **22**(2), 865–875 (2017). https://doi.org/10.1109/TMECH-2016.2641932
12. Harih, G., Kalc, M., Vogrin, M., Fodor-Mühldorfer, M.: Finite element human hand model: validation and ergonomic considerations. Int. J. Ind. Ergon. **85**, 103186 (2021)
13. Lu, T.J., Xu, F.: Overview of mechanical properties of skin. Adv. Mech. (04), 393–426 (2008)
14. Hokari, K., Pramudita, J.A., Ito, M., et al.: The relationships of gripping comfort to contact pressure and hand posture during gripping. Int. J. Ind. Ergon. **70**, 84–91 (2019)

Job Design and Human Productivity

Development and Evaluation of a Knowledge-Based Cyber-Physical Production System to Support Industrial Set-Up Processes Considering Ergonomic and User-Centered Aspects

Nils Darwin Abele[1]([✉]) [iD], Sven Hoffmann[2] [iD],
Aparecido Fabiano Pinatti De Carvalho[3] [iD], Marcus Schweitzer[4] [iD], Volker Wulf[2] [iD],
and Karsten Kluth[1] [iD]

[1] Ergonomics Division, University of Siegen, Siegen, Germany
darwin.abele@uni-siegen.de
[2] Institute of Information Systems and New Media, University of Siegen, Siegen, Germany
[3] Department of Informatics, University of Oslo, Oslo, Norway
[4] Chair of Technology Management, University of Siegen, Siegen, Germany

Abstract. Dynamic markets and constantly changing work practices are causing an increased number of industrial set-up operations on production machines in the wake of a growing demand for customized product requirements. Augmented reality (AR)-based cyber-physical production systems (CPPS) can be used to support complex and knowledge-intensive processes. Resting on a comprehensive ethnographic study, this topic was addressed to identify practices of machine operators in the course of set-up processes on forming or bending machines through a qualitative research approach. Subsequently, a set-up application for an AR-mediated head-mounted display was developed according to a user-centered design approach. For a holistic, objective and subject-related human factors analysis on the handling of AR-based CPPS in the context of assembly or set-up processes, ergonomic sub-studies were conducted. The research work advances the state of the art in the design of digital technologies or CPPS to support operators who are entrusted with set-up processes of industrial production machines.

Keywords: Augmented Reality · Cyber-Physical Production System · Industrial Set-Up

1 Introduction

Due to their central and time-critical character within a production process, industrial set-up operations are elementary from both a scientific and a practical point of view, as they are associated with considerable cost expenditure for the manufacturing companies [1]. Through increasing product individualizations, not only the number of set-up processes to be performed rises, but also the complexity of the individual set-up steps

V. G. Duffy (Ed.): HCII 2023, LNCS 14028, pp. 317–329, 2023.
https://doi.org/10.1007/978-3-031-35741-1_24

because of constantly changing work practices [2]. In order to maintain high-quality and reliable products, efforts are being made to optimize these processes, particularly with regard to the time required and the conservation of resources. Furthermore, it is important to secure and pass on the knowledge of the skilled workers with the help of fast and effective learning procedures. During the technological progress, analog solutions are increasingly being replaced by digital ones [3]. User-centered, ergonomic and knowledge-based support of humans by digital technologies, for example in the form of augmented reality (AR) supported cyber-physical systems (CPS) or cyber-physical production systems (CPPS), has so far received only limited attention, especially with respect to small and medium-sized enterprises.

In the course of the research project "Cyberrüsten 4.0", a prototype application for a mixed reality technology using the Microsoft "HoloLens" first generation was developed using the example of industrial set-up processes on forming and bending machines and evaluated taking into account ergonomic and user-centered aspects. With the help of this head-mounted display (HMD), process-relevant information can be projected holographically and context-specifically into the user's real field of view and enriched with internal and external sensor data and simulations. This article summarizes the main milestones of the research project. Among others, specific information on individual topics can be found in the papers by Abele and Kluth [4, 5], de Carvalho et al. [1, 6] and Hoffmann et al. [2, 7].

2   Related Work

2.1   Technology Development Within Industrial Processes

In order to be able to guarantee experienced and, in particular, inexperienced machine operators comprehensive work support based on theory and the current state of the art, practical, efficient and user-centered methods and tools must be used. The approaches and methods of the "Lean" philosophy and Industry 4.0 or the (Industrial) Internet of Things open up a wide range of possibilities for physical process design, such as AR technologies [3, 8], in the course of the digital transformation and the accompanying variety of highly engineered end devices – especially CPPS and HMD.

Milgram et al. [9] relate the terms "augmented reality" and "virtual reality" together with true reality and augmented virtuality in the form of a reality-virtuality continuum. Augmented virtuality, in which a virtual situation is enriched with information from the real environment, and augmented reality can be described as mixed forms between pure reality and pure virtuality as mixed reality. In the course of these AR research efforts, two main areas of application have emerged: The combination of conventional input mechanisms in the form of keyboard and mouse with displays as output mechanisms [10] and the use of touchscreens and HMDs in conjunction with voice commands [11]. More recent developments focus on the use of gestures as possible interaction mechanisms for AR-based systems [12]. Both application areas aim at the same purpose: The immersive perception of the real world enriched with virtual components.

Cyber-physical systems are systems of tightly coupled physical and digital or cyber-physical components that integrate software, hardware, sensors, and actuators. The general definition of CP(P)S implies that they can connect and manage distributed systems consisting of physical and virtual entities [13]. Their characteristic features are the interconnection of different production components, such as machines or tools and the data sets that characterize them [14]. Interaction with such systems takes place through a human-machine interface, which can be realized by conventional PC interfaces, touch screens or described AR-based technologies. Current and previous research has shown that CPPS can potentially support and facilitate many different processes and expertise in a socio-technical context [1, 2, 7]. Research on the practical application of AR-based cyber-physical production systems, especially in the form of data glasses or head-mounted displays, is still considered underrepresented. At the same time, it shows their potential [15]. Due to the relatively early stage of development, some of them have (interaction-)ergonomic limitations with regard to both the constructive and the application-specific hardware and software design, which inevitably influence user acceptance [5, 16, 17].

2.2 Design of Practical and Knowledge-Based Support Systems

Human practices are actions due to the continuous changes in the environment, often guided by knowledge and mediated by artifacts [18]. In addition, however, non-propositional knowledge, for example in the form of embodied or non-verbalizable actions, also plays a significant role [14]. These mediated mental and physical actions result in routinized patterns, which in turn are used to normatively shape contingent activities [19, 20]. Practice-based computing pays particular attention to the dialogue between knowledge, artifacts and actions that takes place in practice. Within this paradigm, "design" is understood as the result of a creative activity in which knowledge, artifacts and actions work together to create something new [21]. Design emerges as a multi-layered intervention in practice that results in useful and usable tools for users to achieve specific goals or perform specific tasks [18] – for example, to assist machine operators on bending machines.

Augmented reality systems and CPPS, in conjunction with sensor technologies in knowledge-intensive environments, can help to establish fast, unrestricted and context-specific access to information to support learning processes by recording and visualizing knowledge embedded in embodied actions [22]. In this regard, they represent approaches to innovative handling of such processes in favor of efficient work practices [23]. In contrast to the fields of organizational and process management [24–26], the importance of innovative methods for optimizing capture and documentability as well as promoting knowledge transfer among colleagues has been neglected for industrial contexts [27].

2.3 Ergonomics in the Industrial (Set-Up) Context

The prevention of work-related illnesses and the strengthening of employee health promotion entail various challenges and new stress situations in the course of advancing digitalization. Set-up and assembly operations typically feature physical work activities

[5]. Short cycle times and basic work content, sometimes with very narrow process limits, can also have a psychological impact on workers in addition to one-sided physical stress. Among other things, the latter can be triggered by the handling of new types of terminal equipment that are used as tools for performing work [28].

In order to meet these requirements in the best possible way, a specific effects' investigation of direct and indirect work activities is an elementary component of an occupational science analysis. According to Luczak & Volpert [29], it comprises technical, organizational and social conditions of work processes. Objective stress variables and factors act as input variables on a work system. These are to be distinguished from the subjectively perceived strain, which is characterized as the effect of the input variables on humans [30]. The stress-strain concept, which can be traced back to Rohmert [31] represents a theoretical approach that links human-centered aspects of a work system with respect to their causes and effects [32]. Thus, the mutual humans' reactions with their work can be investigated [33]. Procedures for the ergonomic evaluation of work are usually used to analyze a workplace with regard to its risks to human hazards. Depending on the method of the procedure, i.e. metrological, objective or subjective procedures, not only the extent of a possible risk but also suggestions for countermeasures are offered. For example, the task of a machine setter to retrofit a bending machine, which is supplemented by the use of AR-supported data goggles, can be analyzed from an ergonomic point of view through the use of peripheral physiological electromyography (EMG), a thermoregulatory examination, and a global evaluation of the overall strain through workplace assessment procedures. In particular, the electrophysiological measurement method of EMG captures the signals already present in the body without significantly interfering with the performance of work or inconveniencing the work person [34]. The analysis results of the relevant methods and procedures are supplemented by subjective assessments of the worker [35].

In recent years, a large number of studies have been conducted on the use of AR-based data glasses in relation to different research topics, especially with regard to work efficiency and potential knowledge transfer approaches. However, ergonomic studies of potential effects on humans as a result of handling AR-based HMDs have been considered only to a limited extent, especially in an industrial context and in relation to applications that require an increased level of accuracy [36]. On the one hand, relevant studies have identified physical strains, especially in the user's shoulder-neck region [17, 37], and on the other hand, psychological or cognitive strains [38, 39].

3   Methodology

On the basis of a comprehensive ethnographic study, the described subject was addressed in order to be able to identify practices of machine operators in the course of set-up processes on forming and bending machines. In doing so, it was clarified how a methodological transition from qualitative research to the user-centered design of a knowledge-based supporting system can be created in the sense of the research paradigm of "grounded design". This aims to investigate changes in human practices resulting from the use and appropriation of digital technologies [18]. The insights of such studies are used as input for the design of new and innovative digital solutions. In this context, the design case study (DCS), which is divided into three interdependent phases (an empirical (preliminary) study (1), a design of an innovative representation form (2) and a practical evaluation and appropriation of the system (3)), provides a suitable methodological infrastructure for a successful implementation of grounded design [19]. For this purpose, the relevance of modeling the task spectrum and a scenario-based design approach with respect to essential design implications for a CPPS to be used in the set-up context should be highlighted. The study's findings should lead to a comprehensive knowledge transfer model that facilitates and optimizes the derivation of design implications for practical CPPS. Based on a comparison of technical possibilities with the practice-relevant requirements for knowledge and experience transfer captured in the model, a new methodological approach based on augmented reality and sensor technology for the capture and transfer of propositional and procedural knowledge embedded in embodied or practical actions can then be realized in the form of a (prototypical) software application for an AR-based HMD. The practical example further demonstrates to what extent a cyber-physical set-up application complies with or meets the applicable interaction-ergonomic and compatibility-related standards in the context of industrial activities and gesture-controlled, binocular AR systems.

In order to be able to verify or falsify the qualitative findings obtained and finally expand them with quantitative components, the "sequential exploratory design" [40] was used. This mixed-methods approach is based on the analysis of both qualitative and quantitative data that are sequentially collected, prioritized and integrated into one or more phases of the research process. To evaluate the set-up process in an ergonomic and user-friendly manner, quantitative evaluation and measurement methods were also used to expand the qualitative knowledge base. In addition to a screening (Leitmerkmalmethode, LMM) and expert procedure (Ergonomic Assessment Worksheet, EAWS) for the workplace assessment of an industrial set-up operation, selected strain-relevant parameters were investigated based on a comparison between work execution using HoloLens-supported and paper-based instruction within the framework of ergonomic laboratory studies during simple assembly activities and static gaze positioning (sub-study 1) as well as in the course of a set-up process of a rotary draw bending machine (sub-study 2, see Fig. 1).

Fig. 1. Subjects while performing the set-up procedure using the paper instruction (left) and while using the HoloLens (center and right).

Moreover, measurement of muscle physiological parameters of the shoulder-neck area (m. trapezius pars descendens and m. sternocleidomastoideus) by means of surface electromyography (Noraxon TeleMyo 2400T G2) and thermographic parameters in the head area by means of a thermal imaging camera (FLIR T250) were used. Various questionnaire instruments were also consulted, consisting of standardized questionnaires (NASA Task Load Index, Rating Scale of Mental Effort and Visual Fatigue Questionnaire) and qualitative interviews, which also covered aspects of usability in addition to the physiological or psychological experience of strain. Figure 2 shows examples of the measurement methods and techniques used globally and at specific body sites.

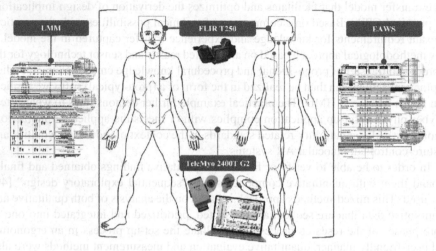

Fig. 2. Measurement methods and evaluation procedures used to objectify work-related stress and strain.

4   Results

The results of the research work show that, in addition to the "workflow" and knowledge-intensive character of an industrial set-up operation, the relationship between dynamic and static process elements with mechanical and non-mechanical work processes, such as the assembly of tools or change processes in the machine program, is also essential for the design of a support system to be used in this context. While some set-up steps, such as the wiper die's assembly of a rotary draw bending machine, can be documented and thus systematized and made explicit due to their simple and quick explanation (e.g. with the help of checklists), others cannot. The latter is particularly due to the fact that machine operators cannot articulate their actions because of supposed banality or too much variability or complexity. The complexity of the tool change is determined in particular by the number of components to be changed and the tool composition of the previous production order. There are also potential challenges in handling or interacting with digital technologies during such activities. Especially, setting up industrial machines requires increased mobility and constant use of both hands to perform the various set-up steps. Therefore, a mobile system for visualizing relevant information should be available at the required different locations in a timely and error-free manner.

A knowledge transfer model based on empirical data has been developed to support the progress and implementation of new and innovative technologies [2, 41, 42]. It presents the empirically collected data with special consideration of knowledge seekers and knowledgeable persons in a situational and organizational context. In addition to the knowledge-based insights gained from the empirical data and channeled through the knowledge transfer model, a set of tool-specific requirements to assist machine operators in industrial set-up operations was identified. These requirements were technically implemented through practice-oriented design implications for CPPS in the described context, taking into account essential ergonomic, compatibility, and user-centric guidelines [1, 4, 6, 41, 42].

Within the scope of the DCS and following a mixed-methods approach, these substantive explanations were first supplemented by an evaluation in natural environments (see Fig. 3 [7]).

Fig. 3. Evaluation of the developed cyber-physical system in different companies or in relation to different set-up processes.

The support of the AR-CPPS based on the transfer of knowledge and expertise manifests itself in the practical (set-up) application in different topics, such as a promotion of independent learning at the workplace and the saving time capacities. It provides a simple and flexible way to record, edit, share and access propositional knowledge embodied in actions. Key interaction requirements and design implications can be divided into four dimensions: The creation and visualization of text-, image-, video-, and holographic-based set-up instructions, the use of sensors (e.g., a 3D camera to check tool positioning), collaborative editing of set-up steps using a set-up editor and dynamic set-up support (e.g. using simulations).

The workplace assessment procedure "Ergonomic Assessment Worksheet" was also used to carry out a weighted risk assessment of the work task using the example of setting up a rotary draw bending machine. From the posture, force and load handling evaluations as well as specific extra points (e.g. short-term special joint positions) it is clear, taking into account the upper extremities, that measures with regard to the reorganization or redesign of the work process are not absolutely necessary, but are recommended. A lower-risk execution of the set-up process with the aid of the HoloLens is justified in comparison to the set-up process execution using a paper instruction by the posture evaluation, which results due to the interaction-related improved overall body posture. The greatest risk factor is posed by action forces during the assembly of individual tools.

Within the two sub-studies, both the objective and subjective strain data did not exceed a moderate level during the experimental procedures. Only measured values of the muscles of the m. sternocleidomastoid, which lie opposite to the direction of gaze and are based on static work components, were clearly above the 15% limit of the maximum capacity of the respective muscles with an average of approx. 23% of the standardized electromyographic activity recorded with the aid of the surface EMG during very strong lateral head movements. Due to the largely natural movements of the test person, dynamic work or set-up activities require constant contraction and relaxation of the muscles, which are thus less stressed than with a purely static muscle load. The differences in the EMG data with and without the use of HoloLens are predominantly significantly minimal overall. However, a significant temperature increase of approx. 1 °C detectable at the contact points of the data glasses poses a potential risk to the user's well-being, e.g. due to pressure points. While the subjective assessment of the test persons with regard to the thermal stress corresponds to the objective measurement results, the muscle physiological strain is occasionally felt to be stronger than could actually be objectively proven. Furthermore, the asthenopic complaints only assumed a moderate level, too. It also became clear that the use of the HoloLens had significant effects on the temporal duration of the set-up process and on the number of assembly errors. It is true that the test subjects required an average of 17.47% more set-up time with the data glasses. However, with the cyber-physical support, a significant error reduction (63.51%) could be realized compared to the paper instruction.

5   Discussion and Conclusion

The research advances the state of the art in the design of digital technologies or CPPS to support people involved in set-up processes of industrial production machines. Progress has been made for the exchange of expertise, especially in terms of contextuality and communication, taking into account collaborative work and social frameworks, while also opening up new research directions on the subject. Due to inevitable limitations of the individual studies, there is still room for further research on the presented topic – especially regarding real and natural conditions where workers are not exposed to controlled environments.

The results take on an important role in practice, since the system supports machine operators in complex, non-automated set-up and assembly processes. The described contents of human factors, knowledge transfer and usability close a research gap with regard to the use of AR-based support systems in the course of industrial set-up processes. Based on the knowledge gained and with the help of further optimization possibilities, the aim is to achieve a process-safe, value-adding and strain-minimizing use of AR-mediated systems in the industrial environment. With the help of CPPS technology and the interplay of contextualized visualizations, sensory support and the combined use of virtual and real process data, the mechanisms of a knowledge-intensive process observed during a set-up procedure can be supported and developed in a new way.

In contrast, however, CPPS also have limitations. In addition to inaccuracies in the sensory detection of the environment and the resulting deviations in the display of set-up instructions, uncertainties can arise with respect to data protection. These technical barriers are not exclusively attributable to the first-generation "HoloLens" but are a general challenge for current AR-based systems. The sensory capturing of set-up processes by the HoloLens and the 3D camera, as well as the options for evaluating set-up data using a set-up editor, increase the transparency of set-up data and the performance of the workers, irrespective of the limitations described.

The extent to which the developed support system or basic infrastructure is actually suitable for everyday, long-term and sustainable practical use will have to be shown by further investigations, for example within a long-term study to be conducted in the sense of a DCS. Regardless, the findings may motivate researchers to transfer the approach to other knowledge areas. Thus, possible comparisons as well as synergies can be established to gain new and insightful knowledge with reference to the promising design possibilities and appropriation of the technology in the industrial context as well as its practice-oriented and knowledge-based effects.

In the best-case scenario, workplace assessment procedures should reveal not only the probabilities of exposure, but also the focal points of exposure. This should reveal to the user the opportunity to derive and implement optimization options. The application of a support system to be used in the present context strives per se for improvements in work organization, which should result in a process that adds as much value as possible and minimizes strain. Only in the case of static gaze positioning and uncomfortable positioning to view holographic or AR-based information, a significantly higher muscle activity is possible compared to a paper-based or analog display of the corresponding information. For dynamic activities, such as the set-up process of a bending machine, this effect is almost unnecessary. Overall, it should be noted that both the objective and subjective strain data in the course of the set-up process do not exceed a moderate level and the differences in the EMG data with and without the use of HoloLens are small. Thus, the interpretability of the objective results is only possible to a limited extent with a simultaneously prevailing very low degree of strain, so that symptoms of fatigue are only likely in the case of repetitive execution without observing breaks. When using the HoloLens, the subjectively perceived additional physical effort results from the subjects' supposed conclusion that the comfort impairments in the head area, which could be objectively proven, are accompanied by a higher muscular effort in the shoulder-neck area. The subjects undoubtedly experience an increased cognitive load at the beginning of the confrontation with new work tasks and terminal devices or novel software. Due to the simple operability paired with an intensive and concentrated examination of the support system, a learning effect sets in quickly regarding the respective work task as well as with reference to the handling of the data glasses and the application. Additionally, repetitive use or execution supports this effect and leads to the fact that the cognitive strain can be reduced. Furthermore, a potentially performance-enhancing influence can be established through the AR application. In the future, familiarization with the system and expected optimization measures for the data glasses and the application will lead to further reductions in set-up times in addition to minimizing the error rate. Therefore, the use of AR technology has the potential to contribute to increasing work effectiveness and efficiency and ultimately to process reliability.

In order to be able to use any of these AR systems in the industrial environment in a way that adds value on the one hand and minimizes strain on the other hand, further acceptance-creating, normative, constructive and technological measures or revisions are indispensable. For example, the latter concerns a reduction of the dead weight, an optimization of the weight distribution, the enlargement of the field of vision or a trouble-free interaction. The support of embodied actions is far-reaching and requires not only the (simple) acquisition of propositional content, e.g. via image and video recordings as well as digital or holographic animations, but also novel technological aids, for example in the form of volumetric or 4D video technology [43]. In this context, complementary to this, little attention has been paid to asynchronous collaboration or remote systematics [44, 45]. These aspects must be fundamentally pursued in addition to the ubiquitous influence of artificial intelligence [46], the advancing mechanization and depending on socio-political developments and decisions in the (further) development and operational implementation of data glasses with regard to the design of an intelligent and yet, at least in the medium term, not completely automated industry. The combination of augmented reality and artificial intelligence represents a promising development for the entire value chain in the coming years, as many industries and research institutions have recognized the importance of their introduction with respect to an increase in production speed and the qualification or training of the workforce. The extent to which these are then actually practicable in everyday practice from an ergonomic and economic point of view must be shown by further investigations.

References

1. De Carvalho, A.F.P., et al.: Of embodied action and sensors. Knowledge and expertise sharing in industrial set-up. Comput.-Supp. Cooper. Work **27**(3–6), 875–916 (2018)
2. Hoffmann, S., de Carvalho, A.F.P., Abele, D., Schweitzer, M., Tolmie, P., Wulf, V.: Cyber-physical systems for knowledge and expertise sharing in manufacturing contexts: towards a model enabling design. Comput. Supp, Cooper. Work **28**(3–4), 469–509 (2019). https://doi.org/10.1007/s10606-019-09355-y
3. Zidek, K., Pitel, J., Adamek, M., Lazorik, P., Hosovsky, A.: Digital twin of experimental smart manufacturing assembly system for industry 4.0 concept. Sustainability **12**(9), 3658 (2020)
4. Abele, N.D., Kluth, K.: Interaktions-ergonomische Gestaltung und Kompatibilität von AR-unterstützten Informationsdarstellungen am Beispiel eines Head-Mounted Displays für industrielle Rüstvorgänge. Zeitschrift für Arbeitswissenschaft (2021)
5. Abele, N.D., Kluth, K.: Strain-related evaluation of an AR-based cyber-physical production system for setting up industrial machines. In: Black, N., Neumann, P. Noy, I. (eds.) Proceedings of the 21st Congress of the International Ergonomics Association, IEA 2021, LNCS, vol. 3, pp. 355–362, Springer, Cham (2021). https://doi.org/10.1007/978-3-030-74608-7_45
6. de Carvalho, A.F.P., Hoffmann, S., Abele, D., Schweitzer, M., Wulf, V.: Designing cyber-physical production systems for industrial set-up: a practice-centred approach. In: Ardito, C., et al. (eds.) INTERACT 2021. LNCS, vol. 12932, pp. 678–701. Springer, Cham (2021). https://doi.org/10.1007/978-3-030-85623-6_38
7. Hoffmann, S., De Carvalho, A.F.P., Schweitzer, M., Abele, N.D., Wulf, V.: Producing and consuming instructional material in manufacturing contexts: evaluation of an AR-based cyber-physical production system for supporting knowledge and expertise sharing. In: Proceedings of the ACM on Human-Computer Interaction, vol. 6, pp. 366:1–366:36 (2022)

8. Birkhan, C.: Smart Production Systems – Intelligente Konzepte zur Gestaltung von Produktionssystemen. Bosch, Kaiserslautern (2008)
9. Milgram, P., Takemura, H., Utsumi, A., Kishino, F.: augmented reality: a class of displays on the reality-virtuality continuum. In: Proceedings of the Society of Photo-Optical Instrumentation Engineers 2351 – Telemanipulator and Telepresence Technologies (1995)
10. Gauglitz, S., Nuernberger, B., Turk, M., Höllerer, T.: In Touch with The Remote World: Remote Collaboration With Augmented Reality Drawings And Virtual Navigation. In: Proceedings of the 20th ACM Symposium on Virtual Reality Software and Technology, pp. 197–205, ACM, New York (2014)
11. Gauglitz, S., Nuernberger, B., Turk, M., Höllerer, T.: World-stabilized annotations and virtual scene navigation for remote collaboration. In: Proceedings of the 27th annual ACM Symposium on User Interface Software and Technology, pp. 449–459, ACM, New York (2014)
12. Pollalis, C., Fahnbulleh, W., Tynes, J., Shaer, O.: HoloMuse: enhancing engagement with archaeological artifacts through gesture-based interaction with holograms. In: Proceedings of the 10th International Conference on Tangible, Embedded, and Embodied Interaction, pp. 565–570, ACM, New York (2017)
13. Lee, J., Bagheri, B., Kao, H.A.: A cyber-physical systems architecture for industry 4.0-based manufacturing systems. Manuf. Lett. **3**, 18–23 (2015)
14. Gallagher, S.: Merleau-Ponty's phenomenology of perception. Topoi – An Int. Rev. Philos. **29**(2), 183–185 (2010)
15. Bhattacharya, B., Winer, E.H.: Augmented reality via expert demonstration authoring (AREDA). Comput. Ind. **105**, 61–79 (2019)
16. Lim, A.K., Ryu, J., Yoon, H.M., Yang, H.C., Kim, S.-k.: Ergonomic effects of medical augmented reality glasses in video-assisted surgery. Surg. Endosc. **36**, 988–998 (2022)
17. Cometti, C., Païzis, C., Casteleira, A., Pons, G., Babault, N.: Effects of mixed reality head-mounted glasses during 90 minutes of mental and manual tasks on cognitive and physiological functions. PeerJ **6**(4), e5847 (2018)
18. Rohde, M., Brödner, P., Stevens, G., Betz, M., Wulf, V.: Grounded design: a praxeological is research perspective. J. Inf. Technol. **32**(2), 163–179 (2016)
19. Wulf, V., Müller, C., Pipek, V., Randall, D., Rohde, M., Stevens, G.: Practice-based computing: empirically grounded conceptualizations derived from design case studies. In: Wulf, V., Schmidt, K., Randall, D. (eds.) Designing Socially Embedded Technologies in the Real-World, pp. 111–150, Springer, London (2015). https://doi.org/10.1007/978-1-4471-672 0-4_7
20. Schmidt, K.: The concept of 'practice': what's the point? In: Rossitto, C., Ciolfi, L., Martin, D., Conein, B. (eds.) Proceedings of the 11th International Conference on the Design of Cooperative Systems, pp. 427–444, Springer, Cham, (2014). https://doi.org/10.1007/978-3-319-06498-7_26
21. Stevens, G., Rohde, M., Korn, M., Wulf, V.: Grounded design: a research paradigm in practice-based computing. In: Wulf, V., Pipek, V., Rohde, M., Stevens, G., Randall, D. (eds.) Socio-Informatics: A Practice-based Perspective on the Design and Use of IT Artifacts, pp. 23–46. Oxford University Press, Oxford (2018)
22. Klopfer, E., Perry, J., Squire, K., Jan, M.: Collaborative learning through augmented reality role playing. In: Proceedings of the 2005 Conference on Computer Support for Collaborative Learning: Learning 2005: The Next 10 Years! pp. 311–315, International Society of the Learning Sciences, Taipei (2005)
23. Paelke, V., Röcker, C.: User interfaces for cyber-physical systems: challenges and possible approaches. In: Marcus, A. (ed.) DUXU 2015. LNCS, vol. 9186, pp. 75–85. Springer, Cham (2015). https://doi.org/10.1007/978-3-319-20886-2_8

24. Hau, Y.S., Kim, B., Lee, H., Kim, Y.G.: The effects of individual motivations and social capital on employees' tacit and explicit knowledge sharing intentions. Int. J. Inf. Manage. **33**(2), 356–366 (2013)
25. Nonaka, I., Toyama, R.: The knowledge-creating theory revisited: knowledge creation as a synthesizing process. Knowl. Manag. Res. Pract. **1**, 2–10 (2003)
26. Argote, L., Beckman, S.L., Epple, D.: The persistence and transfer of learning in industrial settings. Manage. Sci. **36**(2), 140–154 (1990)
27. Clarke, K., et al.: Dependable Red Hot Action. In: Kuutti, K., Karsten, E.H., Fitzpatrick, G., Dourish, P., Schmidt, K. (eds.) Proceedings of the 8th European Conference on Computer-Supported Cooperative Work, pp. 61–80, Springer Netherlands, Dordrecht (2003)
28. Schmauder, M., Spanner-Ulmer, B.: Ergonomie. Grundlagen zur Interaktion von Mensch, Technik und Organisation. Hanser Verlag, München (2014)
29. Luczak, H., Volpert, W.: Arbeitswissenschaft. Kerndefinition – Gegenstandskatalog – Forschungsgebiete. RKW-Verlag, Eschborn (1987)
30. Strasser, H.: Physiologische Grundlagen zur Beurteilung menschlicher Arbeit – Belastung/Beanspruchung/Dauerleistung/Ermüdung/Streß. REFA-Nachrichten **39**(5), 18–29 (1986)
31. Rohmert, W.: Das Belastungs-Beanspruchungs-Konzept. Zeitschrift für Arbeitswissenschaft **38**(4), 193–200 (1984)
32. Schlick, C., Bruder, R., Luczak, H.: Arbeitswissenschaft. Springer, Berlin/Heidelberg/Dordrecht/London/New York (2010)
33. Bubb, H., Schmidtke, H.: Systemstruktur. Kap. 5.1. In: Schmidtke, H. (Hrsg.) Lehrbuch der Ergonomie, S. pp. 305–333, Carl Hanser Verlag, München/Wien (1993)
34. Steinhilber, B., et al.: S2k-Leitlinie zur Oberflächen-Elektromyographie in der Arbeitsmedizin. Arbeitsphysiologie und Arbeitswissenschaft. Zeitschrift für Arbeitswissenschaft **67**(2), 113–128 (2013)
35. Kluth, K.: Physiologische Kosten repetitiver Bewegungen an planzeitorientierten Montagearbeitsplätzen mit sitzender Tätigkeitsausführung. Höpner und Göttert, Siegen (1996)
36. D'Amato, R., et al.: Key ergonomics requirements and possible mechanical solutions for augmented reality head-mounted displays in surgery. Multim, Technol. Interact. **6**(2), 15 (2022)
37. Friemert, D., Ellegast, R., Hartmann, U.: Data glasses for picking workplaces – impact on physical workloads. HCI **22**, 281–289 (2016)
38. Kim, S., Nussbaum, M., Gabbard, J.: Influences of augmented reality head-worn display type and user interface design in performance and usability in simulated warehouse order picking. Appl. Ergon. **74**, 186–193 (2019)
39. Lewis, J., Neider, M.: Through the google glass: the impact of heads-up-display on visual attention. Cogn. Res. Principles Implicat. **1**(13), 1–13 (2016)
40. Creswell, J.W.: Research Design: Qualitative, Quantitative, and Mixed Methods Approaches. SAGE Publications Inc., Los Angeles/London/New Delhi (2014)
41. Abele, N.D., Hoffmann, S., De Carvalho, A.F.P., Schweitzer, M., Wulf, V., Kluth, K.: Design eines praxisorientierten und wissensbasierten Cyber-Physischen Systems für industrielle Rüstvorgänge. Zeitschrift für Arbeitswissenschaft (2021)
42. Abele, N.D., Hoffmann, S., De Carvalho, A.F.P., Schweitzer, M., Wulf, V., Kluth, K.: Knowledge and expertise sharing – designing an AR-mediated cyber-physical production system for industrial set-up processes. In: Black, N.L., Neumann, W.P., Noy, I. (eds.) Proceedings of the 21st Congress of the International Ergonomics Association (IEA 2021). IEA 2021. LNNS, vol, 221, pp. 347–354. Springer, Cham (2021). https://doi.org/10.1007/978-3-030-74608-7_44

43. Cao, Y., Fuste, A., Heun, V.: MobileTutAR: A. Lightweight augmented reality tutorial system using spatially situated human segmentation videos. In: Extended Abstracts of the 2022 CHI Conference on Human Factors in Computing Systems, pp. 1–8, Association for Computing Machinery, New York (2022)
44. Marques, B., Silva, S., Alves, J., Rocha, A., Dias, P., Santos, B.S.: Remote collaboration in maintenance contexts using augmented reality: insights from a participatory process. Int. J. Interact. Des. Manuf. **16**, 419–438 (2022)
45. Irlitti, A., Smith, R.T., Von Itzstein, S., Billinghurst, M., Thomas, B.H.: Challenges for asynchronous collaboration in augmented reality. In: Adjunct Proceedings of the 2016 I.E. International Symposium on Mixed and Augmented Reality, pp. 31–35, IEEE, New York (2017)
46. Devagiri, J.S., Paheding, S., Niyaz, Q., Yang, X., Smith, S.: Augmented reality and artificial intelligence in industry: trends, tools, and future challenges. Expert Syst. Appl. **207**, 118002 (2022)

Evaluating Domain-Independent Small Talk Conversations to Improve Clinical Communication Interaction for Human and Machine

Chloe Aguilar[1], Muhammad Amith[2,5] (iD), Lu Tang[3] (iD), Jane Hamilton[4], Lara S. Savas[4] (iD), Danniel Rhee[4], Tazrin Khan[3], and Cui Tao[4]([envelope]) (iD)

[1] University of Texas, Austin, TX 78705, USA
[2] Department of Biostatistics and Data Science, School of Public and Population Health, Galveston, TX 77555-0128, USA
[3] Texas A&M University, College Station, TX 77843, USA
[4] University of Texas Health Science Center at Houston, Houston, TX 77030, USA
cui.tao@uth.tmc.edu
[5] Department of Internal Medicine, John Sealy School of Medicine, Galveston, TX 77555-0128, USA

Abstract. Conversation as trivial as "small talk" has a significant impact on human relationships, including in clinical care environments. Evidence suggests that small talk can improve health and clinical outcomes. This study aims to analyze the characteristics of domain-independent small talk collected from a sample of conversations. We reviewed the impact of personality factors of the conversation and present our findings on specific factors that are correlated with it. In addition, we discuss the possibility of integrating small talk into our existing ontology-driven dialogue systems, which can assist machines in engaging with and building trust with patients in the clinical environments. Future direction will involve implementing the ontology model and integrating it with a health dialogue engine to test the effectiveness of automated small talk.

Keywords: Small talk · Personality · Patient provider communication · Health care

1 Introduction

Everyday interactions, such as small talk about the current weather, are common part of our daily lives. These types of interactions also happen in health care settings, where small talk can create a relaxed atmosphere and prevent awkward silences. However, some healthcare providers view small talk as unproductive, and most clinics often prioritize efficient use of time. With some among the general public, there is an urgency to avoid small talk to get to the core of a conversation. Nevertheless, small talk is generally distinguishable from essential portions of human interactions, yet could play an important role in human interaction with agents (human or machine).

C. Aguilar, M. Amith and L. Tang—Contributed Equally.

V. G. Duffy (Ed.): HCII 2023, LNCS 14028, pp. 330–343, 2023.
https://doi.org/10.1007/978-3-031-35741-1_25

In the workplace, small talk can be defined as conversation that is not related to workplace business, has a relatively low level of content, and is used for social purposes [1]. In other settings, small talk can refer conversation not related to the context of the interaction, and serving for social and polite purposes. Small talk is often considered "undemanding," and its easy initiation and termination can explain why it is so commonly utilized [2]. Small talk can potentially develop into "social talk," where the participants take more of an interest in the exchange and the other person's responses, and the conversation becomes deeper, yet it may remain brief and routine [1]. Examples of small talk include asking a coworker about the weather, a parent about their children, or a college student about their classes. While the participants may not be deeply invested in the conversation or responses, they still enjoy the act of conversing or feel it necessary in the situation. The main distinction between small talk and "big talk" in social and professional settings is the underlying motivation behind the conversation and the more surface-level topics discussed. Despite this, small talk should not be discounted as unimportant.

Although small talk may seem trivial, it plays several roles in social interactions. Early research on the role of small talk highlight its purpose to create social connections, rather than providing meaning or thought-provoking contents [3]. For example, in workplace, mall talk can help employees feel more at ease while waiting for a meeting to start, breaking the silence and making the situation feel more socially acceptable [1]. Small talk is motivated by a desire to make this situation feel more socially acceptable, not necessarily because the employees desire to make conversation. In addition, since small talk can serve as a segue into more in-depth "social talk," it can also help advance relationships [2]. By helping individuals feel more comfortable around others, small talk can eventually lead to deeper conversations and stronger relationships. Therefore, the impact of small talk goes beyond its ability to make situations flow more smoothly, and extend to it role to developing social bonds.

1.1 Small Talk in Clinical Care

In a clinical setting, small talk is often used to make the patient feel more at ease and open to discuss about health concerns, especially if the patient is concerned about a procedure or health outcome. This type of interaction is also similar in content to small talk in other settings, but may include humor or lighthearted remarks, aimed at reducing stress and increasing interpersonal trust [4]. A study on use of small talk in a neonatal ICU found that nurses who engaged in casual conversation with parents were able to build more trusting relationships compared to those who employed quick and dismissive small talk [5]. Another study observed small talk when used by interpreters in health care situations. A patient that needs an interpreter is likely going to feel very timid and afraid to ask questions, so small talk may be used to help them feel more comfortable. The paper asserts that good practice involves not only interpreting the words of the doctor, but also using small talk to build the patient's trust [6]. Regardless of the content of the small talk, a sincere attempt to engage with the patient can make them feel more comfortable asking questions, help relieve stress, and give them confidence in the care they are receiving.

Another benefit of small talk in clinical settings is it can reveal valuable health information, especially information that would not have otherwise been shared with the provider. Casual questions from the healthcare providers can elicit information that is not directly health related but can provide insight of the patient's overall well-being. For example, in one study, a nurse asked the patient what they had planned for the rest of the day. This not only helped build a connection with the patient, but their response helped the nurse evaluate their mood, energy level, and recovery status [7]. Thus, small talk can help the provider assessing a patient and getting a better understanding of them overall condition. In addition, a nurse in this same study used small talk to avoid "big talk" in a situation where the patient was not using a piece of their needed equipment. She asked the patient if their dog liked the tubing to one of the oxygen-delivering machines, and the patient responded that the dog hates the tubing. This lets the nurse know the reasoning behind why not enough oxygen had been administered, and doesn't put the patient in an uncomfortable situation [7]. In this case, small talk gives the provider better insight into the patient's adherence, and make better recommendations. In short, small talk can help providers assess the patient's well-being and response to illness or treatment.

Despite the potential benefits of small talk in healthcare, questions arise about whether medical providers have the proper training and time to effectively engage in small talk. Some propose that medical providers should receive more training in communication, including small talk, to improve clear communication from both the providers and patients. However, the limited time available for patient interactions may make it challenging for providers to engage in extensive small talk [8]. Nonetheless, the benefits of improving small talk in health care are likely worth the extra training and time needed to execute it.

1.2 Research Objective

In our study, we aimed to explore the relationship between personality and small talk interactions. We collected domain-independent small talk interactions with participants and administrated a personality assessment survey. According to Cuperman and Ickes, personality types are significant factors that influence the quality of the conversation [9]. Different personality types result in various responses that could create a unique conversation between two individuals. Given that personality has shown to have an influence on conversation, our investigation into this relationship will inform the design and implementation of small talk in our development of ontology-driven dialogue systems to improve interactions with users.

By analyzing the interaction data, including the impact of personality, we aim to enhance the development of automated tools, such as dialogue systems or chatbots, to improve communication and provide relevant health information to patients to aid in their shared decision making with their healthcare providers.

2 Methods

2.1 Big Five Personality Model

The Big Five personality traits model is one of the most frequently used and established models that aims to predict an individual's personality. It defines five key traits: *extraversion, agreeableness, openness, conscientiousness*, and *neuroticism* [10]. Understanding an individual's personality traits provides an in-depth understanding of his/her personality, which is crucial to an individual's decision-making process.

Extraversion refers to "the tendency to focus on gratification obtained from outside the self". The extraversion personality traits are characterized by sociable, fun-loving, friendly, spontaneous, active, not lonely, dominant, and bold [11]. *Agreeableness* refers to "a person's ability to put others before their own". The agreeable traits are characterized by trusting, acquiescent, lenient, forgiving, open-minded, flexible, and agreeable [11]. *Openness* refers to one's imagination and insights. People with high openness characteristics are often interested in trying new things, imaginative, creative, broad interests, independent, and original [11]. *Neuroticism* refers to people's negative emotions, including anxiety and depression, such as emotional instability. People with high neuroticism tend to be stressed, nervous, emotional, temperamental, insecure, impatient, and vulnerable [11]. Lastly, *conscientiousness* is defined by a high level of thoughtfulness, organizational abilities, and goal-directed behavior. People with high conscientiousness are often careful of their actions, reliable, well organized, self-disciplined, practical, emotionally stable, and self-reliant [11].

The five personality traits are typically seen as a separate perspectives of personality. However, studies have shown that they are interrelated with each other, where they influence how people converse with each other. For example a study showed that personality traits such as *extraversion* and *agreeableness* positively influenced human bonding and relationships [12]. Moreover, a study found extraversion and neuroticism, which show positive and negative effects, stimulated the tone of communication between individuals [13]. Lastly, a suggested people converse differently by personality types. Regarding Big five personality theory, extraversion and agreeable personality traits were related to people's social behaviors, conscientiousness was related to work behavior, neuroticism was related to affective experience, and openness was related to intellectual life. Thus, people with different personality traits respond by their personality traits, which often influence topics of conversation [9, 14]. However, the extent to which these personality traits and communication factors affect human bonds and trusts in the relationships has not been explored yet. Therefore, the study aims to study how Big Five Personality Traits and communication factors influence human bonds and relationships, including trust, sense of belonging, and affiliation.

2.2 Survey Instrument on Conversation Quality

In order to assess the conversation quality, we adapted the survey questions from a paper that investigates conversation quality in group settings [15]. Videos of the observed conversations were rated based on a five-point Likert scale, ranging from "Disagree Strongly" (1) to "Agree Strongly" (5). The statements ranked on the Likert scale were divided into several categories: *Interpersonal Relationship, Nature of Interaction,* and *Equal Opportunity,* all ranked for both individual and group perceived conversation quality. The first category, *Interpersonal Relationship,* focuses on aspects such as participants' ability to pay attention and get along with others in the group. The next category, *Nature of Interaction,* dissects how enjoyable the conversation is and how well it flows. Lastly, the *Equal Opportunity* category rates how well group members take the lead in the conversation. The questions in our survey instrument were adapted from this study, with eight similar questions assessing aspects such as how well the conversation flows, how comfortable the participant seems, and the warmth of the small talk participant. Two of the eight questions were reverse-scored in our study if agreement to a particular question correlated negatively to good small talk, meaning that "Disagree Strongly" was a score of a 5, and "Agree Strongly" was a score of a 1. The scores from each Likert rating were summed in order to create a total "Small Talk Score" so that this could be compared to their personality scores.

2.3 Data Collection

We recruited participants (n = 44) from the Texas A&M University campus through a recruitment pool in November 2021. Each participant agreed to an informed consent[1], and completed a preliminary demographic and pre-assessment survey online via Qualtrics, measuring their personality traits (*Agreeableness, Conscientiousness, Extraversion, Emotional Stability,* and *Intellect & Imagination*) using the Big-Five personality trait survey instrument tool [16]. Participant later logged on to a virtual meeting space with one of the primary investigators. The two parties engaged in a brief live audio conversation ("small talk") for 10–15 min, with the primary investigator party directing the conversation. The audio of the conversation was recorded and transcribed. Four evaluators reviewed the quality of the conversation on a 5-point Likert scale using a survey that measured conversational exchanges based on eight criteria – *how natural the interaction was, perceived enjoyment, participation through solicitation, equal sharing of the conversation, expression of warmth, signs of anxiety,* or *expression of laughter and humor.* We were interested in whether the overall conversation quality correlated with aspects of different personality types, where the aspects of personality might warrant evaluating to improve "small talk" in patient-provider communication in a clinical environment, either from human-to-human or machine-to-human perspective. For the latter perspective, we intend to investigate the design of a computational ontology model that can help agents in a health care environment to ease patients in a clinical setting.

2.4 Results

Four reviewers rated 44 small talk conversations. The overall quality of the conversation was summation of each factor (i.e., "Small Talk Score"). On average the conversation quality was valued at 30.9. Table 1 shows the mean and median for each of the eight survey questions. For Q1 (*The individual seemed like they had a smooth, natural, and relaxed interaction*), Q4 (*The individual and the interviewer shared the conversation equally*),

---

[1] Exemption status, IRB2021–0017 and HSC-SBMI-21-0230.

Q6 (*The individual showed signs of tension or anxiety*), Q8 (*Some of the individual's remarks made the situation uncomfortable*) exhibited relatively high ratings ($\mu = 4.27$, $\sigma = 0.87$, Mdn = 4; $\mu = 4.23$, $\sigma = 1.10$, Mdn = 5; $\mu = 4.07$, $\sigma = 1.09$, Mdn = 4; and $\mu = 4.53$, $\sigma = 0.92$, Mdn = 5, respectively). While Q7 (*The individual laughs or uses humor during the conversation*) exhibited low rating ($\mu = 2.88$, $\sigma = 1.16$, Mdn = 3). For Q6 and Q8, the ratings were reversed and therefore, a higher score indicated a positive inclination.

Table 1. Aggregate of the conversation quality measurements. *ratings were reversed to indicate positive, than the negative, implication of the question.

Survey questions on conversation quality		Median	Mean(SD)
Q1	The individual seemed like they had a smooth, natural, and relaxed interaction	4	4.27(0.87)
Q2	The individual seemed like they enjoyed the interaction	4	3.88(1.02)
Q3	The individual asked the interviewer questions about themselves or their interests	3	3.05(1.35)
Q4	The individual and the interviewer shared the conversation equally	5	4.23(1.10)
Q5	The individual expressed warmth	4	3.95(0.97)
Q6*	The individual showed signs of tension or anxiety	4	4.07(1.09)
Q7	The individual laughs or uses humor during the conversation	3	2.88(1.16)
Q8*	Some of the individual's remarks made the situation uncomfortable	5	4.53(0.92)

With the Big-Five Factor, the collected results from the participants were summed to give an overall score for each aspect[2] - *Extroversion, Agreeableness, Conscientiousness, Emotional Stability* and *Intellect/Imagination*. On aggregate, Table 2 shows an overview of each factor with average participant scores for mean and median.

From the data presented above, we computed the correlation of the conversational quality with aspects of the Big Five Factor personality using Pearson correlation statistic. The computations were preformed using R [17] with the results presented in Figs. 1, 2, 3, 4 and 5.

The correlation between conversation quality and *Agreeableness*, an aspect involving interpersonal harmony and synergy with others, was found to be negative correlated, but statistically significant with a correlation coefficient of -0.086 ($p = 0.59$). Similarly,

---

[2] https://ipip.ori.org/newScoringInstructions.htm.

Table 2. Aggregate of participant's Big-Five Factor survey measurement

Big-Five Factor Aspect	Median	Mean(SD)
Extraversion	24.50	23.50(8.79)
Agreeableness	30	29.17(5.51)
Conscientiousness	24	23.62(7.02)
Emotional Stability	21	20.55(8.19)
Intellect/Imagination	26	26.93(5.28)

there was no correlation between conversation quality and *Contentiousness*, an indicator of a personality aspect involving persistence and commitment (r(42) = 0.0061, p = 0.7). However, conversation quality and *Emotional Stability* (i.e., *Neuroticism*) had a positive medium correlation and statistical significance, (r(42) = 0.4, p = 0.0081). Conversation quality and *Extraversion*, essentially an indicator of public approach and openness, also had a positive medium correlation with statistical significance (r(42) = 0.41, p = 0.0065). The correlation between conversation quality and Intellect & Imagination (i.e., Openness) was small and not statistically significant, with a correlation coefficient of 0.1 (p = 0.52).

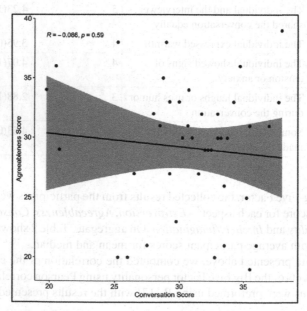

Fig. 1. Pearson correlation for Agreeableness and conversation quality.

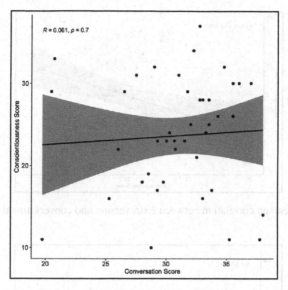

Fig. 2. Pearson correlation between Conscientiousness and conversation quality

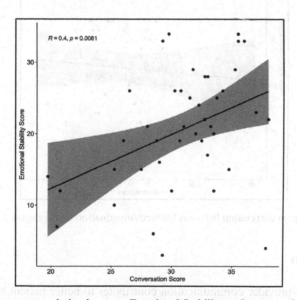

Fig. 3. Pearson correlation between Emotional Stability and conversation quality.

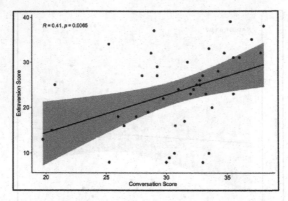

Fig. 4. Pearson correlation between Extraversion and conversational quality.

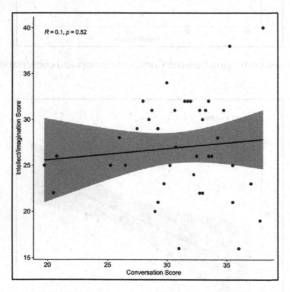

Fig. 5. Pearson correlation between Intellect/Imagination and conversation quality.

3 Discussion

Effective patient-provider communication contributes to better patient satisfaction and clinical outcomes [18, 19]. It contributes to a positive patient-provider relationship by fostering trust, loyalty, and respect between the two parties [20–22]. One aspect of patient-provider communication neglected by researchers is small talk in clinical encounters [23, 24]. Small talk is a type of social-emotional communication [25], and defined as an "off topic chat, not concerned with explicit purpose"[26]. While small talk is not well-researched, there is evidence that small talk has an important role in the healthcare, specifically in patient-provider communication. Small talk in clinical encounters can gather more information about the patient [6, 7, 27], redirect the conversation to a health-related topic [7, 28], improve trust and relationships [5, 8, 25, 29], and reduce any anxiety about a serious health issues [7, 25, 30].

In this study, we aim to understand how utilizing aspects of personalities can improve the quality of "small talk" conversation in clinical settings, and to understand how to apply this knowledge towards computer-based tools that involve speech and dialogue interaction.

From our initial on-going analysis, the Big-Five personality trait of *Extraversion* and *Emotional Stability (Neuroticism)* appear to be positively correlated ($r = 0.41$, $p = 0.01$; and $r = 0.4$, $p = 0.01$, respectively) with the quality of the conversation score (based on an aggregate sum of the eight criteria) where higher scores indicate positive qualities of the conversation. We presume that these two aspects of personality play a strong role in a brief small talk conversation, whereas, the other aspects like *Intellect & Imagination*, *Conscientious*, and perhaps *Agreeableness* are more intrinsic and cerebral in nature, that may require longer interaction duration for these to manifest.

Focusing on quality of the conversation, the evaluators perceive the lack of humor and laughter exchanges with the investigator. Several studies have recognized the importance of humor in building rapport in a dyadic human relationship [31–33]. One possible reason for the low score could be that both parties were strangers to each other, and therefore, the participant is likely to be guarded. Also, there may not have been opportunities for the research investigator to organically interject humor in the small talk conversation without "feeling" forced. In addition, there was a lack of engagement and interest expressed by the participants toward the interview questions. This could be due to the limited time for the participant to ask questions or the participant being reserved. It is also possible that the two parties did not have any common ground despite the small talk conversations being perceived to be comfortable and natural.

Between the participant and researcher, it was perceived that conversation was equally shared in terms of speaking time. This indicates that no party dominated or controlled the conversation. No statements made by the participant were reported as uncomfortable. This could possibly be explained to avoid creating a negative atmosphere since both parties were not well acquainted. Likewise, this might also explain the perception that the two parties had natural and relaxed interaction, and that there were little to no anxiety and tension signaled by the participant.

The factors of *Extraversion* and *Emotional Stability* may play a significant role in improving trust and communication between patients and healthcare providers. These personality traits can be leveraged to tailor messages toward developing intelligent agents that can better connect with the patient in a clinical environment. In addition, with the collection of dialogue interaction between participant and the researcher, we intend to devise lightweight models that can be represented using an ontology using our existing framework for patient-provider communication, as we discuss in the following section.

3.1 Limitations and Future Direction

This study had several limitations. Firstly, we only used a modest sample size and there might be lack of a more diverse and representative population. We presume a large sample with a more generalized population may have provided a validated insight on the impact of conversational quality and cognitive aspects. Secondly, the study only evaluated four ratings for each Big-Five Factor score, limiting the depth of our analysis into the relationship between the elements of conversation quality and personality aspects. we were interested to see specific elements of the conversation quality survey (Q1-Q8 of Table 1) with personality aspects of each individual. Yet, we were also limited to four evaluators - four ratings to each Big-Five Factor score. While we presume that small talk is domain independent irrespective of setting, there may be some benefit to conduct the study in a clinical environment. Lastly, we also did not factor whether the investigator that engaged the participant had an effect by skill and experience on the quality of conversation.

As far as future direction, we intend to extend this study in a clinical care environment and engage random patients. As noted earlier, this could provide further insight in how divergent small talk in a virtual lab setting may differ with face-to-face clinic environment. It may also advance our goals toward understanding and implementing small talk in clinical care environment with humans and machines.

Another future direction is for us to investigate and understand how to improve conversation quality. One area was the lack of humorous engagement by the participant, personal engagement of the participant where the individual is interested in the other party, and relative enjoyment and warmth of the communication on behalf of the participant.

Toward a Computational Ontology-based Model for Patient-centric Healthcare Small Talk. One of the key motivations for this study is our continued work in the use and development of conversational agents ("chatbots") for human papillomavirus (HPV) vaccine using an ontology-based method to drive the interaction. From one of our preliminary Wizard of OZ simulation [34], one type of feedback from users was the lack of "humanization" which may impede on building trust with the agent. We surmised that if small talk were integrated in the counseling and educational procedure of the conversational agent, we could impact this deficiency.

The counseling procedure is driven by the ontology-based method using an application ontology framework called Patient Health Information Dialogue Ontology (PHIDO) [35]. Ontologies are controlled standard terminologies that semantically link terms to express meaning from information and data - essentially giving machines contextual understanding, and the ability to handle complex software tasks [36]. The outcome with ontologies would provide the capacity to build intelligent systems to handle complex tasks. The PHIDO framework used in HPV vaccine counseling implements a type of "chunk and check" [37] for communicating HPV vaccine information to the patients that was adapted from our Wizard of OZ experiments [34, 38]. To integrate the possibility of small talk we would need to develop an integrative ontology-based framework. Currently, our PHIDO framework supports a wide range of identifiable utterances categories (*System Utterance* and *Participant Utterance*) and speech tasks to model complex dialogue interaction and formalize speech communication efforts for health information.

Our immediate next step is to analyze the collection of small talk interaction from this study and devise some basic interaction patterns that can be generalized across the collection. Afterwards, we will use the ontology framework of PHIDO and encode those patterns as a chain of utterances serving multiple speech tasks. The ontology can be integrated to our prototype dialogue engine that can import PHIDO to manage dialogue information and perform autonomously. Also due to the fluid and unpredictable nature of small talk, we will investigate dialogue system mechanism like slots [39] integrated with Semantic Web Rule Language (SWRL) [40] to implement rules for small talk conversation and decision making, and large knowledge graph systems like DBpedia [41]and YAGO [42] that can provide some background contextual information for the utterances.

4   Conclusion

This study aimed to understand the role of personality traits in improving the quality of small talk conversation in clinical care and how to apply this knowledge towards computer-based tools that involve speech and dialogue interaction. From a participant study (n = 44), we revealed a positive correlation between *Extraversion* and *Emotional Stability* with the quality of the small talk according to our analysis. While small talk is domain-independent, we will investigate more direct interaction with patient participants in a clinical environment to further our understanding. Integrating small talk into speech-based conversational agents could possibly improve the conversation quality between human and machines. The outcome of this pilot study could advance the knowledge of patient-provider communication and encourage best practices to improve communication efforts with patients and develop patient-facing tools to improve clinical care.

Acknowledgement. Research was supported by NIH grant under Award Number U24AI163375, the Cancer Prevention Research Institute of Texas Grant # RP220244 and the UTHealth-Houston-CPRIT Innovation for Cancer Prevention Research Training Program Summer Undergraduate Fellowship (Cancer Prevention & Research Institute of Texas Grant #RP210042) and the UTHealth-Houston Prevention Research Center. We thank Mike Garcia for assisting in the evaluation process.

References

1. Holmes, J.: Doing collegiality and keeping control at work: small talk in government departments 1. In: Coupland, J., Coupland, J. (eds.) Small Talk, pp. 32–61. Routledge (2014). https://doi.org/10.4324/9781315838328-3
2. Holmes, J., Stubbe, M.: Power and politeness in the workplace: A sociolinguistic analysis of talk at work. Routledge (2015)
3. Coupland, J., Coupland, N., Robinson, J.D.: "How are you?": Negotiating phatic communion1. Lang. Soc. **21**, 207–230 (1992)
4. McCreaddie, M., Wiggins, S.: The purpose and function of humour in health, health care and nursing: a narrative review. J. Adv. Nurs. **61**, 584–595 (2008)
5. Fenwick, J., Barclay, L., Schmied, V.: 'Chatting': an important clinical tool in facilitating mothering in neonatal nurseries. J. Adv. Nurs. **33**, 583–593 (2001)
6. Penn, C., Watermeyer, J.: When asides become central: Small talk and big talk in interpreted health interactions. Patient Educ. Couns. **88**, 391–398 (2012)

7. Macdonald, L.M.: Expertise in everyday Nurse-Patient conversations: The importance of small talk. Global Qual. Nurs. Res. **3**, 2333393616643201 (2016)
8. Becker, G., Kempf, D.E., Xander, C.J., Momm, F., Olschewski, M., Blum, H.E.: Four minutes for a patient, twenty seconds for a relative-an observational study at a university hospital. BMC Health Serv. Res. **10**, 94 (2010)
9. Cuperman, R., Ickes, W.: Big Five predictors of behavior and perceptions in initial dyadic interactions: personality similarity helps extraverts and introverts, but hurts "disagreeables." J. Pers. Soc. Psychol. **97**, 667–684 (2009). https://doi.org/10.1037/a0015741
10. Costa, P.T., McCrae, R.R.: Normal personality assessment in clinical practice: the NEO personality inventory. Psychol. Assess. **4**, 5 (1992)
11. McCrae, R.R., Costa, P.T.: Validation of the five-factor model of personality across instruments and observers. J. Pers. Soc. Psychol. **52**, 81–90 (1987). https://doi.org/10.1037/0022-3514.52.1.81
12. Jacques, P.H., Garger, J., Brown, C.A., Deale, C.S.: Personality and virtual reality team candidates: the roles of personality traits, technology anxiety and trust as predictors of perceptions of virtual reality teams. J. Bus. Manage. **15** (2009)
13. Bose, N., Sgroi, D.: The role of personality beliefs and "small talk" in strategic behaviour. PLoS ONE **17**, e0269523 (2022). https://doi.org/10.1371/journal.pone.0269523
14. Jaques, N., Kim, Y.L., Picard, R.: Personality, attitudes, and bonding in conversations. In: Traum, D., Swartout, W., Khooshabeh, P., Kopp, S., Scherer, S., Leuski, A. (eds.) Intelligent Virtual Agents. LNCS (LNAI), vol. 10011, pp. 378–382. Springer, Cham (2016). https://doi.org/10.1007/978-3-319-47665-0_37
15. Raj Prabhu, N., Raman, C., Hung, H.: Defining and quantifying conversation quality in spontaneous interactions. In: Companion Publication of the 2020 International Conference on Multimodal Interaction, pp. 196–205 (2020)
16. Goldberg, L.R.: The development of markers for the Big-Five factor structure. Psychol. Assess. **4**, 26 (1992)
17. R Core Team: R: A language and environment for statistical computing (2017). https://www.R-project.org/
18. Hall, J.A., Horgan, T.G., Stein, T.S., Roter, D.L.: Liking in the physician–patient relationship. Patient Educ. Couns. **48**, 69–77 (2002)
19. Ong, L.M., De Haes, J.C., Hoos, A.M., Lammes, F.B.: Doctor-patient communication: a review of the literature. Soc. Sci. Med. **40**, 903–918 (1995)
20. BenSira, Z.: Affective and instrumental components in the physician-patient relationship: an additional dimension of interaction theory. J. Health Soc. Behav. **21**(2), 170 (1980). https://doi.org/10.2307/2136736
21. Cegala, D.J., McGee, D.S., McNeilis, K.S.: Components of patients' and doctors' perceptions of communication competence during a primary care medical interview. Health Commun. **8**, 1–27 (1996)
22. Smith, R.C., Hoppe, R.B.: The patient's story: integrating the patient-and physician-centered approaches to interviewing. Ann. Int. Med. **115**, 470–477 (1991)
23. Miletic, T., Piu, M., Minas, H., Stankovska, M., Stolk, Y., Klimidis, S.: Guidelines for working effectively with interpreters in mental health settings. Victorian Transcultural Psychiatry Unit Melbourne, Australia (2006)
24. Wiener, E.S., Rivera, M.I.: Bridging language barriers: how to work with an interpreter. Clin. Pediatric Emerg. Med. **5**, 93–101 (2004)
25. Maupome, G., Holcomb, C., Schrader, S.: Clinician-patient small talk: comparing fourth-year dental students and practicing dentists in a standardized patient encounter. J. Dent. Educ. **80**, 1349–1356 (2016)
26. Coupland, J.: Small talk: social functions. Res. Lang. Soc. Interact. **36**, 1–6 (2003)

27. Crespo, K.E., Torres, J.E., Recio, M.E.: Reasoning process characteristics in the diagnostic skills of beginner, competent, and expert dentists. J. Dent. Educ. **68**, 1235–1244 (2004)
28. Tiderington, E., Stanhope, V., Padgett, D.: "How do we force six visits on a consumer?": street-level dilemmas and strategies for person-centered care under Medicaid fee-for-service. Am. J. Psychiatr. Rehabil. **21**, 79 (2018)
29. Lu, Y.-L.: How do nurses acquire English medical discourse ability in nursing practice? Exploring nurses' medical discourse learning journeys and related identity construction. Nurse Educ. Today **85**, 104301 (2020)
30. Tracy, K., Naughton, J.M.: Institutional identity-work: A better lens. In: Small talk. pp. 82–103. Routledge (2014)
31. Bogdan, S.: Failed Humour and Its Effects in Conversation: A Case Study. **129**(132), 39–49 (2014)
32. Cooper, C.: Elucidating the bonds of workplace humor: A relational process model. Human Relations. **61**, 1087–1115 (2008). https://doi.org/10.1177/0018726708094861
33. Maki, S.M., Booth-Butterfield, M., McMullen, A.: Does Our Humor Affect Us?: An Examination of a Dyad's Humor Orientation. Commun. Q. **60**, 649–664 (2012). https://doi.org/10.1080/01463373.2012.725006
34. Amith, M., Zhu, A., Cunningham, R., Lin, R., Savas, L., Shay, L., Chen, Y., Gong, Y., Boom, J., Roberts, K., Tao, C.: Early Usability Assessment of a Conversational Agent for HPV Vaccination. Studies in Health Technology and Informatics. 17–23 (2019). https://doi.org/10.3233/978-1-61499-951-5-17
35. Amith, M., Roberts, K., Tao, C.: Conceiving an application ontology to model patient human papillomavirus vaccine counseling for dialogue management. BMC Bioinformatics **20**, 1–16 (2019)
36. Obrst, L., Ceusters, W., Janssen, T.: Ontologies, Semantic Technologies, and Intelligence: Looking Toward the Future. In: Proceedings of the 2010 Conference on Ontologies and Semantic Technologies for Intelligence. pp. 213–224. IOS Press, NLD (2010)
37. Cork, T., White, S.: Exploring community pharmacists' use of health literacy interventions in their everyday practice. Res. Social Adm. Pharm. **18**, 3948–3952 (2022). https://doi.org/10.1016/j.sapharm.2022.06.007
38. Amith, M., et al.: Examining Potential Usability and Health Beliefs Among Young Adults Using a Conversational Agent for HPV Vaccine Counseling. AMIA Summits on Translational Science Proceedings. **2020**, 43 (2020)
39. Jokinen, K., McTear, M.: Spoken dialogue systems. Synthesis Lectures on Human Language Technologies. **2**, 1–151 (2009)
40. Horrocks, I., Patel-Schneider, P.F., Boley, H., Tabet, S., Grosof, B., Dean, M.: SWRL (Semantic Web Rule Language), https://www.w3.org/Submission/SWRL/
41. Lehmann, J., et al.: DBpedia – A large-scale, multilingual knowledge base extracted from Wikipedia. Semantic Web. **6**, 167–195 (2015). https://doi.org/10.3233/SW-140134
42. Suchanek, F.M., Kasneci, G., Weikum, G.: Yago: a core of semantic knowledge. In: Proceedings of the 16th international conference on World Wide Web. pp. 697–706. ACM, Banff Alberta Canada (2007). https://doi.org/10.1145/1242572.1242667

The Impacts of Covid-19 Pandemic on Nursing Workflow in a Medical ICU

Vitor de Oliveira Vargas[1], Jung Hyup Kim[1]($\boxtimes$), Alireza Kasaie Sharifi[1], and Laurel Despins[2]

[1] Industrial and Systems Engineering Department, University of Missouri, Columbia, MO, USA
vdvx55@mail.missouri.edu, kijung@missouri.edu, skdx2@umsystem.edu
[2] Sinclair School of Nursing, University of Missouri, Columbia, MO, USA
despinsl@missouri.edu

Abstract. Within any typical health organization, nurses play a vital role in the quality of care and health promotion. Generally, the nursing workload is determined by the time spent on patient care and nursing activities. Due to the COVID-19 pandemic, ICU nurses might experience much higher physical, psychological, and emotional exhaustion. Hence, this study is focused on analyzing the ICU nurses' workflow and measuring the sequence of nursing tasks under the same subgroup and the frequency of the tasks. In this study, the ICU nurse's workflow data is collected from the Near Field Electromagnetic Ranging (NFER) System.

Moreover, this research revealed significant differences in ICU nurse shift before and during the pandemic. Plus, this study provides the understanding and the tool to cope with the pandemic consequences and optimize nurse's work routines.

Keywords: Nursing · Workflow · Intensive Care Unit

1 Introduction

According to Düzkaya and Kuğuoğlu [1], nurses are the members of the medical team who are with the patient for longer periods of time. Within typical health organizations, nurses are the largest workforce and play a key role in the quality of care and health promotion, making up the majority of the hospital staff [2]. Generally, the nursing workload is determined by the time spent on patient care, nursing activities, and the skills needed to care for the patient. This study is focused on the ICU nurses' workflow, which is analyzed based on three main characteristics: Sequence of tasks under the same subgroup, frequency of the tasks, and tasks duration. According to Moghadam, Chehrzad [2], ICU is an environment that provides care for patients with severe clinical conditions. ICU nurses are exposed to extremely high workloads, both physically and mentally.

In this study, the ICU nurse's workflow data was collected from the Near Field Electromagnetic Ranging (NFER) System and manual observation during two different periods. The first period refers to February and March 2020, a pre-COVID-19 pandemic period, and the second one refers to July 2020, during the COVID-19 pandemic. It is worthwhile to mention that, even during the COVID-19 pandemic, the assessed hospital

ICU is a non-COVID-19 unit. The tasks observed during the data collection were based on the task descriptions in the study by Song, Kim [3].

NFER System is a local positioning system. Kolodziej and Hjelm [4] mentioned several applications to local positioning systems, and particularly to healthcare, they were used to find assets, caregivers, and patients, implying in less time needed to look for people and medical equipment, to reduce inventory and labor, and to increase patient satisfaction. Another healthcare application is for emergency calls, for fast and automatic locating of caller. Schantz, Weil [5] presented results that NFER systems yield an accurate location within 1 m about 83% of the time, which is acceptable for this study.

Pandemics are epidemics in global scale transmission affecting large numbers of people and often resulting in numerous deaths and social and economic upheaval [6]. According to Sagherian, Clinton [7], nursing is physically and mentally strenuous, and performance loss and fatigue are expected during the shift. They concluded that fatigue and performance decrements are safety hazards that have implications for both nurses and patients.

Haas, Swan [8] addressed that a 12-h shift is challenging even in normal conditions. During the pandemic, most nurses have experienced a state of mental, physical, and emotional exhaustion. However, Allison, Doyle [9] found that non-COVID medical emergencies nearly halved during the British lockdown. Other studies show that the pandemic entailed the opposite effect on non-COVID-19 ICU, which tends to be less busy than before. Hence, it is necessary to understand how the COVID-19 pandemic affects the nursing workflow.

This study aims to pinpoint the main differences a 12-h shift (07:00–19:30) presents during pre-pandemic and pandemic periods as a function of the task frequency distribution.

2 Methodology

2.1 Data Collection

Song, Kim [3] used the Near Field Electromagnetic Ranging (NFER) system to record the real-time location of nurses in an ICU, while the observers recorded the start time and end time of each task done by ICU nurses and took notes for any special events during the observation.

The NFER system architecture comprises tracking servers covering the entire ICU area, tracking software installed in an appropriate laptop, and sensors that recognize nurses' location by tags.

The observer followed the nurses and monitored their activity. The observer recorded the start times and end times of each task done by ICU nurses and noted any special events during the observation. Figure 1 shows the ICU layout with the NFER calibration points, and Fig. 2 shows the architecture of the NFER system.

The nurse's activities were organized into seven main categories: Handoff, In-room Activities, Out-of-room Activities, Peer Support, Patient Clinical Processes Conversations, Teaching Residents and/or Students, and Non-nursing Activities.

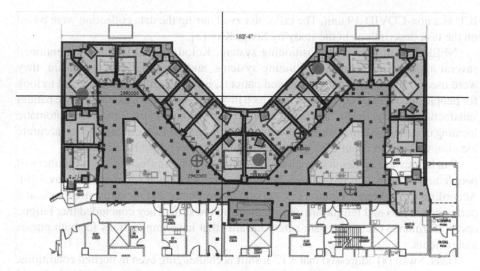

Fig. 1. ICU layout with the calibration points of the NFER system.

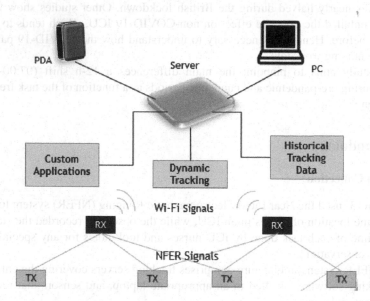

Fig. 2. The architecture of the NFER system.

Handoff consists of a verbal report or verbal report along with the initial patient assessment. The off-going nurse provides the oncoming nurse with a detailed review of the important issues about the patient's health condition (Fig. 3).

In-room Activities are composed of regular primary care activities, the verification of supplies of a room (getting supplies and/or preparing for a procedure and going to stock rooms), interaction with patients, documenting electronic medical records (EMR),

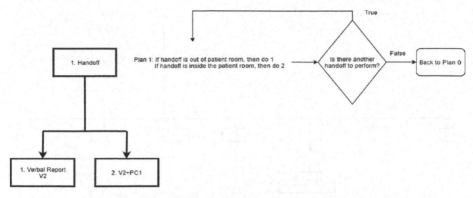

Fig. 3. Hierarchical Task Analysis chart of Handoff activity

cleaning patient's room, attending clinical rounds, and patient transportation. Regular primary care activities consist of medication activities (getting the medication from the station and preparing and administering the medication), performing procedures, patient care, working on monitors and equipment, closed curtain activities, lab specimen activities (taking the patient's specimen and transporting the lab specimen), and patient's assessment (initial or focused assessment). It is important to mention that, to keep the patient's privacy, the observers did not enter a patient room (Figs. 4 and 5).

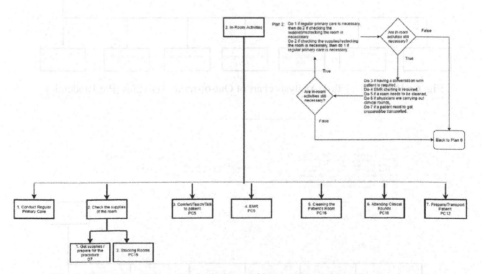

Fig. 4. Hierarchical Task Analysis chart of In-room Activities (Pre-Pandemic)

Out-of-room activities consist of EMR charting, performing a unit task, reviewing documents, washing hands, attending staff meetings, reviewing electrocardiogram (EKG) strips, and taking notes about patients (Figs. 6 and 7).

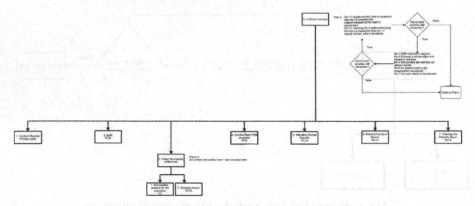

Fig. 5. Hierarchical Task Analysis chart of In-room Activities (Pandemic)

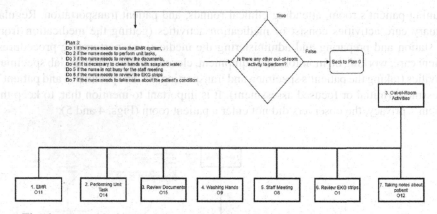

Fig. 6. Hierarchical Task Analysis chart of Out-of-room Activities (Pre-Pandemic)

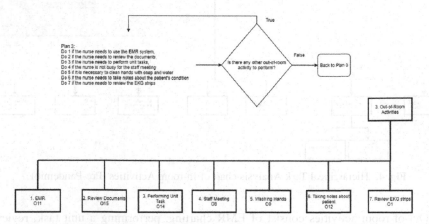

Fig. 7. Hierarchical Task Analysis chart of Out-of-room Activities (Pandemic)

Peer Support is composed of assisting in patient care, assisting in the nurse-led procedure, assisting in physician-led procedure, and assisting in closed curtain tasks. It is also about the activities conducted in the patient rooms, but the observed nurse works as a peer supporter this time (Figs. 8 and 9).

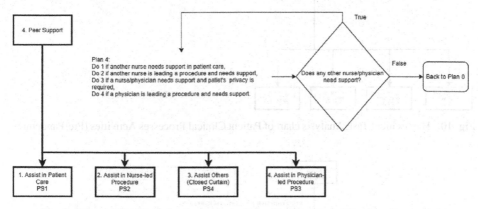

Fig. 8. Hierarchical Task Analysis chart of Peer Support Activities (Pre-Pandemic)

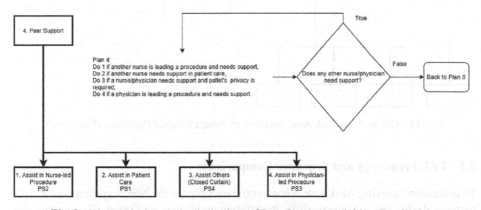

Fig. 9. Hierarchical Task Analysis chart of Peer Support Activities (Pandemic)

Patient clinical processes conversations consist of talking with other nurses, using the room's communication system or table phone, talking with physicians, and talking with patient's family.

Finally, non-nursing activities refer to all activities that are not related to patient care, composed of non-value added (NVA) general activities (Internet Web, phone, etc.), NVA conversation, leaving the unit for restroom or taking a break, lunch break, waiting to report to a next shift nurse, and waiting to receive a report from a previous shift nurse (Figs. 10 and 11).

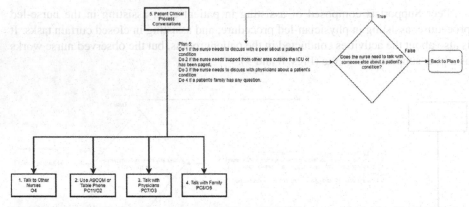

Fig. 10. Hierarchical Task Analysis chart of Patient Clinical Processes Activities (Pre-Pandemic)

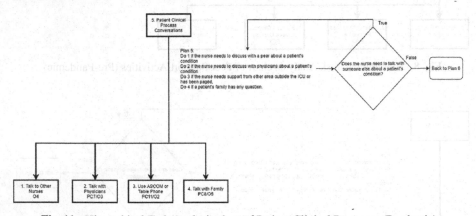

Fig. 11. Hierarchical Task Analysis chart of Patient Clinical Processes (Pandemic)

2.2 Task Frequency and Sequence Comparisons

To understand nursing workflow, it is essential to compare the NFER system output data patterns during the ICU nurse shifts in different conditions and times. To compare the ICU nurse shifts during a pre-pandemic period and pandemic period, this study used a hypothesis test, checking whether there was statistical evidence to support that task frequency and the number of tasks in sequence averages from the different periods are significantly different [10].

3   Results

Table 1 shows that the number of In-room activities was decreased by 18.2% on average during the pandemic. From Table 2, the significant activities are the regular primary care, which dropped 15.7% on average, and EMR, which decreased by 51% in the same period. Within the regular primary care, medication activities fell 28% also during the pandemic. The only activity type that follows the opposite pattern is the verification of supplies of a room that increased on average.

Table 1 also shows that Out-of-room activities are significantly different between periods. During the pandemic period, the numbers decreased on average by 30.5%; EMR decreased by 18.4%, performing a unit Task, 67.4%, and reviewing document tasks, 69% (see Table 3).

Table 1. Differences in task frequencies (# of events) for the main categories of activities.

Main Category of Activities	Period	Mean	SD	F	p-value
In-room Activities	Pre-pandemic	62.143	17.622	7.334	0.009
	Pandemic	50.829	17.331		
Out-of-room Activities	Pre-pandemic	27.886	9.042	21.058	<0.001
	Pandemic	19.371	6.225		

Table 2. Differences in task frequencies (# of events) for In-room Activities.

In-room Activities	Period	Mean	SD	F	p-value
Regular Primary Care	Pre-pandemic	44.743	13.347	5.304	0.024
	Pandemic	37.714	12.160		
Medication Activities	Pre-pandemic	14.134	6.103	8.807	0.004
	Pandemic	10.171	5.017		
Verification of Supplies of a Room	Pre-pandemic	1.171	1.540	27.723	<0.001
	Pandemic	4.514	3.426		
EMR	Pre-pandemic	11.429	5.315	31.457	<0.001
	Pandemic	5.600	3.091		

Table 3. Differences in task frequencies (# of events) for Out-of-room Activities.

Out-of-room Activities	Period	Mean	SD	F	p-value
EMR	Pre-pandemic	20.057	6.028	6.553	0.013
	Pandemic	16.371	6.019		
Performing a Unit Task	Pre-pandemic	2.800	3.846	7.945	0.008
	Pandemic	0.914	0.937		

Table 4 presents the most significant discrepancy in terms of task frequencies during Feb/Mar 2020 (pre-pandemic period) and July 2020 (pandemic period) for patient clinical processes conversations. Talking with the patient's family in person decreased by 74.3% on average during the pandemic.

Table 5 shows that nurses' total number of tasks during the pandemic decreased by 9.6%.

Table 4. Differences in task frequencies for Patient Clinical Processes Conversations.

	Period	Mean	SD	F	p-value
Talking with Patient's Family	Pre-pandemic	2.886	2.945	15.196	<0.001
	Pandemic	0.743	1.380		

Table 5. Differences in the total number of tasks during the shift.

	Period	Mean	SD	F	p-value
Total Number of Activities during the shift	Pre-pandemic	154.46	22.219	8.689	0.004
	Pandemic	139.80	19.278		

4 Discussion

This study aims to compare and pinpoint the pattern differences in nursing workflow during a period before the COVID-19 pandemic and during the pandemic in non-COVID ICUs. According to the results, the pandemic also impacted non-COVID units. The nurses used to perform fewer tasks during their shifts than before. However, there was no significant difference in total nursing care activity times between the two periods. It means that nurses spent more time performing each task during the pandemic than the pre-pandemic.

Table 1 shows that the number of in-room activities decreased during the pandemic. That pattern change should be strongly correlated with avoiding unnecessary contact with patients. Recalling that the ICU in this study is a non-COVID-19 unit, avoiding excessive contact with patients to hinder patient contamination, besides precautionary measures disseminated during the pandemic, such as the article of Huang, Lin [11]. It is reasonable that as nurses carry out a smaller number of in-room activities during the pandemic, they also perform less number of patient's regular primary care, since it represents more than 70% of all in-room activities on average in both periods (see Tables 1 and 2). The same rationale applies to the number of EMR charting, both in- and out-of-room tasks (see Tables 2 and 3). Since the nurses interacted less with patients, they performed fewer electronic recordings. Moreover, the number of medication activities also decreased (see Table 2). It suggests that the patients cared by the nurses during the pandemic period required more time for medications administered through continuous intravenous infusions, while reducing the number of medication administration activities.

Tables 1 and 3 show that EMR activities occupied more than 71% of out-of-room tasks in both periods. The decreased frequency of EMR charting during the pandemic period might impact the number of out-of-room activities (see Table 1).

Other studies also showed that non-COVID units became less busy during the pandemic in some healthcare units around the world, such as Bodilsen, Nielsen [12], which shows that in a hospital in Demark, admissions for all non-covid-19 disease groups decreased compared with the pre-pandemic period. If the nurses are less busy, performing fewer unit tasks (see Table 3) during the pandemic makes sense. Also, the total number of tasks performed by nurses in both periods was compared, reinforcing that nurses are less busy during the pandemic in a non-COVID-19 ICU (see Table 5). Allison, Doyle [9] added that social distancing may have heralded significant reductions in non-COVID and non-pneumonic infections in 2020 compared with 2017. Other studies reported that non-COVID-19 ICUs had been less busy during the pandemic, as changes in working patterns reduce risks associated with long working hours and shift work. It is worth mentioning that this concentrated effort on COVID-19 units could have entailed an increment of out-of-hospital mortality due to non-COVID diseases, particularly during the lockdown weeks, as shown by Santi, Golinelli [13].

On the other hand, the number of times nurses had to go to the supply rooms increased during the pandemic (see Table 2). That result may have come from the pandemic brought extra attention regarding sanitization and disinfection measures for surfaces and equipment.

Finally, on average, the nurse used to talk with the patient's family much less during the pandemic than in the previous period (see Table 4). This data suggests that the family's accessibility to the hospital was limited during the pandemic because of organizational visiting policy changes.

5 Conclusion

According to the results, a non-COVID-19 ICU tended to be less busy during the pandemic because nurses did fewer activities in a shift. And more than identifying those differences and patterns, the main contribution of this study is to advance our understanding of the nursing workflow pattern in a medical ICU in terms of task sequences and task frequency distribution. And combining previous research outcomes, such as the findings of Kasaie, Kim [14, 15] and Camilleri, Henks [16], regarding nurse task duration patterns, and this study findings, will allow us to build models for the nurse ICU shift to optimize it.

It is important to understand other impacts on nursing workload for future work, mainly regarding mental workload and physical fatigue. According to Sagherian, Clinton [7], nursing is physically and mentally strenuous, and performance loss and fatigue are expected during the shift. They concluded that fatigue and performance decrements are safety hazards that have implications for both nurses and patients. So, this study allows a deeper understanding of how the pandemic might affect the nurse workflow in the ICU. The outcomes of the current study findings will allow for building models for the ICU nurse shift to optimize nurses' work routines, maximize nurses' performance, and minimize mental and physical fatigue in any work routine.

References

1. Düzkaya, D.S., Kuğuoğlu, S.: Assessment of pain during endotracheal suction in the pediatric intensive care unit. Pain Manag. Nurs. **16**(1), 11–19 (2015)
2. Moghadam, K.N., et al.: Nursing workload in intensive care units and the influence of patient and nurse characteristics. Nurs. Crit. Care **26**(6), 425–431 (2021)
3. Song, X., Kim, J.H., Despins, L.: A time-motion study in an intensive care unit using the near field electromagnetic ranging system. In: IIE Annual Conference. Proceedings. Institute of Industrial and Systems Engineers (IISE) (2017)
4. Kolodziej, K.W., Hjelm, J.: Local Positioning Systems: LBS Applications and Services. CRC Press, Boca Raton (2017)
5. Schantz, H.G., Weil, C., Unden, A.H.: Characterization of error in a near-field electromagnetic ranging (NFER) real-time location system (RTLS). In: 2011 IEEE Radio and Wireless Symposium. IEEE (2011)
6. Reynolds, T., et al.: Disease control priorities: improving health and reducing poverty. Chapter 13: Strengthening Health Systems to Provide Emergency Care, vol. 9 (2017)
7. Sagherian, K., et al.: Fatigue, work schedules, and perceived performance in bedside care nurses. Workplace Health Saf. **65**(7), 304–312 (2017)
8. Haas, S., Swan, B.A., Jessie, A.T.: The impact of the coronavirus pandemic on the global nursing workforce. Nurs. Econ. **38**(5) (2020)
9. Allison, M.C., et al.: Lockdown Britain: evidence for reduced incidence and severity of some non-Covid acute medical illnesses. Clin. Med. **21**(2), e171 (2021)
10. Montgomery, D.C.: Design and Analysis of Experiments. Wiley, Hoboken (2017)
11. Huang, L., et al.: Special attention to nurses' protection during the Covid-19 epidemic. Crit. Care **24**, 1–3 (2020)
12. Bodilsen, J., et al.: Hospital admission and mortality rates for non-Covid diseases in Denmark during covid-19 pandemic: nationwide population based cohort study. BMJ **373** (2021)
13. Santi, L., et al.: Non-COVID-19 patients in times of pandemic: emergency department visits, hospitalizations and cause-specific mortality in Northern Italy. PLoS ONE **16**(3), e0248995 (2021)
14. Kasaie, A., Kim, J.H., Despins, L.: The impact of Covid-19 pandemic on nurses' behavior for updating assessment results by using the electronic medical record log data in a non-Covid intensive care unit. In: Proceedings of the Human Factors and Ergonomics Society Annual Meeting. SAGE Publications, Sage CA (2021)
15. Kasaie, A., et al.: The impact of nurse experience and sequential organ failure assessment on nurses' workflow in an intensive care unit. In: Proceedings of the Human Factors and Ergonomics Society Annual Meeting. SAGE Publications, Sage CA (2020)
16. Camilleri, N., et al.: EMR usage and nurse documentation burden in a medical intensive care unit. In: Duffy, V.G. (eds.) HCII 2022. LNCS, vol. 13320, pp. 165–173. Springer, Cham (2022). https://doi.org/10.1007/978-3-031-06018-2_11

Human Factors in Manufacturing: A Systematic Literature Review

Fabio Garofalo(✉) and Passawit Puangseree

Purdue University, West Lafayette, IN 47906, USA
{garofalf,ppuangse}@purdue.edu

Abstract. The purpose of this study was to analyze the role human factors play in modern manufacturing systems using a bibliometric approach. The primary method of data collection was using the search function on three well-known academic databases: Scopus, Web of Science, and Google Scholar. Metadata was collected from the results of the searches using the keywords "human factors" and "manufacturing". The resulting data was then analyzed using a variety of tools, such as VOSViewer, MAXQDA, Citespace, and Mendeley. The literature reviewed shows that the arrival of Industry 4.0, and the rapid technological changes accompanying it, have changed human work by challenging existing skills and knowledge. Emphasis is now placed on human-centered work design where workers are given meaningful, autonomous roles as decision makers in a symbiotic relationship with production machinery. Ideas for future research on the topic have been proposed at the end of this report.

Keywords: Manufacturing · Human Factors · Job Design · Bibliometric · VOSViewer · MAXQDA · Citespace · Mendeley

1 Introduction

Academic researchers today have access to a greater amount of information than ever before. The internet has become a vast trove of literature, allowing researchers to study topics of interest in a manner that was not possible in the past. While in many ways this has advanced research at a faster pace than before, having such immense access can make it challenging to extract useful information from a large amount of data. Thankfully, with an increase in the quantity of data on almost all research topics, there have also been improvements in data mining and analysis tools. Academic databases now allow the research to save and analyze metadata from search results, and the metadata can then be analyzed using various bibliometric software tools.

This report discusses the use of the aforementioned tools to research specific topics in the field of human factors and ergonomics (HFE). Two key topics of interest were studied, human factors in manufacturing and workplace design. Both topics were selected due to their importance in job design. Digitization has changed the manufacturing landscape leading to what is now known as the fourth industrial revolution. The fourth industrial revolution, commonly known as Industry 4.0, has brought about rapid technological development to manufacturing systems with the integration of digitized networks in almost all aspects of the manufacturing industry. These developments have rendered manufacturing processes increasingly more complex, with vast improvements to the efficiency and capacity of these systems. While these changes have been beneficial from a supply chain and economic standpoint, it is also increasingly important to consider worker safety and wellbeing as the environments they work in change (Reiman et al. 2021). Beyond manufacturing, workplace design is a broader field of industrial engineering that aims to ensure worker safety, wellbeing, and satisfaction in an increasingly knowledge-based work environment (Chan et al. 2007). A Google Ngram search was executed to understand the emergence of relevant topics over the last ten years (Fig. 1).

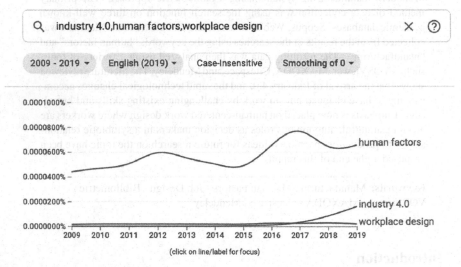

Fig. 1. Google Ngram search comparing relevant topics

The term 'human factors in manufacturing' did not yield any results in Ngram, therefore the search term was changed to 'industry 4.0' since it is a key component of digital manufacturing. This term was then compared to the overarching topic of 'human factors' as well as 'workplace design'. The trendlines show that human factors have been steadily increasing in interest over the last ten years, while industry 4.0 has seen a sharp uptick in the last two years and workplace design has remained constantly low comparatively. While human factors in manufacturing and workplace design were both used in data collection methods, only human factors in manufacturing will be used for data analysis and visualization due to its higher expected relevance in HFE.

2 Purpose of Study

The purpose of this study is to perform a systematic literature review on the topics of human factors in manufacturing and workplace design. The aim is to establish the importance of job and workplace design in manufacturing settings, as this is a topic that is often ignored or subverted when planning business operations. Effective consideration of HFE in manufacturing settings not only benefit the workers' wellbeing but also assist in optimizing production efficiency and costs (Spath and Braun 2021). The execution of this research was assisted with the use of bibliometric tools such as VOSviewer, Citespace, Vicinitas, MaxQDA, and Mendeley.

3 Research Methodology

3.1 Data Collection

The data collection process as part of the systematic literature review was carried out by collecting metadata from three main databases which are Web of Science, Google Scholar and Scopus. These three databases were selected due to them being widely accepted and trusted sources of academic knowledge. Beyond that, they allow the user to extract metadata for further analysis beyond the publications listed in the search results.

Table 1. Keyword Search results from three databases

Database	Search Term	Number of Results
Google Scholar	"Workplace Design"	9,020
Scopus	"Workplace Design"	576
Web of Science	"Workplace Design"	372

Table 2. Keyword search results from three databases

Database	Search Term	Number of Results
Google Scholar	"human factors" AND "manufacturing"	187,000
Scopus	"human factors" AND "manufacturing"	1,568
Web of Science	"human factors" AND "manufacturing"	3,704

The numbers of results are shown for the keywords "Workplace Design" and "'Human Factors" and "Manufacturing'" in Tables 1 and 2. Across the two topics, the databases are consistent with Google Scholar yielding the greatest number of publications. Another consistent factor is that the search term for "'Human Factors" and "Manufacturing'" has a greater number of results compared to "Workplace Design".

This is consistent with the Google Ngram results showing workplace design as having a much lower relevance compared to the topic of human factors. One interesting note is that if the quotation marks are excluded from the search terms, the number of results increases exponentially, as the databases search for articles with any words from the search term rather than the whole term itself. For example, searching for workplace design without quotations will display articles with the word workplace and articles with the word design, but not necessarily articles that include both words together. This can lead to a lower quality of search resultsas often those articles are not relevant to the intended keywords. For the purpose of this literature review, articles resulting from search terms with quotations were used to increase the relevance of the results. Metadata from the results was then downloaded in different formats according to the database specifications and analyzed in the various programs mentioned in the Sect. 2 of this report.

3.2 Engagement Measure

Vicinitas was also used as part of our analysis to assess recent engagement measures on the selected topics. Vicinitas is an online software tool that helps track activities such as engagements, posts, and types of media on a given hashtag or keyword. The program analyzes the data to provide real-time in-depth analytics of user engagement on topics of interest. For this project, we use the keywords "Workplace Design" and "'Human Factors" and "Manufacturing'" with the hashtag and keywords tweets for the data collection and analysis. The results are shown in Figs. 2 and 3.

Fig. 2. Engagement results from Vicinitas for keyword "Workplace Design"

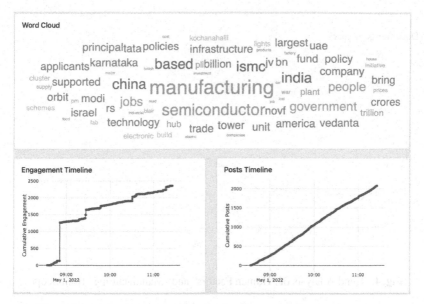

Fig. 3. Engagement results from Vicinitas for keyword "Manufacturing"

The engagement timeline and posts timeline graphs for both the search term show an increase in engagement and interest in the topic, there are significantly more people who discuss or post about "Human Factors" and "Manufacturing" as compared to the keyword "Workplace Design". We were able to come to this conclusion as Vicinitas limits its results to the most recent 2000 tweets. Looking at the posts and engagement timelines for the two search terms, one can see that it took over a week for the term "Workplace Design" to reach 2000 tweets, while it took less than two hours for the term "'Human Factors" and "Manufacturing'" to reach 2000 tweets, confirming yet again the overarching relevance of the latter search term.

3.3 Trend Analysis

The trend analysis from the metadata obtained from the search term on Scopus is generated via the Scopus analyses tab. Trend graphs are created to compare the number of publications of the search term over time, this is done in order to see how the scientific community is interested in Workplace Design and Human Factor in Manufacturing. The diagram is shown in Figs. 4 and 5.

The overall trend from the trend analysis graphs is that the number of publications in both the topics are increasing apart for the slight decline in 1 or two years. At around 2013–2014 both the topics have seen a significant increase in publication which can be link to more public interest in the area. One thing to note however is the fact that the number of publications for "Workplace Design" is much lower than that of "Human Factors" and "Manufacturing".

Documents by year

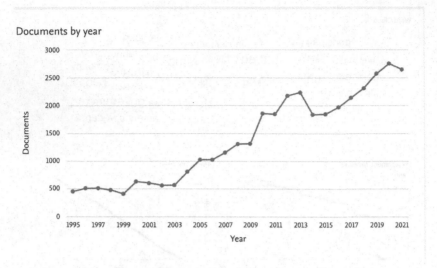

Fig. 4. Trend Analysis of "Human Factors" and "Manufacturing" from Scopus

Documents by year

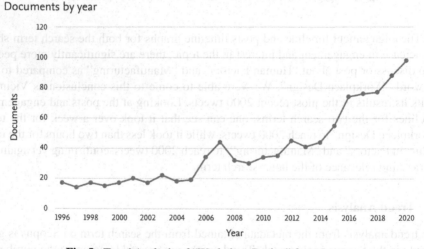

Fig. 5. Trend Analysis of "Workplace Design" from Scopus

4 Results

4.1 Co-citation Analysis

VOSviewer was used to formulate a co-citation analysis from the Scopus search results on "Human Factors" and "Manufacturing". According to IGI Global, "Co-citation is a bibliometric indicator defining the frequency of citing two publications (e.g., journal article, book, and book chapter) together which subsequently highlight the similarity of the cited two documents." Metadata from the 1,569 search results was extracted including bibliographic, citation, abstract and keyword, and reference information. The analysis was limited to articles that had six or more citations, of which twelve articles met the criteria, and the top six of those articles were displayed in the graphic below (Fig. 6).

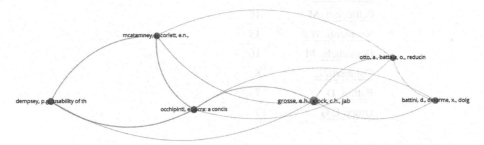

Fig. 6. VOSviewer co-citation analysis

The six articles in the graphic above primarily focus on the ergonomics of worker movement and ensuring worker safety in manual labor related manufacturing environments. These six articles were then saved and stored for further analysis in future work. The Table 3 below lists the six articles and their references.

Table 3. Cited references from co-citation analysis in VOSviewer.

Selected	Cited reference	Citations	Total link strength ⌄
☑	klyatis, l.m., anderson, e.l., (2018) reliability pr...	7	84
☑	klyatis, l.m., (2012) accelerated reliability and d...	6	78
☑	klyatis, l.m., klyatis, e.l., (2006) accelerated qu...	6	78
☑	occhipinti, e., ocra: a concise index for the asse...	7	7
☑	mcatamney, l., corlett, e.n., rula: a survey meth...	6	6
☑	grosse, e.h., glock, c.h., jaber, m.y., neumann, ...	11	5

4.2 Pivot Table

The metadata from Scopus is used to generate the pivot tables for both of our topics. Using the metadata and the built-in data analysis tools on Scopus, we can generate multiple graphs on various topic areas such as documents per year by source and documents by country/territory. In our case, we went with a document by author table which allowed us to identify the top 7 authors that have the most work published on our topic of interest. The results that we received are shown in Tables 4 and 5 below.

The results from the tables above can provide additional insight into future research regarding the topics of interest. Knowing who the leading researchers are in the specified fields under HFE allows for a more in depth analysis into their work and may lead to a larger knowledge base on similar or related topics to our provided search terms.

Table 4. Leading authors table for "Manufacturing" and "Human Factors" generated using Scopus

Author Name	Number of publications
Peruzzini, M	20
Pellicciari, M	16
Neumann, W.P	15
Demichela, M	10
Comberti, L	8
Battini, D	7
Drury, C.G	7

Table 5. Leading authors table for "Workplace Design" generated in Scopus

Author Name	Number of Publications
Caputo, F	6
Greco, A	6
Marras, W.S	6
Gibb, A	5
Gyi, D	5
McDonald, A.C	5
Mertens, A	5

4.3 Cluster Analysis

A cluster analysis was conducted using the Citespace software tool. The cluster analysis uses publication information from the Web of Science search on "Human Factors" and "Ergonomics". The search resulted in 3,708 publications on the topic, and the results were exported as plain text files storing the full record and cited reference of each publication. Web of Science only allows the export of 500 references at a time, therefore the text files had to be manually saved 500 references at a time in a separate folder for processing in Citespace (Fig. 7).

The resulting visualization consists of 49 separate clusters, linked by the orange, yellow, and purple curved lines. The reference information from the clusters is not particularly visible in the graphic above, but the key information that was aimed for extraction was common keywords present in the list of articles. This resulted in five key terms: usability, scheduling, learning, lean production system, and reliability assessment. These key terms are all related to human factors in manufacturing and can be used as search terms in future work. Understanding how these terms play a role in HFE can significantly expand the body of knowledge on the searched topics.

#8 usability

#6 scheduling(15)

#1 learnings (2015)

#3 lean production system

#4 reliability assessment

Lee Jay (2015)

Fig. 7. Keyword cluster analysis in Citespace

4.4   Content Analysis Using MAXQDA

In order to generate a word cloud, we use the program MAXQDA to do a content analysis based on the articles that we have reviewed and deem to be helpful. Word Cloud is a visual representation for text processing and is extremely helpful in helping identify the keywords in the articles uploaded to MAXQDA. The word cloud from MAXQDA can be seen in the Fig. 8 below.

Fig. 8. Word Cloud generated by MAXQDA on articles related to "Human Factors" and "Manufacturing."

MAXQDA, unlike VOSviewer, picks out the key term and information using how many times the words appear in the list of articles. From the word cloud obtained we can see that some of the most common words are lean manufacturing, job design, employee satisfaction, scheduling, and reliability assessments. This is important to the study because we can better focus on the article and look at the area that is the most relevant to us.

5 Discussion

The fourth industrial revolution continues to reconfigure the way manufacturing processes are executed through rapid technical development. The literature reviewed for this report calls attention to the lag of HFE considerations compared to the technological advances that are made in digital manufacturing settings (Reiman et al. 2021). HFE aims to optimize system performance while maintaining the safety and well-being of workers. Even though general worker safety has been an increasingly important aspect of manufacturing business operations, greater emphasis must be placed on ensuring that workers meet the knowledge and skill-based requirements of working in a digitized system. This requires a synergy between management, engineering staff, and operators to ensure that the design of production also factors in the design of the work required by the operator.

The most recent literature places an emphasis on risk prevention and management, as the digital manufacturing emergence presents a plethora of new risks that have no historical precedent. The risks that are emerging as paramount in a digitized manufacturing setting include cybersecurity risks, human oversight of machinery risks, responsibility risks, and a lack of technically qualified employees. More resources should be provided to HFE departments, especially in organizations that are currently transitioning to a highly digitized system. Human work will become less procedural and more cognitive, which will increase employee autonomy and satisfaction, but require a greater level of training and assistance initially. Maturing HFE departments in manufacturing organizations will help to ensure that companies have the personnel required to sustain production excellence.

6 Conclusion

Overall, this systematic literature review has provided a basis of understanding on human factors and ergonomics in manufacturing settings, and how bibliometric analyses can be used to extract more meaningful content on desired topics of interest. Using a variety of sources of information and analysis tools has allowed for a more comprehensive assessment of the current and future knowledge on human factors in today's manufacturing industry. Different databases allow you to extract metadata that can then be processed to gain meaningful diagrams, tables, and figures through statistical methods. This review has consistently shown the importance of including HFE considerations when transitioning or implementing a digital manufacturing system. Even though manufacturing processes are becoming increasingly automated, human oversight and interaction will still be an integral part of manufacturing for the foreseeable future.

7 Future Work

From our literature reviews we were able to identify that there is a lack of studies related to machine, technology, and human interaction in both the topic areas. In a society where new and innovative machines and technology are produced and get integrated in the workplace at a rapid rate, it is crucial to study how this affects human performance. Future work and studies on this topic involve primarily considering how human-machine interaction will evolve as manufacturing workplaces become more digitized. Designing new technology should be done to augment human performance rather than interfere with it. Therefore, future research should place an emphasis on fostering learning and creating meaningful roles for workers.

The keyword for the topic was searched on the NSF.gov website under the award section to grasp what kind of future work the science community is interested in or planning to work on. This gave us a result on how to facilitate human interaction with assistive robots through intent signaling and inference. A screenshot of the future research from NSF is in the Fig. 9 below.

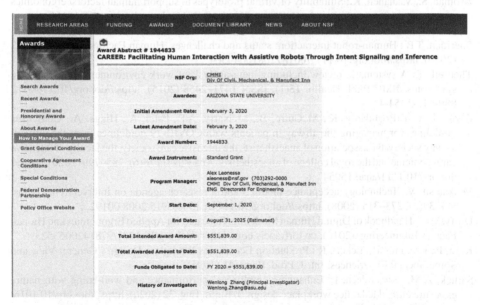

Fig. 9. Screenshot from the NSF website under the awards section which show the future project related to human and machine interaction in manufacturing.

References

Feyen, R., Liu, Y., Chaffin, D., Jimmerson, G., Joseph, B.: Computer-aided ergonomics: a case study of incorporating ergonomics analyses into workplace design. Applied ergonomics (Elsevier) (2000). https://www.sciencedirect.com/science/article/pii/S0003687099000538

Garett, R., Chiu, J., Zhang, L., Young, S.D.: A literature review: website design and user engagement Online J. Commun. Media Technol. 6(3), 1 (2016).https://doi.org/10.29333/ojcmt/2556

Law, R., Qi, S., Buhalis, D.: Progress in tourism management: a review of website evaluation in tourism research. Tour. Manag. (Elsevier) (2010). https://www.sciencedirect.com/science/article/pii/S0261517709002155

Shah, R., Ward, P.T.: Lean manufacturing: context, practice bundles, and performance. J. Oper. Manage. 21(2), 129–149 (2003). https://doi.org/10.1016/S0272-6963(02)00108-0

Finn, R.D.: The Pfam protein families database. Nucleic Acids Res. 36 (2008). ISSN 0305-1048.https://doi.org/10.1093/nar/gkm960

Eaves, S., Gyi, D.E., Gibb, A.G.F.: Building healthy construction workers: Their views on health, wellbeing and better workplace design. Applied ergonomics (Elsevier) (2016). https://www.sciencedirect.com/science/article/pii/S0003687015301058

Safe, S.H.: Polychlorinated biphenyls (PCBs): environmental impact, biochemical and toxic responses, and implications for risk assessment. Critic. Rev. Toxicol. 24(2), 87–149 (1994). https://doi.org/10.3109/10408449409049308

Murphy, S.: 3D bioprinting of tissues and organs. Nat. Biotechnol. 32(8), 773–785 (2014). https://doi.org/10.1038/nbt.2958

Aromaa, S., Vaananen, K.: Suitability of virtual prototypes to support human factors/ ergonomics evaluation during the design. Appl. Ergon. 56, 11-18 (2016). https://doi.org/10.1016/j.apergo.2016.02.015

Sheridan, T.B.: Human-robot interaction: status and challenges. Human Factors. 58(4), 525–532 (2016). https://doi.org/10.1177/0018720816644364

Theorell, T.: A systematic review including meta-analysis of work environment and depressive symptoms. BMC Publ. Health. 15(1), ISSN 1471–2458 (2015). https://doi.org/10.1186/s12889-015-1954-4

Cook, T.M., ElBoghdadly, K., McGuire, B., McNarry, A.F., Patel, A., Higgs, A.: Consensus guidelines for managing the airway in patients with COVID-19 guidelines from the difficult airway society, the association of anaesthetists the intensive care society, the faculty of intensive care medicine and the royal college of anaesthetists. Anaesthesia 75(6), 785–799 (2020). https://doi.org/10.1111/anae.15054

Venkatesh, V.: Technology acceptance model 3 and a research agenda on interventions. Decis. Sci. 39(2), 273–315 (2008). https://doi.org/10.1111/j.1540-5915.2008.00192.x

Duffy, V.G.: Handbook of Digital Human Modeling: Research for Applied Ergonomics and Human Factors Engineering. (2016). taylorfrancis.com. https://doi.org/10.1201/9781420063523

Kern, P., Breining, R., Eckert, R.: Production Economics Workplace Design - General View and Some Special Experiences. Int. J. Prod. Econ. 41 (1995)

Sadick, A.M., Kamardeen, I.: Enhancing employees' performance and well-being with nature exposure embedded office workplace design. J. Build. Eng. 32 (2020). https://doi.org/10.1016/j.jobe.2020.101789

Markkanen, P.,Juuti, E., Herneoja, A.: Exploring ways to study the workplace design in a small knowledge work company. J. Corporate Real Estate (2022). https://doi.org/10.1108/JCRE-01-2021-0006

Lahtinen, M., Ruohomäki, V., Haapakangas, A., Reijula, K.: Developmental needs of workplace design practices. Intell. Build. Int. 7(4), 198–214 (2015). https://doi.org/10.1080/17508975.2014.1001315

Hui, F.K.P., Aye, L.: Occupational stress and workplace design. Buildings. 8(10) (2018). https://doi.org/10.3390/buildings8100133

Chim, J.M.Y.: 6Ws in ergonomics workplace design. In: Bagnara, S., Tartaglia, R., Albolino, S., Alexander, T., Fujita, Y. (Eds.) Proceedings of the 20th Congress of the International

Ergonomics Association (IEA 2018) AISC, vol. 824, pp. 1282–1286. Springer, Cham (2019).https://doi.org/10.1007/978-3-319-96071-5_129

Kačerová, I., Kubr, J., Hořejší, P., Kleinová, J.: Ergonomic design of a workplace using virtual reality and a motion capture suit. Appl. Sci. (Switzerland). **12**(4) (2022). https://doi.org/10.3390/app12042150

Weber, C., Gatersleben, B.: Office relocation: changes in privacy fit, satisfaction and fatigue. J. Corp. Real Estate. **24**(1), 21–39 (2022). https://doi.org/10.1108/JCRE-12-2020-0066

AppelMeulenbroek, R., Janssen, I., Groenen, P.: An end user's perspective on activity based office concepts. J. Corp. Real Estate **13**(2), 122–135 (2011). https://doi.org/10.1108/14630011111136830

Fachrudin, H.T., Fachrudin, K.A., Pane, I.F.: Workplace design concept based on indoor environmental quality analysis to prevent coronavirus transmission. Civil Eng. Architect. **10**(1), 121–130 (2022). https://doi.org/10.13189/cea.2022.100111

SmithJackson, T.L., Klein, K.W.: Open-plan offices: task performance and mental workload. J. Environ. Psychol. **29**(2), 279–289 (2009). https://doi.org/10.1016/j.jenvp.2008.09.002

Brunia, S., de Been, I., van der Voordt, T.J.M.: Accommodating new ways of working: lessons from best practices and worst cases. J. Corp. Real Estate **18**(1), 30–47 (2016). https://doi.org/10.1108/JCRE-10-2015-0028

Tsarouchi, P., Michalos, G., Makris, S., Athanasatos, T., Dimoulas, K., Chryssolouris, G.: On a human–robot workplace design and task allocation system. Int. J. Comput. Integr. Manuf. **30**(12), 1272–1279 (2017). https://doi.org/10.1080/0951192X.2017.1307524

Hair, J.F., Page, M.J., Brunsveld, N.: Essentials of Business Research Methods, 4th edn. Routledge, New York (2020)

Salvendy, G., Waldemar, K.: Handbook of Human Factors and Ergonomics, 5th edn. John Wiley & Sons, Incorporated, Newark (2021)

"VOSviewer. n.d. https://www.vosviewer.com/

Harzing, A.-W.: Reflections on the H-Index. Harzing.com. https://harzing.com/publications/white-papers/reflections-on-the-h-index. Accessed 27 Jan 2022

National Science Foundation - Where Discoveries Begin. Future of Work|NSF National Science Foundation. https://www.nsf.gov/eng/futureofwork.jsp. Accessed 1 May 2022

NSF AWARD SEARCH: Award # 1944833 - CAREER: Facilitating human interaction with assistive robots through intent signaling and inference. https://www.nsf.gov/awardsearch/showAward?AWD_ID=1944833&HistoricalAwards=false

Pre-defined Emergencies on Demand: Simulation-Based Analysis of Information Processing in Emergency Dispatching

Marthe Gruner(✉) ⓘ, Tim Schrills ⓘ, and Thomas Franke ⓘ

University of Lübeck, Ratzeburger Allee 160, 23562 Lübeck, Germany
{gruner,schrills,franke}@imis.uni-luebeck.de

Abstract. Lacking situation awareness is one of the main issues in emergency dispatching that can lead to high uncertainty in decision-making. Automated systems can and will support dispatchers in this process in the future. Yet, the introduction of such systems can place additional cognitive demands on dispatchers and should therefore be tailored to their working routines at an early stage. This is especially true when systems execute tasks that cannot be performed by humans in this form, and thus provide new sources of information. To figure out how to design the integration of new information, it is essential to understand the existing information flow of dispatchers to assess how information processing might change. For this purpose, we propose the combination of simulations and the Critical Decision Method (CDM) with the amplification by psychological experimental design methods as an approach to uncover cognitive processes in decision-making. In a literature review, we identified 10 relevant empirical research papers in which this combination had already been applied in studies. The reviewed papers were analyzed in terms of methodological aspects and takeaways regarding the application of simulations and the CDM. The results show that both the simulation environment and scenarios, as well as the selection of CDM probes, require careful consideration and accurate alignment with the research objectives. In conclusion, we provide and discuss the methodological design, an experimental setup, and an example scenario focused on the emergency dispatching process.

Keywords: Simulation · Critical decision method · Emergency dispatching

1 Introduction

Situation awareness is crucial for emergency dispatchers when responding to incidents. Based on the information provided by the person calling the emergency dispatch center and the contextual information from a computer-aided dispatch (CAD) system, they assess the situation on site and try to predict its development. However, dispatchers' situation assessment might be limited by scarce or unreliable information [1, 2]. For instance, in the case of a forest fire, callers may only be able to smell the fire, but not see it and thus not be able to assess exactly the location or the size of the fire. Based on this restricted information, dispatchers create a situation model (cf. e.g., [3]), which

V. G. Duffy (Ed.): HCII 2023, LNCS 14028, pp. 368–382, 2023.
https://doi.org/10.1007/978-3-031-35741-1_28

may subsequently be flawed. Using the forest fire as an example, they might consider the risk minor at first, due to minimal wind and no other incoming calls. However, they may not be aware that the fire is much larger and close to highly inflammable material. As a result of the prevailing scarcity and unreliability of information, emergency disposition decision-making is fraught with uncertainty. Despite these restrictions, dispatchers must allocate resources rapidly and appropriately, even if that means sending fewer forces to a fire scene than would be necessary.

To improve dispatchers' decision-making, supporting human information processing can be a promising solution [4], as automated systems are beneficial when reliable [5]. In emergency response, such systems may include Unmanned Arial Vehicle (UAV) footage of accident sites (e.g., [6]), emergency calls analyzed by AI (e.g., [7]), or automatic in-vehicle emergency call service (e.g., [8]).

However, in complex and safety-critical areas, it is important that such systems are seamlessly integrated into dispatchers' workflows, for example, to prevent system misuse or additional workload. Especially when supporting tasks where humans depend on automation (e.g., visual assessment of emergency locations), the resulting necessity for human-automation interaction should be considered early in the system's design. This includes a thorough analysis of the information flow involved in emergency dispatching in particularly challenging and complex situations, e.g., when information about on-scene dynamics is lacking or unreliable.

2 Knowledge Elicitation in Safety-Critical Systems

The introduction and embedding of automated systems in safety-critical systems is a sensitive issue and requires a good foundation to minimize disruption to work processes. Cognitive task analysis (CTA) supplies a set of qualitative techniques to analyze cognitive processes (e.g., information processing) in naturalistic environments as a basis for introducing, e.g., technology [9].

Qualitative CTA methods such as observations or interviews offer the possibility to gain insights into work processes to provide early contributions to system design [9]. Observations allow real-time analysis of events but limit the ability to delve into cognitive processes. In contrast, interview-based techniques such as the Critical Decision Method (CDM; [10]) enable effective modelling of cognitive task demands in complex naturalistic environments (see e.g., [11]). Moreover, in the case of situation assessment, CDM was found to provide more and better information than other established methods when the same problem is addressed, and the participants have equivalent expertise [12]. Due to its widespread use, CDM literature provides numerous references to create a comprehensive codebook for data evaluation (cf. [13]). However, retrospection as used in CDM may be constrained by memory distortions, and individual respondents may reference different events [14], hampering generalizable analysis of dispatchers' information acquisition.

To enable a generalizable evaluation of dispatchers' work processes, it would be valuable to expose several dispatchers to the same (standardized) situation. Real cases, however, cannot meet this requirement. Simulations, on the other hand, can, as they allow studying a system's behavior without disrupting it. Importantly, simulations should match the main features and interactions of the actual system [15]. Consequently, a simulated environment in emergency dispatching should allow participants to interact and respond as they would in the real work environment (e.g., reach out to colleagues/supervisors for help or use the CAD- system) to model the actual working system. Such an approach can provide extensive qualitative data without interfering with real-life situations. At this point, it must be mentioned that the use of simulations in qualitative research is not a completely novel approach. Militello and Hutton summarized important aspects of simulation interviews already in 1998 [16]. However, their described approach does not employ structured CDM probes, which we specifically focus on to develop a reliable elicitation approach for cognitive processes in decision-making.

With this work, we aim to highlight the suitability of simulation-based, CDM integrated analysis of challenging, safety-critical situations in emergency dispatching for the optimal design of human-automation interaction. To this end, a systematic literature review was conducted to evaluate methodological criteria to consider when designing a simulation-based CDM.

3 Literature Review

The review of the relevant literature was conducted following the guideline for systematic reviews PRISMA 2020 [17]. The guideline includes a checklist of seven categories with 27 items which were followed at every stage of the review process. Reported data were searched and compiled from various academic research databases (see below) in January 2023.

3.1 Search and Selection Process

The aim of the review was to identify empirical studies on the application of simulations in combination with CDM interviews, regardless of the domain. Emphasis was placed on CDM, as we intended to find studies that explicitly used the proposed probes by Klein et al. [10]. Since the simulation interviews do not explicitly use the CDM probes, we intentionally included CDM as an exact phrase search. The studies identified were compared in their methodological approach and their domain to determine transferability to and relevance for the emergency dispatching. Likewise, the authors' conclusions were reviewed closely to incorporate them in the methodological implementation. The eligibility criteria for the literature search can be found in Table 1.

The databases Scopus, ScienceDirect, and ACM (each last checked on January 14, 2023) served as sources of the data. The search string created based on the review objectives read as followed: ALL ("critical decision method" AND stud* AND interview* AND (simulat* OR scenario*)). The string was adjusted for ScienceDirect since this database does not support wildcards (see Fig. 1 for details). In each database, results were filtered by year (after 1989), language (English), and journal articles as well as

Table 1. Eligibility criteria for the literature review on simulation-based CDM interviews.

	Inclusion criteria	Exclusion criteria
Study type	Empirical and original research study; published in English language and after 1989 (the introduction of the CDM method [10] serves as a chronological reference)	Anything other than journal articles or conference paper, languages of publication other than English
Method	Methodology is described in detail	Method section is not available
	Simulations were conducted and CDM interviews were carried out based on these simulations	No deliberate implementation of simulations with follow-up CDM interviews
	Multiple participants went through the methodological process (i.e., simulation then CDM interviews)	Participants did not experience the simulation firsthand (e.g., hypothetical scenario description)
	Simulation was conducted in a setting that was at least partially controlled	No controlled task setting

conference proceedings. Following flowchart gives an overview of the review process (see Fig. 1).

After retrieving the articles and removing few not accessible articles, all papers were screened in full and manually filtered by original research (to identify and remove reviews not automatically filtered out by the databases), conduction of CDM interviews, level of detail on methodology, and description of conducted simulations. Articles were excluded if no empirical study was conducted or no CDM interviews were reported. This step also included the detailed review of the applied methodology. As mentioned, the aim was to identify papers which conducted simulated tasks with follow-up CDM interviews. For a clearly defined exclusion, the following approach was used in the selection process as a guideline:

1. Inclusion: Predefined incidents were used to conduct CDM interviews based on them.
2. Exclusion: The classical approach of CDM was conducted.
3. Inclusion: Simulations were experienced by the participants first-hand
4. Exclusion: Participants addressed hypothetical cases.
5. Inclusion: Multiple participants engaged in simulated tasks under controlled conditions (i.e., same perspective, same information available, etc.) and were interviewed with the CDM.
6. Exclusion: Single individuals performed a simulated task or were interviewed with the CDM; Specific cases (e.g., industrial accidents) were analyzed or incidents were selected from longer periods of observation without environmental control.

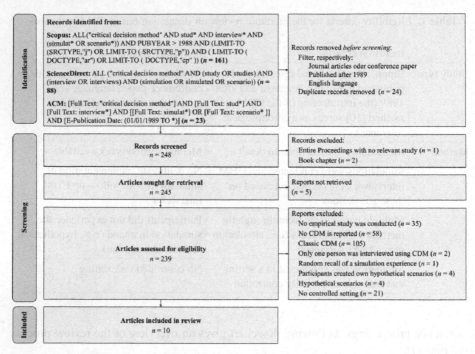

Fig. 1. Flowchart of the literature search on simulation-based CDM interviews.

3.2 Synthesis

Based on these selection criteria, 10 scientific articles were identified, which were then reviewed in detail regarding the domain addressed, the study objective and sample size, and the reported methodological design and discussion (see Table 2).

As the literature discovered shows, the combination of simulations and CDM offers a range of various application opportunities and areas, both with novices and experts. Several conclusions can be drawn from the work reviewed.

Finding 1: Simulations that accurately represent the real system in its complexity provide rich data on decision-making processes.

In the proposed work, the means to realistically represent decision-making processes as conducted by dispatchers in real world is a simulated dispatch environment. In the literature analyzed, several considerations emerged which should be taken into account.

Table 2. Reviewed literature on simulation-based CDM interviews

Authors & Year	Domain	N	Study objective
Crandall, 1989 [12]	Civil Protection	20	Comparison of knowledge elicitation methods (Think aloud and Critical Decision Method)
Elliott et al., 2007 [18]	Civil Protection	20	Investigation of (naturalistic) decision-making in microworlds
Malakis et al., 2014 [19]	Aviation	N/A	Exploration of the capabilities of existing simulator-based training
Mansikka et al., 2021 [20]	Military	39	Development and testing of a new technique for the assessment of Team Situation Awareness
Roose et al., 2018 [21]	Video gaming	17	Introduction of a new method combining of CTA and Eye tracking with proof of concept
Roose & Veinott, 2021 [22]	Video gaming	25	Examination of a team-oriented, first-person shooter game to inform Esports training
Rozzi et al., 2007 [23]	Aviation	4	Investigation of the scope and limits of 3D representations in Air Traffic Control
Salmon et al., 2009 [24]	Military	20	Comparison of Situation Awareness measurement approaches during a military planning task
Stelmaszewska et al., 2010 [25]	Academics	34	Investigation of interaction behavior of users with various electronic resource discovery systems
Walker et al., 2010 [26]	Military	20	Comparison between novices and experts in military command and control tasks

Note. N is Sample size

With their implemented Microworld (i.e., Networked Fire Chief), Elliot et al. [18] demonstrated that appropriate perceptual-cognitive processing for naturalistic decision-making is promoted in the highly controlled setting. However, they also highlight that its abstract nature does not represent the complex factors and their interaction existing in real-world settings (e.g., team and organizational constraints were not included). This subsequently constrains the scope for more in-depth investigation of real-world decision-making and transfer of conclusions to the actual domain.

Mansikka et al. [20] use the example of a training flight simulator, which allows interaction like in an actual airplane. By analyzing cognitive processes (e.g., team situational awareness; TSA) with the CDM, they were able to confirm their assumption that the relationship between SA and performance is most likely to have a curvilinear relationship rather than a linear one as previously assumed. Similarly, using an experimental command-and-control test bed, Salmon et al. [24] demonstrated that CDM can help to capture SA in simulated conditions as it does in real-world environments. However, they also note that the appropriate selection of CDM probes is essential.

Finding 2: Choice of methods for eliciting situation awareness in simulations needs to be considered in regard to participants expertise and desired depth of analysis.

One of the main aspects of the methodology proposed in this paper is the attempt to capture the information processing of the emergency dispatchers to identify root causes of uncertainty in decision-making. As mentioned, this involves the assessment of situation awareness.

In their simulation-based study, Salmon et al. [24] compared three established measures of situational awareness: Situation Awareness Global Assessment Technique (SAGAT; [27]), Situation Awareness Rating Technique (SART; [28]), and the CDM. They conclude that the measures approach the construct from different perspectives and therefore measure it in different ways. SART is easy to apply but elicits subjective perception, which captures, e.g., implicit processing poorly, if at all. SAGAT allows for objective acquisition of SA (i.e., assessment of individuals' perceptions of elements in the environment) but may not be suitable for complex environments where outcomes are not easily predictable. CDM can contribute to determine the information encompassed by situational awareness and how that information is distributed across team and system, making it more suitable for dynamic contexts.

Mansikka et al. [20] point out that, unlike other methods of eliciting cognitive demands to develop and maintain TSA, CDM provides the opportunity to go beyond subjective assessments of SA while avoiding interfering with task performance. Comparing two established knowledge elicitation methods, Crandall found that the CDM (given similar problem sets and participants with equal expertise) resulted in more and better information on situation assessment of experts than the Think-Aloud method.

Differences between novices and experts have likewise been successfully uncovered, for instance, in situation model building [26] and information search strategies [25]. Here, Walker et al. [26] clearly conclude that novices can be engaged as participants in controlled experimental contexts, however, experts are essential for a deeper understanding of, e.g., decision models.

Moreover, the combination of CDM with quantitative analysis methods such as eye-tracking has been introduced [21, 22]. The authors point out that this mixed method allows the analysis of visual attention patterns in decision strategies. The method seems promising as it can help to differentiate between general search strategies and search strategies focusing on crucial decisions, which can be valuable in evaluating problem-diagnostic behavior.

Consistent with the approach of Klein et al. [10], CDM is shown to allow critical decision points to be focused on and analyzed rather than the entire task [21, 22, 24], in simulations as in real-world settings.

Finding: The design of the simulation scenarios and correspond-ing tasks for participants is a key factor valid difficulty.

Not only the simulation environment, but more importantly the task scenarios are crucial to draw valuable conclusions. Therefore, we consider this another aspect that needs to be informed by the existing literature, especially considering that the CDM probes were constructed to help practitioners depict actual experienced events.

Malakis et al. [19] evaluated the capabilities of an air traffic controller training simulator that is used for regular training of controllers to effectively manage emergencies and abnormal situations. To meet these simulation requirements, they point out that experienced pilots design the training scenarios. In comparison, Elliot et al. [18] report that their scenarios, while thoughtfully created by the researchers, may not have been difficult enough for the research purposes.

Comparing TSA accuracy across three different cognitive demands, Mansikka et al. [20] suggest that the high demand condition task may have been too difficult even for experts, based on the considerably weaker TSA accuracy results.

3.3 Review Discussion

The objective of the literature review was to identify relevant papers in which CDM based on simulations was conducted and included reflection on the methodology.

An essential takeaway is that a simulation-based CDM is a valuable method not only to gain deep insights into cognitive processes in decision processes, but also the ability to conduct the analysis in a controlled environment. However, there are aspects that need to be addressed. To represent real-world environments, simulations must be sufficiently complex, i.e., represent all decision-influencing factors, to draw valid conclusions. Equally as important as the design of a simulated system is designing the scenarios required for the simulations to be effective. When it comes to creating the scenarios, experts should be involved to ensure the realism of the events portrayed, but also to ensure the relevance of the scenarios to the domain. Regarding the selection of an appropriate method for the assessment of cognitive processes, the results show that several techniques can be valuable. However, the advantage of the CDM is that it can delve much deeper into data on cognitive processes than alternative methods. Although developed for incident analysis in naturalistic environments, it also demonstrates success in simulated environments.

Ultimately, however, it must be noted that in the papers reviewed, the application of the chosen simulation and the conclusions on CDM integration were not discussed in detail in many cases. Nonetheless, the remarks that can be derived from conducting simulations of safety-critical systems can be considered valuable for the further development of this methodology in future research.

4   Methodology Design

As mentioned above, the general structure of the proposed method is guided by the setup of the CDM [9]. In a combination of high-fidelity simulations and CDM, participants, however, do not recall an event but participate in a realistic simulation analyzed thoroughly using cognitive probes adopted from Klein et al. [10]. Thereby, mainly the first two steps of the CDM are modified (see Fig. 2). The subsequent interview is still intended to follow the samples proposed in the original CDM.

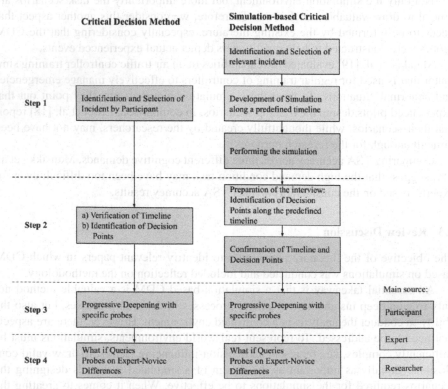

Fig. 2. Comparison of the classic CDM and the modified simulation-based CDM

By simulating a task (e.g., handling an emergency call), realistic behavior of participants can be evoked without creating actual risk situations [29]. Moreover, multiple individuals can be confronted with the same situation, allowing for reliable and comparable elicitation of their information processing. The application of the proposed methodology of simulation-based CDM is further exemplified by the handling of emergency calls.

4.1 Experimental Setup

To demonstrate the applicability of our methodological proposal, a possible experimental setting in the context of emergency dispatching is presented in more detail. In emergency dispatching, dispatchers work in spacious rooms at individual workstations with several screens for operating the CAD system. At these stations, they answer emergency calls and distribute required resources such as emergency services. In the same room, a supervisor monitors the work processes and assists when required. Likewise, the dispatchers help each other when necessary. To ensure a realistic simulation, the following elements are important for the experimental room set-up: (1) the workplace with relevant systems and artifacts, (2) additional dispatchers (with separate workplaces), (3) a supervisor (e.g., see Fig. 3). This ensures that dispatchers have access to every information source that might be available in their daily work environment. Another separate room is typically needed to accommodate individuals who set and monitor the computer system and simulate interactions involving callers and emergency services (i.e., a planning room, see Fig. 3).

Fig. 3. Left: Training room for simulations, Right: Planning room for scenarios; Exemplified by the emergency call center in Harrislee, Germany. ©2013, Leitstelle Nord (Harrislee), Germany.

4.2 Example Scenario

As a starting point for developing a suitable scenario to simulate, we consulted an emergency operations center to determine in which work areas automated support (i.e., in the present case UAV imagery support of emergency locations) would be valuable. One issue that emerged is the uncertainty surrounding forest fires. Problems arising include late discovery of the fire area, poor ability to locate the breakout area, and limited ability to estimate the resources needed to adequately respond to the fire. In the future, two scenarios can be imagined where for instance UAVs could strongly support dispatchers: (1) early detection of potential fire (e.g., if UAVs permanently search for fire sources in dry periods and alert the control center directly) or (2) support in the analysis of an already reported fire source (e.g., by a caller).

The scenario example includes a heavy smoke development around Bordelumer Heide/forest area (North Frisia, Germany). Calling consecutively from different locations, three people report seeing or smelling smoke (development) in the area. Calls are phoned in from the planning room. No specific presets for the computer system are defined. Thus, the dispatchers can dispatch any emergency force they requested. In addition to the main scenario, small scenarios (e.g., hospital transfer calls) are played at irregular intervals to simulate the work routine realistically. The small interim scenarios and the radio communication with the emergency forces on site are also simulated by other dispatchers from the planning room.

4.3 CDM Interviews

As mentioned above, the methodology will be based on the deepening probes proposed by Klein et al. [10]. However, the selection of the employed probes will be guided closely by the objectives of the study. Thus, these include Cues, Information, Options, Assessment, and Decision-Making (see Table 3).

Table 3. CDM deepening probes based on Klein et al. [10] to information processing of emergency dispatchers.

Cues	What were you seeing, hearing, smelling, noticing etc.?
Information	What information did you use in making this decision or judgment? How and where did you get this information, and from whom? What did you do with the information?
Assessment	Suppose you were asked to describe the situation to someone else at this point. How would you summarize the situation?
Options	What other courses of action were considered or were available to you? How was this option chosen or others rejected? Was there a rule that you were following in choosing this option?
Decision-Making	What let you know that this was the right thing to do at this point in the incident?

5 Discussion

With this work, we aimed to present a methodological design to elicit the information processing behavior of emergency dispatchers in challenging emergency call handling situations. The basis for the development was found in the established Critical Decision Method. The basis for the development was an established qualitative method for eliciting knowledge from experts, namely the Critical Decision Method. To avoid bias in knowledge acquisition due to memory bias, we proposed to adapt the method and perform simulations as an initial step. In the literature review conducted, it was shown that attention needs to be paid to the implementation of the simulation, the creation of the scenarios for the simulation, and in the application of CDM to capture cognitive processes such as situational awareness. Therefore, a training simulation environment was chosen that is used in an emergency control center, where technical equipment from the actual workplace is available and communication with colleagues and supervisors is possible during the scenarios. The scenarios were developed in collaboration between an expert (i.e., an incident commander) and the researchers to meet both the requirements of scientific investigation and the practical demands of emergency dispatching. Finally, specific CDM deepening probes were selected to target the goal of capturing the decision-making process and the information flow therein.

5.1 Implications

The proposed methodological approach offers several opportunities regarding scientific quality criteria of data collection: (1) Standardization of the situations analyzed allows multiple dispatchers to experience the same situation [16]. Thus, overlaps and differences in decision-making, e.g., in terms of information processing, can be revealed and design requirements able to serve individual decision processes, can be deducted. (2) Compared to retrospection, it may be easier to guide dispatchers in recalling the incident since the situation is known to the interviewer. Subsequently, the data collected could be more detailed, would be less affected by memory effects, and would thus provide the basis for more accurate analysis. Should participants still have difficulty remembering aspects of the scenario, the interviewer can provide guidance (e.g., by videotaping the performance of the task). (3) This approach allows subsequent interview steps to be prepared in advance, considerably reducing the interview duration, and allowing the interviewer to focus on the details rather than rebuilding the story.

5.2 Limitations and Further Research

When conducting a simulation-based interview study, such as the one addressed in this paper using emergency call handling, some challenges need to be considered. (1) Simulation environment: The construction simulation environment with a high degree of external validity (as seen in Fig. 3) requires a relatively large amount of effort. Consequently, it is not a given in all domains and is not yet a matter of course in all emergency call center. (2) Simulation scenarios: The development of simulation scenarios also demands considerable effort [16]. They need to be created by or at least in cooperation with, if not by, a domain expert [30]. Study and emergency disposition requirements must be defined and aligned, and scenarios are most likely to be created in multiple iterations. Key criteria may include, e.g., domain relevance, realism, situational challenge, and occurrence frequency. (3) The preparation time for the interviewer is rather time-consuming, as the video and audio recording of the simulation must be reviewed before the CDM interviews.

6 Conclusion

As a result of the simulation-based CDM study, a detailed description of the information flow, as well as how missing or unreliable information interferes with the decision-making, could be deduced. The outputs may serve multiple purposes: (1) Requirements for implementing decision support technologies in emergency dispatching can be based on reliable and empirical data to improve validity regarding existing information processing. (2) For future studies, intended to investigate cognitive processes, e.g., situation awareness, the study outcomes will enable the design of realistic laboratory experiments and experimental manipulation of available information. This is particularly beneficial to external validity, which is often severely limited in laboratory settings. The experimental interfaces can be designed close to the dispatchers' CAD system, whilst task scenarios can be created that enable the mapping of existing action and decision processes. Thereby, both aspects allow for realistic and potentially highly valid experimental designs.

Acknowledgment. This work was motivated by scenarios investigated as part of the 5G-TELK-NF project funded by the German Federal Ministry for Digital and Transport (Grant number: 165GU135M). For their support, we would like to thank the team at the Emergency Control Center (Leitstelle Nord) in Harrislee, Germany.

References

1. Artman, H., Wærn, Y.: Distributed cognition in an emergency co-ordination center. Cogn. Technol. Work **1**(4), 237–246 (1999). https://doi.org/10.1007/s101110050020
2. Blandford, A., Wong, W.: Situation awareness in emergency medical dispatch. Int. J. Hum Comput Stud. **61**(4), 421–452 (2004). https://doi.org/10.1016/j.ijhcs.2003.12.012
3. Krems, J.F., Baumann, M.R.K.: Driving and situation awareness: a cognitive model of memory-update processes. In: Kurosu, M. (ed.) Human Centered Design. LNCS, vol. 5619, pp. 986–994. Springer, Heidelberg (2009). https://doi.org/10.1007/978-3-642-02806-9_113
4. Mosier, K.L., Manzey, D.: Humans and automated decision aids: a match made in heaven? In: Mouloua, M., Hancock, P.A., and Ferraro, J. (eds.) Human Performance in Automated and Autonomous Systems. pp. 19–42. CRC Press, Boca Raton, FL : CRC Press/Taylor & Francis Group, 2019. (2019). https://doi.org/10.1201/9780429458330-2
5. Onnasch, L., Wickens, C.D., Li, H., Manzey, D.: Human performance consequences of stages and levels of automation: an integrated meta-analysis. Hum. Factors **56**(3), 476–488 (2014). https://doi.org/10.1177/0018720813501549
6. Dousai, N.M.K., Loncaric, S.: Detection of humans in drone images for search and rescue operations. In: 2021 3rd Asia Pacific Information Technology Conference. pp. 69–75. ACM, Bangkok, Thailand (2021). https://doi.org/10.1145/3449365.3449377
7. Zicari, R.V., Brusseau, J., Blomberg, S.N., Christensen, H.C., Coffee, M., Ganapini, M.B., et al.: On assessing trustworthy AI in healthcare. Machine learning as a supportive tool to recognize cardiac arrest in emergency calls. Front. Human Dyn. **3**, 673104 (2021). https://doi.org/10.3389/fhumd.2021.673104
8. Melcher, V., Diederichs, F., Maestre, R., Hofmann, C., Nacenta, J.-M., van Gent, J., et al.: Smart vital signs and accident monitoring system for motorcyclists embedded in helmets and garments for advanced eCall emergency assistance and health analysis monitoring. Proc. Manuf. **3**, 3208–3213 (2015). https://doi.org/10.1016/j.promfg.2015.07.871
9. Crandall, B.W., Klein, G.A., Hoffman, R.R.: Working Minds: A Practitioner's Guide to Cognitive Task Analysis. The MIT Press, Cambridge, Massachusetts (2006). https://doi.org/10.7551/mitpress/7304.001.0001

10. Klein, G.A., Calderwood, R., MacGregor, D.: Critical decision method for eliciting knowledge. IEEE Trans. Syst. Man Cybern. **19**(3), 462–472 (1989). https://doi.org/10.1109/21. 31053

11. Militello, L.G., Klein, G.: Decision-centered design. In: Lee, J.D., Kirlik, A. (eds.) The Oxford Handbook of Cognitive Engineering, pp. 261–271. Oxford University Press, New York, NY (2013). https://doi.org/10.1093/oxfordhb/9780199757183.013.0016

12. Crandall, B.W.: A comparative study of think-aloud and critical decision knowledge elicitation methods. ACM SIGART Bull. 144–146 (1989). https://doi.org/10.1145/63266.63288

13. Hoffman, R.R., Crandall, B., Shadbolt, N.: Use of the critical decision method to elicit expert knowledge: a case study in the methodology of cognitive task analysis. Hum. Factors **40**(2), 254–276 (1998). https://doi.org/10.1518/001872098779480442

14. Von Thaden, T.L., Wiegmann, D.A.: Improving incident reports using a schematic recall aid: the critical event reporting tool (CERT). In: Proceedings of the Human Factors and Ergonomics Society Annual Meeting, pp. 82–86. SAGE Publications (2001). https://doi.org/10.1177/154193120104500218

15. Thurman, R.A.: Instructional simulation from a cognitive psychology viewpoint. ETR&D. **41**, 75–89 (1993). https://doi.org/10.1007/BF02297513

16. Militello, L.G., Hutton, R.J.B.: Applied cognitive task analysis (ACTA): a practitioner's toolkit for understanding cognitive task demands. Ergonomics **41**(11), 1618–1641 (1998). https://doi.org/10.1080/001401398186108

17. Page, M.J., McKenzie, J.E., Bossuyt, P.M., Boutron, I., Hoffmann, T.C., Mulrow, C.D., et al.: The PRISMA 2020 statement: an updated guideline for reporting systematic reviews. Int. J. Surg. **88**, 105906 (2021). https://doi.org/10.1016/j.ijsu.2021.105906

18. Elliott, T., Welsh, M., Nettelbeck, T., Mills, V.: Investigating naturalistic decision making in a simulated microworld: what questions should we ask? Behav. Res. Methods **39**(4), 901–910 (2007). https://doi.org/10.3758/BF03192985

19. Malakis, S., Kontogiannis, T., Psaros, P.: Monitoring and evaluating failure-sensitive strategies in Air Traffic Control simulator training. In: Proceedings of the 7th International Conference on Pervasive Technologies Related to Assistive Environments. Association for Computing Machinery, New York, NY (2014). https://doi.org/10.1145/2674396.2674462

20. Mansikka, H., Virtanen, K., Uggeldahl, V., Harris, D.: Team situation awareness accuracy measurement technique for simulated air combat - curvilinear relationship between awareness and performance. Appl. Ergon. **96** (2021). https://doi.org/10.1016/j.apergo.2021.103473

21. Roose, K.M., Veinott, E.S., Mueller, S.T.: The tracer method: the dynamic duo combining cognitive task analysis and eye tracking. In: Proceedings of the 2018 Annual Symposium on Computer-Human Interaction in Play Companion Extended Abstracts, pp. 585–593. Association for Computing Machinery, New York, NY (2018). https://doi.org/10.1145/3270316.3271522

22. Roose, K.M., Veinott, E.S.: Understanding game roles and strategy using a mixed methods approach. In: ACM Symposium on Eye Tracking Research and Applications, pp. 1–5. ACM, Virtual Event Germany (2021). https://doi.org/10.1145/3448018.3458006

23. Rozzi, S., Amaldi, P., Wong, W., Field, B.: Operational potential for 3D displays in air traffic control. In: Proceedings of the 14th European Conference on Cognitive Ergonomics Invent! Explore! - ECCE 2007. pp. 179–184. ACM Press (2007). https://doi.org/10.1145/1362550.1362586

24. Salmon, P.M., Stanton, N.A., Walker, G.H., Jenkins, D., Ladva, D., Rafferty, L., et al.: Measuring situation awareness in complex systems: comparison of measures study. Int. J. Ind. Ergon. **39**(3), 490–500 (2009). https://doi.org/10.1016/j.ergon.2008.10.010

25. Stelmaszewska, H., Wong, B.L.W., Bhimani, N., Barn, B.: User behaviour: searching for scholarly material using electronic resource discovery systems. In: Electronic Workshops in

382   M. Gruner et al.

Computing, pp. 1 /–26. BCS Learning & Development (2010). https://doi.org/10.14236/ewic/hci2010.5

26. Walker, G.H., Stanton, N.A., Salmon, P.M., Jenkins, D.P., Rafferty, L., Ladva, D.: Same or different? Generalising from novices to experts in military command and control studies. Int. J. Ind. Ergon. **40**(5), 473–483 (2010). https://doi.org/10.1016/j.ergon.2010.04.003

27. Endsley, M.R.: Situation awareness global assessment technique (SAGAT). In: Proceedings of the IEEE 1988 National Aerospace and Electronics Conference, pp. 789–795. IEEE, Dayton, OH (1988). https://doi.org/10.1109/NAECON.1988.195097

28. Taylor, R.M.: Situational awareness rating technique (SART): the development of a tool for aircrew systems design. In: Salas, E. (ed.) Situational Awareness, pp. 111–128. Routledge, London (2017). https://doi.org/10.4324/9781315087924-8

29. Lipshitz, R., Klein, G., Orasanu, J., Salas, E.: Taking stock of naturalistic decision making. J. Behav. Decis. Mak. **14**, 331–352 (2001). https://doi.org/10.1002/bdm.381

30. Cooke, N.J.: Varieties of knowledge elicitation techniques. Int. J. Hum Comput Stud. **41**(6), 801–849 (1994). https://doi.org/10.1006/ijhc.1994.1083

Design Requirements for Working with Mobile Smart Devices—a Scoping Review

Germaine Haase(✉), Kristin Gilbert, and Ulrike Pietrzyk

Technische Universität Dresden, Arbeitsgruppe Wissen-Denken-Handeln, Dresden, Germany
{germaine.haase,kristin.gilbert,ulrike.pietrzyk}@tu-dresden.de

Abstract. With advancing digitalization, mobile smart devices are becoming more common, supporting numerous work activities in various sectors. When using these digital devices, companies must be aware of work requirements and risk factors. Considering these essential factors, appropriate measures for safe and age-appropriate work design can be implemented. However, more practical support is needed to analyze and design mobile smart devices. To support companies in risk assessment and preventive work design, the German Social Accident Insurance (DGUV) initiated the project "GBU SmarD – Gesunde Arbeit mit Smart Devices (Healthy Work with Smart Devices)." One aim of the project is to compile the current state of research via scoping review on cross-sector requirements and risk factors when using mobile smart devices in the work context. The scoping review (2014 to 2022) includes literature in German and English from the databases PSYNDEX, Web of Science, EBSCOhost, and an extensive hand search. Search criteria consisted of requirements and risk factors of mobile smart devices in general and specifically of "smartphones," "tablets," "smartwatches," and "data glasses." We assigned the work requirements and risk factors provided by the literature to components of the work system and their interactions: employees, work tasks, work organization, workplace, work environment, and work equipment. The classification of the requirements provides the structure for later guidelines to support companies in their mandatory risk assessment working with mobile smart devices. For an extension of the review results, practical experiences of experts are collected in focus groups by the GBU SmarD project and incorporated into the guidelines.

Keywords: risk factors · requirements · mobile smart devices

1 Background

Digitalization has become indispensable both in everyday life and in the workplace. Digital transformation and Work 4.0 have become keywords to characterize the rapid and unstoppable (further) development that is changing old workplace structures. With new interconnected digital technologies, the main goal is to build secure, fast, and flexible networks that allow data transfer and communication anywhere at any time. Mobile smart devices, such as smartphones, tablets, smartwatches, and data glasses are being used more frequently to support work processes in various sectors. Wireless, mobile, and networked electronic devices are designed to support employees in performing their work tasks.

According to the Federal Statistical Office [1], in 2022, employees in Germany were provided with mobile devices with Internet access in 64% of the companies surveyed. Likewise, 60% of full-time employees in Germany used a mobile device with internet access for work [2]. In a study by the Fraunhofer Institute for Industrial Engineering [3], 60% of companies from various sectors reported using mobile devices with touchscreens. However, mobile smart devices of different types are deployed more or less frequently in companies. Smartphones and tablet, for example, are already being used more often in various sectors. According to Deloitte Digital [4] in 2019, tablets and smartphones were used by 51% of German employees. In contrast, technologies such as augmented reality, for example, with data glasses, have been used more rarely. In a survey by the digital association Bitkom [5], 16% out of 604 companies (with 20 or more employees) in Germany stated that they use individual applications for augmented reality.

With the work-related use of mobile smart devices, companies expect not only an increase in productivity and flexibility but also physical and psychological relief for employees. However, there may also be risks associated with digital work equipment, for example, due to higher task complexity [6, 7], task-incompatible assistance systems [8, 9], or increased information density [10, 11, 12]. These risks can represent health-relevant stressors when working with mobile smart devices and shall be considered in the work design process.

Particularly given the proportion of older employees and employees with reduced performance (people who are no longer able to perform in the required manner), modern approaches are needed for a preventive, safe, and health-promoting design for working with mobile smart devices. Therefore, requirements and potential risk factors should be analyzed, especially in the context of the particular needs of impaired employees. The risk assessment should be carried out before introducing new digital work equipment, but it can also be implemented in parallel with its implementation in the company. However, practical guidelines for anticipatory work design are needed first. They form the basis for carrying out a risk assessment, which is required by European law (Framework Directive 89/391/EEC) and national law (e.g., in Germany: Law on the Implementation of Occupational Health and Safety Measures to Improve the Safety and Health of Employees at Work; Arbeitsschutzgesetz).

Protecting employees from potential health risks when working with digital devices by investing in risk assessment is not only a legal and moral obligation but can literally "pay off" for companies. Investments in risk assessment, including potential physical and psychological effects of working with mobile smart devices, can reduce mental and physical stress and cut costs of occupational accidents and work-related illnesses. Absenteeism and disruptions to operational processes can be minimized [13]. In addition, enhanced value can be achieved through increased employee motivation, satisfaction, and an improved corporate image.

The latest survey of the Third European Survey of Enterprises on New and Emerging Risks [14] indicated that about three-quarters of EU-27 companies conduct risk assessments regularly. The routinely conducted risk assessment thus provides a formalized framework for designing healthy, safe, and people-centered work also with regard to the work with smart devices. However, it is, in particular, small and very small enterprises that still face challenges in conducting a risk assessment. In particular, they need practicable guidelines and instructions to properly conduct risk assessments of work with mobile smart devices.

2 Objectives

The project "GBU SmarD – Gesunde Arbeit mit Smart Devices (Healthy Work with Smart Devices)," that is funded by the German Social Accident Insurance (DGUV) combines previous research findings with the experiences of practitioners, for example, producers, software developers, and users. The goal is to develop guidelines to help companies make work with mobile smart devices healthy and safe. This article presents the current state of research on requirements and possible risk factors associated with the work-related use of mobile smart devices. A suitable structure for the essential factors has to be developed to ensure that the guidelines are practical for companies.

3 Method

To compile current research activities on the topic of "working with mobile smart devices," a scoping review was conducted. We selected this method as it provides not only an overview of the current research landscape but also identifies research gaps and highlights issues that require further inquiry [15, 16]. Since scoping reviews are appropriate for examining broader and more descriptive topics, the method was used to summarize requirements for and risk factors in working with mobile smart devices.

We conducted a comprehensive literature search in the databases PSYNDEX, Web of Science, and EBSCOhost and supplemented it with an extensive hand search for German and English publications from 2014 until December 2022. As the topic is relevant to scientists and practitioners, we involved grey literature such as project reports and whitepapers in addition to scientific publications and standards.

The search criteria of the scoping review comprised four string components: on the one hand, "mobile smart devices" in general and "smartphones," "tablets," "smart-watches," and "data glasses" in particular, and on the other hand, "requirements" that are imposed on the use of the new work equipment, and "risks" or "risk factors" which can arise from working with mobile smart devices. The search components incorporated corresponding German and English synonyms. Moreover, we searched for publications in specific domains from the secondary (e.g., production, assembly) and tertiary economic sectors (e.g., services). In a further step, we have restricted the search to older employees and employees with reduced performance capacity to gain further insight into these significant groups of employees.

The scoping review included publications that dealt with mobile smart devices and processes of change in the context of digitization at work and their requirements for (human-centered) work design. Therefore, we excluded articles without work context and topics such as artificial intelligence and working from home. In addition, we excluded articles that focused on using mobile smart devices by clients (e.g., customers and patients). After filtering the results by title and abstract screening, we evaluated the remaining publications in a full-text screening. Figure 1 shows the selection process for this scoping review.

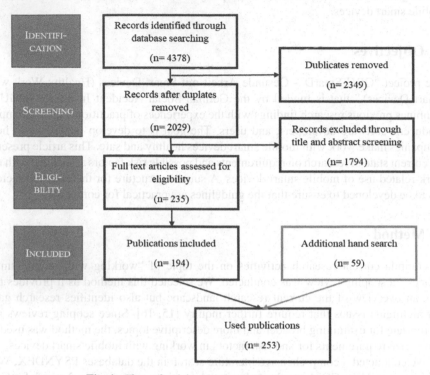

Fig. 1. Flow of article selection in the scoping review

4 Results

Searching the online databases resulted in 4378 articles. After excluding duplication and reviewing (title, abstract, and full-text), 194 remaining papers satisfied all the review's requirements. Together with the results of the hand search, we used 253 publications to filter the requirements for and risk factors in working with mobile smart devices. The extracted publications are primarily empirical and include predominantly experimental research and literature work.

Most articles discuss non-specific mobile smart devices. Most publications that examine specific devices concentrate on tablets [17, 18, 19] and especially on data glasses and the associated augmented reality technology [10, 11]. However, smartwatches have received little attention in the work context so far. Furthermore, most extracted publications concentrate on unspecified work activities. A large part of sector-specific publications mainly focuses on the secondary (especially production and assembly) and parts of the tertiary economic sector (especially logistics, maintenance, and service). Little research was conducted on parts of the tertiary economic sector, like healthcare and social work.

The results of the scoping review revealed that there are two perspectives when considering digital work devices: a "resource perspective," which focuses on requirements for the work-related use of these devices, and a "stressor perspective," which identifies psychological and physical risk factors associated with using mobile smart devices. We combined these two perspectives into design requirements and classified them into different categories. The categorization is based on several significant criteria for work design, such as the work system, the human-centered work design, and the basics of ergonomic work design (e.g., ISO 6385:2016: Ergonomic principles in the design of work systems). The purpose of classifying design requirements is to structure subsequent guidelines. To achieve this structure, the design requirements were assigned to components of a working system that can interact with each other: employees (1), work tasks (2), work organization (3), workplace and work environment (4), as well as work equipment (5). Components (1) to (4) refer to changes in the work system caused by the new work equipment. Component (5) includes the design of mobile smart devices and their interaction with other work equipment (e.g., controllability, task appropriateness, learnability). In terms of preventive work design, companies should ideally consider the design requirements of the components before purchasing mobile smart devices. However, the criteria are still essential during and after implementation.

Implementing new digital work equipment as part of a digital transformation process requires a digitization strategy. For a sustainable introduction of mobile smart devices (or other digital technologies), it is, for example, necessary not only to define the people in charge but also to consider and compare the actual and target conditions [20]. Therefore, the digitization strategy is essential in work organization (3). It addresses various prior considerations, such as the specific need for new digital work equipment and the potential contribution this equipment can provide to achieving the company's goals [21, 22, 23]. Once the needs are clarified, further design requirements should be considered. The most frequently mentioned design requirement for a successful establishment of mobile smart devices relates to the interaction of employees (1), their work tasks (2), and the work organization (3) concerning the new work equipment (5). In the following paragraph, we give examples of the interaction between the design requirements concerning these four components.

It is essential to ensure that the new work equipment and required software is suitable for the existing work tasks to enable a supportive effect in the work process [8, 21, 24]. The device type should be chosen so that its functionality matches the work activities. A smartphone, for example, is a good choice of digital equipment for communicating and displaying or transmitting small messages or signals. However, when the focus lies on text editing tasks, such as documentation or reading instructions for machines, a tablet with a larger screen might be more appropriate [17, 19, 25]. A combination of different mobile smart devices can also be helpful, for example, the integration of smartwatches and tablets. Smartwatches as wearables provide immediate sensory notifications through vibration, for example, about machine errors. However, information can only be displayed in a limited way due to the small screen of a smartwatch. If employees need further information, for example, on the current status or guidelines for error elimination, another information provider is required. Tablets facilitate a more detailed review of information due to their larger screen.

Regarding the human-centered design of work tasks, devices should offer a certain degree of freedom of action [8, 26, 27], decision-making [22, 28] and must not reduce the variety of tasks through their use [5, 23]. Mobile smart devices should therefore be selected and designed to support employees' work tasks. An appropriate selection and design can facilitate sustainable healthy, and productive work processes.

Furthermore, the selected work equipment should ensure that the tasks are not only executable and free of impairments but also promote learning [7, 8, 23]. With increasing digitalization and the growing complexity of processes, competency and qualification requirements, such as digital competencies, human control, and intervention skills, are rising [6, 29, 30]. Sufficient qualifications of the employees are indispensable for a fluent workflow and a sustainable digitalization process of the company [22]. It not only includes introducing the new digital work equipment but also continuously qualifying the employees during the implementation process of this equipment [5, 12, 31]. Moreover, allocating tasks between employees and work equipment should be designed meaningfully. The division of functions between employees and work equipment can, for example, protect against the loss of competence and overloading of employees due to a lack of system knowledge and a reduced repertoire of actions [26, 27, 29]. The apparent relief of employees from (possibly error-prone) routine tasks (activities repeated at short or long intervals) by new digital work equipment can lead to a lower task and system understanding. However, understanding the whole process is often also required for increasing non-routine situations such as monitoring or error diagnosis. If the knowledge and skills wither away because they are rarely needed, they cannot be recalled in non-routine situations [6, 27, 29].

Early and transparent communication about the implementation of mobile smart devices, as well as the prompt involvement of users and their expertise, has been shown essential for enhancing the acceptance of the new work equipment [24, 32, 33]. Employees who feel involved and have a voice in decision-making are more likely to be open to changes, such as using new mobile smart devices. The possibility of participating in the design process enables employees to implement their work-related needs. Participation also supports the perceived usefulness of mobile smart devices and may lead to an increased and correct use of the work equipment [20]. However, not only the digitization concept and process but also the use of personal data need to be communicated to employees in time. Working with mobile smart devices generates process-related and personal data, often allowing conclusions about employees' working methods and efficiency. The opportunity to monitor employees is one of their most common concerns and can lead to increased psychological stress. Therefore, transparent management of personal data is needed to reduce employees' concerns about personnel monitoring [11, 22, 34].

Either way, implementing new work equipment leads to changes in the work system, whether it is the allocation of work tasks, work organization, or the work environment. The change can be intentional, such as the desired performance improvement or the enhanced support of the employees. On the contrary, there is also a possibility of unintentional change, like increased work intensity, time pressure, or interruptions caused by the work equipment. In terms of a healthy work design, these possible unintentional changes and their causes need to be identified and eliminated [7, 35, 36].

Demographic change and the legal framework significantly altered the structure of the working population. The percentage of older employees has increased, and younger newcomers are comparatively rare. For example, labor force participation among 60 – 64-year-olds has increased more than in any other age group. It has risen from 44% (2011) to 61% (2021) in the last ten years [37]. Demographic change causes a more diverse labor force, which requires consideration of general human performance capacities (e.g., limits of working memory) and individual capacity limits (e.g., age- or health-related changes in strength or reaction speed) [11, 24]. The review highlighted the importance of mobile smart devices and their software being customizable for each user to compensate for general and individual performance limitations [8, 11, 24]. If the work equipment is customized, they can provide appropriate support for people with reduced performance capacities and thus integrate them more closely into the work process [6, 38].

The design of mobile smart devices includes the hardware and software, as well as the related handling of work equipment by the employees. The equipment should be selected according to the hardware's suitability for relevant environmental conditions, such as temperature, moisture, or lighting. The functionality of the devices should not be reduced, whether in hot or cold, humid or dusty, and light or dark environments [19, 32]. In terms of software design, there are several design requirements to consider, which can facilitate working with these devices [5, 25]. One crucial aspect is the presentation of information, which should be adapted to the users' needs. The slogan *"The right information at the right time"* summarizes the primary goal in one sentence. Experts, for example, need less information than novices. Therefore, adaptive information supplies help to avoid excessive workloads or interruptions due to information overload and enable good workflow [23, 30, 35].

If the hardware and software are well designed, the handling of the devices should also be unproblematic. Nevertheless, restrictive combinations of mobile smart devices with other parameters (e.g., hygiene requirements in medical facilities or personal protective equipment) shall be considered. For example, working with tablets, smartphones, or smartwatches can cause handling difficulties when wearing work gloves. Likewise, using data glasses with helmets can lead to visual field restrictions [5, 32]. These possible limitations can be quickly detected and considered in the selection and implementation process of new work equipment by involving the employees and their work tasks.

The workplace and work environment component (4) supplements the view to other essential design requirements. Proper digital infrastructure is one of the most vital requirements to enable mobile smart devices or digital transformation in general. However, reduced network coverage, for example, during maintenance work (especially in rural regions) or general network disruptions, might occur at any time. To ensure a fluid work process and reduce employee stress, possible disruption scenarios and how to deal with them should be considered in advance [18, 21, 22].

Digital work equipment, especially data glasses, is not common in everyday life and can be more demanding on employees' attention [5, 9, 24]. It can result in increased distraction, sensory overload, and mental fatigue [6, 9]. Therefore, dangerous workplace situations must be secured even more effectively when using mobile smart devices. For example, signals could be amplified or extended across multiple modalities, such as the visual, auditory, or haptic systems [39]. Furthermore, prohibition and restriction rules should be set for using the equipment, for example, the prohibition of attention-demanding mobile smart devices in certain danger zones.

In addition to the mentioned design requirements concerning the work-related use of mobile smart devices, the scoping review revealed some limitations of current research activities. Like some authors [19, 24], we noted that experimental studies were partly not carried out on actual employees but, for example, on students. The equipment was only used over short periods, which allows little conclusion about the requirements and risk factors during regular work conditions. Moreover, only selected parts of work tasks were considered and thus did not represent the range of activities of the employees. Additionally, we found no long-term studies and rarely publications that paid attention to the needs of older employees and employees with reduced performance capacity.

5 Conclusion

Establishing mobile smart devices in the workplace entails both opportunities and risks. Therefore, design requirements merged from factors of the "resource perspective," and the "stressor perspective" in the work-related use of mobile smart devices should be considered before implementing new digital work equipment. However, since there is a current lack of guidelines for practical support, the German Social Accident Insurance (DGUV) initiated the project "GBU SmarD – Gesunde Arbeit mit Smart Devices (Healthy Work with Smart Devices). The project combines the design requirements from literature with practical experiences to develop helpful guidelines for companies. This article provides an overview of the design requirements that should be considered in a preventive work design when implementing mobile smart devices. The design requirements were selected in a scoping review that examined different publication types from 2014 to December 2022. Considering these different types (e.g., company whitepapers or standards) gave us a deeper insight into the practice of using mobile smart devices.

We identified several design requirements, which can be assigned to different inter-related components: employees, work tasks, workplace and work environment, work organization, and work equipment. These design requirements mentioned in the article represent merely a selection in working with mobile smart devices. The components are not more or less significant; however, the compilation revealed various connections between employees and the other components. These include, for example, employees' early and ongoing involvement and participation in the digitalization process, the needs-based qualification, and a people-oriented division of tasks. Furthermore, the selection of digital work equipment should be based on employees' (individual) needs and the corresponding work tasks, as well as the handling of the devices. Unintended changes caused by the digital work equipment, such as increased work intensity or interruptions, must be avoided or controlled to protect employee health.

However, the scoping review not only provided information about the design requirements but also showed that publications focus more on data glasses and tablets and less on smartwatches. This distribution can be explained on the one hand by the fact that tablets are already frequently used in some work processes. On the other hand, interest in augmented reality technology remains very high and has led to several publications. The great attention might be enhanced because data glasses are rarely applied in professional and everyday life. Besides, smartwatches are used more frequently in everyday life, for example, to measure health parameters. Given their small display, they can only support employees in a few work tasks or in combination with other working equipment, such as tablets. If smartwatches are used in the work context, it is more likely to be used by customers than employees. The low concentration of publications in specific areas of work (health care, social work) may reflect their relative underutilization due to a lack of financial and other resources. Therefore, companies from different sectors with different work activities should be included in further research.

The review results also indicate that little attention has been paid to the particular needs of performance-altered and older employees. When the labor force is constantly aging, and there is a great need for young professionals, it is essential to give more consideration to this age group in further research. In addition, the needs of all employees with reduced performance capacity should be considered. Thus, it can enable a safe, healthy, and human-centered work design. Furthermore, future research has to focus more on the long-term effects of working with mobile smart devices. Additional requirements and risks may be related to working with mobile smart devices if they are used for an extended period or repeatedly. Experimental and field studies are equally important in providing the scientific basis for designing work with mobile smart devices. Field studies, however, can provide more activity-, environment- and employee-specific information.

Integrating mobile smart devices is a complex process in which many factors need to be considered. Practical guidelines should facilitate the identification of new requirements and possible risk factors and help companies eliminate or avoid them optimally. The review results offer a helpful starting point for further research in practice, for example, through focus groups with experts in the GBU SmarD project. Through the exchange of experiences of practitioners, research gaps, such as the lack of long-term effects or the lack of studies in specific sectors (healthcare and social work), can be covered more. The combination of review results and practical experiences makes it possible to develop practical guidelines for health-promoting and safety work design, for example, by a risk assessment. A successful risk assessment of working with mobile smart devices is a prerequisite for companies to implement appropriate measures to promote the safety and health of employees. In addition, preventive work design can contribute to the acceptance and perceived usefulness of mobile digital assistance systems for employees, which may positively affect the use rate and the extent of the perceived digital support in the work process.

References

1. Eurostat: Anteil der Unternehmen in Deutschland, die Beschäftigten tragbare Geräte für geschäftliche Zwecke zur Verfügung stellen, die mobilen Internetzugang über ein Mobilfunknetz ermöglichen, im Jahr 2019 (2020). https://de.statista.com/statistik/daten/studie/221785/umfrage/ausstattung-der-mitarbeiter-von-kmu-mit-mobilen-endgeraeten/. Accessed 11 Jan 2023

2. Eurostat: Erwerbsbeteiligung der Bevölkerung nach Geschlecht und Alter (2022). https://www.destatis.de/DE/Themen/Arbeit/Arbeitsmarkt/Erwerbstaetigkeit/Tabellen/ilo-quartal-geschlecht-alter.html. Accessed 10 Jan 2023
3. Klapper, J., Gelec, E., Pokorni, B., Hämmerle, M., Rothenberger, R.: Potenziale digitaler Assistenzsysteme (2019)
4. Deloitte Digital: Mobile Readiness for Work 2019. Workforce Germany (n.d.). https://www2.deloitte.com/content/dam/Deloitte/de/Documents/technology/enterprise-mobility-booklet-2019.pdf. Accessed 12 Jan 2023
5. Technische Regel für Betriebssicherheit (TRBS) 1151: Gefährdungen an der Schnittstelle Mensch - Arbeitsmittel - Ergonomische und menschliche Faktoren, Arbeitssystem (2015)
6. Kötter, W.: Mensch-Maschine-Systeme. In: Bamberg, E., Ducki, A., Janneck, M. (eds.) Digitale Arbeit gestalten: Herausforderungen der Digitalisierung für die Gestaltung gesunder Arbeit, pp. 59–70. Springer Fachmedien, Wiesbaden (2022)
7. Müller, N.: Digitalisierung und psychische Belastungen – Bilanz und Handlungsperspektiven für Gute Arbeit. In: Schröder, L., Eberhardt, B., Müller, N. (eds.) Gute Arbeit: Arbeitsschutz und Digitalisierung - Impulse für eine moderne Arbeitsgestaltung: Reader 2020, pp. 34–50. Bund-Verlag (2020)
8. Apt, W., Bovenschulte, M., Priesack, K., Weiß, C., Hartmann, E.A.: Einsatz von digitalen Assistenzsystemen im Betrieb. Forschungsbericht 502. Institut für Innovation und Technik, Berlin (2018)
9. Deutsche Gesetzliche Unfallversichung e.V (DGUV) (eds.): DGUV Regel 115-401. Branche Bürobetriebe, Berlin (2018)
10. Grauel, B.M., Terhoeven, J.N., Wischniewski, S., Kluge, A.: Erfassung akzeptanz-relevanter Merkmale von Datenbrillen mittels Repertory Grid Technik. Zeitschrift für Arbeitswissenschaft 68(4), 250–256 (2014)
11. Holz, A., Herold, R., Friemert, D., Hartmann, U., Harth, V., Terschüren, C.: Zentralblatt für Arbeitsmedizin, Arbeitsschutz und Ergonomie 71(1), 24–28 (2020). https://doi.org/10.1007/s40664-020-00394-7
12. Koczy, A., Stahn, C., Hartmann, V.: Mobile Hilfsmittel (Smart Devices) in der Produktion: Auswirkungen auf die Arbeit und Hinweise zur Einführung aus dem Projekt AWA. ifaa — Institut für angewandte Arbeitswissenschaft e. V, Düsseldorf (2020)
13. Eichhorn, D., Schuller, K.: Gefährdungsbeurteilung psychischer Belastung - Reine Pflichterfüllung oder Nutzen für die Betriebe? Sicher ist Sicher 68(10), 428–433 (2017)
14. Irastorza, X., et al.: Third European Survey of Enterprises on New and Emerging Risks 2019 (ESENER-3). GESIS Datenarchiv, Köln (2020)
15. Munn, Z., Peters, M.D.J., Stern, C., Tufanaru, C., McArthur, A., Aromataris, E.: Systematic review or scoping review? Guidance for authors when choosing between a systematic or scoping review approach. BMC Med. Res. Methodol. 18(1), 143–150 (2018)
16. Peters, M.D.J., Godfrey, C.M., Khalil, H., McInerney, P., Parker, D., Soares, C.B.: Guidance for conducting systematic scoping reviews. Int. J. Evid. Based Healthc. 13(3), 141–146 (2015)
17. Debue, N., Oufi, N., van de Leemput, C.: An investigation of using a tablet computer for searching on the web and the influence of cognitive load. Quant. Methods Psychol. 16(3), 226–239 (2020)
18. Lohmann, R., Schrage, T., Rußow, G.: Das Tablet als Standard in der Klinik – mobile digitale Patientenakten und mobiler Workflow. OP-J. 37(01), 10–22 (2021)
19. Tegtmeier, P.: Review zu physischer Beanspruchung bei der Nutzung von Smart Mobile Devices (2016)
20. Moker, A., Brosi, P., Welpe, I.M.: Digitalisierungsstrategie: Der Ausblick. In: Wiesche, M., Welpe, I.M., Remmers, H., Krcmar, H. (eds.) Systematische Entwicklung von Dienstleistungsinnovationen. IT, pp. 609–617. Springer, Wiesbaden (2021). https://doi.org/10.1007/978-3-658-31768-3_31

21. Cortado AG: Integration von Smartphones und Tablet in die Unternehmens-IT. https://www.ucm.de/wp-content/uploads/2015/05/Cortado_Whitepaper_Smartphones-und-Tablets-in-die-Unternehmens-IT.pdf. Accessed 12 Jan 2023

22. Heil, M., Schröder, D.: Digitalisierung im Handwerk. In: Bamberg, E., Ducki, A., Janneck, M. (eds.) Digitale Arbeit gestalten: Herausforderungen der Digitalisierung für die Gestaltung gesunder Arbeit, pp. 133–146. Springer Fachmedien, Wiesbaden (2022)

23. Melzer, M., Rösler, U., Schlicht, L.: Digitale Transformation personenbezogener Arbeit – am Beispiel der professionellen Pflege. In: Bamberg, E., Ducki, A., Janneck, M. (eds.) Digitale Arbeit gestalten: Herausforderungen der Digitalisierung für die Gestaltung gesunder Arbeit, pp. 147–166. Springer Fachmedien, Wiesbaden (2022)

24. Minow, A.: Arbeitsphysiologische Untersuchungen beim Einsatz digitaler Assistenzsysteme für variantenreiche Montageprozesse in der Arbeitswelt 4.0 (2021)

25. Deutsche Gesetzliche Unfallversichung e.V.(DGUV) (eds.): DGUV Information 211-036 Belastungen und Gefährdungen mobiler IKT-gestützter Arbeit im Außendienst moderner Servicetechnik Handlungshilfe für die betriebliche Praxis - Gestaltung der Arbeit, Berlin (2012)

26. Aringer-Walch, C., Besserer, S., Pokorni, B.: Nutzerbedürfnisse an ein digitales Assistenzsystem im Kontext der Industrie 4.0.: Eine explorative Studie im Bereich der Montage (2018)

27. Hacker, W.: Arbeitsgestaltung bei Digitalisierung. Zeitschrift für Arbeitswissenschaft **76**(1), 90–98 (2022)

28. Adolph, L., Rothe, I., Windel, A.: Arbeit in der digitalen Welt - Mensch im Mittelpunkt. Zeitschrift für Arbeitswissenschaft, **70**(2), 77–81 (2016)

29. Rothe, I., Wischniewski, S., Tegtmeier, P., Tisch, A.: Arbeiten in der digitalen Transformation – Chancen und Risiken für die menschengerechte Arbeitsgestaltung. Zeitschrift für Arbeitswissenschaft **73**(3), 246–251 (2019). https://doi.org/10.1007/s41449-019-00162-1

30. Arnold, D., Butschek, S., Steffes, S., Müller, D.: Digitalisierung am Arbeitsplatz: Bericht. Bundesministerium für Arbeit und Soziales; Institut für Arbeitsmarkt- und Berufsforschung der Bundesagentur für Arbeit (IAB); Zentrum für Europäische Wirtschaftsforschung (ZEW) GmbH; Universität Köln, Nürnberg (2016)

31. Kötter, W., Roth, S.: Entwicklung und Gestaltung von Digitaler Arbeit im Handlungsfeld Produktion. In: Bamberg, E., Ducki, A., Janneck, M. (eds.) Digitale Arbeit gestalten: Herausforderungen der Digitalisierung für die Gestaltung gesunder Arbeit, pp. 119–131. Springer Fachmedien, Wiesbaden (2022)

32. Mecke, R., et al.: Gesundes mobiles Arbeiten mit digitalen Assistenzsystemen im technischen Service (ArdiAS). In: Bauer, W., Mütze-Niewöhner, S., Stowasser, S., Zanker, C., Müller, N. (eds.) Arbeit in der digitalisierten Welt, pp. 35–52. Springer, Heidelberg (2021). https://doi.org/10.1007/978-3-662-62215-5_3

33. Müller-Thur, K., Angerer, P., Körner, U., Dragano, N.: Arbeit mit digitalen Technologien, psychosoziale Belastungen und potenzielle gesundheitliche Konsequenzen. Institut für Medizinische Soziologie, Düsseldorf (2018)

34. Nissen, H., Jent, S.: Technologien und Methoden und ihr Einsatz. In: Bamberg, E., Ducki, A., Janneck, M. (eds.) Digitale Arbeit gestalten: Herausforderungen der Digitalisierung für die Gestaltung gesunder Arbeit, pp. 251–266. Springer Fachmedien, Wiesbaden (2022)

35. Bamberg, E., Ducki, A., Janneck, M. (eds.): Digitale Arbeit gestalten. Herausforderungen der Digitalisierung für die Gestaltung gesunder Arbeit. Springer Fachmedien, Wiesbaden (2021)

36. Meyer, S.-C., Meiners, F., Hünefeld, L.: Arbeitsbezogene IKT-Nutzung und Arbeitsintensität: Die Rolle mobiler Geräte. baua: Bericht Kompakt. 1st ed. Bundesanstalt für Arbeitsschutz und Arbeitsmedizin, Dortmund (2022)

37. Statistisches Bundesamt (Destatis): Erwerbstätigkeit älterer Menschen (2023). https://www. destatis.de/DE/Themen/Querschnitt/Demografischer-Wandel/Aeltere-Menschen/erwerbsta etigkeit.html
38. Bovenschulte, M.: Kognitive Assistenzsysteme. Büro für Technikfolgen-Abschätzung beim Deutschen Bundestag (TAB), Berlin (2020)
39. European Committee for Standardization (CEN): ISO 6385:2016-Ergonomic Principles in the Design of Work Systems, 3rd edn (2016)

Implementation of Lean Six Sigma to Improve the Quality and Productivity in Textile Sector: A Case Study

Genett Jiménez-Delgado[1]([⊠]) [iD], Iván Quintero-Ariza[1], Jeremy Romero-Gómez[1], Carlos Montero-Bula[1], Edgar Rojas-Castro[1], Gilberto Santos[2] [iD], José Carlos Sá[3] [iD], Luz Londoño-Lara[4] [iD], Hugo Hernández-Palma[5] [iD], and Leonardo Campis-Freyle[6]

[1] Department of Industrial Engineering, Institución Universitaria de Barranquilla IUB, Barranquilla, Colombia
{gjimenez,iquintero,jeremydromero,cmontero, earojas}@unibarranquilla.edu.co
[2] Design School, Polytechnic Institute Cavado Ave, Barcelos, Portugal
gsantos@ipca.pt
[3] Engineering School, Polytechnic of Porto, Porto, Portugal
cvs@isep.ipp.pt
[4] Civil and Environmental Department, Universidad de la Costa CUC, Barranquilla, Colombia
llondono1@cuc.edu.co
[5] Faculty of Engineering, Industrial Engineering Program, Corporación Universitaria Iberoamericana IBERO, Bogotá, Colombia
hugo.hernandez@ibero.edu.co
[6] Department of Research and Innovation, Soltraf Ingeniería S.A.S, Barranquilla, Colombia

Abstract. The textile industry represents one of the most important economic links worldwide due to its essential generation of direct and indirect jobs, its contribution to the economy, and its ability to reinvent itself and adapt to market trends, government regulations, and the demands of interest groups. However, the textile industry is called upon to continuously improve its capacity to develop efficient, sustainable, and profitable processes in the current complex and volatile environments such as the Covid-19 pandemic, which has generated new challenges for this industry derived from confinement, restrictions trade and the slowdown of the supply chain worldwide and the subsequent reactivation of the economy. In this sense, e-commerce, the design of sustainable products and business models, the optimization of processes, and the improvement of quality have become resilience strategies to face the present and future demands of the market. Lean Six Sigma (LSS) has been proposed to address the challenge of improving productivity and quality since it allows managers to identify the factors that contribute to prolonged lead time throughout the production process. The suggested methodology follows the DMAIC cycle that began with the definition of the Project charter and the mapping of the process through a SIPOC diagram with which the manufacturing process was analyzed, and the critical variables of the process were identified. Then, the measurement system's performance was studied by analyzing essential quality and production indicators, the initial Value Stream Mapping (VSM), and capacity analysis to determine how well the process meets the requirements. Next,

V. G. Duffy (Ed.): HCII 2023, LNCS 14028, pp. 395–412, 2023.
https://doi.org/10.1007/978-3-031-35741-1_30

the potential causes that affect the performance of the process in terms of process times and quality were identified. As the next step, improvement strategies focused on reducing lead time and improving quality were designed and implemented. Subsequently, a comparative analysis was carried out with the before and after to verify the improvements' effectiveness. Finally, a control plan was established to maintain the upgrades obtained after implementing Lean Six Sigma. The proposed framework was validated through a case study of a company in the textile sector with an export profile. The results revealed that the company's average CT went from 62.5 min to 53.1 min, while the long-term sigma level increased from -3.36 to 0.41 and a decrease in the percentage of non-conforming products of 19.43% to 12.38%.

Keywords: Lean Six Sigma (LSS) · Textile sector · Cycle Time (CT) · Quality Control · Non-conforming products

1 Introduction

The textile industry is a constantly growing market worldwide, with essential competitors not only from developed economies such as the United States, China, the European Union, and India but also from developing economies such as Brazil, Argentina, Peru, Colombia, Costa Rica, Dominican Republic, among others. This sector is dedicated to producing textile inputs and garments for domestic consumption and export, with figures showing their importance in the economy. In this regard, growth estimates in global fashion e-commerce, according to Islam et al. [1], were from $549.55 billion in 2020 to $668.1 billion in 2021. This growth was mainly due to companies' reactivation and economic recovery after the Covid-19 pandemic, which restricted operations and interrupted the supply chain but active new digital marketing channels [2]. Recent data from the Textile Global Market Report 2023 [3] show growth figures for the global textile market of $573.22 billion in 2022 and a growth projection of $610.91 billion in 2023, with a compound annual growth rate (CAGR) of 6.6% and growth estimates to 755.38 billion in 2027. Another positive aspect of the sector is the rapid industrialization and evolution of technology, both in developed and developing countries, contributing to improving products and the development of high-efficiency factories [4].

However, the textile sector faces significant current and future challenges, such as the war between Russia and Ukraine, which affects the supply chain and increases the prices of raw materials with an impact on global markets, as well as Technological advances in materials, machinery, and processes for the optimization of resources, the environmental sustainability, innovation and the increasing participation of customers and other interested parties are part of the complex and dynamic environment of the textile industry. In addition to the above, textile companies, especially in low- and middle-income countries, experience problems such as smuggling and the entry of new competitors, as well as the demands for the reduction of contamination resulting from their activities and the adoption of innovative practices. Other challenges not yet widely developed at the research level involve improving operational efficiency, mainly in the process times and the quality problems that generate high production costs, and customer dissatisfaction, negatively impacting companies' growth, competitiveness, and added value. These problems have motivated researchers to develop specific studies and adopt continuous improvement methodologies to provide solutions to the challenges faced by the textile industry [5].

In this sense, the use of Lean Six-sigma (LSS) is proposed as an alternative to close the gaps of the operational inefficiencies since it is a methodological framework that helps in the decision-making process at the managerial level by identifying the factors that do not add value to the process or muda that affect the prolonged times in the production process. In addition, it allows for establishing the most appropriate hard and soft strategies to generate value and increase quality and productivity. The Lean Six Sigma methodology has reported a growing trend in recent years with a wide application in different sectors such as automotive, food, and health. In addition, other objectives have been addressed with implementing LSS, such as reducing lead time and increasing productivity. Still, few studies were found that focused on the reduction of two key objectives: Cycle time (CT) and percentage of non-conforming products. Likewise, more studies are required to demonstrate the practical applications, strategies adopted, and improvements obtained in small textile companies in low- and middle-income countries, which illustrate the need to use the LSS methodology to promote continuous improvement, knowledge management, and the development of synergies between companies in the sector and other interested parties.

This paper proposes using Lean Six Sigma methodology to reduce lead time and increase the main quality performance index of the company, such as long-term sigma level and process productivity, and provides a real case study for laying the groundwork for implementation in other companies. The remainder of this paper is organized as follows. Section 2 presents the literature review of Lean Six Sigma applications in manufacture and textile sector. Section 3 detail the proposed methodology. Section 4 describe the results and discussion of the Lean Six Sigma application in a small textile company. Finally, conclusions and future works are presented in Sect. 5.

2 Literature Review

Lean Six Sigma is a methodology whose objective is to improve processes to increase profitability and productivity. It integrates Lean Manufacturing (LM) and Six Sigma methodologies to reduce losses, minimize process variability that originates quality deviations, and generate value for the stakeholders. The Lean Manufacturing philosophy, also known as Lean Production, is a work organization system that focuses on improving the production system. For this, it is based on eliminating those activities that do not add value to the process or the client. These are called waste or waste and are those tasks that involve overproduction, long waiting times, or damage to the products. Six Sigma is a management program focused on improvement and cost reduction, aiming to optimize a company's production.

For a better understanding of the evidence base related to this topic, a more recent literature review (2009–2023) was developed by scanning the search code "Lean Six Sigma in textile sector" AND "lean six sigma" in the Scopus database. After a detailed screening, authors obtained the following references published in indexed journals were identified, mainly in Medicine, Health Sciences, Computer Science, Engineering, and Multidisciplinary (refer to Fig. 1).

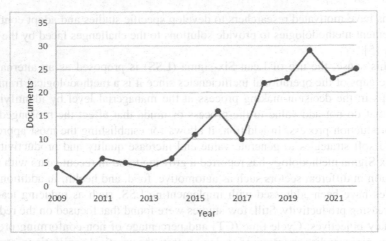

Fig. 1. Documents by year – LSS studies focused on manufacture and textile sector (source: Scopus)

Various applications of integrating both methodologies can be found in the literature to optimize industrial or service processes. In the study developed by [6], the application of LSS in companies in the Moroccan textile sector is shown, finding that only 11 companies have been concerned with improving their processes, highlighting the need to replicate this methodology in a more significant number of companies in the sector. [7] Their study outlines how LSS is a successful strategy to reduce defects along the production line of companies in the textile sector. [8] present a case study in which they integrate LSS with the application of the ISO:9001 standard in a company in the textile sector. An example of a practical application of lean Manufacturing in the textile sector in India is presented by [9]. In the literature review by [10], improvements by applying LSS in various companies in the industrial and service sectors are identified. The typical result, whether for companies from one industry or another, was eliminating unnecessary processes and activities and optimizing Production, quality, and effectiveness levels. In the same literature review, [11] present their study focused on applying LSS in multiple industries, including textiles. Other studies related to the successful implementation of LSS and the optimization of productivity in the textile sector, such as those presented by [12–17].

An example of the increase in quality and productivity of the value chain through Lean Manufacturing of a company in the fishing sector is shown by [18]. Implementing LSS in the educational sector is highly relevant, as seen in the work developed by [19, 20]. But not only the academic or textile sectors (the object of this study) are positively impacted by the integration of lean Manufacturing and Six Sigma optimization methodologies. [21–24] expose the implementation of LSS in various areas and companies belonging to the health sector. The LSS provides healthcare managers with an evidence-based methodological framework for effective decision-making. Indeed, substantial growth in LSS-based studies is evidenced in the scientific literature. LSS has also been implemented in small and medium-sized companies, as explained by [25].

Likewise, LSS has been applied in the aeronautical sector [26] and Manufacturing [27, 28], among others.

Considering the reported literature, the evidence from research to improve cycle times and the percentage of non-conforming products in the textile sector is still limited. In this regard, more LSS applications are developed for designing and improving textile processes adapted to the dynamics and complexities of the fashion market characterized by increased demand, rapid changes in tastes and trends, cost optimization, and high-quality standards. In this sense, the main contribution of this work is the application of LSS in a real scenario of the textile industry with a practical approach focused on the reduction of waste and activities that do not generate added value as well as the reduction of variability and defects in processes, which increases the ability of companies to respond to volatile, uncertain, complex and ambiguous environments (VUCA) as well as the generation of value in business processes and models.

In resume, LM focuses on the factors affecting the organizational system efficiency in terms of process flows, times, quality, and costs. In the meantime, Six Sigma helps to foster continuous process improvement focused on reducing the variability that generates errors or defects through comprehending the root causes of variations and proposing improvement strategies. As [29] mentions in his study, LSS has significantly contributed to increased business excellence.

3 Methodology

To reduce the lead time and increase the quality level in the textile sector, the following five-step methodology is proposed (see Fig. 2).

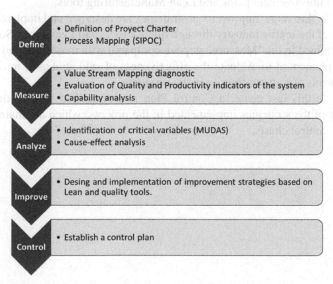

Fig. 2. Proposed Lean Six-Sigma methodology for reducing lead time and increase the quality level in the textile sector

To reduce the cycle time in the garment manufacturing process and increase the level of quality in a company in the textile sector, it is necessary to identify and eliminate activities that do not add value to the production process, as well as optimize process activities that are generating operational inefficiencies or waste, called MUDA in the Lean philosophy and that cause deviations from the quality specifications of the products [18]. In this sense, the methodological framework used for this study is based on the integration of the DMAIC cycle of the Six Sigma methodology (Define, Measure, Analyze, Improve, and Control) with the steps of the Lean Manufacturing methodology (Process Characterization, Identification of MUDA, Improvement Proposals). As a result, the adopted method consists of the following phases [30, 31]:

Define: This phase begins with the definition of the Project Charter, which includes the improvement objectives, the scope, and the execution schedule of the project. This document also allows visualizing of the general operation of the process as well as the exogenous/endogenous variables through the use of the SIPOC diagram.

Measure: In this stage, the objective is to diagnose the current operation of the process in terms of quality and execution times. In this sense, the current behavior of the cycle time (CT) was first estimated using the Value Stream Mapping tool and its comparison against the process indicators. Subsequently, the capacity analysis was carried out to evaluate the actual compliance of the process against the quality specifications.

Analyze: In this phase, the data collected from the textile manufacturing process is analyzed to identify and analyze the leading causes that generate waste or MUDA in the process and process deviations concerning the desired quality level. This phase is critical in the methodology since it seeks to reduce the existing differences between the current behavior of the process in terms of quality and productivity versus the established standards, using tools such as cause and effect analysis, Pareto diagram, groups of experts, 5WH improvement plans and Lean Manufacturing tools.

Improve: In this stage, improvement strategies are designed and implemented in the real scenario of the textile industry through quality tools and Lean tools. Subsequently, the results obtained in the "Measure" step are compared with those obtained through the strategies implemented to evaluate the effectiveness of said strategies in reducing the CT and the levels of non-conformity in the products.

Control: In this last phase, a Control Plan is proposed to support the sustained improvement of the strategies implemented in the process, which are maintained over time through control charts.

4   Results

4.1   Define Phase

This paper presents the application of Lean Six Sigma methodology in a small company in the textile sector dedicated to manufacturing and marketing sportswear for children, youth, and adults. This company is part of the network of small businesses in a low and middle-income country. Currently, the company presents deficiencies in planning its processes and in the standardization of activities, retards on process time, on-time delivery of its orders, quality control process, and non-compliant products. This has increased the costs associated with non-quality, significantly impacting their sales. First, a Lean Six Sigma team of seven experts was established to guide and validate the implementation of the methodology. The team was led by a black belt with experience of more than ten years in the performance of LSS projects. For the project's development, the sports sweater was taken as a product to be analyzed. As a product of the initial diagnosis, an average CT of 62.5 min was estimated, which shows that the goal set by the company was not met (55 min maximum). Another reported finding was non-compliance with the delivery time indicator, whose goal is 90% and was estimated at 67%. On the other hand, non-compliances were identified in the percentage indicator of returned garments (whose goal is a maximum of 5% and the current value is 6.84%) and in the sales data, which revealed a decrease in the percentage of growth −2.25% in sports sweater sales in a two-month analysis period. The above results show that the company requires substantial changes to improve productivity and quality in the process, which significantly impacts the company's operational and financial indicators.

Then, with the results of the initial diagnosis, a Project Charter was defined considering the following profits for the stakeholders: i) compliance in production and delivery times, ii) decrease in the rates of non-conforming products, iii) reduction in costs operations due to poor quality, iv) increase in product sales and four performance indicators (sigma level of the process, defects per million opportunities, lead time and cost per item returned). In addition, the project's objectives were also presented to the sponsor and the company's steering committee for approval and formalization before the start. Next, a SIPOC diagram was produced to detail the main stages of the sportswear manufacturing process and the interrelationships with other internal and external stakeholders (Fig. 3). Through the SIPOC, the steps that do not add value throughout the process and that affect the process and delivery times to the customer, as well as the quality of the products, were initially identified. This is consistent with the findings of Ortíz-Barrios et al. [32], in which reducing process times impacts customer satisfaction, avoids possible penalties for late orders, and increases revenue by improving system performance.

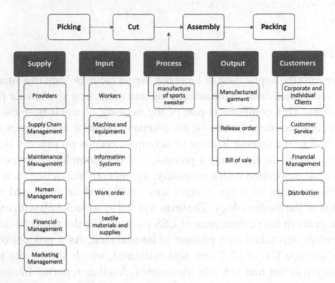

Fig. 3. SIPOC diagram for the manufacture of sports sweater in the textile industry.

4.2 Measure Phase

For the measurement phase, data related to cycle times and non-conforming garments were collected to assess the performance and compliance of the system concerning company standards. Concerning to evaluation of production times, first, the most recent cycle times of the textile process (n = 198 data) were collected. After the data cleaning process, the six-sigma team implemented a normality test where an Anderson-Darling test provided sufficient evidence to accept the normality hypothesis of CT data on the selected (AD = 0.215; p-value = 0.822). Subsequently, Value Stream Mapping (VSM) was used to represent the current flow of the process, from the purchase order, the supply of raw materials, picking, cut, assembly, and packing operations to dispatch of finished garments, considering cycle times, number of shifts, number of operators, and information flow (refer to Fig. 4). The results of the VSM allowed estimating a CT = 62.65 min and identifying bottlenecks in the cutting and ironing sub-process, which are mainly associated with inefficiencies in work methods, human factors, machine and equipment failures, and quality defects, therefore that it is necessary to analyze the causes that generate inefficiencies in the process.

Then, it was verified how far the manufacture of the sports sweater process is concerning the objective CT, and the Six-Sigma team applied a normal-based capability analysis (Fig. 5). The exploratory analysis revealed a process with a CPU of −1.12 which shows that the process cannot meet the maximum accepted CT (55 min). Given the negative nature of CPU, significant interventions are needed to improve the production process. This is also evidenced by the short-term sigma level (−3.36), which, in the meantime, expresses that 999,612 in every 1,000,000 products manufactured in this textile company will have an estimated manufacturing time greater than 55 min.

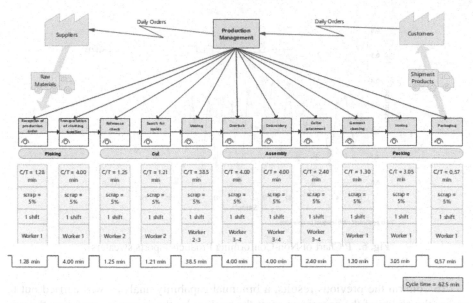

Fig. 4. Value Stream Mapping for the manufacture of sports sweaters in the textile industry

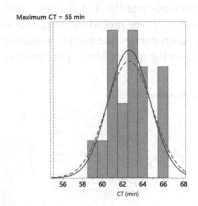

Fig. 5. Capability graph for the CT in the manufacture of sports sweaters process.

On the other hand, regarding the quality evaluation, the data corresponding to the number of non-conforming garments per batch manufactured during 30 days were collected. Subsequently, a control graph by attributes "p" was elaborated to evaluate if the process is in control and identify possible patterns of deviation. The results show that the process is in control; however (see Fig. 6), 53.3% of the data are above the average. Likewise, the process average is above the established goal by the company. The preceding outcomes reveal that the process must be intervened to reduce the proportion of non-conforming garments and the costs of poor quality for garments returned due to quality problems.

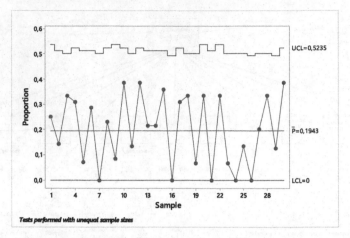

Fig. 6. P Chart of Non-Conforming Products (sports sweaters).

To confirm the previous results, a binomial capability analysis was carried out to assess the ability of the process to meet the goal set by the company regarding the percentage of non-conforming products. The results revealed a defective rate of 19.43 with a sigma level of 0.86, which means that 194,313 in every 1,000,000 manufactured products will be defects (refer to Fig. 7). The preceding, compared to the company's defective percentage goal (d = 5%), corroborates the need to implement strategies focused not only on cycle times but also on the quality level of the process.

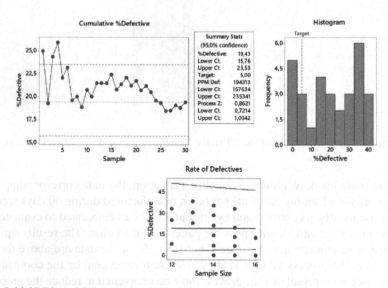

Fig. 7. Initial P Binomial Process Capability Report of No Conforming Products (sports sweaters).

4.3 Analyze Phase

Considering the results obtained from the capacity analysis for the cycle time and the non-conforming garments, the need to design comprehensive intervention strategies to address the productivity and quality problems identified in the company is evident. Therefore, it is necessary to investigate the causes behind the cycle time to improve the performance of the process and get closer to the organization's goal. In this sense, a cause-and-effect analysis was carried out to identify the causes that generate waste or MUDA and are associated with the CT problem (Fig. 8). The possible causes were determined with the support of the Lean Six-Sigma team to provide management and collaborators with a solid framework of causes that supported decision-making that impacts the productivity of the textile industry. Analysis of Variance (ANOVA) tests (alpha level = 5%) were implemented to verify the causes raised in the actual scenario. For example, the results supported the cut time as statistically significant for the increase in CT (p-value = 0.000). There is also evidence of a considerable influence of inadequate work methods and the deficiencies in operator scheduling schemes on the CT of the manufacturing process (p-value = 0.000).

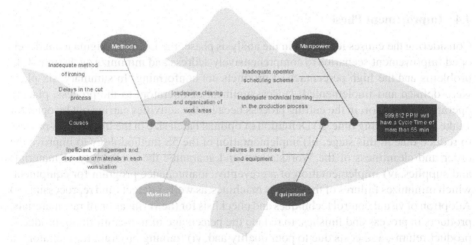

Fig. 8. Cause-and-effect analysis for the CT problem in the manufacture of sports sweaters process

On the other hand, a second cause and effect analysis was carried out to identify the causes that are associated with the problem of the high percentage of non-conforming products NC (Fig. 9). The results of the Analysis of Variance (ANOVA) test (alpha level = 5%) revealed as significant causes in the increase in the percentage of NC to failures in machines and equipment, the deficiencies in the quality verification methods and the inadequate adjustment and enlistment of equipment before operations (p-value = 0.000).

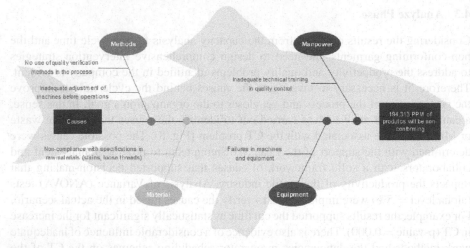

Fig. 9. Cause-and-effect analysis for the Non-Conforming Products in the manufacture of sports sweaters process

4.4 Improvement Phase

Considering the causes identified in the analysis phase, the Lean Six Sigma team developed improvement scenarios to comprehensively address and minimize cycle time (CT) problems and the high percentage of products not conforming. In summary, six plans were defined and implemented: i) Reassignment of operators to the process, placing operator 1 as support in the cutting process because the activities carried out by operator 1 take less processing time, ii) Definition of optimal batch size in the ironing sub-process to reduce time in this stage, iii) implementation of the 5S methodology to improve the order and cleanliness of the Workstations and guarantee the availability of materials and supplies, iv) implementation of a preventive maintenance program for equipment, which minimizes failures of the process machines, as well as defects and reprocessing, v) Adoption of visual control techniques and checklists for the verification of raw materials, products in process and finishes, to reduce the percentage of non-conforming products, product returns, and costs due to poor quality and, vi) training program for operators in textile processes and quality control.

After a 2-month deployment, the new results for CT and the percentage of NC products were analyzed using Minitab 17® software to assess whether the proposed strategies effectively addressed the issues above. For cycle time, the results, described in Fig. 10 and improved Value Stream Mapping (see Fig. 11), revealed a CT = 53.07 min and a CPU value now 0.41, denoting a significant improvement in the CT of the production process, 108,602 of 1,000,000 garments (Reduction: 891,010 PPM) will have an estimated manufacturing time greater than 55 min, which shows that the strategies adopted have been effective. Still, new interventions are required to reduce the TC until the target value is reached. These findings are validated by the long-term sigma level (1.23), which provided sufficient support to continue developing new DMAIC cycles that reduce manufacturing process times to respond to scenarios of growth in demand and company expansion.

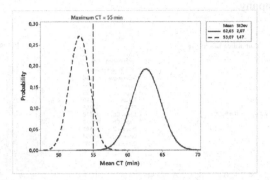

Fig. 10. The comparison between the initial CT performance and the new process status after improvement

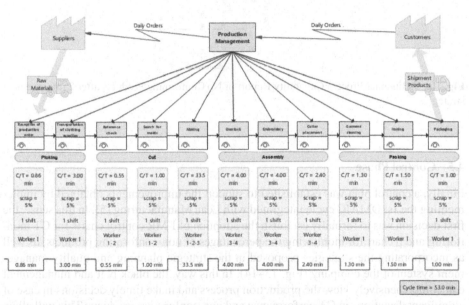

Fig. 11. Improved Value Stream Mapping for the manufacture of sports sweaters in the textile industry

Regarding the percentage of non-conforming products, after two months of implementing the improvement strategies, a new binomial capacity analysis was carried out to evaluate the effectiveness of the adopted methods. The results revealed a defective percentage of 12.38 (Reduction: 7.05% NC products) with a sigma level of 1.15 (see Fig. 12), which means that 123,786 in every 1,000,000 products manufactured will be non-compliant (Reduction: 70,527 PPM). However, it is necessary to continue with the Lean Six-Sigma cycles, to bring the defective percentage of products to the goal established by the company ($d = 5\%$), so new strategies are required to continue with the improvement of this indicator to guarantee customer satisfaction and the financial stability of the company.

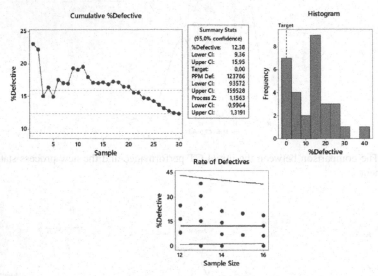

Fig. 12. P Binomial Process Capability Report of No Conforming Products after 2 improvement strategies.

4.5   Control Phase

Finally, a control plan was established to support the improvements obtained by implementing the 1st DMAIC cycle integrated with Lean Manufacturing [5]. In this sense, the first decision was to formally establish the adoption of I-MR control charts for CT monitoring and p chart for monitoring the percentages of non-conforming products, as well as incorporating the strategies proposed in the strategic planning and quality management system of the company (Fig. 13–14). In this way, the black belt and management can comprehensively view the production process and make timely decisions in case of significant deviations in CT performance and non-conforming products. This will allow the company to continuously improve the process through systematic iterations of the integrated Lean Six Sigma methodology.

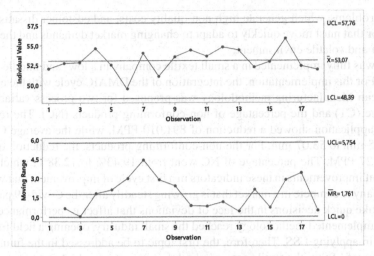

Fig. 13. I-MR p control chart for monitoring the CT after project finalization

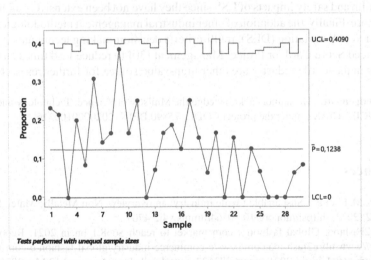

Tests performed with unequal sample sizes

Fig. 14. P control chart for monitoring the percentage of NC products after project finalization

5   Conclusions and Future Work

This study proposes the implementation of the Lean Manufacturing and Six Sigma methodologies under the Lean Six Sigma (LSS) integrated approach to the value chain of the textile industry. Despite being a widely implemented methodology and several successful cases in sectors such as the automotive, food, and manufacturing sectors, LSS is still under development in the textile sector, especially in small companies, as evidenced in the literature review. This is one of the most significant contributions of this study, by presenting the application of LSS concepts, methodology, and tools to improve two essential problems in this industry: operational inefficiencies in process times and quality problems, which generate high non-quality costs, and customer dissatisfaction, in a sector that must move quickly to adapt to changing market demands and the current uncertain and volatile environment.

LSS was fully implemented in a small textile company in a low- and middle-income country. For this implementation, the integration of the DMAIC cycle with the elements of the Lean Manufacturing methodology was proposed for two process variables, the cycle time (CT) and the percentage of non-conforming products (NC). The results of the LSS application showed a reduction of 891,010 PPM, while the average CT went from 62.5 min to 53.07 min. For the non-conforming products, the reduction obtained was 70,527 PPM. The percentage of NC went from 19.43% to 12.38%, which shows significant improvements in these indicators in a first cycle of improvement that will help the company to compete in a market that is growing steadily after the Covid-19 pandemic and to make quick decisions in the face of deviations that affect its performance.

The implemented methodology reached the small industry, opening a field for future research in applying LSS. Therefore, the first topic to be addressed in the future is the application of LSS in the textile sector in both low-income and high-income countries. Other future research would be oriented toward the financial, environmental, and occupational health and safety impacts of LSS since they have not been extensively addressed in the literature. Finally, the adoption of other industrial management methodologies such as Discrete Event Simulation (DES), multi-criteria decision-making techniques (MCDM), the Balanced Score Card, or Project Management [30] to reduce lead times and quality problems in the textile industry are other high-value source for further research.

Acknowledgement. The authors acknowledge the Ministry of Science, Technology and Innovation (MINCIENCIAS), under the project CODE: 75890 BPIN: 2020000100316.

References

1. Islam, M.T., et al.: Sustainable textile industry: an overview. Non-Metallic Mater. Sci. **4**(2), 15–32 (2022). https://doi.org/10.30564/nmms.v4i2.4707
2. Fibre2Fashion. Global fashion e-com market to reach $668.1 bn in 2021: Report. 2021. https://www.fibre2fash-ion.com/news/e-commerce-industry/global-fashion-e-com-market-to-reach-668-1-bn-in-2021-report-273633-newsdetails.htm. Accessed 13 Mar 2023
3. The Business Research Company. Textile Global Market Report 2023 (2023). https://www.the businessresearchcompany.com/report/textile-global-market-report. Accessed 13 Mar 2023
4. Mordor Inteligence. INDUSTRIA TEXTIL: CRECIMIENTO, TENDENCIAS, IMPACTO DE COVID-19 Y PRONÓSTICOS (2023-2028) (2023). Accessed 13 Mar 2023. https://www.mordorintelligence.com/es/industry-reports/global-textile-industry---growth-trends-and-forecast-2019---2024#:~:text=La.industriatextilesun.prendasdevestirenbruto
5. Sá, J.C., et al.: Assessing the impact of lean tools on production and safety by a multicriteria decision-making model and statistical analysis: a case study in textile sector. In: Stephanidis, C., et al. (eds.) HCII 2021. LNCS, vol. 13097, pp. 616–638. Springer, Cham (2021). https://doi.org/10.1007/978-3-030-90966-6_42
6. Elboq, R., Fri, M., Hlyal, M., El Alami, J.: Modeling lean and six sigma integration using deep learning: applied to a clothing company. Autex Res. J.**23**, 1–10, (2021). https://doi.org/10.2478/aut-2021-0043

7. Abbes, N., Sejri, N., Xu, J., Cheikhrouhou, M.: New lean six sigma readiness assessment model using fuzzy logic: case study within clothing industry. Alex. Eng. J. **61**(11), 9079–9094 (2022). https://doi.org/10.1016/j.aej.2022.02.047
8. Karthi, S., Devadasan, S.R., Selvaraju, K., Sivaram, N.M., Sreenivasa, C.G.: Implementation of lean six sigma through ISO 9001:2008 based QMS: a case study in a textile mill. J. Text. Inst. **104**(10), 1089–1100 (2013). https://doi.org/10.1080/00405000.2013.774945
9. Prasad, M.M., Dhiyaneswari, J.M., Jamaan, J., Mythreyan, S., Sutharsan, S. A framework for lean manufacturing implementation in Indian textile industry. Mater Today Proc. (2020). https://doi.org/10.1016/j.matpr.2020.02.979
10. Rosa, A.C.M., Broday, E.E.: Comparative analysis between the industrial and service sectors: a literature review of the improvements obtained through the application of lean six sigma. Int. J. Qual. Res. **12**(1), 227–252 (2018). https://doi.org/10.18421/IJQR12.01-13
11. Kurnia, H., Purba, H.H.: A systematic literature review of lean six sigma in various industries. J. Eng. Manag. Indust. Syst. **9**(2), 19–30 (2021). https://doi.org/10.21776/ub.jemis.2021.009.02.3
12. Nedra, A., Jun, X., Nèjib, S., Jiajia, D.: Effect of ISO (9001) certification and article type produced on lean six sigma application successes: a case study within textile companies. Fibres Text. Eastern Europe **30**(2), 17–22 (2022). https://doi.org/10.2478/ftee-2022-0003
13. Sukwadi, R., Felicia, Y., Muafi, U.: TOC, lean, and six sigma: An integrated model to increase the productivity of the textile industry. J. Mech. Eng. Res. Dev.**44**(1), 327–336 (2021)
14. Ortega, C.G., Parra, D.B.: Método de mejora para incrementar la productividad en la industria maquiladora del vestido en base a la herramienta PHVA , DMAIC , Lean y Six sigma Improvement method to increase productivity in the garment maquiladora industry based on the PHVA, DMAIC. LATAM Revista Latinoamericana De Ciencias Sociales Y Humanidades **44**, 2181–2202 (2023)
15. Mughal, U.K., Khan, M.A., Kumar, P., Kumar, S.: Identification and analysis of stitching defects at the stitching unit: a case study. In: Proceedings of the International Conference on Industrial Engineering and Operations Management, pp. 373–384 (2021)
16. Uluskan, M., Joines, J., Godfrey, A.: Comprehensive insight into supplier quality and the impact of quality strategies of suppliers on outsourcing decisions. Supp. Chain Manag. Int. J. **21**, 92–102 (2016). https://doi.org/10.1108/SCM-04-2015-0140
17. Abad-Morán, J., Montero-Vera, C., Villafuerte-Calderón, A., Barcia-Villacreses, K.: Parametrización e implementación de módulos de un Sistema ERP en una compañía textil utilizando DMADV. In: Proceedings of the LACCEI International Multi-Conference for Engineering, Education and Technology, vol. 2021-July, pp. 1–9 (2021). https://doi.org/10.18687/LACCEI2021.1.1.286
18. Jimenez, G., et al.: Improvement of productivity and quality in the value chain through lean manufacturing - a case study. Procedia Manuf. **41**, 882–889 (2019). https://doi.org/10.1016/j.promfg.2019.10.011
19. Antony, J., Krishan, N., Cullen, D., Kumar, M.: Lean Six Sigma for higher education institutions (HEIs): Challenges, barriers, success factors, tools/techniques. Int. J. Product. Perform. Manag. **61**(8), 940–948 (2012). https://doi.org/10.1108/17410401211277165
20. Isa, M., Usmen, M.: Improving university facilities services using Lean Six Sigma: a case study. J. Facil. Manag. **13**, 70–84 (2015). https://doi.org/10.1108/JFM-09-2013-0048
21. Vest, J.R., Gamm, L.D.: A critical review of the research literature on six sigma, lean and StuderGroup's hardwiring excellence in the United States: The need to demonstrate and communicate the effectiveness of transformation strategies in healthcare. Implement. Sci.**4**(1) (2009). https://doi.org/10.1186/1748-5908-4-35
22. Bhat, S., Gijo, E.V., Antony, J., Cross, J.: Strategies for successful deployment and sustainment of lean six sigma in healthcare sector in India: a multi-level perspective. TQM J. **35**(2), 414–445 (2023). https://doi.org/10.1108/TQM-10-2021-0302

23. Ahmed, S., Manaf, N.H.A., Islam, R.: Effects of lean six sigma application in healthcare services: a literature review. Rev. Environ. Health **28**(4), 189–194 (2013). https://doi.org/10.1515/reveh-2013-0015

24. Singh, M., Rathi, R., Jaiswal, A., Manishbhai, S.D., Sen Gupta, S., Dewangan, A.: Empirical analysis of Lean Six Sigma implementation barriers in healthcare sector using fuzzy DEMATEL approach: an Indian perspective. TQM J. (2022). https://doi.org/10.1108/TQM-05-2022-0152

25. Stankalla, R., Koval, O., Chromjakova, F.: A review of critical success factors for the successful implementation of Lean Six Sigma and Six Sigma in manufacturing small and medium sized enterprises. Qual. Eng. **30**(3), 453–468 (2018). https://doi.org/10.1080/08982112.2018.1448933

26. Elboq, R., Hlyal, M., El Alami, J.: Lean manufacturing and six sigma critical success factors: a case study of the Moroccan aeronautic industry. Int. J. Suppl. Chain Manag. **9**(4), 24–35 (2020)

27. Ahmad, M.F., Zainudin, M.H.H., Hamid, N.A., Ahmad, A.N.A., Rahman, N.A.A., Nawi, M.N.M.: Critical success factors of lean six sigma and its relation on operational performance of SMEs manufacturing companies: a survey result. Int. J. Suppl. Chain Manag. **8**(1), 64–69 (2019)

28. Orji, I.J., U-Dominic, C.M.: Organizational change towards Lean Six Sigma implementation in the manufacturing supply chain: an integrated approach. Bus. Process Manag. J.**28**(5–6), 1301–1342 (2022). https://doi.org/10.1108/BPMJ-04-2022-0169

29. Corbett, L.M.: Lean six sigma: the contribution to business excellence. Int. J. Lean Six Sigma **2**(2), 118–131 (2011). https://doi.org/10.1108/20401461111135019

30. Ortiz-Barrios, M., Coba-Blanco, D., Jiménez-Delgado, G., Salomon, V.A.P., López-Meza, P.: Implementation of lean six sigma to lessen waiting times in public emergency care networks: a case study. In: Stephanidis, C., et al. (eds.) HCII 2021. LNCS, vol. 13097, pp. 83–93. Springer, Cham (2021). https://doi.org/10.1007/978-3-030-90966-6_7

31. Azevedo, J., et al.: Improvement of production line in the automotive industry through lean philosophy. Procedia Manuf. **41**, 1023–1030 (2019). https://doi.org/10.1016/j.promfg.2019.10.029

32. Ortíz-Barrios, M., Neira-Rodado, D., Jiménez-Delgado, G., Hernández-Palma, H.: Using FAHP-VIKOR for operation selection in the flexible job-shop scheduling problem: a case study in textile industry. In: Tan, Y., Shi, Y., Tang, Q. (eds.) ICSI 2018. LNCS, vol. 10942, pp. 189–201. Springer, Cham (2018). https://doi.org/10.1007/978-3-319-93818-9_18

Simulation-Based Training in the Manufacturing Industry: A Suggested Quick Assessment

Tiantian Li(✉) and Kevin J. Kaufman-Ortiz

Purdue University, West Lafayette, IN 47906, USA
{li1596,kaufmano}@purdue.edu

Abstract. Simulation has been widely used as a training tool in multiple industries. Due to the immersive and guided real-life experiences, learners can gain technical and non-technical skills in simulation-based training. However, despite the benefits of simulation-based training, research has shown that knowledge transfer may not be a guarantee. One possible explanation is how learning outcomes are assessed in current training programs using simulations. Therefore, in this report, we conducted a bibliometric analysis to understand the current research landscape related to simulation-based training programs and the learning assessments used in programs both in and outside the manufacturing industry. Based on our findings, more research is needed in simulation-based training in manufacturing and the learning assessment related to these training programs. Future research should focus on expanding the data collection to multiple databases and taking a more qualitative look into the current literature by conducting a systematized literature review.

Keywords: bibliometric analysis · simulation-based training · manufacturing · learning assessment

1 Introduction and Background

1.1 History of Simulation-Based Training

In the 1940s, conversations about engineering psychology and human factors engineering started rising. As part of this conversation, Melton & Briggs [1] emphasized the importance of engineering psychology considerations for training aviation and space shuttle pilots. They studied several psychological stresses, such as physiological, psychological, and task-induced stress. They used these dimensions to clarify the importance of simulations to perform tasks that could induce these stresses in space travel. The theory of skilled performance relates to complex task simulators as important to train people in complex skills. Human factor's role in space travel and exploration was solidified during this time, and the authors clarified that we did not need further specialized fields in psychology.

The authors connect education to human factors engineering in their argument, stating that long-time retention of skills had been neglected in research on human learning. To appropriately design controls and systems, they consider that discrete procedural responses are more prone to being forgotten than long-lasting tasks [2]. The importance of engineering psychology was exacerbated for dangerous and complex tasks such as space travel, reiterating the need for this field and consideration of human factors.

1.2 Types of Simulation-Based Training

Simulation-based training uses simulations to create immersive real-life experiences for learners while offering guidance in these virtual environments. It has a long history of helping in professional development. It has been widely used to aid learners in obtaining both technical and non-technical competencies, such as decision-making and communication skills [3]. Simulation has been widely used as a training tool in fields such as medicine and aviation [3, 4].

We have identified three types of simulation that are relevant to ergonomics and simulation-based training: full-scale mockup models, digital-human modeling, and process/discrete-event simulation. Full-scale mockups are commonly found in the medical field but can also be used to find problems in ergonomic analyses [5]. These mockups can be real-life simulations with objects and rooms designed for training people, but virtual reality has also enabled a more cost-effective way to produce full-scale mockups. Digital-human modeling (DHM) has become more accessible in recent years and is a good way to study ergonomic environments needing high precision. It is a useful tool to train employees and students on ergonomics assessments [6] because of the interactive component of DHM [7]. Lastly, discrete-event simulations are more commonly applied in manufacturing and service settings. They enable an analysis of systems with many variables, are interactive, and help visualize entire processes [8].

Discrete-event simulation benefits training because it lets employees see full-scale processes and modify variables to understand what happens when a part of the process fails or gets delayed. Suppose we incorporate this simulation into training when onboarding new employees; it may help them understand how their task is connected to the larger system. This may promote motivation and connectedness when being trained to execute complex tasks in a manufacturing process, a claim that requires further research. Improving the quality of training programs can impact things like risk management, efficiency, etc. However, research has shown that employees generally experience frustrations about the kinds and amount of training they receive [9]. Training methods such as simulations and games are often used to solve the learner's frustration and make training more engaging and interactive [10].

Benefits of Simulation-Based Training. According to Bell, Kanar, and Kozlowski [11], the benefits simulation-based training programs offer can be summarized into four categories. Firstly, by adopting simulations, information can be presented to learners in multiple formats with increasing richness compared to text and still images [12]. This richness of information is more learner-friendly, provides more scaffolding in learners' sense-making process, and helps to create more realistic learning experiences for learners [13, 14]. Moreover, simulation-based learning offers immersion and a sense of realism, whereas other, more conventional types of learning fail to do so. This sense of immersion has been proven to be especially beneficial in young learners and in cases where emotional arousal and other psychological responses should be incorporated as part of the training experience [15, 16]. The third benefit of simulation-based training is interactivity. Interactivity is the collaborative potential that captures the interaction between different learners, the learner with the learning material, and the learning media [17]. The importance of different kinds of interactivity has long been established in different educational theories and concepts, such as the zone of proximal development by Vygotsky [18] and the Community of Inquiry theory [19]. Lastly, depending on the kind of simulation tools used, simulation-based training allows real-time communication between learners and within teams, creating a more holistic learning experience and developing learners' non-technical skills simultaneously [11].

Areas that Still Need to be Addressed in the Realm of Simulation-Based Training. Despite the benefits of simulation-based training, existing literature also pointed out several areas of improvement that need to be addressed. The fundamental issue regarding simulation-based training lies in the knowledge transfer process of learners. Keys and Wolfe [20] found that good performances in simulation or games do not always translate to actual learning outcomes. This claim can be found in research articles from multiple fields. For example, Baker, Ussher, and Rimes [21] found that despite the real-life, immersive, and guided experience simulations can offer to students; they cannot replicate the stress individuals experience in a clinical setting. This is a major shortcoming of simulation-based training since stress is a vital factor to consider in ergonomics due to its effects on human behaviors, including team interaction, decision-making, and task performance. A group of researchers even went so far as to claim that simulation-based training is no better than problem-based learning, which uses an interactive method and writing prompts of medical cases to help knowledge transfer in the field of anesthesiology in terms of students' performance [22]. Similar studies comparing simulation and video training interventions showed similar results [23].

One possible explanation can be found within the learning assessments embedded in simulation-based training programs [24]. The key to designing a good simulation-based training program, regardless of its target learners (undergraduates or professional learners receiving on-the-job training), is to adopt educational theories in designing and implementing the training program and the associated learning assessments [24]. A literature review expands on this by focusing specifically on the performance assessment of simulation-based training and investigating the theories and methodologies that guide educators in evaluating learning outcomes. After examining the current simulation-based training, the authors compiled a list of best practices, including focusing on assessment processes and outcomes, adopting a multi-level evaluation system, and providing descriptive and diagnostic information about how performances are evaluated, etc. [25].

Most existing literature focuses on medical education and formal training programs such as higher education institutions. Training for professionals, such as on-the-job training, is less discussed but equally important, especially when the problems identified exist theoretically and are not bound by the context in which simulation-based training is used. Therefore, in this report, we conduct a bibliometric analysis of simulation-based training programs in on-the-job training programs in the manufacturing industry.

2 Overview of Report Contents

2.1 Problem Statement

Employees leave companies for a variety of different reasons. In manufacturing alone, the annual separation rate (employees leaving) in the U.S. was 39.9% in 2021 [26], and 32% of these employees quit during the first 90 days of their jobs. Many times, people leave so early because of company culture [27], and the first exposure to this culture is in the onboarding process. An onboarding process containing scheduled trainings helps give a new employee a sense of the company's culture [28]. If companies incorporate manufacturing simulations in their training, it may help give people a sense of a desired company culture.

There is little literature that incorporates manufacturing floor simulations in training programs and little literature that ties it to applied ergonomics. Consequently, there is no literature on learning assessments of training programs incorporating discrete-event simulation into employee onboarding processes.

2.2 Subtopics Covered Within the Report

As our goal is to investigate the current research landscape regarding simulation-based training programs, we plan to approach this goal from two perspectives. Firstly, we need to understand what simulation-based training programs have been created and used in manufacturing. Secondly, to address the knowledge transfer part of our research purpose, we need to explore how learning outcomes are assessed in simulation-based training programs. In the rest of the report, we record the procedures we adopted to conduct the bibliometric analysis, our results, discussions, and future work needed to ensure better performance and learning experiences.

3 Procedure

In this report, we follow the suggested procedures for bibliometric analysis recommended by [29]. As shown in Fig. 1 below, the bibliometric analysis includes steps from identifying the aims and scope of analysis, developing a search string and search method, collecting data, and summarizing results. In the previous sections of this report, we documented our research aim and the scope of this study. To reiterate, we focus on investigating the current literature on simulation-based training programs for on-the-job training in manufacturing and associated learning assessments. We documented our reasons for this particular aim and scope in the "Introduction and Background" section. In Fig. 1, Step 4 listed two parallel paths of conducting bibliometric analysis; we chose performance analysis to examine existing literature.

Step 1	Define the aims and scope of the bibliometric analysis

•i.e. Definition of goals and scope should justify the use of bibliometric analysis.
•**Example:** We aim for high yield in the search rather than a narrow topic.

Step 2	Choose the techniques for bibliometric analysis

•i.e. Choose appropriate bibliometric analysis techniques according to study aims.

Step 3	Collect the data for bibliometric analysis

•i.e Design the search terms based on scope and aims; search database; export
  bibliometric data; clean the data, eliminate duplicates.

Step 4	Run the bibliometric analysis and report the findings

•i.e. Include a performance analysis and science mapping.

Step 5	Organize and write

•Organize and decide subtopics following analysis.
•Write the discussion of the findings and implications.

Fig. 1. Procedures of conducting a bibliometric analysis summarized by Donthu et al. [29] (adapted from Donthu et al. 2021).

We chose Scopus as our database since it is the largest abstract and citation database with articles from multiple international publications and various disciplines such as medicine, engineering, natural sciences, social sciences, etc. [30]. We answered our research question from two perspectives: 1) existing simulation-based training in manufacturing and 2) the current assessment accompanying simulation-based training programs. We developed different search strings and conducted a bibliometric analysis of related articles separately. Refer to Table 1 for our search terms.

Table 1. Search strings used in Scopus to collect data for bibliometric analysis on simulation-based training in on-the-job training programs in manufacturing

Research Purpose	Search Strings	Limiters
Existing simulation-based training in manufacturing	Simulation AND Manufacturing AND Training AND Education	AND NOT (health AND surgery AND officer) AND (LIMIT-TO (DOCTYPE, "ar"))
Current assessments accompanying simulation-based training program	Simulation-based AND Training AND Learning AND Assessment AND Education	(LIMIT-TO (DOCTYPE, "ar"))

Due to a large amount of literature on medical education, military training, and aviation, we decided to eliminate research articles in these fields using limiters. However, in the second research purpose, which is to investigate the learning assessments for simulation-based training programs, we did not include limiters since most learning assessments can be applied to various professional fields. In addition to the search strings, we limited our data to journal papers only as journal papers go through a more rigorous peer-review process. As for results, we used Scopus' built-in result analysis function to acquire tables and graphs and categorize the research articles differently (Fig. 2).

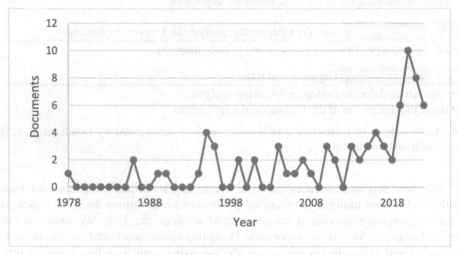

Fig. 2. Number of journal articles related to simulation-based training programs in manufacturing excluding medical and military fields published annually from 1978 to 2022.

4 Results and Discussion

4.1 Existing Simulation-Based Training in Manufacturing

The search string: "Simulation AND Manufacturing AND Training AND Education AND NOT (health AND surgery AND officer)" yielded 269 articles. As a quality consideration, we limited the search to peer-reviewed journal articles, and the total number of papers was reduced to 77. Scopus enables the user to search the number of times an author is cited using this search string (Fig. 3).

Subject area ↓	Documents
Engineering	40
Computer Science	23
Social Sciences	16
Medicine	9
Business, Management and Accounting	6
Dentistry	6
Materials Science	6
Chemical Engineering	5
Mathematics	5
Physics and Astronomy	5

Fig. 3. Number of journal articles on simulation-based training programs in manufacturing excluding medical and military fields, from 1978 to 2022, aggregated by subject area. Areas with less or equal to 3 publications are eliminated from the graph.

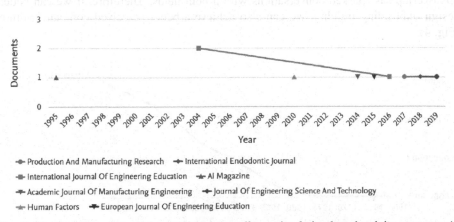

Fig. 4. Number of journal articles published annually on simulation-based training programs in manufacturing excluding medical and military fields, categorized by publication source. Journals unrelated to engineering education with one publication were eliminated from the graph.

From the figures listed above, simulation-based training programs in manufacturing are less commonly explored outside of medical and military applications. Publications in this field started to join the larger research community in 1978 and gained momentum in the 1980s. Company culture is a topic of conversation that began to pick up speed in the

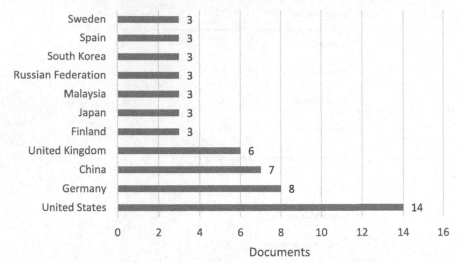

Fig. 5. Number of journal articles published on simulation-based training programs in manufacturing excluding medical and military fields, from 1978 to 2022, aggregated by the countries and territories. Regions with less than two journal publications are eliminated from the graph.

late 1970s. Although not causal, the time that onboarding training and company culture perception happens for new hires coincidentally overlaps. It should be no surprise that this overlap has sparked conversations within both fields. Therefore, if we can better design onboarding training, we can also achieve a better-perceived company culture (Fig. 4).

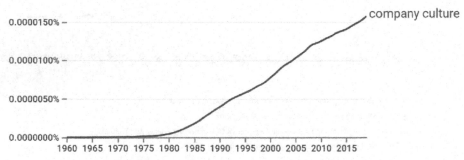

Fig. 6. Number of times "company culture" is mentioned in the literature according to Google nGram

Since medicine and the military were taken out of the search string, we can see that engineers are the leaders in simulation applications. The journal with the most publications (3) is the International Journal of Engineering Education. There is a need to explore this area further in research spaces, even though simulation-based training programs in manufacturing are a more industry-driven field (Fig. 5).

Lastly, among the articles presented in Scopus, they are distributed globally with more concentration in the U.S. and Germany, leaders in digital human modeling. These two countries are some of the only ones with anthropometric data on sample sizes large enough to represent their entire populations, making them leaders in the human factors field. If we can encourage other countries to publish finding commonly found in industry, we can further use simulation for manufacturing onboarding training (Fig. 6).

4.2 Training Example Using FlexSim

Among the many simulation tools available on the market, we focused on using FlexSim to demonstrate how training program can be structured. As we analyze simulation-based training programs, we also incorporate our personal experiences as learners in a class project to use FlexSim to model real manufacturing and service processes. FlexSim is a versatile software that can simulate scenarios in a variety of industries. The training program we participated consists of several lecture demonstrations accompanied by supporting learning materials (in the format of YouTube tutorials videos and reading materials). As shown in Fig. 7 and 8, our learning process of FlexSim can be broken down into several stages: understanding and experimenting with the software, change settings of an existing model for a UPS service counter, and creating a process line from scratch. As learners, we were able to learn about different ways of usage of FlexSim in the industry.

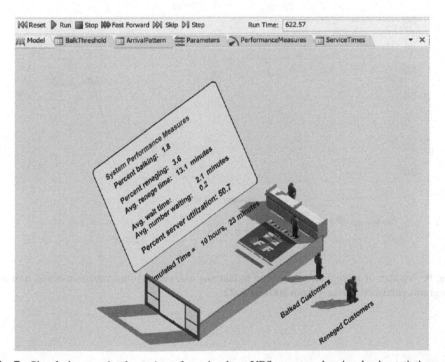

Fig. 7. Simulation results for a day of service in a UPS counter showing basic statistics and customer flows.

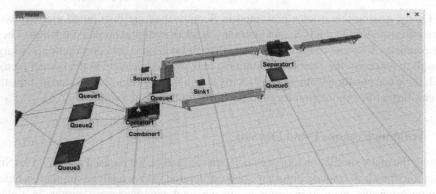

Fig. 8. Screenshot of FlexSim simulation for a process categorizing different colored block.

4.3 Current Assessments for Simulation-Based Training

In total, the search string "Simulation-based AND Training AND Learning AND Assessment AND Education AND (LIMIT-TO (DOCTYPE, "ar"))" produced 503 articles. Publication years for these articles range from 2001 to 2022. Refer to Figs. 9, 10, 11 and 12 for performance analysis of the journal articles on learning assessments of simulation-based training programs.

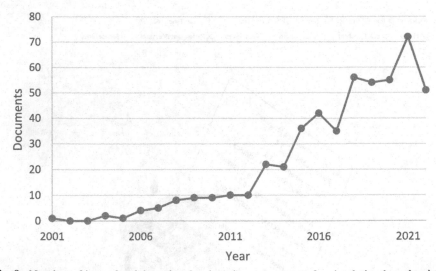

Fig. 9. Number of journal articles related to learning assessments for simulation-based training programs published annually from 2001 to 2022.

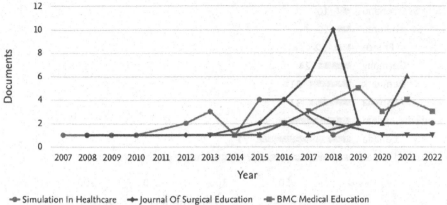

Fig. 10. Number of journal articles published annually on learning assessments for simulation-based training, categorized by publication source. Journals with fewer than ten publications in total were eliminated from the graph.

Subject area ↓	Documents ↓
Medicine	356
Social Sciences	186
Nursing	67
Mathematics	50
Biochemistry, Genetics and Molecular Biology	14
Health Professions	14
Pharmacology, Toxicology and Pharmaceutics	10
Multidisciplinary	8
Computer Science	7

Fig. 11. Number of journal articles on learning assessments of simulation-based training from 2001 to 2022, aggregated by subject area. Areas with less or equal to 5 publications are eliminated from the graph.

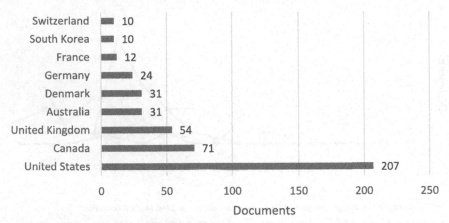

Fig. 12. Number of journal articles published on learning assessments of simulation-based training from 2001 to 2022, aggregated by the countries and territories. Regions with less than ten journal publications are eliminated from the graph.

From the figures listed above, learning assessment of simulation-based training is a relatively new topic. Publications in this field started to join the larger research community in 2001 and gained momentum after 2010. Because simulation has been a large focus of research ever since the 1960s, this delayed development indicates that more emphasis and awareness should be placed on how learning is assessed in this type of learning. Moreover, the drop in publication numbers since 2021 is also an interesting phenomenon, and continuous attention needs to be paid to monitor changes in the future.

Regarding publication outlets and subject areas, medicine continues to be the leading field where discussion on learning assessments in simulation-based training occurs. Four out of five journals are based on health-related professions. Four of the nine subject areas listed in Fig. 11 are related to the health industry. Together, these health- and medicine-related fields produce 89% of the total number of journal papers. There is a larger community in health-related industry and perhaps a lack of awareness in other fields, such as manufacturing, where simulation and simulation-based training is equally important. Calls for action are needed in the manufacturing field to increase research on how to better support and evaluate learning outcomes.

Lastly, among the articles presented in Scopus, countries in the West appear to be leaders in the research effort. The only Asian country that appeared in Fig. 12 in South Korea. This finding may be due to how academia and journal publication systems are structured across different countries/regions. Regardless of the reason for this disparity, a concerted global conversation on related research topics would be greatly beneficial to share knowledge and advancing this field.

4.4 Assessment/Learning Objective Example of FlexSim

Based on our findings in the bibliometric analysis and past literature in educational research, we will provide a brief example of how the associated learning assessments can be developed in a simulation-based training program using FlexSim.

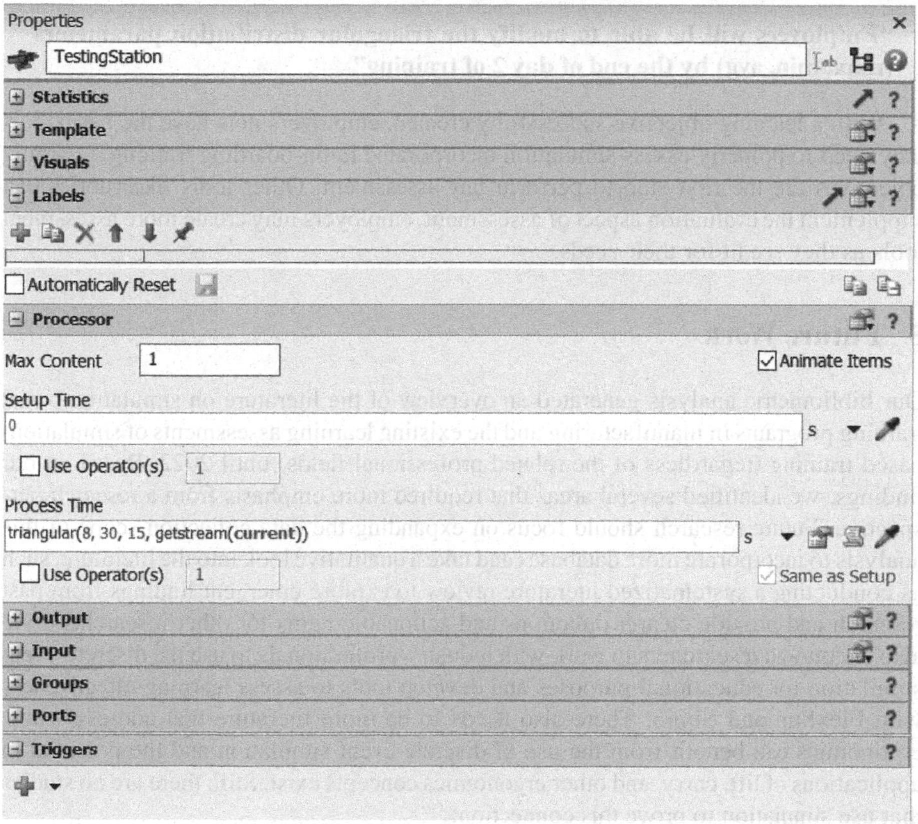

Fig. 13. Example sidebar of one machine within the simulation of a process for a manufacturing line

This given simulation will allow workers to observe and alter the machine times so that new employees can better understand how their jobs can affect the rest of the system. The idea behind this is so that they can understand the system as a whole, their role within the system and where they help if they become cross-trained to avoid delays. Employees do not have to know much about statistics to use a triangular distribution. This distribution uses a minimum, maximum and average to create a distribution that can model how their job works. Figure 13 shows the areas where employees can play around with such as setup time, process time and number of operators for a given process.

The assessment component of using FlexSim requires that trainers develop learning objectives given a full-scale model. Trainers in manufacturing usually lack any sort of education training. Therefore, there are tools that can help trainers develop learning objectives that are in tune with Bloom's Taxonomy [31]. The easygenerator application is the perfect tool for people that have never created learning objectives before and can be found online [32]. A learning objective created for the example in Fig. 13 can be:

"Employees will be able to modify the triangular distribution parameters (max, min, avg) by the end of day 2 of training"

With a learning objective successfully created, employers now have the basic tools they need to properly assess simulation incorporated in on-boarding training. Learning objectives are the first step to perform fair assessment. Other tools like rubrics can supplement the evaluation aspect of assessment, employers may create more assessment tools as they see fit for their needs.

5 Future Work

Our bibliometric analysis generated an overview of the literature on simulation-based training programs in manufacturing and the existing learning assessments of simulation-based training (regardless of the related professional fields) until 2022. Based on our findings, we identified several areas that required more emphasis from a research perspective. Future research should focus on expanding the data collection scope of this analysis to incorporate more databases and take a qualitative look into the literature, such as conducting a systematized literature review to explore emergent findings from past research and provide clearer directions and actionable items for other researchers. We also encourage researchers to work with industry-professionals to use the discrete-event simulation for educational purposes and develop tools to assess learning effectiveness with FlexSim and Simio. There also needs to be more literature that addresses how ergonomics can benefit from the use of discrete-event simulation and the potential in applications of lift, carry, and other ergonomics concepts exist. Still, there are no studies that use simulation to prove this connection.

References

1. Melton, A.W., Briggs, G.E.: Engineering psychology. Annu. Rev. Psychol. 11(1), 71–98 (1960). https://doi.org/10.1146/annurev.ps.11.020160.000443
2. Mengelkoch, R.F., Adams, J.A., Gainer, C.A.: The forgetting of instrument flying skills. Hum. Factors 13(5), 397–405 (1971). https://doi.org/10.1177/001872087101300502
3. Moorthy, K., Vincent, C., Darzi, A.: Simulation based training. BMJ 330(7490), 493–494 (2005). https://doi.org/10.1136/bmj.330.7490.493
4. Lateef, F.: Simulation-based learning: just like the real thing. J. Emerg. Trauma Shock 3(4), 348 (2010). https://doi.org/10.4103/0974-2700.70743
5. Andersen, S.N., Broberg, O.: Participatory ergonomics simulation of hospital work systems: the influence of simulation media on simulation outcome. Appl. Ergon. 51, 331–342 (2015). https://doi.org/10.1016/j.apergo.2015.06.003

6. Anton, N., Duffy, V.G.: Utilizing digital human modeling to optimize the ergonomic environment of heavy earthmoving equipment cabins. In: Duffy, V.G. (eds.) Digital Human Modeling and Applications in Health, Safety, Ergonomics and Risk Management. Anthropometry, Human Behavior, and Communication. HCII 2022. LNCS, vol. 13319, pp. 16–31. Springer, Cham (2022). https://doi.org/10.1007/978-3-031-05890-5_2

7. Chang, Y.H., Miller, C.: Using computer simulation to teach undergraduate engineering and technology students ergonomics. In: 2006 Annual Conference & Exposition Proceedings, Chicago, Illinois, p. 11.1379.1–11.1379.9, June 2006. https://doi.org/10.18260/1-2--1395

8. FlexSim. "Introduction to simulations," Introduction to Simulations. https://docs.flexsim.com/en/21.1/BestPractices/IntroToSimulations/IntroToSimulations.html#example. Accessed 30 Oct 2022

9. Peddle, M.T.: Frustration at the factory: employer perceptions of workforce deficiencies and training needs. JRAP **30**(1), 1–18 (2000)

10. Tannenbaum, S.I., Yukl, G.: Training and development in work organizations. Annu. Rev. Psychol. **43**, 399–441 (1992)

11. Bell, B.S., Kanar, A.M., Kozlowski, S.W.J.: Current issues and future directions in simulation-based training in North America. Int. J. Hum. Resour. Manag. **19**(8), 1416–1434 (2008). https://doi.org/10.1080/09585190802200173

12. Schreiber, D.A., Berge, Z.L.: How Innovative Organizations are Using Technology to Maximize Learning and Meet Business Objectives. Wiley, Hoboken (1998)

13. Mayer, R.E., Anderson, R.B.: The instructive animation: helping students build connections between words and pictures in multimedia learning (1992)

14. Fiore, S.M., Salas, E.E.: Toward a Science of Distributed Learning. American Psychological Association, Washington (2007)

15. Proserpio, L., Gioia, D.A.: Teaching the virtual generation: the rise of a virtual generation (2007)

16. Zantow, K., Knowlton, D.S., Sharp, D.C.: More than fun and games: reconsidering the virtues of strategic management simulations (2005)

17. Kozlowski, S.W.J., Bell, B.S.: A theory-based approach for designing distributed learning systems. In: Fiore, S.M., Salas, E., (eds.) Toward a Science of Distributed Learning, Washington, DC, pp. 15–39. APA (2007)

18. Vygotsky, L.S.: Mind in Society: The Development of Higher Psychological Processes. Harvard University Press, Cambridge (1978)

19. Garrison, D.R., Anderson, T., Archer, W.: Critical inquiry in a text-based environment: Computer conferencing in higher education. Internet High. Educ. **2**(2–3), 87–105 (2000)

20. Keys, B., Wolfe, J.: The role of management games and simulations in education and research. J. Manag. **16**(2), 307–336 (1990)

21. Baker, D.P., Ussher, G.R., Rimes, K.A.: Development of a text-based chatroom HIV prevention and confidence-building intervention for same-sex attracted young males in South England. J. HIV/AIDS Soc. Serv. **20**(3), 262–270 (2021). https://doi.org/10.1080/15381501.2021.1962473

22. Wenk, M., et al.: Simulation-based medical education is no better than problem-based discussions and induces misjudgment in self-assessment. Adv. Health Sci. Educ. **14**(2), 159–171 (2009). https://doi.org/10.1007/s10459-008-9098-2

23. Morgan, P.J., Cleave-Hogg, D., McIlroy, J., Devitt, J.H.: Simulation technology a comparison of experiential and visual learning for undergraduate medical students (2022). http://pubs.asahq.org/anesthesiology/article-pdf/96/1/10/404959/0000542-200201000-00008.pdf

24. Chauvin, S.W.: Applying educational theory to simulation-based training and assessment in surgery. Surg. Clin. North Am. **95**(4), 695–715 (2015). https://doi.org/10.1016/j.suc.2015.04.006

25. Salas, E., Rosen, M.A., Held, J.D., Weissmuller, J.J.: Performance measurement in simulation-based training: a review and best practices. Simul. Gam. **40**(3), 328–376 (2009). https://doi.org/10.1177/1046878108326734

26. U.S. Bureau of Labor Statistics, "Annual total separations rates by industry and region, not seasonally adjusted," Job Openings and Labor Turnover, 10 March2022. https://www.bls.gov/news.release/jolts.t16.htm. Accessed 30 Oct 2022

27. Jobvite, "Job seeker nation study: Researching the candidate-recruiter relationship," Jobvite, Statistical Report (2018). https://www.jobvite.com/wp-content/uploads/2018/04/2018_Job_Seeker_Nation_Study.pdf. Accessed 30 Oct 2022

28. Goddu, J.: Incorporating culture in employee onboarding, Sogolytics Blog, 22 June 2021. https://www.sogolytics.com/blog/how-to-incorporate-culture-in-onboarding/. Accessed 30 Oct 2022

29. Donthu, N., Kumar, S., Mukherjee, D., Pandey, N., Lim, W.M.: How to conduct a bibliometric analysis: an overview and guidelines. J. Bus. Res. **133**, 285–296 (2021). https://doi.org/10.1016/j.jbusres.2021.04.070

30. Scopus, "Scopus," Scopus Preview. https://www.scopus.com/home.uri. Accessed 30 Oct 2022

31. Anderson, L.W., et al.: A Taxonomy for Learning, Teaching, and Assessing: A Revision of Bloom's Taxonomy of Educational Objectives, Complete Longman, New York (2001)

32. easygenerator, "Learning objective maker," easygenerator. https://learning-objectives.easygenerator.com/. Accessed 01 Nov 2022

Analysis of Work-Flow Design Related to Aspects of Productivity and Ergonomics

Sindhu Meenakshi and Santhosh Kumar Balasankar[✉]

Purdue University, West Lafayette, IN 47906, USA
{spanaiya,sbalasan}@purdue.edu

Abstract. All the facility layouts are designed to enhance productivity. Though automation plays a huge role, still manual workers are considered essential for achieving the perfection of the product. In that case, any layout that doesn't consider the ergonomics of the workplace to ensure the worker's health and safety is deemed to be inconsequential. A balanced layout should consider ergonomic variables such as posture, awkward positions, and workstation dimensions. The enhancement of productivity and efficiency in the workflow process along with significant ergonomic improvements can be achieved through simulation. The results obtained are used to validate the procedure and the support methodology. This gives the link between the plant layout variables and ergonomic variables. Amongst the various simulation software, this report discusses FlexSim in detail focusing on the plant and process layout while the ergonomic variable is addressed through the literature survey.

Keywords: Workflow model · productivity · simulation · ergonomics · facility layout

1 Introduction and Background

Engineering may not have been all about simulations during the early 19th century. But, simulation has provided the ability to run operations and foresee events that might arise in the future as a result of various scenarios that we operate in at the moment.

Robotic software such as the ABB robotic studio helps stimulate both simple and complex operations using robots and test and verify their applications. Imagine a situation where we find that a robot is not able to operate at a certain angle because of joint restriction, we can easily figure it out before purchasing the model using the simulation software. The accuracy of simulations depends on how realistic the simulations are.

Flexsim is a simulation software developed by FlexSim Software Products, Inc in 2003. Flexsim operates by modeling and simulating the system to perform discrete sequences of events. Flexsim was initially developed by F&H Simulations, Inc in 2001 mainly to focus on diversified usage in the field of supply chain and its aid in the simulation-based analysis of the work floor (Fig. 1).

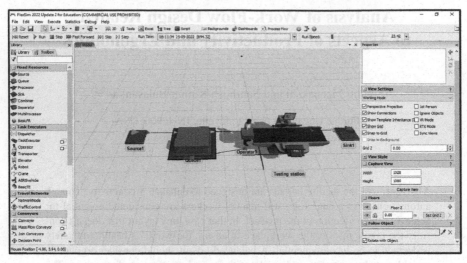

Fig. 1. Simulation inside the Flexsim Software

In a world of growing competition, companies are always developing ways of getting one over another. To do so they minimize time as a constraint in each and every possible scenario. Streamlining the process can lead to a highly optimized facility. However an effective facility layout must consider the needs and accessibility of the employees, thus an ergonomically efficient Facility is the ideal need of every organization [1]. An ergonomically inefficient layout can lead to employee fatigue, repetitive tasks, and skeletal disorders in the workforce [2].

1.1 Factors Considered to Develop Effective Workplace Design

Plant Layout Variables. Cycle time, productive time, Idle time, resource utilization, productivity (units/hr), and units produced are major dependables for any industry to design their production layout [3]. This is addressed in the FlexSim as seen in Fig. 2 by utilizing respective state graphs to analyze the built model.

Ergonomic Variables. The posture of the worker throughout the production cycle and his range of positions pertaining to significant joints such as neck, wrist, shoulder, hip, and knee are the most commonly considered ergonomic variables in this sector. These factors pose the assessment to determine the ergonomic risks related to the workers. The weight handled throughout the work process, the dimensions and the size of the workstations and spaces, and the anthropometry of the workers are essential for a comfortable work environment [4]. The physical attributes of the workplace such as the noise, lighting, ventilation, and temperature also play a significant role in an effective work environment.

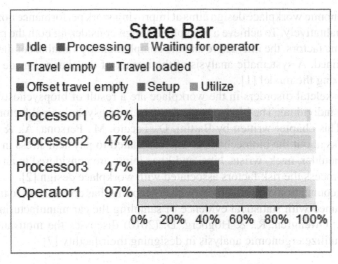

Fig. 2. State bar chart for process variables

Hence, the integration of workers' needs such as health and safety, along with input materials such as machinery and methods are the key determining factors to develop an optimal and effective system.

2   Literature Survey

The optimization of the production system can be achieved by utilizing simulation software that enables efficient creation and testing of the system in a virtual world rather than creating in a physical environment. Simulation of productivity and ergonomics are often carried out in industrial product design. But they are often run by different people with different objectives. This results in a silo effect. The Pascual, A. I., Smedberg, H., Högberg, D., Syberfeldt, A., & Lämkull, D. (2022) discusses the concurrent optimization of the design relating to both ergonomics and productivity [5].

Having a workplace with poor ergonomics not only results in lower sustainable work life for the employees but also results in high costs for the company as they lead to work-related musculoskeletal disorders (WMSDs). The study by Iriondo Pascual, A., Lind, A., Högberg, D., Syberfeldt, A., & Hanson, L. (2022) presents a Digital Human Modelling (DHM) tool to analyze the ergonomics risk along with the parameter of total walking distance and the workstation area which are the factors of productivity [6].

To execute concurrent optimizations of the product or production system design in aspects of productivity and ergonomics, the method of data mining is utilized in addition to various DHM tools. Data mining primarily deals with earlier studies and research providing insight into the problem that is being currently faced by the industry. Knowledge extraction saves time and costs in figuring out the key factors contributing to the risk factors and optimization [4].

The ergonomic workplace design aims at improving work performance both quantitatively and qualitatively. To achieve a workplace design considering both the productivity and ergonomic factors, the interactive and the complementary variables of the design are to be determined. A systematic analysis of the impact of the changes made is required before finalizing the model [1].

Musculoskeletal disorders in the workplace are a result of biopsychosocial factors affecting the individual. The biomechanical, social, and psychological factors are interconnected. This chapter written by Battini, D., Faccio, M., Persona, A., & Sgarbossa, F. (2011) talks about the biomechanical aspects related to physical stress in the human body. The shoulder, neck, wrists, hips, and knee joints are considered in an ergonomic analysis to process the risk factors associated with workplace design [2].

The interconnection of productivity with ergonomics has cost-benefit to the industry. This is explained with statistical evidence of sampling the car manufacturing industry. Falck, A. C., Örtengren, R., & Högberg, D. (2010) discusses the motivation for any company to utilize ergonomic analysis in designing their facility [7].

3   Bibliometric Analysis: Productivity, Ergonomics, and Simulation

Using Scopus [8], a bibliometric analysis of the title keywords (as provided in the abstract section) is studied. The keywords used for the analysis are Productivity, ergonomics, and simulation.

The search yields documents by titles and authors. Using the tab: "Analyze search result" provides a dashboard with many insights such as the documents published years, the sources, countries, universities, etc. It is shown in Fig. 8 for reference. The most relevant categories of the result analysis are discussed in detail here.

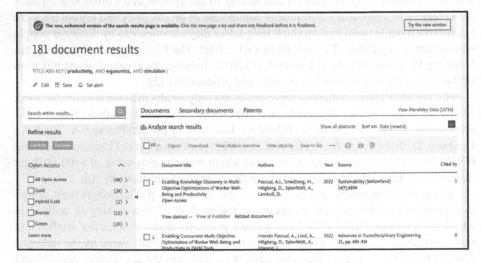

Fig. 3. Scopus search results on the keywords

This analysis as shown in Fig. 3 resulted in 181 documents between the period 1975 and 2023. The frequency of documents published each year between 1975 to 2023 can be seen in Fig. 4 yielding a maximum number of 25 documents published in the year 2021.

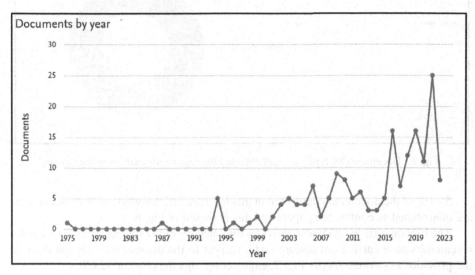

Fig. 4. Documents by year graph obtained through result analysis using Scopus

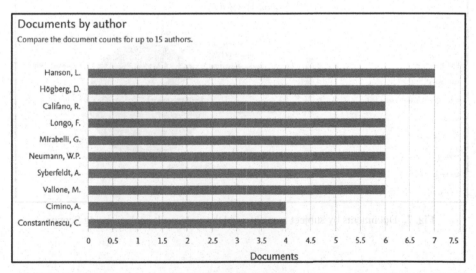

Fig. 5. Documents by Author graph obtained through result analysis using Scopus

As Fig. 5 indicates, Hanson, L. and Högberg, D. have contributed the most number of documents in this field.

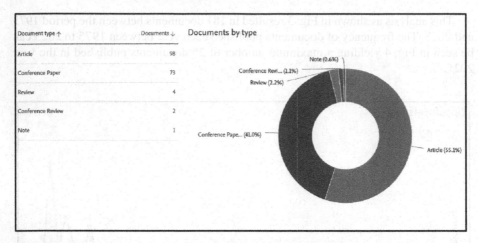

Fig. 6. Documents by type pie chart obtained through result analysis using Scopus

55.1% of the documents published in this field are articles while 41% of documents are contributed as conference papers and this is shown in Fig. 6.

The bibliometric analysis also provides the category of the subject areas in which the researchers have carried out research with respect to the documents searched through the provided keywords. As per Fig. 7, engineering tops the chart at 32.6%.

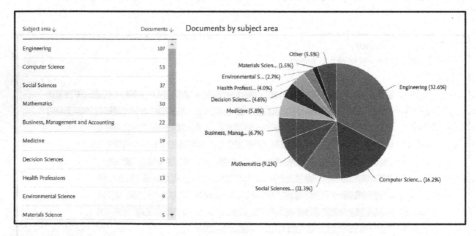

Fig. 7. Documents by subject area obtained through result analysis using Scopus

4   Flexsim

For optimization of the layout design, FlexSim is utilized. As referenced in the introduction section, various plant layout parameters are obtained through the simulation and are optimized for maximum productivity.

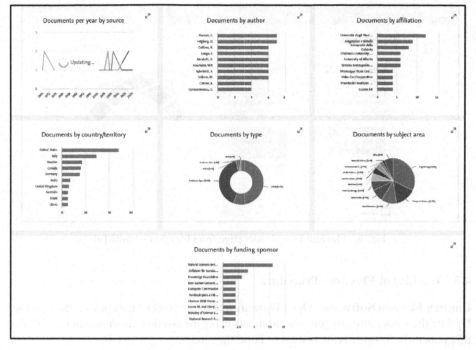

Fig. 8. Analyze search result dashboard

4.1 Installation

1. To install Flexsim head over to the Flexsim website [9] and select Try Flexsim for free.
2. Using your credentials, log in to the webpage and it'll redirect you to the downloads page.
3. Select FlexSim 2022 Update 2 or FlexSim 2022 and your download will start.
4. Install the file on your Windows PC and Flexsim should be up and running.
5. Activate the Flexsim by going to Help > License Activation > Enter the Activation ID and click Activate.

4.2 Version of Flexsim

For this report we have used the 22.2.2 version which was released on 2022–09-13 (Fig. 9).

Fig. 9. FlexSim Downloader page from FlexSim website [9]

4.3   Working of Flexsim - Procedure

Launch FlexSim Software.   Open Flexsim, and in the workspace click on the new file. Update the model units to your requirements using the window as shown in Fig. 10. For this paper, the SI units scale is used to build the model.

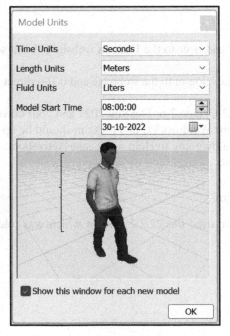

Fig. 10.   Flexsim Model Creation

Build 3D Model. To construct the model as required for the layout, utilize the work objects from the Library panel on the left. A sample of the library toolbox is provided in Fig. 11.

Fig. 11. Library toolbox panel used for FlexSim modeling

Based on the requirements of the process, any complicated system can be achieved with FlexSim. In this paper, a basic model is analyzed. This model is constructed by dragging Source, Queue, Testing station, and Sink and placing them in the workspace from the fixed resources tool panel.

The source object is placed first to create the flow items. The boxed parameter is used and was edited to 15. Queueing station is placed next to the source to get the objects ready for processing. The processor is placed and the processing time of the processor has been changed to triangular for min, max & mode values. The processor is renamed to the testing station. The sink is the end of the model.

Process Flow Model. The simulation could not be run unless the process flow is defined. This is made by connecting one element to another in a sequential manner to obtain the desired performance. The elements of the model are connected by holding on to 'a' and dragging one object onto another. This creates a process flow model as shown in Fig. 12.

Operator Creation. From the Task Executors, an Operator is added to act as an intermediate between the queue and the testing Station. Though the simulation could be run without an operator, we have created one to make the model more realistic and obtain results in regard to operator utilization. Also, the queue needs to have the transport box checked off in the parameters for the simulation to take off with the operator's mobility.

Run Simulation. The motion of boxes from the Queue onto the Testing Station can be observed by clicking on run. The run speed can be changed to observe the motions at a different pace. Graphs and charts can be added for observation.

Analyze Results. In the toolbar, a blank workspace can be opened by clicking on dashboards. A state graph is added to which the processor and the operator are sampled

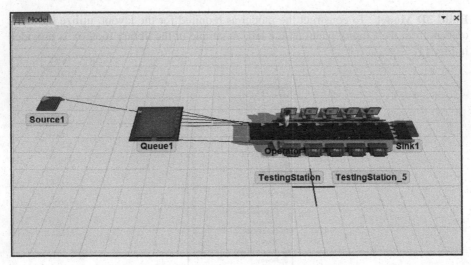

Fig. 12. Process flow model with operator

for utilization. An average content graph is added to sample the queue for the average content. The simulation shall be reset and run. It will be shown that the average content on the queue keeps on increasing as the boxes stack up. To improve the performance parameters, more testing stations are added.

Revise the Model. To tackle the problem found by analyzing the dashboards, more processors could be added. To check on this hunch, the value in the toolbox menu > parameters option > type in the processor is increased to 5. Also, the parameter is changed to an integer and the lower & upper bounds are set with reference to the queue since the output of the queue is a processor.

When we reset and run, an updated dashboard is obtained. The performance measures are utilized to get the average value out of the dashboard charts. Three columns and references are added to each of the respective graphs to end up with values.

Also, Simulink has an experimenter option, which can be utilized to simulate different scenarios to find an optimal solution. In the experimenter, various scenarios are created with testing stations of numbers 1, 2, 3, 4 & 5. The hours are input for which data is evaluated and the experiment is run.

As all turn green, the three parameters graph of the box plot can is seen with varying numbers of testing stations. Analyzing this would help us to decide the optimum number of processors.

The analysis of the created model with the above-mentioned dashboards is shown in Fig. 13.

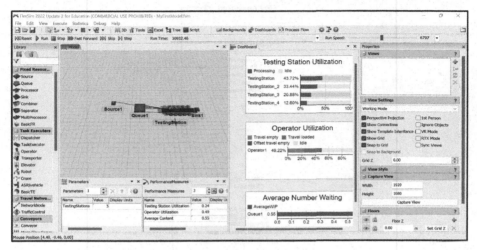

Fig. 13. Analysis of basic model with source, queue, processor, and sink on Flexsim

5 Discussion

The number of requirements that are needed to be met in the plant layout design is very high. When trying to include the ergonomic variables, more often conflicts are faced. The design should be handled in such a way that it includes the most important aspects where comfortness has a significant impact instead of trying to include all the suggestions [1].

Figure 14 shows the basic framework model developed to integrate plant layout design while considering ergonomics for designing an effective layout of the facility aimed at improved productivity [3].

Based on environmental factors and ease of production the following variables are defined with high to low contribution on an ergonomic scale of difficulty [4] (Table 1).

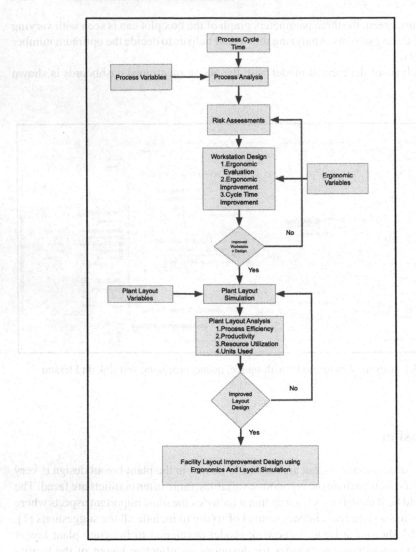

Fig. 14. Facility layout model framework adapted from Delgado & Carlos (n.d)

The consequences of worker discomfort results in direct loss of productivity. When the layout is not designed to match human limitations and characteristics, it leads to ergonomic and safety issues [10]. Both are highly interconnected. This is explained in Fig. 15.

Table 1. List of Ergonomic Variables.

Variable	Effects
Environmental Hazards	Can cause health problems like respiratory diseases, heart disease, and some types of cancer
Neck-related ergonomic risks	Chronic neck pain also can cause fatigue, depression, and irritability
Body Posture	The complications of poor posture include back pain, spinal dysfunction, joint degeneration, rounded shoulders, and a potbelly
Weight Handling, and Muscular load	Excess weight, diminishes almost every aspect of health, from reproductive and respiratory function to memory and mood

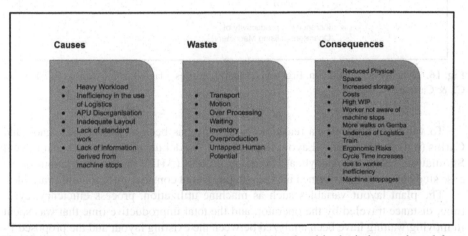

Fig. 15. Causes, wastes, and consequences of the problem faced in the industry adapted from Afonso, T., Alves, A. C., & Carneiro, P. (2021)

6 Results and Conclusion

Both understanding and trust are quick when humans can inspect the processes and interact with a simulation model in action. Effective use of simulation leads to a risk-free environment and provides insight into the dynamics that increases the product's usability and improves the overall design.

The primary objective of this report is to develop a model that is capable of obtaining an improved layout design using ergonomic analysis to resolve the inefficiencies encountered in the system and the layout simulation that eliminates the bottlenecks of production [7]. It results in an improved material handling system that is lean and aims to reduce the wastage in a production process.

This has a direct impact on the production cost as well. It leads to lower material handling costs and reduced cycle time [6]. The synergy between the key factors is explained in Fig. 16.

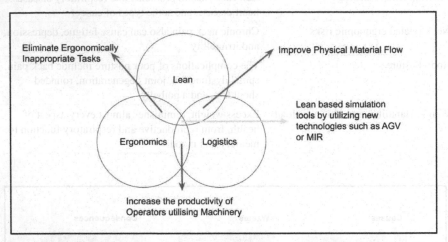

Fig. 16. Synergy between Lean, Ergonomics, and Logistics adapted from Afonso, T., Alves, A. C., & Carneiro, P. (2021)

To validate the results, a real-time case study has been analyzed in Delgado and Carlos (n.d) on the Facility Layout Improvement Model using Ergonomics and Layout Simulation. Using the Analytical Hierarchy Process (AHP), the existing layout in the case study has been transformed into a P-shaped layout considering ergonomic variables.

The plant layout variables such as machine utilization, process efficiency, cycle time, distance traveled by the operator, and the total unproductive time that was spent in moving/waiting have been analyzed between the existing layout and the proposed P-shape layout. The machine utilization of the proposed P-shaped layout has been increased by 16% which led to an increase in process efficiency by 70% when compared with the existing layout. This helped to bring down the cycle time of the process by 84%. The distance traveled by the operator in the P-shape layout has been decreased substantially to 7%, resulting in the lowest unproductive time of just 0.87s/part from 150s/part. This clearly explains that resolving the inefficiencies of workplace ergonomics simulates shorter cycle time, shorter unproductive time, reduced distance traveled, more units produced, and an efficient production process.

For making an effective decision to have a high impact rate on productivity, a good estimate of generic human abilities and limitations along with the specific characteristics of the people working in the designed workplace is essential. A systematic evaluation of the proposed alternatives is a must before implementing any decision. Involving the key stakeholders affected by the decision results in better workplace design.

References

1. Marmaras, N., Nathanael, D.: Workplace design. In: Handbookof Human Factors and Ergonomics, pp. 368–382. Wiley, Hoboken (2021).https://doi.org/10.1002/9781119636113. ch14
2. Marras, W.S., Karwowski, W.: Basic biomechanics and workplace design. In: Handbook of Human Factors and Ergonomics, pp. 303–357. Wiley, Hoboken (2021). https://doi.org/10. 1002/9781119636113.ch12
3. Delgado, J.E., Cecilia, M., Carlos, C.: Facility layout improvement model using ergonomics and layout simulation
4. Battini, D., Faccio, M., Persona, A., Sgarbossa, F.: New methodological framework to improve productivity and ergonomics in assembly system design. Int. J. Ind. Ergon. **41**(1), 30–42 (2011). https://doi.org/10.1016/j.ergon.2010.12.001
5. Pascual, A.I., Smedberg, H., Högberg, D., Syberfeldt, A., Lämkull, D.: Enabling knowledge discovery in multi-objective optimizations of worker well- being and productivity. Sustainability (Switzerland) **14**(9) (2022). https://doi.org/10.3390/su14094894
6. Iriondo Pascual, A., et al.: Multi-objective optimization of ergonomics and productivity by using an optimization framework. In: Black, N.L., Neumann, W.P., Noy, I. (eds.) IEA 2021. LNNS, vol. 223, pp. 374–378. Springer, Cham (2022). https://doi.org/10.1007/978-3-030-74614-8_46
7. Falck, A.C., Örtengren, R., Högberg, D.: The impact of poor assembly ergonomics on product quality: a cost-benefit analysis in car manufacturing. Hum. Factors Ergon. Manuf. **20**(1), 24–41 (2010). https://doi.org/10.1002/hfm.20172
8. Scopus homepage (2023). https://www.scopus.com/home.uri
9. FlexSim Homepage (2023). https://www.flexsim.com/
10. Afonso, T., Alves, A.C., Carneiro, P.: Lean thinking, logistic and ergonomics: synergetic triad to prepare shop floor work systems to face pandemic situations. Int. J. Glob. Bus. Competit. **16**(1), 62–76 (2021). https://doi.org/10.1007/s42943-021-00037-5

Quality of Experience and Mental Energy Use of Cobot Workers in Manufacturing Enterprises

Fabio Alexander Storm[1]([✉]), Luca Negri[2], Claudia Carissoli[2],
Alberto Peña Fernández[3], Carla Dei[1], Marta Bassi[2], Daniel Berckmans[4],
and Antonella Delle Fave[2]

[1] Scientific Institute, I.R.C.C.S. "E.Medea", 23842 Lecco, Bosisio Parini, Italy
`fabio.storm@lanostrafamiglia.it`
[2] Università Degli Studi Di Milano, Milan, Italy
[3] BioRICS NV., 3001 Leuven, Belgium
[4] Department of Biosystems, KU Leuven, 3001 Leuven, Belgium

Abstract. Integrating information on the subjective experience reported by workers operating in collaborative human-machine environments with objective data, collected with wearable sensors capable of monitoring participants' physiological responses, may lead to novel findings regarding the recognition and handling of potentially stressful work situations. To this aim, data were collected from seven participants working in production lines of manufactory companies employing collaborative robots. The experience associated with daily activities by cobot-workers in manufacturing enterprises was investigated for one week through the Experience Sampling Method. Data were analyzed through the Experience Fluctuation Model, relying on the relationship between perceived task related challenges and personal skills to identify eight experiential profiles: arousal, flow or optimal experience, control, relaxation, boredom, apathy, worry and anxiety. Physiological data were continuously collected throughout the same week using a smartwatch and processed to obtain real-time estimation of the mental energy use and recovery. Results showed that flow experience was predominant in tasks involving cobots; production line activities without cobot were instead mostly associated with relaxation. The real-time monitoring of the mental energy levels associated with work corroborated these results by showing that participants were, on average, 2.5 times longer in the focus zone when working with the cobot than when working without it. These findings suggest the heuristic potential of combining psychological and physiological assessment procedures to identify both advantages and areas of implementation emerging from the employment of cobots in industrial settings.

Keywords: Cobots · quality of experience · physiological data · workers' well-being

1 Introduction

1.1 Mental Health and Work-Related Risks

Based on the definition proposed by the World Health Organization [1], mental health is not merely the absence of mental illness, but it rather comprises positive psychological and behavioral dimensions of functioning. The benefits of work for mental health has been investigated widely in the scientific literature [2–5]. However, there is also evidence that physical and mental health problems can be associated with poor psychosocial working conditions: work-related psychosocial risks and stress can cause mental and physical illnesses, resulting in high costs for the individual, the economy, and the whole society [6]. Around 50% of European workers report symptoms of workplace stress, a condition representing a serious concern for nearly 80% of the companies within the EU, contributing to about half of all lost working days [7].

1.2 Industry 4.0 and Collaborative Robotics

The massive introduction of technology, artificial intelligence, and robotics associated to the digital transformation of Industry 4.0 in factories has introduced new challenges to workers' health and well-being, significantly changing the role of the human worker, as well as the way of performing and perceiving job [8]. Robotization of the workplace can have both negative and positive effects on workers' experience: machines can relieve humans from tedious, repetitive, and dangerous tasks, but at the same time they require continuous monitoring. Workers run the risk to perceive themselves as no longer being active contributors to production; on the other hand, the supervision task can be positively perceived as mentally stimulating, because it requires understanding and decision-making capabilities [9].

One of the most rapidly evolving aspects of Industry 4.0 is the significantly advanced collaboration between humans and machines [10]. Collaborative robots, or cobots, are devices enabling direct physical interaction between humans and computer-controlled manipulators [11]. The first passive cobots were quickly replaced by modern devices taking the form of light–weight robotic arms. Cobots are especially advantageous in assembly tasks, where their characteristics of reliability and high payload are combined with the skills and flexibility of human operators [12]. While early cobot implementations often only entailed removal of protective fences, nowadays applications involving full collaboration are increasing (See Fig. 1). This increasing cognitive interaction between operator and cobot may have a significant impact on mental health [13]. On the other hand, thanks to their adaptability to human behavior, they could play a fundamental role in promoting healthy industrial workplaces, reducing job stress, and supporting workers' engagement.

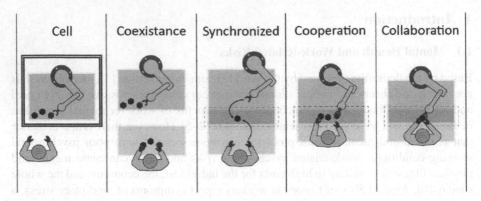

Fig. 1. Types of interaction in the shared workspace: Cell – The cobot is operated in a traditional cage; Coexistence – Human and cobot work alongside each other but do not share a workspace. Synchronized – The human worker and the cobot share a workspace but only one of the interaction partners is actually present in the workspace at any one time. Cooperation – Both interaction partners may have tasks to perform at the same time in the shared workspace, but they do not work simultaneously on the same product or component. Collaboration – Human worker and cobot work simultaneously on the same product or component. Adapted from [14].

1.3 Flow as an Optimal Experience

Evidence derived from psychological research could be exploited to reduce psychosocial risks and their negative consequences on the mental health of workers. In particular, attention should be given to the relationship between the level of challenges and difficulty characterizing job tasks and workers' abilities and skills in facing them.

A large body of evidence has highlighted that the match between appropriate levels of task challenges and adequate workers' skills can lead to Flow, first identified and described by Mihaly Csikszentmihalyi [15] as an optimal experience associated with engaging and intrinsically motivating activities. Flow is "the subjective experience of engaging in just-manageable challenges by tackling a series of goals, continuously processing feedback about progress, and adjusting action based on the feedback" (Nakamura & Csikszentmihalyi, 2002, p. 90, [16]). In the work domain, positive associations were detected between flow and higher work performance [17] and mental health [18–21]. In particular, research suggested that workers' optimal experiences could be facilitated by modifying tasks or the work environment, rather than changing individual dispositional factors [22].

1.4 Estimation of Physical and Mental Energy Expenditure Using Wearables

Although there is available evidence that performing mental tasks can lead to an increase in energy expenditure [23, 24], the component of energy expenditure originating from mental processes is often neglected. Being able to monitor a person's mental energy expenditure can be of great value to study their response to daily life challenges or stressful situations at work [25]. The gold standard for the estimation of whole body energy expenditure is indirect calorimetry. However, this technique is expensive and impractical in daily life situations [26]. Methods based on wearables sensors appear particularly promising as alternatives because of their ecological validity. Researchers have proposed predictive equations based on several physiological signals, especially body acceleration, heart rate, respiration and galvanic skin response [27]. One of the most established approaches is data-based mechanistic modelling [28], in which, using heart rate and movement as inputs, firstly total heart rate is split in different components and, afterwards, the mental energy use and recovery exhibited by an individual while performing a cognitive task is estimated [29, 30]. A real-time algorithm adapting according to the individual data collected for the user can decompose the heart rate of living organisms into three major components: 1) a basal component, linked to basal metabolism and thermoregulation; 2) a physical component which is linked to movement and physical activity; 3) a mental component that is used in mental activity such as concentrating or dealing with a stressful situation.

1.5 Aim

Intervention on technological, relational and organizational aspects of the cobot-based work is urgent, in order to safeguard workers' mental health and job engagement, especially since the global pandemic has accelerated the exposure to this technology. The MindBot project is aimed at developing cobots able to interact with human workers in a flexible and personalized way, both supporting workers' engagement and autonomy, and promoting opportunities for flow experiences during production line activities. A core prerequisite to pursue this aim is to investigate the mental health workers who interact with the typologies of cobots currently employed in manufacturing enterprises. Related findings may lead to a more direct identification and handling of potentially stressful situations in collaborative human-machine environments. The present study represents a first step in this direction, as it is based on the collection of both data on the quality of experience reported by workers during their interaction with cobots, and physiological data collected through a wearable device to estimate in real-time mental energy use and recovery.

2   Methods

2.1   Recruitment and Participants

The experimental protocol was approved by the IRCCS Medea Ethics Committee on the 16th of April 2020. Participants were recruited on a voluntary basis. Before the data collection phase, they signed an informed consent form and received detailed information about the investigation procedure. After the data collection they were invited to a debriefing meeting. Data were pseudonymized before analyses.

2.2   ESM Procedure

To investigate the quality of experience of workers, including its relationship with perceived challenges and skills, data were collected through the Experience Sampling

Method (ESM), a valid and reliable procedure widely used in a variety of studies, including research with workers [31, 32]. ESM is based on repeated assessments of experience in situ during daily activities, allowing to reduce the memory reconstruction bias characterizing single-administration questionnaires [32, 33].

At the beginning of the testing period, workers were briefed about the use of the ESM method by a trained researcher; at the end of the sampling week, they were able to provide comments, observations, and suggestions. Workers were invited to provide answers to short questionnaires (ESM forms) delivered on a mobile app six or seven times a day for seven consecutive days, upon acoustic signals sent to them at quasi-random intervals between 8:00 a.m. and 10:00 p.m. Each form contained a standard set of open-ended questions and Likert-type scales. The open-ended questions investigated participants' present thoughts, activities, locations, social context and the involvement of the cobot during the ongoing activity. The Likert-type scales, ranging from 0 (not at all) to 6 (extremely), assessed the levels of affective, cognitive, and motivational variables. Participants were also asked to assess on the same 0–6 scales their levels of perceived challenges and personal skills in the ongoing activity.

2.3   Real-Time Estimation of Mental Energy Use

Physiological data were also collected throughout the sampling week using a Fitbit smartwatch and processed through Mindstretch, a software developed by BioRICS N.V. The algorithm behind Mindstretch is a real-time adaptive model based on the DBM modelling approach which estimates the mental energy use and recovery exhibited by an individual while performing a cognitive task. The algorithm adapts according to the individual data collected for the user and, when monitoring 24/7, the algorithm will be adapted to the user in 2–3 days. In this project, the wearable devices used are Fitbit Inspire HR activity trackers (Fitbit Inc., USA), which collects heart rate and steps at 1Hz using the Fitbit app for Android as software to collect and store these data from the activity tracker. Averages per minute of these values are the inputs used by the Mindstretch algorithm. The Fitbit and Mindstretch apps run on a Samsung Galaxy tablet with Android OS. Workers are provided with the Fitbit device and data is transferred via Bluetooth to the Fitbit app and shared with the Mindstretch app for processing and estimation of the mental energy levels. Finally, the data is stored pseudonymized in the MindBot repository cloud system (see Fig. 2).

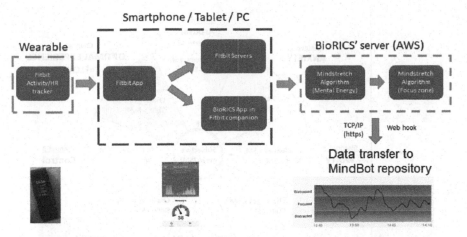

Fig. 2. Schematic representation of the data flow and devices used to collect the raw physiological data (heart rate and steps) via the Fitbit activity tracker, processed via the Mindstretch App and stored in a cloud repository.

2.4 Data Handling and Analyses

Experience Sampling Method. As regards ESM data, forms completed more than 30 minutes after signal receipt were discarded from analysis, in order to avoid distortions due to retrospective recall [34]. Answers to open-ended questions were coded and categorized according to well-established procedures [18, 32, 35, 36]. Given the repeated sampling, the values of each scaled variable were standardized on each participant's weekly mean using z-scores (mean=0 and standard deviation=1). Aggregated mean z-scores for scaled variables were calculated accordingly.

The quality of workers' daily experience was analyzed in relation to perceived challenges and skills through the experience fluctuation model (EFM) [35, 37]. The model is built on a Cartesian plan, in which the standardized values (z-scores) of perceived skill are on the x-axis, while the z-scores of the perceived challenge are on the y-axis. The origin of the two axes corresponds to the average of all participants' means (zero after standardization). Eight experiential profiles, corresponding to sectors or "channels" of the model, can be defined based on the relationship between perceived environmental challenges and personal skills: arousal, flow or optimal experience, control, relaxation, boredom, apathy, worry and anxiety (see Fig. 3).

Physiological Data. The Mindstretch algorithm provides the following outputs:

- Level of Mental energy use/Mental energy recovery (%): This is the primary outcome. It can be understood as the energy needed for mental cognitive tasks. This can either be energy use or energy recovery.
- Balance Score (%): amount of mental energy recovery over the total amount of energy use for the given period or for a specific activity or person. If the value is above 50%, mental energy recovery is higher than mental energy use, and vice versa.
- Average Mental energy for the group [%]: is calculated by adding all the results of each individual worker and dividing the total number of workers.

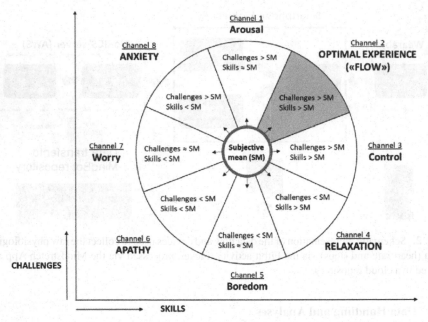

Fig. 3. The Experience Fluctuation Model (adapted from [38]).

- Energy Drainers: activities or situations which give an increase in the mental energy use of a person.
- Energy Refuelers: Activities or situations which give an increase in the mental energy recovery of a person.

The main objective when studying physiological responses in the workers interacting with cobots is to determine the physiological baseline exhibited by a worker who interacts with cobots in the production line. This leads to several secondary objectives. Firstly, the mental energy use and recovery levels needed to perform different tasks by each worker are expected to be defined and monitored. Secondly, relations between these physiological measurements and the ESM data collected are sought. Finally, an estimation of the focus zone for a worker when in the production line, both interacting and not with the cobot and performing other work tasks is defined. This allows monitoring in real-time deviations from this focus zone, which can be used as an early warning to prevent the worker from going out of focus when interacting with the cobot. The analyses were performed using Matlab 2016b (MathWork Inc., USA). For the statistical analysis, the non-parametric Mann-Whitney U test and the Kruskal-Wallis test, were performed, setting the threshold for significance at p-value < 0.05.

3 Results and Discussion

3.1 Workers' Quality of Daily Experience: ESM Results

Descriptive Data. The final data set included 213 valid forms (30.4 self-reports per person on average), corresponding to 66.1% of the 322 scheduled forms. As concerns ongoing activities, participants prominently reported being engaged in job tasks, followed by personal care, interactions with family members, friends, and other acquaintances, and chores. Further activities mapped during the sampling week were reading, using media, watching TV leisure and hobbies.

Thoughts were prominently devoted to work related aspects, followed by daily planning, personal care, leisure and hobbies, chores, and social relations/interactions.

Quality of Experience During Daily Activities. To investigate the quality of experience associated with daily activities, all ESM forms were grouped into three categories: "Work - Production line" comprising all assembly line related activities with or without cobot involvement; "Work – Other" comprising job tasks not performed on the assembly line; "No work" comprising forms in which workers reported activities not strictly related to work. Out of the 47 ESM forms referring to "Work – Production line" activities, 34 (72.34%) included cobot involvement. As Fig. 4 shows, flow or optimal experience was predominant when interacting with the cobot, accounting for half of the ESM forms; the experience of Arousal, also characterized by the perception of high challenges, followed in frequency. Overall, these results clearly show that workers perceived cobot-related activities as highly challenging and involving, as well as mostly manageable through the active investment of personal skills. Conversely, the same activities performed without the cobot were prominently associated with the experience of "Relaxation", namely perceived as low-challenge and easily controllable situations.

Descriptive statistics and tests associated to the ESM experiential variables in the "Work – Production line" category are reported in Table 1. In line with the EFM channel distribution reported above, when working with the cobot participants reported higher levels of Challenges ($p = .003$), Concentration ($p = .04$), and perception of being Active ($p = .02$) compared to their weekly mean. They also reported feeling significantly more Obliged than average ($p < .001$). The perception of time passing slower ($p = .03$) than average was also observed. The experience associated with working on the production line without cobot, instead, was a globally average condition. Only the emotional variable Happy scored significantly lower than average ($p = .003$).

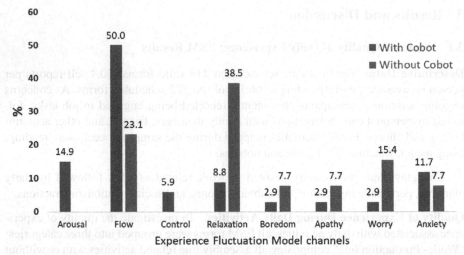

Fig. 4. Experiential profiles of the Experience Fluctuation Model based on ESM data of the participants.

3.2 Workers' Mental Energy Use

Participants were asked to wear the Fitbit activity tracker coupled with the Mindstretch app for a working week. 4 participants were monitored consistently, and another 3 participants were monitored for less than 70% of the total time, because the wearable sensor was not worn overnight.

Mental Energy Levels vs Daily Activities. The activities most commonly reported by the participants were related to the macro categories work, chores and personal care, followed by media and interactions.

Figure 5 shows the average mental energy use and recovery level exhibited by the participants, as a group, per activity. In the group analysis, no statistically significant correlation was found. However, it appears that the most draining activity in terms of mental energy is working in the production line.

Mental Energy Levels While at Work. Following the categories established by the ESM analysis, the same categories were used to evaluate the mental energy use and recovery levels exhibited by the participants. Figure 6 shows the average of these levels for the group in the different work categories. Even though not statistically significant, the mental energy use levels are lower and less variable when working without the cobot than working with the cobot in the production line.

Using the data collected by the ESM, it is possible to establish how the participants are experiencing the working task and in association with a channel of the Experience Fluctuation Model. Due to the low number of ESM forms included in each channel, no statistically significant differences were found. However, as pointed out previously, most events seem to be associated with Arousal and Flow channels when working with the cobot, with a shift to Relaxation when working without it in the production line.

Table 1. Standardized values of the ESM variables in the "Work – Production line" cluster with and without cobot involvement. N_a: number of answers; M: mean; SD: standard deviation; t: Student's t statistic; *:$p < 0.05$; **:$p < 0.01$; ***:$p < 0.001$.

	"Work – Production line" (With cobot) $N_a = 34$			"Work – Production line" (Without cobot) $N_a = 13$		
Variable	M	SD	t	M	SD	t
Challenges	0.39**	0.72	3.17	−0.19	0.93	−0.75
Skills	0.04	0.68	0.37	0.24	1.07	0.81
Concentration	0.22*	0.59	2.14	0.27	0.68	1.41
Control	0.07	0.44	0.92	0.43	1.06	1.45
Happy	−0.25	0.96	−1.53	−0.66**	0.64	−3.69
Lonely	0.05	0.33	0.80	0.29	0.58	1.81
Anxious	0.10	0.66	0.92	−0.03	0.86	−0.12
Sociable	0.08	0.88	0.53	−0.14	0.62	−0.78
Active	0.27*	0.66	2.36	0.16	0.91	0.62
Bored	0.12	0.73	0.93	0.67	1.23	1.95
Involved	−0.01	0.91	−0.06	0.04	0.47	0.34
Stake	0.34	1.01	1.96	−0.01	0.73	−0.07
Time	−0.37*	−2.29	−2.29	−0.57	1.27	−1.63
Satisfaction	0.04	0.61	0.36	−0.29	1.62	−0.65
Physical	0.21	1.01	0.21	0.24	1.44	0.61
Obliged	0.65***	4.93	4.93	0.48	1.00	1.73

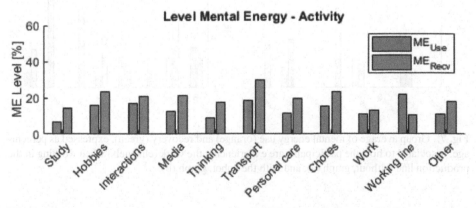

Fig. 5. Group average of mental energy use (orange) and recovery (green), expressed as percentage, while performing the different activities logged via the ESM method.

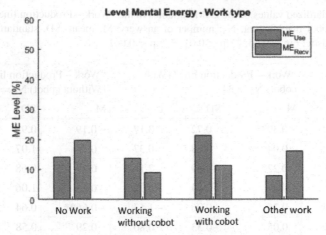

Fig. 6. Group average of mental energy use (orange) and recovery (green), expressed as percentage, while following the different lines of thought logged via ESM.

The mental energy use levels seem to follow the same trend in the participants. When working in the production line with the cobot, the average and standard deviation of the mental energy levels are higher than for the events associated to the Relaxation channel when not working with the cobot (Fig. 7).

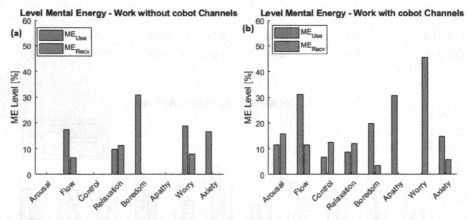

Fig. 7. Group average of mental energy use (orange) and recovery (green), expressed as percentage, associated to how the participants are experiencing the work (channels) when working in the production line without, graph (a), and with the cobot, graph (b).

Focus Zone Analysis. In the present project, where the interest lies in studying the interaction between an individual and a cobot while performing a joint task, ideally the focus zone will be the mental energy level in which the participants are interacting more efficiently with the cobot while getting the job done. Taking advantage of the ESM data, a possibility would be to consider the logged events in which the participant is working in the production line with the cobot perceiving the challenge as neutral and being in congruence. However, due to the exploratory nature of the present analysis, there is not enough data available from all participants to apply this definition of focus zone. Thus, the participant's focus zone was defined as the average mental energy use level when working with the cobot ± the standard deviation.

Results showed a statistically significant difference in the time being in the focus zone when working with the cobot, compared to production line assembly activities with no cobot involvement ($p = .02$). In particular, participants were, on average, 2.5 times longer in the focus zone when working with the cobot than when working without it. Data about real-time mental energy use level also provide information on the dynamics of fluctuations around the focus zone. To exemplify, Fig. 8 shows findings from two participants. In Fig. 8a, the participant is exhibiting time in focus and distracted; in Fig. 8b, the participant starts in focus and finishes in distress.

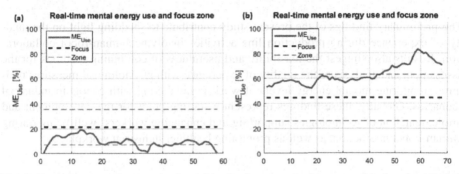

Fig. 8. Real-time mental energy use level (blue line) against the focus zone (black and red dashed lines represent the average value of the focus zone and the boundaries, respectively). In graph (a) the participant is exhibiting time in focus and distracted; in graph (b) the participant starts in focus and finishes in distress.

4   Discussion

In this study, the quality of experience of cobot-workers employed in manufacturing enterprises was investigated with a repeated real-time sampling approach, in combination with physiological data collected through a wearable device to estimate in real-time mental energy use and recovery.

Data confirmed the role of work as a key resource for workers' well-being: in the ESM self-reports it was primarily associated with positive experiences characterized by high challenges, concentration, and cognitive engagement. This is further confirmed by the physiological results provided by Mindstretch: the estimated mental energy levels showed that the most drainer activities and thoughts were those related to the work-related aspects. The estimation of the focus zone and the monitoring in real-time of the mental energy levels associated with work in the different scenarios showed a statistically significant difference in the time being "in focus" when working with the cobot in the production line, compared to working without.

Data inspection also confirmed that Flow experience while working with the cobot represents a positive state of consciousness, characterized by engagement, commitment, as well as satisfaction with one's own achievements. As the results show, production line activities allowed workers to experience high challenges, matched with adequate skills. Nevertheless, a deeper inspection of the ESM findings suggests that activities involving the cobot seem to promote a "bounded" optimal experience. Although–the interaction with cobot was associated with high levels of challenge, concentration, and feeling of being active, workers also felt highly obliged and constrained. The physiological data support these findings through several statistically significant correlations found between the mental energy levels and the variables' z-scores.

5 Conclusion

The preliminary findings of the present study contribute to shedding light on the quality of experience during production line activities involving human-robot collaboration. Results also suggest the feasibility and usefulness of combining methods for the assessment and analysis of the quality of experience with physiological measures real-time monitoring mental energy levels of workers interacting with cobots in industrial scenarios. Globally, these findings represent a starting point for the development and implementation of technologies supporting and enhancing workers' well-being during human-cobot interaction, as well as promoting healthier industrial workplaces.

References

1. WHO: The World Health Report : 2001 mental health. New Underst. New Hope (2001)
2. Kotera, Y., Van Laethem, M., Ohshima, R.: Cross-cultural comparison of mental health between Japanese and Dutch workers: relationships with mental health shame, self-compassion, work engagement and motivation. Cross Cult. Strateg. Manag. (2020). https://doi.org/10.1108/CCSM-02-2020-0055
3. Llena-Nozal, A.: The effect of work status and working conditions on mental health in four OECD countries. Natl. Inst. Econ. Rev. (2009). https://doi.org/10.1177/0027950109345234
4. Memish, K., Martin, A., Bartlett, L., Dawkins, S., Sanderson, K.: Workplace mental health: an international review of guidelines (2017). https://doi.org/10.1016/j.ypmed.2017.03.017
5. Waddell, G., Kim Burton, A.: Is Work Good for Your Health and Well-being? Station. Off. United Kingdom (2006)
6. González, R.C., López, A.M., Rodriguez-Uría, J., Álvarez, D., Alvarez, J.C.: Real-time gait event detection for normal subjects from lower trunk accelerations. Gait Posture. 31, 322–325 (2010). https://doi.org/10.1016/j.gaitpost.2009.11.014
7. EU-OSHA: Second European Survey of Enterprises on New and Emerging Risks (ESENER-2) (2015)
8. Peeters, M.C.W., Plomp, J.: For better or for worse: the impact of workplace automation on work characteristics and employee well-being. In: Digital Transformation - Towards New Frontiers and Business Opportunities. IntechOpen, London, United Kingdom (2022)

9. Smids, J., Nyholm, S., Berkers, H.: Robots in the workplace: a threat to—or opportunity for—meaningful work? Philos. Technol. **33**(3), 503–522 (2019). https://doi.org/10.1007/s13 347-019-00377-4

10. Camarinha-Matos, L.M., Afsarmanesh, H., Antonelli, D. (eds.): PRO-VE 2019. IAICT, vol. 568. Springer, Cham (2019). https://doi.org/10.1007/978-3-030-28464-0

11. Peshkin, M., Colgate, J.E.: Cobots. Ind. Rob. (1999). https://doi.org/10.1108/014399199102 83722

12. Matheson, E., Minto, R., Zampieri, E.G.G., Faccio, M., Rosati, G.: Human-robot collaboration in manufacturing applications: a review. Robotics **8**, 1–25 (2019). https://doi.org/10.3390/rob otics8040100

13. Storm, F.A., et al.: Physical and mental well - being of Cobot workers : a scoping review using the software - hardware - environment - Liveware - Liveware - organization model. Hum. Factors Ergon. Manuf. Serv. Ind., 1–17 (2022). https://doi.org/10.1002/hfm.20952

14. Bauer, W., Bender, M., Braun, M., Rally, P., Scholtz, O.: Lightweight robots in manual assembly – best to start simply! Examining companies' initial experiences with lightweight robots (2016)

15. Csikszentmihalyi, M.: Flow: The Psychology of Optimal Experience. Harper & Row, New York (1990)

16. Nakamura, J., Csikszentmihalyi, M.: The concept of flow. In: Handbook of Positive Psychology, pp. 89–105. Oxford University Press, New York, NY, US (2002)

17. Demerouti, E.: Job characteristics, flow, and performance: the moderating role of conscientiousness. J. Occup. Health Psychol. (2006). https://doi.org/10.1037/1076-8998.11.3.266

18. Finding flow: the psychology of engagement with everyday life. Choice Rev. Online (1997). https://doi.org/10.5860/choice.35-1828

19. Csikszentmihalyi, M., LeFevre, J.: Optimal experience in work and leisure. J. Pers. Soc. Psychol. (1989). https://doi.org/10.1037/0022-3514.56.5.815

20. Fullagar, C., Fave, A.D., Van Krevelen, S.: Flow at work: The evolution of a construct. In: Flow at Work: Measurement and Implications (2017). https://doi.org/10.4324/9781315871585

21. Llorens, S., Salanova, M., Rodríguez, A.M.: How is flow experienced and by whom? Testing flow among occupations. Stress Heal. (2013). https://doi.org/10.1002/smi.2436

22. Fullagar, C.J., Kelloway, E.K.: "Flow" at work: an experience sampling approach. J. Occup. Organ. Psychol. (2009). https://doi.org/10.1348/096317908X357903

23. White, K., Schofield, G., Kilding, A.E.: Energy expended by boys playing active video games. J. Sci. Med. Sport. (2011). https://doi.org/10.1016/j.jsams.2010.07.005

24. Tyagi, A., Cohen, M., Reece, J., Telles, S.: An explorative study of metabolic responses to mental stress and yoga practices in yoga practitioners, non-yoga practitioners and individuals with metabolic syndrome. BMC Complement. Altern. Med. (2014). https://doi.org/10.1186/1472-6882-14-445

25. Piette, D., Berckmans, D., Aerts, J.-M., Claes, S.: Depression and burnout. A different perspective (2020)

26. Ainslie, P.N., Reilly, T., Westerterp, K.R.: Estimating human energy expenditure: a review of techniques with particular reference to doubly labelled water (2003). https://doi.org/10.2165/00007256-200333090-00004

27. Butte, N.F., Ekelund, U., Westerterp, K.R.: Assessing physical activity using wearable monitors: measures of physical activity. Med. Sci. Sports Exerc. **44**, 5–12 (2012). https://doi.org/10.1249/MSS.0b013e3182399c0e

28. Young, P.C.: Data-based mechanistic and topdown modelling. In: Proceedings International Environmental Modelling Software Society Conference (2002)

29. Jansen, F., et al.: Online detection of an emotional response of a horse during physical activity. Vet. J. (2009). https://doi.org/10.1016/j.tvjl.2009.03.017

30. Norton, T., Piette, D., Exadaktylos, V., Berckmans, D.: Automated real-time stress monitoring of police horses using wearable technology. Appl. Anim. Behav. Sci. (2018). https://doi.org/10.1016/j.applanim.2017.09.009

31. Bassi, M., Fave, A.D.: Optimal experience among teachers: New insights into the work paradox. J. Psychol. Interdiscip. Appl. (2012). https://doi.org/10.1080/00223980.2012.656156

32. Hektner, J., Schmidt, J., Csikszentmihalyi, M.: Experience Sampling Method (2007). https://methods.sagepub.com/book/experience-sampling-method, https://doi.org/10.4135/978141 2984201

33. Ebner-Priemer, U.W., Trull, T.J.: Ecological momentary assessment of mood disorders and mood dysregulation. Psychol. Assess. (2009). https://doi.org/10.1037/a0017075

34. Larson, R., Delespaul, P.A.E.G.: Analyzing Experience sampling data: a guide book for the perplexed. In: The Experience of Psychopathology (2010). https://doi.org/10.1017/cbo978 0511663246.007

35. Delle Fave, A., Bassi, M.: The quality of experience in adolescents' daily lives: developmental perspectives (2000)

36. Delle Fave, A., Massimini, F.: Optimal experience in work and leisure among teachers and physicians: Individual and bio-cultural implications. Leis. Stud. (2003). https://doi.org/10.1080/02614360310001594122

37. Carli, M., Massimini, F.: The systematic assessment of flow in daily experience. In: Optimal experience: Psychological studies of flow in consciousness (1988)

38. Delle Fave, A., Massimini, F.: The investigation of optimal experience and apathy: developmental and psychosocial implications. Eur. Psychol. (2005). https://doi.org/10.1027/1016-9040.10.4.264

Something Old, Something New, Something Inspired by Deep Blue?

A Scoping Review on the Digital Transformation of Office and Knowledge Work from the Perspective of OSH

Patricia Tegtmeier(✉) ⓘⒹ, Jan Terhoeven, and Sascha Wischniewski ⓘⒹ

Federal Institute for Occupational Safety and Health (BAuA) Unit Human Factors, Ergonomics, Friedrich-Henkel-Weg 1–25, 44149 Dortmund, Germany
{tegtmeier.patricia,terhoeven.jan,
wischniewski.sascha}@baua.bund.de

Abstract. The nature of work is constantly changing due to digitalization, raising the question about how to design human-centered work in the digital age. Focusing on office and knowledge work, the aim of this study was to conduct a structured literature review of the current state of research on new technologies in information-based tasks, to systematically map the characteristics and identify research topics used in the identified studies. In accordance with the PRISMA extension for scoping reviews, we searched the Web of Science, PubMed, and EBSCOhost databases for peer-reviewed journal articles and reviews published between 1 January 2007 and 31 December 2020. The screening process resulted in a final sample of 267 articles. Most of these articles were published in the second half of the search period, between 2014 and 2020. The charting process revealed three main research themes in the identified studies: (1) flexible workplaces, (2) human-technology interaction, (3) changing work tasks. Along this themes divided into further subtopics, we report the findings with respect to OSH as a short narrative synthesis and discuss the connections between the subtopics in terms of implications for occupational science research.

Keywords: Office work · Knowledge work · Digitalization · Well-being · Job satisfaction · Technology affordances · Occupational safety and health

1 Introduction

The way we work is continuously changing due to the ongoing digitization. The world of work is steadily shifting from physical work toward information and knowledge work [1]. Especially the latter, we can link to the constant evolution of information and communication technologies for more than 40 years [2, 3]. Most of the functionalities of digital work tools used in knowledge work have been around since the mid-1990s [3]. Looking at the possibilities offered by technologies for working with information, the emergence of tablet PCs and smartphones represents another evolutionary stage. Unlike notebooks, which may allow work in defined third locations, e.g., on the train, in a café,

© The Author(s), under exclusive license to Springer Nature Switzerland AG 2023
V. G. Duffy (Ed.): HCII 2023, LNCS 14028, pp. 459–477, 2023.
https://doi.org/10.1007/978-3-031-35741-1_34

or in the departure lounge, the use of smartphones also makes it possible to access work content unplanned and in passing, even in intermediate locations such as the elevator or on the sidewalk [2]. By now, almost 100 percent of information-based tasks at work are computer-aided.

The digital transformation of work is characterized by the mutual interactions between work tasks and the technologies used to perform them [4]: The choice of a specific technology can change task components, add new ones or eliminate them altogether. Equally, the specific activity influences the affordances of the (digital) work tools perceived by the users [5]. In this way, even the use of already established technologies can change given new contexts of use by changing organizational and socio-cultural factors and expectations of functionalities [6].

The resulting changes in the design of work have been a long-standing subject of research in occupational science. As early as 1996, recommendations derived from this research became part of the German Ordinance on Safety and Health Protection at Work with Display Screen Equipment. Since 2016, this has been an integral part of the Ordinance on Workplaces (No. 6 of the annex), extended to include initial requirements for portable display screen equipment for mobile use.

Since its beginnings, research on the digital transformation of office and knowledge work has grown increasingly differentiated. It encompasses various research topics covered by different academic disciplines. The amount of research contributions, each with a very specific focus, increases the danger of ignoring related strands of research, as they may simply use different terminology for their own research subject. Interdependencies of the use of digital technologies on different research strands can also become invisible. Moreover, practitioners in occupational safety and health find it difficult to extract coherent recommendations quickly. A scoping review can provide an overview mapping the volume, nature, and characteristics of a field of research.

Thus, the objectives of this study are: (i) conduct a systematic search of the published literature for empirical studies on the digital transformation of information-related work tasks and work-related outcomes (ii) systematically map the characteristics and identify research topics used in the identified studies and (iii) report findings with respect to OSH as a short narrative synthesis.

2   Study Design

This review was part of a broader research program. Alongside information-based tasks, the focus was also on object-based and people-related tasks as well as managing and leading under the heading of the digital transformation of the world of work. All scientists responsible for these four task components followed a jointly agreed research design.

We conducted a systematic search to identify literature on the digital transformation of information-related work tasks. Our Scoping Review was in accordance with the PRISMA extension for scoping reviews (PRISMA-ScR) [7]. Together, those responsible for the four task components developed parallelized review protocols prior to the start of the respective literature searches. These included the research questions, a description of the individual search steps as well as basic inclusion and exclusion criteria for the selection of publications. The protocol is not publicly available, but can be obtained from the corresponding author upon request.

2.1 Search Criteria

We used an extended version of the PICO (population, intervention, control and outcomes) format to precise the inclusion and exclusion criteria for articles as follows:

- **Population**: A study population relevant for office or knowledge workers or workplaces, aged 18–65 years, main tasks involve professional, managerial or administrative work (VDU users in an office setting, not manufacturing, health care or education). Patients and populations diagnosed with a disease were excluded.
- **Intervention**: Studies reporting the use of digital technologies for knowledge/office work or changes of work tasks associated with digital transformation. Laboratory studies were included if they were conducted in a way that simulated information-related activities in a work context.
- **Comparator:** Any comparator including no intervention
- **Outcomes:** At least one outcome measure described physical or psychosocial outcomes related to OSH. Studies aiming only to measure productivity were excluded.
- **Study Design:** All empirical research designs, both qualitative and quantitative findings. Non-empirical publications such as discussion articles, articles introducing theories/concepts/models/applications/editorials, and non-research-related publications were excluded. Systematic reviews and meta-analysis were included.
- **Others:** Articles published between 1 January 2007 and 31 December 2020 (including online first) in order to portrait contemporary effects of digital transformation on office and knowledge work. Only article written in English or German.

Because smartphones enable ubiquitous computing, we chose the year 2007 as the starting point for the literature review. Databases were Web of Science, PubMed, and EBSCOhost. In January and February 2021, we searched for peer-reviewed journal articles and reviews with the last search performed on 11. February 2021. As the aim of the review was to provide a representative (not fully comprehensive or precise) overview of a broad field of research, we did not include proceedings, reference lists, and gray literature in order to balance breadth with feasibility.

We used variants and combinations of search terms relating to 1) office or knowledge work, 2) various information and communication technologies or digitalization 3) OSH related outcomes, 4) highly interactive professions from the health sector and education/training. The terms within the four string categories were combined using a Boolean OR operator. The work task, technology, and outcome categories were then combined using a Boolean AND operator while the last string was used with a Boolean NOT operator as a criterion for exclusion.

2.2 Publication Selection

First, all references from the three databases were downloaded into Endnote, where duplicates were identified and removed. Studies were then screened first based on title and abstract, then by reading the full text to identify whether the manuscript met the following inclusion criteria: (1) Reference to digitization, (2) Outcome measures directly related to office or knowledge work, (3) Participants in employable age.

Based on the full-text, we excluded studies based on the following criteria: text not in English or German; work task not primarily information-based; missing digitization aspects; technology only as measurement instruments; technology development with usability tests only; development of measurement instruments; prevalence of technology use only; modeling only; methodological contributions; measured outcome productivity only. To increase the relevance for OSH in Germany, studies from countries that not comparable to Germany in terms of economic and social conditions or OSH standards (developing countries) are also excluded.

The lead reviewer (PT) screened the studies for inclusion, with a subsample done by the second author (JT). We resolved any disagreements through discussion, so that all articles had either relevant or irrelevant rating.

2.3 Data Charting and Synthesis

We jointly developed data extraction sheets to capture essential information based on the aims of our scoping review. In addition to predefined data extraction fields, we developed a coding scheme based on the content analysis according to [8] in order to identify recurrent research topics and sub-topics mentioned. Using a multi-stage procedure of category formation and coding, we first identified topics based on titles and abstracts of a randomly selected 1/5 of the articles. In accordance with the process character of qualitative research [9], we coded the entire material in a second run, while differentiating and supplementing the existing categories. In cases where multiple research topics could fit for the same study, we chose based on the main independent variable depicted, so that each study appeared in one topic only. We based the mapping of field of research on publication title and Web of Science categories. In case of multiple categories, we chose the most convenient field. We also selected only one study design per study. If a study measured multiple outcomes, we coded all individually.

Data extraction was performed by the lead reviewer (PT), with a subsample also charted by the second reviewer (JT), partly supported by additional members of the research team (MF, EH). We resolved all discrepancies by discussion and consensus and continuously updated the data-charting form in an iterative process.

The final extraction sheet consisted of seven sections: (1) publication details (author, year, title, aim); (2) research field (measured by publication) and research topic; (3) sample characteristics (sample size, country); (4) study design; (5) outcomes; (6) description of study results.

3 Results

The search of online databases initially retrieved 1130 records. Following de-duplication, we screened 564 records by title, abstract and keyword, of which 289 records continued to full-text screening. This led to a final sample of 267 articles, which we included in the review. Some articles presented the results of different studies. In other cases, separate articles reported different outcomes of the same study. In case of consecutive systematic review articles with the same first author and the same title, we included the most recent version as study. As such, our final sample counted 265 studies. Figure 1 summaries the selection process following the PRISMA flow diagram.

The categorization of the studies into research topics resulted in three content areas, which we further organized into eight subtopics. The first content area focuses on flexible workplaces with the two topics working outside the office and office concepts. The second describes human-technology interaction divided into physical effect of stationary and mobile visual display units (VDU) as well as use patterns as a third subtopic. Third, we subsumed the effects of communication and connectivity, cognitive assistance systems, and sedentary behavior in the theme of changing work tasks. Physical effects of stationary VDU (24.9%), working outside the office (20.4%) and sedentary behavior (19.6) were the most investigated, whereas studies on cognitive assistance systems (1.9%) appeared underrepresented.

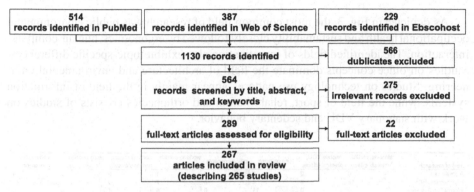

Fig. 1. PRISMA flowchart of the study selection process

3.1 General Characteristics of Included Studies

The majority of the 267 articles date in the second half of the search period. Seventy articles alone date from 2019 and 2020 with specific publication patterns emerging for the eight sub-topics (Fig. 2). For example, studies on working outside the office appear from the beginning of the search period. The number increases sharply in 2015. Studies on office concepts in connection with the digital transformation feature more strongly from 2017 onward. The use of stationary display units is a consistent topic throughout the search period, with the number of studies dropping slightly towards the end. Use patterns (especially with regard to nomadic working) gain momentum as a research topic from 2017 forward. Studies on changing work tasks due to the use of cognitive assistance systems occur sporadically starting in 2016. Studies on sedentary behavior show a strong upswing beginning in 2014, but the number of publications already drops somewhat in 2019.

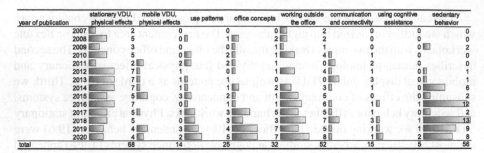

year of publication	stationary VDU, physical effects	mobile VDU, physical effects	use patterns	office concepts	working outside the office	communication and connectivity	using cognitive assistance	sedentary behavior
2007	2	0	0	0	2	0	0	0
2008	5	0	1	2	2	0	0	0
2009	3	0	0	1	0	0	0	2
2010	5	0	2	1	4	1	0	0
2011	2	2	2	1	0	2	0	0
2012	7	1	0	1	4	1	0	1
2013	7	1	1	0	0	3	0	1
2014	7	1	1	2	3	1	0	6
2015	5	3	2	1	5	0	0	2
2016	7	0	1	1	6	1	1	12
2017	5	1	3	5	5	1	0	2
2018	5	0	3	3	7	3	1	13
2019	4	3	4	7	5	1	1	9
2020	4	2	5	7	8	1	2	8
total	68	14	25	32	52	15	5	56

Fig. 2. Years of publication represented by the included articles, by sub topic

As depicted in Fig. 3, the most common field of research was public environmental occupational health and sustainability closely followed by ergonomics, human-computer interaction. The identified fields of investigation also exhibit topic-specific differences. Studies on office concepts dominate the field of architecture and environmental engineering. Studies on technology use patterns appear mainly in the field of information systems, while the field of sport, rehabilitation and orthopedics consists of studies on work with stationary VDU and sedentary behavior.

field of research	stationary VDU, physical effects	mobile VDU, physical effects	use patterns	office concepts	working outside the office	communication and connectivity	using cognitive assistance	sedentary behavior
Architecture	0	0	0	12	1	0	0	0
Ergonomics, HCI	18	6	4	8	7	0	1	23
Information Systems	0	0	11	0	6	7	3	0
Management	0	0	2	1	3	0	0	0
Medicine	12	2	0	1	0	1	0	8
Psychology	0	0	1	3	14	0	0	0
OSH, Sustainability	21	5	4	6	17	3	0	14
Sports, Rehabilitation	13	0	0	0	0	0	0	8
other fields	4	1	3	1	4	1	1	3
total	68	14	25	32	52	15	5	56

Fig. 3. Research fields represented by the included articles, by sub topic

study design	stationary VDU, physical effects	mobile VDU, physical effects	use patterns	office concepts	working outside the office	communication and connectivity	using cognitive assistance	sedentary behavior
RCT	13	6	0	2	2	0	0	18
non-randomized design	5	1	0	4	2	2	1	9
before-after study	8	0	1	6	6	2	0	2
cross-sectional study	19	1	11	7	20	3	1	4
interview study	0	0	9	1	8	2	1	2
observational study	2	2	1	0	1	0	0	1
multi-methods	2	1	5	8	5	6	2	1
narrative review	5	1	0	1	4	0	0	0
scoping review	1	1	0	1	0	0	0	3
systematic review	6	0	1	2	5	0	0	10
meta-analysis	5	0	0	0	1	0	0	2
total	66	13	28	32	54	15	5	52

Fig. 4. Study designs represented by the included studies, by sub topic

Correlational study (cross-sectional) was by far the most common study design and represented in all subtopics (Fig. 4). A total of 49 times a review variant appeared as study design. These mainly related to the subtopics physical effects of stationary VDU use and sedentary behavior. Also most prevalent in these two subtopics were randomized controlled trial or randomized crossover studies. Some form of qualitative study design prevailed in working outside the office, office concepts, use patterns, and communication and connectivity.

The included studies investigate very many different outcome variables (Fig. 5). The subtopics stationary and mobile visual display units (VDU) and sedentary behavior account for the majority of different measures of physical well-being. Although located in specific physical locations, the proportion of studies that have surveyed physical well-being in the subtopics office concepts as well as working outside the office is less than ten percent. The latter look primarily at work characteristics (26.1%), job and workplace satisfaction (22.6%), and mental well-being (20.0%). The top three outcomes measured in office concepts studies are job and workplace satisfaction (35.2%), execution of work tasks (19.7%), and well-being (18.3%).

outcomes	stationary VDU, physical effects	mobile VDU, physical effects	use patterns	office concepts	working outside the office	communication and connectivity	using cognitive assistance	sedentary behavior
mental well-being	3	0	15	13	23	8	0	6
physical well-being	66	11	0	6	4	0	0	42
job satisfaction	2	0	9	25	26	1	0	3
work characteristics	1	2	8	12	30	4	0	8
execution of work tasks	8	0	7	14	21	7	3	15
technology affordances	0	2	15	1	11	5	3	3
total	80	15	54	71	115	25	6	77

Fig. 5. Outcomes represented by the included studies, by sub topic

3.2 Research Topics

We report findings as a short narrative synthesis of the included studies differentiated by sub topics. The sources cited below represent examples. The extraction sheet containing all 267 articles is available as supplemental material on request from the corresponding author.

Working Outside the Office

The research on working outside the office (54 studies including 10 reviews) focuses in particular on the reconciliation of work and private life. With mobile, digital work tools such as notebooks, smartphones, and appropriate network connectivity, employees can perform most office and knowledge tasks from everywhere. The more established the workplace outside the company, the more well founded the studies. As such, studies on working at home are dominant whereas research concerning working while traveling or in third places like hotels or departure areas is sparse (8 studies). Studies of co-working spaces as workplace alternatives are emerging (7 studies). Existing ergonomic findings on mobile work in places, such as trains or hotels, point among other things to the respective environmental conditions and privacy issues as challenges for work design.

The literature reports both positive and negative associations between mobile work and employee well-being. Employees often experience mobile work as inspiring and liberating [10]. It is associated with positive emotions, increased job satisfaction and organizational commitment, and lower emotional exhaustion [11]. On the other hand, employees are easily available outside the company and at unusual times for work-related matters increasing the risk of extended working hours and less detachment from work.

Social and professional isolation are core challenges of mobile working identified in the literature. Direct face-to-face communication is discussed as important for maintaining work friendships and trust, and subsequently for professional exchange and social support. Technical support, organizational support, and potential of digital technologies to support interactions can counteract social and professional isolation. However, technology use can only support planned meetings [12, 13]. There is little or no evidence that working from home has a positive effect on work-life balance in general. With more experience in mobile work, the positive impact of mobile work increases slightly [12].

The temporal extent of working outside the office moderates almost all considered outcomes. Positive effects initially increase with duration, only to decrease again for 2.5 days and more [13]. Furthermore, autonomy and, in particular, time flexibility moderate various outcomes in part or in full [11]. While enhancing flexible, location-independent access to (work-relevant) information as an opportunity for better work-life balance, ICT at the same time pose a risk for losing this flexibility as well as the ability to work without distractions due to constant connectivity [14]. As such, another moderator identified in the literature are organizational culture and a constant availability pressure due to inner obligation and social norms at the workplace. Managing boundaries between work and private life arises as a separate task to avoid role conflicts. Personal preferences for separating or integrating work and private life are evident [15].

Studies of mobile working in co-working spaces indicate a high workplace satisfaction of users. Compared to working at home, co-working spaces offer a clearer separation from private life due to the spatial separation. Fixed opening hours also reduce the necessary self-organization. The reported subjective perception of the working environment is similar to open-plan offices, with unfavorable light, unfavorable climate, and higher noise levels and so on. The nevertheless high satisfaction with the co-working space was associated with a positive self-selection process [16].

Moving and secondary places are complex work environments. Especially in public places, a lack of privacy can hinder certain tasks in connection with data protection. Although similar in terms of many environmental factors, users prefer co-working spaces to working in cafes [17]. For the various activities in diverse environments, mobile workers must carry all their work equipment with them in order to be able to set up their workstation anywhere. Lack of IT support and limited access to networks can limit virtual workspace in mobile conditions. Working in incompatible physical spaces with limited space and behavioral norms of the physical environment such as designated quiet zones for communication needs or higher noise levels for concentration needs can limit tasks performance and influence employees' well-being [10, 18].

Office Concepts
A number of workplace articles (N = 32, including 4 reviews) focus on the flexibility provided by different office concepts, with particular attention to the benefits and risks of activity-based offices. Distinct zones optimized for specific tasks such as concentrated work or interactive exchange are central to this type of office. The activity-based choice of workplace envisaged here, with multiple changes during the working day, is only becoming feasible thanks to the current phase of digitization. In combination with working outside the office, in particular at home, activity-based offices often provide space for only 70 percent of employees. This variant eliminates fixed workstations for

employees (hot-desking). Especially compared with individual offices, these office land-scapes tend to be rated worse by employees in cross-sectional surveys [19]. Longitudinal studies point to an excessive utilization of the existing workplaces and an insufficient number of workplaces for concentrated work as a widespread problem. In this context, the risk of nest-building tendencies is pointed out, in which early arrivers take advantage of the free choice of places and always reserve the same places for themselves and, in some cases, for colleagues [20, 21]. Furthermore, people are more difficult to find due to changing seats. The literature also shows less informal exchange and a loss of team spirit [20]. Employees under hot-desking conditions also express hygiene concerns, especially during the cold season. In general, satisfaction with the new premises is a positive aspect of the changeover. One opportunity is breaking up one's own routine by being able to choose between workplaces and to improve contact and exchange with colleagues from other departments. In this case, it can lead to an expansion of the team feeling to the whole company [22].

In order to realize the benefits of activity-based office design, the subjective fit between activities and available space is crucial. This requires an appropriate mix of areas that promote communication and collaboration and those that allow for concentration and privacy, both for individuals and groups [21, 22]. Activity-based workspaces may be appropriate for work tasks that require a high degree of cross-team communication and collaboration. Intra-team communication and collaboration should occur in traditional combination offices. In addition to the task, social relationships, norms, the effort required to change location, and place attachment potentially influence the use of different workspaces. Here, research indicate that additional organizational support with clear usage rules may be necessary, starting from the very beginning of implementation [21, 23].

Physical Effects of Working with VDU
The majority of the studies included in this review focused on physical effects of working with VDU (N = 79 (66 stationary, 13 mobile VDU), including 19 reviews). With regard to the physical and cognitive ergonomics of stationary VDU work, many scientific findings have already found their way into statutory occupational health and safety.

Musculoskeletal and visual complaints continue to be current topics for ICT-supported information-related activities. Typical musculoskeletal symptoms of computer users include neck, back, shoulder, wrist, and finger pain triggered by posture during computer work. For example, improper positioning of the screen or keyboard can lead to awkward posture and muscular strain [24, 25]. Also mentioned in connection with computer work are visual complaints. Specifically discussed are anomalies in fixation, accommodation and dry eyes. Significant interactions between symptoms of the eyes and in the neck have also been reported [25]. Intervention studies on physical complaints in the context of VDU work indicate varying degrees of effectiveness. For example, storage surfaces to support the forearms and using the mouse in a neutral posture are associated with a lower incidence of neck pain and a reduction in right upper extremity discomfort. Adjusting the workstation and usage of standing desks have no effect on upper limb pain compared to no intervention Additional breaks during data entry can reduce neck and upper limb discomfort. In contrast, training-only interventions show no effect on upper limb pain compared with no intervention. Evidence for an effect of physical activity in the development of neck pain has been insufficient or controversial to date [24].

The use of mobile digital work devices may be associated with further physical stress. In addition to a desktop configuration set up with an external keyboard and mouse, notebooks are also portable devices. Knowledge workers use notebooks cross-legged, lying down, on the lap, or on non-adjustable work surfaces, without external keyboards, pointing devices, or monitors. Depending on the posture considered, studies report severe neck flexion and pain and/or high muscle activity in the shoulder and pain in the upper back and wrist [26, 27]. In general, the use of accessories such as external keyboards, pointing devices and monitors is recommended to improve posture and well-being. However, this may not always be possible depending on the space available in various mobile work locations. Alternatively, when using a notebook in unfavorable postures, it is recommended to work only for short periods [26, 27]. Smartphones and tablets differ from desktop computers in terms of viewing angle, distance, screen size and brightness, method, and usage patterns. Ocular discomfort is discussed along with symptoms similar to those experienced with desktop computer use including changes in accommodation, decreased convergence, or a negative impact on tear stability. In addition, depending on the specific configuration of the users, the use of tablets and smartphones leads to various non-neutral postures that may be associated with risks for musculoskeletal disorders [27]. Different patterns of combined ICT use in the work environment can be identified here, with varying degrees of mobility and total time spent on ICT use. In this context, different patterns of use lead to differences in the incidence of ocular and musculoskeletal complaints [28].

Use Patterns of Technologies

Studies found on use patterns of digital technologies for office and knowledge work (N = 28, including 1 review) describe the use of ICTs as both beneficial and detrimental resulting in a parallel increase in well-being on the one hand and digital-related stress on the other. Categories of stressors that emerged most often are changes in boundaries between work and private life, constant availability (including an inner obligation for availability), connectivity pressure, and increased workload. Work emails and the use of ICT continuing work tasks at home were associated with lower detachment from work. At the same time, employees also describe the use of mobile email devices as a buffer for their availability. Improved communication, instant accessibility, and increased flexibility and independence were benefits resulting of the technologies used [6, 29]. The digital transformation of the world of work thus simplifies access to relevant information related to professional activities; at the same time, it may require increased effort to synthesize and process the large amount of available information [30]. If work is greatly dependent on the technology, non-functioning systems are one of the major constraints for work.

At the office, environment and technology are set up for efficiency as well as personalization in a (semi-)permanent way. Employees cannot easily replicate this away from the office. Reproducing the experience of being in an office needs more time and effort, especially for nomadic employees. The mobile office relies heavily on technological infrastructure resulting in additional things to transport. Notebooks are the primary resource for communication and information work, supplemented by other components such as smartphones, noise-canceling headphones, and various adapters [31].

Communication and Connectivity
A number of studies (N = 15) discuss communication and connectivity in knowledge work. Interruptions and information overload, e.g., through e-mail communication, are already widespread in everyday office life. Mobile workers are even more dependent on various digital ICT for synchronous and asynchronous team communication. The nature of their work tasks influences digitally mediated interruptions even more than in the office. If the work task is independent of other team members, asynchronous communication can reduce the number of interruptions and requests and can thus support, for example, more efficiency and concentration on the tasks in the self-selected work at home. If, on the other hand, tasks of different team members are dependent on each other, communication is already part of the work task. If the team members are distributed across multiple work locations, every communication proceeds via digital media such as e-mail, web conferencing systems, or chat programs. This often results in further communication and the need for clarification. The amount of information conveyed digitally and the interruptions can thus increase significantly. Trying to minimize delays in interdependent tasks increases the risk of constant connectivity, omnipresence of digital technologies and media and a loss of flexibility [32]. Depending on the actual work location, distributed team members may also work in different time zones. This can result in unfavorable working time situations for individuals in the team, especially when using synchronous meetings via web conferencing systems [33].

Using Cognitive Assistance Systems
In view of potential changes in work tasks, some studies research the use cognitive assistance systems for information-based tasks, especially based on artificial intelligence (AI) (N = 5). In this context, AI-assisted automation can range from task substitution to task augmentation to task merging, where AI and humans function as an integrated unit. With the exception of substitution, organizational decisions regarding the division of labor between the algorithm and humans become critical here [34]. Also discussed is the use of algorithms and implications of their use on decision-making processes and associated risks. If sufficiently large training data sets are available, machine learning can produce programs that outperform humans in accomplishing specific tasks. As a result, the share of monitoring tasks may also increase in the area of office and knowledge work. When inconsistencies and malfunctions of AI-supported systems are rare, these becomes very difficult for users to detect [35].

Cognitive assistance and knowledge management systems offer one way to keep the volume and complexity of information manageable for humans. However, algorithm-based assistance systems while showing potential, may not meet the expectations and personal requirements without a high degree of customization and personalization [36].

Sedentary Behavior
The increase in information-related activities increases the proportion of jobs in which the degree of physical task elements decreases. On the topic of avoiding sedentary

behavior (N = 52, including 15 reviews) associated with increased use of digital technologies, a number of studies on various activating interventions and their effectiveness are already available. Compared to conventional office workplaces with a (static) desk, height-adjustable desks or combined sit-stand workplaces can reduce employees' sitting time by up to two hours per workday. However, in contrast to dynamic workstations, e.g., treadmill or bicycle desks, these hardly contribute to increasing energy consumption [37, 38]. Although dynamic workstations can improve physiological parameters and the energy balance of employees, their use also seems to be associated with limitations in work performance [38]. Training and advisory services for employees supported by organizational measures also rate as effective overall. Instead of carrying out physical activities during breaks, it makes more sense to make them an integral part of work. Here, the use of computer, mobile and wearable technologies to reduce sitting time may hold promise for large-scale, cost-effective interventions [39]. In terms of reducing sedentary behavior, interventions related to the work environment and multi-component interventions are more successful compared to interventions related to the individual [38].

4 Discussion

This scoping review aimed at systematically mapping the characteristics and research topics in studies on the digital transformation of information-based work tasks and work-related outcomes including a short narrative synthesis of the findings with respect to OSH. The 265 included studies were from a variety of disciplines and had differences in study design and outcomes measures.

The main theme of the articles is mobile work enabled by digitization. This topic initially links the studies within the identified overarching theme of flexible locations. Under the keyword New Ways of Working, several studies present connections between new office concepts and the possibilities of working outside the office, especially from home. The use of the home as a place for concentrated and quiet work is also outlined here, in cases where this is made more difficult due to the unfavorable design of new office space in the company. This extends the person-environment fit model discussed in the topic area of working from home to include the aspect of work tasks. If the work task takes primacy, the risk arises that the choice of environment may be sub-optimal for the respective person. In particular, the proportion of highly complex tasks that require quiet, undisturbed workspaces should be quantified prior to conversion. With a takeover of routine tasks by algorithms, an increase of this task share is rather expected [23]. Unfavorable conditions that force a particular choice of location should be avoided and genuine freedom of choice of location should be made possible.

Especially working at home can look back on several decades of research tradition. The opportunities and risks of work made possible by ICT listed here are complex and multi-factorial. The focus of the studies is primarily on psychosocial effects on employees. The findings essentially reflect the working situation before the Covid-19 pandemic. Specifically for working from home and its effect on employees, possible changes in the follow-up to the Covid-19 pandemic measures should also be further monitored: Prior, employees working from home were generally a positive self-selection of privileged employees [40]. Due to the lockdown, home office working increased significantly during the pandemic, especially in the knowledge work sector [41]. This trend is expected to continue after the pandemic [42].

The emerging research on co-working spaces as an alternative to working from home also appears significant, especially from the perspective of the New Ways of Working. In combination with new activity-based office concepts, this offers opportunities to cushion social isolation and blurring boundaries between work and private life. However, the selection of co-working spaces should include OSH aspects.

Only a small proportion of studies are available on working in trains and other modes of transportation, as well as public places such as hotels, libraries, and cafes. Although not primarily intended as places for work, this is surprising as working on trains, in airplanes and in waiting areas on business trips is widespread, and digital nomads are described as a new prototype especially in knowledge work [43].

Under the heading of nomadic work, there are several links to human-computer interaction. Use patterns of technologies illustrate the use of a wide variety of ICT for knowledge work outside the office. Employees working at home and other workplaces are heavily dependent on the availability and functionality of ICT. At the same time, personal responsibility for availability is also increasing because employees themselves provide some of the work equipment (such as routers, monitors and printers). Mobile office and knowledge workers carry their digital work tools with them in order to be ready for different situations at different locations. Only if employees are aware of the technical and other affordances available at these locations, they can complete work tasks as planned. Lack of IT support and limited access to networks can limit the virtual workspace in mobile environments. Combined with additional work requirements, this can increase employee strain. This extends the familiar task-technology fit model by the aspect of location to a task-technology-environment fit.

With regard to physical effects of VDU work, tasks that involve prolonged text entries require an external keyboard and mouse. The extensive literature on the ergonomics of stationary VDU work links with working from home or in co-working spaces as semi-stationary places in order to derive recommendations for safe and healthy work design here as well. All the more striking is the small number of studies in the sub-theme of flexible places that have looked at physical outcomes.

The less space the mobile work environment offers, the more likely employees only will use notebooks without external keyboard and mouse or handheld devices such as smartphones and tablet-PCs as indicated in the studies on use patterns of technology. The use of these devices for work results in new, interrelated challenges for occupational health and safety [44]. In traditional VDU work, employees generally have fixed workstations including furniture. Here, a one-time adjustment, e.g. supported by the occupational health and safety specialist, is often sufficient to optimize the workplace. If employees change their workplace more frequently, individual ergonomic advice for each workplace becomes difficult. Being able to work anywhere and at any time means that mobile workers have to design their own working environment. Not all employees have sufficient knowledge or are able to apply this knowledge to their environment and work equipment. The risk increases of adapting to inadequate working conditions [44]. The use of mobile devices in mobile work contexts increases the importance of physical ergonomics. The studies found on the physical effects of mobile VDU work provide initial OSH-related findings here.

Although depicted for years in videos on the office work of the (respective) future, gesture and voice control as well as virtual screens have not yet arrived in the everyday lives of knowledge workers. Studies of immersive technologies in office and knowledge work currently tend to appear in proceedings and were therefore not present in the studies reviewed.

Further interconnections under the overarching theme of mobile work can be found with the sub topics communication and connectivity, use patterns, working outside the office, as well as office concepts. Looking at the timing of the publications, there seems to have been a shift of the communication and connectivity theme towards working outside the office. Because mobile knowledge workers intensively rely on ICT for information gathering and communication at different locations, they are especially prone to interruptions and information overload due to email, web conference systems, instant messages, or chat programs. So far, research has paid little attention to the impact of necessary communication and connectivity in connection with the newly discussed office concepts. The extent to which existing technology in combination with the room concepts avoids disruptions to colleagues who are present could also have an impact here on the "free" choice of workplace. As can be seen in the topic of working outside the office, communication is gaining in importance at the same time in order to counteract professional and social isolation. Face-to-face communication is discussed as an important building block for relationship and trust building in the work environment. Both are important factors for professional exchange and social support. When working outside the office or in activity-based office concepts in distributed teams, the social work space is interrupted. Especially for mobile working, web conferencing systems can be an important tool for virtual team communication and synchronous exchange in projects. However, technology use can only support scheduled meetings. They cannot replace informal meetings in the kitchenette [33, 45]. The question arises as to the extent to which the above-mentioned forms of communication are feasible for distributed teams in different office concepts.

Two of the identified subtopics stand somewhat apart at first glance. The first is research on sedentary behavior. At present, this research is predominantly linked to the physical effects of stationary VDU work, as both focus on the physical consequences of digital office work. Due to the now high number of office and knowledge workers, these effects of increased sitting are significant in the course of the digital transformation of work. However, only stationary VDU workplaces have been considered so far. Especially against the background of increasing local flexibility of employees and the associated work environments and workplaces, a new connection between working outside the office and sedentary behavior opens up.

The second topic with rather little overlap with the other research fields is cognitive assistance systems in the area of office and knowledge work. With the examined outcome of technology affordances, there are some overlaps with the sub topic of use patterns of technology. AI-based assistance systems such as knowledge management systems or chatbots are discussed in terms of their impact within a human-machine collaboration, the degree of automation, the expectation and acceptance of the end users, and the transparency of the systems and the decisions made by them. However, none of the studies found dealt with the outcomes of mental well-being or job satisfaction. Little is known about the impact of AI-based cognitive assistance on employees and organizations, or about generalizable outcomes in terms of principles for design and use [46].

4.1 Implications for Further Research

A central goal of this review on the digital transformation of office and knowledge work was to systematize the research literature in a way that makes cross-connections and research gaps more readily apparent, thereby helping researchers identify research gaps and design future studies. Based on the reported content and characteristics of the included studies, here are first ideas for subsequent research in the area of digital transformation of office and knowledge work and occupational safety and health.

Although there is already a substantial body of research literature on working from home, it remains to be evaluated whether the above findings are still representative in light of the changes following the Covid-19 pandemic. In addition, research linking new office concepts, working from home, and co-working spaces to OSH outcomes seems promising. In the context of this, the view of physical outcomes when working outside of the office could also expand. The success of interventions for more physical activity in different workplaces could also become another topic for research.

Also embedded in the topic of mobile work, research on working while traveling and in third locations could be intensified in order to provide companies and employees with information on the possibilities of work design. Here, links to studies on the physical effects of working with mobile VDUs and findings relevant to occupational health and safety present themselves.

At the junction of the four subtopics communication and connectivity, use patterns, working outside the office, as well as office concepts interdisciplinary research examining the effects on employees under a combined task-technology-person-environment-fit model would be useful for deriving OSH-relevant findings.

Finally yet importantly in the emerging field of cognitive assistance systems for office and knowledge work, an expansion of outcomes measured would be desirable.

4.2 Strengths and Limitations

We see the strength of this review in the breadth of the search, through which, in addition to the eight identified topics on the digital transformation of office and knowledge work, the connections between these topics as well as research gaps became visible. Another strength of this study is the consistent use of transparent methods throughout the process. We initially conducted both the in-depth review of articles for selection and the data charting independently with two reviewers (authors one and two). Only after the independent review revealed very similar data from both reviewers and, in the case of the data charting, extraction sheet was finalized, did one reviewer work on the remaining articles alone.

The study has some limitations that need to be considered. We deliberately limited the literature search to peer-reviewed articles in order to keep the number of articles manageable. However, this leaves out scientific findings from other formats like books, gray literature, and proceedings. Especially in the field of cognitive assistance systems and AI-supported systems in office and knowledge work, these gray literature and proceedings are currently more widely used. A systematic review for this research topic that includes all source formats would therefore be appropriate.

The included studies resulted from database searches only. We added no articles based on forward or backward searches using the reviews and or bibliographies. Some relevant studies were therefore certainly not included if our search string did not match the metadata of the articles. However, our goal was also to provide a representative, if not complete, overview. Due to the total number of studies considered, we anticipated that this would be the case.

Furthermore, we did not assess the quality of the included studies. Therefore, based on this review, no gaps in the literature regarding the quality of the studies are apparent.

5 Conclusions

A current core topic in scientific research on digital change in information and knowledge work is the mobility and flexibility of time and place and the associated opportunities and risks. The more established and integrated into the work organization the digital work equipment and workplaces are, the more likely it is that there are already reliable findings on design recommendations for information-based tasks. Generally known and established design recommendations for occupational safety and health in knowledge work as VDU work, which have already found expression in regulations and ordinances, also retain their significance in the current phase of the digital transformation of work. Here, it is also important to consider VDU workplaces outside the company in a suitable form. In other areas, the impact of digitization on the world of work is already the subject or academic debate, but is still rather at the beginning of the research process in terms of OSH recommendations. For example, there are no scientifically based recommendations on the intensity of use of mobile digital work equipment. Other areas that can be expanded in terms of derivable recommendations for information-related activities are the use of artificial intelligence for decision-making processes and information organization, chatbot support and the effects of VR and AR in knowledge work.

Acknowledgements. We like to thank Mohamed Faily, Eva Heinold, and Tomas Allis for their contributions in the review process.

Contributions. Concept development and Design: PT, JT, SW; Data collection/processing: PT, JT; Literature search: PT; Analysis/interpretation: PT, JT; Writing: PT; Critical review: PT, JT, SW

Funding. No external funding was received for this study.

Conflict of Interests. The authors declare that they have no competing interests.

References

1. van Laar, E., van Deursen, A.J.A.M., van Dijk, J.A.G.M., de Haan, J.: Determinants of 21st-century digital skills: A large-scale survey among working professionals. Comput. Hum. Behav. **100**, 93–104 (2019). https://doi.org/10.1016/j.chb.2019.06.017
2. Messenger, J.C.: Introduction: telework in the 21st century - an evolutionary perspective. In; Messenger, J.C. (eds.) Telework in the 21st century: An evolutionary perspective, pp. 1–34. Edward Elgar Pub., Elgaronline (2019). https://doi.org/10.4337/9781789903751.00005
3. Pliskin, N.: The telecommuting paradox. Inf. Technol. People **10**(2), 164–172 (1997). https://doi.org/10.1108/09593849710175002
4. Hacker, W., Sachse, P.: Allgemeine Arbeitspsychologie. Psychische Regulation von Tätigkeiten. 3., vollständig überarbeitete Auflage. Hogrefe, Göttingen (2014)
5. Norman, D.: The Design of Everyday Things: Revised and, Expanded Basic Books, New York (2013)
6. Mazmanian, M., Orlikowski, W., Yates, J.: The autonomy paradox: the implications of mobile email devices for knowledge professionals. Organ. Sci. **24**, 1337–1357 (2013). https://doi.org/10.1287/orsc.1120.0806
7. Tricco, A.C., et al.: PRISMA extension for scoping reviews (PRISMA-ScR): checklist and explanation. Ann. Intern. Med. **169**(7), 467–473 (2018). https://doi.org/10.7326/m18-0850%m30178033
8. Mayring, P., Fenzl, T.: Qualitative Inhaltsanalyse. In: Baur, N., Blasius, J. (eds.) Handbuch Methoden der empirischen Sozialforschung, pp. 543–556. Springer, Wiesbaden (2014). https://doi.org/10.1007/978-3-531-18939-0_38
9. Lamnek, S., Krell, C.: Qualitative Sozialforschung. Beltz, Weinheim (2016)
10. Koroma, J., Hyrkkänen, U., Vartiainen, M.: Looking for people, places and connections: Hindrances when working in multiple locations: a review. New Technol. Work Employ. **29** (2014). https://doi.org/10.1111/ntwe.12030
11. Charalampous, M., Grant, C.A., Tramontano, C., Michailidis, E.: Systematically reviewing remote e-workers' well-being at work: a multidimensional approach. Eur. J. Work Organ. Psy. **28**(1), 51–73 (2019). https://doi.org/10.1080/1359432X.2018.1541886
12. Suh, A., Lee, J.: Understanding teleworkers' technostress and its influence on job satisfaction. Internet Res. **27**(1), 140–159 (2017). https://doi.org/10.1108/IntR-06-2015-0181
13. Oakman, J., Kinsman, N., Stuckey, R., Graham, M., Weale, V.: A rapid review of mental and physical health effects of working at home: how do we optimise health? BMC Public Health **20**(1), 1825 (2020). https://doi.org/10.1186/s12889-020-09875-z
14. Leonardi, P.M., Treem, J.W., Jackson, M.H.: The connectivity paradox: using technology to both decrease and increase perceptions of distance in distributed work arrangements. J. Appl. Commun. Res. **38**(1), 85–105 (2010). https://doi.org/10.1080/00909880903483599
15. Ciolfi, L., Lockley, E.: From work to life and back again: examining the digitally-mediated work/life practices of a group of knowledge workers. Comput. Support. Coop. Work (CSCW) **27**(3–6), 803–839 (2018). https://doi.org/10.1007/s10606-018-9315-3
16. Robelski, S., Keller, H., Harth, V., Mache, S.: Co-working spaces: the better home office? a psychosocial and health-related perspective on an emerging work environment. Int. J. Environ. Res. Public Health **16**(13), 2379 (2019). https://doi.org/10.3390/ijerph16132379
17. Jarrahi, M.H., Nelson, S.B., Thomson, L.: Personal artifact ecologies in the context of mobile knowledge workers. Comput. Hum. Behav. **75**, 469–483 (2017). https://doi.org/10.1016/j.chb.2017.05.028
18. Janneck, M., Jent, S., Weber, P., Nissen, H.: Ergonomics to go: designing the mobile workspace. Int. J. Hum.-Comput. Interact. **34**(11), 1052–1062 (2018). https://doi.org/10.1080/10447318.2017.1413057

19. Pitchforth, J., Nelson-White, E., van den Helder, M., Oosting, W.: The work environment pilot: an experiment to determine the optimal office design for a technology company. PLoS ONE 15(5), e0232943 (2020). https://doi.org/10.1371/journal.pone.0232943
20. Rolfö, L., Eklund, J., Jahncke, H.: Perceptions of performance and satisfaction after relocation to an activity-based office. Ergonomics 61(5), 644–657 (2018). https://doi.org/10.1080/001 40139.2017.1398844
21. Brunia, S., De Been, I., van der Voordt, T.J.M.: Accommodating new ways of working: lessons from best practices and worst cases. J. Corp. Real Estate 18(1), 30–47 (2016). https://doi.org/10.1108/JCRE-10-2015-0028
22. Gerdenitsch, C., Korunka, C., Hertel, G.: Need-supply fit in an activity-based flexible office: a longitudinal study during relocation. Environ. Behav. 50, 001391651769776 (2017). https://doi.org/10.1177/0013916517697766
23. Hoendervanger, J.G., Van Yperen, N.W., Mobach, M.P., Albers, C.J.: Perceived fit in activity-based work environments and its impact on satisfaction and performance. J. Environ. Psychol. 65 (2019). https://doi.org/10.1016/j.jenvp.2019.101339
24. Jun, D., Zoe, M., Johnston, V., O'Leary, S.: Physical risk factors for developing non-specific neck pain in office workers: a systematic review and meta-analysis. Int. Arch. Occup. Environ. Health 90(5), 373–410 (2017). https://doi.org/10.1007/s00420-017-1205-3
25. Mehra, D., Galor, A.: Digital screen use and dry eye: a review. Asia-Pac. J. Ophthalmol. 9(6), 491–497 (2020). https://doi.org/10.1097/apo.0000000000000328
26. Intolo, P., Shalokhon, B., Wongwech, G., Wisiasut, P., Nanthavanij, S., Baxter, D.G.: Analysis of neck and shoulder postures, and muscle activities relative to perceived pain during laptop computer use at a low-height table, sofa and bed. Work 63, 361–367 (2019). https://doi.org/10.3233/WOR-192942
27. Dennerlein, J.T.: The state of ergonomics for mobile computing technology. Work 52, 269–277 (2015). https://doi.org/10.3233/WOR-152159
28. Soria-Oliver, M., Lopez, J.S., Torrano, F., Garcia-Gonzalez, G., Lara, A.: New patterns of information and communication technologies usage at work and their relationships with visual discomfort and musculoskeletal diseases: results of a cross-sectional study of Spanish organizations. Int. J. Environ. Res. Public Health 16(17), 17 (2019). https://doi.org/10.3390/ijerph16173166
29. Berg-Beckhoff, G., Nielsen, G., Ladekjær Larsen, E.: Use of information communication technology and stress, burnout, and mental health in older, middle-aged, and younger workers - results from a systematic review. Int. J. Occup. Environ. Health 23(2), 160–171 (2017). https://doi.org/10.1080/10773525.2018.1436015
30. Vuori, V., Helander, N., Okkonen, J.: Digitalization in knowledge work: the dream of enhanced performance. Cogn. Technol. Work , 1–16 (2018). https://doi.org/10.1007/s10111-018-0501-3
31. Mark, G., Su, N.M.: Making infrastructure visible for nomadic work. Pervasive Mob. Comput. 6(3), 312–323 (2010). https://doi.org/10.1016/j.pmcj.2009.12.004
32. Dery, K., Kolb, D., MacCormick, J.: Working with connective flow: how smartphone use is evolving in practice. Eur. J. Inf. Syst. 23(5), 558–570 (2014). https://doi.org/10.1057/ejis.2014.13
33. Bosch-Sijtsema, P.M., Fruchter, R., Vartiainen, M., Ruohomäki, V.: A framework to analyze knowledge work in distributed teams. Group Org. Manag. 36(3), 275–307 (2011). https://doi.org/10.1177/1059601111403625
34. Grønsund, T., Aanestad, M.: Augmenting the algorithm: emerging human-in-the-loop work configurations. J. Strateg. Inf. Syst. 29(2), 101614 (2020). https://doi.org/10.1016/j.jsis.2020.101614
35. Sawyer, B.D., Hancock, P.A.: Hacking the human: the prevalence paradox in cybersecurity. Hum. Factors 60(5), 597–609 (2018). https://doi.org/10.1177/0018720818780472

36. Kanza, S., Gibbins, N., Frey, J.G.: Too many tags spoil the metadata: investigating the knowledge management of scientific research with semantic web technologies. J. Cheminf. **11**(1), 1–23 (2019). https://doi.org/10.1186/s13321-019-0345-8

37. Shrestha, N., Kukkonen-Harjula, K.T., Verbeek, J.H., Ijaz, S., Hermans, V., Pedisic, Z.: Workplace interventions for reducing sitting at work. Cochrane Database Syst. Rev. (12), 184 (2018). https://doi.org/10.1002/14651858.CD010912.pub5

38. Backé, E.M., Kreis, L., Latza, U.: Interventionen am Arbeitsplatz, die zur Veränderung des Sitzverhaltens anregen. Zentralblatt für Arbeitsmedizin, Arbeitsschutz und Ergonomie **69**(1), 1-10 (2019). https://doi.org/10.1007/s40664-018-0284-7

39. Huang, Y., Benford, S., Blake, H.: Digital interventions to reduce sedentary behaviors of office workers: scoping review. J. Med. Internet Res. **21**(2) (2019). https://doi.org/10.2196/11079

40. Sostero, M., Milasi, S., Hurley, J., Fernández-Macías, E., Bisello, M.; Teleworkability and the COVID-19 crisis: a new digital divide? (working paper). In: European Commission, JRC121193, Seville (2020)

41. Molino, M., et al.: Well-being costs of technology use during COVID-19 remote working: an investigation using the Italian translation of the technostress creators scale. Sustainability **12**(15), 5911 (2020). https://doi.org/10.3390/su12155911

42. Backhaus, N., Tisch, A., Kagerl, C., Pohlan, L. Working from home in the corona crisis: What's next? (BAuA: Report brief). BAuA, Dortmund (2021). https://doi.org/10.21934/baua:report brief20201123

43. Ciolfi, L., de Carvalho, A.F.P.: Work practices, nomadicity and the mediational role of technology. Comput. Support. Coop. Work (CSCW) **23**(2), 119–136 (2014). https://doi.org/10.1007/s10606-014-9201-6

44. Long, J., Richter, H.: The pitfalls of the traditional office ergonomics model in the current mobile work environment: is visual ergonomics health literacy the remedy? Work **63**, 1 (2019). https://doi.org/10.3233/WOR-192937

45. van der Meulen, N., van Baalen, P., van Heck, E., Mulder, S.: No teleworker is an island: The impact of temporal and spatial separation along with media use on knowledge sharing networks. J. Inf. Technol. **34**(3), 243–262 (2019). https://doi.org/10.1177/0268396218816531

46. Meyer von Wolff, R., Hobert, S., Schumann, M.: Einsatz von Chatbots am digitalen Büroarbeitsplatz – Eine praxisorientierte Betrachtung von Einsatzbereichen, Wirkungen und Handlungsempfehlungen. HMD Praxis der Wirtschaftsinformatik **57**(3), 413-431 (2020). https://doi.org/10.1365/s40702-020-00602-1

Description of Sequential Risky Decision-Making Choices in Human-Machine Teams Using Eye-Tracking and Decision Tree

Wei Xiong [ID], Chen Wang [ID], and Liang Ma [✉] [ID]

Lab of Enhanced Human-Machine Collaborative Decision-Making,
Department of Industrial Engineering, Tsinghua University, Beijing 100084, China
liangma@mail.tsinghua.edu.cn

Abstract. Human-machine collaboration has shown great potential in sequential risky decision-making (SRDM). Human decision-makers made their decisions depending on the condition and their machine teammates. This paper aimed to explore attentional behaviors and decision-making processes under two human-machine collaboration contexts. To this end, 25 participants were asked to complete a modified Balloon Analog Risk Task with a highly accurate machine under different human-machine teams (HMTs). We collected and analyzed task performance, decision-making choices, eye-tracking data and subjective data. We employed the decision tree algorithm to describe decision-making processes and tested the performance through resubstitution validation and train-test validation. We found that both HMTs achieved comparable performance. Participants in the human-dominated team paid more attention to the machine-recommended value while participants in the human-machine joint team paid more attention to the inflation information of the machine. There were significant associations between choice ratios of inflation alternatives and decision choices for most subjects in both HMTs. In the human-machine joint team, we found a correlation between task profits and the fixation count on machine recommended value ($r = 0.40$, $p = 0.05$), and a correlation between the number of total explosions and the fixation count on whether the machine recommending to pump or not ($r = -0.36$, $p = 0.07$). Decision tree algorithm could cover and describe at least 67% of the decision-making choices and performed differently when subjects took different strategies. Our results revealed that eye-tracking and decision tree can be potential tools to describe and understand human SRDM behaviors.

Keywords: Human-machine collaboration · Balloon Analog Risk Task (BART) · Human-machine team (HMT) · Eye-tracking · Decision tree

1 Introduction

Sequential risky decision-making (SRDM) refers to continuous risk-taking, in which the decision-maker makes decisions in uncertain and risky situations, and previous

Supported by the National Natural Science Foundation of China [Grant Nos. 72192824 and 71942005].

decisions and decision outcomes affect the current decision [23]. SRDM is common in investment decision-making, such as in stock exchanges. Our previous research has proven that human-machine teams (HMTs) with different human-machine collaboration modes could achieve superior performance and avoid losses in an SRDM experimental task [24]. Moreover, considerable research has focused on developing and comparing the effectiveness of more equal HMTs in various decision-making situations [5,10,21]. Thus, the development of novel HMTs is promising for facilitating the performance of SRDM.

With the development and increased decision authority of machines, human decision-makers will share decisions with highly accurate machines in different HMTs. This would promote higher requirements for collaboration and introduce more uncertainty [18] and elicit behavioral changes of human decision-makers [20]. Our previous research found that humans became more conservative and fluctuating in SRDM and more sensitive to previous results (loss/gain) of the last trial [24]. In this study, the two HMTs avoided the overconfident behaviors of human decision-makers in different ways. The human-dominated team recommended participants end inflation while the human-machine joint team eliminated overconfidence by using their veto power [24]. Although our previous study focused more on the decision-making behaviors along with the human-machine interaction process than other research did, it did not capture the decision-making mechanism and the attentional behavior associated with each pumping decision. Understanding the underlying human-machine collaboration mechanism helps the machine teammate build a mental model of human decision-makers and enables us to predict human SRDM behaviors in different HMTs.

Attentional behaviors are observable indicators that have been used to display and predict some unobservable decision processes [2]. Eye-tracking is a non-invasive technology and the extracted indicators could reflect different information processing [1]. Studies have shown that the decision to choose one option from multiple alternatives can be predicted by gaze dwell time, which is considered to be a measure of visual attention [2]. These might be related to the fact that gaze dwell time could reflect the thinking time and processing depth of this information [15]. Besides, the number of fixations to certain information could suggest the importance of the subject when making decisions [11,13]. When humans and machines collaborate to make decisions in SRDM, human decision-makers are faced with and need to process multiple information from different sources, such as task information, profit information, the information of machine teammates, etc. As we reported in [24], the preferences for specific alternatives of human decision-makers varied across both HMTs and between HMTs. Thus, it is reasonable to assume that people's attentional behavior will also vary, reflecting their pre-decision cognitive processes. In this study, we attempted to explore the association between attentional behaviors and pumping decisions and the collaboration mechanism of different HMTs.

In order to understand the basis of human SRDM behaviors in two HMTs, we applied a valid and interpretable tool to analyze the multiple factors that influence humans to make decisions. To remain situation awareness and make appropriate decisions, humans should keep the perception of and understand the environment and their machine teammate(s), and form the projection of future outcomes [3]. Human decision-makers change their risk attitude and adjust their decisions according to the external feedback from the task results (loss or gain) [22, 24] and loss attribution (human or machine) in previous trials [4] and the decisions of the machine teammate [6]. Moreover, trust and acceptance of machines have become important drivers when humans are faced with machine-assisted decision-making [10]. A decision tree is a predictive model represented as a set of test conjunctions, where each test compares an attribute with a numerical threshold or a set of possible values [14]. Decision tree has been shown to be interpretable since its graphical model structure and its feature to be transformed into textual descriptions. [17]. Thus, we attempted to employ decision tree to describe and predict the human SRDM behaviors.

Therefore, on the basis of [24], the present study aims to provide a deeper understanding of human SRDM behaviors using eye-tracking and decision tree. In our previous research [24], we collected task performance, behavioral responses and subjective perception when collaborating with a highly accurate machine under different HMTs. In this study, we first collected eye-tracking data and used dwell time ratio and fixation count to examine attentional behaviors of human decision-makers. Then we modelled the SRDM process using decision tree.

2   Method

The experimental task followed our previously conducted study [24] and was set as follows.

2.1   Participants

We recruited 25 participants (13 males, all Chinese) to participate in the within-subject experiment, which included five undergraduates, 19 postgraduates, and one post-doctorate from Tsinghua University in Beijing. Their average age was 24.2 years old ($SD = 1.9$). The average duration of the experiment was 45 min, and the subjects were compensated for their participation and experiment performance. The experiment payoffs included an attendance fee of 45 yuan and a performance fee ranging from 12.5 to 17.5 yuan. In addition, there were zero profits and no additional penalties for exploded balloons. All subjects provided informed consent prior to the experiment. The experiment protocol was approved by the Institutional Review Board of the IE Department, Tsinghua University.

2.2   Sequential Risky Decision-Making Task

We used a modified Balloon Analogue Risk Task (BART) to simulate an SRDM task in two HMTs: the traditional human-dominated team and the human-machine joint team. Figure 1 shows the experiment interfaces for the two groups.

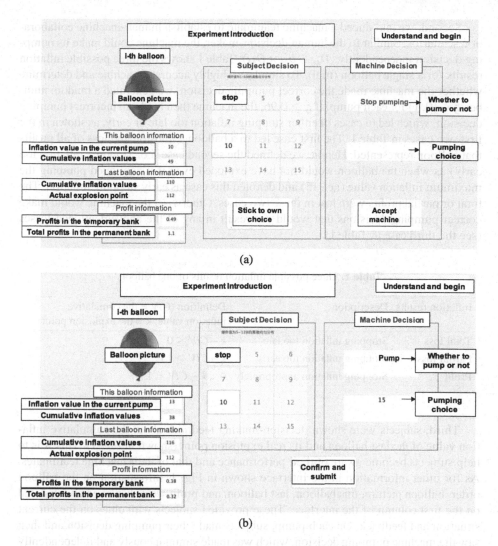

Fig. 1. The experiment interface of two human-machine team collaboration modes: (a) group D; (b) group J

The BART is a classic computerized experimental task that provides an ecologically valid method for measuring risk-taking tendencies [16,23]. We have made the following three adjustments.

First, we added a pumping value variable (Q) and turned the two options ("cash" and "pump", denoted as b_B) into multiple options because classic BART could not represent the change in risk attitude during the sequential process. Thus, the pumping decision was determined using two variables: $D_H = b_H \times Q_H$, where $b_H \in \{0, 1\}$; $Q_H = \{q|5 \leq q \leq 15, q \in \mathbb{Z}\}$. The explosion point followed a discrete uniform distribution on $\{5, 128\}$. The sequence was used for each subject and controlled for each block of 10 balloons.

Second, we introduced a machine teammate to establish human-machine collaboration scenarios. Similar to the human decision-maker, the machine could make its pumping decision independently ($D_M = b_M \times Q_M$). Table 1 shows the three possible inflation results for a single balloon (trial). To simulate a highly accurate machine and determine whether the machine made the correct pumping decision, we generated a random number $\xi \in (0,1)$ for each pump. If $\xi \geq 0.96$, the machine then made an incorrect pumping decision, which led to cases of either stopping inflation too late or early, as shown in the first two cases in Table 1. The first case led to a balloon explosion and loss of all profits that balloon represented. Herein, we defined the second case (i.e., stopping inflation too early) as when the balloon would not have exploded even if it continued pumping the maximum inflation value (i.e., 15) and denoted this case as early stopping inflation. The total or partial profits were lost in these two cases. Otherwise, the machine would make correct pumping decisions that would not result in any of the abovementioned losses (see the third case in Table 1).

Table 1. Three possible inflation results of one balloon.

Inflation results	Description	Definition (CIV = the cumulative inflation value; k = the explosion point)
Total loss	Stopping inflation too late	$k - CIV \leq 0$
Partial loss	Stopping inflation too early	$k - CIV \geq 15$
Profit	Stopping inflation appropriately	$0 < k - CIV < 15$

Third, subjects were shown decision-making feedback about the cumulative inflation value of the last balloon and its real explosion point (shown in Fig. 1). This was to help subjects become aware of their performance and that of their machine teammates. As for other information in the interface shown in Fig. 1, information on the balloon order, balloon picture, this balloon, last balloon, and profit were displayed and updated on the first column of the interface. These provided subjects with clues on the current situation and feedback. On each pump, subjects made their pumping decision and then saw the machine pumping decision, which was made simultaneously and independently (see the two columns on the right of the interface). Then, the final pumping decision of the HMT was generated in the two human-machine team collaboration modes introduced in the next subsection.

2.3 Human-Machine Team Collaboration Mode

We designed two collaboration modes by setting different decision authorities between the human and machine: the machine acting as a subordinate (the human-dominated team, group D) or a partner (the human-machine joint team, group J). In both settings, the human decision-maker and the machine made their pumping decisions independently and simultaneously ($b_H, Q_H; b_M, Q_M$). The final pumping decision of the HMT $D_B = (b_B, Q_B)$ was generated in different ways, as shown in Table 2.

Table 2. The generation of the final pumping decision of the two HMTs

HMT	The way the final decision is generated	Definition
The human-dominated team (group D)	the subject had decision authority for b_B and Q_B	$b_B = b_H$, $Q_B = Q_H$ when the human decision-maker sticked to his own decision; $b_B = b_M$, $Q_B = Q_M$ when the human decision-maker accepted the machine recommendation
The human-machine joint team (group J)	the "one vote veto" and "averaging" mode	$D_B = (b_H = 1 \wedge b_M = 1) \times (Q_H + Q_M)/2$

2.4 Equipment and Data Collection

We used two computers, one display and an eye tracker mounted below the display. The experiment setting was shown in Fig. 2.

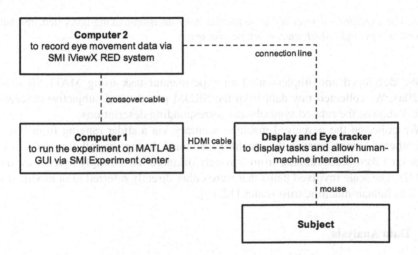

Fig. 2. The equipment and the experiment setting

We recorded, processed and analyzed the raw data was via SMI iViewX RED system, SMI Experiment Center and SMI BeGaze software (SMI, Germany) respectively. We set the recording frequency 60 Hz. Figure 3 showed the Areas of Interest (AOIs), including three parts: the balloon-related information marked in yellow (including balloon picture, inflation information of this balloon, last balloon information, and profit information), the subject behavior-related information marked in blue (including inflation alternatives, response to machine recommendation in group D, submitting choice in group J), and the machine behavior-related information marked in green (including whether to pump or not, pump value). We focused on the length of time and the number of times people pay attention to different AOIs, denoted as dwell time and fixation count. Since each participant took a different amount of decision-making time to make decisions, we calculated and used the dwell time ratio of AOIs. Therefore, we used the dwell time ratio (DTR) and fixation count (FC) to indicate attentional behaviors.

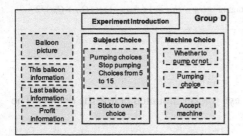 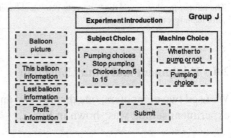

Fig. 3. The experimental interface in sequential risky decision-making tasks (left: the human-dominated team; right: the human-machine joint team)

We developed and implemented an experimental task using MATLAB (version R2020a). We collected raw data from the SRDM process and subjective perceptions. Table 3 showed the related symbols and corresponding descriptions.

We collected the perceived machine accuracy via a slider ranging from 0 to 100. We gathered human trust in the machine teammate during the inflation process using a 7-point Likert scale ranging from 'strongly disagree' to 'strongly agree' (see details in [24]). The scale involved items that were either directly referred to or modified from previous human-machine trust scales [12, 19].

2.5 Data Analysis

Table 4 shows the calculation process of variables from the raw data in Table 3. Further paired comparisons and between-group comparisons could be achieved by averaging the variables of multiple subjects.

For data analysis, we used Mean and SD to describe task performance, human inflation behaviors, attentional behaviors and subjective perceptions. We tested the normality assumption before implementing the statistical tests. All statistical analyses were performed using MATLAB (version R2021b). We set the significance level at 5%.

Table 3. Symbols and corresponding descriptions of raw data in the SRDM process

Symbol	Description
$PT_{i,j}$	Pumping times for the j-th pump in the i-th balloon
$HD_{i,j}$	Pumping decision of the human decision-maker for the j-th pump in the i-th balloon
$\xi_{i,j}$	A random number for the j-th pump in the i-th balloon
$MD_{i,j}$	Pumping decision of the machine for the j-th pump in the i-th balloon
$BD_{i,j}$	Final pumping decision for the j-th pump in the i-th balloon
CIV_i	Cumulative Inflation Value of the i-th balloon
HE_i	Condition of the explosion of the i-th balloon caused by human pumping decisions
ME_i	Condition of the explosion of the i-th balloon caused by machine pumping decisions
E_i	Condition of the explosion of the i-th balloon
k_i	The explosion point of the i-th balloon
TP	Total profits in one group
$pacc_s$	The perceived accuracy of machine after 10 balloons, 30 balloons, 50 balloons (s = 10, 30, 50)
$trust_s$	Human trust in machine after 10 balloons, 30 balloons, 50 balloons (s = 10, 30,50)

Table 4. Variables and the corresponding calculation

Variable	Calculation
Cumulative inflation values of unexploded balloons (CIV)	$CIV = \sum_{ij} E_i \times BD_{ij}$
The number of balloon explosions (E)	$E = \sum_i E_i$
The number of early stopping inflation (ESI)	$ESI = \#(k_i - \sum_j BD_{ij} > 15)$
Choice ratio of inflation alternatives (CRIA)	$CRIA\,(v) = {}^{\#(HD_{i,j} = v)}/{}_{\sum_i PT_i}$

2.6 Procedure

Before the formal experiment, we collected some basic information, such as gender and age. Participants were seated approximately 65 cm away from the eye-tracker and adjusted their chair to ensure their eyes in the center of the screen. The eye-tracker was recalibrated prior to each task.

During the formal experiment, each subject collaborated with a machine teammate in two HMTs (group D and group J). The order was counterbalanced across subjects. Each group included a training stage (10 trials) and two experiment stages (20 trials per stage). In each group, we collected trust in the machine teammate and perceived machine accuracy at the end of the 10th, 30th, and 50th balloon. During this period, the eye-tracker kept recording eye-tracking data.

2.7 Decision Tree

A decision tree is defined as a classification procedure that recursively partitions a data set into smaller subdivisions on the basis of a set of tests defined at each branch (or node) in the tree. In this framework, a data set is classified by sequentially subdividing it according to the decision framework defined by the tree, and a class label is assigned to each observation according to the leaf node into which the observation falls. Decision trees have several advantages over traditional supervised classification procedures such as maximum likelihood classification. First, decision trees are strictly nonparametric and do not require assumptions regarding the distributions of the input data. Second, they handle more diverse relations between input data and output classes, such as nonlinear relations, missing values, and handling both numeric and categorical inputs. Third, decision trees are more intuitive and interpretable [9].

In this study, we used a univariate decision tree (UDT) in which the decision boundaries at each node of the tree are defined by a single feature of the input data. Since each subject would pump several times for each trial (balloon), variables characterizing the decision-making process might be multiple and complex. The features varied in sources: variables of the current balloon, variables of the last balloon(s), variables related to losses (explosions and early stopping inflation) and variables related to the perception and expectation. The dataset we used was composed of 30 features (see Tables 5,6,7,8), including both numeric and categorical variables. The generated decision tree would be pruned based on the best pruning level via the *cvloss* method in MATLAB.

To evaluate the classification performance of the decision tree, we performed a set of ten cross-validations. The behavior data were randomly split into a training set (90%) and a test set (10%), in which the training set was used to generate a decision tree model and the test set was used to evaluate the performance accuracy of the model. To eliminate the effects of different data partition methods, the accuracy of train-test validation is the average of ten-time validations. The decision tree model was built in MATLAB (version R2021b) by *ctree()* and produced predictions for validation by *predict()*.

Table 5. Variables of the current balloon (n = 3)

Variable	Description	Calculation
pumpratio	The ratio of the cumulative inflation value for the $j-th$ pump of the i-th balloon to the maximum inflation value (i.e., 128)	$\sum_{ij} E_i \times BD_{ij}/128$
pumpratio_last	The ratio of the cumulative inflation value for the j-th pump of the i-th balloon to the cumulative inflation value of the (i-1)-th balloon	$\sum_{ij} E_i \times BD_{ij}/CIV_{i-1}$
pumptimes	Pumping times for the j-th pump in the i-th balloon	$PT_{i,j}$

Table 6. Variables of the last balloon(s) (n = 6)

Variable	Description	Calculation
lastk	The explosion point of the (i-1)-th balloon	k_{i-1}
last_totalpump	The cumulative inflation value of the (i-1)-th balloon	CIV_{i-1}
pumpk_diff	The ratio of the difference between the explosion point and the cumulative inflation value to the explosion point of the (i-1)-th balloon	$1 - CIV_{i-1}/k_{i-1}$
last_machhav	Pumping decision of the machine for the (j-1)-th pump in the i-th balloon	$MD_{i,j-1} \ if \ j \geq 2 \ MD_{i-1,j} \ if \ j = 1$
last_mh_diff	The difference between the pumping decision of the machine and human for the (j-1)-th pump in the i-th balloon	$MD_{i,j-1} - HD_{i,j-1} \ if \ j \geq 2 \ MD_{i-1,j} - HD_{i-1,j} \ if \ j = 1$
last_mach_acc	The performance of the machine in the (i-1)-th balloon	$\sum_j (\xi_{i-1,j} < 0.96)/\sum_j PT_{i-1,j}$

Table 7. Variables related to the losses (explosions and early stopping inflation) (n = 18)

Variable	Description	Calculation
explode	Condition of the explosion of the i-th balloon (=0 means balloon explosion)	E_i
earlyend	Condition of the early stopping inflation of the (i-1)-th balloon (=1 means early stopping inflation)	$ESI_{i-1} = \#(k_{i-1} - \sum_j BD_{i-1,j} > 15)$
last5_explode	The number of explosions in the last 5 balloons	$\sum_{i-5}^{i-1} E_t \ if \ i \geq 6$ $\sum_{i-5}^{i} E_t \ if \ i < 6$
last5_earlyend	The number of early stopping inflation in the last 5 balloons	$\sum_{i-5}^{i-1} ESI_t \ if \ i \geq 6$ $\sum_{i-5}^{i} ESI_t \ if \ i < 6$
explode_decay	The temporal effect of one explosion in the i-th balloon	$1 - 0.3 \times (1 - E_i)^{0.316}$
earlyend_decay	The temporal effect of one early stopping inflation in the i-th balloon	$1 - 0.3 \times ESI_i^{0.316}$
explode_machine	The attribution of the explosion of the (i-1)-th balloon (=1 means the explosion attributed to the machine)	$EM_{i-1} = (E_{i-1} = 0 \ \&\& \ \sum_1^{j-1} E_{i-1,t} + MD_{i-1,j} \geq k_{i-1} \ \&\& \ \sum_1^{j-1} E_{i-1,t} + HD_{i-1,j} < k_{i-1})$
earlyend_machine	The attribution of the early stopping inflation in the last balloon (=1 means the early stop attributed to the machine)	$EEM_{i-1} = (k_{i-1} - \sum_j BD_{i-1,j} > 15 \ \&\& \ MD_{i-1,j} = 0 \ \&\& \ HD_{i-1,j} \neq 0)$
last5_explode_machine	The attribution of explosions in the last 5 balloons (=1 means the explosion attributed to the machine)	$\sum_{i-5}^{i-1} EM_t \ if \ i \geq 6$ $\sum_{i-5}^{i} EM_t \ if \ i < 6$
last5_earlyend_machine	the attribution of early stopping inflation in the last 5 balloons (=1 means the early stop attributed to the machine)	$\sum_{i-5}^{i-1} EEM_t \ if \ i \geq 6$ $\sum_{i-5}^{i} EEM_t \ if \ i < 6$
explode_machine_decay	The temporal effect of one explosion caused by the machine in the i-th balloon	$1 - 0.3 \times EM_i^{0.316}$
earlyend_machine_decay	The temporal effect of one early stopping inflation caused by the machine in the i-th balloon	$1 - 0.3 \times EEM_i^{0.316}$
explode_human	The attribution of the explosion in the last balloon (=1 means the explosion attributed to the human)	$EH_{i-1} = (E_{i-1} = 0 \ \&\& \ \sum_1^{j-1} E_{i-1,t} + HD_{i-1,j} \geq k_{i-1} \ \&\& \ \sum_1^{j-1} E_{i-1,t} + MD_{i-1,j} < k_{i-1})$
earlyend_human	The attribution of the early stopping inflation in the last balloon (=1 means the early stop attributed to the human)	$EEH_{i-1} = (k_{i-1} - \sum_j BD_{i-1,j} > 15 \ \&\& \ HD_{i-1,j} = 0 \ \&\& \ MD_{i-1,j} \neq 0)$
last5_explode_human	The attribution of explosions in the last 5 balloons (=1 means the explosion attributed to the human)	$\sum_{i-5}^{i-1} EH_t \ if \ i \geq 6$ $\sum_{i-5}^{i} EH_t \ if \ i < 6$
last5_earlyend_human	The attribution of explosions in the last 5 balloons (=1 means the early stop attributed to the human)	$\sum_{i-5}^{i-1} EEH_t \ if \ i \geq 6$ $\sum_{i-5}^{i} EEH_t \ if \ i < 6$
explode_human_decay	The effect of one explosion caused by the human on subsequent inflations	$1 - 0.3 \times EH_i^{0.316}$
earlyend_human_decay	The effect of one early stopping inflation caused by the human on subsequent inflations	$1 - 0.3 \times EEH_i^{0.316}$

Note: To describe the effect of balloon explosion and early stopping inflation on the subsequent pumps, we employed $1 - 0.3x^{0.316}$, where x refers to the pump times from the event (explosion or early stopping inflation). The parameter was selected based on the Ebbinghaus forgetting curve and theory of working memory (7 balloons).

Table 8. Variables related to the perception and expectation (n=3)

Variable	Description	Calculation
pacc	The perceived accuracy of machine after 10 balloons, 30 balloons, 50 balloons	$pacc_s$
trust	Human trust in machine after 10 balloons, 30 balloons, 50 balloons	$trust_s$
expectk	The perception of the explosion point value in the current balloon (calculated by the average of explosion values of the last 3 balloons)	$\sum_{i-3}^{i-1} k_t/3 \; if \; i \geq 4 \; \sum_1^{i-1} E_t/(i-1) \; if \; i < 4$

3 Results

3.1 Task Performance

We showed the results of task performance in Table 9. We used paired t-tests (or the Wilcoxon signed-rank test when the normality assumption was violated) to compare task performance between the groups. We found that the difference in CIV between groups D and group J failed to reach the usual level of significance ($p = 0.07$). We found an insignificant difference in E ($p > 0.05$) and a significant difference in the ESI ($p < 0.05$) between the groups.

Table 9. Results of task performance in both groups

Variable	group D M (SD)	group J M (SD)
CIV	1861.24 (233.30)	1733 (276.82)
E	9.64 (5.45)	7.96 (4.64)
ESI	6.48 (3.65)	14.32 (4.13)

3.2 Attentional Behaviors

We showed comparison results of the DTR and FC of AOIs in Table 4.

DTR of AOIs Between Groups. We found that subjects paid more attention to cumulative inflation information in the current balloon and inflation information of machines (whether pump or not) but less attention to inflation value information of machine in group J (all $ps < 0.05$). As for DTR of inflation alternatives, participants in group J paid more attention to inflation alternatives with low values (see pump 5, 6, 7, 8, 9 in Table 10) and medium value (see pump 11 in Table 10) while paid less attention to inflation alternatives with high values (see pump 13, 14 in Table 10).

FC of AOIs Between Groups. We found that FC of inflation information of machines (whether pump or not) in group J was significantly higher than that in group D ($p < 0.05$). As for FC of inflation alternatives, participants in group J paid more attention to inflation alternatives with low values (see pump 5, 6, 7, 8, 9 in Table 10) and "stop inflation" (see pump 0 in Table 10) while paid less attention to inflation alternatives with high values (see pump 13, 14, 15 in Table 10).

Table 10. The comparisons of DTR and FC of AOIs between groups

AOI	Dwell time ratio (DTR) (%)		Fixation count (FC)	
	group D M (SD)	group J M (SD)	group D M (SD)	group J M (SD)
Balloon picture	1.0 (2.6)	0.5 (0.5)	21.4 (38.8)	14.9 (14.6)
This balloon information	7.1 (6.5)	9.0 (7.7)*	144.0 (116.0)	168.8 (124.3)
Last balloon information	8.2 (5.0)	8.9 (4.6)	170.6 (89.3)	189.0 (111.0)
Profit information	1.8 (3.0)	1.5 (1.2)	46.4 (91.8)	38.4 (34.3)
Pump 0	0.9 (1.8)	1.1 (1.2)	18.6 (28.5)	26.2 (22.7)*
Pump 5	2.9 (3.9)	7.0 (7.0)*	64.8 (81.6)	150.6 (131.1)*
Pump 6	0.4 (0.6)	1.4 (1.8)*	10.3 (15.1)	33.6 (33.4)*
Pump 7	0.5 (0.7)	1.3 (1.2)*	12.8 (14.1)	32.8 (30.2)*
Pump 8	2.5 (3.1)	5.5 (3.9)*	57.4 (62.1)	122.6 (73.6)*
Pump 9	0.7 (1.0)	1.8 (1.9)*	20.9 (30.7)	43.7 (33.0)*
Pump 10	3.3 (6.6)	2.2 (3.3)	69.5 (124.9)	53.0 (78.5)
Pump 11	2.2 (2.5)	3.2 (2.5)*	56.5 (56.2)	81.0 (71.2)
Pump 12	3.0 (3.7)	2.8 (2.2)	73.9 (83.7)	64.3 (44.8)
Pump 13	0.6 (0.8)*	0.2 (0.3)	17.2 (25.5)*	7.5 (10.5)
Pump 14	1.4 (1.3)*	0.9 (0.7)	41.2 (40.3)*	22.6 (20.5)
Pump 15	8.3 (6.8)	6.2 (6.9)	179.0 (146.7)*	103.8 (66.3)
Machine inflation	1.5 (1.7)	2.7 (2.4)*	44.9 (41.9)	71.3 (64.2)*
Machine inflation value	7.0 (4.3)*	5.3 (3.2)	177.7 (100.3)	144.4 (95.9)
Subject Submit	3.0 (1.9)	2.8 (3.6)	91.8 (58.7)	80.1 (104.5)
Accept Machine	4.5 (3.0)	-	132.8 (91.0)	-

Note: * means the value in this column was significantly higher than that in the other column.

Association Between CRIA and Attentional Behaviors (DTR, FC) of Inflation Alternatives. We found a significant correlation between CRIA and the DTR of attention to corresponding inflation alternatives in 19 of 25 subjects ($r = 0.72$ on average); and a significant association in 16 of 25 subjects between CRIA and the FC of attention to corresponding inflation alternatives ($r = 0.74$ on average) in group D. In the meantime, there were a significant association in 21 of 25 subjects in group J between the DTR of corresponding areas and CRIA ($r = 0.79$ on average); and a significant association in 22 of 25 subjects between FC of corresponding areas and CRIA ($r = 0.77$ on average).

Association Between Attentional Behaviors (DTR, FC.) and Task Performance (TP, E) We found marginally significant correlations between the FC of attention to information on machine pumping choice and task performance in group J. Specifically, there was a positive correlation between inflation value information of machine and TP ($r = 0.40, p < 0.05$) and a negative correlation between inflation information of machine (whether pump or not) and E ($r = -0.36, p = 0.07$).

3.3 Results of Decision Tree

We performed the decision tree for the dataset mentioned in Sect. 2.7 of both HMTs and tested the performance through resubstitution validation and train-test validation. Table 11 showed the validation results of the decision tree. The accuracies (both resubstitution validation and train-test validation) in group D were significantly higher than that in group J (all $ps < 0.01$). In addition, the results (both resubstitution validation and train-test validation) without the training stage were higher than that with the training stage in group D (all $ps < 0.05$). In addition to the average values, we also found the minimum accuracy of both groups was 67%, which indicated that the generated decision tree could cover and describe at least 67% of inflation behaviors in both groups.

Table 11. The result of resubstitution validation and train-test validation

	Resubstitution validation accuracy		Train-test validation accuracy	
	group D M (SD)	group J M (SD)	group D M (SD)	group J M (SD)
balloon 1–50	0.88* (0.09)	0.83 (0.10)	0.73* (0.21)	0.59 (0.23)
balloon 11–50	0.89*† (0.10)	0.83 (0.11)	0.75*† (0.22)	0.59 (0.25)

Note: * means this column was significantly higher than the other column; † means this row was significantly higher than the other row.

We visualized the decision tree and found tree structure of different levels of complexity. Figure 5 showed several cases. Therefore, we compared the results of different decision strategies to further explore the performance of decision tree algorithm (see Figure 4). Results showed that the decision tree performed significantly differently when subjects took different decision strategies in group J (all $ps < 0.05$) while the accuracy of one-choice decision strategy was significantly higher than that of the other two strategies in group D (all $ps < 0.01$).

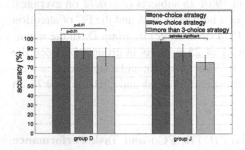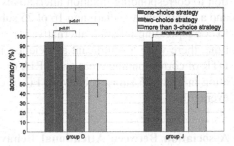

Fig. 4. Result of resubstitution validation and train-test validation of different decision strategies in both groups: (a) accuracy of resubstitution validation; (b) accuracy of train-test validation.

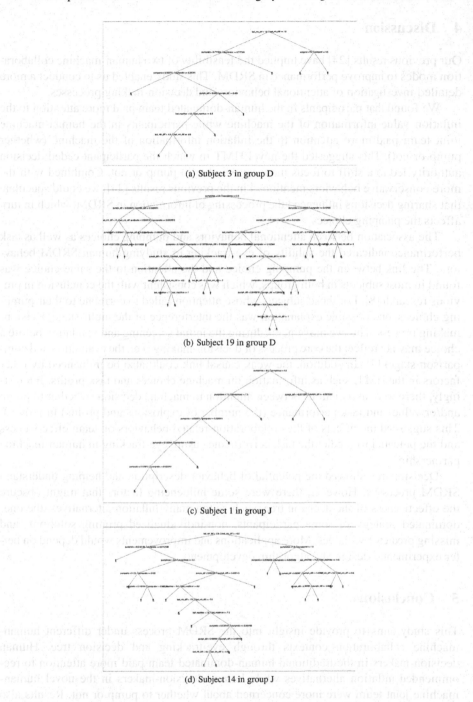

(a) Subject 3 in group D

(b) Subject 19 in group D

(c) Subject 1 in group J

(d) Subject 14 in group J

Fig. 5. Structures of decision trees in group D and group J

4 Discussion

Our previous results [24] have implied the feasibility of two human-machine collaboration modes to improve performance in SRDM. This study enabled us to conduct a more detailed investigation of attentional behaviors and decision-making processes.

We found that participants in the human-dominated team paid more attention to the inflation value information of the machine while participants in the human-machine joint team paid more attention to the inflation information of the machine (whether pump or not). This suggested the novel HMT in which the participant ceded decision authority led to a shift to focus more on whether to pump or not. Combined with the more conservative behaviors mentioned in the previous results [24], we could speculate that sharing decisions influenced the processing of information in SRDM, which in turn affects the pumping choices.

The association between attentional behaviors and pumping choices as well as task performance indicated the validity of eye-tracking in studying human SRDM behaviors. The link between the pumping choice and the attention to the same choice was found in most subjects in both groups, which was consistent with the conclusion in previous research [8]. For those subjects whose attention failed to correlate to their pumping choices, one possible explanation was the interference of the multi-stage decision-making process. The eye movements during the initial screening and validation before a choice may not reflect the core process of decision-making (i.e., the evaluation and comparison stage) [7]. In addition, the weak causal link could also be influenced by other factors in the HMT, such as information on machine choices and task profits. Interestingly, there were associations between attention to machine decision (whether to pump and/or value) and task performance (the number of explosions and profits) in group J. This suggested the effects of the collaboration-related behaviors on team effectiveness and the potential to predict the task performance using eye-tracking in human-machine partnership.

Decision tree showed the potential of behavior description and helping understand SRDM processes. However, there were some influencing factors that might obscure the effectiveness of the decision tree, such as too many inflation alternatives, the one-dominated strategy of some participants, non-individualized pruning solutions, and missing predictor variables. More applications and improvements would depend on better experimental design and algorithm development.

5 Conclusions

This study aims to provide insight into the SRDM process under different human-machine collaboration contexts through eye-tracking and decision tree. Human decision-makers in the traditional human-dominated team paid more attention to recommended inflation alternatives while human decision-makers in the novel human-machine joint team were more concerned about whether to pump or not. Results also showed the potential to use eye-tracking and decision tree to describe the SRDM process. The findings can help uncover decision-making behaviors and human-machine collaboration mechanisms in HMTs

References

1. Causse, M., Lancelot, F., Maillant, J., Behrend, J., Cousy, M., Schneider, N.: Encoding decisions and expertise in the operator's eyes: Using eye-tracking as input for system adaptation. Int. J. Hum Comput Stud. **125**, 55–65 (2019)
2. Cavanagh, J.F., Wiecki, T.V., Kochar, A., Frank, M.J.: Eye tracking and pupillometry are indicators of dissociable latent decision processes. J. Exp. Psychol. Gen. **143**(4), 1476 (2014)
3. Chen, J.Y., Lakhmani, S.G., Stowers, K., Selkowitz, A.R., Wright, J.L., Barnes, M.: Situation awareness-based agent transparency and human-autonomy teaming effectiveness. Theor. Issues Ergon. Sci. **19**(3), 259–282 (2018)
4. Dietvorst, B.J., Simmons, J.P., Massey, C.: Algorithm aversion: people erroneously avoid algorithms after seeing them err. J. Exp. Psychol. Gen. **144**(1), 114 (2015)
5. Dietvorst, B.J., Simmons, J.P., Massey, C.: Overcoming algorithm aversion: people will use imperfect algorithms if they can (even slightly) modify them. Manage. Sci. **64**(3), 1155–1170 (2018)
6. Festinger, L.: A theory of social comparison processes. Hum. Relations **7**(2), 117–140 (1954)
7. France, K.R., Shah, R.H., Park, C.W.: The impact of emotional valence and intensity on ad evaluation and memory. ACR North American Advances . Adv. Consum. Res. **21**, 583–588 (1994)
8. Franco-Watkins, A.M., Mattson, R.E., Jackson, M.D.: Now or later? attentional processing and intertemporal choice. J. Behav. Decis. Mak. **29**(2–3), 206–217 (2016)
9. Friedl, M.A., Brodley, C.E.: Decision tree classification of land cover from remotely sensed data. Remote Sens. Environ. **61**(3), 399–409 (1997)
10. Haesevoets, T., De Cremer, D., Dierckx, K., Van Hiel, A.: Human-machine collaboration in managerial decision making. Comput. Hum. Behav. **119**, 106730 (2021)
11. Hristova, E., Grinberg, M.: Disjunction effect in prisoner's dilemma: Evidences from an eye-tracking study. In: Proceedings of the 30th Annual conference of the cognitive science society. pp. 1225–1230. Cognitive Science Society Austin, TX, USA (2008)
12. Jian, J.Y., Bisantz, A.M., Drury, C.G.: Foundations for an empirically determined scale of trust in automated systems. Int. J. Cogn. Ergon. **4**(1), 53–71 (2000)
13. Kim, B.E., Seligman, D., Kable, J.W.: Preference reversals in decision making under risk are accompanied by changes in attention to different attributes. Front. Neurosci. **6**, 109 (2012)
14. Kotsiantis, S.B.: Decision trees: a recent overview. Artif. Intell. Rev. **39**, 261–283 (2013)
15. Kuo, F.Y., Hsu, C.W., Day, R.F.: An exploratory study of cognitive effort involved in decision under framing-an application of the eye-tracking technology. Decis. Support Syst. **48**(1), 81–91 (2009)
16. Lejuez, C.W., et al.: Evaluation of a behavioral measure of risk taking: the balloon analogue risk task (BART). J. Exp. Psychol. Appl. **8**(2), 75 (2002)
17. Lipton, Z.C.: The mythos of model interpretability: In machine learning, the concept of interpretability is both important and slippery. Queue **16**(3), 31–57 (2018)
18. Liu, B.: In AI we trust? effects of agency locus and transparency on uncertainty reduction in human-Ai interaction. J. Comput.-Mediat. Commun. **26**(6), 384–402 (2021)
19. Madsen, M., Gregor, S.: Measuring human-computer trust. Citeseer
20. Maner, J.K., Gailliot, M.T., Butz, D.A., Peruche, B.M.: Power, risk, and the status quo: Does power promote riskier or more conservative decision making? Pers. Soc. Psychol. Bull. **33**(4), 451–462 (2007)
21. Patel, B., et al.: Human-machine partnership with artificial intelligence for chest radiograph diagnosis. NPJ Digit. Med. **2**(1), 111 (2019)
22. Schmitz, F., Manske, K., Preckel, F., Wilhelm, O.: The multiple faces of risk-taking. Eur. J. Psychol. Assess. **32**(1), 17–38 (2016)

23. Wallsten, T.S., Pleskac, T.J., Lejuez, C.W.: Modeling behavior in a clinically diagnostic sequential risk-taking task. Psychol. Rev. **112**(4), 862 (2005)
24. Xiong, W., Wang, C., Ma, L.: Partner or subordinate? sequential risky decision-making behaviors under human-machine collaboration contexts. Comput. Hum. Behav. **139**, 107556 (2023)

Interacting with Robots and Exoskeletons

Introduction of a Cobot as Intermittent Haptic Contact Interfaces in Virtual Reality

V. K Guda, S. Mugisha, C. Chevallereau, and D. Chablat[✉]

Nantes Université, École Centrale Nantes, CNRS, LS2N, UMR 6004,
44000 Nantes, France
damien.chablat@cnrs.fr

Abstract. Virtual reality (VR) is evolving and being used in industrial simulations, but the possibility to touch objects is missing, for example, to judge the perceived quality in the design of a car. Current haptic interfaces do not make it possible to easily restore texture, therefore an approach is considered as an intermittent contact interface to achieve this. A cobot places a moving surface at the point of contact with a virtual object in order to enable physical contact with the hand of the operator. This paper aims to speak about several challenges: the placement of the robot, the modeling of the operator, the management of the displacement and the speed of the robot, and the detection of the operator's intentions. The placement of the robot is chosen to allow reaching the different working areas and to ensure passive safety by making it impossible for the robot to hit the head and chest of the operator in a normal working position, i.e. sitting in a chair. A user model, consisting of a torso and arms, is designed and tested to track the user's movements in real-time. Interaction is possible with a set of pre-defined poses that the user follows together as desired. Various strategies are proposed to predict the intent of the user. The main aspects of prediction are based on the direction of eye and the position of the hand of the user. An experimental study as well as the resulting analysis demonstrates the contribution by considering the direction of the gaze. The advantage of introducing "safety" points to move the robot away from the operator and allow rapid movements of the robot is emphasized.

Keywords: Safety · intermittent contact interface · human intention prediction · trajectory planning · human-robot collaboration · virtual reality

1 Introduction

Virtual reality technologies allow a user to get immersed in virtual worlds. Haptic technologies born from robotics have increased the immersion in these virtual worlds by providing the sensation of touch.

In a Virtual Reality (VR) simulation, haptic interfaces allow a tangible and physical interaction with the virtual environment, but they must generally be

V. G. Duffy (Ed.): HCII 2023, LNCS 14028, pp. 497–509, 2023.
https://doi.org/10.1007/978-3-031-35741-1_36

constantly held in hand by the user and therefore do not allow objects to be touched in a natural way. At the same time, many applications require hands-on interaction without intermediaries. This is particularly the case for simulations that require tactile exploration of the physical properties of virtual objects.

Classical force feedback interfaces, also called here classic contact haptic interfaces (CHIs), are robotic systems allowing natural motion interactions with virtual or remote environments. They are used in several domains such as design, manufacturing, assembly, scientific visualization, entertainment, education, medicine, space, rehabilitation, micro manipulation and molecular biology. In all cases, they should provide adequate kinesthetic (force) feedback, contributing to enhance the sense of presence in the virtual environment.

With CHIs, the user is usually mechanically linked to the device's end-effector, typically a handle, whose movements, measured by the robot, are used to know the configuration (position and orientation) of his/her hand. This information is necessary to provide force feedback which is consistent with the virtual scene and the mechanical properties of the virtual object (VO) being touched. The mechanical link that is established when the user manipulates the haptic device has however a non-negligible influence since he/she experiences the friction, inertia and vibrations of the mechanical structure, even in free space where he/she is expected to feel nothing. Such unwanted sensations decrease the realism of the interaction since the user feels all the time the presence of the robot. In addition, the difference between free space and contact is less distinctively felt than in the real world.

In order to cope with these issues, several efforts can be made in terms of mechanical design, e.g. use of very lightweight and very stiff structures (even if an optimal trade off is difficult to attain) and more efficient transmission systems. Another approach consists in installing a force sensor at the level of the robot's end-effector in order to measure and compensate any resisting force in the direction of displacement. However, resisting forces can never be totally canceled and none of these approaches completely eliminates the feeling of the presence of the robot in free space.

Years of research on haptics, robotics, and interaction in VR have led to the development of a new generation of haptic devices called intermittent contact interfaces (ICI) [1–3]. Intermittent-contact interfaces (ICIs) represent an original and promising approach aiming to cope with the aforementioned issues. Its principle consists in removing the mechanical link between the human operator and the force feedback interface during manipulations in free space and come at his/her contact only when force feedback is required. This solution implies the need to track and closely follow the user's movements in free space and to prevent him/her to move in the constraint direction when a VO is being touched. This way, the user doesn't feel any force in free space (perfect transparency) and the transitions from free space to contact are deemed to be felt more naturally as the robot really touches the user at the simulated contact moment. This approach aims to improve the realism of the interactions, however it suffers from several shortcomings. First, its efficiency has not yet been proven in terms of user safety. Second, even if IC interfaces are experimentally proven to be stable at low speeds, they tend to become oscillating at higher speeds. Finally, despite the fact that a lot of tasks are performed by the mean of tools in the real world, most of existing ICIs focus on bare finger interactions and are therefore not optimal for simulating tool-mediated tasks.

User safety is central to the implementation of an ICI. To satisfy this constraint, we propose to use a cobot, for which we will develop specific path planning algorithms taking into account its low performance in terms of travel speed in the intrinsically safe mode, as well as all segments of the robot and the user's entire body in interference management. These algorithms will be based on a user activity prediction model that will allow both specifying a final desired location and the constraints to be respected when defining the path to reach this desired location (Fig. 1).

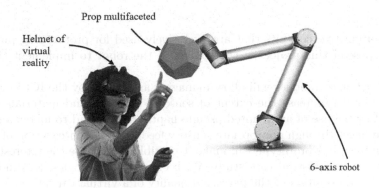

Prop multifaceted

Helmet of virtual reality

6-axis robot

Fig. 1. Conceptual scheme of the experimental platform

This paper summarizes the contribution of [4] which introduces a series of research works aiming to leverage the usability of such a system. This research work is created to deal with the present limits in such a haptic device system.

2   Description of Context

This work was developed under the frame of the French National Research Agency (ANR) LobbyBot Project. The LobbyBot project consisted in developing a system that could be integrated into an industrial application for automotive interior prototyping. The system is intended to be used to recreate an automotive cockpit for faster prototyping in VR for the Renault Group, a French automotive company. In this fast prototyping process, designers had to explore and evaluate the perceived quality of a virtual car interior with their sense of touch of different materials, shapes, and objects that could be arranged in a virtual automotive interior that could be easily configured in VR. This new paradigm was conceived as a means to save the Renault Group costs in budget and time for fabricating

Fig. 2. The LobbyBot project setup.

actual automotive cockpits that are exclusively used for prototyping purposes. The purpose of this project is the control of the robot to implement this ICI (Fig. 2).

Interaction techniques will allow managing any delays by the ICI in relation to the user. To increase the extent of sense of the form and materials can be restored by the use of an adapted pseudo-haptic return, and to follow a surface with the finger through appropriate sensory feedback. The integration of all the results into an ICI prototype will make it possible to validate the interest of the solution on an industrial case study. With current technologies, this industrial application (evaluation of the perceived quality of a virtual car interior) cannot be treated in a fast and low cost way.

3   Applications of ICIs

ICI applications range from industry (Fig. 3a), entertainment (Fig. 3b), medicine (Fig. 3c), and research purposes (Fig. 3d). In all these cases, users expect to "encounter" a surface to touch or manipulate in a Virtual Environment. In the case of industrial applications, these devices are considered for virtual proto-typing that requires to have haptic feedback in several locations to recreate workspace or expected location for objects to be manipulated. In the case of entertainment, they are used to recreate elements that can come in contact with the users when interacting with a virtual environment [5]. In the case of medicine, its often used for remote body-palpation and surgery practice [6]. The use in research purposes often looks for leveraging the device's capabilities for rendering more complex surfaces and objects [7].

4   Challenges

In order to leverage the capabilities of ICI, several challenges must be addressed, these are addressed in different dimensions such as: **User safety and security**

(a) Application in Industry by Lobbybot [8].

(b) Haptic-go-round from one direction to another while fishing in the virtual scene. [5].

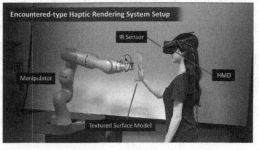

(c) The virtual palpation system. [6].

(d) Synthesizing the Roughness of Textured Surfaces for an Encountered-type Haptic Display [7].

Fig. 3. ICI applications

and **User immersion experience**. The challenges are divided into research questions.

Challenge 1. User safety and security

The concern to avoid unexpected collisions with users has been present ever since the early days of Human-Robot Interaction research. Measures for addressing this issue normally consider path-planning algorithms that help the robot to actively avoid the user in cases where both user and device could come into contact involuntarily. However, the use of path-planning often causes the device to move more slowly. This delay affects response time and user's perceived immersion in the virtual environment, and thus, it has been recognized as an issue to be addressed by the research community.

As an alternative to solutions exclusively relying on path-planning for avoiding collisions with users, we propose additional techniques like the placement of robot to minimize the workspace interaction, and creation of multiple zones for robot motion. Research concerning user safety for ICI systems needs to look for strategies that help to avoid any undesired contact that could break users perceived immersion in the virtual environment. The main objective remains to ensure the safety of the operator. With virtual reality, the operator has a modified perception of the robot and of the risk of collision. A visualization in the virtual world of the robot reduces the immersion but increases the safety. In the intersection zones between the space possibly scanned by the robot and the human, the robot (UR5) will be placed in cobot mode, i.e. it will stop and switch to gravity compensation mode if a contact effort is detected. Thus it cannot injure the operator. However, the speed of the robot is then limited.

Research Question 1. Robot Placement. Robot placement holds the promise of removing the need for a highly dedicated and structured workspace, as well as responding more quickly to environmental changes. Within the systems, dynamic and robust placements are crucial and strategically important, since they are often done in early stages in the process.

A complete set of operations consists in performing a specific task/operation by a robot on a set of task points. Often, after the robot returns to its starting configuration, a user is introduced to the system, and operations are performed. Since these cycles are repeated several times, it is very important that they are executed as fast as possible in order to increase immersion.

Once a set of specific points is assigned to a robot, the layout has limited freedom to optimize the robot workstation:

- robot's base placement (translation and rotation); The orientation of robot TCP at each task points is important as it effects the immersion of the user. So the robot should be able to reach the task points with the required orientations. The study started with no information on the robot base location in the virtual environment.
- visiting order of the work-points; In this approach the user decides the order of interaction with the task points. To improve user safety, the robot has to be closer to the user hands near the task points and as far as possible to the human body (torso, head and especially neck). Major concerns were to restrict the operation of the robot to one aspect to avoid crossing singularities while performing the tasks.
- robot's home configuration in the station (six joints); initial approach is to achieve one single base location and have single aspect of robot to connect and move between all the task point.

The last three ones may be modified by changing the robot program, whereas the first has to be completely decided before installing the robot in the workspace.

Research Question 2. User Model. There is no fixed technique or standard procedure to use a tracking system to explore user actions in VR. Human movement tracking systems are expected to generate real-time data that dynamically represent the pose changes of a human body (or a part of it), based on well-developed motion sensor technologies. Generic tracking systems employed within these systems adhere to the human body in order to collect movement information. These sensors are commonly categorized as mechanical, inertial, acoustic, radio, microwave, and magnetic-based. In such systems, the user is generally equipped with sensors on his hands, that give the sense of interacting with a virtual object. Additionally, these sensors don't give information about the position and orientation of the user's location in the system. Visual marker-based tracking is a technique where cameras are applied to track human movements, with identifiers placed upon the human body.

The whole idea of ICI is to increase immersion and remove the sensation of robot presence in free space. Since the robot has the plan to move between task points without colliding with the user. For safety concerns, the position of the user is very important. However, we cannot have complex tracking systems to locate the user. Normally the use of external cameras and markers are used to locate the user's position. But such systems increase the number of sensors attached to the user, which reduces the immersion. So the goal is to use less additional sensors as possible to give the best immersion experiences while getting the accurate location of the user for planning trajectories of the robot.

Challenge 2. User Immersion Experience

Haptic feedback for ICIs goal is to improve the immersion experience of users. The major idea is to eliminate the mechanical link so as to have perfect transparency in free space. But even trying to achieve this experience comes with the challenges like planning the robot motion between the VO being touched (without colliding with the user), and predicting which VO object the user intends to touch in the environment.

Research Question 3. Robot Motion Planning. In the given scenario the user is immersed in Virtual reality. The user has no information regarding the motion of the robot. The robot's motion has to be safe for the user, experiencing the VR environment. It should avoid collision with the user and also any other obstacles in the environment. The robot's motion should take into consideration collision with the user based on the tracking system used. It's not only for the user's safety, but also to have a better immersion of the user, the robot must place a real object at the place where the user wants to touch the VO as quickly as possible, and before the user's hand reach the contact location.

Research Question 4. Target Object Detection. Since they touch the user only when force feedback is required, intermittent contact interfaces, and in particular close-tracking-type devices, aim to provide more realistic interactions with virtual environments than classical contact haptic interfaces (CHI). User intention prediction in ICI remains a challenge to be properly addressed by the research community.

Previous systems force the user to interact with the VO, selected by it. These systems have to use control algorithms and interaction techniques to make the haptic rendering as efficient as possible. For the new system, we want to give the user freedom to select the VO to interact and the robot system should adapt to align itself w.r.t to the VO. The goal of such a system is to predict the VO the user wants to interact with as soon as possible. However, for these new systems, the two solutions (control algorithms and interaction techniques) are not enough to render the haptic sensation.

5   Roadmap for the Introduction of Cobots

The main research area considered as a contribution to this work is improving user safety and immersive experience for users of a ICI haptic device in human-robot interaction.

The user safety axis is improved by addressing four contributions. The first contribution (C1) consists of a set of safety techniques based on robot placement. The second (C2) creation of a user model for tracking user information, and the third (C3) techniques for robot trajectory planning. Then, the second axis immersive experience is improved by making sure the user does not lose the illusion of the environment. This aspect can be addressed by making sure the user does not wait a long time for the robot to reach the desired interactive location. This is achieved by addressing 2 contributions, the first contribution (C3) techniques in robot trajectory planning and the second contribution (C4) techniques for user goal predictions, designed to optimize the response time in ICI systems.

The relationship between the contributions and the research axis can be seen in Table 1.

Table 1. Contributions to the research axis

Contribution	User safety	Immersive experience
(C1) Safety techniques based on robot placement	x	
(C2) User model for tracking user information	x	
(C3) Techniques for robot trajectory planning	x	x
(C4) Techniques for user goal predictions		x

A set of safety techniques for users based on robot positioning (C1) was presented in [9]. In this paper, a design space for safety techniques was introduced using visuals restricting the interactive workspace of the robot and the user, in order to reduce potential unintended collisions. The dimensions of the workspace are defined by where the user wants to interact with the virtual environment as well as to ensure the safety of the user. Using this design of robot placement, a set of workspaces was developed to explore variations of the prop orientations. An evaluation focusing on the best solution for robot placement is done. Safety was evaluated and the ideal location of the robot was defined. The main constraint is that the robot end effector cannot touch the user's head (Fig. 4).

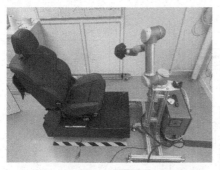 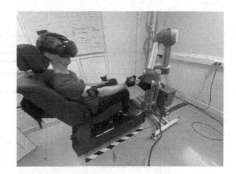

(a) The computed robot placement   (b) Robot interaction with user

Fig. 4. Placement analysis of the base table of the robot.

The model was designed to estimate the user location in the Robot Operating System (ROS) environment [4]. The model created had to have features such as movement of both arms and also the mobility of the user around the hip. These major three moving parts provided better information about the user's location, improving the user's safety in using an ICI system. A user study was designed to assess and test the performance of these motions to test the accuracy and reliability of creating a user model. Results suggested that the model is accurate for the given scenario in locating the user in the environment. Only five sensors are needed to have a good representation of the upper limbs of the user (Fig. 5). This property allows a simplified set up of users while guaranteeing their safety.

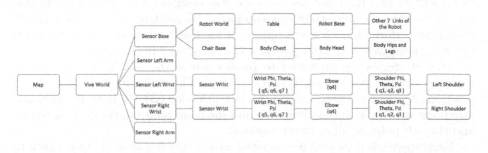

Fig. 5. Structure for both arms to evaluate the joint position of the arms q_i, the position of the hands, and the base position of the robot.

The helmet also adds additional information. The integration of the ROS node into the Unity simulation requires the implementation of a system architecture with elements under Windows and others under Linux (Fig. 6).

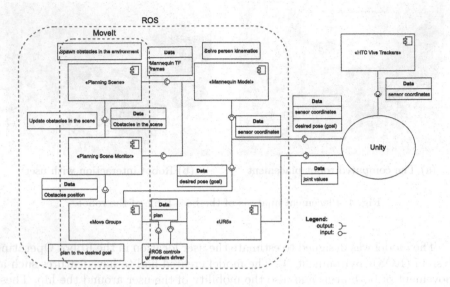

Fig. 6. System's Architecture.

An approach for the trajectory planning of robots was introduced in [10]. The goal is to increase the immersive experience (C3) by reducing the time taken by the robot to reach the contact area. This approach renders large surfaces and multiple textures through the use of a rotating prop, that couples the prop's rotation and position with the users' hand position when exploring a textured surface in VR. A use-case scenario was designed for contextualizing this approach. Later, a user study was conducted to validate the approach haptic rendering performance. A novel approach for the prediction of user intention based on head gaze and hand position was introduced in [11] (Fig. 7).

Four strategies are presented to predict where the user wants to interact with the virtual environment (C4) [11] (Fig. 8). The strategies include the hand position (A), the hand position and the gaze direction (B), the hand position and safe point to allow faster motions (C), and the hand position, the gaze direction, and the safe point to allow faster motions.

Each approach presented is evaluated on four key features: (1) time taken to prediction, (2) time taken by the robot to reach the contact area, (3) distance traveled by the robot, and (4) safety of the user. These approaches integrate an interaction technique for contact area selection and release.

A comparative analysis of data from all the trajectories shows that, if the objective is to maximize safety strategies (C) and (D) would be better. Both strategies (C) and (D) ensure safety by selecting safe points when the hand is

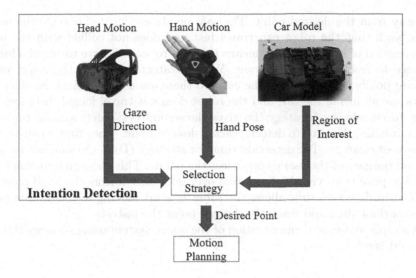

Fig. 7. Diagram of the inputs used to choose a robot movement strategy, hand, and head position with the gaze direction.

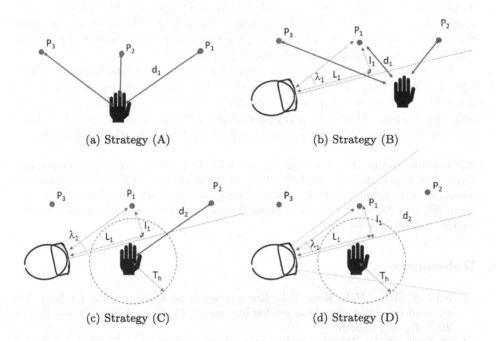

(a) Strategy (A)

(b) Strategy (B)

(c) Strategy (C)

(d) Strategy (D)

Fig. 8. Four strategies to detect human intention

far away from the desired point. The safe points are located outside the user's reach, such that the robot can travel fast and does not collide with the user. The selection of the safe points means that the robot will have to travel a longer distance to reach the desired point. While strategies (A) and (B) select intermediate points that are inside the car and there are no safe points. So since the points are all inside the car, and the robot does not travel longer distances but has reduced velocity. Strategy (D) gives the second-best safety and, at the same time minimize, the time to detect/reach a desired point. Therefore it can be seen as the best strategy. The detection time for strategy (D) is the smallest because we used the gaze of the user to pre-select the points. This plays an important role in giving priority to visual information over information from the hand position. The fastest detection time allows the robot to start moving to the desired point at the earliest time and reach the desired point the fastest.

A simple real-time demonstration of the above system using strategy (D) can be found here[1]

6   Conclusions and Future Work

This paper summarized the context of the introduction of cobot for the implementation of a haptic interface with intermittent contact. The different challenges were presented in order to guarantee the safety of the user and improve the user's immersion. The various stages presented are invariants to be considered for the implementation of similar experiences.

A work of diffusion remains to be done to put on GitHub the functions allowing to define the optimal placement of the robot, the generation of trajectories according to the environment, the position of the user, and his intention for new applications. Moreover, a transfer of the software to ROS2 could improve security by guaranteeing the real-time aspect of the information exchanges.

Acknowledgment. This work was funded under the LobbyBot project: Novel encountered type haptic devices, ANR-17-CE33 [21]. The authors of the article thank the members of the project for their help in carrying out this work, Lionel Dominjon, Sandrine Wullens, Allexandre Bouchet, Javier Posselt, Maud Marchal, Anatol Lecuyer and Victor Rodrigo Mercado Garcia.

References

1. Kim, Y., Kim, H.J., Kim, Y.J.: Encountered-type haptic display for large VR environment using per-plane reachability maps. Comput. Anim. Virtual Worlds **29**(3–4), e1814 (2018)
2. McNeely, W.A.: Robotic graphics: a new approach to force feedback for virtual reality. In: Proceedings of IEEE Virtual Reality Annual International Symposium. IEEE, pp. 336–341 (1993)

---

[1]   https://www.youtube.com/watch?v=wz0dJjk4-qk.

3. Araujo, B., Jota, R., Perumal, V., Yao, J.X., Singh, K., Wigdor, D.: Snake charmer: physically enabling virtual objects. In: Proceedings of the TEI 2016: Tenth International Conference on Tangible, Embedded, and Embodied Interaction. ACM, pp. 218–226 (2016)

4. Guda, V.: Contributions to utilize a cobot as intermittent contact haptic interfaces in virtual reality. Ph.D. dissertation, Ecole Centrale de Nantes (2022)

5. Huang, H.-Y., Ning, C.-W., Wang, P.-Y., Cheng, J.-H., Cheng, L.-P.: Haptic-go-round: A surrounding platform for encounter-type haptics in virtual reality experiences. In: Proceedings of the 2020 CHI Conference on Human Factors in Computing Systems, ser. CHI 2020. New York, NY, USA: Association for Computing Machinery, 2020, pp. 1–10. [Online]. https://doi.org/10.1145/3313831.3376476

6. Filippeschi, A., Brizzi, F., Ruffaldi, E., Jacinto, J.M., Avizzano, C.A.: Encountered-type haptic interface for virtual interaction with real objects based on implicit surface haptic rendering for remote palpation. In: 2015 IEEE/RSJ International Conference on Intelligent Robots and Systems (IROS). IEEE, pp. 5904–5909 (2015)

7. Kim, Y., Kim, S., Oh, U., Kim, Y.J.: Synthesizing the roughness of textured surfaces for an encountered-type haptic display using spatiotemporal encoding. IEEE Trans. Haptics 14(1), 32–43 (2020)

8. Posselt, J., et al.: Toward virtual touch: investigating encounter-type haptics for perceived quality assessment in the automotive industry. In: Proceedings of the 14th Annual EuroVR Conference, 2017, pp. 11–13 (2017)

9. Guda, V.K., Chablat, D., Chevallereau, C.: Safety in a human robot interactive: application to haptic perception. In: Chen, J.Y.C., Fragomeni, G. (eds.) HCII 2020. LNCS, vol. 12190, pp. 562–574. Springer, Cham (2020). https://doi.org/10.1007/978-3-030-49695-1_38

10. Gutierrez, A., Guda, V.K., Mugisha, S., Chevallereau, C., Chablat, DC.: Trajectory planning in dynamics environment: application for haptic perception in safe human-robot interaction. In: Digital Human Modeling and Applications in Health, Safety, Ergonomics and Risk Management. Health, Operations Management, and Design: 13th International Conference, DHM: Held as Part of the 24th HCI International Conference, HCII 2022, Virtual Event, June 26-July 1, 2022, Proceedings. Part II, pp. 313–328. Springer, Cham (2022)

11. Guda, V., Mugisha, S., Chevallereau, C., Zoppi, M., Molfino, R., Chablat, D.: Motion strategies for a cobot in a context of intermittent haptic interface. J. Mech. Robot. 14(4), 041012 (2022)

The Efficiency of Augmented Pointing with and Without Speech in a Collaborative Virtual Environment

Oliver Herbort$^{(\boxtimes)}$ (ID) and Lisa-Marie Krause (ID)

Department of Psychology, University of Würzburg, Würzburg, Germany
`oliver.herbort@uni-wuerzburg.de`

Abstract. Pointing is a ubiquitous part of human communication. However, pointing gestures to distal referents are often misunderstood systematically, which may limit the usefulness of pointing. We examined pointing-based communication in a collaborative virtual environment (CVE) to address three questions. First, we wanted to evaluate the potential of apparently natural but technically augmented pointing in CVEs, such as presenting a warped pointer for increased legibility or the ability to assume the pointer's perspective. Second, we wanted to test whether technical improvements in pointing accuracy also facilitate communication if pointing is accompanied by speech. Third, we wanted to check whether pointing accuracy is correlated with the efficiency of communication involving pointing and speech. An experiment revealed that pointing-based communication has considerable potential to be enhanced in CVEs, albeit the specific augmentation procedure we employed did not improve pointing-based communication. Importantly, improvements in pointing accuracy also facilitated communication when speech was allowed. Thereby, speech reduced but could not rule out misunderstandings. Finally, even a small gain in pointing accuracy allowed participants to agree on a referent faster. In summary, the experiment suggests that augmented pointing may considerably improve interactions in CVEs. Moreover, speech cannot fully compensate misunderstandings of pointing gestures and relatively small differences in pointing accuracy affect the efficiency of communication of speech is allowed.

Keywords: Pointing · Collaborative virtual environment · Speech · Multimodal reference · Deixis

1 Introduction

When people interact, they frequently use pointing gestures to refer to locations or objects in the environment. Pointing gestures appear especially helpful, when verbal descriptions are unlikely to quickly guide the attention of others to the referent. This

---

Supplementary Information The online version contains supplementary material available at https://doi.org/10.1007/978-3-031-35741-1_37.

V. G. Duffy (Ed.): HCII 2023, LNCS 14028, pp. 510–524, 2023.
https://doi.org/10.1007/978-3-031-35741-1_37

may be the case when the object is not salient (e.g., a wild animal hidden in a distant tree line) or when the vocabulary to describe the object is lacking (e.g., shopping pastries in a foreign country). Thus, it comes as no surprise that attempts have been made to facilitate pointing in collaborative virtual environments (CVE) [11, 16, 18, 19]. In the present paper, we want to examine the effectiveness and efficiency of pointing-based communication with and without speech in CVEs.

1.1 Pointing Accuracy

As helpful as pointing may be, pointing does not always guarantee accurate reference in situations, in which a relatively high degree of pointing accuracy would be required while it is not possible to touch the referent. This has mainly two reasons, which result from the necessity to extrapolated from the gesture toward potential referents. First, the process introduces unsystematic errors. That is, the same gesture may be interpreted in different ways in different situations. Second, the interpretations of pointing gestures are typically biased [3] as pointing production and interpretation follow different geometric rules. A pointer typically puts their index finger on the line between their eyes and the referent [6, 17]. Consequently, the eyes of the pointer, index finger, and referent form a line. By contrast, observers typically use a combination of two different visual cues [8]. When beside the pointer, observers typically extrapolate from the arm and index finger, which results in upward biased interpretations.[1] The more observers approach the perspective of the pointer, the more they rely on the vector defined by their (the observers') eyes and the pointer's index finger. This mode of extrapolation typically introduces sideward biases. Additional vertical biases may result when the eye heights of pointer and observer differ. Besides these perspective-induced biases, other biases exist such as non-linearities in human extrapolation [6].

These systematic biases usually contribute considerably to the errors that emerge during pointing-based communication. Hence, different attempts have been made to reduce them. For example, Herbort and Kunde used instructions to improve the legibility of pointing gestures or observers' interpretations thereof [7]. An ingenious method for compensating biases in pointing perception in collaborative virtual environments has been suggested by Sousa and colleagues [16]. They presented a distorted or "warped" version of a pointer in the virtual environment of the observer. The virtual pointer was transformed in such a way, that pointing gestures could be understood better by a naïve observer. This approach has the advantage that the legibility of pointing gestures is improved but the gestures still appear natural – which may be helpful in scenarios that aim for realism. The method has since then been improved to counteract horizontal and vertical biases [11]. By contrast, other methods such as laser pointers, spotlights, and very long arms [19] may be more effective means of reference but lack realism. Thus, one central question of the present paper is to further examine the potential of the presentation of warped virtual pointers.

---

[1] In the current paper, we examine misunderstandings or errors between pointers and observers without considering the individual contributions of both interlocutors. If we use terms such as "biased interpretations", we refer to the mismatch between the pointer's referent and the observer's guess thereof without attributing the misunderstanding to either of the interlocutors.

1.2 Pointing and Speech

In many studies referenced above, pointing was examined in isolation [3, 6–8, 17]. By contrast, pointing is usually accompanied by speech in natural situations. Pointers thus could provide additional verbal descriptions that would allow observers to discern whether they correctly identified the referent. Hence, speech has the potential to eliminate the inevitable inaccuracies of pointing gestures. Moreover, it has been suggested that pointing gestures refer mostly to larger area of space [4] rather than specific locations or small areas [10]. In this case, fine-grained improvement of pointing legibility may be shrouded by verbally conveyed information.

This raises the question whether speech compensate the inaccuracies of pointing and if so, to which extent more accurate pointing nevertheless facilitates communication. With respect to the first question, previous research indicates that pointing per se is a helpful tool for reference, which, however, may be partially compensated by verbal descriptions [9]. The expected accuracy of pointing as such also plays a role. For example, when the distance between interlocutors and an array of potential referents is increased, also more words, especially location descriptions, are used to single out the referent [2, 12]. At the same time, the frequency of pointing gestures decreases.

The second question is more difficult to address because the accuracy of pointing is typically difficult to manipulate in isolation. In previous experiments, changes in pointing accuracy resulted from other changes in the situation (e.g., distance to referents [2]), which in turn affected the types of descriptions used, the prevalence of pointing as such, and the expectations of participants. This makes it difficult to pin-point the effect of pointing accuracy on the effectiveness and efficiency of pointing-based communication. The warping technique allows a unique opportunity to examine the isolated effect of pointing accuracy, because it allows to manipulate pointing accuracy without any apparent changes in the environment. Thus, neither the pointer nor the observer may be aware or even able to detect this type of manipulation.

1.3 The Current Experiment

In the current experiment, we examined pointing-based communication in a CVE. The CVE was modelled after a planetarium, in which one person (pointer) was asked to help another person (observer) find various predetermined planets in an array of similar planets. Our aims were threefold.

First, we wanted to evaluate augmented pointing methods that reduce biases in pointing perception. We evaluated four pointing modes in conditions, in which participants were asked not to speak. In a *naïve mode*, the pointer's body postures were presented veridically in the observer's virtual environment. In a *warping mode*, the pointer's posture was transformed to increase pointing legibility [11, 16]. Both modes were indissociable from the viewpoint of the participants. Next, we used a *pointer perspective mode* in which the observer could assume the perspective of the pointer. It has been shown that this virtually eliminates systematic misunderstandings and reduces unsystematic variability [5]. This mode thus can serve as an upper-bound of the performance that could be achieved with elaborate warping techniques and hence with a natural appearing virtual representation of the pointer. Finally, as a comparison, we included a *laser pointer mode* in which referents can be indicated unambiguously. We expected minimal errors in the laser pointer condition, smaller biases and total errors in the warping and pointer perspective conditions, and larger biases and total errors in the naïve condition.

Second, we wanted to check whether and to which extent the reduction in biases by augmented pointing also affects the accuracy and speed of communication when accompanied by speech. To this end, the different pointing modes were combined with the possibility to speak. If speech fully compensates for misunderstandings, few if any misunderstandings should occur in the speech conditions. If speech is insufficient to rule out misunderstandings, we expect that speech reduces but does not eliminate misunderstandings. In this case, misunderstandings should be largest in the naïve pointing mode, medium in the warping and pointer perspective mode, and smallest in the laser pointer mode. If the accuracy of pointing furthermore affects the efficiency of the communication, we would expect that participants are fastest in the laser pointer mode, slower in the warping and pointer perspective mode, and slowest in the naïve mode. Moreover, the apparent accuracy of pointing is expected to affect how participants communicate verbally.

Third, we were interested in the relationship between overall pointing accuracy and the efficiency in establishing a joint focus of attention based on pointing and speech. To this end, we correlated pointing accuracy in conditions without speech with the speed in the respective conditions across participants.

2 Methods

2.1 Participants

Forty-eight persons (13 male, 34 female, 41 right-handed, 6 left-handed, mean age 28 years range 20 to 67, one participant did not disclose gender, handedness, and age) or 24 pointer-observer dyads from the Würzburg area participated in exchange for course credit or money. The experiment was in accordance with the standards of the ethics committee of the Department of Psychology of the University of Würzburg.

2.2 Stimuli and Apparatus

Both members of a dyad participated in the same room. They saw visual representations of each other in VR but could directly hear the other participant's voice. Both participants were seated on chairs facing the same direction with a lateral distance of 100 cm. The observer always sat to the right of the pointer and in front of a small desk. Both participants were immersed in a virtual environment with a HTC Vive Pro (observer) or HTC Vive Pro Eye (pointer) head mounted display (HMD). Both HMDs have identical displays. The Vive Pro Eye is equipped with an additional eye tracker, which was used to visualize the eye-movements of the pointer. The pointer wielded two HTC Vive wireless Controllers. Additionally, HTC Vive Trackers were attached to the pointer's upper arms. The two PCs controlling the experiment for the pointer and observer were connected via LAN. The experiment was created with the Unity 3D engine.

The VR environment consisted of a virtual planetarium, in which planets were presented on an imaginary sphere with radius 300 cm (Fig. 1, Supplemental Video 1). Planets were arranged in a grid of 37 columns (azimuths of -90° to 90° in 5° steps) and 16 rows (elevations of -15° to 60° in 5° steps). Planets were random combinations of the features diameter (10.0 cm, 12.5 cm, 15.0 cm), texture (Venus, Mars, Jupiter, Saturn, Neptune, Pluto, textures from nasa3d.arc.nasa.gov/images), and moons (none, small moon with texture of Phobos, large moon with texture of Phobos, large moon with texture of Charon, two moons with textures of Phobos and Charon). Planets were presented at random orientations. Hence, planets with identical size, texture, and moon configuration differed with respect to the part of the texture facing the participant, the relative position of the moons, and adjacent planets. The planets were newly generated at the beginning of each block but did not change within blocks. For the pointer, the target planet was indicated by a green square-shaped marker. The observer could move a similar green marker (cursor) with the mouse to select planets. The cursor moved on the planet sphere. Both participants could not see the cursor or marker of the respective other participant.

The avatars were placed on a wooden bench (160 cm x 40 cm x 51 cm) at the center of the planet sphere. The distance of the avatars corresponded to the distance of the participants in the lab. The bench was positioned on a wooden floor. The pointer's avatar was presented as highly stylized figure consisting of a head, a torso, and two arms and hands, which formed a pointing gesture. The observer's avatar only consisted of a head. The position and orientation of the HMDs was mapped on the avatars' heads. In addition, the pointer's avatar reflected the pointer's eye and lid movements. The position and orientation of the pointer's handheld controllers and trackers were mapped onto the pointer's virtual hands, wrists, elbows, and shoulders.

In the laser pointer condition, the pointer's right index finger emitted a red transparent laser ray that ended on the planet sphere. The ray was visible for pointers and observers. In the warping condition, the pointer's arms and hand were presented unchanged to the pointer but were presented rotated to the observer. The rotation was computed as follows.[2] First, the pointed-at position A was estimated by extrapolating the vector defined by the pointer's cyclopean eye and their right index fingertip toward the planet sphere. Next, the observer's naïve guess B was estimated by extrapolating the pointer's right index finger to the planet sphere. The angle between A, the pointer's right shoulder, and B was computed. The arm was then rotated around the shoulder by this angle, so that the positions A and the rotated position B' would be aligned from the observer's viewpoint. Note that this procedure does not use information about the exact referent except for its distance.

---

[2] Our algorithm differed from previously applied warping methods [11,16]. Unlike [16], it takes horizontal errors into account but does not consider the non-linearity of pointing extrapolation. Unlike [11], we used a parameter-free geometric model for simplicity.

2.3 Procedure

Upon providing informed consent, the participants were randomly assigned the role of pointer or observer. Both participants received the HMDs. Next, the pointer was asked to stay in a steady posture while the positions of the shoulders, elbows, wrists, and fingertip relative to the tracker position were determined with a third tracker to allow an accurate mapping of the pointer's posture to their avatar. The experiment was split into eight blocks. At the beginning of each block, the participants were instructed orally by the experimenter. From the view of the pointer, a trial began when a planet was enclosed by the green marker. From the view of the observer, the trial began when the cursor appeared, which could be moved with the mouse. In the first 0.25 s of the trial, cursor and marker zoomed in on their respective positions to facilitate visual detection of the marker or cursor. The trial lasted until the observer had marked one planet with the cursor and pressed the left mouse button. Then marker and cursor disappeared for one second before the next trial was started.

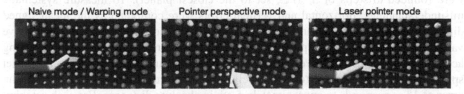

Fig. 1. The different pointing modes from the observer's perspective.

The blocks differed with respect to the modality and the pointing mode. There were two modality conditions. In the *pointing-only* blocks, the pointer was asked to point at the referent and the observer was asked to guess the pointed at planet as good as possible. Participants were instructed not to speak. In the *pointing + speech* blocks, the pointer could point. Both participants were additionally allowed to talk to each other but were asked not to describe the planet with the help of the rows and columns of the planet grid (e.g., "third planet from the right in the fourth row from the top") and to not refer to the planet position of previous trials.

We presented four different pointing mode conditions. In the naïve mode, the avatars of pointer and observer were presented unaltered. In the warping mode, the pointer's right arm was presented unaltered to the pointer but rotated as described above to the observer. In the pointer perspective mode, observers could assume the viewpoint of the pointer by holding down the right mouse button. More specifically, the position of the virtual viewpoint of the observers was aligned to that of the pointer but the observer's head rotations still controlled the direction of the observer's virtual viewpoint. In the laser pointer mode, a laser beam protruded from the pointers finger. The laser beam was visible for pointers and observers.

The experiment was split into eight blocks. For one half of the participants, the first four blocks were *pointing-only* blocks and the remaining blocks were *pointing + speech* blocks. For the other half, this order was reversed. Pointing modes were randomly ordered within the first and second half of the experiment. Each block consisted of two warm-up trials followed by 21 test trials. Targets were presented at azimuths of -45°, -30°, -15°, 0°, 15°, 30°, and 45° and elevations of 0°, 15°, and 30°. Each combination of azimuth and elevation was presented once. Trial order was randomized. The warm-up trials were drawn from the set of possible test trials. During the experiment, the experimenter coded the occurrence of different categories of verbal descriptions using a keyboard. The categories were features (e.g., "It's the *small, red* planet"), locations (e.g., "It's in the *middle*."), deictic expressions ("It's *this* planet."), instructions (e.g., "You need to look left"), and off-topic themes.

2.4 Data Analysis and Reduction

For each trial, the click position of the observer's guesses, the reaction time (defined as the interval from when the marker finished zooming in on the referent and the moment the observer clicked on a planet), and the speech content were recorded. Click positions were recorded in angular coordinates (azimuth, elevation) on the planet sphere and were rounded to steps of 5° (i.e., set to the closest planet). To measure systematic misunderstandings, horizontal and vertical errors were computed as the mean signed difference between referent and guess for azimuth and elevation, respectively. Positive values imply rightward and upward biases of the observer. To measure overall pointing accuracy, we computed the average total angle between guess and referent on the planet sphere (total error) and the percentage of clicks on the correct planet. For comparison, an error of 1° corresponds to approximately 5 cm in absolute distances. For each category of speech content, we coded whether it was used in a trial at least once. After visual inspection of the data, trials were discarded if total errors exceeded 60° (5 trials) or if reaction times were less than 1 s (1). In total, 4026 trials were entered into the analysis. Data were averaged over dyads, modalities and pointing modes. We analyzed the data with R (version 4.2.1[13]) and computed ANOVAS with the afex package (version 1.1–1[14]). Data, scripts and supplemental material are provided on https://osf.io/97xb2/.

3 Results

3.1 Errors and Reaction Times

The 2D-histograms of Fig. 2 give an impression of the errors made in the different conditions. Three things are noteworthy. First, except for the laser pointer mode, errors were frequent and often quite large in the pointing only condition. Second, the possibility to speak reduced but did not eliminate errors. Third, there were no errors in the laser pointer condition. Errors and reaction times were analyzed with within-participant ANOVAs with factors of pointing mode and modality, using a Greenhouse-Geisser correction if applicable. Significant results were followed up with t-tests comparing the naïve condition to the other pointing modes for each level of modality ($\alpha = .05$) . Significant results are indicated by lines in Fig. 3. The full statistics are listed in Supplemental Table 1.

Horizontal Errors
Figure 3A shows systematic horizontal errors. Not surprisingly, horizontal errors were smaller when speech was allowed, $F(1,23) = 7.88$, $p = .010$, $\eta_p^2 = .26$. The pointing

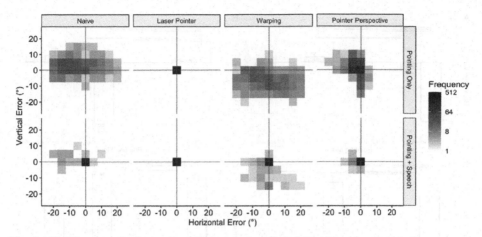

Fig. 2. 2D-Histograms of errors by pointing mode and modality. The blue lines indicate correct interpretations of pointing gestures. The color scale is logarithmic.

mode affected errors, $F(1.6,37.2) = 13.40$, $p < .001$, $\eta_p^2 = .37$. Both factors interacted, $F(1.6,37.7) = 7.69$, $p = .003$, $\eta_p^2 = .25$. Significant (p < .05) results of follow-up t-tests are marked as lines in Fig. 3A. Pointing gestures were interpreted as more leftward in the naïve mode compared to the other modes in the pointing only condition. In the pointing and speech condition, the effect was only preserved when comparing the naïve with the warping mode.

Vertical Errors
There was no significant main effect of modality on vertical errors, $F(1,23) = 13.97$, $p = .217$, $\eta_p^2 = .07$. However, the pointing mode affected vertical errors, $F(2.3,52.6) = 67.88$, $p < .001$, $\eta_p^2 = .75$. Pointing mode and modality interacted, $F(2.5,57.5) = 41.15$, $p < .001$, $\eta_p^2 = .64$. Pointing gestures were interpreted as more upward in the naïve mode compared to the other modes in the pointing only condition. In the pointing and speech condition, the naïve mode resulted in more upward interpretations than the laser pointer mode, warping mode, and marginally also the pointer perspective mode ($p = .083$).

Total Errors
Total errors (Fig. 3C) were considerably smaller when participants could speak, $F(1,23) = 7.95$, $p < .001$, $\eta_p^2 = .93$. In addition, the pointing mode affected total errors, $F(2.5,65.4) = 101.30$, $p < .001$, $\eta_p^2 = .82$. Pointing mode and modality interacted, $F(2.1,47.5) = 65.13$, $p < .001$, $\eta_p^2 = .74$. Observers were more accurate in the laser pointer and pointer perspective mode for both modalities. However, the warping mode resulted in more errors than the naïve mode, regardless of whether speech was allowed.

Percent Errors
In the naïve and warping mode, observers were rarely able to select the correct planet when speech was not allowed (Fig. 4D). Error rates were greatly reduced when speech was allowed, $F(1,23) = 575.39$, $p < .001$, $\eta_p^2 = .96$. The pointing mode likewise affected the percentage of errors, $F(2.1,49.1) = 185.91$, $p < .001$, $\eta_p^2 = .89$. Pointing mode

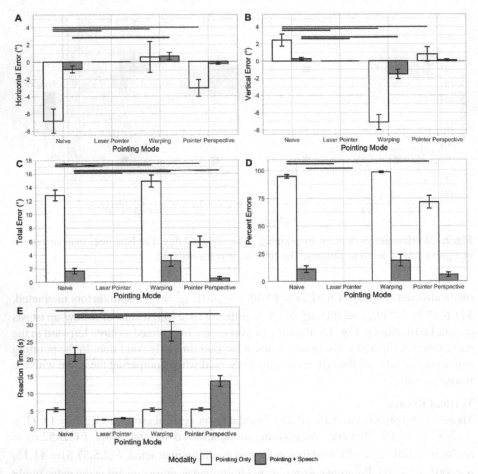

Fig. 3. Mean errors (A-D) and reaction times (E) by pointing mode and modality. No errors were made in the laser pointer mode. The horizontal lines indicate significant differences between conditions. The full statistics of the respective tests are reported as Supplemental Table 1. Positive horizontal and vertical errors are rightwards (A) and upwards (B), respectively.

and modality interacted, $F(2.1, 47.9) = 99.89$, $p < .001$, $\eta_p^2 = .81$. Follow-up t-tests revealed a higher accuracy of the laser pointer mode compared to the naïve mode for both modalities. The pointer perspective mode also helped reducing errors when speech was not allowed. The remaining comparisons approached significance (all $ps \leq .062$).

Reaction Times

Figure 3E shows reaction times. Not surprisingly, reaction times were considerably shorter in the pointing-only condition, $F(1, 23) = 85.41$, $p < .001$, $\eta_p^2 = .79$. Reaction times depended on the pointing mode, $F(2.4, 55.1) = 53.51$, $p < .001$, $\eta_p^2 = .70$. Pointing mode and modality interacted, $F(2.3, 52.6) = 45.85$, $p < .001$, $\eta_p^2 = .56$. Follow-up t-tests revealed that reaction times in the naïve mode were shorter than those in the warping condition but longer than those in the laser pointer and pointer perspective conditions when speech was allowed. In the pointing only condition, only the laser pointer mode yielded faster reactions than the naïve mode.

3.2 Relationship Between Errors and Reaction Time

Next, we address the question how participants benefitted from pointing gestures, by comparing total errors of the pointing only condition with the reaction times in the corresponding pointing and speech condition. We computed repeated measures correlations to assess the relationship of both variables in each dyad across different pointing modes (rmcorr package, version 0.5.4 [1]). Figure 4 shows a scatter plot of both variables for each dyad and pointing mode. The analysis revealed a positive correlation between pointing accuracy and reaction times when all pointing modes were considered, $r_{rm}(71)$ = .78, 95% CI [.67, .86], $p < .001$. A significant correlation was also found when only the data of the naïve and warping mode were entered into the analysis, $r_{rm}(23) = .43$, 95% CI [.04, .71], $p < .032$. In both cases, an increase in total pointing accuracy of 1° shortened reaction times by approximately 1.4 s.

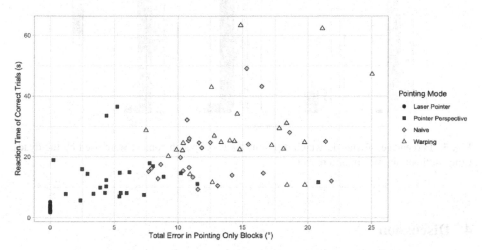

Fig. 4. Relationship between pointing accuracy and reaction time

3.3 Speech Content

Finally, we examined the speech content across pointing modes. Figure 5 shows the percentage of trials in which different types of verbal expression were used. Data was analyzed with an ANOVA with factors of pointing mode and speech content. The category "other" was not included in the analysis. Follow-up t-tests between the naïve mode and the other modes for each type of expression are provided in Supplemental Table 2 and depicted as lines in Fig. 5. The pointing mode affected the prevalence of expressions, $F(2.2, 49.8) = 89.60$, $p < .001$, $\eta_p^2 = .80$. T-tests revealed that overall, features were described more often than locations, locations descriptions were more common than deictic expressions, and deictic expressions were more frequent than instructions, all $t(23) > 4.00$, all $ps < .001$, all $d_zs \geq 0.82$. Likewise, the different types of speech content were used with varying frequencies, $F(1.8, 41.7) = 293.45, p < .001, \eta_p^2 = .93$. Both factors interacted, $F(4.6, 105.5) = 33.35, p < .001, \eta_p^2 = .59$. The interaction can be mainly attributed to location descriptions and deictic expressions being reduced stronger than feature descriptions in the laser pointer mode compared to the other pointing modes. Follow-up t-test revealed that features, locations, deictic expressions, and instructions were less common in the laser pointer condition than the naïve condition. Additionally, more instructions were given in the warping condition compared to the naïve conditions.

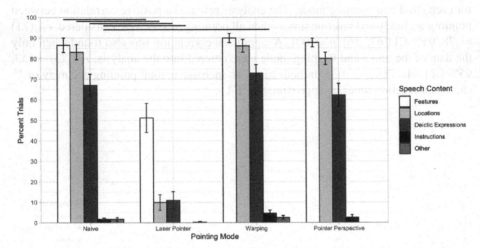

Fig. 5. Percentage of trials in which different types of speech content were used by the dyads. Lines indicate significant differences.

4   Discussion

We studied the efficiency and effectiveness of pointing-based communication with and without speech in a CVE to address three questions. Our first question was whether apparently natural pointing can be augmented to increase pointing accuracy. The answer is mixed. On the one hand, the warping mode reduced horizontal errors but increased vertical errors, resulting in an overall worse performance in our experiment. On the other hand, the presence of systematic errors per se and the decent accuracy of the pointer perspective mode, which indicates the level of accuracy that might be approximated with improved warping techniques, suggests that augmented presentations of pointing gestures may considerably facilitate interactions in CVEs.

Our second question addressed whether accuracy differences between pointing modes are leveled out by speech and whether such differences affect the efficiency when communicating with pointing and speech. Not surprisingly, it became evident that speech allows to greatly reduce the number of errors. However, errors were still made in a substantial percentage of trials (e.g., 11% in the naïve mode) and differed between conditions. Thus, speech can only partially compensate misunderstandings of pointing gestures. Moreover, the accuracy of the different pointing modes without speech were related to the efficiency of communication in the pointing and speech conditions. For example, participants required on average about 14 s to agree on a planet in the relatively accurate pointer perspective mode but twice as long in the warping mode. The different modes of pointing also affected the content of speech. Not surprisingly, locations were rarely described if pointing was unambiguous but frequently used in the other conditions. This supports the notion that pointing as a method of reference is an integral part of otherwise verbal communication [9] and does not only supplement speech with principally redundant gestures.

Thirdly, and related to the previous point, the accuracy of pointing of a specific dyad in a specific pointing mode without speech was tightly correlated with the respective performance in the condition with speech. The analysis showed that even small increments in pointing accuracy directly facilitated verbal interactions.

4.1 Implications for Augmenting Pointing

In the present experiment, pointing interpretations were biased left-ward and up-ward. This result is consistent with the notion that pointers align eye, fingertip, and referent whereas observers extrapolate the pointer's index finger vector [6, 17]. Thus, the behavior in the naïve mode replicates previous findings in real and virtual settings [3, 5–8, 17].

We included a warping mode that was intended to counteract these biases and thus reduce the average magnitude of errors in pointing-based communication. The warping mode indeed shifted systematic errors. In the naïve mode, horizontal errors were relatively large and were considerably reduced by the warping mode. However, vertical errors were smaller than expected and resulted in an overcompensation by the warping mechanism. This led to a strong downward bias and an increment of total errors and the percentage of errors. However, given that vertical errors are typically higher than in our experiment and that the warping technique has been shown to reduce errors elsewhere [11, 16], we would argue that it is – in principle – a feasible technique. However, the parameter-free application in the present experiment may have been an oversimplified approach. First, the present data revealed some variability between systematic errors of the different dyads. Second, different realizations of CVEs and the representation of avatars may also affect biases in pointing interpretations. Hence, a calibration of warping algorithms to different users and environments may proof useful [11]. Third, using elaborate models of pointing perception, which account for other biases, might further improve performance and the generalizability of warping mechanisms [6, 8].

Pointer-observer misunderstandings are mostly rooted in the difference in viewpoints [5]. Hence, we introduced the pointer perspective mode in which both interlocutors assume the same perspective and in which systematic misunderstandings appear to be minimal. As participants rely mostly on the position of the index finger in their visual fields in this condition, visual uncertainty associated with extrapolating the finger is small in this condition [5]. Thus, this mode can be seen as an upper boundary for the accuracy that can be achieved with a sophisticated morphing method. Indeed, accuracy was much higher in this condition than in the naïve mode and participants could agree on a planet much faster if speech was allowed. Thus, given these increments, it seems a worthwhile endeavor to further improve warping techniques.

Finally, we included a simple laser-pointer condition in our experiment, in which reference was unambiguous. This mode was vastly superior to any other mode, including the pointer perspective mode. Hence, the following suggestions can be derived from the data. Virtual interactions could greatly benefit of some means of unambiguous distal reference, such as a virtual laser pointer. In our opinion, this method is unlikely to be rivaled by any warping technique. However, if a CVE setting aims for realism, interactions can be improved with warping techniques. Even if the accuracy of pointing will still be limited, small reductions in pointer-observer biases may facilitate virtual interactions.

4.2 Integration of Speech and Pointing

The experiment showed that speech cannot fully compensate for errors in pointing-based communication. One possibility is, that observers did not wait for the pointers' descriptions in a subset of trials. However, the inspection of the data revealed that reaction times in speech trials that eventually resulted in an error were on average larger than in correct trials and did not differ substantially in speech content (Supplemental Table 3). Thus, it seems that errors were made despite verbal descriptions. Another hypothesis is that observers sometimes selected planets that accidentally corresponded to the pointers' descriptions. This might happen when pointers expect that observers only look for a planet in the vicinity of the pointed-at referent and hence use descriptions that single out the target only locally. Simultaneously, observers might assume that the referent must be close to their incorrect interpretation of the pointing gesture and select a planet that matches the pointer's description. In this case, the misunderstanding remains unnoticed despite speech. If that was the case, one would expect that the total errors in trials in which errors were made do not differ considerably in speech and pointing-only trials. An inspection of the data supported this hypothesis (Supplemental Table 4). This finding is also consistent with the notion that pointing gestures should be considered indicating relatively small areas of space containing the referent [10, 15] and not a precise location.

Finally, the comparison of pointing accuracy without speech and reaction times in condition with speech revealed that small changes in pointing accuracy can considerably affect the time necessary to agree on a referent. In our dataset, an improvement of pointing accuracy of 1° resulted in a 1.4 s shorter reaction time. This effect was corroborated when comparing only the naïve and warping mode. As both modes were indistinguishable for the participants, the effect cannot be attributed to situation-induced changes in the interlocutors' behaviors, such as changed level of caution or verbalization when pointing appears more or less precise [12]. This suggests that interlocutors may try to refer to specific locations or small areas with pointing gestures and not only broader regions of space. Of course, the potential gain associated with improved pointing accuracy can be expected to depend highly on the setting. We deliberately opted for a situation in which precise pointing is required and giving verbal descriptions is difficult. Thus, relatively high gains of more accurate pointing could have been expected. How these effects play out in other situations is an open question.

4.3 Conclusion

The study revealed a close relationship between pointing acuity and the speed and effectivity of establishing a joint focus of attention. Speech could compensate for the limited acuity of pointing perception only partially and at the expense of reducing communication efficiency. Attempts to facilitate pointing-based communication in CVE can potentially have a considerable effect but are not straight forward to implement. Our simple, parameter-free warping mode indeed increased misunderstandings. This suggests that a warped pointer representation might need to consider more information, such as the observer viewpoint, individual factors, or aspects of the CVE. Nevertheless, if such advanced warping techniques could approximate the performance of our pointer perspective mode – which should be theoretically possible – pointing-based interaction with and without speech in CVEs could be improved considerably while still giving the impression of a natural interaction.

Acknowledgments. We thank Anne Hanfbauer and Stefanie Flepsen for their help with the data collection. This work was supported by the German Research Foundation DFG (Grants HE6710/5–1 and HE6710/6–1 to Oliver Herbort).

References

1. Bakdash, J.Z., Marusich, L.R.: Repeated measures correlation. Front. Psychol. **8**(456), 1–13 (2017). https://doi.org/10.3389/fpsyg.2017.00456
2. Bangerter, A.: Using pointing and describing to achieve joint focus of attention in dialogue. Psychol. Sci. **15**(6), 415–419 (2004). https://doi.org/10.1111/j.0956-7976.2004.0069
3. Bangerter, A., Oppenheimer, D.M.: Accuracy in detecting referents of pointing gestures unaccompanied by language. Gesture **6**(1), 85–102 (2006). https://doi.org/10.1075/gest.6.1.05ban
4. Butterworth, G., Itakura, S.: How the eyes, head and hand serve definite reference. Br. J. Dev. Psychol. **18**(1), 25–50 (2000). https://doi.org/10.1348/026151000165553
5. Herbort, O., Krause, L.-M., Kunde, W.: Perspective determines the production and interpretation of pointing gestures. Psychon. Bull. Rev. **28**(2), 641–648 (2020). https://doi.org/10.3758/s13423-020-01823-7
6. Herbort, O., Kunde, W.: Spatial (mis-)interpretation of pointing gestures to distal referents. J. Exp. Psychol.: Hum. Percept. Perform. **42**(1), 78–89 (2016). https://doi.org/10.1037/xhp0000126
7. Herbort, O., Kunde, W.: How to point and to interpret pointing gestures? Instructions can reduce pointer-observer misunderstandings. Psychol. Res. **82**(2), 395–406 (2018). https://doi.org/10.1007/s00426-016-0824-8
8. Krause, L.M., Herbort, O.: The observer's perspective determines which cues are used when interpreting pointing gestures. J. Exp. Psychol.: Hum. Percept. Perform. **47**(9), 1209–1225 (2021). https://doi.org/10.1037/xhp0000937
9. Louwerse, M.M., Bangerter, A.: Focusing attention with deictic gestures and linguistic expressions. In: Proceedings of the 27th Annual Meeting of the Cognitive Science Society (2005)
10. Lücking, A., Pfeiffer, T., Rieser, H.: Pointing and reference reconsidered. J. Pragmat. **77**, 56–79 (2015). https://doi.org/10.1016/j.pragma.2014.12.013

11. Mayer, S., et al.: Improving humans' ability to interpret deictic gestures in virtual reality. In: Proceedings of the 2020 CHI Conference on Human Factors in Computing Systems, pp. 1–14. Association for Computing Machinery, New York (2020). https://doi.org/10.1145/3313831. 3376340

12. Pechmann, T., Deutsch, W.: The development of verbal and nonverbal devices for reference. J. Exp. Child Psychol. **34**(2), 330–341 (1982). https://doi.org/10.1016/0022-0965(82)90050-9

13. R Core Team R: A language and environment for statistical computing. R Foundation for Statistical Computing, Vienna, Austria (2022)

14. Singmann, H., Bolker, B., Westfall, J., Aust, F., Ben-Shachar, M.S.: afex: Analysis of factorial experiments (2022)

15. van der Sluis, I., Krahmer, E.: Generating multimodal references. Discourse Process. **44**(3), 145–174 (2007). https://doi.org/10.1080/01638530701600755

16. Sousa, M., dos Anjos, R.K., Mendes, D., Billinghurst, M., Jorge, J.: Warping DEIXIS: distorting gestures to enhance collaboration. In: Proceedings of the 2019 CHI Conference on Human Factors in Computing Systems, pp. 1–12. CHI 2019, Association for Computing Machinery, New York (2019). https://doi.org/10.1145/3290605.3300838

17. Wnuczko, M., Kennedy, J.M.: Pivots for pointing: visually-monitored pointing has higher arm elevations than pointing blindfolded. J. Exp. Psychol.: Hum. Percept. Perform. **37**(5), 1485–1491 (2011). https://doi.org/10.1037/a0024232

18. Wong, N., Gutwin, C.: Where are you pointing? The accuracy of deictic pointing in CVEs. In: Proceedings of the ACM Conference on Human Factors in Computing Systems (CHI 2010), pp. 1029–1038 (2010). https://doi.org/10.1145/1753326.1753480

19. Wong, N., Gutwin, C.: Support for deictic pointing in CVEs: still fragmented after all these years. In: Proceedings of the 17th ACM Conference on Computer Supported Cooperative Work & Social Computing, pp. 1377–1387. ACM (2014). https://doi.org/10.1145/2531602. 2531691

Does the Form of Attachment Have an Impact on Occupational Thermal Comfort? A Study on the Spinal Exoskeleton

Yang Liu, Yanmin Xue(✉), Chang Ge, Yihui Zhou, and Wen Yan

School of Art and Design, Xi'an University of Technology, Xi'an 710049, China
{105388,gechang,yanwen}@xaut.edu.cn, 915728096@qq.com

Abstract. The motivation of this study is to investigate the effects of exoskeleton attachment on parcel-collector who undertake lifting work in temperature steps. With the rapid growth of China's economy and e-commerce, the domestic courier industry has gained fast development. The interaction effect of exoskeleton attachment and temperature steps on the human body will be studied to help people understand the physiological mechanisms that trigger thermoregulatory behaviour and thermal sensation in such situations. In total, 30 male subjects were examined under 26 °C (Warm), 16 °C (Mild cold) and 6 °C (Cold) environments in a thermal chamber. Their metabolic rate (MR) and mean skin temperature (MST) were measured. The subjects' thermal sensation votes (TSV), thermal comfort votes (TCV) and sweat feeling index (SFI) were also collected. The results reveal that when people are engaged in exoskeleton assistance, the activation of thermoregulation decreases. The spinal exoskeleton attachment form can improve work's thermal comfort and capacity. Ambient temperature significantly influences MST rather than regional skin temperature (RST). The study reveals the interaction influence of exoskeleton and temperature upon workers' thermoregulatory and thermal sensations.

Keywords: temperature steps · thermoregulatory · workloads · metabolic rate · thermal sensation

1 Introduction

With the rapid growth of China's economy and e-commerce, the domestic courier industry has gained fast development. According to the data from 2015, the volume of handling was 20.6 billion parcels [1]. The highest daily handling exceeded 160 million parcels. Since parcel collectors perform parcel classification, collection, delivery, and information record tasks mostly in express stations [2], both work intensity and climate characteristics affect couriers' health, as they spend most of their daily time in such workplaces.

The research and development of wearable exoskeletons are used to prevent musculoskeletal injuries of workers under different working conditions. Wearing comfort is critical for exoskeletons to be widely promoted and safe for use. Existing studies of

V. G. Duffy (Ed.): HCII 2023, LNCS 14028, pp. 525–538, 2023.
https://doi.org/10.1007/978-3-031-35741-1_38

exoskeletons have shown that they can reduce muscle fatigue and thus have benefits for preventing WMSDs [3–5]. However, these advantages can easily make people ignore the impact of environmental factors on ergonomics in exoskeleton applications. Unlike other wearable devices, the exoskeleton can cause changes in muscle activity, but wearability also makes the exoskeleton impact the heat exchange between the body and the environment.

The interaction between humans and the environment is usually studied without external assistance [6–9]. Working in a hot environment can contribute to physical and mental disorders [10, 11]. Luo et al. found a significant association between exposure to ambient heat (about 25.9 °C to 28.6 °C) and urolithiasis among workers in Guangzhou, China. Decreased ambient temperature and work intensity were associated with a drop in heart rate and blood flow, which could prevent the worker from generating heat stress [12]. Nevertheless, workers in the mild cold workshop (17.2 °C to 19.2 °C) had more abnormal symptoms than those in the office, such as repeated pain in the musculoskeletal system, disturbance throughout the body and respiratory symptoms, etc. [13–17]. The exoskeleton increases the complexity of heat exchange between the human body and the environment. There is still a lack of research on the influence of the exoskeleton's assistance and attachment mode on the thermal cycle.

This paper aims to study the effects of a passive exoskeleton on the thermal response of the human body. The exoskeleton is mainly used to reduce the lower back load of the human body during repeated operations. Although previous studies have shown that exoskeletons can provide good assistance, they did not explain the impact of the structure on human thermal response [18, 19]. This study analyzes other thermal responses, including thermal sensation and comfort, which help evaluate wearability under environmental variables. Also, this study explored the improvement of thermal comfort by optimizing the exoskeleton-wearing structure.

2   Method

This study was approved by the Institutional Review Board at Xi'an Jiaotong University (No: 2017–697) and followed the ethical standards of the 1964 Declaration of Helsinki (2008). Participants gave their written informed consent to participate.

2.1   Subjects and Environment

To exclude the impacts of gender, age and weight, thirty healthy male college students were equally assigned into three groups. To ensure the validity of experimental data, the subjects were reminded to avoid caffeine and alcohol ingestions, smoke and strenuous activities, and to sleep well the day prior to the experiment. Mean values (standard error of the mean, SEM) of age, height, body mass and BMI were 23.1(1.6) yrs, 1.74 (0.09) cm, 66.0 (11.3) kg, and 21.6 (1.9) kg/m^2, respectively. All subjects were required to wear long underpants, straight trousers, a long-sleeved sweatshirt, socks, boots and a jacket. The total insulation value calculated was approximately 1.27clo [20].

Simulation of handling work was conducted in a thermal chamber (L × W × H = 5 × 4.5 × 3.5 m). Xi'an is one of the major cities in Northwest China. The temperature in

Spring, Winter and Summer in Xi'an are 5.6 °C, 17.0 °C, 26.1 °C, respectively. Relative humidity in these seasons is 53%, 37%, and 52%, respectively.

Accordingly, temperature points were set at 26 °C (Warm), 16 °C (Mild cold) and 6 °C (Cold). The relative humidity and air velocity were strictly kept at 50% and 0.1 m/s, respectively.

2.2 Test Procedure

Figure 1 shows the detailed experiment procedure. On arrival, subjects entered the room at a thermoneutral air temperature (20 °C), preparing for about 10min to calm down, change clothes, get familiar with the questionnaire, and wear physiological sensors. After that, subjects entered the chamber and remained seated (Sedentary) for 25 min, then performed a 5kg handling work with two exoskeleton techniques (T1: spinal attachment, T2: chest support). Each group was randomly assigned to one of the three thermal conditions. Subjects only underwent one technique on the first day of the experiment and underwent the second after three days. All subjects were not permitted to eat or drink three h before the experiment.

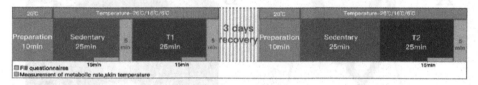

Fig. 1. Test procedure

According to a previous study, the metabolic rate increased progressively in the first 2–3 min of exercise, and then a steady-state metabolic rate was obtained from 3–8 min [21]. Furthermore, according to another study, human thermal sensation and skin temperature tended to be steady within 15–20 min when the metabolic rate changed [22]. Based on these findings, in this study, the subjects were asked to maintain 25min for each workload and finish the questionnaires during the last 5 min. Their metabolic rate and skin temperature were measured every 1 min during the last 10 min of handling work as steady-state physiological responses to the activity. For the Sedentary condition, physiological parameters and subjective questionnaires were obtained before T1.

2.3 Exoskeleton

In the study, a passive chest support exoskeleton (Mile Bot, Shenzhen, China) and a spinal exoskeleton developed by Xi'an Jiaotong University were used, as presented in Fig. 2. The chest support exoskeleton shown in Fig. 2(A) is designed to protect high-frequency repetitive bending workers. It includes a spacer for the chest and two spacers for the thighs. The two parts are connected by a supporting structure containing a damping mechanism that provides support at hip joints. The exoskeleton is adjusted and fixed to the body by straps on the back and crotch. During work, the upper body of the human body is supported by the spacers on the chest and thighs, and the damping mechanism in the middle provides the support force, thereby reducing the muscle activity of the lower back. The weight of this exoskeleton is 3.0kg, and the maximum support torque is 38N/m.

The spine assist exoskeleton developed by Xi'an Jiaotong University is shown in Fig. 2(B), which is designed to prevent the musculoskeletal injury of workers caused by repeated operations, especially the excessive shear force at L5/S1. In the way of wearing, the exoskeleton is fixed on the torso of the human body through the back strap and the waist strap. The back flexible unit assists. Seven elastic units connect the spine to form a passive assistance structure. The interior of each unit is composed of a spherical hinge and a spring. It is stretched and twisted with the movement of the spine during the movement. A single unit can produce a maximum torque of 2.7Nm. It provides elastic support in the bending movement of the human body and ensures flexibility in the movement. The back assist mechanism can be disassembled and adjusted according to the task. In this study, a flexible unit with a width of 8cm, 6cm and 4cm was designed to study the thermal comfort of the human body and the degree of conscious exertion.

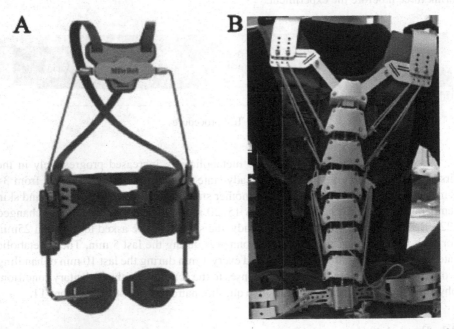

Fig. 2. Exoskeleton in the experiment ((A). The passive spinal exoskeleton was used in the experiment. (B)The optimized exoskeleton.)

2.4 Physiological and Subjective Measurements

Metabolic Rate (MR)

The METAMAX metabolic device (CORTEX, Germany) was used to measure oxygen consumption and carbon dioxide production. In the system, captured gas is analyzed in a micro-dynamic mixing chamber, outputting oxygen consumption rate (V O2), carbon dioxide output (VCO2), ventilation (VE), and respiratory exchange ratio. The metabolic rate was determined by the measured $\dot{V}O2$, $\dot{V}CO2$, respiratory quotient (RQ), and Ad according to Eqs. (1), (2), (3), as follows:

RQ is respiratory quotient, which is the molar ratio of VCO_2 (L/min) exhaled to VO_2 (L/min) inhaled. VCO_2 and VO_2 is the volumetric rate of carbon dioxide production and oxygen consumption respectively (ml/s, at conditions of 0 °C, 101.3 kPa).

$$RQ = VCO_2 / VO_2 \tag{1}$$

And A_d is the Dubois surface area (m^2). It can be determined by following empirical equation [12]:

$$A_{Du} = 0.202H^{0.725}W^{0.425} \tag{2}$$

where H is height (m) and W is weight (kg).

Then, the metabolic rate was calculated by the following equation [12]:

$$M = \frac{21(0.23RQ + 0.77)VO_2}{A_{Du}} \tag{3}$$

where M is metabolic rate (W/m^2).

Mean Skin Temperature (MST)

RST were recorded using eight iButton skin thermochrons (Maxim Integrated, CA, USA) which were placed on the forehead, chest, upper arm, forearm, hand, anterior thigh, anterior calf and foot of the right side of the body. Skin temperature of each site was recorded every 1 min throughout the experimental session. MST was calculated using Gagge/Nishi's equation [23]:

$$T_{sk} = 0.07T + 0.175T_{chest} + 0.175T_{upperarm} + 0.07T_{forearm} + 0.07T_{hand} +$$
$$0.05T_{calf} + 0.19T_{thigh} + 0.2T_{foot} \tag{4}$$

Questionnaires

Subjects were required to fill out a questionnaire about their thermal sensation and thermal comfort during the last 5 min of experiment in each chamber condition when the skin temperature and hence thermal sensation and comfort were stable so as to avoid the temporal alliesthesia. As shown in Fig. 3, thermal sensation vote (TSV) was divided into ASHRAE seven-point scales: hot (+3), warm (+2), slightly warm (+1), neutral (0), slightly cool (-1), cool (-2), and cold (-3). Thermal comfort vote (TCV) is divided into 6 scales: very comfortable (+2), comfortable (+1), just comfortable (+0.1), just uncomfortable (-0.1), uncomfortable (-1), and very uncomfortable (-2). Sweat rate is one of the significant characteristics of body temperature regulation. People can judge about whether they sweat and how strongly sweating they are by using sweat feeling index (SFI) to investigate the influence of sweat activity on skin temperature and thermal sensation [24]. SFI is scaled as 0, 1, 2 and 3, which indicates that subjects have no feeling of sweating, slight feeling of sweating, moderate feeling of sweating and strong feeling of sweating respectively.

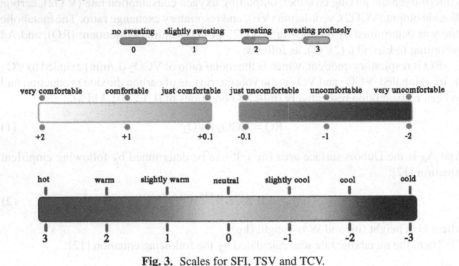

Fig. 3. Scales for SFI, TSV and TCV.

3 Statistical Analysis

Three factors, repeated-measures ANOVA, were performed to compare the dependent variables from temperature conditions, both with and without the exoskeleton. All data were assessed for approximation to a normal distribution and sphericity, and when necessary degrees of freedom were adjusted using the Greenhouse-Geisser adjustment. When an ANOVA revealed a significant F test, Neuman-Kuels post hoc pair-wise comparisons were conducted. All data were performed using SPSS statistical software (V22, Chicago, IL, USA). When the test result showed significance of difference, it was labeled as "p < 0.05" or "p < 0.01", otherwise, "p > 0.05" was labeled. All data are reported as mean ± SE.

3.1 Result

3.2 Results of MR

The statistics of the MR during graded workloads in Warm, Mild cold and Cold are shown in Fig. 4. MR values for each group were relatively close, as is shown Fig. 4A (Warm: 73.9 ± 13.2 W/m^2; Mild cold: 68.8 ± 17.5 W/m^2; Cold: 71.2 ± 19.1 W/m^2; p > 0.05). For instance, MR was higher than the classification of Sedentary MR in ASHARE Handbook. Reduced heat loss caused by large clothing insulation might be a main reason for the above results. No significant difference was observed among three groups in T1 (p > 0.05) (Fig. 4B). However, Fig. 4C revealed that the MR in Cold was higher than in Warm and Mild cold in T2 (Warm: 275.4 ± 23.7 W/m²; Mild cold: 267.1 ± 20.1 W/m²; Cold: 319.9 ± 26.5W/m², p < 0.05), which indicates that there might be a combined effect of temperature and work activity on metabolic heat production. According to the MR calculated by RQ, VO_2 and Ad, the activity level of Sedentary, T1 and T2 condition were approximately 1.2, 2.4 and 4.0 Met respectively, which is correspondingly defined by ASHRAE (2010).

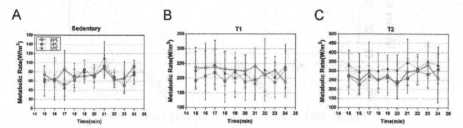

Fig. 4. Steady-state MR over time in temperature steps and graded workloads ((A) shows MR under Sedentary, (B) shows MR under T1 task, (C) shows MR under T2).

3.3   Results of Skin Temperature

MST

Figure 5 compares the MST among three temperature steps under Sedentary, T1 and T2 conditions. The result for MST showed a decreasing tendency along with the temperature change from warm to mild cold to cold. For Sedentary conditions (Warm: 33.7 ± 0.2 °C; Mild cold: 32.3 ± 0.1 °C; Cold: 31.9 ± 0.2 °C), the differences of the MST between Warm and Mild cold, Warm and Cold were both significant (p < 0.05). No significant difference was found between Warm and Mild cold. For T1 and T2, MST decreased from 34.5 ± 0.3 °C in Warm to 30.0 ± 0.2 °C in Cold and from 34.4 ± 0.2 °C in Warm to 31.1 ± 0.2 °C in Cold, respectively. Neuman-Kuels post hoc pair-wise comparisons revealed a significant difference in MST among three temperature points under T1 and T2 conditions (p < 0.05). In terms of handling work in each temperature step, a sustained increase of the MST was observed in Warm and Mild cold. In the cold, however, MST in sedentary was higher than T1 and T2 (p > 0.05).

RST

With the decrease in temperature, the RST excluding thigh temperature presented a gradient change. In the Sedentary condition (Fig. 6A), the chest skin temperature showed the smallest (35.4–34.4 °C, 1 °C) range of temperature change among all skin temperature measurements throughout the experiment. Hand and forehead skin temperatures showed a significant decline with direct mild cold and cold exposures. In T1 and T2 (see Fig. 6B and Fig. 6C), hand skin temperature showed a continuous decline with direct cold exposures. However, forearm (Warm: 35.0 °C ± 0.2 °C; Mild cold: 33.1 °C ±

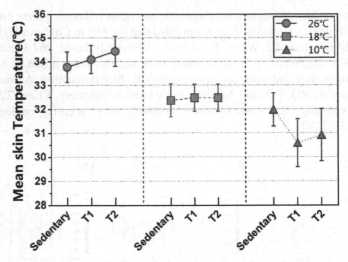

Fig. 5. MST under exoskeleton and temperatures steps.

0.1 °C; Cold: 32.6oC ± 0.2 °C) and upper arm skin temperatures (Warm: 35.66 °C ± 0.1 °C; Mild cold: 33.47oC ± 0.2 °C; Cold: 33.18oC ± 0.2 °C) showed a significant increase compared with in Sedentary and T1 (p < 0.05).

A 0.38 °C decline occurred for chest skin temperature when subjects from T1 proceeded into T2 condition in Warm. A similar tendency was found for forehead skin temperature between Sedentary and T1 conditions, which indicated that the rise of skin temperature brought by handling work tended to be slackened by sweating. A steady state of thigh skin temperature was observed at 26oC temperature (Sedentary: 32.2 ± 0.2 °C; T1: 32.9 ± 0.1 °C; T2: 33.0 ± 0.1 °C). Calf and foot skin temperatures under each exoskeleton condition showed the same tendency among the three groups. However, foot skin temperature presented a significant rise tendency when the workload increased. In addition, foot skin temperature was significantly higher than calf in Warm.

3.4 Results of TSV and TCV

Figure 7 shows the comparison of thermal sensation and thermal comfort in Warm, Mild cold and Cold under Sedentary, T1 and T2 conditions. For Sedentary, the TSV in Warm was 0.40 ± 0.51 (neutral), which was significantly higher than in Cold (p < 0.001), which was -2.00 ± 0.66 (cool). TCV was also significantly improved in Mild cold [0.57 ± 0.99 (just comfortable)] than in Cold [-0.86 ± 0.98 (just uncomfortable)] (p = 0.004). Although no significant difference was found between Warm and Mild, TCV was 0.38 units higher in Mild cold than in Warm. Under the T1 condition, TSV was improved from "slightly cool" (-0.30 ± 0.82) in Cold to "warm" (2.00 ± 0.81) in Warm (p < 0.001). However, TCV declined from "just uncomfortable" (-0.02 ± 0.10) in Cold to near "uncomfortable" (-0.86 ± 0.98) in Warm (p < 0.05). For the T2 condition, TSV increased from Cold to Warm. A significant difference was found between Warm and

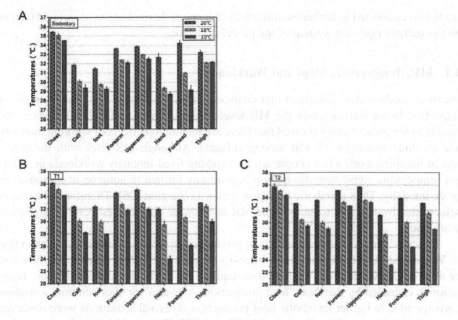

Fig. 6. RST in temperatures steps and graded workloads ((A) shows RST under Sedentary, (B) shows RST under T1 task, (C) shows RST under T2 task).

Cold (p = 0.002) and between Mild cold and Cold (p < 0.05). However, TCV under T2 showed an inverse tendency. TCV in Warm and Mild cold was critically lower than in Cold (p < 0.05).

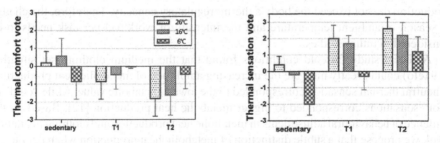

Fig. 7. TSV and TCV in temperatures steps and graded workloads.

4 Discussion

Despite the enormous employment opportunities associated with the courier industry, the effects of the task environment on the physiological health of Parcel-collectors cannot be ignored. With intense workloads from collection or distribution, parcel-collecting activities in various temperature steps cause thermal stress and working fatigue. This study was conducted to further examine the influence of thermal and work-related factors on the thermoregulation system of the parcel-collector.

4.1 MR, Temperature Steps and Workloads

Previous studies have confirmed that change in season and climate temperature is an important factor that increases the MR level of non-active people [25]. However, the results of the present study showed that there are interaction effects of working intensity and clothing insulation on MR among subjects. Although MR rises with the intensity of handling work when people are undertaking fixed-intensity workloads in different temperature steps, heat dissipation is primarily limited to autonomic responses as work intensity. Thus metabolic heat production is constant [26]. Therefore, this paper selects steady-state MR to analyse the MR level under different temperature steps and workloads.

This study found that metabolic heat production in Cold was much higher than that in Warm and Mild cold under high-intensity works (T2). When subjects are in warm or mild cold environments, the heat loss required for environmental temperature regulation is exceeded by metabolic heat production. A "warm" or "hot" thermal sensation corresponded to higher metabolic heat production. Thermal sensations were observed near a "slightly warm" and increased MST and SFI. This could imply that increasing heat loss in cold environment was effective in improving metabolic heat production to keep the body's thermal balance when people are undertaking heavy workloads. Our study found a 2.7W/m2 increase from Warm to Cold under Sedentary conditions, while metabolic heat production was lowest at mild cold temperatures. In the previous study, voluntary neuromuscular activation was lower in a hot environment (35 °C) than in a cool environment (15 °C) during a cycling time trial [27]. These neuromuscular alterations corresponded with a decrease in exercise work rate to ensure that metabolic heat production did not exceed the body's thermoregulatory capacity. Therefore, the change of season or ambient temperature and the intensity of workload per task needs to be considered in future studies.

A recent study on cold conditions found that the medium clothing set situation (0.91clo) could greatly mitigate the increasing amplitude of metabolic heat production. A neutral thermal sensation corresponded to the lowest metabolic value, while "cold" or "hot" sensations corresponded to higher metabolic heat production [12]. Based on the evidence of behavioural adjustments in metabolic heat production and clothing insulation level, we propose that a subtle distinction of metabolic heat production when people are sedentary is reasonable. For instance, a recent study revealed that when people wore clothes with high insulation, their metabolic rate would increase due to elevation in physiological strain [28]. This may explain why MR is relatively higher in our study.

Based on the findings of the present and previous studies, it is effective that parcel-collector with thick clothes keep the body warm when doing light work in cold environments. However, increased clothes may increase the metabolic burden under heavy workloads in other climates. Therefore it is suggested that the regulator should improve the working temperature, which is a better choice for reducing metabolic energy expenditure.

4.2 Thermoregulatory

The results for MST and RST emphasize the interaction between the body's mechanisms of thermoregulatory and environmental conditions and the effects of working intensity on thermoregulatory. As T1 was performed in Warm and Mild cold, vasodilation occurred in skin blood vessels so that the heat was lost from the skin and sweat glands became more active to increase evaporative heat loss. Thus, subjects obtained a 'warm' sensation. More prominently, phenomena were presented under the T2 condition. In contrast, during cold exposure, vasoconstriction occurred in skin blood vessels, and less heat was lost in the environment. It can be deduced that the decrease in MST at 6oC was caused by the work intensity, which was not high enough under the T1 condition.

Further information can be inferred from Fig. 6, showing the RST responses to the handling work. In agreement with the previous finding [29], for both constant handling works, the skin temperature change was slightly pronounced in the most peripheral regions (for instance, forehead and thigh), which are less involved in loading tasks. Conversely, the skin over-exercising muscle mass (for instance, forearm and upper arm) exhibited drastically increase in temperature and tended to be warmer than the skin over other structures as the exercise progressed, especially for the T2 condition; this result is probably related to the increasing delivery of blood flow to the working muscles for metabolic needs and to the heat conduction from the muscles to the skin surface. Therefore, the body surface temperature increases as the work intensity. In a previous study, a lifting risk was revealed when workers feel cold, which may lead to muscle and skin symptoms. Due to uneven workload in parcel collection, the activity of body-surface thermoregulatory alternate with inactivity of that will generate cold stress which may also harm limbs of parcel-collector.

4.3 Combined Effects of Workloads and Ambient Temperature on TSV and TCV

This study further found the influence of workloads and temperature on improving subjective thermal sensation among subjects during the experiment. The comparison between the sedentary and handling work indicated that subjects under loading conditions felt neutral and more comfortable than at 6 °C without workloads. In comparison, at 26 °C or 16 °C, subjects felt warm and uncomfortable under loading conditions. It was also found that changes in workload would cause significant differences in thermal sensation in cold environments rather than in warm, as subjects' TSV values increased from T1 to T2 when at 6 °C. Comparing the TCV in warm and cold conditions under handling work, a lower bias ratio in cold environment was presented under both T1 and T2 conditions. Both heat and cold stress can affect work capacity and ultimate health [30]. Despite that, high-intensity work could counteract the increase in cold stress. Therefore workers may obtain thermal comfort. Athletic capacity was reduced in hot environments (35 °C) than in cool (15 °C) or moderate (25 °C) environments [17]. It can be deduced that lower ambient temperature positively promotes heavy manual labour workers' work capacity. Our study suggests that ambient temperature is not independent when evaluating thermal sensation and comfort. When a worker with lower workload in cold conditions, thermoregulatory becomes inactivity, so cold stress is still possibly generated.

5 Conclusion

This paper investigates the effect of exoskeleton attachment on the parcel collector in a well-controlled thermal chamber. The results revealed the combined effects of exoskeleton and temperature on physiological and subjective parameters. Improving the working environment is critical to ensuring the overall health and preventing heat or cold stress among parcel collectors in Northeast China. The following conclusions could be obtained:

Compared with the chest support, the exoskeleton in the spine mode is more effective in reducing the metabolic rate. Though high clothing insulation with the exoskeletons may mitigate the increasing amplitude of MR in sedentary, when working in cold environment, MR sharply increases to keep the thermal balance.

Exoskeleton and temperature have a combined effect on thermal sensation and comfort. Chest support exoskeleton in the experiment is associated with improved thermal sensation in cold conditions. However, TCV is significantly worse than the spine exoskeleton. Cold stress is still possibly generated while working with low workloads in cold condition.

MST significantly decreases with the temperature drop in sedentary and two exoskeleton conditions. The effect on RST caused by regional workloads was larger than that caused by ambient temperatures. More attention should be paid to protecting the parcel collector's hands.

It should be noted that the exoskeleton attachment form has a significant interactive effect on thermal balance and thermal acceptability. In order to fully understand the mechanism, further experiments need to be conducted to measure acute sweat rate with graded clothing insulation under different workloads.

References

1. Wang, J.J., Xiao, Z.: Co-evolution between etailing and parcel express industry and its geographical imprints: the case of China. J. Transp. Geogr. **46**, 20–34 (2015). https://doi.org/10.1016/j.jtrangeo.2015.05.005
2. Zhuo, J., Wei, J., Liu, L.C., Koong, K.S., Miao, S.: An examination of the determinants of service quality in the Chinese express industry. Electron. Mark. **23**, 163–172 (2013). https://doi.org/10.1007/s12525-013-0133-7
3. Schmalz, T., et al.: Biomechanical and metabolic effectiveness of an industrial exoskeleton for overhead work. Int. J. Environ. Res. Public Health **16**, 4792 (2019). https://doi.org/10.3390/ijerph16234792
4. Baltrusch, S.J., et al.: Spexor passive spinal exoskeleton decreases metabolic cost during symmetric repetitive lifting. Eur. J. Appl. Physiol. **120**, 401–412 (2020)
5. Troster, M., Wagner, D., Muller-Graf, F., Maufroy, C., Schneider, U., Bauernhansl, T.: Biomechanical model-based development of an active occupational upper-limb exoskeleton to support healthcare workers in the surgery waiting room. Int. J. Environ. Res. Public Health **17**, 16 (2020)
6. Yang, Y., Li, B., Liu, H., Tan, M., Yao, R.: A study of adaptive thermal comfort in a well-controlled climate chamber. Appl. Therm. Eng. **76**, 283–291 (2015). https://doi.org/10.1016/j.applthermaleng.2014.11.004

7. Morabito, M., Crisci, A., Moriondo, M., Profili, F., Francesconi, P., Trombi, G., et al.: Air temperature-related human health outcomes: current impact and estimations of future risks in central Italy. Sci. Total Environ. **441** (2012). https://doi.org/10.1016/j.scitotenv.2012.09.056

8. Luo, M., Ji, W., Cao, B., Ouyang, Q., Zhu, Y.: Indoor climate and thermal physiological adaptation: Evidences from migrants with different cold indoor exposures. Build. Environ. **98**, 30–38 (2016). https://doi.org/10.1016/j.buildenv.2015.12.015

9. Guéritée, J., Tipton, M.J.: The relationship between radiant heat, air temperature and thermal comfort at rest and exercise. Physiol. Behav. **139**, 378–385 (2015). https://doi.org/10.1016/j.physbeh.2014.11.064

10. Lee, S., Lee, H., Myung, W., Kim, E.J., Kim, H.: Mental disease-related emergency admissions attributable to hot temperatures. Sci. Total Environ. **616–617**, 688–694 (2018). https://doi.org/10.1016/j.scitotenv.2017.10.260

11. Nunfam, V.F., Adusei-Asante, K., Van Etten, E.J., Oosthuizen, J., Frimpong, K.: Social impacts of occupational heat stress and adaptation strategies of workers: A narrative synthesis of the literature. Sci. Total Environ. **643**, 1542–1552 (2018). https://doi.org/10.1016/j.scitotenv.2018.06.255

12. Luo, M., Zhou, X., Zhu, Y., Sundell, J.: Revisiting an overlooked parameter in thermal comfort studies, the metabolic rate. Energy Build. **118**, 152–159 (2016). https://doi.org/10.1016/j.enbuild.2016.02.041

13. Thetkathuek, A., Yingratanasuk, T., Jaidee, W., Ekburanawat, W.: Cold exposure and health effects among frozen food processing workers in eastern Thailand. Saf. Health Work **6**, 56–61 (2015). https://doi.org/10.1016/j.shaw.2014.10.004

14. Oliveira, A.V.M., Gaspar, A.R., André, J.S., Quintela, D.A.: Subjective analysis of cold thermal environments. Appl. Ergon. **45**, 534–543 (2014). https://doi.org/10.1016/j.apergo.2013.07.013

15. Cheshire, W.P.: Thermoregulatory disorders and illness related to heat and cold stress. Auton. Neurosci. **196**, 91–104 (2016). https://doi.org/10.1016/j.autneu.2016.01.001

16. Bortkiewicz, A., Gadzicka, E., Szymczak, W., Szyjkowska, A., Koszadawłodarczyk, W., Makowiecdabrowska, T.: Physiological reaction to work in cold microclimate. Int. J. Occup. Med. Environ. Health **19**, 123–131 (2006). https://doi.org/10.2478/v10001-006-0020-y

17. Sormunen, E., Rissanen, S., Oksa, J., Pienimaki, T., Remes, J., Rintamaki, H.: Muscular activity and thermal responses in men and women during repetitive work in cold environments. Ergonomics **52**, 964–976 (2009). https://doi.org/10.1080/00140130902767413

18. Cachon, G., Gallino, S., Olivares, M.: Severe weather and automobile assembly productivity. SSRN Electron. J. (2012). https://doi.org/10.2139/ssrn.2099798

19. Liu, Y., et al.: The effects of a passive exoskeleton on human thermal responses in temperate and cold environments. Int. J. Environ. Res. Public Health **18**, 3889 (2021). https://doi.org/10.3390/ijerph18083889

20. Committee A. S.: Ansi/ashrae/ies standard 55-2010: Thermal environmental conditions for human occupancy. American Society of Heating, Refrigerating and Air-Conditioning Engineers, Atlanta, GA (2010)

21. Miyachi, M., Yamamoto, K., Ohkawara, K., Tanaka, S.: METs in adults while playing active video games: a metabolic chamber study. Med. Sci. Sports Exerc. **42**, 1149–1153 (2010). https://doi.org/10.1249/mss.0b013e3181c51c78

22. Goto, T., Toftum, J., de Dear, R., Fanger, P.O.: Thermal sensation and thermophysiological responses to metabolic step-changes. Int. J. Biometeorol. **50**, 323–332 (2006). https://doi.org/10.1007/s00484-005-0016-5

23. Nishi, Y., Gagge, A.P.: Direct evaluation of convective heat transfer coefficient by naphthalene sublimation. J. Appl. Physiol. **29**, 830 (1970). https://doi.org/10.1152/jappl.1970.29.6.830

24. Wang, H., Hu, S.: Experimental study on thermal sensation of people in moderate activities. Build. Environ. **100**, 127–134 (2016). https://doi.org/10.1016/j.buildenv.2016.02.016

25. van Ooijen, A.M.J., van Marken Lichtenbelt, W.D., van Steenhoven, A.A., Westerterp, K.R.: Seasonal changes in metabolic and temperature responses to cold air in humans. Physiol. Behav. **82**, 545–553 (2004). https://doi.org/10.1016/j.physbeh.2004.05.001

26. Schlader, Z.J., Stannard, S.R., Mündel, T.: Human thermoregulatory behavior during rest and exercise — a prospective review. Physiol. Behav. **99**, 269–275 (2010). https://doi.org/10.1016/j.physbeh.2009.12.003

27. Tucker, R., Rauch, L., Harley, Y.X.R., Noakes, T.D.: Impaired exercise performance in the heat is associated with an anticipatory reduction in skeletal muscle recruitment. Pflugers Arch. **448**, 422–430 (2004). https://doi.org/10.1007/s00424-004-1267-4

28. Borg, D.N., Costello, J.T., Bach, A.J., Stewart, I.B.: Perceived exertion is as effective as the perceptual strain index in predicting physiological strain when wearing personal protective clothing. Physiol. Behav. **169**, 216–223 (2017). https://doi.org/10.1016/j.physbeh.2016.12.009

29. No, M., Kwak, H.-B.: Effects of environmental temperature on physiological responses during submaximal and maximal exercises in soccer players. Integr. Med. Res. **5**, 216–222 (2016). https://doi.org/10.1016/j.imr.2016.06.002

30. Cheung, S.S., Lee, J.K., Oksa, J.: Thermal stress, human performance, and physical employment standards. Appl. Physiol. Nutr. Metab. **41**, S148 (2016). https://doi.org/10.1139/apnm-2015-0518

A Multimodal Data Model
for Simulation-Based Learning
with Va.Si.Li-Lab

Alexander Mehler[1]([✉])(iD), Mevlüt Bagci[1](iD), Alexander Henlein[1](iD),
Giuseppe Abrami[1](iD), Christian Spiekermann[1], Patrick Schrottenbacher[1](iD),
Maxim Konca[1](iD), Andy Lücking[1](iD), Juliane Engel[1](iD), Marc Quintino[1](iD),
Jakob Schreiber[1](iD), Kevin Saukel[1](iD), and Olga Zlatkin-Troitschanskaia[2](iD)

[1] Goethe University Frankfurt/M, Frankfurt am Main, Germany
`mehler@em.uni-frankfurt.de`
[2] Johannes Gutenberg-Universität Mainz, Mainz, Germany

Abstract. Simulation-based learning is a method in which learners
learn to master real-life scenarios and tasks from simulated application
contexts. It is particularly suitable for the use of VR technologies, as
these allow immersive experiences of the targeted scenarios. VR methods are also relevant for studies on online learning, especially in groups,
as they provide access to a variety of multimodal learning and interaction
data. However, VR leads to a trade-off between technological conditions
of the observability of such data and the openness of learner behavior. We
present VA.SI.LI-LAB, a *VR-Lab for Simulation-based Learning* developed to address this trade-off. VA.SI.LI-LAB uses a graph-theoretical
model based on hypergraphs to represent the data diversity of multimodal learning and interaction. We develop this data model in relation
to mono- and multimodal, intra- and interpersonal data and interleave it
with ISO-Space to describe distributed multiple documents from the perspective of their interactive generation. The paper adds three use cases
to motivate the broad applicability of VA.SI.LI-LAB and its data model.

Keywords: multimodal learning · simulation-based learning ·
distributed multiple documents · critical online reasoning · visual
communication · VA.SI.LI-LAB

1   Introduction

Collaborative learning in *Virtual Reality* (VR) has gained much popularity over
the last years [24,41,61,78,83]. In particular, it is highlighted that collaborative
learning in VR leads to higher learning gains than under textbook conditions,
at least with respect to visually/spatially complex learning topics [6]. VR environments lend themselves to the presentation of visual information, with added
benefits from immersive, embodied interaction and gamification (*op. cit.*). This
is even more so when visual settings are linked to a narrative, i.e., meaningful

V. G. Duffy (Ed.): HCII 2023, LNCS 14028, pp. 539–565, 2023.
https://doi.org/10.1007/978-3-031-35741-1_39

storytelling ([63], although the authors address augmented reality). Last but not least, VR allows collaboration among geographically distant agents [66].

The relevance of this technological development for education science can be explained by the experimental study of *Critical Online Reasoning* (COR) [89], under conditions as real as possible. COR refers to the ability to evaluate the credibility of online information in the context of learning ([85] cited after [60]). To date, COR is primarily studied as an ability or process carried out by individuals. However, even though students are increasingly learning online, they are not necessarily learning in isolation. Rather, this learning also takes place in groups by sharing information, recommending texts, or discussing them. In addition, students interact in learning forums and platforms, e.g., write or read lesson-specific wikis, and create shared learning spaces through linguistic interaction that lifts them out of isolation as passive recipients of web content. In this regard, there is considerable potential for critical online learning or the use of online media in interactions with learners to challenge one's own point of view or views adopted by these media. This happens in dialogs or multilogs, in synchronous or quasi-synchronous communication, where one has to deal with the views, criticisms, perspectives, etc. of others to strengthen, profile or revise one's own position. This potential can impact all facets of COR [59], e.g., information acquisition (what media and sources are searched), evaluation (how is the information assessed or credited), and reasoning (what is it used for).

From this perspective, a kind of *Interactive Critical Online Reasoning* (InCOR) emerges that challenges a central theoretical concept in educational science, namely that of multiple documents [10,14,32,33,47,73]. A multiple document is the textual manifestation of a reading process that includes several texts. Consequently, it may consist of mutually incoherent text segments arranged, graph-theoretically speaking, in different *walks* (*trails* if no text link or so is used multiple times, or *paths* if no text segment is consulted more than once) as a model of their reading order and possibly manifesting different genres, registers, topics, authorships, credibilities, etc. InCOR calls for an extension of this concept with respect to cooperative learning processes. That is, by analogy with the notion of distributed cognition [38], we may speak of *Distributed Multiple Documents* (DMD) whose constitutive segments and structure are due to decisions made by cooperating learners.[1] This extension continues in the levels of multiple document modeling, that is, at the level of the so-called *Intertext Model* (IM) and its counterpart in terms of a mental model as distinguished in the documents model of [13,64]: let us assume with [13] that the IM, as an analogue to the textbase in single text comprehension [44], consists of so-called document units as conceptual representations of text segments of the underlying multiple document plus meta-information (e.g., on trustworthiness or authorship). DMDs then confront us with the task of modeling the extent to which these units are distributed, or the extent to which they are cooperatively constituted, shared, or aligned among cooperating learners. This challenge becomes greater at the level of mental models, with their greater distance from the originating DMD.

---

[1] For an earlier approach to this concept, see [52].

Thus, DMDs challenge us to represent the cooperation of learners (e.g., their social networking) and its outcomes in terms of (short-term) conceptual alignment [65]. That is, to properly model InCOR, we need to capture DMDs, the reading processes that are constitutive of them (which are in part a consequence of learner interactions) and the resulting mental representations at least at the level of the IM. While VR systems are the first choice for the former (since they integrate eye-tracking and other behavioral observation methods), the latter are best represented by language models based on neural networks so far. However, modeling the comprehension of multiple documents induced by single persons is already a technological challenge, as it requires the observation of (online) reading behavior, the accurate detection of eye movements, the focusing of corresponding text segments, and the tracking of text links, text switching, text embeddings, and the like. How much more difficult then is it to make observable collective behavior based on distributed decision making that relies on extensive conversational behavior and other collaborative processes that underlie the creation of distributed multiple documents? How does a VR system look like that makes this possible? And how can the different model dimensions (VR-based and neural network-based) be integrated in such a system; what does this integration look like formally? Put differently: *How can external behavioral information be interleaved with internal representational information in a single formal model?* This paper aims to provide an answer especially to the latter question.

The study of COR is just one of the many application areas for which there is a need for openly designed and widely deployable VR systems that use AI methods to make linguistic and multimodal data analyzable for social science purposes. These applications require the comprehensive and integrated collection of behavioral data across all modalities involved. Subjects should be studied under conditions that are as natural as possible, i.e., in contexts in which they can interact largely freely and naturally according to their communication abilities. From this point of view, we arrive at a trade-off between *observability* and *behavioral openness*. That is, a system is needed that allows the observation of a variety of multimodal information *without constraining the (inter-)actions of the agents generating that information* The complexity of a comprehensive and flexible VR system for social science purposes that addresses this trade-off is apparently reflected in the observation that there are still few implementations of suitable systems in the educational science context [7].

We present VA.SI.LI-LAB, a *VR-Lab for Simulation-based Learning* that addresses the requirements presented so far. VA.SI.LI-LAB combines AI methods and methods from *Natural Language Processing* (NLP) with the analysis of multimodal and interactive data from VR as a source for grounding multimodal semantics. The main use case of VA.SI.LI-LAB concerns VR-based [12] multiplayer role-playing games [27] (in the sense of serious games [17]) for the purpose of simulation-based learning and training [8,39,87] through highly interactive experiential learning [27] (rather than pure observation), partly augmented by artificial agents [46]. VA.SI.LI-LAB is developed as an open, broadly applicable system that can be used in particular for VR-based COR studies and related research scenarios. Its applicability to COR studies is based on the reuse of VANNOTATOR's [1,51,79] virtual browser and the annotation functions provided by it. VA.SI.LI-LAB collects and models data along the modalities shown in Fig. 2. These include language-related data, manifesting the spoken or written contributions of the agents involved, and a range of motion-related data. Regarding speech, this involves the lip movements of agents, which are simulated as corresponding movements of their counterparts in the form of Meta Avatars – for which the speech contributions of the agents are processed. Using the same technology, data about facial expressions is recorded. In addition to spoken language, VA.SI.LI-LAB captures data generated by reading or writing actions: the former by means of eye-tracking technology in conjunction with VANNOTATOR's browser, the latter by integrating VANNOTATOR's annotation functionalities [79].[2] In this way, extensive semantic annotations (e.g., of semantic roles) can be made starting from automatically preprocessed texts. In all of these cases, speech data are converted into text data (using Whisper [70]), which are further processed using NLP pipelines (e.g., spaCy [40]) mediated by TextImager [35], which is used to process any text data in VA.SI.LI-LAB.

Besides language-related data, VA.SI.LI-LAB makes a range of movement data accessible: data generated by manual gestures (freehand in the case of Meta Avatars) or hand movement data concerning the use of controllers and head movement data related to gaze (where gaze is captured using Meta's VR glasses). VA.SI.LI-LAB also collects data about the agents' movements in space, their distances from each other, from objects located in these spaces, and from the corresponding space- or room-forming boundaries. Figure 1 exemplifies several of the scenarios and spaces currently supported by VA.SI.LI-LAB. These scenarios were designed following current theoretical discussions in educational science (see Subsect. 3.2). They aim to translate pedagogical challenges such as economization [80], diversity and heterogeneity [49], uncertainties and ambiguities of pedagogical interactions [34], and the use of (institutionalized) power [30] into playable VR settings.

Last but not least, VA.SI.LI-LAB captures simultaneous manipulations of the same objects by different agents. Similarly, data on social interactions (e.g., group formations) is derived from core observational data. In this way, VA.SI.-LI-LAB is suitable for the analysis of multimodal interaction in the context of simulation-based learning and InCOR. This concerns dialogic communication as well as the cooperative manipulation, processing or generation of (e.g., semiotic) aggregates, especially of (interactive) multiple documents.

The VR system outlined by the example of VA.SI.LI-LAB is reminiscent of the trade-off between observability and behavioral openness mentioned above. But this trade-off now appears to be exacerbated by a third moment. This moment concerns the combinatorial explosion of the range of information types

---

[2] VANNOTATOR's browser enables immersive visualization of multimedia information units. These include texts, images, and videos that can be mapped to linkable discourse referents as meaning representations of entities manifested in these information units that can themselves be manipulated as 3D objects.

Fig. 1. Two application scenarios of VA.SI.LI-LAB: left: organizational work environment; right: social work in the context of career counseling.

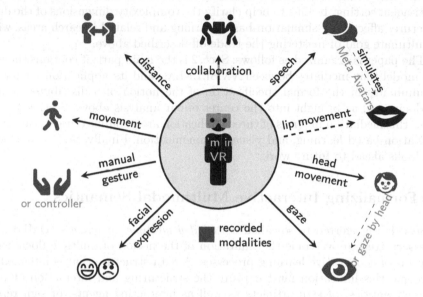

Fig. 2. The range of modalities captured by VA.SI.LI-LAB.

that a system like VA.SI.LI-LAB must cover to meet the requirements of simulation-based learning. More precisely, a multiplicity of multiplicities must be covered, which consists of multiple agents interacting multimodally by processing and integrating a multitude of information sources, so that ephemerally emerging aggregates (e.g., distributed multiple documents) become observable and analyzable according to a mixed-methods approach, possibly through competing (AI and NLP) methods for their processing. Secondly, the system should be open in opposite directions: (1) inward, by ensuring a kind of multiperspectivity on the object of study (by distinguishing, e.g., intra- and intermodal, intra- and interpersonal perspectives; and (2) outward, by ensuring a kind of multi-usability, after which the system bridges different application domains (e.g., simulation-based learning, visual communication, InCOR, etc.). Thirdly, the system should exploit automation potentials as much as possible, e.g., regarding the detection of spatial and temporal relations of the actions, spaces, objects, and agents involved, the language they use, the anchoring of their utterances in the situations they describe, and the formation of a shared language between these agents in the course of a simulation, of shared cognitive maps, social relations etc. Implementing this requirements analysis demands modeling at the three levels distinguished by [50], i.e., the conceptual, formal, and physical level. This should be done in such a way that the formal model mediates between the rather dynamic conceptual model and the comparatively static implementation by ensuring algorithmic transparency and interpretability. This is the task of the present paper, which develops a formal model of distributed multiple documents that bridges interaction modeling and multimodal communication in a multi-agent setting. It aims to help clarify the complexity dimensions of the data structures affected by simulation-based learning and related research areas, with the ultimate goal of mastering the trade-off described above.

The paper is organized as follows: Sect. 2 is the main part; it contains the formal model that mediates between VA.SI.LI-LAB and its application scenarios. It culminates in the formal specification of the notion of a distributed multiple document, as brought into the center of our analysis above. Section 3 illustrates this mediation in terms of three application areas: online critical reasoning, simulation-based learning, and visual communication. Finally, Sect. 4 concludes and looks ahead to future work.

2   Formalizing Interactive Multimodal Semantics

In Sect. 1, we referred to so-called *distributed multiple documents* (DMD) as a necessary step to overcome the limitation of the notion of multiple documents in terms of cooperative learning processes. A data structure that is intended to overcome this limitation must capture the structuring and interaction of very different entities: of sign artifacts as well as interacting agents, of sign representations as well as social networks, to name a few.[3] We need to integrate structural models of relevant entities (agents, objects, semiotic artifacts, etc.), their compositions and aggregations, and models of their emergence over time. Moreover, we need to take into account the self-similarity of these structurings and therefore emphasize generic aspects more than specificities. To meet this requirements analysis, we refer to hierarchical hypergraphs as an expressive model for describing structures and their temporal ordering to gain access to generative aspects. The generality of our model will be ensured by recursively using the same generic structure to derive increasingly specific models. More precisely, we use the following definition of hierarchical hypergraphs as a starting point (see [11, 77] for related approaches in software engineering and robotics[4])

---

[3] This requirement is somewhat reminiscent of multimodal time-aligned network series introduced by [54,56,57], but goes beyond them, as will be shown by reference to hypergraphs.

[4] We refer to the notion of directed hypergraphs of [28].

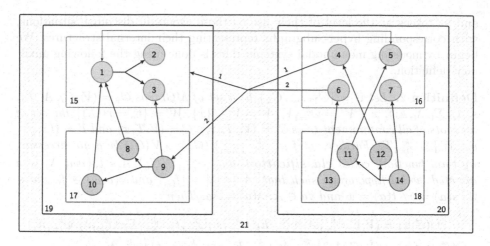

Fig. 3. Visualization of an MGraph where containment is visualized by an inclusion hierarchy rather than by arcs or hyperarcs. The example contains multiple hyperarcs, but no hyperedge. It includes an ordered hyperarc with two source and two target vertices that end at vertices at different levels of the containment tree.

and develop this notion in five steps to arrive at so-called *course of event graphs*, which finally give us access to the notion of DMDs as conceived here:

Definition 1. *An **attributed hierarchical labeled mixed multiple ordered hypergraph** or **MGraph** is a hypergraph*

$$G = (V, C, A, E, s, t, \Sigma, \lambda, \mathbb{A})$$

consisting of

1. *a set $V = V(G) = \{v_1, \ldots, v_m\}$ of vertices,*
2. *a so-called **containment tree** $C = (V, T, r)$, $T \subseteq V^2$, rooted in $r(C) = r(G) = r$, such that for each $(v, w) \in T$: v is said to **contain** w,*
3. *a set $A = \{a_1, \ldots, a_n\}$ of hyperarcs and two functions $s, t: A \to 2^V \setminus \{\emptyset\}$ such that for $a \in A$: $s(a)$ is called the **source** and $t(a)$ the **target** of a,*
4. *if $a \in A$ is ordered, the functions $s_o, t_o: A \to 2^{\mathbb{N} \times V} \setminus \{\emptyset\}$ are used instead of s, t to refer to a's ordered source and target;*
5. *a set $E = \{e_1, \ldots, e_o\} \subseteq 2^V \setminus \{\emptyset\}$ of hyperedges,*
6. *a set Σ of labels together with a labeling function $\lambda: V \cup A \cup E \to \Sigma$,*
7. *a set $\mathbb{A} = \{x_1, \ldots, x_l\}$ of vertex, hyperarc and hyperedge attributes x_i with domains $\mathrm{dom}(x_i)$ such that $x_i: X \to \mathrm{dom}(x_i), X \in \{V, A, E\}$, is not necessarily a total function.*

Definition 1 is intentionally kept abstract, hiding its later use for the purpose of interaction modeling. Based on it, we define graph models of (1) mono- and multimodal structures, (2) single- and multi-agent systems, (3) and their anchoring in (courses of) events. For simplicity, we assume that mono- and multimodal signs are addressable as types at the level of agents' long-term memory and as tokens at the level of their use by those agents in discourse situations, with corresponding hyper-subgraphs representing their internal structures. We begin by modeling monomodal systems. This is done using the following auxiliary definition.

Definition 2. *Let* $\mathbb{G} = \{G_1, \ldots, G_k\}$ *be a set of MGraphs* $G_i = (V_i, C_i, A_i, E_i, s_i, t_i, \Sigma_i, \lambda_i, \mathbb{A}_i)$, $x \notin V' = \cup_{i=1}^k V_i$, $V = V' \cup \{x\}$, $W = \{r_i = r(C_i)\}$ *the set of all roots of all containment trees* $C_i = (V_i, T_i, r_i)$, $C = (V, T, x)$ *and* $T = \{(x, y) \mid y \in W\} \cup \cup_{i=1}^k T_i$. *Further, let* $f_{G_i}: \cup_{n=1, n \neq i}^k V(G_n) \to V(G_i)$ *be a not necessarily total function, called* ***classification***, *and* $(\cup_{n=1}^k V(G_n), A, s, t, \{isa\}, \lambda)$ *be a directed labeled hypergraph such that* $|A| = |\lambda| = |f_{G_i}|$ *and* $\forall (v, w) \in f_{G_i} \exists! a \in A: s(a) = v \wedge t(a) = w$ *and* $\forall a \in A: \lambda(a) = isa$. *Then*

$$\cup(\mathbb{G}, x) = (V, C, \cup_{i=1}^k A_i, \cup_{i=1}^k E_i, \cup_{i=1}^k s_i, \cup_{i=1}^k t_i, \cup_{i=1}^k \Sigma_i, \cup_{i=1}^k \lambda_i, \cup_{i=1}^k \mathbb{A}_i)$$

$$\cup(\mathbb{G}, x, f_{G_i}) = (V, C, A \cup \cup_{i=1}^k A_i, \cup_{i=1}^k E_i, s \cup \cup_{i=1}^k s_i, t \cup \cup_{i=1}^k t_i,$$
$$\{isa\} \cup \cup_{i=1}^k \Sigma_i, \lambda \cup \cup_{i=1}^k \lambda_i, \cup_{i=1}^k \mathbb{A}_i)$$

are both called the ***graph union of the MGraphs*** *in* $\mathbb{G}$.

Using the notion of a union of MGraphs, we recursively define nested graph structures that model mono- and multimodal single- and multi-agent interaction systems. For monomodal systems, we assume two types of token-level entities and three types of type-level entities to distinguish between sign *production* and sign *processing* per agent. This will allow us to distinguish between fusion and fission processes and to differentiate corresponding association relations.

Definition 3. *Let* $\mathbb{G} = \{G_1, G_2, G_3, G_4, G_5\}$ *be a set of five MGraphs* $G_i = (V_i, C_i, A_i, E_i, s_i, t_i, \Sigma_i, \lambda_i, \mathbb{A}_i)$, $\mathfrak{m} \notin \cup_{i=1}^5 V(G_i)$ *a constant, called* ***mode***, *used to span a containment tree and* $f_{4.2}: V_4 \to V_2$, $f_{5.3}: V_5 \to V_3$, $f_{2.1}: V_2 \to V_1$, $f_{3.1}: V_3 \to V_1$ *be total functions. Further, let* $\mathfrak{m}^{G_\mathfrak{m}}$, $\top_{G_\mathfrak{m}}^\forall$, $\bot_{G_\mathfrak{m}}^\forall \notin \cup_{i=1}^5 V_i$. *A* ***unimodal graph of mode*** $\mathfrak{m}$ *is an MGraph*

$$G_\mathfrak{m} = (V, C, A, E, s, t, \Sigma, \lambda, \mathbb{A}) \supset G_\mathbb{I}, C = (V, T, \mathfrak{m}^{G_\mathfrak{m}})$$
$$G_\mathbb{I} = \cup(\{G_\bot, G_\top\}, \mathfrak{m}^{G_\mathfrak{m}}, f_{4.2} \cup f_{5.3})$$
$$G_\top = \cup(\{G_1, G_2, G_3\}, \top_{G_\mathfrak{m}}^\forall, f_{2.1} \cup f_{3.1})$$
$$G_\bot = \cup(\{G_4, G_5\}, \bot_{G_\mathfrak{m}}^\forall)$$

satisfying the following conditions and naming conventions:

1. $V^{\top_{G_\mathfrak{m}}^\forall} = V_1 \cup V_2 \cup V_3$ *is called the set of* $\mathfrak{m}$-***types***;
2. $V^{\top_{G_\mathfrak{m}}^\pm} = V_1$ *is called the set of* ***merged*** $\mathfrak{m}$-***types***;
3. $V^{\top_{G_\mathfrak{m}}^+} = V_2$ *is called the set of* ***produced*** $\mathfrak{m}$-***types***;
4. $V^{\top_{G_\mathfrak{m}}^-} = V_3$ *is called the set of* ***processed*** $\mathfrak{m}$-***types***;
5. $V^{\bot_{G_\mathfrak{m}}^\forall} = V_4 \cup V_5$ *is called the set of* $\mathfrak{m}$-***tokens***;
6. $V^{\bot_{G_\mathfrak{m}}^+} = V_4$ *is called the set of* ***produced*** $\mathfrak{m}$-***tokens***;

7. $V^{\perp \bar{G}_{\mathsf{m}}} = V_5$ is called the set of **processed** m-**tokens**;

8. $\{V_i \mid i \in \{1, \ldots, 5\}\}$ is a partition of $V \setminus \{\mathsf{m}^{G_\mathsf{m}}, \top_{G_\mathsf{m}}^\forall, \perp_{G_\mathsf{m}}^\forall\}$;

9. $r(C_1)$ is denoted by $\top_{G_\mathsf{m}}^\pm$, $r(C_2)$ by $\top_{G_\mathsf{m}}^+$, $r(C_3)$ by $\top_{G_\mathsf{m}}^-$, $r(C_4)$ by $\perp_{G_\mathsf{m}}^+$ and $r(C_5)$ by $\perp_{G_\mathsf{m}}^-$;

10. λ is an injective function on each of the three sets V_1, V_2, V_3 (each type occurs at most once);

11. there are attributes in $\mathbb{A}$ that map vertices onto static (cf. [36]), contextualized (cf. [86]), distributional (cf. [57]), ontological (cf. [15]) or mixed (cf. [37, 74]) embeddings; these mappings are called **symbolic associations** (cf. [75]);

12. $\top_{G_\mathsf{m}}^\forall$ and $\perp_{G_\mathsf{m}}^\forall$ are called **long** and **short term** m-**memory** (cf. [4]).

We assume that the association of vertices $v \in V$, hereafter called m-**expressions** or simply **expressions**, by hyperarcs $a \in A$ or hyperedges $e \in E$ depends in part on their symbolic associations.

Following the terminology of [72] and of [75], Definition 3 allows for mapping syntagmatic and paradigmatic associations of unimodal expressions. However, this is done by distinguishing between produced and processed m-expressions and their associations. In this way, Definition 3 allows modeling associations related to sign production (along fission processes) and sign processing (along fusion processes), initially still separately for each agent, while an additional layer ($\top_{G_\mathsf{m}}^\forall$) provides for modeling merged associations that resolve the difference between fusion and fission. Figure 4 shows a visualization of such a unimodal graph, focusing on the type and token layers as well as fusion (right) and fission (left) stages. The next step is to move beyond the realm of monomodal associations towards their multimodal counterpart and multimodal ensembles [53, 55].

Definition 4. Let $\mathbb{G} = \{G_{\mathsf{m}_1}, \ldots, G_{\mathsf{m}_k}\}$ be a set of unimodal graphs $G_{\mathsf{m}_i} = (V_i, C_i, A_i, E_i, s_i, t_i, \Sigma_i, \lambda_i, \mathbb{A}_i)$, $r(G_{\mathsf{m}_i}) = \mathsf{m}_i^{G_i}$, and $x \notin \cup_{i=1}^k V_i$. A k-**modal** or **multimodal graph of modes** $\mathfrak{M} = \{\mathsf{m}_1, \ldots, \mathsf{m}_k\}$, $|\mathfrak{M}| = k$, is an MGraph

$$G_{\mathfrak{M}}^x = G(\mathbb{G}, x) = (V, C, A, E, s, t, \Sigma, \lambda, \mathbb{A}) \supset \cup(\mathbb{G}, x)$$

satisfying the following conditions and naming conventions:

1. all sets V_i, V_j, $i, j \in \{1, \ldots, k\}$, $i \neq j$, are disjoint,

2. any arc $a \in A_i$ is called **intramodal**, as is any edge $e \in E_i$;

3. any $a \in A$ for which $\exists V_i, V_j, 1 \le i < j \le k$: $s(a) \cap V_i \neq \emptyset \neq s(a) \cap V_j \vee t(a) \cap V_i \neq \emptyset \neq t(a) \cap V_j \vee s(a) \cap V_i \neq \emptyset \neq t(a) \cap V_j$ is called **intermodal**, as is any $e \in E$ such that $\exists V_i, V_j, 1 \le i < j \le k$: $e \cap V_i \neq \emptyset \neq e \cap V_j$;

4. let $e \in E$ and $L(e) = \{l \in V \mid \exists v \in e \exists v_1, \ldots, v_o, (v_i, v_{i+1}) \in T, 1 \le i \le o-1, v_1 = v, v_o = l\}$ be the set of all leaves in C that are dominated by a vertex $v \in e$ and $G_{\mathfrak{M}}^x(e) = (e, A^e, E^e, s^e, t^e, \Sigma^e, \lambda^e, \mathbb{A}^e) \subseteq (V, A, E, s, t, \Sigma, \lambda, \mathbb{A})$ be the subgraph of $G_{\mathfrak{M}}^x$ induced by e; then, e is called an **ensemble**, if $G_{\mathfrak{M}}^x(e)$ is connected and $|L(e) > 1|$; for ensembles, we assume an attribute $\varepsilon \in \mathbb{A}$,

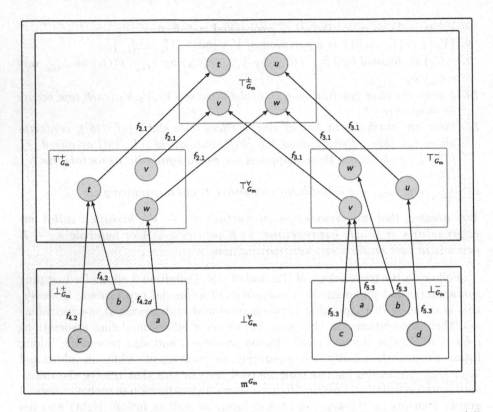

Fig. 4. Visualization of a monomodal graph showing only classification hyperarcs (all other hyperarcs are omitted). The upper layer is type-related, the lower token-related. The left part is fission related, the right fusion related.

$\varepsilon : E \rightarrow G(G_{\mathfrak{M}}^x)$, where $G(G_{\mathfrak{M}}^x)$ is the set of subgraphs of $G_{\mathfrak{M}}^x$ and $\varepsilon(e) \subseteq G_{\mathfrak{M}}^x(e)$ such that $\varepsilon(e)$, the so-called **graph realization** of e, is connected; let $\dot{C}(v) = \{i \mid \exists w \in e \cap V_i\}$; then, for $|\dot{C}(v)| > 1$ e is called a **multimodal ensemble** and for $|\dot{C}(v)| = 1$ a **monomodal ensemble**; further:

i. for $L(e) \subseteq \cup_{i=1}^k V^{\top^\vee_{G_{m_i}}}$ e is called a **type-level ensemble** collected by the set $\varepsilon^{\top^\vee}(G_{\mathfrak{M}}^x)$;

ii. for $L(e) \subseteq \cup_{i=1}^k V^{\top^\pm_{G_{m_i}}}$ a **merged type-level ensemble** collected by the set $\varepsilon^{\top^\pm}(G_{\mathfrak{M}}^x)$;

iii. for $L(e) \subseteq \cup_{i=1}^k V^{\top^+_{G_{m_i}}}$ a **produced type-level ensemble** collected by the set $\varepsilon^{\top^+}(G_{\mathfrak{M}}^x)$;

iv. for $L(e) \subseteq \cup_{i=1}^k V^{\top^-_{G_{m_i}}}$ a **processed type-level ensemble** collected by the set $\varepsilon^{\top^-}(G_{\mathfrak{M}}^x)$;

v. for $L(e) \subseteq \cup_{i=1}^k V^{\perp^\vee_{G_{m_i}}}$ a **token-level ensemble** collected by the set $\varepsilon^{\perp^\vee}(G_{\mathfrak{M}}^x)$;

vi. for $L(e) \subseteq \cup_{i=1}^{k} V^{\perp^{+}_{G_{\mathfrak{m}_i}}}$ a **produced token-level ensemble** collected by the set $\varepsilon^{\perp^{+}}(G_{\mathfrak{M}}^{x})$ and

vii. for $L(e) \subseteq \cup_{i=1}^{k} V^{\perp^{-}_{G_{\mathfrak{m}_i}}}$ a **processed token-level ensemble** collected by the set $\varepsilon^{\perp^{-}}(G_{\mathfrak{M}}^{x})$;

viii. if e is neither a token-, nor a type-level ensemble, it is called **mixed** and collected by the sets $\varepsilon^{\top}(G_{\mathfrak{M}}^{x})$, $\varepsilon^{\top^{+}}(G_{\mathfrak{M}}^{x})$ and $\varepsilon^{\top^{-}}(G_{\mathfrak{M}}^{x})$;

ix. additional ensemble sets are defined by intersections and unions of the sets introduced so far;

x. we omit the argument $G_{\mathfrak{M}}^{x}$ if it follows from the context;

$\deg(e) = |\dot{C}(e)|$ is the **degree of multimodality** of the ensemble e; for monomodal ensembles $\deg(e) = 1$;

5. there are attributes in $\mathbb{A}$ that map ensembles onto static (cf. [45]), contextualized, distributional (cf. [57]), ontological or mixed embeddings; this mapping is called **multimodal symbolic association**.

We assume that the association of vertices $v \in V$ by hyperarcs $a \in A$ or hyperedges $e \in E$ depends in part on multimodal symbolic associations.

For a visual representation of the data underlying the spanning of a multimodal graph, see Definition 5.

Uni- and multimodal MGraphs allow the representation of uni- and multimodal long- and short-term memory contents of individual agents. To account for multimodal interactions between different agents and thus for interpersonal structure formation (e.g., alignment), we need to extend our list of definitions as follows:

Definition 5. Let $\mathbb{G} = \{G_1(\mathfrak{M}, x_1), \ldots, G_n(\mathfrak{M}, x_n)\}$ be a set of k-modal graphs $G_i(\mathfrak{M}, x_i) = (V_i, C_i, A_i, E_i, s_i, t_i, \Sigma_i, \lambda_i, \mathbb{A}_i)$ with pairwise disjoint vertex sets and $x \notin \cup_{i=1}^{k} V_i$. A k-**modal** or **multimodal multi-agent graph of modes** $\mathfrak{M}$ is an MGraph

$$G_{\mathfrak{M}}^{x} = G(\mathbb{G}, x) = (V, C, A, E, s, t, \Sigma, \lambda, \mathbb{A}) \supset \cup(\mathbb{G}, x)$$

satisfying the following conditions and naming conventions:

1. Any arc $a \in A_i$ is called **intrapersonal**, as is any edge $e \in E_i$.
2. Any $a \in A$ for which $\exists V_i, V_j, 1 \le i < j \le k: s(a) \cap V_i \ne \emptyset \ne s(a) \cap V_j \lor t(a) \cap V_i \ne \emptyset \ne t(a) \cap V_j \lor s(a) \cap V_i \ne \emptyset \ne t(a) \cap V_j$ is called **interpersonal**, as is any $e \in E$ such that $\exists V_i, V_j, 1 \le i < j \le k: e \cap V_i \ne \emptyset \ne e \cap V_j$.
3. Hyperarcs or hyperedges over $Y = \{r(G_i(\mathfrak{M}, x_i)) \mid i \in \{1, \ldots, n\}\}$ are called **social**.
4. There exist attributes in $\mathbb{A}$ that map vertices from Y onto static, contextualized, distributional, ontological or mixed embeddings; this mapping is called **social association**.
5. We assume that social arcs and edges depend in part on social associations.

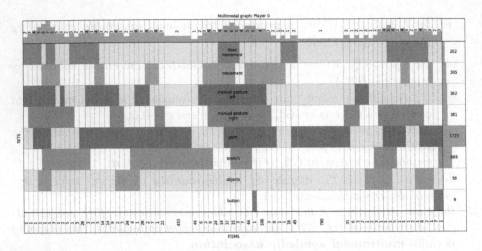

Fig. 5. Visualization (by means of supervenn [26]) of a multimodal MGraph based on 8 modalities, including object and button manipulations. The underlying MGraph represents data from a single agent participating in an organizational work environment task (cf. Figure 1). Button-related actions concern, e.g., a control button that allows subjects to signal their desire to remain in or leave the experiment, or to be advised by the experimenters. Objects concern virtually manipulable objects (e.g., a virus model in a school context) in the virtual spaces that the participants enter. Items (horizontal axis) encode time slices in which the corresponding events and their co-occurrences are measured. Rows correspond to the modalities depicted in Fig. 2. Columns code multimodal ensembles.

Definition 4 defines the sets $\varepsilon^{\top^\vee}$, $\varepsilon^{\top\pm}$, $\varepsilon^{\top^+}$, $\varepsilon^{\top^-}$, $\varepsilon^{\perp^\vee}$, $\varepsilon^{\perp^+}$, $\varepsilon^{\perp^-}$, $\varepsilon^{\mathcal{I}}$, $\varepsilon^{\mathcal{I}^+}$ *and* $\varepsilon^{\mathcal{I}^-}$*, which are all based on single agents. To distinguish them from their multi-agent counterparts, we refer to the sets* $\ddot{\varepsilon}^{\top^\vee}$, $\ddot{\varepsilon}^{\top\pm}$, $\ddot{\varepsilon}^{\top^+}$, $\ddot{\varepsilon}^{\top^-}$, $\ddot{\varepsilon}^{\perp^\vee}$, $\ddot{\varepsilon}^{\perp^+}$, $\ddot{\varepsilon}^{\perp^-}$, $\ddot{\varepsilon}^{\mathcal{I}}$, $\ddot{\varepsilon}^{\mathcal{I}^+}$ *and* $\ddot{\varepsilon}^{\mathcal{I}^-}$*.*

The next step is to account for pragmatic associations [75]. To this end, we additionally consider extra-personal situations or events consisting, e.g., of places [68] and the objects (e.g. spatial named entities in the sense of [68] and semiotic artifacts such as online texts) located within them, in which agents manipulate these objects while communicatively coordinating their actions. We again use MGraphs to model such settings. In this way, hypergraphs are generated in which multimodal signs are associated with objects that agents refer to or describe when they cooperatively manipulate these objects or perform actions with their help.

Definition 6. *Let* $G^x_{\mathfrak{M}} = (V_i, C_i, A_i, E_i, s_i, t_i, \Sigma_i, \lambda_i, \mathbb{A}_i)$ *be a multimodal multi-agent graph and* $G = (V_j, C_j, A_j, E_j, s_j, t_j, \Sigma_j, \lambda_j, \mathbb{A}_j)$ *an MGraph, henceforth called **object graph**. Let further* $y \notin V_i \cup V_j$ *and* $\mathfrak{b}, \mathfrak{e} \in \mathbb{R}^+_0$*,* $\mathfrak{b} < \mathfrak{e}$*, be time-stamps. An **event graph** is an MGraph*

$$\mathcal{E} = (V, C, A, E, s, t, \Sigma, \lambda, \mathbb{A}, \mathfrak{b}, \mathfrak{e}), (V, C, A, E, s, t, \Sigma, \lambda, \mathbb{A}) = \cup(\{G^x_{\mathfrak{M}}, G\}, y)$$

satisfying the following conditions and naming conventions:

1. $\{V_{eventuality}, V_{event\text{-}path}, V_{motion}, V_{obj}, V_{path}, V_{place}, V_{motion_s}\}$ *is a partitioning of V_j where:*
   - $V_{eventuality}$ *is a set of entities denoting* **non-motion eventualities**,
   - $V_{event\text{-}path}$ *is a set of entities denoting* **event paths**[5],
   - V_{motion} *is a set of entities denoting* **motions**,
   - V_{obj} *is a set of* **no-locational spatial entities**, *hereafter called* **objects**,
   - V_{path} *is a set of entities denoting* **paths**,
   - V_{place} *is a set of entities denoting* **places**, *all in terms of ISO space 2.0;*
   - $V_{sive} \subseteq V_{obj}$ *is a subset of entities denoting* **sign vehicles** *(e.g., string streams or documents, audio signals, images, video streams etc.);*
   - V_{motion_s} *is a set of entities denoting* **sign processes** *that affect or are related to elements of V_{sive}.*

   For each vertex in $V_j \setminus (V_{sive} \cup V_{motion_s})$, we assume attributes in $\mathbb{A}$ that model the corresponding attributes from ISO-Space for these entities.[6]

2. *Each $v \in V_{event\text{-}path} \cup V_{path}$ is a hypergraph in the form of a directed hyperpath*[7] $p = v_0, a_1, v_1, a_2, \ldots, v_k$ *such that for each $v_i \in \{v_0, \ldots, v_k\}$ there exists an arc $b_i \in A$ with $s(b_i) = \{v_i\}$ and $t(b_i) \in [V_{obj} \cup V_{place} \cup V_{agent}]^1$, $V_{agent} = \{v \mid (r(G_{\mathfrak{M}}^x), v) \in C_i\}$. We say that v resp. p are* **anchored** *by $\{b_0, \ldots, b_k\}$ as is v_i by b_i and assume that $\lambda(b) = $ instance of $\in \Sigma$. We also say that p* **manifests** *v.*

3. *There exists a subset of* **sign production or processing-related event paths** *$V_{s\text{-}event\text{-}path} \subset V_{event\text{-}path}$ manifested by paths consisting only of vertices, all anchored in sign vehicles from V_{sive}.*

4. *We adopt ISO-Space links and extend them by so-called semioLinks:*
   - **qsLinks** *(qualitative spatial links), which denote binary topological relations according to RCC8+ (cf. [71]), are arcs $a \in A_{qs} \subset A$ that connect two vertices $v, w \in s(a) \cup t(a) \in [V_{location}]^1$, $V_{location} = V_{path} \cup V_{place}$.*
   - **oLinks** *(orientation links), which denote non-topological absolute (bird's eye view), intrinsic (orientation), or relative (point of view) relations, are arcs $a \in A_o \subset A$ that connect in the same way as qsLinks.*
   - **qsLinks**^{e} *$a \in A_{qse} \subset A$ and* **oLinks**^{e} *$a \in A_{oe} \subset A$ connect an eventuality $s(a) \in [V_{eventuality}]^1$ with one or more locations $t(a) \subseteq 2^{V_{location}} \setminus \{\emptyset\}$.*
   - *Arcs $a \in Z = A_{qs} \cup A_{qse} \cup A_o \cup A_{oe}$ are connected with two attributes $tri_1, tri_2 \in \mathbb{A}$, $tri_1 : Z \to 2^{V_i}$, $tri_2 : Z \to 2^{V_{sive}}$ indicating subsets of so-called triggers distinguished as follows:*[8]

---

[5] "[...] event-paths are trajectories created by motions." [42, 12], although not every description of a motion involves a description of an event path [42, 17].

[6] This can lead to redundancy in our model, since some of these attributes are explicitly modeled using hypergraph structures (see below), but this saves us from enumerating all the attributes that do not create redundancy.

[7] For hyperwalks see [2, 18]; for directed hypergraphs see [5]; for directed hyperpaths see [28]. We refer to hyperpaths to map the linear structure of such events, and use anchoring arcs to map repeating vertices.

[8] Here we leave ISO-Space by allowing multiple triggers for the same link. This is necessary, for example, to account for alignment between interlocutors.

- a is said to be **externally triggered**, if $tri_2(a) \neq \emptyset$,
- a is said to be **internally triggered**, if $tri_1(a) \neq \emptyset$; more precisely, for $\mathcal{X} \in \{\varepsilon, \ddot{\varepsilon}\}$, a is said to be triggered by a
  - i. **type-level ensemble** for $tri_1(a) \subseteq \mathcal{X}^{\top^\vee}(G^x_{\mathfrak{M}})$,
  - ii. **merged type-level ensemble** for $tri_1(a) \subseteq \mathcal{X}^{\top^\pm}(G^x_{\mathfrak{M}})$,
  - iii. **produced type-level ensemble** for $tri_1(a) \subseteq \mathcal{X}^{\top^+}(G^x_{\mathfrak{M}})$,
  - iv. **processed type-level ensemble** for $tri_1(a) \subseteq \mathcal{X}^{\top^-}(G^x_{\mathfrak{M}})$,
  - v. **token-level ensemble** for $tri_1(a) \subseteq \mathcal{X}^{\perp^\vee}(G^x_{\mathfrak{M}})$,
  - vi. **produced token-level ensemble** for $tri_1(a) \subseteq \mathcal{X}^{\perp^+}(G^x_{\mathfrak{M}})$,
  - vii. **processed token-level ensemble** for $tri_1(a) \subseteq \mathcal{X}^{\perp^-}(G^x_{\mathfrak{M}})$,
  - viii. **mixed ensemble** for $tri_1(a) \subseteq \mathcal{X}^{\mathcal{I}}(G^x_{\mathfrak{M}})$,
  - ix. **processed mixed ensemble** for $tri_1(a) \subseteq \mathcal{X}^{\mathcal{I}^+}(G^x_{\mathfrak{M}})$,
  - x. **produced mixed ensemble** for $tri_1(a) \subseteq \mathcal{X}^{\mathcal{I}^-}(G^x_{\mathfrak{M}})$;
- for $\mathcal{X} = \ddot{\varepsilon}$, a is called **multi-agent-based** and for $\mathcal{X} = \varepsilon$ **single-agent-based**;
- for $tri_1(a) = tri_2(a) = \emptyset$, a is said to be **untriggered**.

In ISO-Space, qsLinks and oLinks are triggered by spatial relations called sRelations. Here, triggering occurs by short- or long-term memory representations of agents or through sign vehicles (e.g., verbal expressions that manifest sRelations). To capture sRelations from ISO-Space, we assume an XML Schema attribute sRelation $\in \mathbb{A}$ assigned to qsLinks a that uses the IDs of the vertices involved to refer to them. That is, we let links be triggered directly by what would be called a markable in ISO-Space.

- **mLinks** (measure links), which denote distances, are modeled by arcs $a \in A_{dist} \subset A$ connecting two vertices $v, w \in s(a) \cup t(a) \in [V_{obj} \cup V_{agent} \cup V_{location}]^1$.

- For each $a \in A_z$, $z \in \{dist, o, oe, qs, qse\}$, we adopt its ISO-Space attributes by corresponding attributes in $\mathbb{A}$; especially, there are attributes $\phi_z, \gamma_z : A_z \to V_{location}$, $\{\phi_z(a), \gamma_z(a)\} \subseteq s(a) \cup t(a)$, $\phi(a) \neq \gamma(a)$; $\phi(a)$ is called the **figure** and $\gamma(a)$ the **ground** of a.

- **moveLinks**, which denote motion events where a mover in the role of the figure is linked to an event path in the role of the ground of the underlying motion, are arcs $a \in A_{move} \subset A$ connecting $s(a) \in [V_{obj} \cup V_{agent}]^1$ and $t(a) \in [V_{event\text{-}path}]^1$. Let $a \in A_{move}$, $t(a) = \{w\}$ and $p = v_0, a_1, v_1, a_2, \ldots, v_k$ be the manifestation path of w. Then, we assume an attribute $tri_3 \in \mathbb{A}$, $tri_3 : A_{move} \to V_{motion}$, such that for $v = tri_3(a)$ there exist two attributes $\tau \in \mathbb{A}$ whose attribute value $\tau_v = \tau(v)$ is a function $\tau_v : \{v_0, \ldots, v_k\} \to \mathbb{R}_0^+$ that maps all vertices v_i of w resp. p to *timestamps* $\tau_v(v_i) \in \mathbb{R}_0^+$ *such that* $\forall i, j \in \{0, \ldots, k\} : i < j \Rightarrow \tau_v(v_i) \leq \tau_v(v_j)$.[9] *Further, we assume an attribute* $\sigma \in \mathbb{A}$ *whose attribute value* $\sigma_v = \sigma(v)$ *for* v *is a function* $\sigma_v : \{v_0 \ldots, v_k\} \to 2^{V_i}$ *mapping each sign vehicle from* p *to* 2^{V_i} *analogous to* tri_1.[10] *Finally, we assume:* $\forall a \in A_{move} \exists \phi_{move} : A_{move} \to V_{obj} \cup V_{agent}, \gamma_{move} : A_{move} \to V_{event\text{-}path} : \phi_{move}(a) \in s(a) \wedge \gamma_{move}(a) \in t(a).$

- *semioLinks, which do not exist in ISO-Space, are arcs* $a \in A_{sem} \subset A$ *connecting vertex sets* $s(a) \in 2^{V_{agent}} \setminus \{\emptyset\}$ *with sign-processing related event paths* $t(a) \in [V_{s\text{-}event\text{-}path}]^1$. *Let* $a \in A_{sem}$, $t(a) = \{w\}$ *and* $p = v_0, a_1, v_1, a_2, \ldots, v_k$ *be the manifestation path of* w. *Then, we assume an attribute* $tri_4 \in \mathbb{A}$, $tri_4 : A_{sem} \to V_{motion_s}$, *such that for* $v = tri_4(a)$ *there exists an attribute* $\tau \in \mathbb{A}$ *whose attribute value* $\tau_v = \tau(v)$ *for* v *is a function* $\tau_v : \{v_0 \ldots, v_k\} \to \mathbb{R}_0^+$ *that maps all vertices of* w *to timestamps* $\tau_v(a) \in \mathbb{R}_0^+$ *such that* $\forall i, j \in \{1, \ldots, k\} : i < j \Rightarrow \tau_v(v_i) \leq \tau_v(v_j)$. *Further, by analogy to moveLinks, we assume an attribute* $\sigma \in \mathbb{A}$ *whose attribute value* $\sigma_v = \sigma(v)$ *for* v *is a function* $\sigma_v : \{v_0 \ldots, v_k\} \to 2^{V_i}$ *mapping each sign vehicle from* p *to* 2^{V_i} *analogous to* tri_1. *Finally, we assume:* $\forall a \in A_{sem} \exists \phi_{sem} : A_{sem} \to V_{agent}, \gamma_{sem} : A_{sem} \to V_{motion_s} : \phi_{sem}(a) = s(a) \wedge \gamma_{sem}(a) = t(a).$

- *For* $z \in \{dist, move, o, oe, qs, qse, sem\}$, *we say that* $a \in A_z$ *is figured by* $\phi_z(a)$ *and grounded by* $\gamma_z(a)$.

5. $\mathfrak{b}, \mathfrak{e}$ *denote the begin and end time of* $\mathcal{E}$.

The subset of sign vehicles referred to in Definition 6 needs clarification. Definition 6 is abstract and therefore leaves open what these objects are: they are only specified by what they are not: elements of V_i, etc. Any computational operationalization of this definition needs to elaborate on this. For example, it could specify that, starting from a VR application such as VA.SI.LI-LAB, a sign vehicle corresponds to a segment of an online text delimited by a reading action of at least one agent represented by a multimodal graph. Such demarcations can result, e.g., from indirect actions identified by eye-tracking, or from explicit text selection, highlighting, or segmentation by agents who extract text segments from 3D browsers to make them manipulable as 3D objects. In fact, such a browser already exists (see [1,51]), and is part of VA.SI.LI-LAB.

Since Definition 6 extends the definition of MGraphs, we need to adjust the notion of MGraph union:

---

[9] TIMEX3 values according to ISO-TimeML [69] are an alternative here, but since we consider measurement operations using VA.SI.LI-LAB, we restrict ourselves to timestamps in this definition. We also deviate from ISO-Space 2.0 in that we refer to (s-)motions as entities that allow us to relate, e.g., the type or manner of motion and its temporal structure to (s-)event paths: the same path can then be related to different motion events. Since our task here is not to annotate spatial relations in utterances or texts, but to capture spatial relations using motion and behavioral data in VA.SI.LI-LAB, we take this route of adapting ISO-Space.

[10] Of course, σ_v goes beyond the realm of ISO-Space.

Definition 7. *Let* $\mathbb{G} = \{G_1, \ldots, G_k\}$ *be a set of event graphs* $G_i = (V_i, C_i, A_i,$ $E_i, s_i, t_i, \Sigma_i, \lambda_i, \mathbb{A}, \mathfrak{b}_i, \mathfrak{e}_i)$, $\mathbb{G}' = \{G_1', \ldots, G_k'\}$, $G_i' = (V_i, C_i, A_i,\ E_i, s_i, t_i, \Sigma_i, \lambda_i,$ $\mathbb{A})$, $\bot = \min\{\mathfrak{b}_1, \ldots, \mathfrak{b}_k\}$, $\top = \max\{\mathfrak{e}_1, \ldots, \mathfrak{e}_k\}$ *and* x *and* f_{G_i} *be given according to Definition 2 – that is,* f_{G_i} *is a classification. Then*

$$\dot{\cup}(\mathbb{G}, x) = (V, C, A, E, s, t, \Sigma, \lambda, \mathbb{A}, \bot, \top)$$
$$(V, C, A, E, s, t, \Sigma, \lambda, \mathbb{A}) = \cup(\mathbb{G}', x)$$
$$\dot{\cup}(\mathbb{G}, x, f_{G_i}) = (V, C, A', E, s', t', \Sigma', \lambda', \mathbb{A}, \bot, \top)$$
$$(V, C, A', E, s', t', \Sigma', \lambda', \mathbb{A}) = \cup(\mathbb{G}', x, f_{G_i})$$

*are called the **graph unions of the event graphs** in* $\mathbb{G}$.

Event graphs as defined by Definition 6 can be considered as models of utterance and embedding situations in the sense of [9, 20], but not generally of resource situations that become accessible via (shared) memory content. They model single events that may differ in their temporal extent and in the depth of structure formation they capture. It remains to define time series of such event graphs as models of courses of events:

Definition 8. *Let* $\mathbb{G} = \{\mathcal{E}_0, \mathcal{E}_1, \ldots, \mathcal{E}_s\}$ *be a set of event graphs* $\mathcal{E}_i = (V_i, C_i, A_i,$ $E_i, s_i, t_i, \Sigma_i, \lambda_i, \mathbb{A}_i, \mathfrak{b}_i, \mathfrak{e}_i)$ *such that* $\forall i, j \in \{1, \ldots, s\} \colon \mathfrak{b}_i \leq \mathfrak{b}_j$, $\mathfrak{b}_0 = \min\{\mathfrak{b}_1, \ldots,$ $\mathfrak{b}_s\}$ *and* $\mathfrak{e}_0 = \max\{\mathfrak{e}_1, \ldots, \mathfrak{e}_s\}$. *Further, let* $x \notin \cup_{i=1}^{k} V_i$ *and* $f_{\mathcal{E}_0} \colon \cup_{i=1}^{s} V_i \to V_0$ *be a classification in the sense of Definition 2 and Definition 7. A **course of events graph** is an MGraph*

$$G(\mathbb{G}, x) = (V, C, A, E, s, t, \Sigma, \lambda, \mathbb{A}, \mathfrak{b}, \mathfrak{e}) \supset \dot{\cup}(\mathbb{G}, x, f_{\mathcal{E}_0})$$

By $f_{\mathcal{E}_0}$, *vertices in* $\cup_{i=1}^{s} V_i$ *are classified by vertices in* V_0 *so that vertices of different event graphs can be considered as instances of the same class.*

Based on the constitutive classification of course of event graphs, the embedding of the same entities or processes in different, "successive" event graphs can be mapped.

According to our series of definitions introduced so far, course of events graphs are defined recursively by applying a series of five unions at different levels of representational resolution (MG stands for MGraph):

$$f_5(\dot{\cup}(\{\ldots, f_4(\cup(\{f_3(\cup(\{\ldots, f_2(\cup(\{\ldots, f_1(\cup(\{\ldots, \underbrace{G_i}, \ldots\}, \mathfrak{m}_i)), \ldots\}, \cdot)), \ldots\}, \cdot)), \ldots\}, \cdot)), O_j\}, \cdot)), \ldots\}, \cdot))$$

with braces labeled (from innermost to outermost): *MG*, *unimodal graph*, *multimodal graph*, *multimodal agent graph*, *event graph*, *course of events graph*

What does the formal model presented so far do for us? It allows for precisely modeling, e.g., intra- and intermodal intra- and interpersonal processes of alignment among interacting agents, thereby distinguishing (the routinization of shared or private) syntagmatic, paradigmatic, and pragmatic associations – the latter due to the fact that we embed multi-agent graphs in event graphs and their temporal ordering according to Definition 8. At the present stage, we do this in terms of spatial relations according to ISO-Space. This brings us to the second significant achievement of our formal model: by operationalizing Definition 8 using VR technologies such as VA.SI.LI-LAB, it is possible to *automatically* capture a part of the spatial and representational (long- and short-term, fusion or fission-related) relations involved and make them accessible for modeling the grounding of shared, aligned association relations. Thirdly, starting from the documents model of [13,64], we can now precisely define *distributed multiple documents* (DMD) which become accessible as measurable objects by means of VA.SI.LI-LAB. The focus is on the question of the representation model of DMDs that are delimited and networked in multi-agent sign processing and production processes, whose boundaries and compositions are thus not determined by a single reader but by a group of more or less interacting agents such as a learning group.

More precisely, based on the concept of course of event graphs, multiple documents are captured at multiple levels. First, of all, they are modeled by hyperarcs a that connect a number of entities: the formal side of multiple documents – *so to speak their sign vehicles structured as walks* – are modeled by sign processing-related event paths (see $V_{s\text{-}event\text{-}path}$). While these paths are token-related, their vertices are each anchored in sign vehicles V_{sive} – with the help of this anchoring we can reconstruct the underlying (hyper-)walks. The agents who generate these walks by the sign processes they perform (e.g., by reading, writing or discussing) are modeled by subsets $s(a) \in 2^{V_{agent}}$: for $|s(a)| > 1$, the respective multiple documents are *distributed*. At this level, our model captures which sign vehicles are processed in a multiple-document-generating way by whom in which cooperation. Additional information about the temporal structure of a DMD and the way it is *internally* anchored by single or multiple agents, by mono- or multimodal ensembles, by processes of sign production or reception etc., is obtained using the V_{motion_s}-related attribute of a:

1. First, this concerns the function τ_v for $v = \text{trig}_4(a)$, which determines the temporal structure of a sign processing- or production-related event path with respect to a motion$_s$ event.
2. Second, this concerns the function σ_v for $v = \text{trig}_4(a)$, which determines how the motion$_s$ event is anchored by internal representations of the agents involved.

And since we distinguish association-related embeddings at multiple levels, such as mono- and multimodal or intra- and interpersonal associations, we arrive at a representational model of DMDs that encompasses their internal, conceptual and external, sign-vehicle-related structure as the object of event-related short-term alignment processes. These models are in turn referable as components of course of event graphs, so that, e.g., discontinuous learning processes that continue the same DMDs can be modeled. This can be seen as a starting point for modeling, e.g., long-term processes of alignment [65]. VA.SI.LI-LAB takes the role of providing the elementary observations necessary to populate this model. VA.SI.LI-LAB thus ultimately aims to establish DMDs as formalized, observable entities that help overcome the limitations of the concept of multiple documents in the context of cooperative learning.

3   Three Usage Scenarios

In this section, we briefly describe three application scenarios that can benefit from the capabilities for observing interactive learning behavior provided by VA.-SI.LI-LAB. This concerns critical online reasoning, simulation-based learning, and visual communication.

3.1   Interactive Critical Online Reasoning

To validly assess student learning and performance in online environments and in interaction with media and information they use, innovative Internet-based assessments and simulations for diagnostic purposes as well as digital training tools with feedback for instructional purposes in (post-)university education have been developed and tested within and across many disciplines (e.g., medicine, economics; [76,88]). Using online assessments and learning platforms, students' online behavior has been tracked and logged in real time (e.g., using wearable sensors, mobile (eye) tracking, smartphone applications) [23,76,84]. Recent analyses have focused on an indicator-based representative sample of information. Indicators include domain-specific epistemology, inquiry practices, COR strategies, overarching concepts and principles including misconceptions, forms of information representation (e.g., through texts, images, videos, sounds), and discourse and language structures, e.g., with varying degrees of complexity in different modalities and structural differences [23,33,47,76]. In this way, an information and learning landscape of digital and analog sources that are available to and used by students in formal and informal learning environments is quantitatively and qualitatively mapped and described. Moreover, students' actual learning paths through this landscape are tracked in real time [88].

In this context, VA.SI.LI-LAB offers the possibility to further develop online assessments and learning simulations to include more interaction and collaboration or communication information. Analyses based on an integrative model such as VA.SI.LI-LAB target interaction of individuals (e.g., between learners and subgroups depending on group-specific characteristics) in different constellations (such as online learning platforms or university seminars). In addition, macro characteristics, such as output measures that depend on the number and type of learning agents, available materials, soft- and hardware, and the distribution of specific entity roles, including the presence of intermediaries, gatekeepers, and filter bubbles and their influence on learners' access to information, may fall within the scope of measurement operations that become accessible with VA.-SI.LI-LAB. Findings are expected to indicate, e.g., students' use of only partially reliable information from diverse (un)trustworthy sources depending on group characteristics, the extent to which machine-generated representations can produce trustworthy sources, and the extent to which human characteristics matter for the learning environment. Based on such analyses, students can eventually be supported through various types of information sources, experts, and media.

3.2 Simulation-based Learning

Teamwork concerns a skill that is required of pedagogues in their future work. However, it also forms a social and cultural practice of the collective construction of knowledge through the negotiation of epistemological and normative facticity [25,48]. In this context, simulation-based learning can be viewed as a technique that aims to recreate real-world scenarios and make learners approximately familiar with the subject matter. This approach is widely used in nursing, medicine [21] and law [3] to introduce novices to the procedures and practices of these fields. More recently, social work [22] and education [19] have also embraced simulation-based learning as a means of preparing students for their careers [16], where VR technologies enable immersive learning experiences [43]. This development has been accelerated by the decrease in cost and accessibility of VR technologies. However, VR has hardly been used in language-based professions due to technical limitations [81]. Thus, there is an untapped advantage, as simulation-based learning related to teamwork aims to enable learners to creatively exercise conflicting positions and roles in social networks. Here, VR scenarios can support learners how to have a productive impact on a discursive work environment through different roles. This is precisely one of the contexts of application of VA.SI.LI-LAB, namely to create a learning environment open to learners' creative practices and epistemological, cultural and social conflicts based on their social roles and communicative interactions. So instead of giving learners fixed roles and goals, our design encourages, e.g., negotiation and creativity as integral parts of developing pedagogical professionalism. To this end, we developed several simulation-based learning scenarios (cf. Fig. 1) which show that this openness offers students the opportunity to practice different forms of co-creative pedagogical teamwork in a playful way. From a theoretical perspective, this openness not only offers learners the opportunity to shape interactions according to their individual beliefs, but also provides fruitful empirical insights into the tacit knowledge that informs their construction of professionalism. Therefore, VA.SI.LI-LAB's embedding of agent-related language models into graph-theoretical models of social networks shaped by the interactions of learners is of central interest for teamwork-related simulation-based learning.

3.3 Visual Communication

It is not yet fully understood if interlocutors monitor each others manual gestures, respectively under which conditions they do (not) [82]. Letting a virtual avatar perform a fixed set of multimodal stimuli (speech and co-speech gesture in, say, a question–answer game) and thereby systematically vary the avatar's gaze (other gaze, gaze at gesture, gazing somewhere else) would provide repeatable settings. Tracking the gazing direction of interlocutors (the experiments' participants) provides the needed evidence of whether the stimulus gesture is observed at all, at least within visual focus. Note that such an experiment is difficult to carry out outside an immersive environment: a confident participant presenting the stimulus will not be able to produce it without changes, even if well-trained. And using prerecorded stimuli on a screen changes the visual perception conditions. Note that such experiments contribute to visual grounding [58] and attention [62] in HCI. In this sense, VA.SI.LI-LAB can also be considered an experimental environment for the study of visual communication (see https://vicom.info for further information, and [31] for a broader perspective).

4   Conclusion

We presented VA.SI.LI-LAB, a VR lab for simulation-based learning that enables experimental investigation of multimodal communication in learning scenarios, including *interactive online critical reasoning* (iCOR). VA.SI.LI-LAB targets the embedding of agent-related language models into graph-theoretical models of social networks shaped by the interactions of interlocutors. VA.SI.LI-LAB is currently being evaluated in the context of three application areas, including organizational work environments and school environments. In the context of iCOR, we focused on extending the notion of multiple documents in terms of their distribution among groups of collaborative learners. To overcome limitations of this notion, we developed a formal model that integrates a variety of concepts such as interactive multimodal semantics, communicative alignment, distributed multiple documents, and embeddings of linguistic and social entities. The formal model, which is recursively based on attributed hierarchical, labeled, mixed, multiple ordered hypergraphs, essentially designs a model for integrating these and a variety of other information entities. It uses ISO-Space to simultaneously develop a model of interactive processing or generation of distributed multiple documents. In this way, the model may serve as a starting point for multimodal representation learning in the context of communication scenarios such as those studied here. It integrates situational components and artifacts and is therefore also of interest for reference semantic approaches. To this end, however, it should be extended to characterize objects by their affordances [29,67], which make them amenable to different manipulations by agents. This is where the notion of a port comes into play, making nodes in hierarchical hypergraphs accessible to various operations while encapsulating vertex behavior in an object-oriented manner. This extension will be future work.

Author contribution

Author	Sect. 1	Sect. 2	Sect. 3	Sect. 3.1	Sect. 3.2	Sect. 3.3	Sect. 4	Prog	Exp	Fig. 1	Fig. 2	Fig. 3	Fig. 4	Fig. 5
AH									•	•				
AL	o				•						•			
AM	•	•	o	o	o	o	•	o	•	o	•	•	•	o
CS									•					
GA									•	•				
JE	o				•					•				
JS	o				•					•				
KS										•				
MB									•	•	•	•		•
MK											•			
MQ									•					
OZ	o		•											
PS									•					

•: main work; o: minor contribution. Prog. concerns conceptualizing and programming of VA.-SI.LI-LAB; Exp. concerns design of simulation-based learning scenarios and experimentation.

Acknowledgement. We especially thank all participants involved in the experiments with the help of VA.SI.LI-LAB for their support. This work was co-funded by *Bundesministerium für Bildung und Forschung* (BMBF), grant 01JD1906B, as well as the "Digital Teaching and Learning Lab" (DigiTeLL) at the Goethe University Frankfurt. Furthermore, this work was supported by the *Deutsche Forschungsgemeinschaft* (DFG) [grant numbers ME 2746/10-1 and LU 2114/2-1].

References

1. Abrami, G., Henlein, A., Kett, A., Mehler, A.: Text2scenevr: generating hypertexts with vannotator as a pre-processing step for text2scene systems. In: Proceedings of the 31st ACM Conference on Hypertext and Social Media, pp. 177–186 (2020). https://doi.org/10.1145/3372923.3404791
2. Aksoy, S.G., Joslyn, C., Ortiz Marrero, C., Praggastis, B., Purvine, E.: Hypernetwork science via high-order hypergraph walks. EPJ Data Sci. **9**(1), 1–34 (2020). https://doi.org/10.1140/epjds/s13688-020-00231-0
3. Apel, S.B.: No more casebooks: using simulation-based learning to educate future family law practitioners. Fam. Court. Rev. **49**(4), 700–710 (2011). https://doi.org/10.1111/j.1744-1617.2011.01406.x
4. Atkinson, R.C., Shiffrin, R.M.: Human memory: a proposed system and its control processes. In: Psychology of Learning and Motivation, vol. 2, pp. 89–195. Elsevier (1968). https://doi.org/10.1016/S0079-7421(08)60422-3
5. Ausiello, G., Laura, L.: Directed hypergraphs: introduction and fundamental algorithms–a survey. Theoret. Comput. Sci. **658**, 293–306 (2017). https://doi.org/10.1016/j.tcs.2016.03.016
6. de Back, T.T., Tinga, A.M., Nguyen, P., Louwerse, M.M.: Benefits of immersive collaborative learning in CAVE-based virtual reality. Int. J. Educ. Technol. High. Educ. **17**(1), 1–18 (2020). https://doi.org/10.1186/s41239-020-00228-9

7. Back, T.T.D., Tinga, A.M., Louwerse, M.M.: Learning in immersed collaborative virtual environments: design and implementation. Interactive Learning Environments , 1–19 (2021). https://doi.org/10.1080/10494820.2021.2006238
8. Baker, S.C., Wentz, R.K., Woods, M.M.: Using virtual worlds in education: second life® as an educational tool. Teach. Psychol. **36**(1), 59–64 (2009). https://doi.org/10.1080/00986280802529079
9. Barwise, J., Perry, J.: Situations and Attitudes. MIT Press, Cambridge (1983). https://doi.org/10.2307/2219775
10. Barzilai, S., Zohar, A.: Epistemic thinking in action: evaluating and integrating online sources. Cogn. Instr. **30**(1), 39–85 (2012). https://doi.org/10.1080/07370008.2011.636495
11. Bildhauer, D.: Verteilte hierarchische Hyper-TGraphen: Definition und Implementation eines ausdrucksstarken Graphenkonzepts. Logos-Verlag (2012)
12. Bradley, P.: The history of simulation in medical education and possible future directions. Med. Educ. **40**(3), 254–262 (2006). https://doi.org/10.1111/j.1365-2929.2006.02394.x
13. Britt, M.A., Rouet, J.F., Braasch, J.L.: Documents as entities: Extending the situation model theory of comprehension. In: Britt, M.A., Goldmann, S.R., Rouet, J.F. (eds.) Reading-from words to multiple texts, pp. 161–179. Routledge (2012). https://doi.org/10.4324/9780203131268
14. Britt, M.A., Rouet, J.F., Durik, A.M.: Literacy Beyond Text Comprehension: A Theory of Purposeful Reading. Routledge, New York (2018)
15. Budanitsky, A., Hirst, G.: Evaluating WordNet-based measures of lexical semantic relatedness. Comput. Linguist. **32**(1), 13–47 (2006). https://doi.org/10.1162/coli.2006.32.1.13
16. Chernikova, O., Heitzmann, N., Stadler, M., Holzberger, D., Seidel, T., Fischer, F.: Simulation-based learning in higher education: a meta-analysis. Rev. Educ. Res. **90**(4), 499–541 (2020). https://doi.org/10.3102/0034654320933544
17. Clark, R.E.: Learning from serious games? Arguments, evidence, and research suggestions. Educ. Technol. **47**(3), 56–59 (2007). https://www.jstor.org/stable/44429512
18. Contreras, I., Loeb, S., Yu, C.: Hyperwalk formulae for even and odd Laplacians in finite CW-hypergraphs. arXiv preprint arXiv:1708.07995 (2017). https://doi.org/10.48550/arXiv.1708.07995
19. De Coninck, K., Valcke, M., Ophalvens, I., Vanderlinde, R.: Bridging the theory-practice gap in teacher education: The design and construction of simulation-based learning environments. Kohärenz in der Lehrerbildung: Theorien, Modelle und empirische Befunde, pp. 263–280 (2019). https://doi.org/10.1007/978-3-658-23940-4_17
20. Devlin, K.: Logic and Information. Cambridge University Press, Cambridge (1991)
21. Dieckmann, P., Friis, S.M., Lippert, A., Østergaard, D.: Goals, success factors, and barriers for simulation-based learning: a qualitative interview study in health care. Simul. Gaming **43**(5), 627–647 (2012). https://doi.org/10.1177/1046878112439649
22. Dodds, C., Heslop, P., Meredith, C.: Using simulation-based education to help social work students prepare for practice. Soc. Work. Educ. **37**(5), 597–602 (2018). https://doi.org/10.1080/02615479.2018.1433158
23. Drachsler, H., Goldhammer, F.: Learning analytics and eassessment—towards computational psychometrics by combining psychometrics with learning analytics. In: Burgos, D. (ed.) Radical Solutions and Learning Analytics. LNET, pp. 67–80. Springer, Singapore (2020). https://doi.org/10.1007/978-981-15-4526-9_5

24. Drey, T., et al.: Towards collaborative learning in virtual reality: a comparison of co-located symmetric and asymmetric pair-learning. In: Proceedings of the 2022 CHI Conference on Human Factors in Computing Systems. CHI 2022 (2022). https://doi.org/10.1145/3491102.3517641
25. Engel, J., Göhlich, M., Möller, E.: Interaction, subalternity, and marginalisation: an empirical study on glocalised realities in the classroom. Diaspora, Indig. Minor. Educ. 13(1), 40–53 (2019). https://doi.org/10.1080/15595692.2018.1490717
26. Fedor: gecko984/supervenn: add some tests for supervenn(), September 2020. https://doi.org/10.5281/zenodo.4016732
27. Frasson, C., Blanchard, E.G.: Simulation-based learning. In: Seel, N.M. (ed.) Encyclopedia of the Sciences of Learning, pp. 3076–3080. Springer, US, Boston, MA (2012). https://doi.org/10.1007/978-1-4419-1428-6_129
28. Gallo, G., Longo, G., Pallottino, S., Nguyen, S.: Directed hypergraphs and applications. Discret. Appl. Math. 42(2–3), 177–201 (1993). https://doi.org/10.1016/0166-218X(93)90045-P
29. Gibson, J.J.: The theory of affordances. Hilldale, USA 1(2), 67–82 (1977)
30. Gilbert, R., Low, P.: Discourse and power in education: analysing institutional processes in schools. Aust. Educ. Res. 21(3), 1–24 (1994). https://doi.org/10.1007/BF03219572
31. Goldin-Meadow, S., Brentari, D.: Gesture, sign, and language: the coming of age of sign language and gesture studies. Behav. Brain Sci. 40, e46 (2017). https://doi.org/10.1017/S0140525X15001247
32. Goldman, S.R., Braasch, J.L., Wiley, J., Graesser, A.C., Brodowinska, K.: Comprehending and learning from internet sources: processing patterns of better and poorer learners. Read. Res. Q. 47(4), 356–381 (2012). https://doi.org/10.1002/RRQ.027
33. Goldman, S.R., Brand-Gruwel, S.: Learning from multiple sources in a digital society. In: International Handbook of the Learning Sciences, pp. 86–95. Routledge (2018). https://doi.org/10.4324/9781315617572
34. Helsper, W.: Antinomien und paradoxien im professionellen handeln. Handbuch Professionsentwicklung 1, 50–62 (2016)
35. Hemati, W., Uslu, T., Mehler, A.: TextImager: a distributed UIMA-based system for NLP. In: Proceedings of the COLING 2016 System Demonstrations. Federated Conference on Computer Science and Information Systems (2016). https://aclanthology.org/C16-2013
36. Herbelot, A., Baroni, M.: High-risk learning: acquiring new word vectors from tiny data. In: Proceedings of the 2017 Conference on Empirical Methods in Natural Language Processing, pp. 304–309. Association for Computational Linguistics, Copenhagen, Denmark, September 2017. https://doi.org/10.18653/v1/D17-1030
37. Hirst, G., Mohammad, S.: Semantic distance measures with distributional profiles of coarse-grained concepts. In: Mehler, A., Kühnberger, K.U., Lobin, H., Lüngen, H., Storrer, A., Witt, A. (eds.) Modeling, Learning and Processing of Text Technological Data Structures. Studies in Computational Intelligence, Springer, Berlin/New York (2011). https://doi.org/10.1007/978-3-642-22613-7_4
38. Hollan, J., Hutchins, E., Kirsh, D.: Distributed cognition: toward a new foundation for human-computer interaction research. ACM Trans. Comput. Human Interact. 7(2), 174–196 (2000). https://doi.org/10.1145/353485.353487
39. Hollan, J.D., Hutchins, E.L., Weitzman, L.: STEAMER: an interactive inspectable simulation-based training system. AI Mag. 5(2), 15–15 (1984). https://doi.org/10.1609/aimag.v5i2.434

40. Honnibal, M., Montani, I., Van Landeghem, S., Boyd, A.: spacy: Industrial-strength natural language processing in python (2020). https://doi.org/10.5281/zenodo.1212303
41. Inoue, Y.: Virtual reality learning environments. In: Seel, N.M. (ed.) Encyclopedia of the Sciences of Learning, pp. 3407–3410. Springer, US, Boston, MA (2012). https://doi.org/10.1007/978-1-4419-1428-6_651
42. ISO: ISO 24617-7 - language resource management - semantic annotation framework - part 7: Spatial information. https://www.iso.org/standard/76442.html (2020)
43. Kerres, M., Mulders, M., Buchner, J.: Virtuelle realität: Immersion als erlebnisdimension beim lernen mit visuellen informationen. MedienPädagogik: Zeitschrift für Theorie und Praxis der Medienbildung 47, 312–330 (2022). https://doi.org/10.21240/mpaed/47/2022.04.15.X
44. Kintsch, W.: Comprehension. A Paradigm for Cognition. Cambridge University Press, Cambridge (1998)
45. Krishnaswamy, N., Pustejovsky, J.: Affordance embeddings for situated language understanding. Front. Artif. Intell. 5 (2022). https://doi.org/10.3389/frai.2022.774752
46. Lester, J.C., Stone, B.A., Stelling, G.D.: Lifelike pedagogical agents for mixed-initiative problem solving in constructivist learning environments. User Model. User-Adap. Inter. 9, 1–44 (1999). https://doi.org/10.1023/A:1008374607830
47. List, A., Alexander, P.A.: Toward an integrated framework of multiple text use. Educ. Psychol. 54(1), 20–39 (2019). https://doi.org/10.1080/00461520.2018.1505514
48. Lyotard, J.F.: The postmodern condition. Mod. Critic. Concepts. 4, 161–177 (1999)
49. Markic, S., Abels, S.: Heterogeneity and diversity: a growing challenge or enrichment for science education in German schools? Eurasia J. Math. Sci. Technol. Educ. 10(4), 271–283 (2014). https://doi.org/10.12973/eurasia.2014.1082a
50. Marr, D.: Vision: a computational investigation into the human representation and processing of visual information. Freeman, New York (1982). https://doi.org/10.7551/mitpress/9780262514620.001.0001
51. Mehler, A., Abrami, G., Spiekermann, C., Jostock, M.: VAnnotatoR: A framework for generating multimodal hypertexts. In: Proceedings of the 29th ACM Conference on Hypertext and Social Media, pp. 150–154. HT 2018, ACM, New York, NY, USA (2018). https://doi.org/10.1145/3209542.3209572
52. Mehler, A., Hemati, W., Welke, P., Konca, M., Uslu, T.: Multiple texts as a limiting factor in online learning: Quantifying (dis-)similarities of knowledge networks. Front. Educ. 5 (2020). https://doi.org/10.3389/feduc.2020.562670
53. Mehler, A., Lücking, A.: A structural model of semiotic alignment: The classification of multimodal ensembles as a novel machine learning task. In: Proceedings of IEEE Africon (2009). https://doi.org/10.1109/AFRCON.2009.5308098
54. Mehler, A., Lücking, A.: A graph model of alignment in multilog. In: Proceedings of IEEE Africon (2011)
55. Mehler, A., Lücking, A.: Pathways of alignment between gesture and speech: assessing information transmission in multimodal ensembles. In: Giorgolo, G., Alahverdzhieva, K. (eds.) Proceedings of the International Workshop on Formal and Computational Approaches to Multimodal Communication under the auspices of ESSLLI 2012 (2012)
56. Mehler, A., Lücking, A., Menke, P.: Assessing cognitive alignment in different types of dialog by means of a network model. Neural Netw. 32, 159–164 (2012). https://doi.org/10.1016/j.neunet.2012.02.013

57. Mehler, A., Lücking, A., Weiß, P.: A network model of interpersonal alignment. Entropy **12**(6), 1440–1483 (2010). https://doi.org/10.3390/e12061440
58. Mehlmann, G., Häring, M., Janowski, K., Baur, T., Gebhard, P., André, E.: Exploring a model of gaze for grounding in multimodal HRI. In: Proceedings of the 16th International Conference on Multimodal Interaction, pp. 247–254. ICMI 2014 (2014). https://doi.org/10.1145/2663204.2663275
59. Molerov, D., Zlatkin-Troitschanskaia, O., Nagel, M.T., Brückner, S., Schmidt, S., Shavelson, R.J.: Assessing university students' critical online reasoning ability: a conceptual and assessment framework with preliminary evidence. In: Frontiers in Education, p. 258. Frontiers (2020). https://doi.org/10.3389/feduc.2020.577843
60. Nagel, M.T., Schäfer, S., et al.: How do university students' web search behavior, website characteristics, and the interaction of both influence students' critical online reasoning? In: Frontiers in Education, vol. 5, p. 565062. Frontiers Media, SA (2020). https://doi.org/10.25358/openscience-5542
61. Nur Affendy, N.M., Ajune Wanis, I.: A review on collaborative learning environment across virtual and augmented reality technology. IOP Conf. Ser. Mater. Sci. Eng. **551**(1), 012050 (2019). https://doi.org/10.1088/1757-899X/551/1/012050
62. Oertel, C., Jonell, P., Kontogiorgos, D., Mora, K.F., Odobez, J.M., Gustafson, J.: Towards an engagement-aware attentive artificial listener for multi-party interactions. Front. Robot. AI 8 (2021). https://doi.org/10.3389/frobt.2021.555913
63. Park, S.-B., Jung, J.J., You, E.S.: Storytelling of collaborative learning system on augmented reality. In: Camacho, D., Kim, S.-W., Trawiński, B. (eds.) New Trends in Computational Collective Intelligence. SCI, vol. 572, pp. 139–147. Springer, Cham (2015). https://doi.org/10.1007/978-3-319-10774-5_13
64. Perfetti, C.A., Rouet, J.F., Britt, M.A.: Toward a theory of documents representation. In: van Oostendorp, H., Goldman, S.R. (eds.) The construction of mental representations during reading, pp. 99–122. Erlbaum, Mahwah, NJ (1999). https://www.taylorfrancis.com/chapters/mono/10.4324/9781410603050-9/toward-theory-documents-representation-herre-van-oostendorp-susan-goldman
65. Pickering, M.J., Garrod, S.: Toward a mechanistic psychology of dialogue. Behav. Brain Sci. **27**, 169–226 (2004). https://doi.org/10.1017/S0140525X04000056
66. Prasolova-Førland, E., McCallum, S., Estrada, J.G.: Collaborative learning in VR for cross-disciplinary distributed student teams. In: 2021 IEEE Conference on Virtual Reality and 3D User Interfaces Abstracts and Workshops (VRW), pp. 320–325 (2021). https://doi.org/10.1109/VRW52623.2021.00064
67. Pustejovsky, J.: Dynamic event structure and habitat theory. In: Proceedings of the 6th International Conference on Generative Approaches to the Lexicon (GL2013), pp. 1–10 (2013). https://aclanthology.org/W13-5401
68. Pustejovsky, J.: ISO-Space: Annotating static and dynamic spatial information. In: Handbook of Linguistic Annotation, pp. 989–1024 (2017). https://doi.org/10.1007/978-94-024-0881-2_37
69. Pustejovsky, J., Lee, K., Bunt, H., Romary, L.: ISO-TimeML: an international standard for semantic annotation. In: LREC 2010, pp. 394–397 (2010). https://aclanthology.org/L10-1027/
70. Radford, A., Kim, J.W., Xu, T., Brockman, G., McLeavey, C., Sutskever, I.: Robust speech recognition via large-scale weak supervision. arXiv preprint arXiv:2212.04356 (2022). https://doi.org/10.48550/arXiv.2212.04356
71. Randell, D.A., Cui, Z., Cohn, A.G.: A spatial logic based on regions and connection. KR. **92**, 165–176 (1992). https://doi.org/10.5555/3087223.3087240

72. Rieger, B.B.: Semiotic cognitive information processing: Learning to understand discourse. a systemic model of meaning constitution. In: Kühn, R., Menzel, R., Menzel, W., Ratsch, U., Richter, M.M., Stamatescu, I.O. (eds.) Adaptivity and Learning. An Interdisciplinary Debate, pp. 347–403. Springer, Berlin (2003). https://doi.org/10.1007/978-3-662-05594-6_24

73. Rouet, J.F., Britt, M.A., Potocki, A.: Multiple-text comprehension. In: Dunlosky, J., Rawson, K.A. (eds.) The Cambridge Handbook of Cognition and Education, pp. 356–380. Cambridge University Press, Cambridge (2019). https://doi.org/10.1017/9781108235631.015

74. Saedi, C., Branco, A., Rodrigues, J., Silva, J.: Wordnet embeddings. In: Proceedings of the third workshop on representation learning for NLP, pp. 122–131 (2018). https://doi.org/10.18653/v1/W18-3016

75. Schmid, H.J.: A blueprint of the entrenchment-and-conventionalization model. Yearbook German Cogn. Linguist. Assoc. **3**(1), 3–26 (2015). https://doi.org/10.1007/978-3-642-22613-7_4

76. Schmidt, S., et al.: Undergraduate students' critical online reasoning–process mining analysis. Front. Psychol. **11**, 576273 (2020). https://doi.org/10.3389/fpsyg.2020.576273

77. Scioni, E., Hübel, N., et al.: Hierarchical hypergraph for knowledge-centric robot systems: a composable structural meta model and its domain specific language NPC4. JOSER: J. Softw. Eng. Robot. **7**(11), 55–74 (2016). https://hdl.handle.net/10446/87779

78. Sedlák, M., Šašinka, Č., Stachoň, Z., Chmelík, J., Doležal, M.: Collaborative and individual learning of geography in immersive virtual reality: an effectiveness study. PLOS ONE. **17**(10), 1–18 (2022). https://doi.org/10.1371/journal.pone.0276267

79. Spiekermann, C., Abrami, G., Mehler, A.: VAnnotatoR: a gesture-driven annotation framework for linguistic and multimodal annotation. In: Pustejovsky, J., van der Sluis, I. (eds.) Proceedings of the Eleventh International Conference on Language Resources and Evaluation (LREC 2018). AREA, European Language Resources Association (ELRA), Paris, France (2018)

80. Spring, J.: Economization of Education: Human Capital, Global Corporations, Skills-based Schooling. Routledge (2015)

81. Stavroulia, K.-E., Lanitis, A.: On the potential of using virtual reality for teacher education. In: Zaphiris, P., Ioannou, A. (eds.) LCT 2017. LNCS, vol. 10295, pp. 173–186. Springer, Cham (2017). https://doi.org/10.1007/978-3-319-58509-3_15

82. Streeck, J.: Gesture as communication I: its coordination with gaze and speech. Commun. Monogr. **60**(4), 275–299 (1993). https://doi.org/10.1080/03637759309376314

83. Tataru, M., Berzescu, S., Vert, S., Mihaescu, V., Stamatoiu, R., Vasiu, R.: Designing applications for collaborative learning in virtual reality. In: 2022 International Symposium on Electronics and Telecommunications (ISETC), pp. 1–4 (2022). https://doi.org/10.1109/ISETC56213.2022.10010175

84. Wineburg, S., Breakstone, J., McGrew, S., Smith, M.D., Ortega, T.: Lateral reading on the open internet: a district-wide field study in high school government classes. J. Educ. Psychol. 893–909 (2022). https://doi.org/10.1037/edu0000740

85. Wineburg, S., McGrew, S., Breakstone, J., Ortega, T.: Evaluating information: the cornerstone of civic online reasoning (2016). http://purl.stanford.edu/fv751yt5934

86. Xu, P., et al.: Optimizing deeper transformers on small datasets. In: Proceedings of the 59th Annual Meeting of the Association for Computational Linguistics and the 11th International, Joint Conference on NLP, pp. 2089–2102 (2021). https://doi.org/10.18653/v1/2021.acl-long.163

87. Ziv, A., Small, S.D., Wolpe, P.R.: Patient safety and simulation-based medical education. Med. Teach. **22**(5), 489–495 (2000). https://doi.org/10.1080/01421590050110777
88. Zlatkin-Troitschanskaia, O., et al.: Performance assessment and digital training framework for young professionals' generic and domain-specific online reasoning in law, medicine and teacher practice. J. Supranatl. Polic. Educ. **13**, 9–36 (2021). https://doi.org/10.15366/jospoe2021.13.001
89. Zlatkin-Troitschanskaia, O., Beck, K., Fischer, J., Braunheim, D., Schmidt, S., Shavelson, R.J.: The role of students' beliefs when critically reasoning from multiple contradictory sources of information in performance assessments. Front. Psychol. **11**, 2192 (2020). https://doi.org/10.3389/fpsyg.2020.02192

TWINMED T-SHIRT, a Smart Wearable System for ECG and EMG Monitoring for Rehabilitation with Exoskeletons

Paolo Perego[1]([⊠]) [iD], Roberto Sironi[1], Emanuele Gruppioni[2] [iD],
and Giuseppe Andreoni[1] [iD]

[1] Design Department, Politecnico Di Milano, Via Candiani 72, 20158 Milan, (MI), Italy
paolo.perego@polimi.it
[2] Centro Protesi Inail, Via Rabuina, 14, 40054 Vigorso, (BO), Italy

Abstract. Wearable devices have become increasingly popular in recent years and have been utilized in a range of different fields, including healthcare, fitness, and entertainment. In particular, the development of smart textiles has been a major breakthrough in the wearable technology industry. This paper discusses the design and development of a wearable system for muscular and cardio-respiratory evaluation for rehabilitation with exoskeleton.

The paper is focus on the Twinmed system which consists in an exoskeleton and a smart t-shirt that records cardiac and muscle signals through silver-based 3D textile electrodes. The t-shirt has been designed tailored onto the patient's measurements for optimal sensor placement, and each sensor is connected to a device that can monitor the two main signals: muscular and cardiac.

The system was developed with a focus on evaluating the progress of rehabilitation and proper use of crutches during exoskeleton walking. All the design features have been selected through collaboration and interaction with project stockholders: patients, therapists, and engineers. The system has been pretested in laboratory both without and with the exoskeleton and have been shown to be effective for monitoring EMG signals and provide physicians with a clearer view of the cardiovascular exertion required, while allowing patients to have quantitative feedback on their health status.

Keywords: Rehabilitation · Wearable device · Exoskeleton

1 The Twinmed System

1.1 The System

Wearable devices for rehabilitation are quickly becoming an integral part of modern health care. These devices can provide users with accurate data and feedback on their physical condition and progress, allowing medical professionals to better track and monitor their patient's progress. Wearable devices can be used to track movement, posture, and range of motion, as well as other important health metrics [1]2.

V. G. Duffy (Ed.): HCII 2023, LNCS 14028, pp. 566–577, 2023.
https://doi.org/10.1007/978-3-031-35741-1_40

Physical rehabilitation can include helping with physical therapy, as well as helping patients recover from injuries or surgery. Additionally, wearable devices can help to provide patients with more motivation to take part in their rehabilitation, as they can see their progress and results in real time [3, 4].

Wearable devices are also becoming more personalized, with some devices being specifically designed for certain conditions [5]. For example, devices designed for physical rehabilitation can measure more specific metrics related to a patient's specific condition, allowing medical professionals to track progress more accurately.

In this paper authors report the design and test process for a new wearable system based on a smart t-shirt. The system has been designed specifically for supporting and evaluating the patient during the rehabilitation process with an exoskeleton.

This research is part of a project funded by INAIL (National institute for insurance against industrial injuries) which starts from a previous project who seen the development of a new modular exoskeleton by Rehab Technologies Lab IIT-INAIL (Genova, Italy). The project TWIN [6] consist in a novel modular lower limb exoskeleton for personal use of spinal-cord injury (SCI) subjects. The exoskeleton was designed based on features requested by users during participatory investigation which were attended by patients, engineers, designers and therapists. The TWIN exoskeleton was therefore designed to have the following characteristics (lightweight and portability, quick and autonomous wearing and setup, cost effectiveness, long battery life, comfort and safety, and especially stability during standing and walking). Figure 1 shows the TWIN exoskeleton in action.

Fig. 1: The exoskeleton Twin without the smart t-shirt

In the last years, the use of robots and exoskeletons for rehabilitation is becoming more common, but very often only the orthopedic and neurological aspects are considered, leaving out the whole cardiovascular aspect instead.

In this kind of rehabilitation, it is important to consider the potential risks to the cardiovascular system. When individuals use exoskeletons, they are often engaging in physical activity that they might not be able to perform unassisted; this can lead to an increase in heart rate, blood pressure, and cardiac output, which can put additional stress on the cardiovascular system, which in most cases comes from periods of inactivity due to post-surgery or post-disease course. Mulroy et al. [7] that patients with spinal cord injuries who used exoskeletons for walking experienced an increase in heart rate and blood pressure. The study also found that the patients had a higher cardiac output during exoskeleton-assisted walking compared to walking without the exoskeleton. These findings suggest that the use of exoskeletons for rehabilitation can put additional stress on the cardiovascular system; the authors concluded that the use of robots for rehabilitation should be carefully monitored to avoid any adverse effects on the cardiovascular system.

It is important to note that while the use of robots and exoskeletons for rehabilitation can be beneficial for patients, it can also pose risks to their cardiovascular health. Patients with pre-existing cardiovascular conditions, such as hypertension or heart disease, may be at higher risk for adverse effects. Therefore, it is important to carefully evaluate patients before using these devices and to monitor their cardiovascular health throughout the rehabilitation process. Medical professionals should also be aware of the potential risks and take appropriate precautions to ensure patient safety.

It has also been pointed out that in many cases, during the use of rehabilitation robots or exoskeletons on patients with spinal injuries there is an increase in extrasystoles that go to further highlight the danger of using these systems if not properly supervised.

2 Design the T-shirt

As described in the previous section, cardio-respiratory monitoring during rehabilitation exercise with robots and exoskeletons is of paramount importance to prevent risky events for patients. On the other hand, another critically important aspect in rehabilitation is clinical adherence to therapy, that is, in case of rehabilitation, how committed the patient is to continue with the exercises assigned to him or her by the therapist over time. The issue that most often plagues those who do home rehabilitation, or tele-rehabilitation, is dropout: on the one hand because progress is not always immediately visible, and on the other hand because the exercises that are usually offered are repetitive and boring.

The wearable system described in this paper has the main goal of heuristic patient monitoring. To optimize the type of measurements and the number of signals acquired, the system was designed by considering the users from the first stages.

By user we mean not only the end users, i.e., patients, but all stakeholders who are part of the group of people who design, configure, install, and use the system.

To do this, the so-called double diamond methodology, or rather, in this case, triple diamond [8] was tapped, which is especially applicable to hardware and software design context.

The Triple Diamond methodology is a design thinking approach that builds on the Double Diamond methodology. The key difference between the Triple and Double Diamond models is that the Triple Diamond places a greater emphasis on implementation and delivery, whereas the Double Diamond focuses more heavily on ideation and problem-solving. The Double Diamond model consists of two main stages: discover and define, with a focus on exploring the problem and generating ideas. The Triple Diamond model adds a third stage, deliver, which emphasizes the importance of implementing and delivering a solution that meets the needs of the users and the business.

The Triple Diamond model consists of three main stages: discovery, define, and deliver. Each of these stages is further broken down into specific steps [9].

The first stage, discovery, is about understanding the problem and the context in which it exists. This stage involves research, observation, and empathy to gain insights into the problem and the people affected by it. The goal is to identify the real problem to be solved and the opportunities for innovation. As described above, in this stage patients and therapist who use exoskeleton were observed in order to extract information and main problems during all the phase of the rehabilitation: preparation, execution and conclusion.

The second stage, define, is about synthesizing the information gathered in the discovery stage to define the problem statement and create a clear design brief. This stage involves analyzing the data collected in the discovery stage and identifying patterns and themes. The goal is to create a clear and actionable problem statement that will guide the ideation and prototyping phases. In order to better understand user's needs, in this second stage we involved all the stakeholder directly in the process by means of focus groups. The focus group was held at a clinical rehabilitation institute and involved physical therapists, physicians, engineers, and patients, for a total of 8 people. During the focus group, physicians stressed the importance of having available, in addition to the electrocardiographic signal, a respiratory signal that can immediately highlight possible fatigue problems.

They also emphasized the need to acquire muscle signals (through surface electromyography) for the upper body only, to highlight how well the patient is walking correctly with the exoskeleton or not, a kind of biofeedback. This last part was the most discussed during the focus group because it needed a trade-off between engineers and clinicians; while from the clinician point of view a lot of EMG signals is necessary to have an optimal analysis of all body movement, there is also a trade-off with the need to make the system portable, small, and wearable. Moreover, another technical problem is related to the type of data transmission to integrate; in fact, if the most widely used technology in wearables is Bluetooth LE, this allows up to a maximum of 7 devices connected simultaneously, thus limiting the number of wearable devices that can be used, and consequently the signals acquired.

The third stage, deliver, is about creating and implementing a solution based on the problem statement and design brief. This stage involves ideation, prototyping, testing, and iteration to create a viable solution. The goal is to create a solution that meets the needs of the users and the business requirements. This last stage, combined with the outcomes from the focus group, emphasized the importance of having the wearable system developed on two fronts: a design related to comfort while using the exoskeleton, and a design related to monitoring.

2.1 Comfort Design

Figure 2 shows the first analysis outcome on the patient using the lower limb exoskeleton. The figure shows a first approach to the design of the wearable system where the positioning for EMG signal acquisition, positioning for ECG and breathing signal acquisition, pressure sensors for measuring discomfort at the thoracic level, and soft parts to decrease discomfort in some areas where the exoskeleton might be uncomfortable are visible.

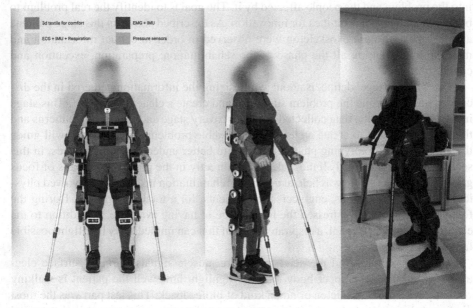

Fig. 2. First design for the wearable design. On the left the signal parts, on the right the comfort part

As visible in the figure, the red rectangle indicates the possible positions underline during the ghosting phase in which the contact of the exoskeleton can be in contact with the patient's body and create discomfort or injuries. After a more thorough analysis with who designed the exoskeleton, thanks in part to modifications built into the braces that hold exoskeleton in place, the points where contact discomfort is possible have decreased. However, the parts below the knee and on the back remaining of possible interference.

Different solutions can be used to minimize discomfort due to the contact between exoskeleton and skin. The pressure generated by this contact may change depending on the size of the patient who wear the exoskeleton. However, having the goal of designing a sensorised t-shirt/suit, the most suitable choice turns out to be the implementation of "special" fabric in the garment that can absorb pressure and work as a protection.

A 3D textile is a fabric that has a three-dimensional structure, usually created by using fibers or yarns of different lengths or by using a variety of weaving or knitting techniques. In garment design, 3D textiles can be used to provide additional protection or cushioning in areas that are prone to impact or wear. They can also be used to provide structural support or to create unique aesthetic effects.

Figure 3 shows and example of 3d textile; the thickness of the fabric is generated by a weave made from fabric with a high polyamide component. Although the fabric is composed mainly of plastic material, a surface finish can be given to make it comfortable. In addition, the texturing of the fabric allows air circulation, so as to avoid heavy sweating that occurs when the worn fabric is synthetic.

Fig. 3. Example of 3d textile applied as comfortable cushion for exoskeleton joint

2.2 Smart T-shirt Design

The second design phase for the smart garment consist in the development of a solution for data acquisition. During the focus group mentioned earlier, a qualitative analysis was carried out regarding what characteristics the garment should have and what signals to acquire. Starting from a design brief shown to the participants in which many more signals than were needed were included (see Fig. 2), the focus group participants opened a discussion by comparing technical and medical needs in order to define a solution that was feasible and at the same time able to monitor the patient optimally. No longer a technology driven design, but a user's-driven design, in which users lead development, focusing resources on what is really needed for the project.

This open discussion among all stakeholders in the project also led to drastic decisions such as removing the sensors from the lower limb, as they were deemed unnecessary for performance monitoring since they are linked to residual or passive activity generated by limb movements via the exoskeleton.

During the focus group, all participants were able to actively be part of the discussion on all the features of the system, including the more technical ones, thanks to the presence of engineers, and designers trained on technology. This made it possible to draft from the first iteration the characteristics that the system should have, including the technological point of view and its feasibility.

The main features are listed below, while Fig. 4 shows the final structure of the wearable system:

1. ECG channel on the 10th rib;
2. Thoracic breath sensor (if possible, also diaphragmatic);
3. Six channel EMG:
   a. Right and left triceps
   b. Right and left deltoid
   c. Right and left middle (or upper) trapezius
4. ECG sample frequency 1 kHz;
5. EMG sample frequency 1 kHz;
6. At least 4 h battery life;
7. Bluetooth connection;
8. Small size;
9. Light weight;
10. Ease of connection with the garment;
11. LED for status.

The wearable system shown in Fig. 4 consists of three devices each capable of measuring two EMG signals, and a fourth device for measuring the ECG signal and respiration. The ECG device also records, through an inertial motion unit, the patient's trunk position. The devices are connected to the T-shirt by means of four snaps buttons each. The snap buttons were preferred over a connection with spring and magnetic probes in order to be able to optimize the measurement of signals, especially EMG signals which are much more sensitive to noise than ECG ones.

Each device has a button for control and an LED that identifies status through color change and flashing. The devices can be connected to a hub through the Bluetooth connection. However, since the signals are acquired with a fairly high sampling rate, the Bluetooth connection is over-used and requires high performance hub with specific characteristics that can support this kind of transmission (e.g.. Bluetooth 5.2 with at least 247 byte MTU, 2M Physical Layer and < 15 ms priority).

The sensorized T-shirt is made of highly elastic fabric, in order to maintain a strong adhesion to the skin and optimize the acquired signals, minimizing disturbances due to movement and rubbing of the electrodes with the skin. The electrodes are made of 3D conductive fabric based on silver. It was chosen to use a 3D conductive fabric instead of a more common plain conductive fabric for two main reasons:

• being three-dimensional and having the component that generates the three-dimensionality also conductive, the characteristics of an electrode made with this fabric approach those of a classic Ag-AgCl electrode (the impedance is much lower than the plain fabric).

- the three-dimensionality creates a sponge effect, which retains water/sweat or electrode gel; this further improves the conductivity of the electrodes and therefore the quality of the signal.

The size of the electrodes is optimized based on the measurement to be taken. The two ECG electrodes (the right leg drive is removed) have a size of 20 × 30 mm. The electrode then narrows to a strip of thickness 10 mm, which is used to transmit the ECG signal from the actual electrode to the automatic button used for connection with the electronic device. The breath sensor is instead composed by a special fiber of TPU charged with graphene ponder. The graphene add conductivity to the fiber that, when subject to stretching or squashing, change. This change in conductivity can be used to monitor fiber elongation; if this fiber is applied to a shirt in the thoracic or diaphragmatic region, the enlargement of the rib cage or diaphragmatic breathing cause a lengthening of the fiber thus making it possible to monitor respiration.

Unlike the ECG signal, the position, shape, and dimension of EMG electrodes are important factors which can affect the signal quality and accuracy of the measurement [10].

The position of EMG electrodes is crucial for obtaining accurate and meaningful data. The electrodes must be placed over the muscle of interest, as close as possible to the motor endplate zone, where the muscle fibers are innervated by the motor neuron. Placement of the electrodes in the optimal position ensures that the recorded signal is representative of the activity of the muscle fibers. The muscle length and orientation of the fibers can also affect the recorded signal. Therefore, it is important to standardize the placement of the electrodes for each muscle group.

The electrode should be large enough to capture the electrical activity of the muscle, but not so large that it picks up signals from neighboring muscles. An electrode that is too small may not pick up enough signal, while an electrode that is too large may pick up signals from other muscles or from the skin. The shape of the electrode can also affect the signal quality, with rounded electrodes being preferred over square or rectangular ones.

Another choice to make when dealing with EMG is whether to use a unipolar or bipolar system. Bipolar EMG consist of three electrodes: two are placed on the skin over the muscle of interest. The third electrode is placed at fixed distance apart from the other two and used as reference.

Unipolar EMG electrodes consist of only two electrodes, one for the measurement and one for the reference. The recording electrodes is placed over the muscle of interest, while the reference electrode is placed on a nearby bone or tendon. This kind of configuration allows for using less electrodes, which is essential when designing a smart garment because it allows to minimize the number of electrodes and, in the case of this specific project, the number of connections between device and garments. Moreover, this type of EMG recording provides more spatial resolution than bipolar ones.

The electrodes on the t-shirt follow the unipolar configuration; the shape, size and position are based on Seniam [11] guidelines.

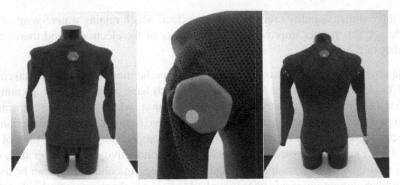

Fig. 4. The sensorised t-shirt. The devices are connected on the back for trapezius EMG, on the arm for deltoids and triceps, and on the front for ECG and respiration measurement.

3 System Test

To verify the correct functioning of the system, three different types of tests were implemented.

The first test was carried out to verify the feasibility of measuring EMG through textile electrodes in a unipolar configuration, structured according to the Seniam guidelines [11]. To simplify the test operations, instead of monitoring the muscles listed above, it was preferred to measure the EMG on the brachioradialis and ulnar flexor muscles. To do this, a sleeve was made inside which the textile electrodes were positioned, connected to a medical snap button with the possibility of connecting a commercial EMG device. The test protocol involved two consecutive measurements, the first with the sensorised sleeve, and the second with the classic Ag-AgCl electrodes positioned like those present in the sleeve. The subject was asked to isometrically flex and extend the wrist in order to collect the activation of the two muscles. The two signals were subsequently compared to check if the textile electrodes were able to record muscle activation, and fatigue.

The second test was carried out with the aim to verify the correct position of the electrode on the t-shirt. Figure 5 show this test and the EMG signal acquired during gait with crutches. The protocol foresaw the subject wore the sensorized shirt connected to a commercial EMG (FREEMG Wireless surface EMG by BTS Bioengineering) while walking with crutches. The healthy subject simulated a correct walk with crutches and a walk instead with incorrect support of the crutches. The two types of walking activate the muscles in different ways, giving the possibility to have feedback on the correct use of the exoskeleton.

The third test was performed with the exoskeleton. The objective of this latest test was to verify the interferences between the exoskeleton and the smart T-shirt, in order to possibly optimize the position of the electrodes on the shirt. The protocol envisaged the use of EMG devices developed ad-hoc for the project. The test was carried out in two different phases: a first phase with isometric contractions to verify the correct functioning of the system; a second phase in which all signals were acquired during the use of the exoskeletal. All the data have been than processed by means of specific algorithm in order to verify the quality of the signals.

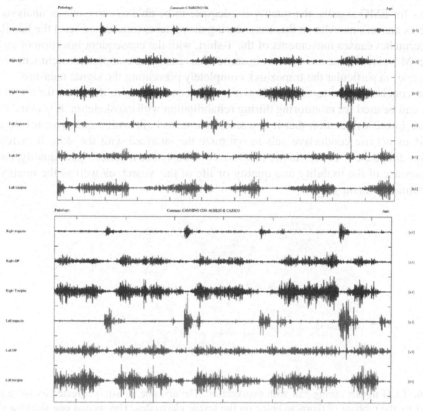

Fig. 5. EMG acquired with the sensorised T-shirt. The first chart shows the activation of the six muscles during the correct use of crouches; the second chart show the activation of the same muscle with wrong support of the crutches.

4 Conclusion

The data recorded during the first two test sessions made it possible to optimize the size and especially the production process of sensors in order to obtain clean signals comparable with the ones recorded through classic modes. The third test has allowed to check if the sensorized T-shirt developed was able to detect the signals during the use of the exoskeleton. The acquired data show an excellent signal quality when the subject uses the exoskeleton but in a static position. During the gait, on the other hand, the exoskeleton interferes with the correct functioning of the sensorised T-shirt. In particular, the signal that is more affected by noise is the cardio-respiratory one. The exoskeleton is in fact anchored to the body by means of a thoracic brace that has the edges exactly near the textile electrodes and the strain gauge. This involves many disorders on the two signals that prevent the correct measure of cardio-respiratory parameters. The modification of the brace or the repositioning of the electrodes in such a way that they are completely covered by the brace, significantly improves the quality of the signal (Fig. 6).

As for EMG signals, the quality is adequate to be able to carry out an analysis on muscles activations. Also in this case, during movements (raised and seat) the handling with crutches causes movements of the T-shirt, with the consequent insertion of signal noise. Moreover, these movements in some cases cause the complete detachment of the electrode (in particular the trapezius), completely preventing the signal measure.

In conclusion, the tests have shown how a sensorised shirt, designed for a specific goal, can be used for monitoring during rehabilitation with exoskeleton. It is mandatory to take into consideration that it is a smart garment, built with conductive textile and that does not use conductive gels to optimize the interface with the skin. It therefore follows that the use of the classic measures obviously has a better signal quality, but at the expense of the usability and quality of life of the wearer, as well as the quality of rehabilitation therapy.

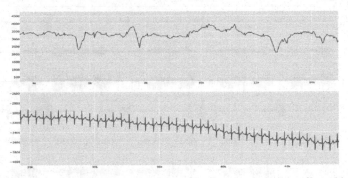

Fig. 6. ECG signals during gait with exoskeleton. The first one is visibly affected by noise generated by the rubbing of thoracic brace on the textile electrodes. The second one shows a clear ECG when electrodes are completely covered by the brace.

References

1. Rodgers, M.M., Alon, G., Pai, V.M., Conroy, R.S.: Wearable technologies for active living and rehabilitation: current research challenges and future opportunities. J. Rehabil. Assist. Technol. Eng. **6**, 2055668319839607 (2019)
2. Bonato, P.: Advances in wearable technology for rehabilitation. In: Advanced Technologies in Rehabilitation, pp. 145–159. IOS Press (2009Kindly)
3. Maceira-Elvira, P., Popa, T., Schmid, A.C., Hummel, F.C.: Wearable technology in stroke rehabilitation: towards improved diagnosis and treatment of upper-limb motor impairment. J. Neuroeng. Rehabil. **16**(1), 1–18 (2019)
4. Bowman, T., et al.: Wearable devices for biofeedback rehabilitation: a systematic review and meta-analysis to design application rules and estimate the effectiveness on balance and gait outcomes in neurological diseases. Sensors **21**(10), 3444 (2021)
5. Wang, Q., Markopoulos, P., Yu, B., Chen, W., Timmermans, A.: Interactive wearable systems for upper body rehabilitation: a systematic review. J. Neuroeng. Rehabil. **14**(1), 1–21 (2017)
6. Awolusi, I., Marks, E., Hallowell, M.: Wearable technology for personalized construction safety monitoring and trending: review of applicable devices. Autom. Constr. **85**, 96–106 (2018)

7. Laffranchi, M., et al.: User-centered design and development of the modular twin lower limb exoskeleton. Front. Neurorobot. **15** (2021)
8. Mulroy, S.J., Thompson, L., Kemp, B., Hatchett, P., Newsam, C.J., Lupold, D.G.: Cardiac monitoring during exoskeleton-assisted walking in patients with spinal cord injury: a case series. Arch. Phys. Med. Rehabil. **97**(8), S216–S223 (2016)
9. Chen, M.: The Zendesk Triple Diamond (2020). https://medium.com/zendesk-creative-blog/the-zendesk-triple-diamond-process-fd857a11c179
10. Design Council UK. The principles of the triple diamond (2018). https://www.designcouncil.org.uk/news-opinion/principles-triple-diamond
11. Campanini, I., Merlo, A., Degola, P., Merletti, R., Vezzosi, G., Farina, D.: Effect of electrode location on EMG signal envelope in leg muscles during gait. J. Electromyogr. Kinesiol. **17**(4), 515–526 (2007)
12. Hermens, H., Freriks, B.: The state of the art on sensors and sensor placement procedures for surface electromyography: a proposal for sensor placement procedures. Enschede, The Netherlands: Roessingh Research and Development (1997)

Evaluating Multimodal Behavior Schemas with VoxWorld

Christopher Tam(✉) , Richard Brutti , Kenneth Lai ,
and James Pustejovsky

Brandeis University, Waltham, MA, USA
{christophertam,brutti,klai12,jamesp}@brandeis.edu

Abstract. The ability to understand and model human-object inter-actions is becoming increasingly important in advancing the field of human-computer interaction (HCI). To maintain more effective dialogue, embodied agents must utilize situated reasoning - the ability to ground objects in a shared context and understand their roles in the conversation [35]. In this paper, we argue that developing a unified multimodal annotation schema for human actions, in addition to gesture and speech, is a crucial next step towards this goal. We develop a new approach for visualizing such schemas, such as Gesture AMR [5] and VoxML [33], by simulating their output with VoxWorld [21] in the context of a collaborative problem-solving task. We discuss the implications of this method, including proposing a novel testing paradigm using the generated simulation to validate these annotations for their accuracy and completeness.

Keywords: Multimodal dialogue · AMR · Gesture annotation ·
Non-verbal behavior · Meaning representation

1 Introduction

Collaborative problem-solving tasks, used in educational contexts to facilitate the development of critical thinking and teamwork skills, are a rich source of multimodal behavior. We believe that efforts toward developing a unified multimodal annotation schema for these and similar tasks will yield practical insights for modeling multi-party dialogue, and inform a greater range of expression for multimodal interactive virtual agents (IVAs).

In this paper, we first address the challenge of annotating multiple modalities in videos of two subjects engaged in task-based interactions. Then, to test and validate both the completeness and the expressiveness of the ensemble annotations, we use them to generate animated simulations of the interactions in the Unity-based VoxWorld platform [21].

This work was supported in part by NSF grant DRL 2019805, to Dr. Pustejovsky at Brandeis University. We would like to express our thanks to Nikhil Krishnaswamy for his comments on the multimodal framework motivating the development of the simulation platform, FibWorld. The views expressed herein are ours alone.

The VoxWorld platform enables the deployment of embodied agents with contextual awareness, allowing them to interact and communicate from their virtual environments through speech and gesture [35]. Our research proposes a new approach for validating multimodal annotation schemas, such as VoxML [34] and Gesture AMR [5], by simulating their output with VoxWorld.

Our approach focuses on the *Shared Weights Task* [3], a collaborative task that involves deducing the weights of physical blocks using a scale. We capture several videos of participants performing this task, and develop a simple multimodal annotation schema to encode the speech, gestures, and physical actions performed within them. We model the environment and equipment for the Shared Weights Task digitally in Unity3D using the VoxWorld platform, with IVAs (*Diana* and *Apollo*) standing in as proxies for the human participants. The video annotations are then imported into Unity as a series of timestamped events, which can be executed sequentially to generate a real-time simulation of the annotated video, with the IVAs generating the corresponding behaviors to complete the task. Because this method succeeds at replicating the speech, select non-verbal behaviors (gestures), and actions of the task videos, it provides an informative visualization of the range of behaviors captured by the annotation schema. We plan to apply this method to a variety of candidate annotation schemas involving additional nonverbal modalities (such as gaze, pose, and sentiment), and then collect crowdsourced judgments of the simulation results to achieve the most accurate representation of the ground truth. The resulting framework, we believe, will help evaluate annotation schemas for multimodal interactions, both for their accuracy and their completeness.

2   Related Work

As multimodal interactive systems continue to become more commonplace and more sophisticated, users expect that their interactions will resemble interactions with other humans. A major challenge of human-robot interaction (HRI) and HCI involves communicating intentions, goals, and attitudes through simultaneous modalities in addition to language, including gesture, gaze, facial expression, and situational awareness [6,9,20,26,39,42]. This in turn brings a need for capturing, representing, and annotating the data that encodes these various non-verbal modalities.

There are very few meaning representations that have been designed for or deployed in the context of true situated multi-party interaction that are both adequately expressive of the multimodal content and compact enough for corpus development. This is partially due to the fact that empirical evidence is often lacking for arriving at a data-based understanding of the nature of multimodal constructions in conversation [46]. Many existing approaches to annotating meaning representation treat verbal and nonverbal components as distinct and autonomous, while those that do address the interaction between them generally focus on form rather than meaning [17,20]. For example, the Behavior Markup Language (BML) [19] is an exchange language originally intended to describe an agent's communicative actions along a range of temporally marked behaviors, including gesture, pose, facial expressions, head movements, and gaze, among others. However, BML is not designed to represent the intents that give rise to such actions.

Embodied HCI systems must necessarily have an understanding of the objects in their environment and their associated affordances to achieve physical goals in their interactions. This requires the annotation of *actions* that result in the manipulation or transformation of objects in the environment. There has been significant interest in how encoding affordances might be used to improve the accuracy of human-object interaction (HOI) recognition and scene understanding models [12]. Modern annotation schemes for such affordances and actions range from general classification of human-object interactions in movie clips [10] to affordance annotation with the Gibsonian/telic (conventional) distinction [14]. An additional, critical layer to this task is visual semantic role labeling (VSRL) [11,45] - the identification of how entities in an image fulfill the thematic roles of the events they are involved in; work has been done to apply this to cooking clips [44] and movie scenes [38].

After developing a satisfactory annotation scheme, the process of annotating and reviewing the various tracks of the multimodal data can be challenging and time-consuming. It is worthwhile to investigate methods to efficiently inspect and validate them beyond the software initially used to create them. Visualizing symbolic multimodal data has different requirements from simulating numerical data, such as mapping points from motion capture or pose tracking. Though previous studies have attempted to translate these annotations into visual images, such as finite state machines [30], another interesting approach is to instead directly use them to drive the behavior of embodied conversational agents (ECAs) [17]. In addition to being used to annotate the general form of gestures, this *copy-synthesis* approach [27] was also used to interpret emotional annotations to inform facial expression and gesture activity. To our knowledge, however, there has been little research on using ECAs to model changes of environment state as a result of actions, as situated reasoning has only been a recent area of focus in the field.

We use the VoxWorld platform to experiment with this visualization problem: it is the joint product of the VoxML modeling language [34] and its real-time Unity interpreter VoxSim [24], resulting in an environment based on rigorously defined interaction semantics. This architecture easily lends itself to action annotation interpretation, as annotation descriptions converted to linguistic entities defined in VoxML have a explicit correspondence in the simulation. Within VoxWorld, the Diana agent has been developed as an interface to recognize user speech and gesture [22], distinguishing itself from other IVAs with its ability to reason and act on a variety of objects with a well-defined affordance structure. It is equipped with a rig that can perform basic operations on simulated objects, like pointing, grabbing, lifting, and moving, and has achieved success at collaborating with users on a paired block structure-building task [23]. We use this agent as a starting point to directly model human behavior.

3   Method

3.1   Source Data: The Shared Weights Task

Collaborative problem-solving tasks are specifically designed to promote student intercommunication and mutual learning, and their participants are often in constant interaction with the materials at hand. These tasks can thus be a prime candidate for dense multimodal annotation. However, we note that the collaborative aspect of these tasks is greatly diminished in the presence of what is known as *social loafing* [16], where a participant is inclined to make fewer contributions if they perceive that the other participants can complete the task on their own.

To ensure that the human interactions in our data are productive and meaningful, we require that the observed task promote equal interaction and communication. To meet these requirements, we introduce the *Shared Weights Task*, based off the classroom task described in [3]. This is a two-person problem, in which the objective is to determine the relative weights of six colored blocks using a provided scale. The block weights follow the Fibonacci sequence pattern, which the participants must deduce during the task. The participants are seated opposite each other at a table, with three blocks placed immediately in front of each of them, and the scale placed between the two sets of blocks. The participants are told the weight of one of the unit blocks (e.g., "The red block weighs one unit."), and are instructed to determine the relative weights of the rest of the blocks. The task is considered completed when each participant can relay the relative weights of their own blocks.

The Shared Weights Task imposes the additional constraint that each participant may only interact with the subset of blocks on their respective side of the table. This restriction is useful for several reasons. First, both participants must necessarily take a roughly equal number of actions, as it is impossible for either participant to complete the task on their own. Second, it introduces imperfect information. In our formulation, participants cannot directly compare blocks of different sets against each other by weighing them with both hands; they must communicate using language to coordinate use of the provided scale.

3.2   Data Collection

An initial set of data was collected at the Brandeis University Lab for Linguistics and Computation, with various lab members as participants. Video was captured with a Microsoft Azure Kinect mounted above and behind the left shoulder of one of the seated participants. Audio was captured with a Realtek conferencing microphone placed on the edge of the table. The video and audio were synchronized using the OBS Studio software.

The combined audio and video were imported into ELAN [4], and annotated by the authors. Each modality was annotated on a separate track for each participant. We refer to the collected array of tracks as an annotation *score*. An example of the ELAN annotation interface is shown in Fig. 1.

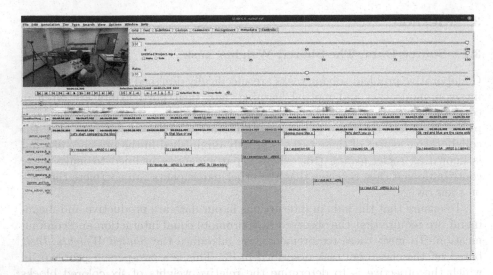

Fig. 1. ELAN annotation environment.

3.3 Annotation Schema

To capture both the physical and communicative acts in these videos, we develop the following annotation schema:

Speech. First, the speech is transcribed, speaker-diarized, and segmented into utterances; this was done manually for our initial data set. We add the utterance strings to the appropriate tracks in ELAN, one track for each speaker. In addition to recording the form of each utterance, we also annotate its meaning using Abstract Meaning Representation (AMR) [1,18]. AMR represents the predicate-argument structures of sentences in the form of graphs. Compared to other meaning representation systems such as Discourse Representation Theory [15] or Minimal Recursion Semantics [7], AMRs are designed for ease of annotation and parsing.

Specifically, we use Dialogue-AMR, an extension of AMR developed to represent meanings in task-based dialogues [2]. For example, an utterance "Is that blue or purple?", could be annotated as follows:

```
(q / question-SA
  :ARG0 (p1 / participant-1)
  :ARG1 (t / that
          :ARG1-of (a / amr-choice
                    :op1 (b / blue-01)
                    :op2 (p / purple-02)))
  :ARG2 (p2 / participant-2))
```

The above Dialogue-AMR is rooted by a speech act, here a question, and the ARG0 and ARG2 represent the speaker and addressee, respectively. The ARG1 is

Fig. 2. Deictic gesture towards a blue block. (Color figure online)

Fig. 3. Action of putting the blue block on the left side of the scale. (Color figure online)

the semantic content of the utterance, similar to how it would be represented in standard AMR.

Gesture. We also use AMR to annotate gestures in our data; in this case, we use Gesture AMR [5]. Similarly to Dialogue-AMR, Gesture AMR classifies content-bearing gestures into four kinds of "gesture acts": deictic, iconic, emblematic, and metaphoric; and marks the gesturer, addressee, and semantic content of the gesture. For example, the situation in Fig. 2, involving a deictic, or pointing, gesture towards a blue block, can be represented like so:

```
(d / deixis-GA
  :ARG0 (p1 / participant-1)
  :ARG1 (b / blue-block)
  :ARG2 (p2 / participant-2))
```

Action. In addition to speech and gesture, we also annotate the actions performed by the participants, again using an AMR-style template. We create a taxonomy of actions by adapting relevant predicates from PropBank [29], that can be interpreted in VoxML. For instance, an action of putting a blue block on the left side of a scale, as shown in Fig. 3, is assigned the following annotation:

```
(p / put-ACT
  :ARG0 (p1 / participant-1)
  :ARG1 (b / blue-block)
  :ARG2 (o / on
          :op1 (1 / left-scale)))
```

The argument structure of the action follows that of the corresponding Prop-Bank predicate, in this case, put-01.[1]

---

[1] We are currently developing a much richer specification for action annotation (Action AMR), for both collaborative tasks as well as procedural texts and narratives.

Alignment. Because agents can potentially use multiple modalities to communicate some piece of information, it is important to align the various modalities both temporally and semantically, so that we know (and can reconstruct) not only what is being communicated, but how it is done [25]. Temporal alignment is done within ELAN, as each annotation is stamped with its begin and end times. Semantic alignment, i.e., coreference relations between entities across tracks, is done using Uniform Meaning Representation (UMR) [41]. UMR is a meaning representation that adds document-level coreference annotation to AMR, along with aspect and scope relations, temporal and modal dependencies, and support for morphologically complex languages. This annotation is currently done outside of ELAN. As an example, the following annotation combines the previous three examples, and indicates that the object referred to as "that" in the speech, pointed to in the gesture, and moved in the action, are identical, as are the mentions of "participant-1" and "participant-2".

```
(s2q / question-SA              (g1 / gesture
  :ARG0 (s2p1 / participant-1)    :coref ((g1p1 :same-entity s2p1)
  :ARG1 (s2t / that                       (g1b :same-entity s2t)
    :ARG1-of (s2a / amr-choice            (g1p2 :same-entity s2p2)))
      :op1 (s2b / blue-01)
      :op2 (s2p / purple-02)))   (a1 / action
  :ARG2 (s2p2 / participant-2))    :coref ((a1p1 :same-entity g1p1)
                                           (a1b :same-entity g1b)))
(g1d / deixis-GA
  :ARG0 (g1p1 / participant-1)
  :ARG1 (g1b / blue-block)
  :ARG2 (g1p2 / participant-2))


(a1p / put-ACT
  :ARG0 (a1p1 / participant-1)
  :ARG1 (a1b / blue-block)
  :ARG2 (a1o / on
    :op1 (a1l / left-scale)))
```

3.4   Environment Modeling

To model the environment and participant actions in the Shared Weights Task, we use the VoxWorld platform to develop FibWorld, a virtual translation of the real-world task that embodied agents can fully interact with. The scene includes the original set of six colored blocks, arranged and assigned weights in the same way as in the physical setup. The scale is converted to a digital representation, with physics implemented so that when the combined weight of blocks on one side of the scale is heavier, a yellow indicator lights up on that side. This modified representation avoids the time-consuming "bouncing effect" of the physical scale when a weight is placed on either end.

To represent the participants, we modify the Diana paradigm from its user-centric model, introducing multiple IVAs into the simulation to function as proxies interacting with each other. To achieve this, we duplicate the original Diana avatar, as well as its underlying cognitive architecture and event management systems, to serve as the second proxy. To differentiate the two avatars, we additionally replace the model of the second IVA with a male avatar designed in Reallusion Character Creator 4 [37], which we name "Apollo". The underlying keys in VoxWorld's blackboard architecture are adjusted to allow for separate streams of event messages to be assigned to each individual agent.

3.5   Annotation Import and Execution

This annotation score is exported from ELAN in tab-separated value (TSV) format, then converted to JSON as a list of annotation objects. The participant subject of each act is either marked as such in the AMR annotation, or implicitly suggested from the annotation track it is associated with. We assign one of the participants to the Diana avatar, and one to the Apollo avatar. The JSON objects are sent to the corresponding IVA in the simulation, sorted by starting timestamp, and read into annotation event queues, with each queue corresponding to a specific modality (speech, gesture, action). As the simulation runs, the annotation event at the head of each queue is automatically interpreted and executed when the current elapsed time exceeds its starting timestamp.

Speech utterance strings are fed directly into Diana's (or Apollo's) text-to-speech module, requiring no further interpretation. Gestures do not result in manipulation of the environment, and thus are handled separately from actions. For deixis, we simply trigger a pointing interaction for the duration of the timestamp, and utilize Diana's interruption-handling ability to undo previous actions to stop the interaction at the end of the timestamp. Other gesture types (icon, emblem, metaphor), did not appear in the data and were therefore not annotated, though future work will investigate how these gestures will be represented in VoxWorld.

For events, we rely on the internal mechanisms of VoxWorld to handle the recognition of object affordances, the situational habitats they require, as well as event satisfaction conditions. The composition and execution of events in VoxWorld are determined by their underlying specification in VoxML. Before interpretation, action AMR annotations must first be converted to VoxWorld event strings, which are predicate-argument structures of the following form:

```
PREDICATE(ARG1,ARG2,...)
```

For example, the action of putting a red block on the right side of the scale is converted to:

```
put(RedBlock,on(RightScale))
```

The main predicate corresponds to a VoxML program key, and the arguments to that predicate are listed out in sequence. As the event string is interpreted, it is broken down into compositions of primitive events, defined by a subevent structure in the main predicate's VoxML entry. For instance, the VoxML entry for the program *put* is:

Fig. 4. Simulation snapshot of Apollo putting a red block on the right side of the scale. (Color figure online)

$$
(1) \quad
\begin{bmatrix}
\textbf{put} \\
\text{LEX} = \begin{bmatrix} \text{PRED} = \textbf{put} \\ \text{TYPE} = \textbf{transition\_event} \end{bmatrix} \\
\text{TYPE} = \begin{bmatrix} \text{HEAD} = \textbf{transition} \\ \text{ARGS} = \begin{bmatrix} A_1 = \textbf{x:agent} \\ A_2 = \textbf{y:physobj} \\ A_3 = \textbf{z:location} \end{bmatrix} \\ \text{BODY} = \begin{bmatrix} E_1 = grasp(x,y) \\ E_2 = [while((\neg at(y,z) \wedge hold(x,y)), move(x,y)] \\ E_3 = [at(y,z) \rightarrow ungrasp(x,y)] \end{bmatrix} \end{bmatrix}
\end{bmatrix}
$$

Here, the agent must first *grasp* the block, *move* it to the given location until it is at the given location, and finally *ungrasp* the block. Thus when we execute a given action annotation, it is interpreted in VoxML as a series of subevents that drive behavior in the Unity simulation. Figure 4 shows the result of Apollo putting the red block on the right side of the scale.

4   Discussion and Future Work

The resulting simulation created upon execution of an annotation score is a faithful replay of the multimodal behavior in the source video, as defined by the combination of our chosen annotation schema and the behavioral generation capabilities of the VoxWorld platform. As a consequence of precisely modeling the locational transformations of objects with action annotations, the simulation provides useful state tracking for the task itself - the positions of the blocks and the current value of the scale reading are accurate for any given point in time. Future modifications of FibWorld could conceivably keep track of problem-solving status, and provide predictions or suggestions for the next step towards the goal state. We anticipate this method being potentially useful in knowledge tracing and counterfactual (alternate outcome) simulations to better understand learning outcomes for the Shared Weights Task and other similar collaborative problem-solving tasks.

A visual inspection of the simulation provides valuable insight into each of its individual components: the annotation score; the annotation schema; and the IVA interpretation layer, as described below.

4.1 Annotation Score Validation

For researchers developing novel natural language annotation schemes, it is common practice to review exemplar documents in order to pilot early versions of the scheme. The typical early phase of annotation development takes place during the MAMA (Model-Annotate-Model-Annotate) sub-cycle [36], part of the larger MATTER annotation development methodology (Model, Annotate, Train, Test, Evaluate, Revise) [32].

Open source text annotation tools, such as BRAT [40], Doccano [28], and TreeAnnotator [13] all have clear visual interfaces for verifying and reviewing annotations. However, performing an "eyeball test" on a multimodal annotation scheme is much more difficult with video data, where the modalities are commonly separated by distinct tracks in the annotation environment and simple errors such as mislabeling a participant or an object under manipulation become difficult to detect.

Our simulation makes this analysis considerably more straightforward, especially for the assignment of semantic roles. Issues with under-generation can be identified by an evaluation of the alignment between the simulated speech, gesture and action. For instance, a missing action or deictic gesture often entails the associated object being underspecified in speech (e.g., saying "This block is heavier" without pointing to anything). On the other hand, missing speech utterances will be associated with objects being interacted with for no reason. Finally, any mislabeling of semantic roles in the action annotation will surface as clear state mismatches between the simulation and the video (e.g., a block being placed in an invalid location).

This validation process can easily be crowd-sourced given a user interface that displays both the simulation and the accompanying utterance content side-by-side. An annotation validator can highlight problems such as missing antecedents for demonstratives, excessive gestures and actions, and incorrect semantic role labeling. All feedback can then be used to adjust the annotation, and thus the simulation, resulting in a self-improving feedback loop.

4.2   Annotation Schema

Natural language annotation schemes are commonly developed using an iterative approach [36], and are heavily dependent on machine learning goals or corpus objectives. Annotation schemes and annotator guidelines tend to evolve as corpora are annotated and as exceptions and edge cases are discovered in the data. Annotation schemes based on well-studied linguistic phenomena, such as named entities or semantic roles, will likely encounter fewer edge cases and therefore less modification to the original annotation specifications.

The primary goal of our pilot annotation schema, composed of speech utterances alongside verbal and nonverbal AMR, was to adequately capture the semantics of the Shared Weights Task to accurately model the problem state. It mostly succeeded in this aspect, allowing for a straightforward assignment of participant actions to agents and semantic role labels to VoxML arguments.

Beyond semantics, we note that AMR annotation does not capture the specific form of more abstract gestures, like icon, symbol, and beat gestures, as they do not encode quantitative pose data. As a result, the best pose estimations we can currently generate for icon gestures, for instance, would be predefined gestures based off the VoxML-defined geometry of the referenced object in question. Future work will investigate improvements and alternatives to our current annotation schema to handle these gesture types accurately: whether the AMR representations require additional expressive or timing markers, or if pose can be encoded and integrated alongside these annotations using markup languages focusing on form.

4.3   IVA Expression

Even provided with an adequately expressive annotation schema, our method equally relies upon the subsequent interpretation and execution of these annotations by the IVA. Accurately representing nonverbal behavior is an especially crucial component in fostering positive human-computer interactions, and the field is currently moving towards a standardized evaluation of their quality [43].

A side-by-side comparison between the video and our simulation highlights distinctions between the ground truth and Diana's current capabilities. This contrasts with approaches that display trained model output alongside the participants' behaviors as in [25]. The Diana avatar treats all events as a strict interpretation of its VoxML definition, and does not currently consider the speed, handedness or manner of particular gestures or actions. The current implementation of the VoxML *put* program, for instance, takes a set amount of time to complete, and as a result the avatar struggles to relay drawn-out or rapid-fire actions. Additionally, we noticed that due to the mathematical nature of the task, gestures would often refer to multiple objects as a group. Though these gestures could easily be modeled in Gesture AMR, the particular manner of gesturing towards multiple objects at once could have had numerous potential interpretations with Diana (point averaging, back-and-forth gesturing, using two hands). These observations provide interesting avenues of exploration for expanding Diana's expressiveness, involving iterative adjustments to the event primitive programming aimed at bridging the gap between video and simulation.

5 Conclusion

In this paper, we argue that, in the context of the evolving notion of embodied HCI [8,31], there is a serious need to develop a unified multimodal annotation scheme, one that includes human-object interactions, in addition to speech and gesture. To this end, we introduced the Shared Weights Task, an collaborative problem-solving task involving deducing the weights of blocks, as a subject for multi-party dialogue investigation. To visualize the developing state of the interaction as captured by an annotation score on example Shared Weights Task videos, we used the VoxWorld platform to develop FibWorld, a virtual recreation of the task that allows embodied IVAs to stand in for human task participants, recreating their behavior across multiple modalities. Finally, we discussed how this simulation visualization can be used to intuitively correct and validate multimodal annotation schemas, as well as provide insight into expanding the ranges of expression of the associated embodied IVA agents.

References

1. Banarescu, L., et al.: Abstract meaning representation (AMR) 1.0 specification. In: Parsing on Freebase from Question-Answer Pairs. In Proceedings of the 2013 Conference on Empirical Methods in Natural Language Processing, Seattle: ACL, pp. 1533–1544 (2012)
2. Bonial, C., et al.: Dialogue-AMR: abstract meaning representation for dialogue. In: Proceedings of the 12th Language Resources and Evaluation Conference, pp. 684–695 (2020)
3. Bradford, M., et al.: Challenges and opportunities in annotating a multimodal collaborative problem-solving task (2022)
4. Brugman, H., Russel, A.: Annotating multi-media/multi-modal resources with ELAN. In: Proceedings of the Fourth International Conference on Language Resources and Evaluation (LREC 2004). European Language Resources Association (ELRA), Lisbon, Portugal (2004). http://www.lrec-conf.org/proceedings/lrec2004/pdf/480.pdf
5. Brutti, R., Donatelli, L., Lai, K., Pustejovsky, J.: Abstract meaning representation for gesture. In: Proceedings of the Thirteenth Language Resources and Evaluation Conference, Marseille, France, pp. 1576–1583. European Language Resources Association (2022). https://aclanthology.org/2022.lrec-1.169
6. Cassell, J., Sullivan, J., Churchill, E., Prevost, S.: Embodied Conversational Agents. MIT Press, Cambridge (2000)
7. Copestake, A., Flickinger, D., Pollard, C., Sag, I.A.: Minimal recursion semantics: an introduction. Res. Lang. Comput. 3(2–3), 281–332 (2005)
8. Evans, L., Rzeszewski, M.: Hermeneutic relations in VR: immersion, embodiment, presence and HCI in VR gaming. In: Fang, X. (ed.) HCII 2020. LNCS, vol. 12211, pp. 23–38. Springer, Cham (2020). https://doi.org/10.1007/978-3-030-50164-8_2
9. Foster, M.E.: Enhancing human-computer interaction with embodied conversational agents. In: Stephanidis, C. (ed.) UAHCI 2007. LNCS, vol. 4555, pp. 828–837. Springer, Heidelberg (2007). https://doi.org/10.1007/978-3-540-73281-5_91
10. Gu, C., et al.: Ava: a video dataset of spatio-temporally localized atomic visual actions. In: Proceedings of the IEEE Conference on Computer Vision and Pattern Recognition, pp. 6047–6056 (2018)

11. Gupta, S., Malik, J.: Visual semantic role labeling. arXiv preprint arXiv:1505.04474 (2015)
12. Hassanin, M., Khan, S., Tahtali, M.: Visual affordance and function understanding: a survey. ACM Comput. Surv. (CSUR) **54**(3), 1–35 (2021)
13. Helfrich, P., Rieb, E., Abrami, G., Lücking, A., Mehler, A.: Treeannotator: versatile visual annotation of hierarchical text relations. In: Proceedings of the Eleventh International Conference on Language Resources and Evaluation (LREC 2018) (2018)
14. Henlein, A., Gopinath, A., Krishnaswamy, N., Mehler, A., Pustejovsky, J.: Grounding human-object interaction to affordance behavior in multimodal datasets. Front. Artif. Intell. **6**, 1084740 (2023)
15. Kamp, H., Van Genabith, J., Reyle, U.: Discourse representation theory. In: Gabbay, D., Guenthner, F. (eds.) Handbook of Philosophical Logic, pp. 125–394. Springer, Dordrecht (2011). https://doi.org/10.1007/978-94-007-0485-5_3
16. Karau, S.J., Williams, K.D.: Social loafing: a meta-analytic review and theoretical integration. J. Pers. Soc. Psychol. **65**(4), 681 (1993)
17. Kipp, M., Neff, M., Albrecht, I.: An annotation scheme for conversational gestures: how to economically capture timing and form. Lang. Resour. Eval. **41**, 325–339 (2007)
18. Knight, K., et al.: Abstract meaning representation (AMR) annotation release 1.2.6. Web download (2019)
19. Kopp, S., et al.: Towards a common framework for multimodal generation: the behavior markup language. In: Gratch, J., Young, M., Aylett, R., Ballin, D., Olivier, P. (eds.) IVA 2006. LNCS (LNAI), vol. 4133, pp. 205–217. Springer, Heidelberg (2006). https://doi.org/10.1007/11821830_17
20. Kopp, S., Wachsmuth, I.: Gesture in Embodied Communication and Human-Computer Interaction, vol. 5934. Springer, Heidelberg (2010). https://doi.org/10.1007/978-3-642-12553-9
21. Krishnaswamy, N., et al.: Situational awareness in human computer interaction: Diana's world (2020)
22. Krishnaswamy, N., et al.: Diana's world: a situated multimodal interactive agent. In: Proceedings of the AAAI Conference on Artificial Intelligence, vol. 34, pp. 13618–13619 (2020)
23. Krishnaswamy, N., Pickard, W., Cates, B., Blanchard, N., Pustejovsky, J.: The voxworld platform for multimodal embodied agents. In: Proceedings of the Thirteenth Language Resources and Evaluation Conference, pp. 1529–1541 (2022)
24. Krishnaswamy, N., Pustejovsky, J.: Voxsim: a visual platform for modeling motion language. In: Proceedings of COLING 2016, the 26th International Conference on Computational Linguistics: System Demonstrations, pp. 54–58 (2016)
25. Lücking, A., Bergmann, K., Hahn, F., Kopp, S., Rieser, H.: The bielefeld speech and gesture alignment corpus (SaGA) (2010). https://doi.org/10.13140/2.1.4216.1922
26. Marshall, P., Hornecker, E.: Theories of embodiment in HCI. In: The SAGE Handbook of Digital Technology Research, vol. 1, pp. 144–158 (2013)
27. Martin, J.C., Niewiadomski, R., Devillers, L., Buisine, S., Pelachaud, C.: Multimodal complex emotions: gesture expressivity and blended facial expressions. Int. J. Humanoid Rob. **3**(03), 269–291 (2006)
28. Nakayama, H., Kubo, T., Kamura, J., Taniguchi, Y., Liang, X.: doccano: text annotation tool for human (2018). https://github.com/doccano/doccano
29. Palmer, M., Gildea, D., Kingsbury, P.: The proposition bank: an annotated corpus of semantic roles. Comput. Linguist. **31**(1), 71–106 (2003)

30. Podlasov, A., Tan, S., O'Halloran, K.: Interactive state-transition diagrams for visualization of multimodal annotation. Intell. Data Anal. **16**, 683–702 (2012). https://doi.org/10.3233/IDA-2012-0544

31. Pustejovsky, J., Krishnaswamy, N.: Embodied human computer interaction. Künstliche Intelligenz (2021)

32. Pustejovsky, J.: Unifying linguistic annotations: a timeml case study. In: Proceedings of Text, Speech, and Dialogue Conference (2006)

33. Pustejovsky, J., Krishnaswamy, N.: Voxml: a visualization modeling language. In: Proceedings of LREC (2016)

34. Pustejovsky, J., Krishnaswamy, N.: Voxml: a visualization modeling language. arXiv preprint arXiv:1610.01508 (2016)

35. Pustejovsky, J., Krishnaswamy, N.: Multimodal semantics for affordances and actions. In: Kurosu, M. (ed.) HCII 2022. LNCS, vol. 13302, pp. 137–160. Springer, Cham (2022). https://doi.org/10.1007/978-3-031-05311-5_9

36. Pustejovsky, J., Stubbs, A.: Natural Language Annotation for Machine Learning: A Guide to Corpus-Building for Applications. O'Reilly Media, Inc. (2012)

37. Reallusion Inc.: Character Creator 4 (2022). https://www.reallusion.com/character-creator/

38. Sadhu, A., Gupta, T., Yatskar, M., Nevatia, R., Kembhavi, A.: Visual semantic role labeling for video understanding. In: Proceedings of the IEEE/CVF Conference on Computer Vision and Pattern Recognition, pp. 5589–5600 (2021)

39. Schaffer, S., Reithinger, N.: Conversation is multimodal: thus conversational user interfaces should be as well. In: Proceedings of the 1st International Conference on Conversational User Interfaces, pp. 1–3 (2019)

40. Stenetorp, P., Pyysalo, S., Topić, G., Ohta, T., Ananiadou, S., Tsujii, J.: Brat: a web-based tool for NLP-assisted text annotation. In: Proceedings of the Demonstrations at the 13th Conference of the European Chapter of the Association for Computational Linguistics, pp. 102–107 (2012)

41. Van Gysel, J.E., et al.: Designing a uniform meaning representation for natural language processing. KI-Künstliche Intelligenz, pp. 1–18 (2021)

42. Wahlster, W.: Dialogue systems go multimodal: the smartkom experience. In: Wahlster, W. (ed.) SmartKom: Foundations of Multimodal Dialogue Systems, pp. 3–27. Springer, Heidelberg (2006). https://doi.org/10.1007/3-540-36678-4_1

43. Wolfert, P., Robinson, N., Belpaeme, T.: A review of evaluation practices of gesture generation in embodied conversational agents. IEEE Trans. Hum.-Mach. Syst. (2022)

44. Yang, S., Gao, Q., Liu, C., Xiong, C., Zhu, S.C., Chai, J.: Grounded semantic role labeling. In: Proceedings of the 2016 Conference of the North American Chapter of the Association for Computational Linguistics: Human Language Technologies, pp. 149–159 (2016)

45. Yatskar, M., Zettlemoyer, L., Farhadi, A.: Situation recognition: Visual semantic role labeling for image understanding. In: Proceedings of the IEEE Conference on Computer Vision and Pattern Recognition, pp. 5534–5542 (2016)

46. Ziem, A.: Do we really need a multimodal construction grammar? Linguist. Vanguard **3**(s1) (2017)

Robust Motion Recognition Using Gesture Phase Annotation

Hannah VanderHoeven[✉][iD], Nathaniel Blanchard[iD],
and Nikhil Krishnaswamy[iD]

Colorado State University, Fort Collins, CO 80523, USA
{hannah.vanderhoeven,nathaniel.blanchard,
nikhil.krishnaswamy}@colostate.edu

Abstract. Robust gesture recognition is key to multimodal language understanding as well as human-computer interaction. While vision-based approaches to gesture recognition rightly focus on detecting hand poses in a single frame of video, there is less focus on recognizing the distinct "phases" of gesture as used in real interaction between humans or between humans and computers. Following the semantics of gesture originally outlined by Kendon, and elaborated by many such as McNeill and Lascarides and Stone, we propose a method to automatically detect the preparatory, "stroke," and recovery phases of semantic gestures. This method can be used to mitigate errors in automatic motion recognition, such as when the hand pose of a gesture is formed before semantic content is intended to be communicated and in semi-automatically creating or augmenting large gesture-speech alignment corpora.

Keywords: Gesture semantics · Gesture annotation · Gesture phases

1 Introduction

A key requirement in modeling the behavior of humans in interaction with each other and with intelligent agents is the ability to model and recognize gestures. Not only is this crucial to creating multimodal corpora [16,17], it is also a critical component of intelligent systems that communicate multimodally with humans [11–13]. The technical solution for most modern gesture recognition systems is some form of computer vision algorithm. As these are usually large neural networks, successful vision systems depend on a sufficient volume of high-quality training data.

In order to create effective training data for machine learning tasks, as well as for robust modeling of human gestures, accurate annotation is necessary to establish correct ground truth values. This often involves identifying the key frames where the semantics of the gesture are expressed. For instance, a difficulty in automatic recognition may arise if an algorithm focuses only on individual frames, such as when a distinct hand pose is formed (e.g., a pointing gesture) before the semantic denotatum of the gesture is intended to be communicated (cf. [10]). Therefore, correct identification of key frames helps reduce noise and aids accurate identification of gestures, but manually sifting through

V. G. Duffy (Ed.): HCII 2023, LNCS 14028, pp. 592–608, 2023.
https://doi.org/10.1007/978-3-031-35741-1_42

video data to identify when exactly a gesture of interest starts and stops can be time-consuming and labor-intensive. In this paper, we propose an approach to automatically identify the key phases of gestures to aid in semi-automatic detection and annotation of gesture semantics. Following the gesture semantics originally formulated by Kendon [8] and elaborated by McNeill [21] and Las-carides and Stone [15], among others, we focus on automatic identification of key frames that comprise the *pre-stroke*, *stroke*, and *post-stroke* phases of a ges-ture unfolding across multiple frames. We present our methodology, qualitative and quantitative outputs, and evaluate the utility of the entire pipeline on a gesture recognition task, showing very promising results.

2   Related Work

2.1   History of Gesture Semantics

There is a wealth of foundational and theoretical work in gesture semantics that informs our research. In this section, a small selection of key contributions in this area follow.

Adam Kendon [8] pioneered an approach that models gestures as simple schemas consisting of distinct sub-gestural *phases*. Of these, the *stroke* phase is regarded as the content-bearing phase. David McNeill [20,21] treated gesture and speech as sharing "the same psychological structure" and "a computational stage." This position set the stage for interpretations of gesture to be modeled using similar semantic structures as verbal language. McNeill's formulation [19] extends Kendon's to include "preparation" and "retraction" phases.

According to Lascarides and Stone [14,15], gesture is interpretable in the direct visual context if and only if the denotation of its interpretation function is also directly co-perceptible by both the gesture-making agent and said agent's interlocutor. An example of this would be the object intended to be denoted by a deictic gesture; namely, the deixis is only fully interpretable when its pointing "cone" [9] aligns with the object, while in the case of an iconic gesture (say, holding thumb and forefinger together to indicate "smallness"), the directly-perceptible visual denotatum is the gesture itself. However, in both cases, the physical act of making the gesture involves a pause or *hold* on either side of the stroke phase, along with the initial preparation and final retraction phases.

Lücking et al. [18] similarly adopt McNeill's gesture phase scheme for a study of deixis, which models a pointing cone that extends outward from the extended digit. The intersection of the cone and the objects in the environment becomes the region that contains the denotatum, but only during the stroke phase. This makes automated detection of the stroke phase critical for intelligent systems that model and interpret gesture.[1]

The work that most closely approaches ours is Gebre et al. [5], on automatic stroke phase detection. But, where the authors approach detecting stroke phases

---

[1] A similar formulation that models deictic precision decreasing with distance is adopted by van der Sluis and Krahmer [25].

as an end in itself, we utilize detection of holds along with sequence-based segmentation techniques to implicitly segment stroke phases from other phases by utilizing the aforementioned foundational semantic frameworks [8,15,19].

2.2 Real World Applications

Over time, gesture recognition has become an increasingly ubiquitous method to facilitate humans interaction with computers. Multimodal interactive agents, e.g., [11-13], can use gesture along side speech, but typically require gestures to held still for a short period for the gesture recognition algorithm to achieve the requisite confidence, which leads to lag.

Hand detection tools, such as MediaPipe, an open source library developed by Google [27], can aid in gesture recognition by returning joint locations, or *landmarks*, of detected hands on a frame-by-frame basis [27] that can be used to train custom gesture recognition models with a wide range of applications. In prior studies and HCI applications, these tools have proven to be an effective foundation on which to develop custom models that classify generally static, standalone gestures that are identifiable in a single frame. For example, using a model trained to recognize a collection of simple gestures, a user can interact with a graphical user interface hands-free [6]. Additionally, gesture recognition models have been utilized as an effective simple solution to control various robotic systems [1]. In both of these examples, a dataset containing multiple static gestures is used to develop a recognition model, allowing the user to change between various gestures and commands in real time. However, in most studies the change in motion of a hand between gestures is not important to the intended command—once the user settles on a new gesture, the shape of the hand is static and identifiable in a single frame. In this paper, we present a pipeline to recognize gestures that extend across multiple frames, thus allowing more granularity in the gestures that can be used to command a system, and allowing more intuitive movements to represent a command from the user's perspective (i.e., pinching to zoom.)

Tools like MediaPipe can reduce the inherent ambiguity present in single still images of a gesture, but a collection of frames may still contain redundant information. Thus, we propose to filter out surplus information by identifying key frames. The combined use of landmark detection and key frame identification has enabled model success for other complex (non-gestural) movements [23]. Our model, driven by effective features for robust motion detection, both aids recognition and, by smart segmentation, will cut down on time and effort that researchers spend manually annotating video data.

3   Methodology

The pipeline presented in this paper aims to automatically identify the key phases of gestures to aid in semi-automatic annotation of gesture semantics through identifying the sub-gestural phases. Specifically, we focus on the automatic detection of "key frames," which we define as frames comprising the union of the pre-stroke, stroke, and post-stroke phases, where the most of the semantically significant movement takes place. Our pipeline consists of three stages that aid in reducing noise and distilling videos down to these key frames, and we evaluate it over a collection of complex, multi-frame gestures in two datasets. Key components of the pipeline include a classification model whose main purpose is to recognize the general static shape of complex gestures when in a hold phase (Sect. 3.3), a movement segmentation routine which aids in breaking down a video into segments of similar movements (Sect. 3.4), and a phase markup annotation which uses the classification model and the video segments in order to identify and annotate the segments and frames that are in a "hold" phase, and thus most semantically significant, or adjacent to the most semantically-significant frames. Figure 1 shows an overview of the major components and the order in which they work together. In this section we will walk step by step through each piece of the pipeline and tools used in more detail.

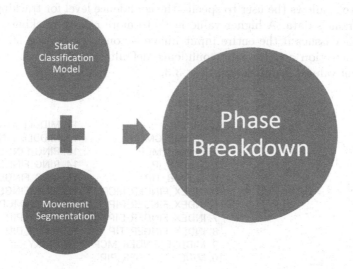

Fig. 1. Complex gesture annotation pipeline

3.1   MediaPipe

Categorizing gestures inherently involves a focus on hand poses and movements. This is key to the gesture semantics approaches discussed in Sect. 2.1, as well as to computer vision approaches to gesture recognition [22]. Therefore, extraction of features of hand location is critical. We use MediaPipe to return joint locations, or landmarks, of detected hands on a frame-by-frame basis, which are used to help identify key frames. MediaPipe tracks hands using 21 landmarks that consist of x, y, and z (relative depth) coordinates. It uses a two-stage pipeline: 1) the palm is detected using the full input image, and a bounding box is formed around the hand that marks its initial location; 2) more precise hand landmarks (joint positions) are located and modeled based on the location of the hand bounding box. Figure 2 shows the location of hand landmarks and indexes returned by MediaPipe. This process is optimized by using the hand bounding box from the previous frame to help track the bounding box in the next frame. The entire input image is only used again if tracking confidence drops below a defined threshold [27].

Google's API includes a handful of user definable parameters that can be configured when using MediaPipe. We use a few of these, including maximum number of hands, minimum detection confidence, and minimum tracking confidence. Maximum number of hands allows the user to define the number of hands expected in the frames and defaults to 2. Minimum detection confidence, which is on a scale of 0 to 1, allows the user to specify the confidence value required to consider a hand detected, higher values require clearer images but also reduce false positive values. In addition minimum tracking confidence, which is also on a scale of 0 to 1, allows the user to specify the confidence level for tracking via the previous frame's data. A higher value leads to more robust tracking but could cause latency issues if the entire input image is consistently used for tracking. Both the detection and tracking confidence default to 0.5. For annotation, we use different values, mentioned in Sect. 3.3.

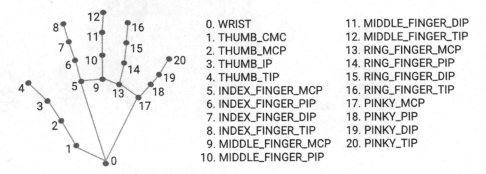

Fig. 2. MediaPipe Hand Landmarks (reproduced from [27])

3.2 Datasets

Microgesture Dataset. Microgestures are a category of small, subtle hand gesture requiring less gross motion [26]. The overall goal of such gestures is to reduce the fatigue of a user interacting with a system long-term. The "Microgesture dataset" is a collection of short single-gesture videos, focusing on a single hand. 49 gestures are included in this dataset, each unique and identifiable, fitting into categories including: taps, rotations, move, snap, numbers, zoom, open/close, and slide. Using 3 Microsoft Azure Kinect cameras positioned at 3 different angles, 72 videos were collected for each gesture, spanning 10 participants [7]. Each video consists of approximately 60–81 frames with different start and end points for each gesture, thus making the data a good candidate to test our phase detection solution.

Weights Task Dataset. The Weights Task dataset provides data that can be used to test our gesture phase segmentation pipeline on a more realistic scenario. This dataset is a collection of audio-visual recordings data where triads perform a task involving correctly identifying the weights of various colored blocks using a balance scale. Unknown to the participants, the weights of the blocks follow a specific pattern, and the task involves participants collaboratively uncovering this pattern. This shared collaborative task involves multimodal communication using speech, gesture, gaze, and action in context, making the identification of key gesture semantics important for automated analysis. The dataset spans 10 groups of 3, and includes videos from 3 different camera angles [2]. The videos include many potential gestures of interest, including pointing, grasping and placing blocks on a scale, which are good candidates for automatic phase segmentation and annotation. Because there are multiple hands in these videos, there are processing issues that need to be overcome to make our solution more robust, which we discuss further in Sect. 6.

3.3 Static Classification Model

The first step of our pipeline is a classifier that runs over individual frames to identify frames where the hand appears in the shape identifiable as the gesture of interest. In this section we outline the annotation method used to create data for the classifier and the details of the classifier itself.

Annotation. Some manual annotation is required to create a static classification tool for any given complex gesture. In order to create this data, we developed an annotation script for the Microgesture and Weights Task datasets. Using this script we step frame by frame through a sample video using OpenCV. For any selected frame of the Microgesture data we save off the *phase type*, *gesture type*, *participant ID*, and normalized landmarks returned from MediaPipe. For the Weights Task dataset we include additional fields such as *hand index* and *group ID*. *Phase type* can be one of two values: "hold," which signifies a frame in which the hand shape is similar to the shape of the gesture in any of the stroke phases, and "no hold" which represents a noise shape (dissimilar from stroke) that should be ignored. *Gesture type* maps directly to the index of the gesture in the Microgesture dataset, and in the case of the Weights Task data can be user-defined to map to a predefined gesture of interest. Figures 3 and 4 show examples of annotated data from each of the datasets used in this paper.

For annotation using the Microgesture dataset, we used the default tracking and detection values for MediaPipe (cf. Sect. 3.1), and set the maximum number of hands to 1. For the Weights Task data both tracking and detection values were set to 0.6 with maximum hands set to 6, thus allowing us to annotate any combination of hands returned from MediaPipe.

Fig. 3. Annotation examples from Microgesture dataset

Fig. 4. Annotation examples from Weights Task dataset

Classification Model. To test our pipeline we experiment on a subset of gestures from the Microgesture dataset and created a classification model for each. To generate this subset we selected one gesture from a handful of the hierarchical categories of the Microgesture dataset [7]. We selected one gesture from the following categories: *move, snap, number, zoom, open/close*. The categories were with the intent to create a diverse selection of gestures across multiple categories. From here we selected one specific gesture from each category, including *two* for number, *index finger swipe right* for move, *hand close* for open/close, *zoom in with palm* for zoom and *snap* for snap. Because each gesture comes from a different category, we expect each to be distantly identifiable using key frames. Figure 5 shows samples of each of the 5 gestures of interest selected for evaluation.

Using the annotated values for each frame in the sample data for each gesture, we create a random forest binary classifier using the scikit-learn library for

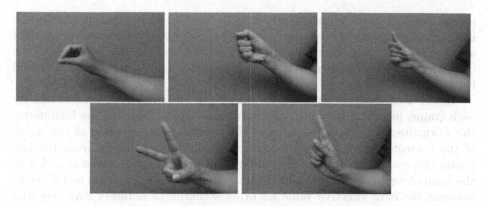

Fig. 5. Hold phase stills (from top left): *zoom in with palm, hand close, snap, two,* and *index finger swipe right*

each gesture of interest. A random forest classifier is made up of a collection of independent decision-tree classifiers generated from a randomly selected subset of training data. These classifiers then vote on the most probable classification for any given input [3]. Random forest classifiers have been used in other MediaPipe based classification projects (e.g., [4] and [24]). The overall purpose of this model is to identify if a hand is in a "hold" phase or not. Table 1 shows the accuracy metrics, Cohen's Kappa, and AUROC values of each of the random forest classifiers generated. The high values for all metrics on each gesture shows that we can use landmarks to identify the general shape of the hold in a single frame, however as mentioned before this is not enough to identify key frames and additional processing is required.

Table 1. Overall accuracy, balanced accuracy, Kappa, and AUROC. Gestures of interest come from the Microgesture Dataset.

Gesture	Accuracy	Balanced Accuracy	Kappa	AUROC
Two	0.92	0.93	0.92	0.92
Index finger swipe right	0.91	0.87	0.89	0.89
Hand close	0.87	0.78	0.84	0.82
Zoom in with palm	0.83	0.91	0.88	0.87
Snap	0.94	0.95	0.95	0.95

3.4 Movement Segmentation

Our pipeline's second phase involves grouping similar individual frames into like movements. For each frame, we compute a value representing the hand's general location in the frame, representing the average (x, y) values in pixel space, using the 21 landmarks returned from MediaPipe. Figure 6 shows an example of average hand location determined from the individual landmarks. Hereafter we define a collection of frames with a difference in average location under a defined threshold as a "segment."

In order to generate segments for a video, we first cache off information for each frame, including the video number, frame number, MediaPipe landmarks, the normalized landmark values, and the average (x, y) location of the hand. If the current frame's average location is significantly different from the last frame this marks the start of a new segment, otherwise the frame is added to the current segment. The threshold value used in our experiments is 0.8 pixels, however the most effective value for other scenarios or datasets may very and thus the value is user-definable. Figures 7 and 8 show a visualized example of these steps on a subsection of *zoom in with palm* frames.

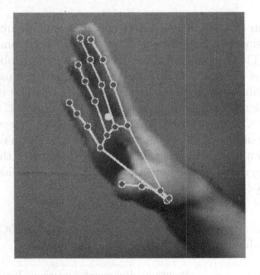

Fig. 6. Example of average hand location, shown by the yellow dot. (Color figure online)

Fig. 7. Movement Segmentation: cached frame values

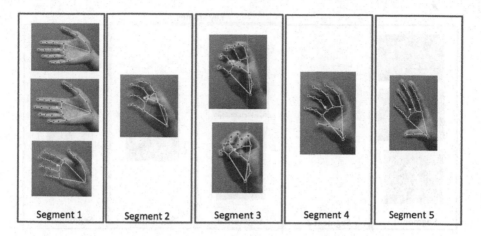

Fig. 8. Movement Segmentation: creating segments

3.5 Phase Breakdown

After the video has been broken down into segments, we analyze the segments using our classification model to identify segments with a significant percentage of frames in *hold*. For each segment in the video we run our static shape classifier on each frame in the corresponding segment. If at least 80% of the frames are in *hold*, we mark that entire segment in *hold*. During this process we look for the following pattern: the first *hold* segment found marks the potential start of the key frames interval, or a "section of interest." After a hold is found, the next "no hold" segment marks the end of the section of interest. The entire detected section should span the pre-stroke, stroke and post-stroke phases. For each section of interest found in a video, we also calculate the total frames. The user can define the number of frames required to mark the section as significant or key frames and thus as a candidate for automatic annotation. Figure 9 shows a visualized example of this grouping, continuing the example from the previous section.

Once key frames are identified a few values are saved off that can then be utilized to help extract key frames from a video subsequently to train additional models to classify a collection of gestures in real time. These values include the first and last frame of the key frame section, and the first and last frame of the peak segment, also defined as the segment that contained the most frames. In addition, the frame count for each segment can be plotted to show the pattern of motion for any gesture of interest. It is worth noting that the pattern of peaks and valleys on this chart can be used to map the occurrence of the stroke phase, and for some gestures this could take place in or around the peak segment. Figures 10, 11 and 12 show example plots of the distributions for each of the five gestures examined. It is worth noting that for each gesture the start location and length of the key frames vary, showing the importance of dynamic key frame selection.

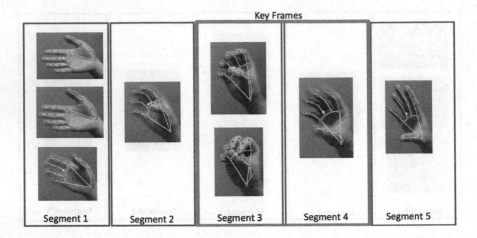

Fig. 9. Phase Breakdown: locating key frames

Selecting one static key frame location across all values in the dataset would lead to noise in training inputs. The "peaks" shown in these charts indicate a section of frames where motion was relatively small (that is, a high concentration of similar frames), whereas valleys show locations where change in motion is more significant.

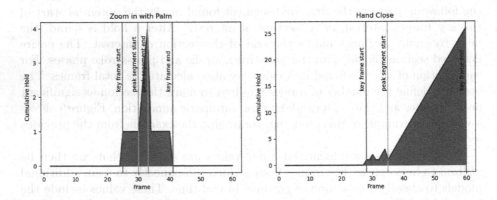

Fig. 10. Key frame examples from *zoom in with palm* and *hand close*

4   Evaluation

Our major motivation in this paper has been to develop a way to automatically pinpoint the exact locations of key frames for any given gesture. Success in this

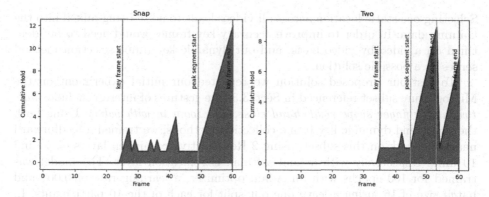

Fig. 11. Key frame examples from *snap* and *two*

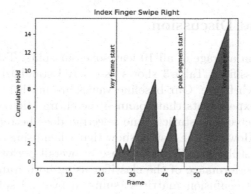

Fig. 12. Key frame examples from *index finger swipe right*

aim means that automatically extracted key frames should be more informative of a gesture to a recognition system than a naive or random baseline. We demonstrate our success on such a recognition task.

Our initial goal application was to train a classifier to recognize multi-frame gestures across the entire Microgesture dataset using MediaPipe's landmark data. In an initial attempt, where all frames in each video were gathered and fed into a simple classifier, the resulting accuracy that was equivalent to a random guess. To reduce noise and trim down the number of frames being fed into our classifier, we gathered 10 frames starting at the 20th frame for each video. This resulted in performance very similar to the first attempt. Various additional attempts were made to select a number of frames from the same static location in each video that best fit the entire dataset. Through our experiments we were able to improve accuracy slightly only to an accuracy of about 20%. This value using naive or static key frame selection serves as a baseline. We hypothesize this occurred because the true location of the key frames varied greatly for each gesture, and no single starting position would be effective across the entire dataset.

Selecting one static location across all videos leads to noise being mixed into the training data. In order to improve accuracy key frames would need to be identified on a video by video basis, and our dynamic key frame selection method serves as a possible solution.

To test our proposed solution we repeated our initial experiment on the Microgesture subset referenced in Sect. 3.3 (the gestures of interest include *snap*, *two, index finger swipe right, hand close*, and *zoom in with palm*). Using both the static and dynamic key frame collection methods, we trained a feedforward neural network on this subset, using 2 ReLU-activated hidden layers of 20 and 10 units respectively with a final softmax classification layer. The model was trained for 100 epochs with an Adam optimizer, a learning rate of 0.001 and batch size of 16, using a leave one out split for each of the 10 participants. In both cases we gathered 10 frames from each video.

5   Results and Discussion

Our results show an average of all 10 leave-one-out splits. Table 2 shows statistics from both classifiers. Table 3 shows associated standard deviations across all 10 splits for each figure. Our baseline values are much higher then the values in our initial experiments that spanned the entire Microgesture dataset, as for the subset selected, the static frame selection does better at selecting relevant information. However our results show that when using dynamic key frame selection, there is still a significant increase in overall performance. Figures 13 and 14 show the performance of the classifier using both frame selection methods in the form of confusion matrices (summed over all splits). It is evident from Fig. 14 that dynamic key frame selection does significantly better over all the gestures of interest. Our experiments show that our pipeline and dynamic key frame selection is a promising solution to reduce visual noise in a dataset by focusing on segmenting gestures using semantically-informed key inflection points, thus improving the performance of models tasked with identifying complex multi-frame gestures.

Table 2. Average reported metrics: precision, recall, F1, and top-k accuracy. 10 frames were gathered for both methods. Static collection started at frame 20 of each video. Dynamic started at the unique key frame location for each individual video.

Method	Precision	Recall	F1	Top-1	Top-3
Static	35.28	39.16	33.86	41.48	83.49
Dynamic	66.35	66.48	62.78	69.10	89.10

Table 3. Standard deviation of reported metrics: precision, recall, F1, and top-k accuracy.

Method	Precision	Recall	F1	Top-1	Top-3
Static	23.99	20.36	21.97	21.16	9.78
Dynamic	22.80	19.00	22.00	18.28	9.86

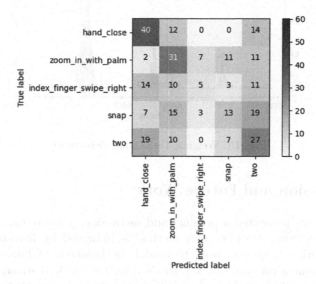

Fig. 13. Classification results using static key frame selection

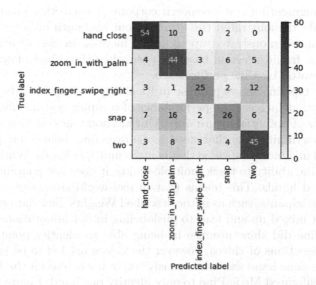

Fig. 14. Classification results using dynamic key frame selection

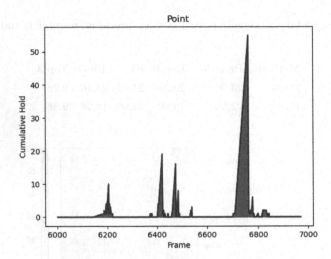

Fig. 15. Weights Task, point detection

6   Conclusion and Future Work

In this paper we presented a pipeline and methodology for dynamic key frame selection of gestures in video. Our method is informed by foundational work on the semantics of gesture used to model the behavior of humans in multi-modal communication, and our key frame selection method strongly correlates to segmentation of the hold and stroke phases of a gesture. Our methodology is expected to aid in the semi-automatic annotation of gesture, e.g., for the purposes of augmenting gesture-speech corpora or correcting errors in gesture recognition. We demonstrated the utility of our approach on a gesture classification task, and demonstrated up to a 30% increase in classification accuracy against a static frame selection baseline, even when the subset of gesture chosen artificially elevated baseline performance.

While our pipeline shows promise in its ability to help identify the location of key frames that increase the performance of complex gesture classifiers, there are a few areas of potential future work. Our method relies on MediaPipe, which itself has a few limitations that need to be overcome before our pipeline is a feasible to aid in annotating video that contain multiple hands. While MediaPipe does provide the ability to track multiple hands, it does not guarantee the order of the returned hands. This means that in real-world situations with multiple hands and participants, such as in the described Weights Task dataset (Sect. 3.2), hands can get mixed up and lead to mislabeling in our annotations.

Our pipeline did show promise in being able to identify pointing gestures in various subsections of videos, however the videos needed to be vetted first to make sure the same hand was continuously tracked, whereas for the Microgesture dataset we configured MediaPipe to only identify one hand. Figure 15 shows the output of our segmentation pipeline over a subsection of one of the Weights Task videos. The figure shows that our pipeline could detect deictic pointing gestures (cf. the video stills in Fig. 4) in a group work scenario and return meaningful output, however to make our solution more robust to this type of dataset additional work needs to be done to consistently associate a hand with a participant. One potential solution for this could involve rendering the Kinect body locations on each frame, along with the MediaPipe output. That way the wrist location of the body closest to a hand could be tracked to potentially make hand tracking more consistent.

Finally, our experimental results, while demonstrating promise and also computational efficiency by relying not on one large model but a series of small ones, were presented only a subset of gestures from the Microgesture dataset. Our pipeline needs to be evaluated over a full dataset, such as the entire Microgesture dataset or a more complex scenario, such as the Weights Task dataset.

Acknowledgements. This work was partially supported by the National Science Foundation under awards CNS 2016714 and DRL 1559731 to Colorado State University. The views expressed are those of the authors and do not reflect the official policy or position of the U.S. Government. All errors and mistakes are, of course, the responsibilities of the authors.

References

1. Allena, C.D., De Leon, R.C., Wong, Y.H.: Easy hand gesture control of a ROS-car using google mediapipe for surveillance use. In: Fui-Hoon Nah, F., Siau, K. (eds.) HCII 2022. LNCS, vol. 13327, pp. 247–260. Springer, Cham (2022). https://doi.org/10.1007/978-3-031-05544-7_19
2. Bradford, M., Khebour, I., Blanchard, N., Krishnaswamy, N.: Automatic detection of collaborative states in small groups using multimodal features. In: International Conference on Artificial Intelligence in Education (under review)
3. Breiman, L.: Bagging predictors. Mach. Learn. **24**, 123–140 (1996)
4. Bugarin, C.A.Q., Lopez, J.M.M., Pineda, S.G.M., Sambrano, M.F.C., Loresco, P.J.M.: Machine vision-based fall detection system using mediapipe pose with IoT monitoring and alarm, pp. 269–274 (2022). https://doi.org/10.1109/R10-HTC54060.2022.9929527
5. Gebre, B.G., Wittenburg, P., Lenkiewicz, P.: Towards automatic gesture stroke detection. In: LREC 2012: 8th International Conference on Language Resources and Evaluation, pp. 231–235. European Language Resources Association (2012)
6. Indriani, M.H., Agoes, A.S.: Applying hand gesture recognition for user guide application using mediapipe. In: 2nd International Seminar of Science and Applied Technology (ISSAT 2021), pp. 101–108 (2021)
7. Kandoi, C., Jung, C., Mannan, S., VanderHoeven, H., Meisman, Q., Krishnaswamy, N., Blanchard, N.: Intentional microgesture recognition for extended human-computer interaction. In: HCII 2023. LNCS. Springer, Cham (2023)
8. Kendon, A., et al.: Gesticulation and speech: two aspects of the process of utterance. In: The Relationship of Verbal and Nonverbal Communication, vol. 25, no. 1980, pp. 207–227 (1980)

9. Kranstedt, A., Lücking, A., Pfeiffer, T., Rieser, H., Wachsmuth, I.: Deixis: how to determine demonstrated objects using a pointing cone. In: Gibet, S., Courty, N., Kamp, J.-F. (eds.) GW 2005. LNCS (LNAI), vol. 3881, pp. 300–311. Springer, Heidelberg (2006). https://doi.org/10.1007/11678816_34

10. Kranstedt, A., Wachsmuth, I.: Incremental generation of multimodal deixis referring to objects. In: Proceedings of the Tenth European Workshop on Natural Language Generation (ENLG 2005) (2005)

11. Krishnaswamy, N., Alalyani, N.: Embodied multimodal agents to bridge the understanding gap. In: Proceedings of the First Workshop on Bridging Human-Computer Interaction and Natural Language Processing, pp. 41–46 (2021)

12. Krishnaswamy, N., et al.: Diana's world: a situated multimodal interactive agent. In: Proceedings of the AAAI Conference on Artificial Intelligence, vol. 34, pp. 13618–13619 (2020)

13. Krishnaswamy, N., et al.: Communicating and acting: understanding gesture in simulation semantics. In: IWCS 2017–12th International Conference on Computational Semantics-Short papers (2017)

14. Lascarides, A., Stone, M.: Formal semantics for iconic gesture. Universität Potsdam (2006)

15. Lascarides, A., Stone, M.: A formal semantic analysis of gesture. J. Semant. 26(4), 393–449 (2009)

16. Lücking, A., Bergman, K., Hahn, F., Kopp, S., Rieser, H.: Data-based analysis of speech and gesture: the bielefeld speech and gesture alignment corpus (SaGA) and its applications. J. Multimodal User Interfaces 7, 5–18 (2013)

17. Lücking, A., Bergmann, K., Hahn, F., Kopp, S., Rieser, H.: The bielefeld speech and gesture alignment corpus (SaGA). In: LREC 2010 Workshop: Multimodal Corpora-Advances in Capturing, Coding and Analyzing Multimodality (2010)

18. Lücking, A., Pfeiffer, T., Rieser, H.: Pointing and reference reconsidered. J. Pragmat. 77, 56–79 (2015)

19. McNeill, D.: Hand and mind. In: Advances in Visual Semiotics, p. 351 (1992)

20. McNeill, D.: Language and Gesture, vol. 2. Cambridge University Press, Cambridge (2000)

21. McNeill, D.: Gesture and thought. In: Gesture and Thought. University of Chicago Press (2008)

22. Narayana, P., Beveridge, R., Draper, B.A.: Gesture recognition: focus on the hands. In: Proceedings of the IEEE Conference on Computer Vision and Pattern Recognition, pp. 5235–5244 (2018)

23. Roygaga, C., et al.: APE-V: Athlete Performance Evaluation using Video, pp. 691–700 (2022)

24. Singh, A.K., Kumbhare, V.A., Arthi, K.: Real-Time Human Pose Detection and Recognition Using MediaPipe, pp. 145–154 (2022). https://doi.org/10.1007/978-981-16-7088-6_12

25. van der Sluis, I., Krahmer, E.: Generating multimodal references. Discourse Process. 44(3), 145–174 (2007)

26. Wolf, K., Naumann, A., Rohs, M., Müller, J.: A taxonomy of microinteractions: defining microgestures based on ergonomic and scenario-dependent requirements. In: Campos, P., Graham, N., Jorge, J., Nunes, N., Palanque, P., Winckler, M. (eds.) INTERACT 2011. LNCS, vol. 6946, pp. 559–575. Springer, Heidelberg (2011). https://doi.org/10.1007/978-3-642-23774-4_45

27. Zhang, F., et al.: Mediapipe hands: on-device real-time hand tracking. arXiv preprint arXiv:2006.10214 (2020)

Short Intervention of Self-study-Videos in a Safety Engineering Learning Arrangement: An Investigation of Effects on Learning Performance and Motivation

Julia Waldorf[1,2]($\boxtimes$), Florian Hafner[1], Marina Bier[1], Nina Hanning[1], Lucia Maletz[2], Carolin Frank[2], and Anke Kahl[1]

[1] Chair of Occupational Safety, University of Wuppertal, Wuppertal, Germany
[2] Chair of Didactics of Technology, University of Wuppertal, Wuppertal, Germany
waldorf@uni-wuppertal.de

Abstract. Several publications claim positive effects of learning videos - in addition to indications of increased motivation among learners, studies suggest that learning performance can be increased [1–3]. With a focus on digital transformation, this paper will consider a self-study-video in the field of university education. The content of the investigated self-study-video is a central model of occupational safety: the design model of protective measures. The presented short intervention was designed as self-study-video based on an existing textbook chapter. Besides the evaluation of design elements, it was investigated which effects learning videos may have on the motivation and learning performance of students learning the design model. Students of the University of Wuppertal were the sample for the intervention. The study population were Safety Engineering students, who visit the lecture "basics of occupational safety". Ninety students attended all steps of the experiment (treatment group n = 44; textbook-group n = 46). The self-study-video has a significant effect on the increase of knowledge and the video-group seems to be more successful than the textbook-group in the post-test. However, the self-study-video is not as motivating as expected, caused by the design of the self-study-video with a computer-generated voice.

Keywords: Occupational safety models · Learning performance · Self-study-video

1 Introduction

Transferring theory to applied knowledge is fundamental for the qualification of professionals, including the field of occupational safety. The central concern of occupational health and safety is to design safe and healthy working conditions for employees. A systematic and holistic assessment of activity-specific hazards and stresses, such as noise and hazardous substances, is based on methodological principles and models. Therefore, it is necessary to teach and practice different models as a systematic basis for operational knowledge. As a key model for application, the design model of protective measures plays a central role in the conception and prioritisation of measures across all hazard potentials [4]. Understanding this central model is a core competency of students in Bachelor's programme in Safety Engineering at the University of Wuppertal, Germany [5]. There is some indication that the students perceive the knowledge input in the lecture "Basics of occupational safety" as too extensive and therefore there is a desideratum for improving education. An aim of the courses is to support students in the initial phase to assess the central role of methodological models for problem-solving, which are often understood as abstract and very theoretical. Therefore, it can be helpful to use different teaching formats to facilitate access.

Even before the SARS-CoV-2-pandemic the supplemental use of learning videos was popular among young adults [6]. Because of the recent pandemic, universities have been rapidly adapting their educational formats such as lectures to digital alternatives. Positive aspects of digital teaching have been recognised and are prompting universities to further implement digital learning content in presence teaching [7]. As a part of these digitalisation strategies, dynamic and audio-visual learning media are finding further relevance in learning offers [8]. Several publications point out positive effects of learning videos, in addition to indications of increased motivation among learners, studies suggest that learning performance can be increased [1–3]. In addition, there are calls for the digitalisation of university lectures at federal state level [9], which the University of Wuppertal concretises in its digitalisation strategy [10]. In this strategy, the use of supporting digital tools is required, especially in fields where they can increase the transfer of knowledge. For achieving the aim of this strategy, it is crucial to improve digital transformation approaches.

Due to the strive for improvement of education and digitalisation, the Chair of Occupational Safety at the University of Wuppertal carried out the short intervention as presented in the following. For the short intervention, an excerpt from an existing textbook "Arbeitssicherheit - Fachliche Grundlagen" (eng.: Occupational Safety - Specialized Fundamentals) was digitally transformed into a self-study-video [4]. In the framework of the lecture, the students were randomly divided into two groups. The intervention group received the self-study-video and the other group the book excerpt. Embedded in the learning opportunity, knowledge and motivational aspects were evaluated. In literature, there are no comparable publications on a learning media comparison in an occupational safety context.

The aim of the study is to investigate whether the use of self-study-videos in self-learning phases can increase motivation and learning success in the field of occupational safety compared to traditional media. A further aim is to improve learning performance of the design model of protective measures.

2 Theoretical Background and State of Research

2.1 Occupational Safety

Bachelor Programme "Safety Engineering". As this study was conducted within the Bachelor of Science programme "Safety Engineering", this programme is presented below. The students can gain safety-engineering expertise in a wide variety of fields, such as environmental protection, fire protection, civil protection or occupational safety. After the scientific basics, students of safety engineering get an overview of the different fields in their third semester in the form of basic lectures. In the following semester, students choose between specialisation modules in these fields.

Contents of the Lecture "Basics of Occupational Safety". Occupational safety characterises a relevant social and operational field. Based on the risk assessment, the discipline of occupational safety forms an interface between human and technology. It combines modern and effective technical protective measures with behavioural aspects to form holistic operational design concepts. The primary objective of occupational safety is to reach no or only acceptable work-related hazards and strains [4]. In one of the basic lecture series, called "Grundlagen der Arbeitssicherheit" (eng.: Basics of occupational safety), the students learn conceptual and legal basics as well as the history of occupational safety. They are also taught important methods, models and tools, which can be classified into analysis, valuation, and design approaches, followed by specific hazard factors [4]. At the end of the lecture series, the goal is for the students to have fundamental technical and methodological knowledge in the field of occupational safety. They should be able to apply the taught methods, models and tools [5].

Design-Model of Protective Measures. As one of the design approaches, the design-model of protective measures (see Fig. 1) is a basic model in occupational safety methodology and has two overarching aims [4]:

- The design and market release of a safe product and
- Safe operational utilisation of this product.

Therefore, two sides are considered in this model, see Fig. 1: product safety and occupational safety. On the side of product safety, the producer's aim is to introduce a safe product to the European market [11]. For this purpose, a product-related risk assessment must be conducted and on this basis, the product design has to be adapted. On the side of occupational safety, the employer has to protect his employees when they are carrying out their tasks by designing the working conditions according to the German Occupational Safety Act. For this purpose, it is necessary to conduct a task-related risk assessment [12]. The residual risks resulting from the product-related risk assessment are included in the task-related risk assessment. This results in various design options, which represent an effective and permanent prevention or minimisation of hazards with decreasing effect regarding the variety of solutions. Demonstrates the six decreasing design options D1–D6.

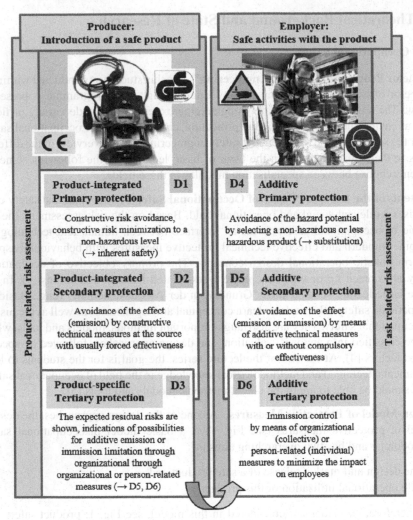

Fig. 1. Design model of protective measures [4]

To achieve the aims of both sides, measures are developed according to the rank-order oriented STOP-model, according to German Occupational Safety Act. This hierarchy of measures, consisting of substitution (S), technical (T), organisational (O) and personal (P) measures, can be assigned to three design levels as shown in Fig. 2: primary protection, secondary protection and tertiary protection. [4, 12].

The STOP-model with the three design levels is applied to the product safety and occupational safety sides of the design model, resulting in the six design options (D1–D6). The effectiveness of one or more protective measures and the achievement of the required design option decreases from design option D1 to D3 and from D4 to D6. Table 1 illustrates examples for each design option.

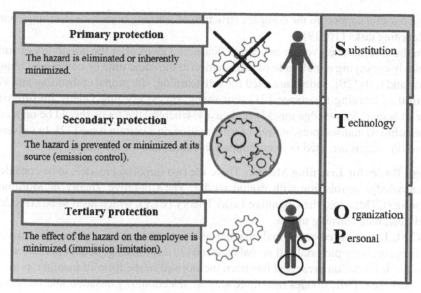

Fig. 2. Design levels compare to the STOP-model [4]

Table 1. Examples for the design levels [4, 13]

Design option	Example	Design option	Example
D1	Bevelling of gears to reduce inherent noise emission	**D4**	Paint removal with an infrared device instead of chemicals
D2	Direct and integrated extraction, e.g. on an angle grinder	**D5**	Technical lifting aids, e.g. for barrels, boxes or tools
D3	Packaging and container labelling (e.g. gas bottles)	**D6**	Personal protective equipment

2.2 Learning Media Background

Digital Transformation in Education Using Videos. Learning success is based on the method and the learning media [14]. Learning media are those means which are used for supporting the learning process and for conveying content in an educational context [15]. The wide-ranging field of learning media is continuously developing. Digital learning media is associated with advantages compared with traditional learning media, such as multimedia representational opportunities [16, 17].

Digital transformation is not just about transforming analogue data, but also about the intention to open up new opportunities and initiate positive change by setting concrete objectives [18]. A variety of media presentation forms of information in digital format can be described as digital media [19], they include for example videos or podcasts. Digital media with the purpose of knowledge transfer such as the investigated self-study-video can be a useful support in the complex structure of learning objectives, learning content and learning tasks [16, 19].

In the context of university education, learning videos offer the possibility of simultaneously conveying a multitude of information at the same time by combining images, audios and texts [20]. Videos are used for self-learning, situational embedding and visualisation of learning assistance [21]. For many topics, learning videos are offered in order to acquire knowledge quickly and easily, whereby the focus should be on a comprehensible, visualised presentation of information on a certain issue [22]. In university education, videos are used in many flipped, blended, and online classes [23].

Design Basics for Learning Media. There are two important models to be considered for knowledge acquisition with digital media: The Cognitive Theory of Multimedia Learning (CTML) and the Cognitive Load Theory (CLT), which need to be considered when designing learning media.

The CTML is based on the dual-channel-assumption that humans have different channels for processing pictorial and verbal material [24]. Knowledge acquisition takes place when the information presented has been memorised in the form of mental representations and the CTML divides into three stages: selection, organisation and integration. During learning processes, an individual has to select from the various verbal and visual information in order to achieve his learning objective. Due to the limited capacity of the working memory, it is important not to cognitively overload learners with a large amount of information [19].

The CLT describes that due to its limited capacity, humans can effectively process only a certain amount of information at a time. This theory differentiates between three types of processes that occur among learners. The germane load processes describe that knowledge success can be successful if the mental resources can be allocated mostly for learning schemes. Extraneous load processes describe those processes that are necessary for the acquisition of current information, but which are not supportive of understanding (e.g. a poorly legible font). While the mode of presentation describes the external cognitive load, the intrinsic cognitive load processes refer to the cognitive load. This load is caused by the intrinsic nature of the learning tasks themselves. In order to consider CLT in the design of learning media, the aim is to avoid those processes that cause extraneous load and to promote those that cause germane load [19, 25, 26].

Based on the theories presented there are various instructional design rules, for example to reduce the cognitive load to a minimum by avoiding unnecessary elements such as background music [27]. In order to prevent an overload effect between viewing the video and reading a text, audio instructions can be used instead of readable text [24].

Effects of Learning Videos. Learning videos can increase the cognitive load for students, for example if audio and visual elements are used simultaneously, which should be considered when developing self-study-videos [28]. Nevertheless, learning with videos is predicted to have predominantly positive effects, especially on motivation and learning performance. Motivation as an indicator of interest and understood here in the sense of actualised individual interest or situational interest [29] and describes the current psychological state of a person. A meta-analysis showed that the correlation between interest and performance is .30 on average [30].

Several studies describe positive effects of appropriately used learning videos on learning success or motivation [1–3, 15]. A meta-analysis on the occasion of the recent pandemic-related remote teaching from 2021 investigated more than 100 higher education use cases in which learning videos led to an improved learning effect [31]. However, in order to achieve the positive effects, some design principles must be taken into account, for example that videos must be embedded in a didactic framework [16, 32]. The impact of learning videos is higher if the videos are interactive, if skills are developed in the videos and if they are used as a supplement to existing learning material [31]. Furthermore, the self-study-videos are more effective when including an assessment, for example by integrating control questions [32, 33]. Also videos can have a positive impact on motivation. For example, in comparison with text instructions, a study among students in engineering drawing showed videos to enhance learners' motivation [34].

3   Research Questions

The following research questions are examined in this paper. With regard to motivation, the (1) difference in motivation of the test persons with the self-study-video compared to the test persons with the textbook is investigated. Afterwards, the (2) difference in the knowledge increase using the self-study-video compared to learning with textbook is examined by choosing a study design based on knowledge tests.

Based on the research questions (1) and (2) the following hypotheses need to be investigated:

- *H1: There is a difference in motivation of the test persons with self-study-video compared to the test persons with textbook.*
- *H2: There is a difference in knowledge increase using the self-study-video compared to learning with textbook.*

4   Methods

4.1   Study Design and Experimental Procedure

To test the two hypotheses, an experimental intervention-control group design in which students were randomly divided into two groups was implemented. The experimental procedure is described below.

In the two previous dates of the weekly lecture „Basics of Occupational Safety", the students were already informed about the implementation of the short intervention during the regular lecture hours on 18.11.2022 and it was announced that this event would take place online via ZOOM. After a short welcome and a presentation of the research project, the students were assigned to two groups (breakout sessions) in the ZOOM meeting, which the students are used to.

For each group, a password-protected Moodle course was created. Here, documents and questionnaires/items were unlocked one after the other. In order to prevent students from exchanging documents with the respective other breakout session, the documents were always released simultaneously in both groups. The set-up is illustrated in Fig. 3.

First, the socio-demographic data of the students was requested. Then the students had to answer entry questions to determine their current level of knowledge.

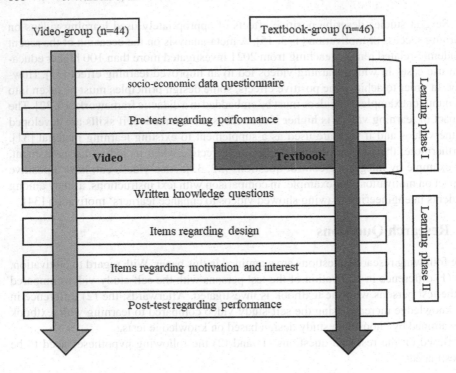

Fig. 3. Experimental set-up

After the level of knowledge was determined, learning phase I began. Here, one group was provided with the self-study-video (in the following referred as "video-group") and the second group with an extract from the textbook "Occupational Safety: Specialized Fundamentals" (in the following referred as "textbook-group"). After viewing once, the media were hidden again and the learning material was evaluated via a questionnaire.

Subsequently, in learning phase II, the media were made available again. This time, the students had to answer knowledge questions for cognitive activation with the help of the self-study-video/textbook excerpt. These were not evaluated for this study.

Finally, items regarding motivation and interest were asked as well as a post-test. During the two breakout sessions, two research assistants from the Chair of Safety Engineering/Occupational Safety were available at all times to answer questions and help with technical problems.

In order to inspire as many students as possible for the task, 0.5 ECTS points were awarded in the form of laboratory points as a reward for active participation.

4.2 Material

As topic for the short intervention, the design model was selected, as it represents a fundamental basis for occupational safety. Furthermore, this model is included in the curriculum of the lecture "Fundamentals of Occupational Safety", which is held in the third semester of the Bachelor's degree programme [5]. The basis for the material prepared for this short intervention forms Sect. 4.7 of the textbook "Occupational Safety: Specialized Fundamentals", which covers a holistic design approach out of the methodical basis [4]. The textbook is a comprehensive compendium in occupational safety for students and for all others who would like to deal more intensively with occupational safety topics.

For comparability, we ensured that essential content and illustrations of the self-study-video and textbook excerpt were identical. In the following, it is described how the self-study-video and the textbook excerpt were created.

When creating the self-study-video, the CLT and CTML were taken into account by reducing the content to the necessary minimum and avoiding for example a poorly legible font or background music. Audio tracks are played parallel to the content they refer to. To maintain concentration, the duration of digital learning media should also be considered [35]. It can be assumed here that a 20-min self-study-video and text material of a comparable length is appropriate, since students are used to longer learning units, for example 90-min-lectures.

The self-study-video was created with the platform Animaker [13]. This browser-based DIY video animation software allows to create videos using pre-built characters and templates [36]. The self-study-video created for the short intervention displays an excerpt from the textbook "Occupational Safety: Specialized Fundamentals" in animated form [4]. The self-study-video has a length of 19:51 min and can be started and stopped independently. For the study, the self-study-video was provided via the media platform Moodle.

The content of the chapter "holistic design approach" from the textbook was shortened for the intervention to the essential components on the topic of the design model [4]. The 16 pages were provided to the students in the form of screenshots via the media platform Moodle.

4.3 Data Collection Methods

Hypothesis. The hypothesis "H1: There is a difference in motivation of the test persons with self-study-video compared to the test persons with textbook" uses the items adapted from Deci and Ryan's Intrinsic Motivation Inventory (IMI) [37]. The hypothesis "H2: There is a difference in knowledge increase using the self-study-video compared to learning with textbook" is based on the learning objectives. In order to investigate effects on performance, a knowledge test is used and group characteristics are included. Furthermore, design elements for learning media are evaluated. The data collection methods described below are intended to confirm the hypotheses.

Measurement of Group Characteristics. To describe the sample, several socio-demographic and characterising questions were asked at the beginning of the short intervention. In addition to semester, sex and age, participants were asked before the intervention whether they are attending the lecture for the first time and whether they know the design model. This question was added to identify differences in prior knowledge about the design model. The measurement of the group characteristics is intended to verify if the randomization has been successful and the groups can be considered as comparable.

Measurement of Design. As the design of the learning material has an impact on motivation and the results of the knowledge transfer, several design-related items were used to investigate to what extent a design compliant with CTL and CMTL was achieved.

In the section "Evaluation of learning materials", items were questioned on the structure and comprehensibility of the learning materials. These items were created based on the evaluation questionnaire (EvaSys) for the lectures at the University of Wuppertal. The items investigate "structure", "meaningfulness", "preparation", "perceived learning gain", "interest", "overall satisfaction" and "clarity of learning objectives" of the learning media. For the purpose of comparability, items from EvaSys, which is used to evaluate a course at the end of each semester, were adapted to the learning material. The aim is to compare the evaluation of the new learning material provided in the short intervention with the evaluation of the course "Basics of Occupational Safety" from previous semesters.

At the end of the questionnaire, the students were given the opportunity to respond open-ended to the question: "Do you have any other annotation on the learning materials?". This qualitative question was evaluated by two objective interrater not involved in this study using the categories for encoding in Table 2. The interrater-reliability is proved by Cohen's kappa [38].

Measurement of Motivation and Interest. To investigate motivation, sub-scales from the IMI (Intrinsic Motivation Inventory) were used [37]. Based on the self-determination theory, the IMI is a multidimensional questionnaire and its reliability and validity have been proven in several studies [39–41]. The IMI includes the following seven sub-scales: 1. Interest/Enjoyment, 2. Perceived choice, 3. Perceived competence, 4. Pressure/Tension (negative predictor), 5. Value/Usefulness, 6. Effort, 7. Relatedness. Each subscale consists of several items. Each item is a statement, which is rated on a Likert scale ($1 \triangleq$ not at all true, $7 \triangleq$ very true).

For this study the sub-scales of the "text material questionnaire I" (TMQ I), which includes the following three dimensions of the IMI is used: 1. Interest/Enjoyment, 2. Perceived competence, 3. Pressure/Tension and is a subset of the IMI [37]. All Items of the TMQ I were translated to German, slightly adapted to the learning situation and included in this study.

Table 2. Categories for encoding

Category	Positive aspects			Negative aspects					Others
Code	PG	PC	PD	NG	NC	NV	ND	NA	O
Sub-category	General aspects	Content	Design	General aspect	Content	Visual design	Design of dialogue	Design of audio	Note without reference to learning media

In addition to the above-mentioned three sub-scales from the TMQ I, the sub-scales "perceived choice" and "value/usefulness" from the IMI were used for this study, see Table 3. These two sub-scales were added as perceived choice is a basic psychological need and value/usefulness measures the value-related dimension of interest [42]. Also the items from the IMI were translated to German and adapted to the learning situation if necessary.

To validate the internal consistency of the individual sub-scales of intrinsic motivation, Cronbach's α is calculated. For two-item scales the Pearson correlation coefficient is chosen and assessed according to Cohen [38]. Eight respondents are excluded after converting the reversed items. This results in a change of respondents in the video-group of n = 42 and in the textbook-group of n = 40. The overall internal consistency reliability is good (>.70, [43]), with Cronbach's α = .80.

As demonstrated in Table 3 regarding the items from the TMQ I, the Interest/Enjoyment sub-scale showed excellent consistency. The other two sub-scales (Perceived Competence and Pressure/Tension) consisted of only two items each in accordance with the TMQ I. The Pearson correlation was strong for the Pressure/Tension sub-scale, but only moderate for the perceived competence scale.

With regard to the added sub-scales from the IMI, the consistency is good for perceived choice and acceptable for value/usefulness.

Table 3. Sub-scales used to measure Motivation and Interest

Sub-scale	Definition	Items used in this study	Cronbach's α / Pearson correlation
Interest/Enjoyment (IEEnj)	This sub-scale is a self-report measure for intrinsic motivation	5 items from TMQ I (5 items in TMQ I)	Cronbach's α: .90 (excellent)
Perceived competence (IEComp)	This sub-scale measures the perceived competence (basic psychological need)	2 items from TMQ I (2 items in TMQ I)	Pearson correlation: .43 (moderate)
Pressure/Tension (IETens)	This sub-scale measures the perceived stress level	2 items from TMQ I (2 items in TMQ I)	Pearson correlation: .78 (strong)
Perceived choice (IC)	This sub-scale measures the autonomy (basic psychological need)	3 items from IMI (7 items in IMI)	Cronbach's α: .76 (good)
Value/Usefulness (IV)	This sub-scale measures the value-related valence of interest	5 items from IMI (7 items in IMI)	Cronbach's α: .65 (acceptable)

The results and rating of the individual sub-scales are shown in Table 3. The two-item sub-scale IETens has a strong Pearson correlation value of .78, p < .001 according to Cohen [38]. Meanwhile, the correlation of IEComp (.43, p < .001) is moderate.

Measurement of Learning Performance. A further aspect investigated in this study is performance. While often, the self-assessed level of safety knowledge [44] is used, it is more objective to use test-performance as an indicator for safety knowledge. A knowledge test was developed to measure the performance. The items investigated theoretical as well as applied competences in the field of the design model.

To develop the test, five learning objectives were defined using Bloom's taxonomy [45]. For each learning objective, one to three items were defined. The complexity of the items correspond to the complexity of the learning objective. Each item was constructed with a ≤ 25% probability for guessing the correct answer. The items were implemented in Moodle using Multiple-Choice, drag and drop on picture and drag and drop on text formats.

The total test has 13 items of varying complexity. The items are in line with the needed difficulty levels of the learning objectives as well as the range of the ability of the students' ranging from basic knowledge items to difficult and complex items which required deeper understanding of the design-model and prior knowledge, see Table 4. The Cronbach's alpha of all 13 items is .79, which indicates an acceptable (close to good) internal consistency.

4.4 Evaluation Methods

For the evaluation of the measurements, the answers are checked for missing values and outliers. Data sets without any answers in every questionnaires are not considered in the results. Outliers are excluded in the relevant parts, but not for the entire analysis. The exact exclusion is described in the results section. Reversed items (n = 3) were converted. Thereby, it is checked whether the respondents had taken into account the change in direction of the answers. This is seen as an indication of thoughtful editing of the questionnaire. Respondents for whom the difference between the reversed item and the item in the same construct was greater than three are excluded for further consideration in the relevant questionnaire.

5   Results

5.1 Sample Description

The sample consisting of students enrolled in the Bachelor's programme in safety engineering at the University of Wuppertal (n = 94) was divided into two groups for the purpose of scientific comparability. The short intervention was carried out in the context

Table 4. Items used to measure Learning Performance

Type of knowledge	# Items	Item	Extracts of exemplary items
Prior knowledge (Applied knowledge about the hazard-exposition model)	1	Q1	Is "corrosive property" considered a hazard or an exposition in the hazard-exposition model?
Theoretical knowledge about the design model and STOP-model	5	Q2, Q4–7	What do the letters S, T, O and P in the STOP-model stand for? For P: "Periodic", "Personal" or "Primary Safety"?
Applied knowledge about the design and STOP-model	5	Q3, Q9–12	To which design level does a protection door on a milling machine correspond?
Applied knowledge about the design model including the limits of the design model	1	Q13	To which design level does appointment of an emission control officer correspond? Correct answer: to none of the design levels
Applied knowledge about the design model linked with prior knowledge (applied knowledge about the hazard-exposition model)	1	Q8	To which design level does the removal from a hazard correspond?

of the lecture "Basics of Occupational Safety", which is compulsory for all students of the study programme in the third semester. The average age of the sample is 22.97 years. On average, the students are in their 4.59th semester. 72% of the total sample are male, 26% female and 2% did not indicate their gender.

The questionnaires on socio-demographic data were completed by 44 subjects in the video-group. In the textbook-group are 46 subjects. Table 5 shows the distribution of age, academic semester and gender in the randomised groups.

Table 5. Characteristics of the investigation group

	Video-group	Textbook-group
	44	46
Average age (years)	23.35	22.70
Average semester	4.52 (SD = 1.99)	4.65 (SD = 2.35)
Male/female/not specified	64%/32%/4%	80%/20%/0%
Previous lecture attendance	55%	54%
Prior knowledge of design model	28%	37%

5.2 Design of Learning Materials

Even though the design-related items do not make a substantial contribution to answering the hypotheses, they are presented for exploratory reasons. In addition, the evaluation provided important insights into the comparison of the media. In context of the design-related items both groups were not normally distributed, as assessed by the Shapiro-Wilk test ($p < .001$). For this reason not a t-test but a Mann-Whitney-U-Test is calculated to determine if there were differences in the perception of the design between both groups. The distributions differ between both groups, Kolmogorov-Smirnov $p < .05$. No statistically significant difference is elicited in the structure ($U = 795.50, Z = -1.95, p = .051$), meaningfulness ($U = 862.0, Z = -1.310, p = .190$), preparation ($U = 873.0, Z = -1.208, p = .227$), perceived learning gain ($U = 901.5, Z = -.956, p = .339$), interest ($U = 893.0, Z = -1.02, p = .308$), overall satisfaction with the form ($U = 855.0, Z = -1.356, p = .175$) of the learning material.

However, for the item "the learning objectives were clear and comprehensible" a statistically significant difference between the video-group ($M_{Rang} = 51.56$) and the textbook-group ($M_{Rang} = 39.71$) can be identified, $U = 745.50, Z = -2.358, p = .018, r = -.260$. It can be concluded that in the self-study-video, the learning objectives were perceived as clearer than in the textbook with a slight effect.

The question "Do you have any other annotation about the learning materials?" provided an open-ended response option. This item was answered by 36 respondents: 24 persons from the video-group and 12 persons from the textbook-group. There is a moderate interrater reliability all over the categories (Cohen's Kappa = .57). In the video-group, 12 of 15 negative comments included the computer-generated voice as a disturbing factor, see Table 6. For this subcategory the two interrater agreed almost perfect (Cohen's Kappa = .88). Additional, there are seven positive and two other comments related to the general process of the intervention. The textbook had the most comments on the negative visual presentation followed by positive aspects on the content.

Table 6. Encoding Results of the question: "Do you have any other annotation about the learning materials?"

Category	Code	Video-group	Textbook-group	Total
Positive aspects	PG	4	0	4
	PC	0	3	3
	PD	3	1	4
Negative aspects	NG	0	1	1
	NC	1	2	3
	NV	0	4	4
	ND	2	-	2
	NA	12	-	12
Others	SO	2	1	3
Total		24	12	36

5.3 Motivation and Interest

Because of the good internal consistence, the answers of each sub-scale-item are summarised to an average value of the whole sub-scale. Group differences are tested with a t-test, see Table 7. For IEEnj, IEComp and IC the values in the video-group are higher than in the textbook-group, but without significance.

Table 7. T-test for equality of means between both groups

| | Equal variance | Levene test of variance equality | | T-test for equality of means | | | | | | | | |
| | | F | Sig | T | df | Significance | | Average difference | Difference for standard error | 95% confidence interval | | |
						One-sided p	Two-sided p			Lower value	Upper value
IEENj	Yes	.09	.76	.43	80.00	.33	.67	.10	.23	-.36	.56
IETens	No	8.90	.00	-1.78	71.80	.04	.08	-.61	.34	-1.30	.08
IEComp	Yes	.35	.56	1.44	80.00	.08	.15	.34	.17	-.09	.58
IV	Yes	3.94	.05	-.59	80.00	.28	.56	-.10	.16	-.42	.23
IC	Yes	.01	.92	1.96	80.00	.03	.05	.53	.27	-.01	1.08

5.4 Learning Performance

Before testing the hypotheses, it is checked whether both learning media have fulfilled their purpose of knowledge transfer. A review of the overall results of the pre- and post-tests shows that both groups have increased their knowledge: Video-group $t(43) = -8.43$ ($p < .001$, Cohen's $d = 1.27$) and textbook-group: $t(45) = -8.47$ ($p < .001$, Cohen's $d = 1.25$). At the same time, it can be noticed that the two groups present a crucial difference in the results of the pre-test, despite randomization, as shown in Fig. 4. The four outliers in the post-test of the video-group, marked with an asterisk or circle in Fig. 4, are excluded for further analysis.

The textbook-group has a higher mean and a smaller interquartile range in the pre-test. After the intervention, the results of the post-tests have experienced an alignment. In order to find out the reasons for the large variations in the pre-test and thus possible influencing factors, a further analysis.

To avoid that the groups already differ significantly in their knowledge before the short intervention, the group was homogenised by forming twin pairs so that both groups start the experiment in the same way (video-group and textbook-group n = 21). The single factor analysis of variance with repeated measures (pre- and post-test) shows that

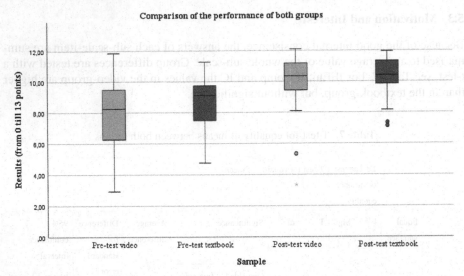

Fig. 4. Comparison of the performance of both groups as boxplot-diagram

both groups learned significantly with a large effect of .80 according to Cohen [38]. The following Fig. 5 shows the performance increase over the pre- and post-test of both groups.

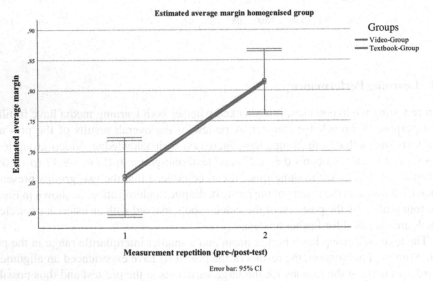

Fig. 5. Estimated average margin homogenised group

Since both homogeneous groups learn approximately equal amounts (see Fig. 5), no differences in the learning medium can be observed. A possible cause could be the high level of prior knowledge of the test persons.

Table 8. Descriptive statistics of the adjusted sample

	Pre-test		Post-test		
	M	SD	M	SD	N
Video-group	6.39	.67	10.29	0.96	16
Textbook-group	6.99	.90	9.75	1.14	16

Therefore, the sample is adjusted by regarding the previous knowledge in order to show the effects of the learning medium. Only probands below the total average of 8.27 (n = 90) are considered and outliers with a score below 5.0 (n = 5) were eliminated. The following Table 8 shows the descriptive statistics of the adjusted group. The video-group shows a larger increase of performance ($\Delta M = 3.73$) than the textbook-group ($\Delta M = 2.76$).

A single factor analysis of variance with repeated measures (pre- and post-test) is carried out with the adjusted data. It is determined that there was a significant performance increase of both groups over the time (p < .001 < .05; Cohen's d = 1.9). In the comparison of the two media, the video-group also shows a significant increase of performance (p = .038 < .05; Cohen's d = .0137). The following Fig. 6 shows the increase in performance of the adjusted groups.

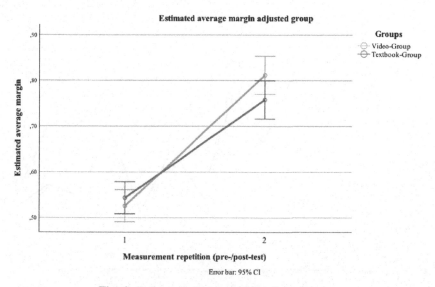

Fig. 6. Estimated average margin adjusted group

In the following, the groups are compared across the 13 performance items, as illustrated in Table 9.

The following Fig. 7 shows the average values of the groups for the individual items in the pre- and post-test. Questions Q8, Q10 and Q11 are particularly to be emphasised

Table 9. Average values of the groups for the individual items in the pre- and post-test

	Q1	Q2	Q3	Q4	Q5	Q6	Q7	Q8	Q9	Q10	Q11	Q12	Q13
Video-group (Pre-test), n = 16	.78	1.00	.63	.89	.67	.88	.27	.44	.17	.53	.13	.31	.15
Textbook-group (Pre-test), n = 16	.69	1.00	.70	.93	.55	.79	.27	.52	.19	.63	.27	.33	.21
Video-group (Post-test), n = 16	.83	1.00	.98	1.00	.84	1.00	.83	.75	.67	.97	.75	.56	.36
Textbook-group (Post-test), n = 16	.66	.94	.97	1.00	.84	.98	.81	.64	.64	.81	.65	.64	.28
Δ Video-group	.06	.00	.35	.13	.19	.13	.57	.32	.53	.44	.61	.28	.18
Δ Textbook-group	-.03	-.06	.27	.07	.30	.19	.54	.13	.45	.19	.38	.31	.06

for the video-group as there is a high increase in knowledge compared to the textbook-group. These three items have in common that they measure application knowledge, see Table 4.

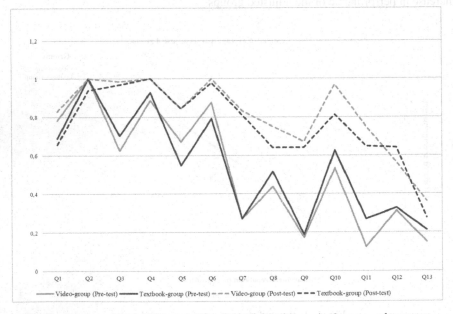

Fig. 7. Average scores of the groups for the individual items in the pre- and post-test

An analysis of variance was carried out with the adjusted data. It was determined that there was no significance between the groups.

6 Discussion

During the analysis of the findings of this short intervention, several aspects emerged which are discussed in the following section.

Regarding the sample, receiving 0.5 ECTS-point might lead to the fact that the sample also includes people who do not belong to the total population. Moreover, the randomization did not take into account the prior knowledge of the design model, which led to differences in the groups in the pre-test, so that adjusted groups were defined for the further analysis in this paper. It is therefore difficult to transfer the results to the general population.

The lack of influence of previous lecture attendance for the pre-test is an indication that knowledge transfer in relation to the design model needs to be improved. Thus, it was a good decision to design a self-study-video as a new learning medium. At the same time, it is noticeable that mostly those people attend a lecture twice who were unsuccessful in the corresponding examination.

The literature points out some design principles that should be considered when creating learning videos. For example, in this short intervention, the following were not considered sufficiently: Videos should be interactive, they can be successful if skills are developed in the videos and if they are used as a supplement to existing learning material [31]. Furthermore, the self-study-video would be more effective when including an assessment, for example by integrating control questions [32, 33]. By using digital storytelling - the processing of knowledge in the form of a story - as a tool, the design can also bring additional enjoyment and increase motivation [46]. Adding appropriate embedded gamification elements and interactive components to learning videos can also be helpful [47].

The CLT has been taken into account in general, but the computer voice can lead to further load, which can have a negative effect on motivation and performance. This is revealed by the analysis of the open question, because the computer-generated voices were found to be inconvenient. However, these voices are necessary to keep the effort to create the self-study-video proportionate to reduce barriers to future educational approaches. As a positive aspect, the guiding through the self-study-video by the virtual characters makes the learning objectives clearer than written sentences. This can be deduced from the greater values of the video-group for the item "the learning objectives were clear and comprehensible".

Overall, considering the design, it is important that learning media encourage the students to an intensive cognitive engagement [48].

In the context of the short intervention, part of the intrinsic motivation is measured, but extrinsic motivation cannot completely be excluded by the achievement of half an ECTS point. This might be a reason, why no significant differences between the groups regarding intrinsic motivation were achieved.

Regarding the measurement of motivation, it needs to be taken into account that despite the use of a validated construct, only a few items were asked. However, this is necessary in order to fit to the self-study-video. The measurement of value-based valence (IV) can be considered as successful based on the acceptable value of Cronbach's α. For IEEnj, IEComp and IC the values in the video-group are greater than in the textbook-group, but without significance. This implies that the enjoyment, competence and self-determination are perceived as larger in the video-group.

The aim of the short intervention was to improve the model-related safety knowledge of occupational safety, which was investigated via the learning performance. In the following, this measurement is critically reviewed.

Adjusting the sample according to prior knowledge reduced the sample and must be regarded as a limitation. For further evaluation of the performance, other effects could be excluded through this adjustment. However, a significant increase in performance for the video-group was observed in this short intervention. The video has particular strengths in relation to application-oriented knowledge items.

Based on the results, H1 cannot be verified due to the low significance. According to the results of the performance items in the adjusted sample, H2 can be verified with a significance.

Although the examined video was a singular digitalisation of analogue data, it is apparent that for digital transformation and taking into account design elements, didactic principles and the results of this study, further approaches are worthwhile.

7   Conclusion and Outlook

University teaching is still dominated by frontal teaching [20]. The aim of this study is to improve learning performance of the design model of protective measures, examining the increase in knowledge and motivation.

The self-study-video has a positive effect for the increase of knowledge and the adjusted video-group is more successful than the textbook-group in the post-test, especially for application-related topics. With regard to the intention to improve the teaching of safety-relevant models, this has been a success and can therefore also be considered for other models in the future.

However, the self-study-video is not as motivating as expected. This may be due to the disturbing computer-generated voices. Therefore, this study should be repeated with a human voice for the audio track. When repeating this study, the groups must be homogeneously readjusted after the pre-test. Thus, only participants who can show an increase in knowledge are considered. Furthermore, by integrating control questions into the video, motivation could be increased.

The fact that digital media alone does not improve the learning performance can be confirmed by general studies what requires a content-related foundation for the use of media [48]. Learning media should be systematically embedded in an adequate learning arrangement.

Since this is only a short-term intervention, no long-term results are available, which results in a demand for future research.

In addition, further research is needed regarding teaching efficiency for safety-related concepts and models. The potential of digital transformation regarding learning media to improve model-related safety knowledge should also be further investigated.

Acknowledgement. We would like to thank Peer Leske[2] for his support in the statistical analysis.

References

1. Bravo, E., Amante, B., Simo, P., Enache, M., Fernandez, V.: Video as a new teaching tool to increase student motivation. In: Global Engineering Education Conference, pp. 638–642 (2011)
2. Findeisen, S., Horn, S., Seifried, J.: Lernen durch Videos – Empirische Befunde zur Gestaltung von Erklärvideos. MedienPädagogik, pp. 16–36 (2019). https://doi.org/10.21240/mpaed/00/2019.10.01.X
3. Marx, R.D., Frost, P.J.: Toward optimal use of video in management education: examining the evidence. J. Manag. Dev. **17**(4), 243–250. https://doi.org/10.1108/02621719810210154
4. Kahl, A. (ed.) Arbeitssicherheit. Fachliche Grundlagen. Erich Schmidt Verlag, Berlin (2019)
5. Bergische Universität Wuppertal: Modulhandbuch zu der Prüfungsordnung Studiengang Sicherheitstechnik mit dem Abschluss Bachelor of Science (2020). https://bscw.uni-wuppertal.de/pub/bscw.cgi/d11908678/20200818_MH_Sicherheitstechnik_BSc.pdf
6. Jugend / YouTube / Kulturelle Bildung. Horizont 2019. Studie: Eine repräsentative Umfrage unter 12- bis 19-Jährigen zur Nutzung kultureller Bildungsangebote an digitalen Kulturorten, Essen (2019). https://www.bosch-stiftung.de/sites/default/files/publications/pdf/2019-06/Studie_Jugend%20Youtube%20Kulturelle%20Bildung%202019.pdf. Accessed 18 Jan 2023
7. Breitenbach, A.: Digitale Lehre in Zeiten von Covid-19: Risiken und Chancen (2021)
8. Merkt, M., Schwan, S.: Lernen mit digitalen Videos. Psychologische Rundschau (2016). https://doi.org/10.1026/0033-3042/a000301
9. MKW NRW: Vernetzte Hochschulen: Digitalisierung von Studium, Lehre und Forschung. https://www.mkw.nrw/digitalisierung. Accessed 18 Jan 2023
10. Bergische Universität Wuppertal: Digitalisierungsstrategie der Bergischen Universität Wuppertal (2022). https://uniservice-dt.uni-wuppertal.de/fileadmin/uniservicedt/Strategie_Digitalisierung.pdf. Accessed 1 Dec 2022
11. Das Europäische Parlament und der Rat der Europäischen Union: Richtlinie 2006/42/EG des Europäischen Parlamente und des Rates. Maschinenrichtlinie (2006)
12. Bundestag: Gesetz über die Durchführung von Maßnahmen des Arbeitsschutzes zur Verbesserung der Sicherheit und des Gesundheitsschutzes der Beschäftigten bei der Arbeit. ArbSchG (1996)
13. Kahl, A.; Grzegorski, E.; Waldorf, J.; Bier, M.; Hafner, F.; Hanning, N.: Das Gestaltungsmodell. Ergänzendes Video zum Lehrbuch "Arbeitssicherheit - Fachliche Grundlagen" (2022). https://www.arbeitssicherheit.uni-wuppertal.de/de/lehre/lehrvideos/
14. Ramdhani, M.A., Muhammadiyah, H.: the criteria of learning media selection for character education in higher education. In: International Conference of Islamic Education in Southeast Asia (2015)
15. Puspitarini, Y.D., Hanif, M.: Using learning media to increase learning motivation in elementary school. Anatol. J. Educ. (2019). https://doi.org/10.29333/aje.2019.426a
16. Petko, D.: Neue Medien -- Neue Lehrmittel? Potenziale und Herausforderungen bei der Entwicklung digitaler Lehr- und Lernmedien. Beiträge zur Lehrerbildung (2010). https://doi.org/10.25656/01:13730
17. Tulodziecki, G.: Entwicklung von Medienkompetenz als Erziehungs- und Bildungsaufgabe. Pädagogische Rundschau (1998). https://doi.org/10.25656/01:1482
18. Harwardt, M.: Digitalisierung und digitale Transformation. In: Management der digitalen Transformation, pp. 1–16. Springer, Wiesbaden (2019). https://doi.org/10.1007/978-3-658-27337-8_1
19. Brünken, R., Seufert, T.: Wissenserwerb mit digitalen Medien. In: Online-Lernen. Handbuch für Wissenschaft und Praxis, pp. 105–114. Oldenbourg, München (2009)

20. Kandlbinder, K.: Lehr- und Lernvideos – Medieneinsatz und -produktion. In: Noller, J., Beitz-Radzio, C., Kugelmann, D., Sontheimer, S., Westerholz, S. (eds.) Studierendenzentrierte Hochschullehre. PH, pp. 169–177. Springer, Wiesbaden (2021). https://doi.org/10.1007/978-3-658-32205-2_10

21. Vollstädt, W.: Die zukünftige Entwicklung von Lehr und Lemmedien. In: Vollstädt, W. (ed.) Zur Zukunft der Lehr - und Lernmedien in der Schule, pp. 39–82. VS Verlag für Sozialwissenschaften, Wiesbaden (2003)

22. Schön, S.: Klappe zu! Film ab! – Gute Lernvideos kinderleicht erstellen. In: Pauschenwein, J. (ed.) Lernen mit Videos und Spielen. Tagungsband zum 12. E-Learning Tag der FH Joanneum am 18.9.2013, pp. 3–10. FH Joanneum, Graz (2013)

23. Brame, C.J.: Effective educational videos: principles and guidelines for maximizing student learning from video content. CBE Life Sci. Educ. (2016). https://doi.org/10.1187/cbe.16-03-0125

24. Mayer, R.E., Moreno, R.: Nine ways to reduce cognitive load in multimedia learning. Educ. Psychol. (2003). https://doi.org/10.1207/S15326985EP3801_6

25. Sweller, J., Ayres, P., Kalyuga, S.: Cognitive load theory. In: Explorations in the Learning Sciences, Instructional Systems and Performance Technologies Ser. Springer, Heidelberg (2011). https://doi.org/10.1007/978-1-4419-8126-4

26. van Merriënboer, J.J.G., Sweller, J.: Cognitive load theory and complex learning: recent developments and future directions. Educ. Psychol. Rev. (2005). https://doi.org/10.1007/s10648-005-3951-0

27. Clark, R.C.: E-learning and the science of instruction. In: Proven Guidelines for Consumers and Designers of Multimedia Learning. Wiley (2016)

28. Homer, B.D., Plass, J.L., Blake, L.: The effects of video on cognitive load and social presence in multimedia-learning. Comput. Hum. Behav. (2008). https://doi.org/10.1016/j.chb.2007.02.009

29. Krapp, A.: Interest, motivation and learning: an educational-psychological perspective. Eur. J. Psychol. Educ. **14**, 23–40 (1999)

30. Schiefele, U., Krapp, A., Schreyer, I.: Metaanalyse des Zusammenhangs von Interesse und schulischer Leistung. Zeitschrift für Entwicklungspsychologie und Pädagogische Psychologie, pp. 120–148 (1993)

31. Noetel, M., et al.: Video improves learning in higher education: a systematic review. Rev. Educ. Res. (2021). https://doi.org/10.3102/0034654321990713

32. Sailer, M., Figas, P.: Umgedrehte Hochschullehre. Eine Experimentalstudie zur Rolle von Lernvideos und aktivem Lernen im Flipped Teaching. die hochschullehre, pp. 317–337 (2018)

33. Gross, D., Pietri, E.S., Anderson, G., Moyano-Camihort, K., Graham, M.J.: Increased preclass preparation underlies student outcome improvement in the flipped classroom. CBE Life Sci. Educ. (2015). https://doi.org/10.1187/cbe.15-02-0040

34. Ismail, M.E., Irwan Mahazir, I., Othman, H., Amiruddin, M.H., Ariffin, A.: The use of animation video in teaching to enhance the imagination and visualization of student in engineering drawing. IOP Conf. Ser. Mater. Sci. Eng. (2017). https://doi.org/10.1088/1757-899X/203/1/012023

35. Hattermann, M., Salle, A., Bärtl, M., Hofrichter, R.: Instruktionale Texte und Lernvideos – Konzeption und Evaluation zweier multimedialer Lernformate. In: Biehler, R., Eichler, A., Hochmuth, R., Rach, S., Schaper, N. (eds.) Lehrinnovationen in der Hochschulmathematik. KSHLM, pp. 399–436. Springer, Heidelberg (2021). https://doi.org/10.1007/978-3-662-62854-6_17

36. Animaker Inc.: Animaker. Swiss Army knife of creativity. https://www.animaker.com/features. Accessed 2 Feb 2023

37. Deci, E.L., Ryan, R.M.: Intrinsic motivation inventory (IMI) Scale description (2010). https://selfdeterminationtheory.org/intrinsic-motivation-inventory/. Accessed 5 Jan 2023

38. Cohen, J.: Statistical Power Analysis for the Behavioral Sciences. Routledge (1988)
39. Tsigilis, N., Theodosiou, A.: Temporal Stability of the Intrinsic Motivation Inventory. PMS (2003). https://doi.org/10.2466/PMS.97.4.271-280
40. McAuley, E., Duncan, T., Tammen, V.V.: Psychometric properties of the Intrinsic Motivation Inventory in a competitive sport setting: a confirmatory factor analysis. Res. Q. Exer. Sport (1989). https://doi.org/10.1080/02701367.1989.10607413
41. Monteiro, V., Mata, L., Peixoto, F.: Intrinsic motivation inventory: psychometric properties in the context of first language and mathematics learning. Psicol. Reflex. Crit. (2015). https://doi.org/10.1590/1678-7153.201528302
42. Ryan, R.M., Deci, E.L.: Overview of self-determination theory: an organismic dialectical perspective. In: Deci, E.L., Ryan, R.M. (eds.) Handbook of self-determination research, Kapitel 1. University of Rochester Press, Rochester (2004)
43. Blanz, M.: Forschungsmethoden und Statistik für die Soziale Arbeit. Kohlhammer-Verlag, Grundlagen und Anwendungen (2021)
44. Griffin, M.A., Neal, A.: Perceptions of safety at work: a framework for linking safety climate to safety performance, knowledge, and motivation. J. Occup. Health Psychol. (2000). https://doi.org/10.1037//1076-8998.5.3.347
45. Bloom, B.S., Engelhart, M.D., Furst, E.J., Hill, W.H., Kratwohl, D.R.: Taxonomy of Educational Objectives. Handbook 1 - Cognitive Domain (1956)
46. Jahn, D., Tress, D., Attenberger, C., Chmel, L.: Lernvideos können mehr als nur Erklären: Eine Studie zum Einsatz von narrativen Film-Ankern in einer hochschuldidaktischen Online-Weiterbildung. In: Buchner, J., Freisleben-Teutscher, C.F., Haag, J., Rauscher, E. (eds.) Inverted classroom. Vielfältiges Lernen: Begleitband zur 7. Konferenz Inverted Classroom and Beyond 2018, FH St. Pölten, 20. & 21. Februar 2018, pp. 149–164. ikon VerlagsGesmbH, Brunn am Gebirge (2018)
47. Weinert, T., Benner, D., Dickhaut, E., Janson, A., Schöbel, S., Leimeister, J.M.: HMD Praxis der Wirtschaftsinformatik **58**(6), 1483–1503 (2021). https://doi.org/10.1365/s40702-021-00798-w
48. Kerres, M.: Medienentscheidungen in der Unterrichtsplanung. Zu Wirkungsargumenten und Begründungen des didaktischen Einsatzes digitaler Medien. Bildung und Erziehung **53**, 19–39 (2000)

An AI-Based Action Detection UAV System to Improve Firefighter Safety

Hong Wang[1], Yuan Feng[2], Xu Huang[2], and Wenbin Guo[3]([✉])

[1] School of Construction Machinery, Chang'an University, Xi'an 710064, China
hong.wang@chd.edu.cn
[2] Department of Mechanical and Aerospace, University of Missouri, Columbia, MO 65203, USA
{yfzc8,xuhuang}@mail.missouri.edu
[3] Digital Worlds Institute, University of Florida, Gainesville, FL 32611, USA
wenbin@digitalworlds.ufl.edu

Abstract. Human hazardous fires can inflict massive harm to life, property, and the environment. Close contact with fire sources threatens firefighters' lives who are critical first responders to fire suppression and rescue. Unmanned aerial vehicles (UAVs) are recently introduced to improve firefighters' performance by monitoring fire characteristics and inferring trajectory. Some UAVs studies used artificial intelligence (AI) for pattern recognition for wildfire prevention and other relevant tasks. However, how to coordinate firefighters is equally important and needs to be explored. Therefore, this research offers an analysis and comparison of AI-based computer vision methods that can annotate human movement automatically. This study proposes to use UAVs combined with AI-based human motion detection to recognize firefighters' action patterns. Based on existing human motion datasets of firefighting videos, we have successfully trained a supervised machine learning algorithm recognizing firefighters' forward movement and water splashing actions. The trained model was tested in the existing video and reached an 81.55% accuracy rate. Applying this model in the UAV system is able to improve firefighters' functioning and safeguard their lives.

Keywords: Artificial intelligence · Human motion classification · Laban movement analysis

1 Introduction

Human hazardous fires can inflict massive harm to life, property, and the environment [1]. According to National Fire Protection Association (NFPA), the United States had more than 1.35 million fires responded by local fire departments in 2021, which caused 3,800 death, 14,700 injuries and a property damage cost of $15.9 billion [2]. From 2001 to 2020, more than 68,000 wildfires were recorded and they caused average of 7 million acres burned per year. Large amounts of fine particulate matter and carbon monoxide are emitted by wildfires, resulting in air pollution and leading to many health issues [3]. Fires fighting is considered crucial preserving natural resources and ensuring personal and property safety.

V. G. Duffy (Ed.): HCII 2023, LNCS 14028, pp. 632–641, 2023.
https://doi.org/10.1007/978-3-031-35741-1_44

Close contact with fire sources threatens firefighters' lives who are critical first responders to fire suppression and rescue. Early fire detection and ongoing monitoring of fires can offer great help to firefighters and reduce casualties. With advancements of technologies, the detection and monitoring system now primarily rely on ground-based systems, human piloted aircrafts, and satellite-based systems [4]. Ground monitoring system is constrained by the terrain so the surveillance ranges are limited. Aircraft crews must include people with fire monitoring or detection experiences. And hazardous fire environment can be a risk for human pilots [5]. Satellites can quickly acquire images of fires in a wide area, but the image resolution and frequency of images taken are too low [6].

Unmanned aerial vehicles (UAVs) are recently introduced to improve firefighters' performance by monitoring fire characteristics and inferring trajectory [7, 8]. Compared with the three systems mentioned above, UAVs have advantages in better deployment flexibility, lower cost, long detection range, no pilot risk, live and high-resolution images.

Some UAVs studies used artificial intelligence (AI) for pattern recognition for wildfire prevention and other relevant tasks [9–11]. However, how to coordinate firefighters is equally important and needs to be explored. Communication and coordination are critical for firefighters since their work environments are dangerous and dynamic. Their skills of gathering information, optimizing coordination and sensemaking are learned mainly through their experience [12]. To increase the safety and efficiency of firefighters' work, cognitive system engineering focuses more on information flow to make efficient decisions [13].

In this study, we propose to use UAVs combined with AI-based human motion detection to recognize firefighters' action patterns. Based on existing human motion datasets of firefighting videos, we have successfully trained a supervised machine learning algorithm recognizing firefighters' forward movement and water splashing actions. The trained model was tested in the existing video and reached an 81.55% accuracy rate. Applying this model in the UAV system is able to improve firefighters' functioning and safeguard their lives.

2 Related Works

2.1 AI Applications in Firefighting

AI can learn from experience and help solve problems in various scenes, especially in pattern recognition areas. To boot, more and more researchers make AI-based methods play an important role in improving the safety and efficiency of firefighters' work and protecting their lives. DHS and NASA's Jet Propulsion Laboratory developed an AI platform, the Assistant for Understanding Data through Reasoning, Extraction, and Synthesis (AUDREY), which is a real-time system to help firefighters know more information about the environment, receive danger signals and recommendations through sensors, and also get good team communication and collaboration [14, 15]. Another study aims to predict the number of firefighters' interventions between emergency and non-emergency with machine learning methods. They applied XGBoost and LightGBM algorithms for the dataset to predict the type of deployment from 14 different categories in order to help firefighters to be well prepared and assign work efficiently [16]. In addition, the research attempted to analyze the stress of firefighters during a rescue mission and display the alerts to protect their lives. The author proposed that AI methods can study and predict stress among firefighters beforehand further [17]. Moreover, firefighters' action patterns reflect plenty of helpful information during the rescue mission. However, limited research focus on this. With the development of AI-based methods in motion detection, lots of work can be applied in recognizing firefighters' movements.

2.2 UAV Assistance in Firefighting

With the advantages of flexibility, stability, convenience, low cost, multiple functions and without danger to personnel safety, UAVs are competent for difficult tasks in more and more fields. For example, in [18] the author mentioned that one challenge firefighters face is accessing the upper floors of tall buildings, but UAVs can quickly and efficiently reach these areas. They developed a Firefighting UVA with a mechanism for shooting and dropping fire extinguishing balls that helps firefighters decrease the spread of fire. Applying UAVs for forest fire detection and monitoring have make a great progress recent years. One notable study generated a powerful UAV which is long-range, long-endurance, solar-powered, and with flight autonomy and pattern recognition. The real-time images and advice of fire could be provided to firefighters [19]. In order to diversify the functions of UAVs and make them more accurate, researchers try to combine them with other sciences to derive functions for more scenarios. One study applied optical remote sensing techniques and UAVs to detect the forest fire. Image processing with color and motion features from the camera on a UAV and color-based fire detection algorithm shows good performance in improving the accuracy of fire detection [11]. Along with, in [20] the author proposed an automatic forest firefighting monitoring system based on the combination of UAV and remote sensing. Their system with remote sensing algorithms and image processing techniques shows good performance on fire prediction and response. Moreover, the applications of UAVs combined with AI-based methods become more and more popular.

2.3 AI-Based UAV Applications

Combining UAVs and AI techniques together can achieve higher efficiency and safety during the difficult rescue tasks. Several research papers in last three years have compassed the topic to design and develop smart UAVs assistance for firefighters. A study developed in [21] construct a UAV with AI and image processing to monitor and estimate people stuck by fire, and support firefighters. Their study contributes to decrease loss of lives. Another study aims to detect early wildfire with deep learning-based computer vision algorithms and UAVs in order to prevent and reduce the loss of lives and resources. In their research, the author tried and compared many different computer vision algorithms and showed the great potential of the applications in firefighting combined with UAVs [22].

Hence, the contribution and novelty of this work lies in the combination of popular studies, by using AI-based motion detection algorithms and UAV to detect firefighters' different actions in order to provide useful information for firefighters to protect their safety and improve the rescue efficiency.

Several researches focus on the fire detection, environment monitor and analysis with the combination of AI and UAVs, while few of present studies focus on firefighters' motion detection, which could be meaningful during the rescue. In this research, we intend to build a UAV system, which includes software part and hardware platform, to realize real-time image collection and the identification of firefighters' action. In this paper, we mainly introduce the software part, which include the models we built with different machine learning and deep learning methods. In our further work, we will build a hardware platform, which will be built on Nvidia Jetson Nano, which is a microcomputer with powerful cores, a mini camera and STM32 Nucleo board, which is used for controlling the response of UAV. Then, we will apply the models we built in this paper on our UAV hardware platform to realize whole pipeline of real-time detection.

3   Methods

Like most AI-based methods, our approach comprised of three key stages: 1) Data preparation, 2) Training and testing, 3) Automated annotation.

In this project, we trained five traditional machine learning models and one deep neural network to receive a video sequence as input and recognize the firefighter action changes. A total of 95 videos were collected in the publicly available datasets, including two actions moving forward and water splashing. The dataset was split into a 90:10 ratio, 85 videos were used for training the model, and 10 videos were tested for models' accuracy. Table 1 shows the video distribution for train and test sets.

Table 1. Dataset

Action	Train set videos	Test set videos
Moving Forward	35	5
Water Splashing	50	5

Mediapipe is a framework to detect the human key points of skeleton joints and a total of thirty-three key points for the human skeleton [23]. The human skeleton is detected frame by frame and classified into two actions to test the model performance.

Five traditional machine learning models include Naïve Bayes, Support Vector Machines (SVM), Logistic regression, Decision tree and Random forest.

Naïve Bayes can be used for various tasks, including classification and text classification. There are different variations of the algorithm, including the Gaussian Naive Bayes, Multinomial Naive Bayes, and Bernoulli Naive Bayes.

SVM is a type of supervised learning algorithm that can be used for classification, regression, and outlier detection. The algorithm aims to find the hyperplane in a high-dimensional feature space that best separates the data into classes, or predicts the target value for regression.

Logistic regression is used for binary classification problems. Logistic regression is a fast and simple algorithm to implement and can provide good results in many practical problems, especially when the relastionship between the independent variables and the target variable is approximately linear.

Decision tree is a tree-like model used for supervised learning and decision making. It is a type of algorithm that splits the data into smaller subsets based on certain conditions, with each split represented as a node in the tree. The splits are chosen based on the feature that maximizes the information gain, which measures the reduction in entropy or uncertainty of the target variable. Decision Trees can handle both categorical and numerical features, and can be used for classification and regression tasks.

Random forest is an ensemble learning method that combines multiple decision trees to make a prediction. It is a type of algorithm used for both classification and regression tasks. This combination of individual trees helps to reduce the variance and overfitting that can occur in a single decision tree, leading to improved accuracy and stability of the model.

Deep neural network is feed forward neural network that consists of an input layer, one or multiple hidden layers, and an output layer. The information flows only in one direction, from input to output, without forming a cycle. Each layer processes the input data and passes it on to the next layer, until the final output is produced. Each layer is composed of multiple neurons, and each neuron performs a simple computation on the weighted sum of its inputs and produces an output. The weights of the connections between neurons and the biases of each neuron are learned through the training process using an optimization algorithm, such as gradient descent.

For our training dataset, we sourced firefighter training and live videos from online resources for evaluation and testing purposes. 85 randomly selected videos from the collected dataset were used for supervised learning, while the remaining 10 were reserved for testing. To streamline the prototyping phase, the annotation system was coded in Python utilizing the Scikit-learn library. The system was developed and tested on a 2080 Ti GPU.

The performance was evaluated based on precision, recall, accuracy, and F1 scores. Precision reflects the classifier's ability to correctly identify negative samples, while recall represents its ability to detect positive samples, with a maximum score of 1. The F1 score, calculated as the harmonic mean of precision and recall, gives equal weight to both metrics and ranges from 0–1. The formulas are as follows:

$$\text{Precision} = \text{TP}/\left(\text{TP} + \text{FP}\right) \tag{1}$$

$$\text{Recall} = \text{TP}/\left(\text{TP} + \text{FN}\right) \tag{2}$$

$$\text{Accuracy} = \left(\text{TP} + \text{TN}\right)/\left(\text{TP} + \text{TN} + \text{FP} + \text{FN}\right) \tag{3}$$

TP = True Positive, TN = True Negative,
FP = False Positive, FN = False Negative

$$\text{F1 score} = 2 * \left(\text{precision} * \text{recall}\right)/\left(\text{precision} + \text{recall}\right) \tag{4}$$

Finally, the automated annotation was visualized using the Matplotlib library, which is a comprehensive tool for creating dynamic and interactive visualizations.

4   Results

Figure 1 compares the results of six machine learning algorithms, including Naïve Bayes, SVM, logistic regression, decision tree, random forest, and deep neural network. The results demonstrate that the deep neural network achieves the highest accuracy, 81.55%.

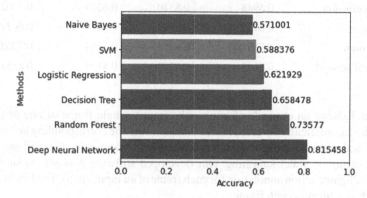

Fig. 1.   Machine learning algorithms comparison

Figure 2 shows the confusion matrix for each machine learning method. The diagonal elements are correctly predicted actions. Deep neural network has the advantages in the true positive compared with other traditional machine learning models (Table 2).

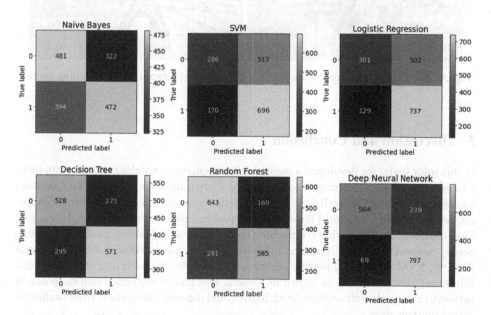

Fig. 2.   Confusion matrix of each Laban movement dimension

Table 2. Firefighter action annotation using six machine learning algorithms

Algorithms	Precision	Recall	Accuracy	F1 score
Naïve Bayes	0.5945	0.5450	0.5710	0.5687
SVM	0.5738	0.8037	0.5884	0.6696
Logistic regression	0.5948	0.8510	0.6219	0.7002
Decision tree	0.6749	0.6594	0.6585	0.6671
Random forest	0.7852	0.6755	0.7358	0.7263
Deep neural network	0.7693	0.9203	0.8155	0.8381

Figure 3 shows an example of our results from a single frame of one of the input videos. The automatically detected human skeleton and the corresponding key points are superimposed on the image. For the left frame annotation is moving forward and the right frame annotation is water splashing. Our developed software was able to successfully produce firefighter action annotation for each frame of an input video. The labels reflected the firefighter action in each frame.

Fig. 3. The automated annotation on videos. Left = Moving forward, Right = Putting out fire

5   Discussion and Conclusion

In this pilot study, we developed a method for recognizing firefighter actions from input videos using machine learning algorithms. The study trained and compared six machine learning algorithms (Naïve Bayes, SVM, logistic regression, decision tree, random forest, and deep neural network) through supervised learning on existing firefighter action video datasets. By comparing six machine learning and deep learning methods, the deep neural network had the highest accuracy of 81.55% compared with Naïve Bayes at 57.10%, SVM at 58.84%, logistic regression at 62.19%, decision tree at 65.85%, and Random forest at 73.58% as shown in Table 2. Our results suggested that deep neural networks can work well on high-level, hidden, and meaningful features from firefighter action classification.

In our observation of the confusion matrix, the deep neural network only had 69 false negatives (true label 1 with predicted label 0) and 239 false positives (true label 0 with predicted label 1). Both false negative predictions were lower than those of other five machine learning methods. In addition, SVM had 170 false negatives and 517 false positives. Logistic regression had 129 false negatives and 502 false positives. Besides having the highest false rate, these two methods also had an imbalanced matrix. The other three methods (Naïve Bayes, random forest, SVM, logistic regression, and decision tree) performed relatively well on the confusion matrix of firefighter action detection. The mechanism of these models needs to be further analyzed in future works.

Moreover, we analyzed the false prediction. The phenomenon might be explained by multiple firefighters in the same frame image. What's more, some images in the frames show the firefighters' feet or arms covered by equipment, fire engines and other firefighters' body. These may lead to zero value with movement analysis. It is difficult for feature extraction if firefighters with covered persons.

However, despite these limited data, our proposed deep neural network still has relatively high accuracy for AI-based human motion detection to recognize firefighters' action patterns (forward and putting out fire movement). These results demonstrated that firefighter action analysis could be potentially automated using machine learning algorithms. These algorithms operate on raw input videos and AI-driven standardized human motion evaluation systems can be developed.

Our results indicated that such AI-driven movement classification could enable fully automated reporting in firefighter action classification.

6 Future Work

The next step includes applying the action detection model on Jetson Nano. Jetson Nano is a small, powerful computer that can be installed on a UAV and runs CNN. Online action detection with user feedback may further improve performance. Moreover, the object tracking and path planning model can be extended to the UAV as sequences of actions. Further applications like multi-task allocation and trajectory planning can be applied to a fleet of UAVs. These works are involved in complex fire rescue situations and show the full potential of saving firefighters' lives by improving putting fire efficiency.

References

1. Seraj, E., Silva, A., Gombolay, M.: Safe Coordination of Human-Robot Firefighting Teams (2019). https://arxiv.org/abs/1903.06847
2. Hall, S., Evarts, B.: Fire loss in the United States during 2021. National Fire Protection Association (2022)
3. NOAA National Centers for Environmental Information, Monthly Wildfires Report for Annual 2022, published online January 2023. https://www.ncei.noaa.gov/access/monitoring/monthly-report/fire/202213. Accessed 10 Feb 2023
4. Den Breejen, E., et al.: Autonomous forest fire detection, pp. 2003–2012. ADAI-Associacao para o Desenvolvimento da Aerodinamica Industrial, Coimbra (1998)
5. Merino, L., Caballero, F., Martinez-de Dios, J.R., Ollero, A.: Cooperative fire detection using unmanned aerial vehicles. In: Proceedings of the 2005 IEEE International Conference on Robotics and Automation, pp. 1884–1889. IEEE (2005)

6. Sujit, P.B., Kingston, D., Beard, R.: Cooperative forest fire monitoring using multiple UAVs. In: 2007 46th IEEE Conference on Decision and Control, pp. 4875–4880. IEEE (2007)

7. Hrabia, C.E., Hessler, A., Xu, Y., Brehmer, J., Albayrak, S.: EffFeu project: efficient operation of unmanned aerial vehicles for industrial fire fighters. In: DroNet 2018 - Proceedings of the 2018 ACM International Conference on Mobile Systems, Applications and Services, pp. 33–38 (2018). https://doi.org/10.1145/3213526.3213533

8. Seraj, E., Gombolay, M.: Coordinated control of UAVs for human-centered active sensing of wildfires. In: Proceedings of the American Control Conference, 2020-July, pp. 1845–1852 (2020). https://doi.org/10.23919/ACC45564.2020.9147613

9. Luna, M.A., Refaat Ragab, A., Ale Isac, M.S., Flores Pena, P., Cervera, P.C.: A new algorithm using hybrid UAV swarm control system for firefighting dynamical task allocation. In: Conference Proceedings - IEEE International Conference on Systems, Man and Cybernetics, pp. 655–660 (2021). https://doi.org/10.1109/SMC52423.2021.9659275

10. Yfantis, E.A.: A UAV with autonomy, pattern recognition for forest fire prevention, and AI for providing advice to firefighters fighting forest fires. In: 2019 IEEE 9th Annual Computing and Communication Workshop and Conference, CCWC 2019, pp. 409–413 (2019). https://doi.org/10.1109/CCWC.2019.8666471

11. Yuan, C., Liu, Z., Zhang, Y.: Aerial images-based forest fire detection for firefighting using optical remote sensing techniques and unmanned aerial vehicles. J. Intell. Rob. Syst. **88**(2–4), 635–654 (2017). https://doi.org/10.1007/s10846-016-0464-7

12. Toups, Z.O., Kerne, A.: Implicit coordination in firefighting practice: design implications for teaching fire emergency responders. In: Proceedings of the SIGCHI Conference on Human Factors in Computing Systems, pp. 707–716 (2007)

13. Seraj, E., Silva, A., Gombolay, M.: Safe coordination of human-robot firefighting teams. arXiv preprint https://arxiv.org/abs/1903.06847 (2019)

14. Castro, D., New, J.: The promise of artificial intelligence. Center Data Innov. **115**(10), 32–35 (2016)

15. Horowitz, M.C., Allen, G.C., Saravalle, E., Cho, A., Frederick, K., Scharre, P.: Artificial intelligence and international security. Center for a New American Security (2018)

16. Mallouhy, R.E., Guyeux, C., Abou Jaoude, C., Makhoul, A.: Machine learning for predicting firefighters' interventions per type of mission. In: 2022 8th International Conference on Control, Decision and Information Technologies (CoDIT), vol. 1, pp. 1196–1200. IEEE (2022)

17. Raj, J.V., Sarath, T.V.: An IoT based real-time stress detection system for fire-fighters. In: 2019 International Conference on Intelligent Computing and Control Systems (ICCS), pp. 354–360. IEEE (2019)

18. Zadeh, N.R.N., Abdulwakil, A.H., Amar, M.J.R., Durante, B., Santos, C.V.N.R.: Fire-fighting UAV with shooting mechanism of fire extinguishing ball for smart city. Indones. J. Electr. Eng. Comput. Sci **22**, 1320–1326 (2021)

19. Yfantis, E.A. A UAV with autonomy, pattern recognition for forest fire prevention, and AI for providing advice to firefighters fighting forest fires. In: 2019 IEEE 9th Annual Computing and Communication Workshop and Conference (CCWC), pp. 0409–0413. IEEE (2019)

20. Sherstjuk, V., Zharikova, M., Sokol, I.: Forest fire-fighting monitoring system based on UAV team and remote sensing. In: 2018 IEEE 38th International Conference on Electronics and Nanotechnology (ELNANO), pp. 663–668. IEEE (2018)

21. Thakur, A., Kate, O., Malhotra, T.: Design and Development of smart UAV assistance for Firefighters (2021)

22. Bouguettaya, A., Zarzour, H., Taberkit, A.M., Kechida, A.: A review on early wildfire detection from unmanned aerial vehicles using deep learning-based computer vision algorithms. Signal Process. **190**, 108309 (2022)
23. Lugaresi, C., et al.: MediaPipe: A Framework for Building Perception Pipelines (2019). http://arxiv.org/abs/1906.08172

The Effect of Transparency
on Human-Exoskeleton Interaction

Yilin Wang[1] ⓘ, Jing Qiu[2]([⊠]) ⓘ, Hong Cheng[3], Xiuying Hu[1], Peng Xu[4], Jingming Hou[5], and Hongqin Xie[3]

[1] Innovation Center of Nursing Research, Nursing Key Laboratory of Sichuan Province, West China Hospital, Sichuan University, Chengdu 610041, China
[2] School of Mechanical and Electrical Engineering, University of Electronic Science and Technology of China, Chengdu 611731, China
qiujing@uestc.edu.cn
[3] School of Automation Engineering, University of Electronic Science and Technology of China, Chengdu 611731, China
[4] School of Life Science and Technology, University of Electronic Science and Technology of China, Chengdu 611731, China
[5] Department of Rehabilitation, The Southwest Hospital, Third Military Medical University, Chongqing 400038, China

Abstract. The exoskeleton robot is a new type of cooperative robot that forms a typical human-robot system with its wearer. In order to achieve a common task goal, human-exoskeleton cooperative tasks need to integrate natural cooperation. Exoskeleton robots must not only predict the task goals of human partners but also make human partners anticipate their own intentions and perceive the execution of tasks during cooperation. Therefore, studying the transparency of exoskeleton robots plays a very important role in improving the mutual understanding between humans and exoskeletons and enhancing the interoperability and naturalness of human-robot cooperation. In previous studies, we investigated the human-exoskeleton behavioral information transfer path given the lack of an efficient communication mechanism between the wearer and the exoskeleton named AIDER. A tactile feedback method based on the change of vibration intensity was proposed to transmit the current walking state of the human-exoskeleton system to the wearer, and a voice-based interaction method was proposed to express the human-robot behavioral intention. To verify the effectiveness of the above methods, this study analyzed the wearer's mental workload using functional near-infrared spectroscopy while performing the human-exoskeleton walking tasks in the different modes. The results showed that the mental load of the transparency mode (TM) was similar to that of the normal walking mode (NWM). However, the data fluctuated more than in the other two modes in the NTM (non-transparency mode), indicating that the mental workload is heavier than in the other groups. Therefore, transparency can help reduce the mental workload of the wearer. It was shown that transparency plays an important role in the collaboration between humans and robots, which can improve efficiency and trust between the exoskeleton and the wearer.

Keywords: Exoskeleton · Transparency · Human-robot collaboration · Functional near-infrared spectroscopy · Mental workload

V. G. Duffy (Ed.): HCII 2023, LNCS 14028, pp. 642–652, 2023.
https://doi.org/10.1007/978-3-031-35741-1_45

1   Introduction

Transparency was early defined as a physical term. In robotics, transparency refers to the intuitive and explicable principles exhibited by machines to their users. Moreover, it encapsulates the notion that machines are capable of informing their operators in a way that is readily accessible, comprehensible, and effortless. In other words, transparency in robotics is about enabling users to easily manage and interact with complex, automated systems. Machine transparency refers to the ability of humans to effectively communicate information with an agent in order to accurately understand the agent's current goal principle and future state [1, 2]. As humans and robots become more complex themselves and their interactions, so do the decisions they make. As part of a research effort on robots, researchers aim to understand how robots can work collaboratively with humans rather than simply replacing them [3]. Therefore, it becomes more and more difficult for humans and machines to understand each other in highly dynamic environments and complex tasks [2]. As robots transition from tools to human teammates, their models need to be expanded to better support human-machine collaboration, which requires two-way transparency [4]. The U.S. Defense Science Board published a report in 2016 called the Summer Study on Autonomy [5], in which "Observability, predictability, guidance, audibility" and "mutual understanding" are the key problems that cause communication barriers between humans and intelligent systems was proposed. In August 2016, the Defense Advanced Research Projects Agency (DARPA) announced a project called XAI (eXplainable Artificial Intelligence) that highlighted the importance of making intelligent systems easier for humans to understand [6]. In addition, the fourth principle of EPSRC Robotics [7] also mentioned that "Robots are man-made objects. They should not be designed in a deceptive way to take advantage of vulnerable users. Instead, their mechanical nature should be transparent". Therefore, as robots become more intelligent, their self-explanatory mechanisms become more and more important [8]. It is an important task of man-machine collaboration to promote the common understanding of the team. Therefore, in order to realize efficient cooperation between humans and robots, it is necessary not only for the robot to understand what humanity is doing but also for the robot's behavior to be understood by humans. The characteristics of robot communication have a positive impact on the outcome of human-robot interaction, such as the degree of trust situation perception, and the human-robot task performance [10]. Although humans are born with a limited ability to understand others, this ability has evolved and developed in an environment where humans and other animals live together and do not apply to artificial intelligence products [11]. Therefore, the design of intelligent systems such as intelligent robots needs to be transparent to human users [11], which is especially important for specific user-oriented (such as the disabled and elderly) robots [12].

Several types of research indicated that adding transparency to the robot's action selection can help users understand the robot more accurately [11], and at the same time avoid wrongly attributing errors to robots [13]. In our previous research, transparency design for exoskeleton robots was carried out, including auditory feedback [14, 15] and vibration-tactile feedback methods [16], respectively representing the behavioral intention and walking state of the exoskeleton robot, to assist the wearer in understanding the exoskeleton and reducing mental workload. However, how to evaluate machine transparency has not been studied in detail.

Human intelligence combined with an exoskeleton allows the robotic system to perform tasks through human-robot interaction. During the operation of an exoskeleton for the lower limb, we also found an insufficient consideration for the condition of the user, such as mental workload. It is possible to determine the mental workload from mental fatigue measurements, where a high cognitive workload is associated with a higher state of mental fatigue. Roy et al. famously hypothesized in 1890 that when the brain is stimulated locally, the blood flow of the corresponding cortex will increase, resulting in an increase in oxygenated hemoglobin [17]. Therefore, the changes in cerebral blood oxygen can be measured to infer the functional regions of brain nerve activity and to analyze the function and role of each brain region in different tasks. The motor cortex is an area of the cerebral cortex involved in planning, controlling, and executing voluntary movements [18]. The prefrontal cortex is involved in higher cognitive functions such as attention, memory, and problem-solving [19]. Therefore, we theorize that only the motor cortex is involved when a normal person performs a simple, voluntary movement such as walking. When the wearer uses the exoskeleton robot to walk, operation method, machine function, proficiency, task difficulty, and other aspects may stimulate the wearer's "attention", "memory", "problem-solving" and other cognitive functions, which may increase activity in the prefrontal cortex. In order to evaluate the effectiveness of transparency design for the exoskeleton on reducing mental workload, functional near-infrared spectroscopy (fNIRs) was used in this paper to obtain brain activation changes without invasive methods.

2 Method

2.1 Subjects

There were ten male subjects paid for participating in the experiment (mean age 24 ± 2.0 years, height 173 ± 2.5 cm, mean weight 62.0 ± 5.9 kg). None of the subjects suffered from or had a history of psychiatric diseases, hearing impairment, comprehension impairment, or organ injury. This study was approved by the University of Electronic Science and Technology of China's research ethics committee. An informed consent form was signed by all participants after they received written and verbal instructions about the study.

2.2 Material and Devices

The exoskeleton was named AIDER (Fig. 1), and developed by the *Center for Robotics, University of Electronic Science and Technology of China*. It can assist the wearer in complete sitting-to-standing, standing, keeping balance, and walking in community environments.

The fNIRs data of this paper was collected by the device named NirSmart (Fig. 2(a)) of Danyang Huichuang Medical Equipment Co., LTD. The data was processed via NirSpark. In the human brain, the motor cortex is responsible for motor function. The

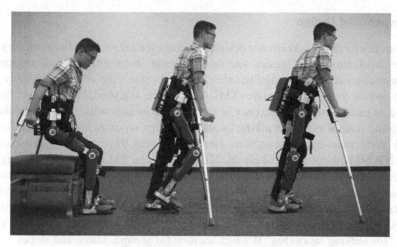

Fig. 1. The exoskeleton AIDER.

prefrontal cortex area is associated with higher cognitive functions such as attention, memory, and problem-solving. Therefore, we selected the motor and prefontal cortex (Fig. 2(b)) to detect the changes in brain hemoglobins during human-robot collaboration tasks. 'S' represents the transmitting probe, and 'D' represents the receiving probe. A transmitting probe and a receiving probe form a channel. A total of 35 channels were set up in our experiment with 16 in the motor cortex and 19 in the prefrontal cortex. The transmitting probe emits a beam of near-infrared light, which is absorbed by the brain and received by the receiving probe. Activation of brain functions is manifested by increased concentration of Oxyhemoglobin (HbO).

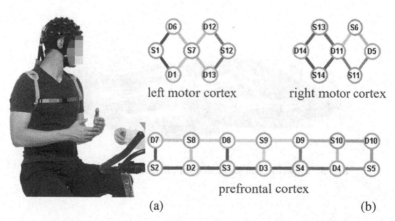

Fig. 2. The NirSmart and detector location. (a) The NirSmart. (b) Detector location.

2.3 Experiment Design

Transparency for the exoskeleton is designed to make the interactions between the wearer and the exoskeleton safer, easier, and more efficient. To evaluate the effectiveness of the transparency design, the significant difference between the non-transparency mode (NTM) and the transparency mode (TM) needed to be analyzed. Furthermore, the final purpose of exoskeleton transparency is to make the wearer walk with an exoskeleton close to the state of normal walking (without wearing an exoskeleton). Therefore, the validity verification experiments were carried out under three modes: normal walking mode (NWM) without an exoskeleton, NTM mode, and TM mode. The walking tasks included three different terrains, which are walking on flat ground, going up and down the stairs, and slopes. The following Table 1 gives a summary of the experiment scheme. The subjects were required to complete walking tasks wearing the exoskeleton on different terrains. Because of the limitations of the laboratory environment, we chose typical terrains for walking tasks (Fig. 3) which include flat ground, stairs, and slopes.

Table 1. The experiment schemes.

Mode	Feature	Terrains	Repetitions
NWM	normal walking (without an exoskeleton)	flat ground, stairs, and slopes	3
NTM	walk with the exoskeleton AIDER without the transparency design		
TM	walk with the exoskeleton AIDER with the transparency design		

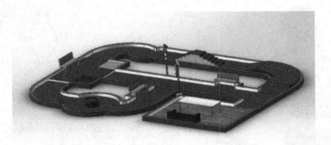

Fig. 3. Experimental scene diagram in laboratory environment

2.4 Data Analysis

The degree of brain activation was calculated from the difference between the near-infrared light density of the transmitting probe and the near-infrared light density of the receiving probe. Firstly, the collected data are preprocessed, including motion arti-fact removal, filtering, blood oxygen calculation and block average. Secondly, *HbO* concentration was calculated via fixed-value modified beer-lamber law [20] (1).

$$\Delta OD^{\lambda_i} = (\varepsilon_{HBO}^{\lambda_i} \Delta C_{HBO} + \varepsilon_{HBO}^{\lambda_i} \Delta C_{HBR}) \times r \times DPF^{\lambda_i} \tag{1}$$

where *OD* was the light density. λ_i was the wavelength that penetrates an optical fiber. ε was the extinction coefficient. C_{HBO} was the oxygenated hemoglobin density. C_{HBR} the deoxyhemoglobin density. *r* was the distance between transmitting and receiving probes. *DPF* was the differential path factor, which was set in [666] in this paper. $r \times DPF$ was how far the light travels.

In order to analyze whether the measured value of the blood oxygen response of a channel is significantly correlated with one of the design variables in the experimental design, the Generalized Linear Models (GLM) were used to generate a task-related design matrix, and then parameter estimation and hypothesis testing were performed on oxygen data. In this paper, the significance level is set at 5%. If $P < 0.05$, the corresponding cortex was significantly activated. The red areas represent significant activation in the cortex ($P \leq 0.05$), where dark red represented the most active ($P \leq 0.01$).

3   Results

After processing the raw data, the changes in *HbO* concentration in each channel during NWM, NTM, and TM were shown in Fig. 4, Fig. 5, and Fig. 6, respectively.

The vertical axis was the concentration of *HbO*, and the abscissa was normalized time. We used color curves to represent changes in *HbO* concentration of each channel. The results showed that when walking in NWM, HbO concentration fluctuates within the range of -0.2 to $0.2\, mmol/L * mm$, which was -0.6 to $0.5\, mmol/L * mm$ in the NTM and -0.25 to $0.25\, mmol/L * mm$ in the TM. It indicated that mental load of the wearer in the NTM is greater than that in the TM. What's more, the mental load in transparency mode is closer to NWM.

We selected the channel with the largest change in *HbO* concentration in the three modes for quantitative analysis. The selected channel of NWM was S2-D2, NTM was S5-D4, and TM was S3-D3. The outliers of the three channels were removed. The *HbO* concentration ranges under the three modes were shown in Fig. 7(a). The median of *HbO* concentration in NWM, NTM, and TM were 0.01722, -0.02833, $-0.007365\, mmol/L*mm$, respectively. In NWM and TM, *HbO* concentration changes were more concentrated, while in NTM, *HbO* concentration distribution was more discrete. The spectrum of *HbO* concentration in three modes is shown in the Fig. 7(b). In NWM and TM, the frequency spectrum periodic variation rule was similar, and the amplitude is close. In the opac-ity mode, the amplitude is relatively large. The *HbO* concentration in the three modes was statistically analyzed by paired sample t-test (Table 2). No difference was found in *HbO* concentration between NWM and TM ($P > 0.05$), which indicated that the mental workload was similar in the two modes. However, a significant difference was observed in NTM - TM and NWM - NTM ($P < 0.05$). The mental load of wearers in the NTM is significantly higher than that in the TM.

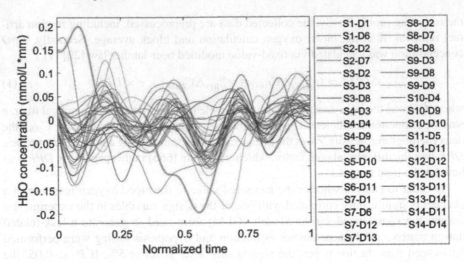

Fig. 4. The changes of *HbO* concentration in NWM.

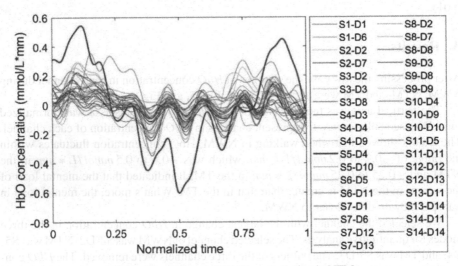

Fig. 5. The changes of *HbO* concentration in NTM.

We analyzed the correlation between brain regions and tasks via GLM analysis (Fig. 8). When the subjects walking in NWM and TM, the most task relevant cortex was the motor cortex (Fig. 8(a) and (c), the deepest red area means significant correlated to tasks), which indicated that the task correlation of the cortex was similar in the two modes. However, the most relevant cortex in NTM (Fig. 8(b)), expressing a high mental workload.

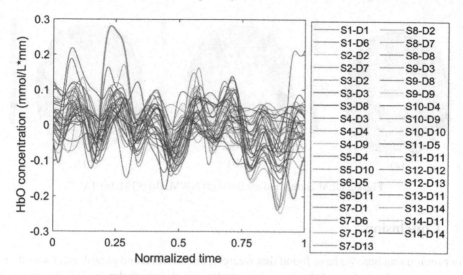

Fig. 6. The changes of *HbO* concentration in TM.

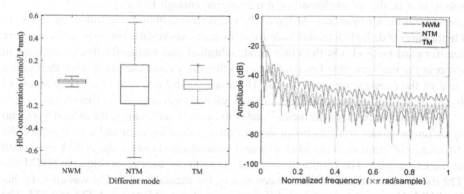

Fig. 7. The channel with the largest change in *HbO* concentration of three modes.

Table 2. The experiment schemes.

Paired samples	Pairing difference			t value	significance
	mean value	standard deviation	mean standard deviation		
NWM-TM	0.002298	0.110063	0.005217	0.440	0.660
NWM-NTM	0.030129	0.248350	0.004639	6.495	0.000
NTM-TM	0.013974	0.251692	0.004701	2.972	0.003

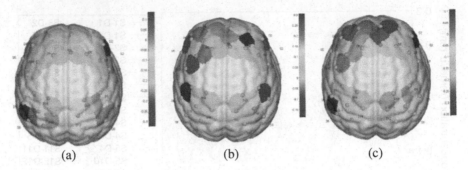

Fig. 8. GLM correlation analysis. (a) NWM. (b) NTM. (c) TM

4 Conclusion

In previous studies, we have found that wearers, both normal and paraplegic, focus their attention on the surface of the foot while walking in the exoskeleton [21]. We guessed that this phenomenon is due to the wearer's lack of understanding of the exoskeleton robot, that is, the exoskeleton is not transparent enough to the wearer. Therefore, we carried out the transparency design of the exoskeleton robot in the follow-up research. On the one hand, the behavioral intention of human-exoskeleton is expressed by auditory feedforward method. On the other hand, vibration and tactile feedback was used to express the man-machine behavior state, so that the wearer can know what the current state of the exoskeleton was [14, 16]. However, we did not verify the effectiveness of transparency design in a real human-exoskeleton system but only in theoretical.

This paper focused on the mental load of the wearer, and analyze the mental workload in different modes via functional near-infrared technology. In order to compare the difference of brain working load with and without exoskeleton, the NWM was added in the experiment. The results showed that the subjects' mental workload in NWM and TM did not have statistical differences, that is, the mental load in TM was close to that in NWM. However, a significant difference was observed between NTM and TM. The GLM analysis results indicated the correlation between the brain cortex and tasks. We found that the most correlated cortex in TM and NWM was the motor cortex, while the prefrontal cortex was most correlated with tasks in the NTM. Therefore, it can be considered that the transparent design of the exoskeleton robot is helpful to enhance the mutual understanding between the wearer and the exoskeleton, thus reducing the mental workload of the wearer.

5 Discussion

In this paper, normal people are recruited as subjects, because we need to detect the brain workload without wearing exoskeleton to compare with TM. At the same time, in order to exclude other factors as much as possible, we recruited male subjects of similar age. Because the male subjects were considered had stronger upper limbs than the females, they might perform better when wearing the exoskeleton robot to complete the walking task. In the future work, we will further validate the effectiveness of the transparency design for the exoskeleton in clinic studies, and recruit subjects with different ages and genders.

fNIRs can measure the changes in oxygenated hemoglobin levels of the human brain. Functional near-infrared technology can detect changes in the concentration of oxygenated hemoglobin in the brain and reflect the extent to which brain regions are related to tasks. Here we found that the most related brain cortex in NWM and TM was the same (motor cortex), and there was no significant difference in HbO concentration in these two modes. However, fNIRs observations can only reflect the effectiveness of transparency design from one level, namely the mental workload. We hope that the transparent design of the exoskeleton can achieve natural human-exoskeleton understanding, efficient human-exoskeleton collaboration, and better performance. Therefore, in addition to reducing wearers' mental workload when using an exoskeleton, the transparency design would also be validated from various aspects, such as subjective feelings, human-exoskeleton effectiveness, behavior analysis, etc.

Acknowledgments. This research project was supported by the key project of the Joint Foundation of the National Natural Science Foundation of China (No. U19A2082) and the National Natural Science Foundation of China (No. 62103081).

References

1. Schaefer, K. E., Brewer, R.W., Putney, J., et al.: Relinquishing manual control: collaboration requires the capability to understand robot intent. In: International Conference on Collaboration Technologies and Systems, Orlando, pp. 359–366. IEEE (2016)
2. Chen, J.Y.C., Barnes, M.J.: Human-agent teaming for multirobot control: a review of human factors issues. IEEE Trans. Hum.-Mach. Syst. **44**(1), 13–29 (2014)
3. Ali, A., Azevedo-Sa, H., Tilbury, D.M., et al.: Heterogeneous human-robot task allocation based on artificial trust. Sci. Rep. **12**(1), 1–15 (2022)
4. Chena, J.Y.C., Lakhmanib, S.G., Stowersb, K., et al.: Situation awareness-based agent transparency and human-autonomy teaming effectiveness. Theor. Issues Ergon. Sci. **19**(3), 259–282 (2018)
5. David, R.A., Nielsen, P.: Defense science board summer study on autonomy. Defense Science Board Washington United States, Washington DC (2016)
6. Gunning, D., Aha, D.: DARPA's explainable artificial intelligence (XAI) program. AI Mag. **40**(2), 44–58 (2019)
7. Boden, M., Bryson, J., Caldwell, D., et al.: Principles of robotics: regulating robots in the real world. Connect. Sci. **29**(2), 124–129 (2017)
8. Roncone, A., Mangin, O., Scassellati, B.: Transparent role assignment and task allocation in human robot collaboration. In: IEEE International Conference on Robotics and Automation, Singapore, pp. 1014–1021. IEEE (2017)
9. Chen, L., Zhou, M., Wu, M., et al.: Three-layer weighted fuzzy support vector regression for emotional intention understanding in human-robot interaction. IEEE Trans. Fuzzy Syst. **26**(5), 2524–2538 (2018)
10. Guznov, S., Lyons, J., Pfahler, M., et al.: Robot transparency and team orientation effects on human-robot teaming. Int. J. Hum.-Comput. Interact. **36**(7), 650–660 (2020)

11. Wortham, R.H., Theodorou, A.: Robot transparency, trust and utility. Connection Sci. **29**(3), 242–248 (2017)
12. Sharkey, A., Sharkey, N.: Granny and the robots: ethical issues in robot care for the elderly. Ethics Inf. Technol. **14**(1), 27–40 (2012)
13. Ramaraj, P., Sahay, S., Kumar, S.H., et al.: Towards using transparency mechanisms to build better mental models. In: Advances in Cognitive Systems, Cambridge, Massachusetts, vol. 7, pp. 1–6 (2019)
14. Qiu, J., Wang, Y., Cheng, H., et al.: Auditory movement feedforward for a lower-limb exoskeleton device (AIDER) to increase transparency. Int. J. Hum. Factors Model. Simul. **7**(3–4), 247–261 (2022)
15. Qiu, J., Wang, Y., Cheng, H., Wang, Lu., Yang, X.: A pilot study on auditory feedback for a lower-limb exoskeleton to increase walking safety. In: Black, N.L., Neumann, W.P., Noy, I. (eds.) IEA 2021. LNNS, vol. 223, pp. 325–334. Springer, Cham (2022). https://doi.org/10.1007/978-3-030-74614-8_39
16. Wang, Y., Qiu, J., Cheng, H., Wang, L.: A prospective study of haptic feedback method on a lower-extremity exoskeleton. In: Gao, Q., Zhou, J. (eds.) HCII 2021. LNCS, vol. 12786, pp. 253–261. Springer, Cham (2021). https://doi.org/10.1007/978-3-030-78108-8_19
17. Roy, C.S., Sherrington, C.S.: On the regulation of the blood supply of the brain. J. Physiol. **11**(1–2), 85–158 (1890)
18. Ma, R., Xia, X., Zhang, W., et al.: High gamma and beta temporal interference stimulation in the human motor cortex improves motor functions. Front. Neurosci. **15**, 1743 (2022)
19. Cools, R., Arnsten, A.F.T.: Neuromodulation of prefrontal cortex cognitive function in primates: the powerful roles of monoamines and acetylcholine. Neuropsychopharmacology **47**(1), 309–328 (2022)
20. Asgher, U., Ahmad, R., Naseer, N., et al.: Assessment and classification of mental workload in the prefrontal cortex (PFC) using fixed-value modified beer-lambert law. IEEE Access **7**, 143250–143262 (2019)
21. Wang, Y., Qiu, J., Cheng, H., et al.:Analysis of human-exoskeleton system interaction for ergonomic design. Hum. Factors 0018720820913789 (2020)

Author Index

Printed in the United States
by Baker & Taylor Publisher Services